Crossroads, Directions,
and a New Critical Race Theory

Crossroads, Directions, and a New Critical Race Theory

EDITED BY

Francisco Valdes, Jerome McCristal Culp,
and Angela P. Harris

TEMPLE UNIVERSITY PRESS

PHILADELPHIA

Temple University Press, Philadelphia 19122
Published 2002
Printed in the United States of America

⊖ The paper used in this publication meets the requirements of the American National Standard for Information Sciences—Permanence of Paper for Printed Library Materials, ANSI Z39.48-1984.

Library of Congress Cataloging-in-Publication Data

Crossroads, directions, and a new critical race theory / edited by Francisco Valdes, Jerome McCristal Culp, and Angela P. Harris.
    p.   cm.
    Includes bibliographical references and index.
    ISBN 1-56639-929-7 (alk. paper)—ISBN 1-56639-930-0 (pbk. : alk. paper)
    1. Race discrimination—Law and legislation—United States.   2. United States—Race relations—Philosophy.   I. Valdes, Francisco. II. Culp, Jerome M., 1950- III. Harris, Angela P., 1961-

KF4755.A75 C76 2002
305.8'00973—dc21

2001042448

Dedication

Remembering Trina Grillo

Stephanie M. Wildman

TRINA GRILLO, one of the founding sisters of Critical Race Theory, died in July 1996, a few days before what would have been her forty-eighth birthday, after a battle with Hodgkin's disease. Trina was a spiritual person. She was a brilliant analytical thinker with a keen legal mind, known best for her work about race and for her contributions to the field of mediation. Trina also understood that more informs our human wholeness than simply our brains.

The work of Critical Race Theory—and, perhaps more important, the people associated with it—meant a great deal to Trina. She was buried in her Critical Race Theory T-shirt. I wish I could give you a sense of the joy she felt being at Critical Race Theory workshops over the past decade. This feeling is perhaps best exemplified by the glowing way she described singing gospel songs at one early workshop. All those powerful minds joined in the unity of prayerful song.

Trina was committed to including everyone in that unity; she saw the interconnectedness of humanity and took diversity seriously. Diversity meant having everyone in the room, the atheists and the prayerful ones, newcomers and veterans, across many lines of difference, able to sing and talk together.

In the months following Trina's death, I had a dream in which she appeared. She arrived at the door of my office, bundled up in the black corduroy jacket she often wore. Needless to say, I was stunned to see her, because I knew she had died.

"Trina," I exclaimed, giving her a hug. "How are you?" I managed to blurt out, ushering her in to sit in my desk chair. She looked beautiful. "I'm fine," she said, making it clear this visit was not for chit-chat. She looked at me intently and said, "We have a lot of work to do."

All I could think was about how tired I felt (after all, I was trying to sleep), wondering whether we really had to start right then. "How can I help you?" I managed to ask.

She replied, "What I really need is a flashlight, so that I can read in the darkness."

I nodded as she hurriedly left.

Warm, energetic, committed, and caring are only some of the words that describe Trina Grillo. She had a vision of pedagogy that recognized difference when such a notion was minimized or discarded. Using student collaboration, active learning, and student voices, she created a learning community where students who differed from other law students because of class, race, gender, sexual orientation, physical ability, or cognitive processing ability could thrive. Her legacy, incorporating diversity into the curriculum and into our institutions, continues to be at the cutting edge of legal education.

We can best honor her memory by carrying on this work. Many people, from many identity categories, could say about her, "She was my best friend." Remember Trina Grillo; make a friend across lines of difference. Shine a flashlight into the darkness, and continue the work.

Contents

     AND FAMILY IN/JUSTICE   345
        Berta Esperanza Hernández-Truyol

16. CRITICAL RACE THEORY AND POST-COLONIAL DEVELOPMENT   366
        Enrique R. Carrasco

Part III: Directions

17. CRITICAL COALITIONS: THEORY AND PRAXIS   379
        Julie A. Su and Eric K. Yamamoto

18. BEYOND, AND NOT BEYOND, BLACK AND WHITE: DECONSTRUCTION
     HAS A POLITICS   393
        Mari Matsuda

19. OUTSIDER SCHOLARS, CRITICAL RACE THEORY, AND "OUTCRIT"
     PERSPECTIVITY: POSTSUBORDINATION VISION AS
     JURISPRUDENTIAL METHOD   399
        Francisco Valdes

     AFTERWORD: THE HANDMAID'S TRUTH   411
        Derrick A. Bell

     ABOUT THE CONTRIBUTORS   413

Foreword

Who Are We? And Why Are We Here?
Doing Critical Race Theory in Hard Times

Charles R. Lawrence III

Editors' note: This Foreword is a slightly edited transcript of a speech given by Charles Lawrence at the opening session of the November 1997 Critical Race Theory Conference at Yale University, where many chapters of this book were first presented as panel presentations and working papers. We have published Professor Lawrence's speech as he spoke it to preserve its intimacy and energy, as well as its historical context.

WHEN HARLON DALTON asked me to give the opening remarks at this conference, and I asked him what I should talk about, he said something like, "Just be your warm, wise self." My first reaction to Harlon's typically playful and generous response was ambivalence. It was the same feeling I had experienced when I first received the announcement of the conference in the mail. The flyer described the meeting as a tenth birthday celebration for Critical Race Theory and named my Stanford article on unconscious racism[1] among the genre's foundational canon. I felt honored by this generous acknowledgment of my work. I knew it was a gesture of love and respect by the conference organizers. But I wasn't at all sure I liked Harlon's undisguised pleasure in calling me an "old man" and getting away with it. He even suggested that when I gave this talk I might wear an old brown leather jacket—a favorite of mine that was fashionable, even hip, in the early days of Critical Race Theory but would now look quaint. Harlon swears that he was but a child when he first saw me wear it.

But as the day drew closer, my primary emotion was anxiety. What I was experiencing was something more than the ordinary jitters that always accompany public presentations of self. This was not a lecture to students or colleagues who would judge me on terms I had learned to mediate and master, even as I held the judges at arms length. This would be a conversation with friends and comrades. I do not know you all, but there are many of you who know me well—who have shared my joys and sorrows, stood with me against my enemies, and covered my back. And I know that many of you whom I do not know well have been with me, too, because I have seen your work and it is work that teaches, nourishes, and shelters me and reminds me that I am not crazy—or maybe it is that I am not the only crazy one. So fast and facile footwork with theory and text will not do. I must speak the truth, as best I can, about things that matter to me. Now what I feel is not primarily anxiety but exhilaration and pride at the sight of you and in the beauty of my chosen family.

I remember feeling the same way ten years ago. There were only forty, maybe fifty, of us then. We were gathered in a large upstairs room that looked like a combination auditorium/gymnasium. Folding chairs were arranged in a large circle around the room's perimeter. It was the first session of the tenth National Critical Legal Studies Conference. A small group of us had been attending CLS meetings for several years, seeking intellectual community in what was then the dominant progressive movement in the legal academy. There were more of us at this CLS conference than ever before. Our numbers were larger because the conference, entitled "Sounds of Silence: Racism and the Law," had placed us momentarily at the center of the CLS agenda. Although in its initial incarnation it was a conference planned by and for white folks, we had, in the end, played a significant role in its creation. Ultimately, it was a genuine response by our friends and collaborators in CLS to our personal experiences of alienation and marginalization in their community and to our challenge that their work contained insufficient attention to and understanding of the issues we considered central to the work of combating racism.[2] We were also asking them to examine their own racism (never an easy request to make or respond to) and trying to figure out for ourselves where we fit in—how to situate ourselves as progressive people of color in law teaching.[3]

The organizers of the conference had decided that the colored people and white folks should meet in separate "minority" and "non-minority" caucuses for the opening evening session. We hoped that this would allow the white folks to take responsibility for dealing with their own racism (the help said we wouldn't do windows that evening), and we wanted an opportunity to speak to one another with candor, and without posturing, about our own condition as people of color on the left. This was a chance to sit down with family and really talk.

Kimberlé Crenshaw had asked me to chair the colored caucus. Kimberlé was only in her first year of law teaching, but she had been a moving force in putting the conference on the right track, and would soon become one of Critical Race Theory's founding sisters. I had been in the teaching business longer than Kimberlé and thought of myself as a big brother, but even then, when Professor Crenshaw said "We need you to do this," there was no saying no.

Because we were a much smaller group then, I could do what I wish were possible here—that is, listen instead of talk. I suggested that we proceed by going around our large circle, with each of us speaking briefly, so that we could hear from everyone in the room. I asked each person two questions: "Who are you?" and "Why are you here?" I wanted to know where we were from, who our people were, and by what route we had come to this place. What had attracted us to critical legal studies, and what made us feel alienated? What were our frustrations, and what were our hopes?

The stories we told one another that night were wonderful and richly complex. We had lots to say, and suddenly it could all be said: our anger, pain, and even joy; our strength and vulnerability; the ambivalence of our roles as outsiders on the inside; the schizophrenia that comes with mastering the master's language while struggling to maintain fluency in languages that are expressive of liberating themes. We were lonely souls seeking community and refuge from the white worlds where we worked. We looked less diverse than we do now. Most of us were African Americans, but the clear and vibrant voices of Native, Latino, and Asian American brothers and sisters presaged the considerable gifts and important work that they represent among us today.

What we had most in common was a genealogy. On the second day of the conference, Harlon Dalton described our shared biography in an eloquent and irreverent speech. Contrasting us with the "typical crit" who "lived in his head disconnected from much of the richness of the surrounding world," he said this of us,

> No matter how smart or bookish we were, we could not retreat from the sights, sounds, and smells of the communities from which we came. We learned from life as well as from books. We learned about injustice, social cruelty, political hypocrisy and sanctioned terrorism from the mouths of our mothers and fathers and from our very own experiences. . . . And from the beginning we learned, not as an article of political faith but rather as a simple fact of life, that our fate and that of all persons of similar hue were inseparably intertwined. That fundamental connectedness, together with our distinctive subcultures, nourished and sustained us, created in us an unshakable sense of community. The lucky ones among us reveled in that community, fed on it. Others of us resented it or tried to hide from it. But escape was not possible, for the community was within us, and we were branded forever.[4]

Those of us who were most senior, and even *we* were young people then, had come of age in the midst of the rushing river of the Civil Rights Movement.[5] In 1966, the summer of my first year in law school, I traveled to southwest Georgia to work with C. B. King.[6] When we drove to court in Baker County or Americus, the brothers in the movement would meet us at the county line and escort us to the courthouse, with the barrels of their shotguns sticking out the window. The following summer, I dropped out of law school for a year to teach and organize in North Philadelphia. High-school kids were reading Malcolm and Fanon and Harold Cruz—or, at least, they were carrying the books around and quoting from them. In 1970, I dropped out again, leaving a legal-services job to become the principal of a parent-run community school in Roxbury, a poor Black neighborhood in Boston. Mary Helen Washington, in her presidential address to the American Studies Association, describes this period in her own professional history, when she was a young assistant professor in the English Department at the University of Detroit,

> Besides teaching a full load, fighting to increase the pitifully small number of black students on campus, negotiating with the traditional departments for their reluctant acceptance, we were under a great deal of pressure, in the Black Power climate of Detroit, to be politically involved; you had to read Mao and Marx and Malcolm; you had to be "in struggle." I remember one meeting at Wayne State, where I went to hear the fiery Ron Dellums speak, that featured the entire spectrum of black political thought in Detroit: There were Black Muslims, Black Panthers, Pan-Africanists, black cultural nationalists, black Christian nationalists, Marxist-Leninists, and communists; I was there as a closeted integrationist. In my journals I reported coming home that night and becoming deeply involved in cleaning my house so I could restore my sense of order.[7]

Like the young Professor Washington, I do not remember so much choosing to be an activist as being pulled along by the current of the times: trying to understand and keep up with an onrushing river of liberation, trying to do the practical work of representing jailed freedom fighters and drafting resolutions at neighborhood meetings and Black political conventions. I embarked on my professional career at the high point of the long, forward-moving doctrinal march from *Sweatt* to *Griggs*.[8]

Many of the folks in that room ten years ago were a decade younger than I, and it was this generation of law teachers who first called themselves critical race theorists. Kimberlé Crenshaw locates Critical Race Theory's conception in the late 1980s when she began law school.[9] It was a period of retrenchment, an initial assault against the gains made during the Civil Rights Movement. This somewhat younger group of progressive colored law teachers were part of the militant resistance to that retrenchment. Their political consciousness and intellectual agenda were forged in the activism that opposed visions of race, racism, and law that were dominant in this post–civil-rights period. The *Bakke* case is the doctrinal marker of the times that shaped this generation of critical race theorists. They were part of an organized grassroots movement that waged an effective fight against the backlash embodied in *Bakke*. The result of this struggle was an uneasy compromise: watered-down affirmative-action programs remained in place alongside a new rhetoric of "reverse discrimination."[10]

If the youthful biographies of early critical race theorists were shaped by the movements that culminated in *Griggs* and *Bakke*, the biographies of our younger brothers and sisters, and the middle passage of my contemporaries, are marked by *Croson, Adarand, Hopwood,* Propositions 187 and 209,[11] the confirmation of Justice Clarence Thomas, and the Million Man March. How do we do Critical Race Theory in these perilous times? How do we define ourselves when there is no ideologically grounded mass movement to define us? How do we resist an organized and well-funded ideological assault from the right that has been vicious and successful beyond anything we anticipated?[12] How do we talk to one another about the hard stuff—sexism, heterosexism, nationalism, class privilege, internalized racism—moving beyond the Black–white paradigm and still understanding its special place in the construction of American racism?[13] "Who are we? And why are we here?"

In the remainder of this talk I want to say some things about how we might begin to talk with one another about the answers to these questions. I start with a list of things that keep coming up in the conversations I have been having with myself as I struggle to find, or define, a place and way to work, and a community to work with, in this season of my life. I offer this short and tentative list not as answers to my questions but as places to begin our conversations:

1. Speaking simple truths to power.
2. Making our own communities our first audience.
3. Creating a homeplace for refuge and hard conversations.
4. Defining boundaries (knowing who is us and who is them).
5. Starting small (knowing that small is important and good).
6. Remembering that we are beautiful and that we are bad (or "the bomb").

Speaking Simple Truths

Mari Matsuda and I recently spoke on a panel at the American Studies Association annual conference. The conference organizers had asked us to speak about our book *We Won't Go Back: Making the Case for Affirmative Action.*[14] Roger Wilkins, the historian, journalist, and long-time civil-rights activist, was the respondent to our papers. He gave a wonderful talk that was at once penetrating, thoughtful, and inspiring. Two things that he said stand out for me. First, he reminded us that Proposition 209, the anti–affirmative-action initiative in California, and *Hopwood*, the Fifth Circuit Court decision holding a race-based affirmative-action program at the University of Texas unconstitutional, are reenactments of those provisions of the slave codes that made it a crime to teach a slave to read or cipher; and second, both the eighteenth- and late-twentieth-century versions are products of the slave masters' fear of revolt. "It doesn't surprise me," said Roger, "that when white folks read Matsuda and Lawrence's work, they say, 'We better stop teaching these folks to read and write.'"

When a member of the audience asked Wilkins why the children of middle-class Black folk like him should benefit from affirmative action, he answered, "Because fighting racism in white institutions is hand-to-hand combat. And if my daughter is among the best-trained and most committed freedom fighters, we must have her here with us. We need every warrior we can muster."

These are simple truths, simply said. The dismantling of affirmative action is segregation. Its purpose and meaning are the same as the Jim Crow laws. We need to call Pete Wilson and Orrin Hatch what they are—old-fashioned segregationists. When our liberal colleagues stand by and wring their hands, saying, "Now that these measures are law, nothing can be done," we need to ask, "Which side are you on?" and tell them that we will judge them by the results of their actions. Law faculties determine the standards by which we judge who is qualified to attend our schools, and if we are unwilling to reexamine measures of merit that replicate white privilege, we must explain our collaboration with segregationists.[15] Just as respectable white folks in Birmingham, Alabama, and Jackson, Mississippi, were responsible for the bombings and lynchings by the Klan, because they had the power to put a stop to them, we and our colleagues are responsible for the crime that is done by the resegregation of our law schools, and that simple truth must be told.[16]

These are truths that have been lost and forgotten amid the revisionist rhetoric of "color blindness" and "racial preferences." When our colleagues accuse us of "being polemical and lacking balance" or engaging in "identity politics" and "vulgar racial essentialism" or being "radical nihilists" when today's political climate calls for pragmatism and compromise, or when they attack our scholarship as "unanalytic," "unsophisticated," "untruthful," "Beyond All Reason," and even "anti-Semitic,"[17] we must know that these are words designed not just to discredit and defame but to intimidate and pressure us to self-censor. I am worried that our enemies have achieved some success in this project, that too often we seek the safety of abstract theory and avoid the narratives that implicate our colleagues. I do not mean in saying this that we should not be doing erudite meta-theory and complex deconstruction. Nor is this a call to abandon the openness, empathy, and reconciliation that have been such an important part of our work. But we must also speak the simple and radical truths of white supremacy and patriarchy and class oppression and heterosexism, even when we know we will pay a price for speaking them.

Speaking to Our Own

Critical Race Theory was born as part of the resistance to retrenchment, and it is not surprising that we and our work have been subject to relentless attack throughout the past ten years. We know the colleagues who have established careers and gained name recognition by critical-race–bashing. More important, impugning our ideas and silencing our message is central to the ideological war that is being waged by the right. Most of us live and work in a largely white world, and our work is paid for and judged by a white audience. Powerful white folks and their non-white allies, such as Ward Connolly and Justice Clarence Thomas, have the power to make and enforce law, and it is natural that, as lawyers and law professors, we so often find ourselves speaking to them first and foremost: responding to attacks, seeking to influence legislation, writing articles for white tenure committees, lecturing and writing in venues where few in our audience are colored or poor. This is often important work. Much of it is the hand-to-hand combat that Roger Wilkins spoke of. But I want to suggest that in these times of backlash and retrenchment, it is especially important that we find ways to speak to and with the folks from our own communities.

There are several reasons for this. I want to mention four and save for another time a discussion of each. The first is that our lack of control of or access to mainstream media has forced us into a reactive posture. In a recent column in *The Nation*, Patricia Williams described the frustration and futility of defending against the stream of caricature of Critical Race Theory in such places as the *Wall Street Journal* and the *New Republic*:

> They take a fluidly left-leaning group and depict it as an idiotically "separatist" right wing monolith. This "why did you beat your wife" strategy means that real debate of issues posed by a serious, responsible left is eternally circumvented as we sacrifice precious time to the kind of simple-minded but necessary refutation that only sets you up for more: I am not a neo-Nazi! I can so tell the difference between fantasy and fact! And of course, some of my best friends are white....
>
> Critical Race Theory is treated as a conceptual ghetto filled with dangerous low-income scholarship unworthy of reading, never mind careful reading. From there, it is easy to believe whatever misquoted, misconstrued blather is said to stream from the mouths of those ... anti-intellectual thugs with "blood" on their Singular Mind—theirs being, of course, the True Black Mind that fabricates faster than Madame Defarge could knit.[18]

What makes Patricia Williams's piece most poignant is that it is an exercise in the very futility she describes. Moreover, our rejoinder to these libelous falsehoods can never adequately redress the injuries they inflict. Precious souls such as Patricia Williams should not be subjected to the personal assault and abuse that goes with participating in this anything-but-intellectual debate.

The second reason to spend less time talking to white folks and more to our folks is that the latter conversations are important to our own continuing education. We learned the best of our theory in conversations with our own communities and within the context of activism with those communities. The remarkable chapters in this volume are evidence that this continues to be so.

Third, there is much teaching to be done in communities of color, both the teaching of the skills that are denied our children in the public schools (each of us should find a young person to tutor) and the teaching of politics—helping young Black people put the lie of their inferiority outside of them, helping men of color understand how patriarchy harms them as well as their sisters, teaching colored professionals the importance of coming out of the closet as beneficiaries of affirmative action.

And fourth, we would not be here but for the ideologically informed struggles of the communities from which we come, and we will not be here for long if the folks in those communities do not know that they belong here and that they must fight for our inclusion and theirs. George C. Wolfe, who produced *The Colored Museum* and *Bring in 'Da Noise*,

Bring in 'Da Funk sees as one of his central missions building new audiences among young Black people. He is setting aside large groups of tickets for Black schools and marketing deep discounted tickets on cable TV's Black Entertainment Television (BET) and in the hiphop magazine *Vibe*. Wolfe says: "You are building an audience, because audiences are mostly old and white, and that perception is a fact. And when they die, there is a possibility that audiences could die."[19]

Creating Homeplace

bell hooks, a keynote speaker at that Critical Legal Studies Conference ten years ago, has said: "Home, however fragile and tenuous (the slave hut, the wooden shack), had a radical dimension. Despite the brutal reality of racial apartheid, of domination, one's homeplace was the site where one could freely confront the issue of humanization, where one could resist."[20]

In hard times, it is especially important to create homeplaces: safe places among trusted friends to seek refuge and dress the wounds of battle and places for hard conversations, where differences can be aired and strategy mapped, where we can struggle with and affirm one another. As we have increased our numbers, it has become more difficult for Critical Race Theory meetings to be a homeplace for us all. From the beginning, we have also been about coalition-building. That wondrous musical/political voice Bernice Reagon Johnson has said of coalition: "Coalition work is not done in your home. Coalition work is done in the streets. It is some of the most dangerous work you can do. And you shouldn't look for comfort."[21]

Critical Race Theory has always lived with this tension. Folks have come seeking refuge from hostile workplaces, and often they have encountered the unsafety of coalition-building. We have struggled to teach one another about the intersections that gender and race and heterosexism make and to confront our own internalization and participation in those subordinations. Some of us have said, "I am marginalized or made invisible or even dehumanized by this discussion." And we have not always heard them. Inevitably, I will hear gossip about some falling-out or a faction forming, but I take this news of Critical Race conflict as evidence of growing pains. I am reassured that we are alive and not unlike other families. I also believe it is not necessarily a bad thing that, as we grow in number, we form smaller, more intimate groups of younger and older Lat-Crits and queer-race-Crits and Midatlantic-women-of-color-Crits, homeplaces within a collective too large now to be a homeplace itself. I think this is good because some wonderful work is produced in these smaller groups and because I do not experience them as excluding or divisive. Many of us move freely among them and identify with more than one.[22]

Defining Boundaries

There is another tension that has been with us always. This is the tension between our desire to create a community of kinship and safe harbor for all people of color who self-identify as progressive and our need to define our politics with sufficient clarity to make that politics meaningful and functional. In hard times, I think it is more important than ever to define clearly who we are and what we stand for. I am not talking about the silly debate over whether certain individuals have been, or should be, barred from attending

Critical Race Theory workshops. I am not advocating the adoption of a party platform or the recitation of an apostles' creed. I believe that our work suffers when we are not prepared to engage in serious criticism of ourselves and of one another. But in a time in which we are misrepresented and caricatured by our enemies, when there are people of color who are misogynist, homophobic, or anti-other but still call themselves progressive race-men, we must be clear about what we stand for. We must know who is us and who is them. For me, an important starting point in this project of self-definition is our commitment to the end of eliminating racial oppression as part of the broader goal of ending all forms of oppression. The end of racial oppression requires fundamental social transformation, not just adjustments within established hierarchies, and those who would claim Critical Race Theory without a commitment to challenging hierarchy and subordination in all its many intersecting forms should not find community with us.

Starting Small

What do we do when there is no mass movement, when the river of liberation is not pulling us along in a rushing torrent but only moving in its deep streams? I have been thinking about those who went before us, earlier generations of radical teachers who kept the flames of freedom alive in hard times. There is a poster on my office wall at home with a picture of the brothers of the Niagara movement, all in fancy hats. When I look at that picture, I am always struck by what a small group they were. I think of Ida Wells mounting an anti-lynching campaign, at first almost single-handedly. Spike Lee interviews Andrew Young in his movie *Four Little Girls,* a retrospective documentary about the infamous Easter Sunday bombing of the Sixteenth Street Church in Birmingham, Alabama. Young reflects on the massive Civil Rights Movement that rose up in that city, so long known for the brutality of its racism. He says, "Everybody always thinks of the movement as hundreds and thousands of people marching and going to jail, but when we first came to Birmingham, we'd have ten or twelve people show up for a march."[23] In hard times, we must continue to be activists. In hard times, it is important and necessary and good to start small.

We cannot teach about liberation without actively engaging in its politics. As Paulo Freire has said, "There is no true word that is not at the same time praxis."[24] Many among us are doing this important work. Julie Su is helping immigrant garment workers in Los Angeles sweatshops to fight the big names of American fashion and learning from them what it means to fight.[25] Gerald Torres is quietly working behind the scenes to mount a political fight-back against the Fifth Circuit's *Hopwood* decision. Kendall Thomas is putting together cross-racial coalitions in New York to fight homophobia. Sumi Cho, Margaret Montoya, Margalynn Armstrong, and Angela Harris are meeting with student and community activists at Boalt to organize an action campaign and march against the resegregation of the University of California. I have named just a few of you. Surely there is no need to despair, because there is still a movement as long as we continue to act up.

Remembering That We Are Gorgeous

One morning about a month ago, Mari Matsuda walked into her office. Scrolling across the screen of her computer in three-inch-high letters were the words, "Professor Matsuda

Is the Bomb." Was this a threat or a not-so-funny practical joke? Had some member of a hate group found a way to write this message on her computer? Thinking it was better to be safe than sorry, Mari called the associate dean, and the dean called security. It was the security guard, a young brother, who said, "Professor Matsuda, I think someone is trying to pay you a compliment."

Mari tells this story on herself, laughing in good-humored self-deprecation at how out of touch she is with youth culture. Her very hip Afro-Asian research assistant, Ms. Susan Epps, had put the message on the screen, and she does think her professor is "the bomb." For me this story is not just an artifact of the generation gap. It is a reminder that in hard times it is important to remember that we are "the bomb," or "bad," as we first-generation critical race theorists used to say when we were young. Each of you is "the bomb," and collectively we are a nuclear explosion of beauty.

Why am I here? Mainly because this is the smartest, best-looking, sweetest bunch of people in law teaching. Judge Richard Posner says you are bad role models for minority youth, that you reinforce all the pejorative stereotypes of colored folks.[26] But if he's right that white folks will think that all colored folks look and act like you, that's just fine with me. I want Kimi and Pauli to grow up to be just like you.

Derrick Bell says that racism is permanent. One thing is for certain: None of us will live long enough to know whether he is right. So we're in this fight for the long haul, and Derrick is certainly right when he says we struggle because that is what gives life meaning, that is what gives us joy.[27] I for one am glad I'm in this struggle with all of you.

Notes

1. Charles R. Lawrence III, "The Id, the Ego, and Equal Protection," *Stanford Law Review* 39 (1987): 317.

2. For a discussion of the history of Critical Race Theory and its relationship to the critical legal studies movement, see Mari J. Matsuda, Charles R. Lawrence III, Richard Delgado, and Kimberlé W. Crenshaw, *Words That Wound: Critical Race Theory, Assaultive Speech, and the First Amendment* (Boulder, Colo.: Westview Press, 1993); Kimberlé Crenshaw, Neil Gotanda, Gary Peller, and Kendall Thomas, eds., *Critical Race Theory: The Key Writings That Formed the Movement* (New York: New Press, 1995); Jose A. Bracamonte, "Foreword—Minority Critique of the Critical Legal Studies Movement," *Harvard Civil Rights–Civil Liberties Law Review* 22 (1987): 297.

3. Charles R. Lawrence III, "The Word and the River: Pedagogy as Scholarship as Struggle," *Southern California Law Review* 65 (1992): 2231.

4. Harlon Dalton, "The Clouded Prism," *Harvard Civil Rights–Civil Liberties Law Review* 22 (1987): 435.

5. Vincent Harding, *There Is a River: The Black Struggle for Freedom in America* (San Diego: HarBac, 1981), xviii–xix. Harding uses the river as metaphor in writing the history of Black radicalism in America. He says of his chosen metaphor: "I wanted and needed to write . . . a narrative, analytical, and celebrative history of the freedom struggle of black people in this country, beginning before there was a country. I was especially concerned to try to convey its long, continuous movement, flowing like a river, sometimes powerful, tumultuous, and roiling with life; at other times meandering and turgid, covered with the ice and snow of seemingly endless winters . . . the river of black struggle is people, but it is also hope, the movement, the transformative power that humans create and that creates them, us, and makes them, us, new persons."

6. C. B. King was one of the small army of civil-rights attorneys in the deep South. At the height of the Civil Rights Movement, he was the only African American attorney within an eighty-mile radius of Albany, Georgia. A brilliant lawyer and orator, King rode the circuit of back-country courthouses in southwestern Georgia representing the young freedom fighters of the Student Nonviolent Coordinating Committee (SNCC) and the Southern Christian Leadership Conference (SCLC) and the local folk who rose up in a

mass movement around them. An outstanding figure in his own right, he was also a mentor to an impressive corps of young civil-rights attorneys, including Dennis Roberts, Paul Harris, and Robert Cover.

7. Mary Helen Washington, "Disturbing the Peace: What Happens to American Studies If You Put African American Studies at the Center? Presidential Address to the American Studies Association," *American Quarterly*, sec. 50.1 (October 29, 1997), 1–2.

8. *Sweatt v. Painter*, 339 U.S. 629 (1950), holding that a Black law-school candidate had to be admitted to the University of Texas Law School, despite the existence of a local Black law school, because the latter was not equal to the University of Texas in faculty, resources, or reputation, among other criteria. I name *Sweatt* as the beginning of this progressive doctrinal march because it contained the revolutionary seeds of *Brown v. Board of Education of Topeka*, 347 U.S., 483 (1954). In finding that a segregated law school for Negroes could not provide them with equal educational opportunities, the Supreme Court relied in large part on "those qualities which are incapable of objective measurement but which make for greatness in a law school," thus recognizing the intangible injuries of stigma and racial isolation that became the foundation of *Brown* and the 1964 Civil Rights Act. *Griggs v. Duke Power Company*, 401 U.S. 424 (1970), holding that the Civil Rights Act prohibits an employer from requiring certain tests, such as a high-school diploma, when such tests are not significantly related to job performance, when the tests disqualify Blacks at much higher rates than whites, and when whites previously had received such jobs by preference to the point of excluding Blacks. I name *Griggs v. Duke Power Company* as the high point of this progressive doctrinal movement because it was *Griggs* that required a justification of ostensible neutral practices that produced racially discriminatory results. In *Griggs*, the court momentarily transformed antidiscrimination law by shifting the emphasis on bad intent to one on consequences, thus adopting what Alan Freeman called the "victim perspective"—that there is no equality until the conditions associated with slavery and segregation have changed: Alan David Freeman, "Legitimizing Racial Discrimination Through Antidiscrimination Law: A Critical Review of Supreme Court Doctrine," *Minnesota Law Review* 62 (1978): 1049.

9. Professor Kimberlé Crenshaw discusses the politics and legal ideology that characterized the retrenchment of the post-Civil Rights era in "Race, Reform, and Retrenchment: Transformation and Legitimation in Antidiscrimination Law," *Harvard Law Review* 101 (1998): 1331. For a discussion of Critical Race Theory's historical, intellectual, and political origins, see Matsuda et al., *Words That Wound*, 1–15, and Crenshaw et al., *Key Writings*, xiii–xxxii.

10. *Regents of the University of California v. Bakke*, 438 U.S. 265 (1978). For a discussion of the history of the politics of backlash against remedial racial remedies and affirmative action that culminated in the *Bakke* case, and of the politics of resistance to that backlash, see Charles R. Lawrence III and Mari J. Matsuda, *We Won't Go Back: Making the Case for Affirmative Action* (Boston: Houghton Mifflin, 1997). See also Joel Dreyfuss and Charles R. Lawrence III, *The Bakke Case: The Politics of Inequality* (New York: HarBac, 1979).

11. *City of Richmond v. J. A. Croson*, 488 U.S. 469 (1989), striking down Richmond's plan requiring prime contractors awarded city construction contracts to subcontract at least 30 percent of the dollar amount to one or more minority enterprises; *Adarand Constructors, Inc. v. Pena*, 515 U.S. 200 (1995), holding that a federal program designed to provide highway contracts to disadvantaged business enterprises must withstand strict scrutiny; *Hopwood v. University of Texas*, 78 F. 3d 932 (5th Cir.), cert. denied, 116 S. Ct. 2581, holding that the goal of achieving a diverse student body is not a compelling interest justifying racially preferential admission policies. California's Proposition 187 prevents illegal aliens from receiving social services, health-care services, and public education. *League of United Latin Citizens v. Wilson*, 908 F. Supp. 755 (C.D. Calif. 1997), held that portions of Proposition 187 were pre-empted by federal laws regulating immigration. Thus, the portions of the proposition that required state officials to verify an immigrant's status, notify authorities that he may be here unlawfully, and publicly report his immigrant-status information were struck down. California's Proposition 209 prohibits the use of affirmative action in public employment, public education, and public contracting. In *Coalition for Economic Equity v. Wilson*, 110 F. 2d 1431 (9th Cir. 1998), the court affirmed and upheld Proposition 209, holding that it did not deny citizens equal protection.

12. See, for example, Jeffrey Rosen, "The Bloods and the Crits: O. J. Simpson, Critical Race Theory, the Law, and the Triumph of Color in America," *New Republic*, December 9, 1996, 27; Richard A. Posner, "The Skin Trade" (book review), *New Republic*, October 13, 1997, 40; Daniel A. Farber and Suzanna Sherry, *Beyond All Reason: The Radical Assault on Truth in American Law* (New York: Oxford University Press, 1997).

13. See, for example, the chapters by Sumi Cho and Robert Westley, Catharine A. MacKinnon, Mari Matsuda, Francisco Valdes, and Eric Yamamoto and Julie Su in this volume.

14. Lawrence and Matsuda, *We Won't Go Back.*

15. The LSAT remains the primary determinant of admission at Boalt and UCLA, and the primary cause of the exclusion of African American and Latino students. The failure of these faculties, and almost all others, to abandon this heavy reliance on the LSAT has little to do with their confidence in its infallibility as an accurate predictor of performance in law school, much less the profession. Rather, it is evidence that they are more concerned about preserving their ranking in the *U.S. News and World Report* pecking order and the privilege that hides in the myth of meritocracy than they are with racial justice. For a discussion of how the liberal defense of affirmative action fails to challenge the manner in which traditional standards of merit perpetuate race and class privilege and ignores substantive defenses of affirmative action that articulate the need to remedy past and ongoing discrimination, see Charles R. Lawrence III, "Two Views of the River: A Critique of the Liberal Defense of Affirmative Action," *Columbia Law Review* 101 (2001): 928.

16. Martin Luther King chastised white religious leaders who stood silent while Blacks' homes and churches were bombed and then called his campaign of nonviolent direct action "extreme" and counseled compromise with and acceptance of segregation. Dr. King wrote, "I have almost reached the regrettable conclusion that the Negro's great stumbling block in the stride toward freedom is not the White Citizens 'Councilor' or the Ku Klux Klanner, but the white moderate who is more devoted to 'order' than to justice; who prefers a negative peace which is the absence of tension to a positive peace which is the presence of justice": Martin Luther King, Jr., "Letter from Birmingham City Jail," in *Eyes on the Prize: Civil Rights Reader,* ed. Clayborne Carson et al. (New York: Penguin Books, 1991), 153, 156.

17. Posner, "Skin Trade," uses the following words and phrases to describe critical race theorists and their ideas: "identity politics," "paranoid," "rational fringe and lunatic core," "goofy," "irresponsible," "childish," "loony Afrocentrism," "disgrace to legal education," "extremism," and "hysteria." Rosen, "Bloods and the Crits," has employed phrases such as "vulgar racial essentialism" and accused critical race theorists of being polemical and lacking balance. Farber and Sherry, *Beyond All Reason,* 52–71, devote an entire chapter to the alleged "anti-Semitism" of critical race theorists.

18. Patricia J. Williams, "De Jure, De Facto, De Media . . . ; Diary of a Mad Law Professor," *New Republic,* June 2, 1997, 10.

19. Jacqueline Trescott, "'Da Noise' of a Full House: National Tour Strives to Reach Diverse Audience," *Washington Post,* November 9, 1997, G1.

20. bell hooks, *Yearning: Race, Gender, and Cultural Politics* (Boston: South End Press, 1990), 42.

21. Bernice Reagon Johnson, "Coalition Politics: Turning the Century," in *Home Girls: A Black Feminist Anthology,* ed. Barbara Smith, 1st ed. (New York: Kitchen Table–Women of Color Press, 1983), 356, 359.

22. See the chapter by Francisco Valdes in this volume.

23. Spike Lee, *Four Little Girls* (New York: HBO Home Video, 1998), audiovisual (40 Acres and a Mule Fireworks, 1997).

24. Paulo Freire, *Pedagogy of the Oppressed* (New York: Continuum, 1982), 75.

25. See the chapter by Julie A. Su and Eric K. Yamamoto in this volume.

26. Posner, "Skin Trade": "The ironic consequence is that the critical race theorists are poor role models. Instead of exemplifying in their careers the potential of members of their groups for respected achievement in the world outside the ghetto of complaint—the kind of exemplification that we find in the career of Colin Powell—critical race theorists teach by example that the role of a member of a minority group is to be paid a comfortable salary to write childish stories about how awful it is to be a member of such a group."

27. See generally Derrick A. Bell, Jr., *Faces to the Bottom of the Well: The Permanence of Racism* (New York: Basic Books, 1992).

Crossroads, Directions, and a New Critical Race Theory

INTRODUCTION

Battles Waged, Won, and Lost: Critical Race Theory at the Turn of the Millennium

Francisco Valdes, Jerome McCristal Culp, and Angela P. Harris

THE EMERGENCE of Critical Race Theory (CRT) in the legal academy of the United States during the late 1980s has had a galvanizing effect not only within the narrow world of legal academia, but also on the public discourse on race more generally. In part, this impact has been due to what CRT has to say. CRT, like critical legal studies (CLS) before it, rejects the basic premises of American legal liberalism.

Critical race theorists have not placed their faith in neutral procedures and the substantive doctrines of formal equality; rather, critical race theorists assert that both the procedures and the substance of American law, including American antidiscrimination law, are structured to maintain white privilege. Neutrality and objectivity are not just unattainable ideals; they are harmful fictions that obscure the normative supremacy of whiteness in American law and society. Ten or so years ago, critical race theorists set out to expose and dismantle this social and legal status quo from an explicitly race-conscious and critical "outsider" perspective. Since then, as this anthology attests, our work collectively has accomplished both much and not nearly enough.

Today, at the opening of the millennium, CRT continues to reject at least three entrenched, mainstream beliefs about racial injustice. The first belief—and still the most powerful despite more than a decade of challenge from critical scholars—is that "blindness" to race will eliminate racism. This belief, in turn, stems from the deep-rooted individualism that leads most American scholars and lawmakers, even liberal ones, to abhor all forms of group-based identity. Critical race theorists have challenged this belief, asserting instead that self-conscious racial identities can be—and have been—the source of individual fulfillment, collective strength, and incisive policymaking.

The second popular belief about racial injustice that CRT challenges is that racism is a matter of individuals, not systems. The goal of antidiscrimination law, as understood historically and currently by courts, was to search for perpetrators and victims: perpetrators could be identified through "bad" acts and intentions, while victims were (only) those who could meet shifting, and increasingly elusive, burdens of proof. Instead, critical race theorists have located racism and its everyday operation in the very structures within which the guilty and the innocent were to be identified: not individual "bad-apple" police officers, but the criminal justice system; not bigoted school-board members, but the structures of segregation and wealth transmission. In its first decade, CRT described and critiqued not a world of bad actors, wronged victims, and innocent bystanders, but a world in which all of us are more or less complicit in sociolegal webs of domination and subordination.

The third popular belief about racial injustice that CRT challenges is that one can fight racism without paying attention to sexism, homophobia, economic exploitation, and other forms of oppression or injustice. From the beginning, CRT has been dedicated to antiracist social transformation through an antisubordination analysis that would be "intersectional" or "multidimensional," taking into account the complex layers of individual and group identity that help to construct social and legal positions. As CRT developed, scholars began to see "race" itself as the product of other social forces—for example as the product of heteropatriarchy in a post-industrial, post-colonial, capitalist society—or, as in the United States, in a Euro-American heteropatriarchy.[1]

These three oppositional stances—an insistence on progressive race consciousness, on systemic analysis of the structures of subordination, and on multi-intersectional or multidimensional critiques of power relations—also are embraced and

advanced by the works collected here. Today, as in earlier times, these tenets and their articulation give to CRT much of its discursive edge and transformative potential. However, subjecting the concept of "race" itself to critical scrutiny—while maintaining political and intellectual commitments to antiracist color-consciousness—has created another set of tensions within which critical race theorists struggle.

During the first decade, one key manifestation of this struggle has been "antiessentialism." The crux of this "problem" can be simply stated: We are all antiessentialists now. For instance, it now has become almost de rigeur for feminists, critical race theorists, and queer theorists to use antiessentialism to argue that the traditional categories of race, class, and sexuality, and the identity warriors within those categories, are defined in ways that exclude or subordinate the voices of the non-privileged, in turn reproducing historic injustices that skew antisubordination analysis and antiracist politics. This antiessentialist critique began as the product of a leftist commitment to antisubordination crossed with postmodern, poststructuralist, and post-colonial analysis,[2] but the antiessentialist bandwagon now prominently includes individuals on the political right. In a supremely ironic co-optation, conservatives have learned to argue that right-leaning non-whites are victims of essentialists on the left who equate a "voice of color" with progressive politics.

For example, conservatives could—and did—support Clarence Thomas's nomination to the Supreme Court for antiessentialist reasons. His supporters claimed that Thomas's black identity could be used to de-essentialize the political image of black people, and argued that Thomas's opponents had an essentialist agenda in assuming that any "true" black justice would be liberal, much less progressive. Using antiessentialist arguments, conservatives and backlashers also fiercely continue to contest the principle that racial "diversity" in higher education should be treated as a kind of proxy for diversity of viewpoints and experiences, taking exception to any correlation of color to social experience and, hence, to social understanding, viewpoint, or conscience. In this colorblind scheme, racial–ethnic diversity can mean nothing because race cannot be essentialized—that is, used as a rough barometer of experience and, perhaps, outlook. To believe that any "voice of color" can or does exist is, in this reactive view, the rankest essentialism.[3] As these examples indicate, it now has become possible to interject an antiessentialist argument in just about any setting. Yet it remains hard to be clear about what this means, or should mean, as a matter of principle because "antiessentialism" is not one concept but many.[4]

Indeed, "antiessentialism" has become a kind of theoretical *Rashomon*, meaning different things to everyone and often different things to individuals at the same time. This multiplicity of meanings sometimes has created an appearance of consensus that masks actual disagreement, and can inhibit clarity of critical thought and the substantive exchange of ideas or priorities. At other points, this *Rashomon* effect simply means that antiessentialism has, or may, become a convenient club with which anyone can be beaten over the head. Not only has it become a mainstream means of bashing progressive theories and politics generally, but it can also sow confusion, uncertainty, and hesitation within critical race discourse about foundational commitments to identity-conscious analysis. Antiessentialism can be, and perhaps has become, a way of not only co-opting CRT externally but also of distracting us internally from the bottom line: antisubordinationist social transformation.

The struggle over antiessentialism underscores CRT's need for a well-grounded and capacious theory of subordination. If antiessentialism has no necessary political implications—or limits—then it is theories of subordination that must do the work of locating and combating injustice. At the same time, all struggles based on identity must acknowledge that identities always are deeply contested, even as they also are socially constructed. The trick is to forge a potent theory *and* praxis through a critical and self-critical melding of identity-conscious analysis, antiessentialist politics, and antisubordination principles.

The chapters in this volume both reflect CRT's continuing critique of structural racism and colorblind individualism and mark new theoretical forays into identity, antiessentialism, and subordination, which ideally will help further to pluralize and globalize CRT and enhance its law and policymaking impact. This collection of original writings brings together a range of critical race "generations" in one body of work through a careful blending of varied contributions by established critical race scholars and up-and-coming younger scholars. It represents a conscious effort to assemble a rich balance of topics, identities and methodologies that fairly represents the state, and likely trajectories, of critical race theorizing as the first decade gives way to the second. Toward this end, the volume is divided into three major sections that engage and link CRT's past, present, and future: "Histories," "Crossroads," and "Directions."

For a small band of scholars whose ideas are set out in multisyllabic words and who travel with armies of footnotes, CRT has had, as noted at the outset, an extraordinary impact on popular as well as on legal discourse. Yet most of the media attention given CRT has been negative, as Kimberlé Crenshaw's contribution to this volume notes. In part, CRT has hit a nerve because of the way it has confronted and rejected the central myths of American legal culture and race relations. Critical race theorists demand not only simple legal reform but also actual social transformation; the prize has become social, economic, and political equity, not formal equality.

In part, however, CRT has inspired such intemperate public reaction because of who critical race theorists were and are. As Crenshaw explains, the architects of CRT were and are a new breed in the legal academy: young faculty, mostly African American, Asian American, and Latino/a with progressive politics, who were and are appalled and angry at the racial backlash politics of the century's twilight and who remain ready, able, and willing to challenge the sweep of retrenchment throughout the nation. This new breed has not only challenged the structural status quo of law and society, but of necessity also has changed the monochromatic complexion and cozy arrangements of law schools from coast to coast. Thus, CRT's challenge to historic arrangements, liberal curatives, and backlash politics has addressed not only the practices of far-away courts and mighty corporations but also the very make-up of our own profession.

Hitting closest to home, CRT challenges not only the premises and practices that dispense power throughout society but also those that disempower people of color in law school and in law practice—including, specifically, the premises and practices that structure the legal professorate of the United States. These challenges not only have implicated complacent understandings of "standards" and "scholarship"; they have also disturbed structurally racist approaches to appointments and admissions criteria, to teaching and pedagogy, and to curricular reform and updating. In this sense, critical race theorists not only have theorized and critiqued the dynamics and effects of white privilege. We have also practiced in the workplace the insights and imperatives that

our first decade of work collectively has yielded. In this first decade, *applied* CRT oftentimes has amounted to hand-to-hand combat in and for the corridors of academic power in the United States.

As the practitioners of CRT increase in number, in ethnic, gender, and sexual diversity, and as they continue to speak their perceived heresies in a "voice of color," they—we—increasingly are likely to be regarded as a threat by the traditional guardians of economic and social power, both within and beyond the legal professions. Not surprisingly, this volume reflects this larger and ongoing public struggle over knowledge—its production and its dissemination. This book, then, is a testament to the battles waged, both won and lost, in the decade-long struggle to establish, through critical legal scholarship, a race-conscious structural prescription for antiracist policy and social transformation from an explicitly non-white perspective.

Despite the doubts, sneers, and attacks, CRT has not only survived but is also flourishing as it enters its second decade. Critical race feminists, critical race queers, and Latino/a critical theorists (LatCrits) have added sexual oppression, transnationality, culture, language, immigration, and social status to our original understanding of racism and class stratification as central to racial injustice. While foregrounding a race-conscious-identity perspective, these diverse outsider scholars continue to deepen and broaden CRT's substantive reach, excavating doctrinal and social domains that range from "traditional" areas to more recent explorations of religion and spirituality, transitions to democracy, the means of mass communication, and other sociolegal terrain.[5] CRT's battles not only have tested and proved our immediate or short-term capacity for discourse and community; they also have contributed to longer-term resistance struggles and to historic aspirations of liberation.

Institutionally, CRT also has begun to have a profound impact on legal education: law-school courses on race, ethnicity, culture, and the law have risen both in number and in quality during the past ten years or so.[6] Not coincidentally, the professorate of color also has grown substantially during this time, as Sumi Cho and Robert Westley note in their joint chapter. In this way, a new generation of law students—perhaps especially those of color—have been intellectually engaged and newly politicized by their interrogation of critical race theorists' writings, even as those writings proliferate from year to year. Indeed, the work of pioneers such as Patricia Williams and Derrick Bell increasingly is being read by students as undergraduates, before they reach the law schools. And as Julie Su and Eric Yamamoto suggest, legal practice itself may be on the brink of profound changes as CRT's insights reach into the practicing bar. At the same time, CRT is crossing both national and disciplinary boundaries, as scholars from other disciplines and countries begin more and more actively to engage our accumulated record. The chapters in this book thus display both the enduring utility of CRT's earliest interventions and the movement's remarkable progress and present-day vitality.

But these chapters also point to the work that remains to be done. These chapters remind us not only of hard-won gains but also of their constant fragility—especially in times of culture war and backlash lawmaking. These chapters not only contain insight and inspiration. They also provide a salutary reminder of our pending challenges, human limitations, and substantive commitments. They show how far we have come, but they also demand that we ensure, collectively, that the first decade will not be the best. In our view, the works collected here effectively serve as a rebuttal to the determined skeptics of the first decade.

Rather than become distracted or disheartened by the attacks of critical race detractors, this book shows that generations of scholars and activists have kept busy advancing CRT's original agenda and extending its antisubordination reach and insights. By featuring the previously unpublished work of newer scholars and activists, as well as key contributions from "first-generation" authors, this book helps to consolidate CRT's vigor and status in critical legal theory while providing a new teaching resource that allows faculty around the country—and beyond—to share these exciting developments directly and in a timely way with today's students, whether in law or in other disciplines. To capture this remarkable sense of progress, we have sought to craft a collection of essays and other contributions that both showcases and contextualizes the remarkable expansion and evolution of CRT during its first decade. With this volume, we aim to both share and celebrate the past and present of this vibrant jurisprudential movement while also anticipating, and seeking to help secure, the future and its challenges.

Notes

1. See Francisco Valdes, "Unpacking Hetero-Patriarchy: Tracing the Conflation of Sex, Gender and Sexual Orientation to Its Origins," *Yale Journal of Law and Humanities* 8 (1996): 161, describing some of the sex/gender and sexual-orientation norms that underlie and animate androsexism and heterosexism to produce the patriarchal form of homophobia—heteropatriarchy—that still prevails in Euro-American societies, including the United States, today. This effort to conceptualize and name the multi-intersectional architecture and operation of subordination represents a lively strain within outsider jurisprudence. See, for example, e. christi cunningham, "The Rise of Identity Politics I: The Myth of the Protected Class in Title VII Disparate Treatment Cases," *University of Connecticut Law Review* 30 (1998): 441, on wholism; Berta E. Hernández-Truyol,

"Building Bridges—Latinas and Latinos at the Crossroads: Realities, Rhetoric and Replacement," *Columbia Human Rights Law Review* 25 (1991): 369, on multidimensionality; Darren Lenard Hutchinson, "Out Yet Unseen: A Racial Critique of Gay and Lesbian Legal Theory and Political Discourse," *Connecticut Law Review* 29 (1997): 561, on multidimensionality; Peter Kwan, "Jeffrey Dahmer and the Cosynthesis of Categories," *Hastings Law Journal* 48 (1997): 1257, on cosynthesis; Francisco Valdes, "Sex and Race in Queer Legal Culture: Ruminations on Identities and Inter-Connectivities," *Southern California Review of Law and Women's Studies* 5 (1995): 25, on interconnectivity.

2. See generally Angela P. Harris, "Foreword—The Jurisprudence of Reconstruction," *California Law Review* 82 (1994): 741, introducing the first symposium devoted specifically to CRT in an American law review.

3. Whether a "voice of color" exists has been made controversial by the reactions to CRT's early interventions in legal scholarship. See, for example, Randall L. Kennedy, "Racial Critiques of Legal Academia," *Harvard Law Review* 102 (1989): 17456; Colloquy, "Responses to Randall Kennedy's Racial Critiques of Legal Academia," *Harvard Law Review* 103 (1990): 1884. See also Jerome McCristal Culp, Jr., "Autobiography and Legal Scholarship: Finding the Me in the Legal Academy," *Virginia Law Review* 77 (1991): 539; Alex M. Johnson, Jr., "Defending the Use of Narrative and Giving Content to the Voice of Color: Rejecting the Imposition of Process Theory in Legal Scholarship," *Iowa Law Review* 79 (1994): 803.

4. See Katherine T. Bartlett and Angela P. Harris, *Gender and Law: Theory, Doctrine, Commentary* (New York: Aspen Press, 1998): 1007-9.

5. One reflection of this diversity can be found in the myriad approaches taken to the capitalization of words such as "black" and "white" in this volume. We have retained the authors' original capitalization in deference to the many theories of antiracist rhetoric that these practices represent.

6. The gains, though impressive, are limited. For a current study focused on Latina/o-oriented law courses, see Francisco Valdes, "Barely at the Margins: Looking for Latinas/os in the Law School Curriculum—A Survey with LatCritical Commentary," *University of Oregon Law Review* 80 (2001) (forthcoming).

PART I

Histories

CHAPTER ONE

The First Decade: Critical Reflections, or "A Foot in the Closing Door"

Kimberlé Williams Crenshaw

IN THE INTRODUCTION to *Critical Race Theory: The Key Documents That Formed the Movement*,[1] Gary Peller, Neil Gotanda, Kendall Thomas, and I framed the development of Critical Race Theory as a dialectical engagement with liberal race discourse and with critical legal studies. We described this engagement as constituting a distinctively progressive intervention within liberal race theory and a race intervention within CLS. As neat as this sounds, it took almost a decade for these interventions to be fleshed out fully. Reflecting on the past ten years of CRT, this essay explores the course of these interventions from the personal perspective of an organizer and early participant of CRT. Looking forward, I offer some speculative and aspirational views about our future.

It should be noted at the outset that this dialectical engagement occurred not in the abstract but in a context shaped by specific institutional struggles over concrete issues that were set in motion by certain individuals. While the broad ideological trajectory of CRT was set forth in the introduction to *Key Documents*, here I amplify that analysis by setting forth more of a social narrative of CRT's origins: a series of interactions, events, personal relationships, and institutional engagements that prefaced a conscious recognition of CRT. Some of these interactions were undertaken consciously to develop CRT as a movement; others were only later revealed to have contributed significantly to the formation of CRT as a movement.

Though aimed at setting forth a social narrative of CRT's first iterations, this account is inherently a personal narrative that reflects the multiple positions from which I have related historically to the events I tell. From the vantage point of a student, a young professor, an organizer, and now a first-generation participant of a multigenerational project, I recall events that not only inspired CRT's formation but that also shaped me. It thus is a personal narrative in the sense that the author and narrative tell each other. No doubt many of the events I discuss here are especially memorable because they shaped my perspectives about a number of things, including the teaching profession, institutional politics, organizing and leadership—particularly its gender and race dimensions—the media, and, of course, the functional dynamics of race in post–civil-rights society.

Consequently, there are as many different points of departure in the narrative of early CRT as there are people associated with it. In this account, the contributions of one scholar stand out, a scholar whose academic insurgency lit the path toward Critical Race Theory and one to whom we owe an enormous intellectual debt: Derrick Bell.

Derrick Bell: From "Race, Racism, and American Law" to the "Alternative Course"

Bell was at the center of the germination of CRT in at least two important ways. Institutionally, it was his (first) departure from Harvard Law School (HLS) in 1981 that prompted a group of students to struggle with the dean over the curricular marginalization of race. As students of the post-integration generation, many of us were close enough to an activist tradition to question certain institutional arrangements—specifically, the dearth of minority law professors and the relative complacency of those who were convinced that this problem lay outside the discourse of desegregation and antidiscrimination. As the Civil Rights Movement segued into various liberationist movements, students and young activists were confronting the reality that formal segregation was not the only mechanism through which racial power would find expression in American institutions. These realities were readily apparent in the hallowed halls of HLS, where many of us found ourselves in the midst of a struggle over the curricular and personnel consequences of Bell's departure. We understood that Bell's

departure was in part a consequence of his long and only partly successful struggle with the law school on issues relating to the recruitment of professors of color. In the wake of his departure, the school failed to put in place any plans to have Bell's courses taught. In our view, not only should Bell's courses be taught, but this curricular vacuum provided the school with an important opportunity to desegregate the faculty by hiring a person of color.

The articulated resistance to our demands was enlightening. Not only did our dean question the value that a course such as "Constitutional Law and Minority Issues" would add to our curriculum, but he also made the rather startling claim that there were few if any people of color in the country "qualified" to be hired at HLS. This framing of the issue gave many of us involved in that struggle a clear sense about how conceptions such as colorblindness and merit functioned as rhetorics of racial power in presumptively race-neutral institutions. Bell's resignation thus set in motion a chain of events that ultimately would erupt into a controversy surrounding affirmative action that drew national attention. The ensuing struggle would provide fertile ground for the emergence of a critical discourse around contemporary forms of race and social power. The ensuing struggle would also provide the occasion for scholars across the country to gather in the heat of this contest and to develop important intellectual relationships that would strengthen and grow in a series of subsequent connections.

Professor Bell was influential not only in setting the context for contesting the exclusionary practices of elite law schools, but also in helping to establish a scholarly agenda that placed race at the center of intellectual inquiry rather than at the margins of constitutional theory. Bell's bold departure from the discursive conventions of legal scholarship laid down an analytical track that would satisfy our quest for new ways of framing the complex relationships between law and our everyday experiences of race in America. This was no small undertaking.

At a long-overdue tribute to Bell in 1992,[2] I recounted how I had come to understand Bell's stance in academe as analogous to that infamous image of Tommy Smith and John Carlos, two African Americans who raised their black-gloved hands in a Black Power salute while the National Anthem played in their honor at the 1968 Olympics.[3] I was a child at the time, yet I remember vividly the near-hysteria that overtook the country at the very sight of these sleek athletes imposing this powerful symbol of the Black liberation at such an august occasion. Although the labeling of and debate about identity politics was not fully articulated at the time, critics condemned the act as a dangerous and ill-conceived performance of racial grievance that tragically undermined and fractured the presentation of the American subject. That this explicit critique of America was performed on the world stage at precisely the moment that America's pluralistic superiority was to be celebrated struck some as virtually treasonous. To critics, this reckless decision to insert racial politics into that pristine patriotic moment had embarrassed the country in front of the world. For this act, Smith and Carlos were certain to be punished.

There was a lot that I didn't understand about race at the time, but I certainly knew from the angry reports at the time that Smith and Carlos were in serious trouble for performing something Black in front of the world.[4] In explaining to me why so many people seemed to be so angry, my parents likened such reactions to how they themselves would respond if I had decided to act out in church. (Interestingly enough, my mother's term for such misbehavior was "performing in public," and the punishment for such transgressions was severe.)

Given my family's own rules about acting outside the family's approved public script, it struck me that, unlike many Americans, my family was not at all mad at Smith and Carlos. My brother, a Panther wanna-be (actually, I'd really have to say that Panther politics were shared by my mom, as well), said "Right on!" when he saw the replay of the raised-fist salute. My mother said something about the fate of Jesse Owens, an earlier "colored" Olympian who apparently had done what he was supposed to do at Hitler's Olympics—win—and in return was rewarded with the opportunity to race against horses following his heroic homecoming. My father, impressed by the courage of Carlos and Smith, talked about how everything was going to "hit the fan" as a result of that raised-fist salute. "They're tellin' it like it is," they all agreed with pride.

Maybe that vivid memory was why I immediately resonated with Bell's text *Race, Racism and American Law*[5] when first I opened the pages to find that sketch of Smith and Carlos. It was 1981, and I was one of many students who had chosen Harvard because the renowned Derrick Bell was there, only to be disappointed to find that he had departed a few months earlier. I bought the book nonetheless, eager to see whether the pages of his text filled in the gaps between what our very expensive education offered and what many of us felt we needed to know.

From the very first chapter it was apparent that Bell's approach diverged from standard fare in several important respects. Traditional scholarship on race was at this point firmly grounded in the liberal individual-rights model. The objective was to get these second-class citizens some rights, but the efforts to secure these rights had to be reconciled with other important interests, such as federalism, the free-market economy, institutional stability, vested expectations, and the like. Anticipating a conservative counter-critique, early scholarship around race sought to legitimize a certain amount of judicial "activism" in the face of concerns about judicial overreaching, social engineering, political agenda setting, and recommitting the interventionist errors of *Lochner*.[6]

Bell's approach diverged from this conventional orientation in at least two important ways. First, for Bell, the question was not how to justify judicial interventions on behalf of the interests of racial equality against independent, pre-existing interests. These interests themselves often functioned as repositories of racial subordination. Nor, in his view, should success in achieving constitutional protection be measured solely in terms of individual rights. The point was to understand how laws contributed to the systemic disempowerment of African Americans more broadly. Moreover, Bell understood that the measure of civil-rights law is its concrete effectiveness in helping to contest the actual conditions of racial domination. Bell, therefore, was a realist in that he looked at legal rules in terms of their function in a racial world; he was a Crit in that he understood the indeterminate and frequently contradictory character of law.[7] Bell was thus not only a racial realist but an early critical race theorist.

No one, of course, was using the "Critical Race Theory" label at the time—it would be years before that term would be coined. But it was clear that Bell marched to a different beat, and a lot of us wanted more exposure to that rhythm through a course that the school was prepared to let slip into obscurity. We students felt that it was unfortunate that Professor Bell had left HLS, but we did not understand why his course had been dropped from the curriculum and why no plans were in the offing to use this curricular need as an opportunity to recruit

minority professors. Pressing the matter against an initially uninterested administration, nearly 500 students signed a petition urging HLS to reinstate "Constitutional Law and Minority Issues" and to hire tenure-track professors to teach this and other courses addressing minority issues. At a follow-up meeting to underscore our concerns, Dean Vorenberg asked a startled student delegation whether we wouldn't prefer "an excellent white teacher" to a "mediocre black one." To emphasize his point, the dean contrasted a leading white civil-rights lawyer with a nameless mass of unqualified minorities. This stunning invocation of one of the principle justifications for the dearth of minority professors set the terms for the protracted contest over affirmative action that would eventually spill over into the national arena.

Although the dean's inartful articulation of the "pool problem" was more than enough to make the meeting significant, the dean also articulated a more subtle challenge to our demands that would eventually generate a powerful response. What was it, he queried, that was unique about a specific course on constitutional law and minority issues that required such a specific course? Why couldn't we students distill what we wanted from existing courses—say, Constitutional Law—in conjunction with a legal-aid placement? We knew we lacked the language to explain what was unique and important about such a course. We also knew that if burden remained on students to articulate what we *would* learn in a course that had not yet been offered, the school was poised to win by default.

The Black Law Student Association (BLSA) responded to the pool problem by generating a list of more than thirty minority professors around the country whom it urged HLS to consider as candidates to teach the course. Yet at year's end, the course remained unstaffed. In the midst of growing tension about HLS's apparent reluctance to engage any of the available minority law professors to teach the course, the school announced that ten white male professors had been hired. This announcement served to sharpen the conflict and broaden the coalition of students demanding affirmative action, but it was HLS's next move that tipped agitation into active protest. In response to students' demands for the course "Constitutional Law and Minority Issues," the school offered a three-week mini-course on civil-rights litigation, an inadequate response on numerous fronts. First, we wanted a full-semester course—something that would constitute a sustained treatment of race throughout the entire term. Second, we wanted a course with a broader scope than one that focused on civil-rights practice as such. We understood that the course being offered was a review of remediation structures. Although we know that remediation was important, we wanted to ground our studies in a thorough understanding of how law constituted the problem of race in the first place. At this time, we were encountering heavy silence about race throughout the curriculum, even though we knew that it lay just beneath the surface of many of our courses.

Finally, we wanted the school to use the course opening as a target of opportunity to recruit a full-time minority law professor. Harvard certainly was behind the eight-ball in terms of integrating its faculty: At the time, there was one tenured and one untenured faculty of color among HLS's seventy-plus professors. Thus, the crux of the difficulty between we students and the administration was that we saw racial experience as a "plus" factor, whereas conventional and widely held opinion dictated that such considerations be rejected as discriminatory and backward. Nevertheless, we remained convinced that we needed more professors of color at Harvard, not simply

because of the superficial "color" they would bring to the halls, but because we valued the varying perspectives on law that would be brought into the classroom by those who have lived lives as non-white in American legal culture.

Clearly, other criteria mattered as well, but it was obvious to us that traditional criteria did not begin to value a range of experiences that we thought were qualifying while the administration did not. To the considerable extent that the school's down-to-the-wire decision to offer a mini-course taught by two visiting civil-rights lawyers was grounded in the assertion that there were no qualified people of color to be hired by HLS to teach race-related courses, we felt it was imperative to demonstrate our deep rejection both of that logic. But our student boycott was neither a rejection of the importance of studying civil-rights practice nor a rejection of the well-respected men who were coming to teach it. Rather, it was a rejection of the mini-course as a completely inadequate response to our pedagogical demands and of the institutional rhetoric through which our demands were distorted and ultimately dismissed.

Necessity is the mother of all invention, and so it was with the dean's refusal to have the course taught. The Third World Coalition decided to organize an "Alternative Course."[8] The coalition was made up of representatives of all the student-of-color organizations. We worked with the support of other students groups as well. We pooled our resources and raised money from other sources to invite academics of color to come to Harvard to teach a chapter out of Bell's book. We saw our efforts not only as an attempt to create for ourselves the educational experience the school had denied us, but also as an opportunity to provide a showcase of intellectual talent that effectively would counter the dean's claim that the pool of qualified scholars of color was prohibitively shallow. Among the scholars who answered our request to participate were several who would become central figures in CRT: Chuck Lawrence, Richard Delgado, Linda Greene, Denise Carty-Bennia, and Neil Gotanda. Other participants in the course who were similarly engaged in a critical project were John Brittain, W. Haywood Burns, Robert Coulter, Harold MacDougall, and Ralph Smith. There were students, too, who would later contribute to the development of a new intellectual moment, including Mari Matsuda and myself. CLS faculty members at Harvard contributed to the effort as well by attending lectures and by giving students independent-study credit for papers written in conjunction with the course.

With a registered enrollment of more than two hundred students and the participation of a dozen faculty throughout the country, the Alternative Course was a success. It would also be a gift to the future that keeps on giving. It served as an important precursor to CRT having brought legal scholars and students together from across the country to address race from a self-consciously critical perspective. The Alternative Course, and the institutional struggle that created it, produced a critical mass of people of color who were intellectually and politically connected to one another and to a particular transformative moment. This critical mass of academics would now have in common an institutional *text* from which to decipher the institutional rhetorics of racial exclusion, and a collective engagement with an alternative *textbook* that provided a sustained counter-critique to prevailing conceptions of equality. Of course, at the time we did not fully appreciate the opportunity that the law school had given us to ground a future movement. To be sure, we were sorely disappointed by Harvard's reaction to our demands. Yet in terms of future dividends, the school's rejection may

have been the best thing to have happened to us. Indeed, it could be that CRT was conceived in the very moment we were challenged to articulate what was compelling and unique about an inquiry focused on the relationship between race and law.

Of course, the Alternative Course was just an embryonic consequence of our determination to exercise political will against institutional resistance; its viability as a sustained enterprise was scarcely imaginable at the time. Yet the intellectual muscle many of us gained from being forced to create a meaningful dialogue about race and law in the teeth of institutional resistance was apparent even then, and it has served us well since. We gained proficiency in negotiating the institutional politics of race, including the ability to nurture cross-racial coalitions. We learned to decipher the institutional language through which racially subordinating values and preferences would be encoded, whether intentional or not. We learned to anticipate gross distortions of our viewpoints through the sometimes vicious attacks we received from the media, especially from liberal spokespeople.[9] More important, we each found support in our rejection of discursive conventions that typically forced us to think and talk about racial injustice in ways that distanced us from our own experiences.[10]

That there were others—dozens of others—who believed one could think meaningfully and legitimately as a legal "scholar" while remaining committed to progressive racial transformation gave us the liberty to think creatively and to write boldly. Perhaps as a consequence of this inception, CRT has been able to eschew and transcend racial convention. For many of us who later became critical race theorists, the Alternative Course made possible a sustained interaction with one another while foregrounding a text and an interpretive framework on civil-rights law that was as different from the norm in legal education as was Smith and Carlos's symbolic salute at the 1968 Olympics.

Although we scattered after the course, the momentum continued. Some participants in the Alternative Course—including its instructors, organizers, students, and sponsors—would come together in various venues over the next few years, many at CLS conferences and summer camps. Students at Stanford, Berkeley, Columbia, and other law schools took up the demands to desegregate the faculty and curriculum, some drawing inspiration from the events at Harvard.[11] Lawrence, Gotanda, Delgado, and others continued to expand the parameters of race scholarship and, by so doing, opened the terrain to subsequent scholars, some of whom included students exposed to these openings through these very desegregation struggles. Mari Matsuda, for example, returned to Hawaii to become the first Asian American woman to teach at the University of Hawaii Law School and there began to shape a pathbreaking career in legal education. Several other participants in the course wound up in legal education, including the late Muhammad Kenyatta (Buffalo), Tony Thompson (New York University), George Bisharat (Hastings), Ibrahim Gassama (Oregon), Glenn Morris (University of Colorado), and F. Burnette Carter (George Washington University).

For me, the Alternative Course confirmed that there was an answer to the question the dean had put before us: There was indeed substantive content and pedagogical value to be derived from a focused study of the relationship between race and law. Neither could be appreciated by any course on constitutional law, any placement with legal aid, or even a three-week seminar on civil-rights litigation. This much was clear. What wasn't clear, however, was the sometimes contentious relationship between the emerging perspectives of scholars of color and those of our progressive allies in CLS. The limita-

tions of traditional liberal discourses on race that we encountered at Harvard had firmly convinced me that we weren't fish, but it also seemed to me from some of the emerging rhetoric on race within CLS that perhaps we weren't fowl, either. I left Harvard and headed for the University of Wisconsin—some would say the "official" birthplace of CLS—with a goal of thinking more about this double marginality.

The CLS Conferences of the Mid-1980s

The events described in the previous section constituted one dialectical engagement: the critical intervention in conventional institutional rhetorics of race. CRT, however, also reflects a simultaneous encounter of people of color with CLS. Since the inception of CLS, a few people of color have always been present to varying degrees. Some have maintained a sustained presence. Neil Gotanda, for example, participated in the founding meeting of CLS at Madison, Wisconsin, in 1977. Others cycled through at various points, attending meetings and retreats during some of the more dynamic moments of CLS's early formation. Some were professors, such as Regina Austin, Denise Carty-Bennia, Chuck Lawrence, Gerry Spann, Patricia Williams, Linda Greene, and Gerald Torres. Others first visited CLS as students, including Mari Matsuda, Stephanie Phillips, Teri Miller, and me. Regardless of our status as professor or student, newcomer or veteran, at each meeting or retreat we usually found ourselves off in someone's room, engaged in animated discussion about the racial politics of CLS. These "off-stage" meetings gave us an important opportunity to talk about what attracted us to CLS and what held us at bay.

Our meetings had a furtive quality about them, crowded as we were in those little hotel rooms like revelers at a Depression-era speakeasy. Yet for some of us, those all-too-quick conversations were the highlight of whatever conference we were attending, and we began to look forward to them. These adjuvant meetings created substantive connections that helped to ground our gradual emergence as a loosely organized caucus in CLS. A pivotal event during this time that signaled the beginning of the "race turn" in CLS occurred at the 1985 CLS conference organized by the feminist wing of CLS, more popularly known as the Fem-Crits. Prompted by Regina Austin's call to women of color to discuss how we might want to participate in the conference, several of us began discussing how to facilitate a discussion about race at this FemCrit conference. We ultimately decided to organize a workshop on racism in which the conference attendees could be divided into breakout groups to facilitate greater discussion. There, participants would be invited to turn CLS's critical lens inward.

The provocative question that launched the workshop—"What is it about the whiteness of CLS that keeps people of color at bay?"—foreshadowed the eventual recognition that interrogating whiteness is an important dimension of any critical discourse on race. Unfortunately, this cutting-edge intervention was not well received, particularly by some of the white male heavies of CLS. Amid the vocal resistance was the charge that we were "mau-mauing" CLS and that the framework we had introduced certainly would tear the organization apart.[12]

As the dust was settling from the 1985 conference, plans were under way to shift the CLS stage to California. A contingent from the UCLA, USC, and Loyola law schools began planning the 1987 conference, with the goal of focusing on race. By 1986, I was also headed west to join the faculty at UCLA. There, I joined the ongoing dialogue about the focus of the upcoming conference.

Although this 1987 conference promised to move the discussion of race to the center of CLS, a number of factors tempered the enthusiasm of many people of color associated with CLS. Many harbored serious reservations about the value of such a conference in light of the maelstrom prompted by the 1985 race workshop. Those of us who had experienced such resistance to the internal dialogue about race in CLS were concerned that the upcoming conference would sidestep the more controversial discourse and focus instead on developing a CLS critique of race in legal institutions "out there." Neil Gotanda, for example, had participated in the initial discussions of the conference-planning committee and perceived early on reluctance to build on the previous workshop and other work related to race and racism that already had occurred within.[13] Indeed, the initial orientation of the conference was to examine race within legal institutions and even more broadly—race within the larger society. The goal of examining race within CLS was noticeably absent as a conference objective.

Deep ambivalence about the promise of further engagement with CLS was fueled by other high-profile events that had heightened the frustration level among people of color associated with CLS. A stunning controversy involving Derrick Bell's visit at Stanford Law School deepened the recognition among many minority scholars that we would remain vulnerable to patterns of unconscious racism from students and colleagues, despite our achievements in the profession. In short, the administration at Stanford, heeding complaints of white students unhappy with Professor Bell's approach to constitutional law, arranged a series of supplemental lectures to be given by other faculty members. Bell was invited to participate as well, but the fuller story behind the creation of the supplemental lectures was revealed only when BLSA students prepared a written statement of protest. Minority law professors across the country were aghast that Stanford would subject a pathbreaking scholar such as Bell to this type of disrespectful treatment. Those of us closer to CLS were particularly disappointed that such a debacle would happen at Stanford, thought to be a CLS stronghold, with a dean and prominent faculty members who long had been associated with CLS.

In struggling to understand how students' complaints against Bell possibly could have persuaded the administration to pursue such an insulting, institutionally embarrassing strategy, there were, of course, the obvious possibilities that many professors of color report confronting on a daily basis. An additional factor was found in the possibility that there was sympathy for at least one allegation apparently made by students—that Bell's approach to constitutional law, grounded as it is in the breathtaking contradiction between the constitutional rhetoric of freedom and the reality of slavery, illegitimately foregrounded race. This inference dovetailed with criticisms that were beginning to emerge from Stanford quarters in the form of a counter-critique to our early work, characterizing it as essentialist. Whether intended or not, in that critique some of us heard a crude characterization of our work as theoretically unsophisticated and politically backward.

If these events were not enough to cloud the horizon, yet another piece of evidence emerged to suggest that behind CLS's hip irreverence lurked an element of racial condescension. In the CLS newsletter, *The Lizard,* an account of a conference in Bremen, West Germany, included a remark that deployed a racial stereotype of Mexicans.[14] The remark—"Don't you realize that telling a German he has no theory is like telling a Mexican he has no gun?"—was apparently thrown in to add "color" to the conference report. As Jose Bracamonte, Richard Del-

gado, and Gerald Torres would later write, what was amazing about the inclusion of the remark was that no one in the editorial process apparently deemed it to be inappropriate for publication.

All of this made the reactions of those resistant to the internal racial gaze in CLS even more indefensible: Racial power was exerting itself within CLS, just as it had in other legal institutions. The question remained whether anything could be gained by participating fully in the conference and contesting the terms of the group's racial discourse.

Troubled by these events, a small group of us teleconferenced to discuss "how those of us who struggled through the racism workshop (in 1995) [might] share that experience with the others . . . and what, if anything, that experience suggest[ed] regarding our participation in the upcoming conference."[15] We had before us textbook illustrations on how to "read" race, and the spirit of contestation was part of our own civil-rights history as well as that of CLS. Coming on the heels of the annual meeting of the American Association of Law Schools (AALS), the 1987 conference also presented us with an excellent opportunity to gather together scholars of color to talk about race scholarship and politics not only within CLS but also in the nation's law schools more generally. The 1987 CLS conference in Los Angeles indeed provided us with a crucial staging ground to push our presence and projects further.

The final format of the 1987 conference reflected a negotiation among various objectives, providing us with the opportunity to meet as a caucus, to air and respond to the minority critique of CLS, and to discuss and develop critical approaches to articulating race within substantive legal topics. The 1987 conference became the site of the first formal meeting of the minority caucus within CLS, which necessitated, in turn, an all-white caucus held concurrently. Whiteness was again on the agenda, but this time the discussion would not be facilitated by us.

Dozens of professors of color attended the minority caucus, most of them eager to discuss the climate, our scholarship, and the need to create a more sustained interaction. Cornel West, bell hooks, and Rodolfo Acuña were invited as plenary speakers to provide an interdisciplinary perspective on race. Some of us hoped that our invited guests would help grease the wheels of the "race turn" in CLS by effectively speaking to the various constituencies within CLS, challenging pockets of resistance to race-conscious scholarship in the very language that was sometimes used against us. But we didn't leave all the heavy lifting to our guests.

In a panel entitled "The Minority Critique of CLS Scholarship (and Silence) on Race," Denise Carty-Bennia, Harlon Dalton, Richard Delgado, Mari Matsuda, Gerald Torres, and Pat Williams spoke out from the inside on the racial politics of CLS. Their comments focused on the racially specific culture of CLS, the critique of rights, and on the silencing of voice of color in the legal academy more broadly. Attendees at that conference found the session memorable for any number of reasons, not the least of which was the airing of Randall Kennedy's very public challenge to the embryonic movement, a challenge that would find its way onto the pages of the *Harvard Law Review* a few short years later.[16]

Looking back at the "Sounds of Silence" conference crystallizes for me that this 1987 gathering was a watershed moment for CRT. Within the space of a few years, we had progressed from a loose group of colored folk at the margins of CLS to an experienced group of insurgents who occupied center stage at a national CLS conference. Clearly, there were disappointments—there was little resolution to some of the central points of contention between CLS and its

minority critics, and there is reason to believe that some of the negative reaction to the "race turn" continued well into the next decade. Some white male heavies never returned—whether because of the coincidental appeal of other interests or an organizational "tipping" problem remains unclear. What was clear by the end of that conference was that we had exercised some institutional muscle: We had staked out an intellectual project by giving voice to a range of our institutional experiences living in a post-apartheid legal culture.

It was also clear, however, that the anterooms of CLS would no longer be sufficient to build on this momentum. To consolidate this race turn, we would have to find a way to institutionalize ourselves. That opportunity would come the following year.

The Birth of the Critical Race Theory Workshop

In 1988, while on research leave from UCLA, I returned to the University of Wisconsin as a visiting fellow. Stephanie Phillips was also at Wisconsin as a Hastie Fellow, and together we began discussing ways to convene the usual suspects in a manner that went beyond hotel-room caucusing. We were both veterans of CLS summer camps— smallish meetings that drew together a core group of Crits to explore a range of topics— and we thought it might serve as a useful model to facilitate the more sustained intellectual interaction we sought. Richard Delgado was by that time on the Wisconsin faculty, and together we approached David Trubek, director of the Institute of Legal Studies, seeking financial support for a workshop tentatively entitled "New Developments in Race and Legal Theory." The purpose of this workshop was to gather together our motley crew of marginal types—people of color who were attracted to and frustrated by CLS—to a several-day summer camp.

Although there were undoubtedly many objectives to be served by such a retreat, foremost in my mind was determining whether something substantive held the group together, something that constituted a distinctive contribution to the discourse on race and the law. More specifically, I wondered whether it could be said that there was a "there" somewhere in the interstices of conventional civil-rights discourse and conventional critical legal studies. We had launched simultaneous critiques of CLS, on the one hand, and of liberal race theory on the other; in doing so, were we actually setting forth something that could be fashioned into a theory in its own right? Could some common threads be found in our collective work that might be woven together to form an intellectual whole?

It was clear that we were inviting folks to something formative, but the "New Developments" tag that appeared in the initial call for papers didn't fully capture the aim. Somewhere in the process, we made what essentially amounts to a marketing decision: We jettisoned the generic title and sought something more provocative. Stephanie and I, now joined by the summer-camp veterans Neil Gotanda and Teri Miller, wanted to attract a specific audience of other "misfits" who were looking for both a critical space in which race was foregrounded and a race space where critical themes were central. We wanted the conversation to start at a point beyond questioning critical theory, on the one hand, or race on the other. We wanted to play with folks who would not be dissuaded from the association with a leftist project, who were interested in defining and elaborating on the lived reality of race, and who were open to the aspiration of developing theory.

Having participated in the FemCrits' West Coast meetings, I had been thinking about how useful it had been to organize

our work around the framework of "feminist legal theory" rather than the considerably narrower category of "sex-discrimination law." Feminist legal theory laid claim to a broader undertaking than a mere study of rules governing sex discrimination: Contained within the broader feminist concept was the project of unpacking law's relationship to gender. What would be the parallel concept for critical scholars of color seeking to lay claim to the broader study of law's relationship to race? What was to civil rights what feminist legal theory was to sex-discrimination law?

Turning this question over, I began to scribble down words associated with our objectives, identities, and perspectives, drawing arrows and boxes around them to capture various aspects of who "we" were and what we were doing. The list included: progressive/critical, CLS, race, civil rights, racism, law, jurisprudence, theory, doctrine, etc. Mixing them up and throwing them together in various combinations, one combination came together in a way that seemed to capture the possibility we were aiming to create. Sometime toward the end of the interminable winter of 1989, we settled on what seemed to be the most telling marker for this peculiar subject. We would signify the specific political and intellectual location of the project through "critical," the substantive focus through "race," and the desire to develop a coherent account of race and law through the term "theory."

But the work wasn't quite done yet. Was this an independent thing or merely a descriptive or generic term? Should we capitalize it or leave it as two modifiers and a noun? We decided to go for broke. If we were going to give this inchoate thing a name, let it be a proper sign on the intellectual landscape: *Critical Race Theory*. (I had this preoccupation at the time with the politics of proper nouns, having just won a battle with the *Harvard Law Review* about capitalizing

"Black" when used as a racial identifier.)[17] So the name Critical Race Theory, now used as interchangeably for race scholarship as Kleenex is used for tissue, was basically made up, fused together to mark a possibility.

It was far from clear at the time whether the name would stick, and there were discussions at the first workshop about what, if anything, the name actually meant. In fact, participants at the first workshop kicked around several other possibilities, including the idea of calling our project "Reconstruction Theory." It so happened, however, that a new periodical edited by Randall Kennedy was called *Reconstruction*, and concerns about the potential confusion generated by two similarly named projects with very different ideological premises may have contributed to the somewhat greater appeal of the name "Critical Race Theory." In any case, the name stuck. The task remained to define it.

After naming the project, we set out to gather souls to join us in Madison. Aside from the usual suspects, we had no idea who else would be attracted to a "Critical Race Theory" workshop. What exactly was the profile of the scholar who would be interested in our project? We began to generate a list of people whom we had met, read, or heard about—folks whose work was similarly situated at the margins of traditional race scholarship. We wrote letters, solicited recommendations, and cold-called people, often with the awkward inquiry of whether they would like to apply to a workshop that they had never heard of previously. Oddly enough, dozens of people did agree to apply, and on July 8, 1989, the twenty-four participants of the first Critical Race Theory Workshop gathered in Madison, Wisconsin.[18]

The first couple of workshops were designed to get at the question of what constituted CRT, and we structured the program with this goal in mind.[19] Borrowing models derived from both Martha Fineman's "Feminism and Legal Theory" workshops and a CLS–German workshop on critical theory in Bremen, we created a blend of paper writers, presenters, and commentators. Although the production and presentation of written work was, of course, the focal point of our meeting, our sense was that we would benefit more as a potential movement if someone other than the author presented the key themes of each paper and yet another person was responsible for weaving those key themes together with the themes from all of the other papers.

This scheme played out with varying degrees of success. Some common themes did emerge, and we honed them further in the next workshop. Yet we remained fundamentally eclectic in many respects. We eventually achieved some degree of intellectual coherence down the road, but the notion of CRT as a fully unified school of thought remains a fantasy of our critics. Many participants yearned for a space apart from law faculties, conferences and the like where we could explore ideas and express ourselves in ways that were not constrained by the expectations of our colleagues or the established parameters of race discourse in our respective institutions.

The safe-space interests and the intellectual-coherence objectives were occasionally pitted against one another. For example, some disagreement developed in the second workshop over the relationship between resisting racism and resisting patriarchy and homophobia. Some of us felt that patriarchy and homophobia were intertwined in racial power and thus were inseparable from the scope of CRT. Others felt that racial subordination was distinct and should be theorized as such. Some participants framed the issue as a conflict over whether CRT would have a theoretical "line" or whether, as a safe space, it was a big tent open to all comers. Yet others pointed out that, in some respects, the debate was really about competing visions over what was necessary to make CRT a safe space. If CRT resisted acknowledging and theorizing the intersection of racism with patriarchy and heterosexism, could it really be considered a safe space for all members of this diverse group of men and women of varying sexual identities?

One also could recalibrate other debates that were pitched as tension between the call for safe space and the call for substantive content as, in fact, a tension between competing conceptions of substantive content. For example, the organizational goal of "safe space" served as the provisional justification for the initial inclusion of people of color only.[20] One might frame the issue as safe-space values having trumped substantive content: Identity rather than substantive criteria won out as a defining factor in determining participation in the workshop. However, this, too, could be reframed as competing substantive perspectives. Was CRT a product of people of color, or was CRT a product of any scholar engaged in a critical reflection of race? Because I subscribe to the latter proposition, I regard the traditional exclusion of whites from our workshops as an unfortunate development. But, of course, opinions on this and similar issues vary considerably among original and subsequent workshop participants.[21]

While safe space clearly was a value that developed out of the first workshop, we were not bereft of specific themes that captured in some way the group's interest. Critiques of neutrality, objectivity, colorblindness, meritocracy, and formal equality constituted the most common themes that linked our work. Because these critiques were informed in part by critical theory and other intellectual traditions, organizers decided to devote the second workshop to developing a clear theoretical grounding for CRT. Thus, in the next workshop, hosted by

Stephanie Phillips at Buffalo Law School, we shifted to a format that mixed paper presentations with substantive seminars. With the able assistance of Kendall Thomas, who had joined the organizing committee along with Linda Greene and Mari Matsuda, we organized four critical-theory seminars in addition to discussed papers. Topics included "Liberalism and Its Critics," "Post-Structuralism and the Concept of Race," "Race and Political Economy," and "Intellectuals, Race and Power."

With this foundation, CRT was off to a running start. Of course, in the intervening years, the format, focus, and personnel would continue to be debated along with efforts to establish the substantive parameters of the work. Questions about the role of identity and the inclusiveness of the tent remain ripe, particularly in light of the emergence of Asian American Jurisprudence and LatCrit Theory. Yet to be fully fleshed out is the question of how wide the space is between a race-conscious intellectual project informed by experiential particularities and a project grounded in successive turns of identity politics. If the legacy of CRT has in fact crystallized into identity formations, then questions about whether it was so at its inception, or whether it became so at particular moments for particular reasons, remain ripe for discussion. Surely these are vexing questions around which there is ample room for debate. But true to their genealogy, all these contemporary questions bear a striking resemblance to the debates and struggles that shaped the early years of CRT.

This narrative of the early years of CRT would not be complete without a word about our sponsors. Although the development of CRT has been framed as emerging out of the overlapping of various oppositions with liberal race theory and CLS, it is also quite clear that without specific support of individuals within each of those spheres, CRT would not have developed in that time and space. David Trubek, a founding member of CLS, funded the first workshop, despite, as I mentioned earlier, some faculty opposition and some of his own reservations about the minority critique of CLS that was developing at the time.[22] Buffalo Law School, the host of the second annual CRT workshop, also boasted several CLS adherents among its faculty who supported the project. And Jim Jones, a true civil-rights visionary, supported the CRT workshop despite his deep reservations about CLS. I think this type of support suggests that many non-CRT scholars saw CRT as continuous in important ways with their own projects. Perhaps CRT had a different focus and endorsed approaches to solving equality issues that may have made some in the traditional civil-rights community uncomfortable. However, in the broad scheme of things, traditional civil-rights adherents saw CRT as fundamentally "on the same side" as they were.

Critical Race Theory Then and Now: From Birth to Backlash

On the basis of this brief overview, I will note some points of comparison between CRT at its birth and CRT now. I think the overarching point of comparison is the fundamental difference in the historical and institutional context. CRT came into existence in the twilight of what had been a transformative social period. The grassroots movement for civil rights was, by most accounts, a distant memory by the mid-1980s, and although we believed we were in a full-scale retrenchment by that point, we were really just seeing its prologue. Nevertheless, there were still vestiges of the movement (preserved perhaps by the rarefied air of the academy), vestiges of the old insurgency that constituted a loosely defined sensibility about the imperative of social change. Sociologists might describe this in terms of expectations that were still rising throughout the academy and within civil-rights practice. On the books, there were still favorable precedents, cases we might call remnants of Alan Freeman's "victim perspective" that remained good law.[23] Affirmative action was still hotly contested, and most people had not heard yet of Clarence Thomas.

There was also a sense that there was something to a left-liberal reform discourse, something worth struggling for. Students thus fought to expand these vague commitments into specific curricular and hiring objectives: Constitutional scholars such as Charles Lawrence fought to extend the liberal opprobrium toward race-dependent decisions to include unconscious racism; civil-rights lawyers fought to include race-neutral exclusionary practices within the liberal rejection of white supremacy. On the left angle, CLS was alive and vibrant, and many of us struggled to expand its critique of social power and illegitimate social hierarchy to address the social power and illegitimate hierarchy of race as well. In sum, there were live contestations, both within the mainstream and in the margins, that contributed to the generation and incorporation of new ideas.

Today, by contrast, we are in the throes of a powerful, tightly organized, almost evangelical movement. It is well-organized and highly visible, and it boasts a string of impressive victories to call its own. It has friends in high places: the media, Congress, the White House, and the Supreme Court. It has a political strategy, a research agenda, and a grassroots and propaganda campaign that are among the most sophisticated and efficient in today's cyberbolic society. It has no known rival, and its resources seem to be endless. Unfortunately, this movement is not ours.

In fact, to the extent that we are in the picture, it is only as cannon fodder. As a result, the interests we champion have been under attack for some time. We managed to survive the first round of crude "P.C." hysteria, yet the ideas with which we are associated have made us subject to more sophisticated modes of censure. In short, we have been race-baited.

Although it has been in the making for some time, this moment constitutes a significant shift in the intellectual and political terrain. Now, the very effort to expand doctrinal categories or to argue about the broader scope of what constitutes racial discrimination presumptively disqualifies able candidates from holding positions of responsibility, whether in government or elsewhere.[24] The vestiges and remnants of the 1960s grassroots movements, already anachronistic in the 1980s, are now repackaged alternatively as the source of all contemporary social ills or as noble movements for an equality that has already been won. The left is itself demobilized, demoralized, and disorganized.

This moment obviously presents a challenge of a different magnitude for CRT scholars. Our story has always been one of a struggle to survive, but while the earlier struggle was one of coming *into* existence, the question then being whether this motley crew could last long enough to become viable, the question now is whether the movement can survive in the face of a more complex and better-organized counter-resistance. While people once puzzled over whether we were fish or fowl, now they brand us easily; indeed, they can draw on a veritable casebook of racially inflected insults. Moreover, as Patricia Williams has noted, as in the case of the man who is asked whether he still beats his wife, there is no response that doesn't confirm the charge.[25]

Our critics' reconstruction of who we are and what we do is so complete that we can barely recognize ourselves in the mass media. Indeed, if we were to read more about ourselves in the media, we would find out that we are a pretty amazing bunch. We would learn from the *New Republic,* for example, that CRT is part of the the "lunatic fringe" of the academy.[26] (Duncan Kennedy and Catharine MacKinnon will be relieved to know that they are exempted from this exclusive category; they represent the rational fringe.) Richard Delgado might be amused to know that Judge Richard Posner has passed to him the hand of fellowship to the white race, remarking that Delgado,

> claims to be a member of, and a spokesman for, a group that he calls "people of color." The group seems to be more a state of mind than a race. I have met Professor Delgado. He is as pale as I am, has sharply etched features in a long face, speaks unaccented English, and, for all that appears upon casual acquaintance, could be a direct descendant of Ferdinand and Isabella. He lives and teaches, contentedly so far as I know, in an "Enlightenment-based democracy," namely the United States. Delgado's whiteness lends an Evelyn Waugh touch to critical race theory.[27]

Similarly, we would learn from Jeff Rosen, writing also for the *New Republic,* that we apparently have connections in Hollywood—that artists from rappers to movie executives have bowed to our influence.[28] And it will come as a surprise to those of us who took strong positions against the Million Man March and Louis Farrakhan that the logical conclusion of our work "leads to Farrakhan."[29]

Indeed, we would learn from Daniel Farber and Suzanna Sherry that we are anti-Semitic because our support of disparate impact theory and our critique of exclusion from colleges and universities, taken to its logical conclusion, implicitly suggests that the over-representation of Jews in American law schools is the work of a conspiracy.[30] This last item is curious for a number of reasons, not the least of which is that our apparent interest in wresting a greater share of law-school slots from privileged whites is at odds with Neil Lewis's claim that "critical race theory is providing an intellectual foundation for black separateness."[31]

Despite what we may have thought we have written, our critics now inform us that we do not support the Civil Rights Movement, that we believe that nothing is better today than it was thirty years ago, and that we think law is utterly useless as a means of social reform. Puzzlingly, despite all this apparent madness, CRT has enormous influence. Our jurisprudence in law reviews "reigns supreme" (take that, you impressionable student editors!), and even judges have been "taken in" by us. The flurry of bias studies in the court system across the country was actually "prodded by feminist and critical race theorists."[32]

Although we have spent so much time mesmerizing lawyers, deans, producers, students, and judges, surprisingly our newfound influence seems to have done little to soften our rough edges. We are "loud and militant," and we "wage open warfare over appointments and tenure."[33] Although we are a minority, we apparently can kick up quite a fuss in law schools. Indeed, Daniel Farber and Suzanna Sherry are sympathetically presented as anguished members of the great majority of white liberals in legal academe. Our critics, it seems, have adapted racial profiling to the ivory tower. Apparently, these two traditional liberals have been mugged by their "radical colleagues in the ivory tower,"[34] and we intellectual gangbangers are presumptively guilty.

Critical race theorists, we're told, are not only rude; our work is beyond all reason. To readers of the *Toronto Sun*, we represent "the most embarrassing trend in American publishing."[35] We offer no analysis, we just tell stories—bad ones, at that—and we don't do law. Because our movement "has achieved influence and dominance within any num-ber of the country's most prestigious universities," we have to be dealt with severely. We replicate like a virus. Says one authority on problems like us: "Unless you challenge them at their source, you will always be fighting a rear-guard action when their influence spreads into broader American society."[36]

Make no mistake about it: We are in a full-scale race-baiting campaign. It is well organized, and it could be effective if we fail to mine the lessons of Crit-bashing in the 1980s and red-baiting in the 1950s. Indeed, the structure of the assault is virtually identical: The baiters identify some threat to our cherished institutions or way of life, tie it to some "pointy-headed intellectuals," and then claim that ruthless suppression is the only way to be sure the threat has been contained.

Consider the classic baiting technique used by Jeffrey Rosen. Rosen is fully aware that many whites were apoplectic about O. J. Simpson's acquittal. "There's anger there, a sense that something cherished has been lost." Rosen points this anger at CRT. What seems to scare him is that critical race theorists are theorizing relations that many Americans do not want to think about yet must encounter occasionally when they want something very badly and have to engage the sensibilities of people of color to get it. Take, for example, his portrayal of the acquittal of O. J. Simpson. Here Rosen's message goes: If you didn't like the verdict, then you really won't like these CRT folks— they gave members of the jury the idea; the Simpson verdict is nothing but Critical Race Theory *applied*.[37]

Of course, we really are not alone in being targeted in all this hysteria. This reaction has the contours of all other baiting campaigns, including its implicit disciplining of liberals for having allowed us into the legal academy in the first place—evidence of their lack of resolve. It's all of a piece, a new line in an old chorus: "Liberals are soft on communism, soft on crime, soft on Crits, soft on RaceCrits." Ultimately, it may not mat-ter that in some ways we may be in the trenches with liberals as targets of a con-servative assault. First, some liberals have joined the fray, as evidenced by *Beyond All Reason*.[388] And the jury truly is out on the question of whether we can count on our colleagues more broadly for support as the heat turns up. If the institutional reaction to resegregating policies in California, Texas, and Washington is any indication, the road ahead may be bumpy indeed.[39]

Where We've Been, Where We're Going

So what should we critical race theorists do now, facing the second decade? I think we need to take up a war of maneuver against racial entrenchment, on the public and on the private front. As to the public front, I think we need more organized intervention. Patricia Williams and Richard Delgado have responded courageously, yet they can't go this alone.[40] Conventional wisdom about the nature of ideological attack says that there is little we can do—"take the high road; don't give them the satisfaction of a response." I have some sympathy for this view. If we were to respond to all of our detractors, we would probably do little else. But the truth is more complicated than that.

I learned this the hard way from a call I received from a government-service worker in St. Louis. It was somewhat of an apology, actually. The caller had simply assumed from various media reports that CRT truly is the backward, racist, unsophisticated assortment of half-baked scholarship that he had heard about. Luckily, he said as much to someone who knew better and began to read us for himself. I realized while listening to his "discovery" that the days when we could expect people from our very own com-munities to read between the lines of an

attack were long gone. To paraphrase an old saying, "A distortion travels around the world before the truth puts its boots on."

These developments have reminded us that the days when different communities are exposed to fundamentally different information sources are dwindling. To speak to a mass community often means speaking in mass media. We need to determine how to translate our work better, to intervene in ways that help model interventions at the local level, to show people what a difference critical race thinking makes in their own workplaces and communities. And we need to learn how to demand popular space and make good use of it when we get it.

At the local level, back in the academy, I think we have to remember the basic les-sons of indeterminacy and put energy into fighting battles in the trenches of interpre-tation. Unlike some colleagues I respect, I see nothing immoral or amoral about press-ing the malleability of legal interpretation into service to defend affirmative action and other equity policies against assault. For example, the battle over the elimination of "preferences" presumes an agreed-upon baseline from which to measure. But what is a "preference," and what is "discrimina-tion"? There is much work to be done in our own institutions to rethink and chal-lenge this baseline, and fundamentally to rethink how legal education should be dis-tributed. We may have some time to stem the tide, but not much.

Finally, I think the times require a re-engagement with our colleagues. What seems to be lacking among both our liberal colleagues and our Crit colleagues is a spirit of confronting exclusionary policies, a familiarity with our own basic texts, and a contemporary critique of the standard oper-ating procedures in our institutions. In this sense, perhaps we've come full circle. As I place the genesis of CRT in a confrontation within institutions of higher learning over curricular and hiring matters, it seems that the lessons we learned from a course of study focusing on race, racism, and American law continue to resonate throughout a new decade.

Yet these lessons have not penetrated the outer periphery of institutional consciousness within American law schools. We have been afforded pluralistic (tokenistic?) inclusion within the academy, but one wonders whether this, too, will go the way of "diversity" in the face of wholesale external assault. If our colleagues cannot defend a set of programs against competing institutional constraints that pit the edict against "preferences" with the prohibition against "discrimination," do we think they (or we) will fare better when and if the organized cabal that has attempted to discredit us in the media manages to turn up the heat on our own institutions? What can and should we do to recapture our sense of identity, struggle, and empowerment? These are the questions I think we must put to ourselves as we think about the future.

Conclusion: In Search of a Caption

In assessing the first decade of Critical Race Theory I asked myself: If I were to gather it all up into a snapshot, what caption would I inscribe beneath? I thought of several, ranging from the mundane ("A Good Start," "Against All Odds") to the noble ("Keeper of the Flame," "Bridge from the Past"). I settled on one that is far less poignant but descriptively apt: "A Foot in the Closing Door." I truly believe that what separates this period of retrenchment and counter-assault from that which transpired in the nineteenth century is the wealth of resources—institutional, organizational, intellectual, and the like—represented by the people who do Critical Race Theory. We have managed to keep alive a spirit, diffuse

though it may be, that resists all attempts to declare the project of ending white supremacy a done deal.

Now, if I were to gather up all my hopes for our future into a snapshot, what would its caption say? Again, my thoughts ranged from the truly trite ("New and Improved," "Bigger and Better," "Smarter and Wiser") to the buzzword of today's mega-trend ("Critical Race Theory Turns Global!"). In the end, I settled on a retrieval from the past, brought back to the future.

Ten years ago, I wondered: Where do we take our sit-ins when the WHITE ONLY signs come down, when Kresge closes its lunch counters and moves out of town, when power doesn't live where it used to anymore? What happens when the contemporary configuration of power doesn't have an address; when dogs and water hoses are traded in for numbers and tests; when gatekeepers are automated, and exclusion is formulaic; when ideas are red-lined, and people are warehoused? These days, colorblind discourse is the virtual lunch counter, the rationalization for racial power in which few are served and many are denied. Thus, in my fantasy, ten years from now, the caption reads: "Discursive Disobedience: Critical Race Theory Stages a Virtual Sit-in in American Consciousness."

The task ahead is to pull up a seat and stake out our positions in large and small ways, as individuals and as groups, as discrete formations and as broad coalitions. Frederick Douglass said something about the ways of power that holds true even a century after it was first uttered: "If there is no struggle, there is no progress. . . . Power concedes nothing without a demand. It never did, and it never will."[41] In this spirit, and in light of the daunting tasks we face and the remarkable resources we bring to bear, I hope our journey onward in the coming decades is provocative, productive, and proactive.

Notes

Acknowledgments: This essay was delivered as a plenary talk at the 1997 CRT conference in New Haven, Connecticut. I am grateful to the several colleagues who have offered helpful comments and reactions to the various iterations of this narrative, before and after the 1997 conference, including Neil Gotanda, Luke Harris, Duncan Kennedy, Charles Lawrence, Cecil McNab, and Stephanie Phillips. Thanks also to Gulgun Ulger for research assistance; Duncan Alford for reference assistance; and the editors for their enormous, patient support. As always, but especially here, all errors are my own.

1. Kimberlé W. Crenshaw, Neil Gotanda, Gary Peller, and Kendall Thomas, eds., *Critical Race Theory: The Key Writings That Formed the Movement* (New York: New Press, 1995).

2. Organized by Charles Ogletree, the tribute to Bell drew numerous colleagues and former students to Harvard. For a published tribute to Bell, see Charles R. Lawrence III, "Doing the 'James Brown' at Harvard: Professor Derrick Bell as Liberationist Teacher," *Harvard Blackletter Journal* 8 (1991): 263.

3. See generally Mark Conrad, "Major Legal Events of the Century: 1961-1972," *New York Law Journal* (August 1999): 5, describing the events and their aftermath; Howard Manly, "A Powerful, Two-Fisted Documentary," *The Globe* (Boston), August 8, 1999, D4, introducing a documentary made about Torres and Smith.

4. See generally Paul Gallaway, "Whose Olympics?" *Chicago Tribune*, July 16, 1996, 1, discussing the interaction between the Olympic Games and politics; Larry Platt, "They Bad," *New York Times Magazine*, November 14, 1999, sec. 6, 114, discussing the making over of Black athletes for white America.

5. Derrick A. Bell, Jr., *Race, Racism and American Law*, 2nd ed. (Gaithersburg, Md.: Aspen Publishers, 1980).

6. See, for example, Paul Brest, "The Supreme Court, 1975 Term—Foreword: In Defense of the Antidiscrimination Principle," *Harvard Law Review* 90 (1976): 1; John Hart Ely, *Democracy and Distrust* (Cambridge, Mass.: Harvard University Press, 1980); Jesse H. Choper, "Thoughts on State Action: The 'Government Function' and 'Power Theory' Approaches," *Washington University Law Quarterly* (1979): 757. For a critique of the assertion that judicial intervention on behalf of racially subordinated groups constitutes a revisiting of Lochner's sins, see Gary Peller, "Neutral Principles in the 1950s," *University of Michigan Journal of Law Reform* 21 (1988): 561; see also Cass R. Sunstein, "Lochner's Legacy," *Columbia Law Journal* 87 (1987): 873-4 ("The received wisdom is that Lochner was wrong because it involved 'judicial activism': an illegitimate intrusion by the courts into a realm properly reserved to the political branches of government. This view has spawned an enormous literature and takes various forms"). For an excellent critique of liberal race jurisprudence, see Alan David Freeman, "Legitimizing Racial Discrimination Through Antidiscrimination Law: A Critical Review of Supreme Court Doctrine," *Minnesota Law Review* 62 (1978): 1049, reprinted in Crenshaw et al., *Key Writings*, 29. Among the more provocative critiques of traditional liberal scholarship is Richard Delgado, "The Imperial Scholar: Reflection on a Review of Civil Rights Literature," *University of Pennsylvania Law Review* 132 (1984): 561, reprinted in Crenshaw et al., *Key Writings*, 47.

7. See, for example, Bell, *Race*, xxiii, noting that for all the "furor" of the civil-rights cases and laws dealing with racial problems in the three decades before the second edition of his casebook in 1980, "these civil rights cases and laws are today [1980] increasingly regarded as either obsolete or insufficient . . . before they could be enforced effectively. In a nation dedicated to individual freedom, laws that never should have been needed face neglect, reversal, and outright repeal, while the discrimination they were designed to eliminate continues in the same or a more sophisticated form." For a more recent account of the same themes, see Derrick A. Bell, Jr., "Racial Realism," *Connecticut Law Review* 24 (1992): 363, reprinted in Crenshaw, *Key Writings*, 302, noting that "every civil rights lawyer has reason to know—despite law school indoctrination and belief in the 'rule of law'—abstract principles lead to legal results that harm blacks and perpetuate their inferior status." Bell recognized that "legal precedents we thought permanent have been overturned, distinguished, or simply ignored," and "precedents, rights theory, and objectivity merely are formal rules that serve a covert purpose; even in the context of equality theory, they will never vindicate the legal rights of black Americans."

8. The Third World Coalition was an umbrella committee made up of representatives from organizations representing African American, Arab, Asian American, Chicano, Native American, and Puerto Rican law students. Founded in 1979 as the united voice of students of color at HLS, the coalition sought to "forge the shared hopes and frustrations

of its member groups into affirmative policy expressions which bring to the fore the legal needs and legal injustices which characterize the daily lives of men and women of color in this country and in the world. A critical part of [the coalition's] efforts has been devoted to providing a meaningful and realistic critique of legal education in this country: What is taught; how it is taught, and who is teaching": Third World Coalition, letter, February 8, 1983, on file with the author. Some of the members of the coalition involved in the events described herein are George Bisharat, F. Burlette Carter, Kimberlé Crenshaw, Jose Garcia, Ibrahim Gassama, Mari Mayeda, Cecil McNab, Glenn Morris, and Nick Sheats. For a contemporaneous account of the Alternative Course, including a chronology, syllabus, position papers, and sample letters, see Kimberlé Crenshaw, "The Case for an Alternative Course," unpublished ms., 1983, on file with the author.

9. The magnitude of the attack against the boycott was as crushing as the media's distorted coverage of the controversy. See, for example, Carl T. Rowan, "Blind Pride at Harvard," op-ed, *New York Times,* August 11, 1982, A22 ("There is little point of pride if its price is ignorance"), and "Bad Behavior at Harvard," op-ed, *Washington Post,* August 20, 1982, A15 ("Now we have black students in the exalted climes of Harvard declaring all whites guilty of something—because they are white"). Martin Kilson, "Ethnic Arrogance at Harvard," August 13, 1982, accused BLSA of intellectual infantilism and banal ethnocentricism and declared that "Black students who require ethnocentric crutches as part of their academic regime have to start growing up, and soon, or they will be overwhelmed by the intellectual sophistication and scholarly rigor associated with good and superior levels of learning and performance at places such as Harvard Law School." A letter to the editor (Bayard Rustin, "A Misguided Protest by Blacks at Harvard," *New York Times,* August 17, 1982, A26) called the objection that Jack Greenberg, a civil-rights lawyer and visiting professor at Harvard, was white nothing more than blatant racism.

The full-scale denunciation, coming on the heels of Dean Vorenberg's decision to release all correspondence between BLSA President Muhammad Kenyatta, Dean Vorenberg, Julius Chambers, and Greenberg to second- and third-year students over the summer, caught the coalition and BLSA off guard. Dean Vorenberg's decision to go public with the threatened boycott introduced the issue in a manner that stressed the points of least agreement within the coalition while obscuring the deeper

issue of the school's abysmal hiring record and its resistance to students' demands for a course taught by a full-time instructor. Reporters for the *Post* and the *Times* quickly ceased on the dog-bites-man aspect of Kenyatta's letter, in which he criticized Greenberg for his leadership of the Legal Defense Fund. See for example, "Minority Students at Harvard Protest Boycott," *New York Times,* August 9, 1982, A9 ("Black students at HLS are calling for a boycott of a course on race and legal issues that is to be taught in part by a white civil rights lawyer"); "Blind Pride," A22 ("Black law students are calling for a boycott of a course in race and legal issues because one of its teachers, Jack Greenberg, is white"); and Rustin, "Misguided Protest" ("Students are calling for a boycott of a course on race and legal issues because it will, in part, be taught by a white civil rights lawyer").

Because students involved in the boycott were away for the summer, Dean Vorenberg's spin on the issue went largely uncontested. The broader issue regarding the school's unwillingness to offer "Constitutional Law and Minority Issues" and the inadequate response to the coalition's affirmative-action demands were entirely lost in the media fracas over the boycott as the debate became reduced to one of "reverse discrimination." Lost, too, in the media's coverage of the controversy was the multiracial makeup of the coalition. Despite many efforts to clarify what the boycott was and was not about, the media persisted in framing the controversy as a contest between Dean Vorenberg and BLSA President Muhammad Kenyatta. This distortion was only heightened by Kenyatta's letter to the dean citing Greenberg's leadership of the NAACP-LDF as an additional reason for boycotting the course, and Dean Vorenberg's decision to release that correspondence to support the claim of "reverse racism." Although the letter neither represented the coalition's position nor reflected the substance of the negotiations between the coalition and the HLS administration, it became the lightning rod that drew the wrath of many in the civil-rights community.

Although the issue was tragically distorted in the media, there was a question about whether it was legitimate to assume that race would in any significant way shape the content of a course or should be considered as a factor in making academic appointments. Many of the most vocal critics of the boycott in fact supported affirmative action. When faced with what they viewed as racial discrimination against a man who had devoted his entire career to fighting for civil rights, however, these critics embraced a colorblind rhetoric that framed the students' demand for a full-time minority law professor to teach Bell's course as patently absurd. An interesting version of the tension in viewing this matter as reverse racism versus affirmative action is embodied in two op-ed pieces by Carl Rowan. In the first ("Blind Pride"), Rowan excoriated BLSA for racist, anti-intellectual, anti–civil-rights behavior: "Many black people of my generation have faced death in defense of the idea that people are to be judged on their own merits." In the second ("Bad Behavior"), he continued to criticize BLSA, this time for "letting Harvard off the hook by causing the press to focus on extraneous issues." The real issue had become the "surprisingly pathetic list of excuses as to why so few minority professors are appointed." Rowan went on to criticize Harvard's President Derek Bok for not valuing intrinsic educational benefits that diversity provides. For a thoughtful and balanced insider's view of the events leading up to the boycott and a pedagogical defense of race as a factor in hiring decisions, see Christopher Edley, Jr., "The Boycott at Harvard: Should Teaching Be Color-blind," *Washington Post*, August 18, 1982, A23 ("Race remains a useful proxy for a whole collection of experiences, aspirations and sensitivities, in that it is at least as strong a way as anyone's ethnic heritage or professional experiences [in shaping] the way he understands and explains life. It's not just a matter of having a particular slant on things; it's a question of what kind of glasses you've been wearing as the years roll by"). Edley also revealed that negotiations were under way with several minority candidates, but several were still mulling over their offers. As was traditional, this information was not shared with the students. Despite his public defense of Harvard's poor hiring record as reflecting a dearth of qualified minority candidates, Dean Vorenberg apparently targeted select candidates to recruit, some of whom were eventually hired by HLS. This duality—the public rhetoric declaring the pool of qualified minorities to be virtually nonexistent and the tremendous support Vorenberg gave to some minority candidates—no doubt accounts for his simultaneous legacy as a pioneer in integrating select people of color into law teaching as well as the embodiment of institutional resistance to broadening HLS's hiring criteria to assess more fairly the potential of scores of other minority law candidates. Whether this limited hiring effort would have occurred in the absence of sustained student struggle is anyone's guess, but some think not. See generally Derrick Bell, *Contesting Authority* (Boston: Beacon Press, 1994).

10. For a critique of the racial self-denial involved in learning to "think like a lawyer," see Kimberlé W. Crenshaw, "Foreword: Toward a Race-Conscious Pedagogy in Legal Education," *National Black Law Journal* 11 (1989): 1.

11. See, for example, Ruth Marcus, "Black Law Group Supports Boycott of Harvard Course," *Washington Post*, August 18, 1982, A3. The National Association of Black Law Students also passed a resolution supporting the actions of the Third World Coalition and calling for broad measures to increase the presence of professors of color at Harvard and all American law schools. See Cynthia Muldrow and Donald Tyler, "Goal of a Boycott at Harvard Law," letter to the editor, *New York Times*, August 20, 1982, 26. See also, "Stanford Rights Class Dropped After Black Protest," *New York Times*, March 20, 1983, 27, 20. The National Board of BLSA also convened a special task force on affirmative action to which I was appointed as co-chair. The task force was charged with the responsibility of examining affirmative-action policies in various law schools and formulating strategies to effect change. In this capacity, I prepared a report detailing the events leading up to the course, offering a critique of exclusionary hiring policies and providing a guide on how to mount such an undertaking. The report was made available to all chapters at BLSA's 1983 annual convention.

12. Some would say that this dire prediction was accurate in that many of the white male heavies did eventually pull away from CLS after the FemCrit and RaceCrit turn. I must confess that although I expected some degree of resistance from the old guard, I remained mystified by the visceral nature of the reaction. I had witnessed some amazingly confrontational interventions by white feminists in CLS, yet none prompted the emotional intensity that our workshop elicited. I was struck not simply by the apparent contradiction between the CLS rhetoric extolling local contestation and its own resistance to the interrogation we were demanding, but also by the dismissive rejection of the discourse as something that they had already done and were not going to do any more. As some folks explained it, this "been there, done that" attitude was a contemporary response to various offenses suffered by white radicals at the hands of African American activists in the 1960s. However accurate this account of lingering white angst from the 1960s may have been, the extent to which this claim reflected real lived experiences of our CLS colleagues remained unclear. So, too, did the question of whether the

narrative was appropriated as a parable about the hazards of racial contestations on the left. A provocative take on the dynamics of the 1960s racial encounters on the left can be found in Gary Peller, "Black Rage Confronts the Law," *Tikkun*, November 21, 1997, which argues that the rhetorical politics of Black Power constituted a psychosexual threat that continues to cast a shadow over the white left, suppressing any meaningful critique of race from its quarters. For an argument that links the disintegration of the left to the destructive emergence of identity politics, see Todd Gitlin, *The Twilight of Common Dreams* (New York: Henry Holt, 1995). The debate continues in various forms today. See for example, Vanessa Daniel, "Ralph Nader's Racial Blindspot," *Colorlines Magazine*, Internet edition (August 17, 2000), available from: <http://www.arc.org/C_Lines/CLArchive/story_web00_01.html>.

13. Neil Gotanda to Carrie Menker-Meadow, memorandum, July 24, 1986, on file with the author (critiquing the planning committee for its "unwillingness to build from previous panels and work . . . unwillingness to deal with Black women . . . [and] inability to talk about race within the organizing committee.")

14. The remark prompted Bracamonte, Delgado, and Torres to write an open letter to CLS, unpacking the messages conveyed in the cartoonlike stereotype and arguing that the unfortunate event suggests the possibility that Crits "focus so closely on the hegemonic tactics of liberals that [they] fail to notice [their] own." See "Statement by Jose Bracamonte, Richard Delgado, and Gerald Torres, Minority Critique Panel," CLS Annual Meeting, Los Angeles, January 1987, on file with the author.

15. Kimberlé W. Crenshaw to Regina Austin, letter, August 3, 1986.

16. Randall L. Kennedy, "Racial Critiques of Legal Academia," *Harvard Law Review* 102 (1989): 1745. That was not the only surprising challenge in store for conference attendees. While some of the conference organizers imagined hooks making a race intervention within feminist discourse in CLS, and West making a parallel intervention within the ranks of the critical theory wing, all bets were off when hooks critiqued West for speaking a language that was inaccessible and mystifying. Needless to say, the moment was electric: Its complexity and surprise represented precisely the kind of charge that kept many of us coming back to CLS events, despite some of the more predictable problems.

17. See Kimberlé W. Crenshaw, "Race, Reform and Retrenchment: Transformation and Legitima-

tion in Antidiscrimination Law," *Harvard Law Review* 101 (1988): 1331.

18. Answering the call to Madison were Anita Allen, Taunya Banks, Derrick Bell, Kevin Brown, Paulette Caldwell, John Calmore, Kimberlé Crenshaw, Harlon Dalton, Richard Delgado, Neil Gotanda, Linda Greene, Trina Grillo, Isabelle Gunning, Angela Harris, Mari Matsuda, Teresa Miller, Philip T. Nash, Elizabeth Patterson, Stephanie Phillips, Benita Ramsey, Robert Suggs, Kendall Thomas, and Patricia Williams

19. In the letter announcing the first Annual Workshop, a provisional definition of CRT suggests that "critical race scholarship generally challenges the legitimacy of dominant approaches to race and racism by positing values and norms that have traditionally been subordinated in the law. Critical race theorists thus seek to validate minority experiences as an appropriate grounding for thinking about law and racial subordination. . . . Many approach antidiscrimination law as ideological discourse which does not so much remedy racial subordination as provide continuing rationalizations for it. Traditional notions of civil rights are simply conceptual starting points to explore the limitations of civil rights reforms and the possibilities of developing a more deeply grounded transformative practice. Others are interested in examining implicit racial assumptions that exist beneath the surface of dominant discourse and in revealing how language conveys meanings beyond its ordinary legal sense. Included also in critical race scholarship are critiques of the political sociology of our profession and its embedded racial implications": see "Invitational Letter," April 19, 1989, on file with author.

20. This policy was not without some controversy. Indeed, some faculty members at the University of Wisconsin were not entirely comfortable with the all-minority make-up of the group and sought a review of Trubek's decision to fund it. The decision would not be easily replicated in today's environment.

21. The issue is somewhat academic at this point in light of the growing body of critical articles on race written by white colleagues. Alan Freeman, Gary Peller, Barbara Flagg, and Duncan Kennedy are just a few Anglo scholars whose articles are key texts within CRT.

22. Trubek's support was notable, as he was at the time fully aware of the emerging critique of CLS, having been an adviser on my graduate thesis and a colleague of Patricia Williams and Richard Delgado. All three of us were critics of CLS, and our

critiques were eventually published. See Crenshaw, "Race, Reform and Retrenchment": 1331; Richard Delgado, "The Ethereal Scholar: Does Critical Legal Studies Have What Minorities Want?" *Harvard Civil Rights–Civil Liberties Law Review* 22 (1987): 301; Patricia J. Williams, "Alchemical Notes: Reconstructed Ideals from Deconstructed Rights," *Harvard Civil Rights–Civil Liberties Law Review* 22 (1987): 401.

23. See Freeman, "Legitimizing Racial Discrimination": 1049.

24. See, for example, Clint Bolick, "Clinton's Quota Queens," *Wall Street Journal*, April 30. 1993, A12. For descriptions of President Clinton's efforts to distance himself from Lani Guinier, his onetime nominee for the head of the Civil Rights Division of the Justice Department, see Michael Isikoff and Ruth Markus, "Administration Leaves Guinier in Limbo," *Washington Post*, June 3, 1993, A1, and Michael Putzel, "Rights Nominee Digs in as Clinton Backs Off," *The Globe* (Boston), June 3, 1993, 1. See also Lani Guinier, *Lift Every Voice* (New York: Simon and Schuster, 1998), describing her nomination and nomination-revocation processes. Guinier quotes Yale Professor Harlon Dalton as saying, "Her Senate hearing would have been a conversation about what democracy looks like in a multicultural society in the 1990s, and I think that's a conversation we need to have. Instead, the Senate and the president ran away from it": Guinier, *Lift Every Voice*, 130. Though less publicized than Guinier's nomination, the planned nomination of Gerald Torres to head the Justice Department's Environment and Natural Resources Division was criticized because of his association with the CLS movement: see Michael Isikoff, "2 Withdraw Justice Department Candidacies," *Washington Post*, December 18, 1993, A1.

25. Patricia J. Williams, "De Jure, De Facto, De Media," *The Nation*, June 2, 1997, 10.

26. Richard A. Posner, "Beyond All Reason: The Radical Assault on Truth in American Law," *New Republic*, October 13, 1997, 40.

27. Ibid.

28. Jeffrey Rosen, "The Bloods and the Crits: O. J. Simpson, Critical Race Theory, the Law, and the Triumph of Color in America," *New Republic*, December 9, 1996, 27.

29. Heather Mallick, "Danger: Critical Race Theory Approaching from the South," *Toronto Sun*, February 16, 1997, C10.

30. Daniel A. Farber and Suzanna Sherry, *Beyond All Reason: The Radical Assault on Truth in American Law* (New York: Oxford University Press, 1997), 52–71.

31. Neil A. Lewis, "Race Theory Challenges Goal of a Colorblind Society," *Austin American-Statesman*, June 8, 1997, J1.

32. Heather MacDonald, "Law School Humbug," *City Journal* (Fall 1995), 46

33. Alex Kozinski, "Bending the Law," *New York Times*, November 2, 1997, 46.

34. Ibid.

35. See Mallick, "Danger," C10.

36. Andrew Sullivan, "Truth and Lies in the Language Class," *Sunday Times* (London), January 12, 1997, 8.

37. See Rosen, "Bloods and the Crits," 27.

38. See Farber and Sherry, *Beyond All Reason*, 52–71.

39. Proposition 209 is a 1996 amendment to the California Constitution banning racial and gender preferences in public hiring, contracting, and education. See Larry D. Hatfield, "High Court: 209 Stands," *San Francisco Examiner*, November 3, 1997, A1. For a more comprehensive analysis of the proposition, see Girardeau A. Spann, "Proposition 209," *Duke Law Journal* 47 (1997): 187.

40. See Williams, "De Jure," and Bracamonte et al., "Statement."

41. Frederick Douglass, "Speech Before the West Indian Emancipation Society (August 4, 1857)," in Philip S. Foner, *The Life and Writings of Frederick Douglass, Volume II* (New York: International Publishers, 1950), 426.

CHAPTER TWO

Historicizing Critical Race Theory's Cutting Edge: Key Movements That Performed the Theory

Sumi Cho and Robert Westley

IN THIS CHAPTER, we attempt to retrieve an obscured history that we believe was central to the development of Critical Race Theory—the history of student activism for diversity in higher education from the 1960s to the 1990s. To do so, we focus on one longitudinal case study in particular, that of the University of California at Berkeley's Boalt Coalition for a Diversified Faculty (BCDF). This local movement, which became national in 1989 with the BCDF-coordinated Nationwide Law Student Strike for Diversity, embodied and practiced many of the insights theorized by CRT; it was a movement that performed the theory. This retrieval thus may help critical race theorists not only to understand CRT's first decade better, but also to draw key lessons for its second.

This retrieval is especially valuable because existing accounts of CRT's development as a movement tend to emphasize

This chapter appeared earlier in *UC Davis Law Review* 33 (Summer 2000): 1377–427.

the agency of individual scholars. To be sure, these individual stories are important because they map the intellectual history of a movement formed by the courageous actions of people who were dissatisfied with both critical legal studies (CLS) and traditional civil-rights paradigms. We applaud such historicization of the movement's origins in the major CRT anthologies but hope to supplement the origin stories in the following two ways.

First, we strive to demonstrate more closely the linkages between the 1960s Civil Rights Movement and student activism with the 1980s legal-intellectual movement. According to the introduction in one of the leading anthologies on Critical Race Theory, CRT became a "self-conscious entity" in 1989, when the first CRT workshop was convened. The editor acknowledges the intellectual influence of CLS and the political inspiration of the Civil Rights Movement and other national movements. We believe the CLS–CRT genealogy has been well developed in the popular understanding of CRT's origins and therefore aim in this essay to draw a closer nexus between student activism and CRT.[1]

Second, we seek to offer a more nuanced political history of CRT's birth that can help explain, for example, why CRT burst onto the legal academic scene at the time that it did. The other leading CRT anthology contains a detailed description of CRT's origins in its Introduction. Like the first anthology's origin story, this description of CRT's development notes the importance of the Civil Rights Movement for "inspiration" and "direction," as well as the CLS leftist intervention into legal discourse, as "elements in the conditions of [CRT's] possibility." The editors then identify two events central to the development of CRT as a movement—a student protest at Harvard Law School in 1981 over an alternative course on race and law, and the 1987 National Critical Legal Studies Conference on race and silence.[2] The emphasis placed on the Harvard protest is suggestive and, from our perspective, very useful, but still incomplete. Why such protest emerged in 1981 and why there was a six-year gap between the two central events remain unexplained. It remains unclear how the 1981 protest played a developmental or catalytic role in CRT's rise.

On the whole, therefore, genesis stories of the movement now known as Critical Race Theory are focused mostly on the scholarly writings that "formed the movement." We strive in this essay to complete the story and counter, to an extent, the "super-agency" approach to collective action that movement histories sometimes adopt.[3] We attempt to ground CRT in resistance movements not to proliferate competing genesis stories but, rather, to contextualize politically CRT's birth and growth. What follows is our attempt to pursue a more politicized and multi-factored historiography in explaining the conditions of possibility behind the intellectual projects that became CRT.

This chapter also analyzes the cross-pollination of movement and theory, assessing both achievements and shortcomings. By historicizing the efforts of the initial critical-race proponents against the larger background of communal struggle, we demonstrate how antiracist practices and antiracist theorizing were metabolically intertwined. In the course of making this linkage, we credit not only the BCDF movement, but other local and national struggles that employed race-consciousness in their problem-and-goal-definition, action strategies, and organizational structure.

In doing so, we also use as our point of departure insights from the recent critical-race–praxis literature that underline the significance of progressive lawyering to critical-race theorizing. We extend this praxis analysis by highlighting the importance of *political organizing* for the past, present, and future of the CRT antisubordination project, and vice versa.[4] This broadened understanding of CRT's roots, status, and prospects is timely and valuable because it has significant implications for our appreciation of the mutual obligations between progressives in the academy and political communities. We utilize the methodology of longitudinal case study to illuminate and ground a discussion of the current conjuncture, when the Race-Crit community sometimes seems uncertain as to the meaning and necessity of coalition building, praxis, activism, and, indeed, self-historicization.

The activism at Boalt Hall School of Law for faculty diversity in the late 1970s and late 1980s was part of a tradition of race-conscious resistance at UC Berkeley. Because UC Berkeley is a public, land-grant institution, it is subject to far greater community scrutiny and public pressure than its private counterparts. In addition, as an elite state university in one of the most racially diverse states of the country, its applicant pool yielded a mix of students that could form the basis for effective political coalitions—coalitions that would not be so easily dismissed or ignored. These unique circumstances led to some of the earliest, and most sustained, race-plus[5] coalitional efforts. This Berkeley tradition, beginning with the Free Speech Movement of 1964, valorized political self-actualization and thereby promoted a positive culture and historical memory of coalitional activism among its student body—a positive culture that embraced diversity to promote coalitions and that can aid an increasingly diversified CRT to retain its momentum in the coming decades.

As we will show, student-diversity activism at Boalt Hall constituted itself as a membership organization committed to diversity in three primary spheres: faculty, student body, and curriculum. The focus on law-faculty diversity was driven in part by particular events—that is, the consistent refusal by Boalt's faculty over a long period of time to hire, tenure, or even seriously consider candidates other than openly heterosexual white men who had benefitted structurally and personally from the historical exclusion of women, people of color, and openly lesbian/bisexual/gay people from legal education and the legal profession.

Yet the struggle for a more open legal education at Boalt was waged not only at the level of the substantive goal of faculty diversity, but also at the level of self-determination and empowerment of marginalized groups through race-conscious organizational and leadership structures. As a result, a group-based–coalition model developed among student groups active on the issue—the Black Law Students Association (BLSA; later Law Students of African Descent [LSAD], the La Raza Law Students Association (LRLSA), the Asian American Law Students Association and Pacific Islander Law Student Association (AALSA/PILSA), and the Boalt Hall Women's Association, among others. Under this model, each BCDF demand on the administration was first vet-

ted and ratified among a membership that was made up primarily of members of these groups. Thus, diversity within BCDF's own ranks and leadership, as well as in its agenda, was a core operational principle. The BCDF's tactics effectively represented a kind of mobile coalition that required students to bridge lines of difference through self-education, cooperation, and risk-taking.

The substantive themes that this essay explores relate largely to continuing tendencies within some CRT scholarship to separate theory from activism, and we seek through this exploration to show how this separation can defeat the antisubordinationist aspirations of outsider activists and scholars such as CRT scholar–activists. Our analysis will show that the gesture toward separation of theory from activism assumes both methodological and thematic forms. From a methodological standpoint, separation entails individualist strategies at the level of organizing resistance; intertextual approaches at the level of writing scholarship; and sublimation at the level of doing theory. From a thematic standpoint, separation has meant an impolitic and ahistorical infatuation with unmodified antiessentialism and the critique of identity politics. The separation of theory from activism, we argue, spells defeat by promoting theoretical extravagance and reactive strategies that permit external co-optation.

To pursue alternatives to these defeatist strategies and tendencies within CRT, this essay explores the history of student-led diversity activism with an eye toward revealing and drawing the lessons of productive linkages between theory and activism. We propose to show that maintaining productive linkages between theory and activism in the context of CRT movement politics, from a methodological standpoint, leads to the following preferred options: race-conscious collective action rather than individualism at the level of organizing resistance;

intersubjective rather than intertextual method at the level of writing scholarship; and synergism rather than sublimation at the level of doing theory. Thematically, this analysis implies rejection of "unmodified antiessentialism" as an overall ethic of outsider discourse. This analysis also embraces a general reclamation project that retrieves histories of resistance that help create the conditions of solidarity necessary to minimize theoretical extravagance and to promote progressive community formation. We believe that this retrospective understanding of CRT's first decade is pivotal to the prospective fulfillment of CRT's potential in the second decade.

The chapter proceeds in two parts. In part one, we review the historical significance to CRT of student-of-color activism. By focusing on the unique role and qualified successes of student-of-color activism in the rise of CRT as an intellectual movement, we hope that the necessary linkage between race-conscious antisubordination theory and practice will surface. In part two, we offer thoughts on the need to understand movement history as part of a valuable yet suppressed body of knowledge. In this part, we explain how the modes of interaction between CRT and movement history may either sublimate and repress subjugated knowledge of student-of-color movements or pursue synergistic strategies with them. Because sublimation entails underestimating the importance of political structures and the need for solidarity between theory and activism, and because it overestimates the level of regressive disposition within activist communities of color, we argue that CRT in its next decade should adopt synergistic strategies in relation to movement history and join with other justice-minded communities to develop a coalitional, race-plus organizational structure for the advancement of antisubordination transformation through legal theory and praxis.

Linking Antiracist Organizing and Antiracist Theorizing: Race-Conscious Models of Political Organizing: A Case Study (1964–86)

Historical Significance of Race-Conscious Student Movements

There are quite a few students who have attended school at Berkeley who went South to work with the Student Nonviolent Coordinating Committee, and who have been active in the civil rights movement in the Bay Area.... I was one of these returning students. We were greeted by an order from the Dean of Students' Office that the kind of on-campus political activity which had resulted in our taking part in the Summer Project was to be permitted no longer.
... This is what gave the Free Speech Movement its initial impetus.
—Mario Savio, June 1965[6]

This fight now is ours as much as it is yours. If there had been no students, we would have had no Freedom Rides.
—James Farmer, national director of the Congress of Racial Equality (CORE)[7]

We begin this genealogical tracing in 1964 with the rise of the Free Speech Movement at UC Berkeley, an event that marks the beginning of the mass student-movement era. The Free Speech Movement, known primarily as a student rebellion against the university's attempts to restrict students' speech, had a definitive but largely overlooked racial origin. When a police squad car summoned by the university administration attempted to arrest a member of CORE for violating a new regulation curbing education and recruitment efforts on Sproul Plaza by student organizations, it was spontaneously surrounded by hundreds of students who prevented the car from leaving for the next thirty-two hours. Although destined to be abstracted from its origins and construed as a battle only or chiefly over freedom of expression, the Free

Speech Movement is significant to this inquiry because it is one of the first post-World War II campus movements to originate substantively from antiracist student organizing. Although the movement's adherents were mostly white students, its racial roots persisted and laid the political groundwork for the earliest collective UC Berkeley student-of-color organizing effort—the Third World Strike of 1969.[8]

The Third World Strike at UC Berkeley was the longest, costliest, and arguably the most institutionally significant student strike of UC Berkeley's history. It is also one of the least known movements of the 1960s. This strike did not originate at the Berkeley campus, but Berkeley students of color responded to the call by their counterparts across the bay at San Francisco State University, where a racial coalition of groups calling itself the Third World Liberation Front (TWLF), was demanding educational change. The Third World Strike of 1969 is significant as a paradigmatic moment of late-or post–civil-rights activism undertaken by multiple communities of color in historically white educational institutions because it led to the creation of the ethnic studies departments at UC Berkeley, affirmative-action admissions and recruitment, and other racial-justice reforms.[9]

Apart from their notable success in achieving institutional reform, the ensuing student strikes were particularly noteworthy for providing a model for student-of-color organizing. The TWLF, which organized and led UC Berkeley's Third World Strike, was a coalition of student organizations representing the Afro-American Student Union, Asian American Political Alliance, Mexican American Student Confederation, and Native American Students Association. The TWLF was composed of a steering committee with two representatives from each member organization to promote egalitarian cross-racial coalition. The TWLF's race-con-

scious, group-based approach to coalitional leadership and decision-making ultimately would become the model for successful race-plus coalitions organized by student movements in the subsequent decades.[10]

After the Third World Strike victory in 1969, two issues dominated 1970s protest politics: apartheid and affirmative action. The Soweto uprisings in 1976 brought international attention to the inhumanity of the South African racial regime, and student organizers began developing coalitions that reflected connections between antiracist organizing at home—in the context of the *Bakke* case—and abroad. The *Bakke* decision, rendered in 1978, was seen at the time as a setback, which demoralized affirmative-action organizers. In time, civil-rights organizations discovered the "silver lining" of Justice Lewis Powell's opinion permitting race-conscious admissions. However, the "promise" of *Bakke* would be quietly realized not by activists, but by administrators and staff who implemented affirmative-action admissions. In addition, competition and sectarianism among rival leftist organizations—often expressed as vanguardism—further fractured the diversity coalition.[11] Thus, although these 1970s movements enjoyed peak periods of activity, they had waned by the time of Ronald Reagan's election to the presidency in 1980.

Due to these developments, student-of-color antiracist activism on the whole slowly would subside from the late 1970s to early 1980s, with most campus political activity focusing on anti-nuclear protests, Central American solidarity work, and environmental issues. However, the anti-apartheid movement regained momentum in the watershed year of 1984. Three important factors contributed to this revival: 1) the November 1984 protests at the South African embassy in Washington, D.C.; 2) Jesse Jackson's first 1984 bid for the presidency and the work of the Rainbow Coalition; and 3) the twenty-year commemoration of the Free Speech Movement, observed in the fall of 1984. These events once again spotlighted continuing racial injustice, both domestically and internationally, thereby recalling and re-energizing Berkeley's role as a site of student social-justice activism. In this setting, students of color also established two important political structures in 1984.

Borrowing from the 1969 example of the TWLF, one structure took the form of a *"race-plus" coalition* model known as Cal-Students for Equal Rights and Valid Education (Cal-SERVE). This coalition united students of color and les/bi/gay organizations interested in slating candidates for student-government positions. These groups united in the context of Cal-SERVE in part because they had been marginalized by previous progressive coalitions. Tellingly, this electoral coalition remains as the oldest campus political party to this day. The other structure involved an *individual-member–based organization of progressives of color* known as United People of Color (UPC), discussed in greater detail later. With these two political structures in place—Cal-SERVE's electoral race-plus coalition and UPC's individual-member–based organization of progressives of color—organized students of color were poised to assume leadership on campus issues. In fact, UPC would become the leading organization in the anti-apartheid movement during the next few years, until the Board of Regents of the University of California voted finally to divest funds in the summer of 1986.[12] But with the ascendance of student-of-color leadership, friction with the white left arose—tensions not unlike those encountered by early RaceCrits vis-à-vis CLS scholars.

As in CRT's early history, and specifically in its dialogue with CLS, this contestation during the mid-1980s with the white left at Berkeley was a formative experience for organizers in UPC, including the engage-ment of similar debates on "formality" and "informality" in the political as well as the intellectual arena. For example, one key conflict between UPC and the predominantly white anti-apartheid group Campaign Against Apartheid (CAA) was over the decision-making process to be followed in coalitional meetings. The CAA insisted on an informal, consensus-oriented decision-making process that rejected any hierarchical leadership structure. While reasonable, if not ideal, in theory, this approach in operation empowered those who had the most discretionary time on their hands to persevere through hours of discussion, and it effectively excluded or limited participation by those who had competing time pressures. Unfortunately, the impact of this process worked to the detriment of students of color, who found they generally had less time on their hands for such open-ended meetings and less inclination for this sort of exercise in consensuality by attrition. As a result, planning meetings and political actions, such as the protest on the steps at Sproul Plaza against University of California investments in South Africa, became virtually devoid of student-of-color participation in the name of radical hyperdemocratic (consensus-only) decision-making.[13] Ironically, for both CLS and the CAA, what was considered "radical" took precedence over the substantive and structural inclusion of people of color in antiracist resistance.

The UPC and CAA were the principal organizers of a vibrant anti-apartheid campus movement in the last half of the 1980s. However, as the anti-apartheid movement wound down after important victories such as the UC regents' vote to divest the university system's funds from South Africa, a clear and open split between the CAA and the UPC became more and more evident because the former group was relying increasingly on "radical" tactics of confrontation and sensationalism to highlight the urgency of the struggle. The CAA's lack of discipline and non-commitment to non-violence meant that joint activities of the CAA and the UPC would be unduly hazardous for UPC members. When, for example, an anonymous CAA member would spit or throw bricks at police from a crowd, those police would invariably seek targets—usually tall men of color from the UPC—on whom to focus their disciplinary wrath. Beyond placing students of color unnecessarily at physical risk, such activities under the guise of radicalism were problematic for most UPC members because the tactics were designed not to build and grow the movement, but simply to "defy authority." Moreover, that authority often was rather removed from the stated target of the movement—that is, the South African apartheid regime. Thus, akin to CLS's critique of rights as legitimation, the CAA's overriding commitment to radical defiance and its insistence on informal, non-hierarchical processes grossly underappreciated and obscured the dynamics of racial oppression as a lived experience. In this way, the allegedly egalitarian make-up and radical stance of both the CAA and CLS bespoke white perspectivalism and privilege.[14]

The highs and lows of these two decades of race-conscious organizing at UC Berkeley illustrate how the design of political structures to ensure the effective participation and leadership of students of color was central to the success of antiracist student movements. Absent such structures, the majoritarian bent of politics-as-usual systematically relegated students of color to a supporting role and failed to produce meaningful, institutional change for racial justice. However, with the formation of the TWLF of 1969, an effective race-conscious political structure that shared power equally between and among African Americans, Asian Americans, Chicanos/Chicanas, and Native Americans was put into place. This structure was

adopted and modified in the 1980s to form Cal-SERVE as a race-plus campus electoral coalition, which remains effective to this day. At the same time, the UPC, an organization of progressives of color, also emerged to lead the anti-apartheid movement and, subsequently, the diversity movements of the late 1980s and early 1990s, to successful institutional reforms. These lessons are corroborated by the more recent experience focused on law schools.

Converging Histories: Applying the Race-Conscious Infrastructure for Resistance to Mainstream Legal Education (1986–91)

> *Aquí, ayar, apartheid morirá!*
> —1980s UPC chant

The success of the Berkeley anti-apartheid movement, measured by the end goal of divestment, validated the race-conscious organizing developed through the UPC as well as the race-plus coalitional model adopted by Cal-SERVE. Because this organizational infrastructure was squarely in place, this victory also opened up the vista of political possibilities for future student activism and cultural contestation. In addition, the anti-apartheid movement had established the UPC as a student-of-color organization with members who were seasoned organizers and who understood, and were committed to, a principle of political self-determination.

The linkage, well established in the 1970s and highlighted during the 1980s, between apartheid "there" and "here" made natural for those student activists a transition from the focus on divestment to an engagement of racism closer to home. Therefore, anti-apartheid veterans next focused on two areas of unfinished business left over from the 1969 Third World Strike agenda: 1) curricular reform, including the specific demand for an ethnic-studies graduation requirement; and 2) affirmative action, in terms of employment (tenuring junior faculty of color, pursuing affirmative action in faculty hiring) and in admissions (undergraduate, graduate, and law school).[15] These race-conscious efforts (in both form and substance) at Berkeley and across the country became known more broadly as "diversity movements." And it was in this historical context of close lineage to the antiracist struggle against apartheid that the diversity student movement specifically at Boalt Hall would come into being. Indeed, Berkeley's 1969 Third World Strike provided the catalyst for Boalt student activism on racial-justice issues at the law school and inspired a Boalt student strike in 1972 to secure the reformation of admissions policies.

Affirmative-action admissions to law school for African American, Asian American, Latina/Latino, and Native American students had begun in the first fall following the successful campuswide Third World Strike of 1969. Reflecting that success, the first two years of post-strike affirmative-action admissions to law school yielded 12 percent and 18 percent students of color in the incoming fall classes of 1969 and 1970, respectively. In the fall of 1971, the proportion of special-admissions students increased to 31 percent of the entering class due to an unexpectedly high "show-up rate" among those admitted. The Boalt admissions committee had clearly underestimated the pent-up demand among California's communities of color for low-cost, high-quality legal education.

According to Linda Greene, a student leader of the BLSA at the time, this sudden change of student demographics was experienced as a "traumatic event" by Boalt faculty, who had not expected such a large enrollment in part because the school had not made a commensurate increase in financial aid to support minority admittees. In response to this trauma, the Boalt faculty proposed eliminating the special-admissions program altogether, thus prompting the 1972 law-student strike organized by the BLSA and joined by the LRLSA, AALSA, and the one Native American student enrolled at the school. The 1972 strike lasted two weeks before the faculty proposed to continue the special admissions program, but with a lowered target goal of 28 percent for "Third World" students. The BLSA and AALSA accepted the faculty proposal, effectively ending the strike.[16]

Although that strike produced a successful result, its lack of an organizational structure fostered disunity among students of color, as substantive and strategic decisions were made seemingly without regard to the needs or views of other allied groups, much less with proactive intergroup coordination of complex issues. Thus, for instance, Chicano students refused to end the strike after the BLSA and the AALSA reached agreement, continuing to press for "parity" between law-school admissions and state population percentages. Pursuing parity, the LRLSA organized a separate sit-in at the Boalt admissions office as part of the 1972 strike, which was unsuccessful in part because it was unilateral. Without any coalitional structure from 1972 to 1977, separate groups organized various activities on an ad hoc basis, and with limited success, as issues arose.

During this fluid period and into the early 1980s, student-of-color input into the Boalt admissions process was significantly curtailed. During these years, student participation in admissions shrank incrementally from full organizational voting rights on the admissions committee, to formal but perfunctory advisory rights for student-of-color organizations, to the most limited advisory role for individual committee appointees selected from (not by) student-of-color organizations.[17] Thus, although the power of student-of-color organizing clearly was evident in the early to mid-1970s, as was the influence of earlier movements, the failure of Boalt student groups during this time to build an effective political structure and to coordinate antiracist efforts permitted the administration to contain individual and organizational demands on a case-by-case basis. This period of decline, like earlier (and later) lows, correlated to choices over design and structure in the formation and operation of antiracist movements.

The Formation of the Coalition for a Diversified Faculty:

> In terms of hiring, the school's affirmative-action record is good.
> —Phillip Johnson, chair of Boalt faculty appointments committee, March 1978[18]

Responding to the mounting frustration engendered by this ongoing decline, the next significant race-based organization at Boalt emerged in fall of 1977 as the Coalition for a Diversified Faculty (CDF). Like the TWLF before them, seven organizations representing the "old" race-plus coalition of earlier times issued a position paper with a number of proposals to rectify the racial problems that students perceived. The proposals were neither discussed nor mentioned at subsequent faculty meetings. Meetings between CDF members and the the law school's administration proved fruitless. Dean Sanford Kadish refused to permit CDF members to address a faculty meeting to discuss the issues raised in the position paper. After determining that no substantive dialogue with the institution was possible, the CDF called for an all-day teach-in and strike on March 21, 1978, which was supported by 75 percent to 90 percent of Boalt students.[19] This action revitalized antiracist student activism.

The late 1970s CDF activity peaked with a student-drafted Title VI and Title IX complaint filed with the U.S. Department of Housing, Education, and Welfare (HEW) on April 9, 1979. The complaint alleged that Boalt's hiring policies resulted in a lack of minority and women faculty (see Table 2-1) and contended that the faculty's composition denied students differing perspectives on important legal issues, especially in the areas of public-interest law and poverty law. To the CDF's surprise, HEW officials decided to investigate the students' complaint. However, using the standard of other elite law schools' hiring as a guide, the federal report concluded that Boalt's faculty was no less diverse than the non-diverse faculties of top law schools across the country. Following this setback, and like the political activity on the main campus, antiracist organizing at the law school faded at the close of the 1970s and early 1980s, perhaps as a result of the same meta- and micro-forces: the increasing national political and cultural conservatism, internal divisions, student turnover, and political retrenchment.[20]

The Reformation of CDF in the 1980s:

The reinvigoration of the diversity movement at Boalt in the mid- to late 1980s originated with the formation of United Law Students of Color (ULSC) in the fall of 1985, when law students in the campuswide UPC came to the realization that a similar organization would benefit diversity specifically at the law school. Various subcommittees were formed to address specific law-school issues, among which was a subcommittee on faculty diversity. Although the ULSC was short-lived as an organization due to its

---

TABLE 2-1

1978 Boalt Faculty Composition

---

1 Asian American male
1 African American male
3 white females
37 white males

---

overly ambitious initial agenda, competing time demands, and established strength of student-of-color organizations the faculty-diversity subcommittee prospered and grew, expanding to include white allies. With the decline of ULSC, the subcommittee on faculty diversity reorganized itself, coincidentally under the name Boalt Coalition for a Diversified Faculty (BCDF), without any awareness that such a group with the same name had existed in the previous decade.[21]

Spearheaded by this new formation, the Boalt diversity movement became reinvigorated in the mid- to late 1980s. Gaining political and popular momentum from the galvanizing successes of the campuswide divestment movement, which culminated in the 1986 regents' vote, this reinvigoration also was spurred on by negative actions of Boalt's faculty in their decision to deny

tenure to two faculty members, Marjorie Shultz in 1985 and Eleanor Swift in 1987. The denial of tenure to these two popular, white, female law teachers brought human faces to the struggle for diversity at Boalt and propelled the BCDF into a focal organizational role at the law school. In the fall of 1987, the BCDF highlighted the lack of progress over the decades in diversifying the law faculty by publicizing widely and graphically the appalling racial and gender caste system that had seen but one tenured faculty member of color from 1967 to 1987, while increasing the number of tenured (white) female faculty from one to two-and-one-half over the same twenty-year period (see Figure 2-1).

In the following year, 1988, an unprecedented four diversity hires out of five total hires (including an African American man

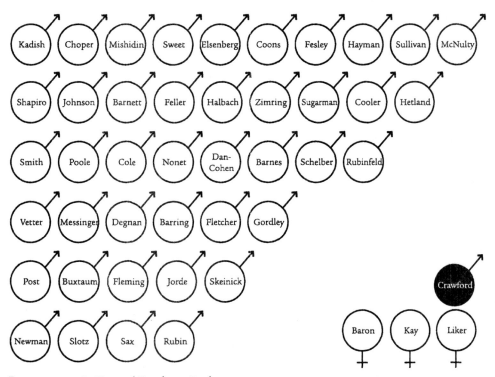

FIGURE 2-1   1987 Tenured Faculty at Boalt.

and woman, a Latino, and a white woman) were made in response to the movement's diversity hiring demands, and in implicit acknowledgment of the school's embarrassment over the BCDF's public documentation of its monolithic straight-white-male faculty identity.

Adding to this pressure to diversify was the threat of Eleanor Swift's pending lawsuit, which she had filed alleging sex-based discrimination after her negative tenure vote. The public pressure on the law school became acute when Professor Swift held a press conference in the fall of 1988 to announce that the Privilege and Tenure Committee of UC Berkeley had made an unprecedented prima facie finding of sex-based discrimination in her case. Two weeks after Swift's press conference, the Boalt faculty abruptly voted to reverse its denial of tenure to Marjorie Shultz.[22] However, another year would pass before Swift also received tenure.

While the BCDF was organizing this external struggle for diversity against the Boalt administration and faculty, an internal struggle for power was developing within the coalition. Students of color generally had felt relegated to the margins by the BCDF organizational structure, which was largely an individual-membership organization. Unlike the campuswide UPC, the BCDF at the time was open to anyone enrolled at Boalt. Outnumbered and alienated by white liberals who approached the problem without an understanding of institutionalized forms of racism, and who combined this ignorance with a considerable dose of white paternalism and maternalism, students of color reduced their participation in the BCDF dramatically and quickly. In recognition of the internal contradiction caused by white domination of the BCDF, the remaining students of color active in the organization called for a reorganization of the leadership structure to a more group-based coalitional model that would initially include on the steering committee representatives from the BLSA, LRLSA, AALSA, and Boalt Hall Women's Association.[23] The elements of a race-plus coalitional structure within the BCDF thus were assembled.

This restructuring was a key to the BCDF's continuing momentum because it allowed a new internal balance, which shifted the BCDF's culture, consciousness, and strategy to students of color and their racial perspectives and experiences on the nature of power and struggle. Generally at that time, the liberal and predominantly white students who had come to dominate the BCDF before its restructuring had manifested a different orientation toward the white faculty than the more disaffected students of color. Principally, liberal white students at first believed in the sincerity of the administration and some faculty members when they said that the institution really wanted to hire faculty of color but just could not find any. Accordingly, liberal BCDF members had advocated a kind of "constructive engagement," while progressive students (disproportionately students of color) were ready to engage in direct action by the spring of 1987. These social and strategic differences, which led to the restructuring of the organization, were also racialized in the sense that they flowed in large part from the gap between the lived experiences of white versus racial-minority students in contending with daily power negotiations. After the BCDF was restructured as a minority-organization–based coalition, the participation and leadership of students of color changed the organization's direction dramatically and led to important victories.

Crucially, early CRT works offered theoretical tools that proved useful to organizers during this time. The first positive theoretical intervention was a *Harvard Civil Rights–Civil Liberties Law Review* volume devoted to

"Minority Critiques of Legal Academe," published in 1987.[24] Although white members of the BCDF at the time were more liberal than leftist, this classic volume's naming of white paternalism, which too often has characterized relations between the white left and communities of color, resonated with alienated students of color in the BCDF. Reading critical analyses of similar paternalistic dynamics occurring within legal academe, students of color gained insight and confidence to insist on political structures that would help preclude, and create means to ensure accountability for, any further perpetuation of deeply ingrained patterns of racial subordination within antiracist political movements.

Similarly, a second CRT intervention important to the BCDF's work occurred simultaneously within the civil-rights community: the move designed to insert a more progressive politic into traditional rights-oriented movements. The attempt by CRT to radicalize our understanding of civil-rights strategies was useful to student-diversity movements contending with liberal factions for influence over agenda-setting and strategizing priorities because of the general tendency to internalize negative conceptions of counter-majoritarian, progressive politics—particularly when asserted by people of color. The incisive CRT (and CLS) critiques of the limitations of traditional civil rights emboldened students of color who were challenging not only the law school's daily operations, but also the expectation of liberal white students to lead protest movements—even those focusing on the exclusion of people of color. Under this new structure, the BCDF continued its numerous educational events (often involving critical-race, feminist, and critical-legal scholars) and organizational meetings, but it also presented demands to the faculty and administration that fit within a direct-action strategy. After building a base of support among student groups through these activities, and having received no commitments to include students in the faculty-hiring process, the BCDF called for a student strike and teach-in (coincidentally, almost ten years to the day after the 1978 CDF strike). On March 22, 1988, that call was honored by 80 percent of the Boalt student body, as well as by significant numbers of students from the rest of the campus. The event culminated in twenty-eight arrests in Dean Jesse Choper's office.

This action announced a clear break within the BCDF both with the substance of "constructive engagement" as a viable strategy for faculty diversification and with the process of white paternalism as a viable strategy for self-determination and political empowerment within and through antiracist movements. As a result of the 1988 strike, the administration entered into protracted negotiations that proved inconclusive. Nevertheless, this strike invigorated the student movement for success in upcoming battles.

After another year of administrative non-action and ongoing educational efforts, the BCDF called for a nationwide strike of law students on April 6, 1989. Law schools across the country observed the day of action with various activities, sending a clear message to their faculties to diversify.[25] As discussed in the next section, this first Nationwide Law Student Strike was even more successful than the 1988 Boalt strike, as measured by its impact on legal education nationally. In retrospect, the 1989 nationwide strike represented the crest of the BCDF's resurgence, culminating that summer in the central administration's overriding of the Boalt faculty's denial of tenure to Eleanor Swift.

This high point was followed in 1990 by another nationwide effort that effectively marked the beginning of the movement's decline. In fact, the next year's Nationwide Law Student Strike probably would have been a failure at the originating school

(Boalt Hall) had a main campus diversity strike (the first campuswide strike since the Third World Strike) not been effective in funneling students to aid the Boalt effort. Both local and national conditions contributed to this weakening of student activism at Boalt.

Locally, a strategic over-emphasis on direct action for action's sake and a concomitant abdication of base-building through education led to a significant erosion in the membership of the BCDF. In addition, the perceived success of the movement reduced the sense of urgency that underpinned the once widespread popular support of the BCDF among the student body and community. Perhaps most significantly, the organization-based coalitional structure in place at Boalt was soon abandoned after the anemic 1990 National Law Student Strike. To compensate for its inability to sustain group-based support, the BCDF leadership (which now included a former CAA member) chose to dissolve the coalitional structure and reinstate the individual-membership organization that was "race-neutral." From that point on (until the BCDF's revival in the late 1990s), the protests organized by the coalition enjoyed little popular support, nudging the reorganized BCDF to undertake progressively more dramatic actions to compensate for its diminished stature and influence.[26]

This renewed decline of the BCDF in the 1990s can be traced in part to its failure to heed the centrality of race-consciousness being forwarded at that time by critical race theorists. The race-plus model of the mid-1980s BCDF, rooted in the Third World Strike of 1969, responded to the problems of racism, white privilege, and white paternalism/maternalism externally as well as within progressive coalitions. By affirmatively designing a coalitional structure that did not permit internal marginalization of racial-minority groups, the BCDF coalitional model of the mid-1980s grounded the movement in experiences and insights of out-group students. This form of "affirmative action" in the design and operation of coalitional structures could also be applied within other formations that arise from out-groups that historically have faced similar marginalization.

Nationally, other and larger forces contributed to the decline of the diversity movement at Boalt and elsewhere—namely, the organized right's effective strategy to delegitimate diversity movements through its "political correctness" campaign, and the Supreme Court's avid retrenchment on race jurisprudence. Following what would be the peak of the student-diversity movements in 1989, a pivotal *New York Times* article, "The Rising Hegemony of the Politically Correct," was published in fall of 1990. The article popularized the term "political correctness" to taboo the articulation of demands for racial, gender, and sexual justice. To illustrate, in Nexis database searches, only seventy citations indicating the use of the term "political correctness" appeared in newspapers and magazines in 1990, the year the *Times* article ran, whereas in the next year, the number of citations increased to 1,532 and reached a peak of more than 7,000 references in 1994.[27] This recasting of diversity activism as political correctness served to undermine the moral claims of such movements, previously a difficult task for conservatives and institutions in the face of both the ample data and the obvious skews of race and gender exclusion.

This assertion of majoritarian backlash was validated by the other key macro-event of those times: judicial retrenchment. It is likely that every generation of law students experiences a legal development that shapes its disposition toward law and legal practice in a profound, possibly career-altering way. For the BCDF generation, it was *Croson*. Not so much for what it said but for what it symbolized, the 1989 *Croson* ruling dropped like psychological napalm onto Boalt's burgeoning diversity movement, which by that time, and after years of frustrated efforts to diversify the faculty, was beginning to enjoy successes at home as well as national recognition of the problems associated with the lack of diversity in law-school faculties. As students were arrested for "trespassing" on law-school property in acts of civil disobedience, *Croson* seared the political imagination, demoralizing and debilitating diversity constituencies. The case was dispiriting because it symbolized retrenchment at a higher level of authority within the legal profession and the system of justice, a retrenchment that stood in stark contradiction to the diversity principles that only recently had guided the student movement to its modest successes.[28]

Not long after *Croson* came *Adarand*, and then *Podberesky* and *Hopwood*. Then the University of California regents voted in 1995 to end affirmative action. Finally, in 1996 Proposition 209 was passed by a majority of California voters. In light of these events, the Boalt administration's old slogan—"Our Hands Are Tied"—now seemed like a self-fulfilling prophecy. Today, faculty committed to diversity at Boalt and elsewhere in California are in the position of "managing the resegregation" of public education. In this context, it is of course sobering to recall and contrast the militant official resistance to *Brown v Board of Education* throughout the South and other parts of the nation with the current institutional acquiescence to the dismantling of affirmative action, which in recent years has wrought a kind of collective sigh of relief from much of the legal profession and from law-school administrations.[29]

Despite the movement's latest dormancy and unfulfilled potential, the student challenge to "business as usual" at one of the nation's top public law schools forced into the open the heretofore informal hiring and promotion practices that tended to exclude outsiders from membership within the elite, white, openly heterosexual men-only club of law faculty. Despite the shortcomings of race-plus student organizing, the message sent by student organizing for diversity at Berkeley and elsewhere was heard loud and clear across the nation. The material gains of the diversity movement, assisted in part by CRT insights and interventions, would in turn reinforce the emergence and development of CRT. By helping to effect a change in legal-academic culture, and specifically by helping to bring about dramatic increases in the hiring of faculty of color nationwide, race-plus student coalitions helped to set the stage and open the door for CRT's growth and popularity.

Outcomes

The organized student activism recounted here challenged the structure, substance, and culture of U.S. legal education, helping to fertilize the proliferation of institutional-cultural[30] resistance to the reigning (non-)analyses of race and law. Thus, prior to its spread as a form of critical legal scholarship, race-consciousness in the form of student activism already had proved itself as a viable approach to law-school organizing. This record of contemporary and historical struggle thereby stood ready to serve as a living reference point upon which to ground a race-conscious jurisprudence. Moreover, the vibrant political contestation in law schools across the country specifically in the late 1980s and early 1990s directly and positively affected critical race scholars' access to top law reviews—access that is crucial to their legitimacy and popularity and, subsequently, to their placement in top law schools.[31] Although our objective in this essay is to acknowledge student activism as a factor in these developments, we recognize that a multitude of actors, including organizations and individuals, worked to bring about law faculties that today are relatively *more* representative of this society.[32] In this fluid and intricate milieu, the positive relationship of student activism to antiracist legal theory and culture is borne out by the following empirical sketch of material gains attributable to diversity-movement politics.

According to a Society of American Law Teachers (SALT) survey conducted in 1981, 30 percent of the nation's law schools belonged to the "Zero Club" in that they had not yet hired even one person of color onto their faculties. Another 34 percent had made one (token) hire.[33] In other words, almost two-thirds of the law schools that responded to the survey had none or just one law faculty of color in 1981. From the mid-1970s throughout the 1980s, faculty of color thus hovered around 4–6 percent of full-time law teachers. The record for hiring women was similarly dismal. Ninety percent of law schools responding to a 1982 SALT survey recorded that they had 0–20 percent female faculty who were tenured or on the tenure track. More than one-third of those respondents had 0–10 percent women on the tenured or tenure-track faculty at that time.[34] And as late as 1988–89, full-time law teachers of color made up only 5.4 percent, with women composing only 23 percent of the total number of full-time law professors.[35]

Moreover, the spurious "pool argument"—that no diverse pool of qualified law-school graduates existed from which to hire—was not credible given the fact that people of color and women represented at the time 11.8 percent and 42 percent, respectively, of all enrolled J.D. students—approximately twice the levels reported for faculty members.[36] At some schools, such as Boalt, the disjuncture between student and faculty diversity was particularly appalling. In 1986, when the BCDF became active, UC Berke-

ley's law faculty included but one tenured man of color and two-and-one-half tenured white women—out of approximately forty-five tenured faculty. Yet students of color and female law students made up 25 percent and 40 percent of Boalt's students, respectively.[37] Subsequent events strongly suggest that this disjuncture became increasingly difficult for law administrations to justify in the face of determined student pressure, as sketched earlier.

In the first hiring year (1989–90) following the successful 1989 Nationwide Law Student Strike, the percentage of full-time law faculty of color shot up to 8.7 percent of the total, a 61 percent increase *in one year* (see Table 2-2 and Figure 2-2). This rise occurred in a year of nominal increase in overall faculty size, which grew at a rate of only 2.5 percent. Seemingly overnight, the pool appeared to have become much deeper and better than previously imagined. The following year (1990–91), the percentage of full-time faculty of color increased again to 10 percent, or 662 of 6,638 total law faculty. Thus, within two years of the first nationwide strike, the percentage of people of color teaching in law schools increased by 85 percent. The percentage continued to increase steadily for the next six years, to a

TABLE 2-2

Percentage of Full-time Law Teachers of Color (1975–97)

Year	Percentage
1975–76	3.78
1980–81	3.8
1982–83	5.63
1986–87	5.4
1988–89	5.4
1989–90	8.7
1990–91	10
1992–93	11.4
1996–97	13

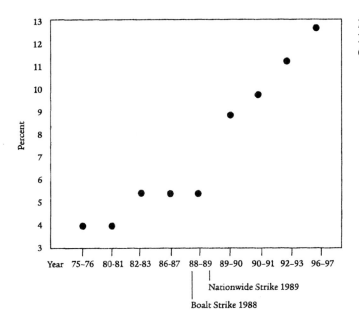

FIGURE 2-2   Percentage of Full-time Law Teachers of Color.

1996–97 high of 13 percent full-time faculty of color—a 141 percent increase from the 5.4 percent of the 1988–89 status quo.[38]

While the simple correlation reflected in Figure 2-2 does not "prove" that student activism "caused" the contemporaneous spate of diversity hires, these statistics, combined with the retrieval of political history offered earlier, make a case that the correlation reflects more than mere coincidence.

Student-diversity movements contributed to faculty diversification across race and gender lines in part because the closed system of hiring and promotion in law schools had never before been subjected to such sustained public scrutiny. The public gaze cast on the formerly secretive, arbitrary, and cronyist process of hiring and tenuring disrupted the equilibrium of power on law faculties and brought about leadership crises that led to changes. For example, in 1987, the BCDF's organizational demands to the faculty emphasized student inclusion in the faculty-hiring process and that the next five hires be diverse. Amid broad-based student and some faculty support, the BCDF would strike classes, sit in at the dean's office, take over the law library, and undergo arrest to bring about change. In the face of such turbulence, the dean's firm grip on the reins of power had to give way to more liberal or moderate actors, who could negotiate between protesting students and an entrenched old guard that was momentarily losing its balance. Understanding the negative publicity generated by such "impact agitation," many institutions of legal education undertook proactive measures to avoid Boalt's turmoil, incorporating at least token representation into their faculty ranks.

It was in this political context that CRT as a scholarly movement proliferated and achieved its initial national publicity and acclaim. The rise of CRT was aided by newly hired law teachers of color, including successive hires of "junior" RaceCrits who supported CRT scholarship in part by canonizing the early works of those we now consider "senior" RaceCrits. To be sure, the quality of work by early RaceCrits was impressive for its theoretical insight, methodological innovation, and analytical depth and breadth. But the popularization and legitimation of the intellectual movement through publication in premier student-operated law journals, and the installation (and retention and promotion) of leading RaceCrits into top law schools a few years later, was fostered in no small part by the student-catalyzed transformation of the institutional culture of legal education.

To overlook the role of local and national student organizing in bringing about these changes is dangerous to CRT as a long-term project. Such oversight buttresses the liberal myth of self-correcting societal institutions, such as law faculties, that respond to social injustice and "better argument." In this telling, law schools diversified when exceptional candidates of color miraculously presented and proved themselves worthy. Thus, the sudden arrival of academic non-white "stars" precipitated social change; sustained and heated political activism was merely incidental, maybe even detrimental, to the diversification process. However, in our view, this myth of self-correcting institutions not only masks actual workings of sociological power; it can also lead to strategies among progressives that easily may be coupled and turned against progressive politics. In our view, a more appropriate and antisubordinationist history would not lose sight of the centrality of collective agency in the rise of CRT.

Our analysis of various movement structures suggests that individualistic or race-neutral strategies at the level of organizing resistance are not as effective or empowering as race-conscious structures. The next part of the essay attempts to show that intersubjective, rather than intertextual, method at the level of writing scholarship, and synergism rather than sublimation at

the level of doing theory, help to avoid co-optation of progressive politics. Moreover, as we will show in the following arguments, radical separation of theory from activism not only encourages progressive strategies that permit external co-optation but also promotes theoretical extravagance. In particular, we focus on how unmodified antiessentialism and the outsider critique of identity politics not only overlook the lessons to be drawn from race-plus, group-based student coalitions, but also fail to meet the challenges posed to activist communities of color by two ongoing developments: retrenchment on the right and attacks on identity politics by the allegedly progressive/radical left.

Movements and Critical Theory

In the first half of this essay, we considered the development of a race-conscious, race-plus, group-based infrastructure for political resistance in higher education and highlighted points of articulation between this resistance and CRT. We now offer some thoughts on the need to understand movement history as part of a valuable body of subjugated knowledge—knowledge considered illicit, crude, and low-ranking. Throughout, we remain convinced of the possible synergism between movement politics and critical theory. In so doing, we register a warning against the dangers of sublimating movements.

Subjugated Knowledge and Movement Histories

The new student [African American, other minority, women's and radical white] groups changed the atmosphere at Boalt Hall, not only because many of them tended to be militant and distrustful, but because they often did not respond to traditional law school teaching methods. . . .

The strained relationships of the 1980s were confirmed in faculty interviews. . . . Whatever the contrasts in motivation or approach, it was generally agreed that the dozens of confrontations that had occurred over the previous 20 years had taken a heavy toll on the environment at Boalt Hall and that the warm, collegial atmosphere of earlier days had been replaced with formality, distrust and hostility.
—Sandra Epstein[39]

Since its foundation in 1882, the School of Law (Boalt Hall) has demonstrated through progressive admissions policies its commitment to diversity in legal education.
—Cecilia V. Estolano et al.[40]

Instead of shutting down the school or protesting at the dean's office, we are doing heavy duty lifting of policy analysis.
—*Chicago Tribune*[41]

The work of student-diversity activists constitutes a form of subjugated knowledge as defined by Michel Foucault: "a whole set of knowledges that have been disqualified as inadequate to their task or insufficiently elaborated: naive knowledges, located low down on the hierarchy, beneath the required level of cognition." One task of critical opposition to supremacy and subordination is to disinter such knowledge in order to "establish a historical knowledge of struggles and to make use of this knowledge tactically today." Subjugated knowledge challenges unitary theories, from both the right and the left, that purport to offer a totalizing picture of how societies are ordered.[42]

A recent work on the "history of Boalt Hall" shows the process by which a dominant discourse absorbs and invisibilizes the illicit knowledge produced by movements of resistance. In that history, Sandra Epstein writes about the 1980s student movements only briefly in her lengthy celebration of Boalt's past, and without citing a single member of the BCDF. Instead, the story is told through the eyes of faculty and admin-istrators who resisted the student challenge to Euroheteropatriarchy. Epstein describes "angry students" for whom "confrontation became a way of life" crafting "manifestos" and "disrupt[ing] classes," caricaturing the broad-based movement that was able to garner 80–90 percent student support for its nonviolent boycotts of Boalt classes and to change, at least for a time, faculty-hiring policies. She characterizes negatively the UC Berkeley central administration's closer scrutiny of Boalt's hiring and tenuring policies and "blames" not the law school's concerted intransigence against faculty heterogeneity in the face of an increasingly diverse society, state, and campus, nor the targeting of women in two denials of tenure that later were reversed, but student protesters who "seemed to be setting the law school agenda."[43] In reifying the narrative of privilege, this account revises rather than recounts events and insights during a key moment in the institution's history. And in doing so, this revisionism seeks to subjugate movement history and knowledge.

Perhaps a more disappointing example of the erasure and disparagement of student activism in service of a self-correcting institution narrative appears in "New Directions for Diversity," a report written by Boalt students. In this otherwise critical report on the Boalt admissions process in the wake of Proposition 209, the authors imagine an institution that they claim has demonstrated "commitment to diversity in legal education" by virtue of the 40 percent student-of-color enrollment in pre-Proposition 209 California. The report presents a history of admissions at Boalt that fails to note the 1972 admissions strike, the 1977–79 HEW investigation, or the BCDF struggles of the 1980s. Not surprisingly, this account concludes by extolling Boalt's pro-diversity tradition. While extremely useful for its policy analysis and concrete recommendations, this report plays a dangerous game by stipulating to a sanitized institutional history, presumably in exchange for greater currency with the administration and faculty. Such a "policy not protest" approach may produce short-term gains but at the cost of doing a potential violence to the very culture of movement politics that makes possible meaningful student input toward progressive reform policies. Put plainly, a "good cop–bad cop" reform strategy can work only if the "good" cop does not begin to believe that the "bad" cop actually is bad and expendable. An institutional history that offers no account of political struggles fought over the institution's identity and future is not only seriously incomplete. It also aids other apologist discourse that elides subjugated knowledge.[44] CRT's sense of self and its antisubordination purpose mean that it must deny this aid.

Generally, CRT scholarship seeks transformation through recovery of, and emphasis on, excluded and marginalized elements of the body politic. CRT participates in the production of knowledge through the creation of a counter-discourse that documents and disseminates the knowledge and experience of the oppressed and silenced.[45] The antisubordination counter-discourse of CRT consequently stands opposed to powerfully entrenched systems of totalizing knowledge that function in part through the selection and exclusion of data, such as the administration's version of Boalt's history. But the systems of domination that CRT opposes cannot bear having their histories told. History is dangerous territory for oppressors because it cannot sustain their shopworn alibis, which legitimate unjust power arrangements through the purgation of history and the subjugation of illicit knowledge produced in resistance experiences. Thus, CRT from its inception has taken seriously the power–knowledge coupling recognized by critical theory. For this reason, we should bear in mind that social movements long

have been a primary effect, as well as a constituent of, power–knowledge configurations.

To engage in relevant and effective antisubordination theorizing, CRT therefore must not lose sight of the histories of resistance. These histories orient the collective intellectual project toward combating the danger of internal disunity. These histories also may help create the conditions of solidarity necessary for progressive political-community formation. And indeed, key CRT texts also subscribe to this commitment, claiming it as foundational to CRT from the outset. Proceeding from this commitment to community formation, we next urge that the internal antagonisms and solidarities lived by movements become both sites of critical intervention and places from which we speak as counter-discursive subjects. In order to account for social movements more seriously in our work, we will turn to two methods that can be adopted by CRT scholars attempting reclamation of resistance histories to advance CRT's antisubordination project: the methods of synergy and sublimation.

Between Synergism and Sublimation

We have tried to establish closer developmental linkages in this essay between CRT and contemporary race-conscious political struggles, suggesting how the latter have been foundational to the former. In this final section, we explore two models for relating movement histories to CRT "synergism" and "sublimation." We conclude that CRT's next decade should adopt more synergistic modes of interacting with movements and movement histories because synergism, unlike sublimation, is congruent with CRT's commitments to community formation and social transformation.

The Benefits of Synergism: Theory, Practice, and Politics: Synergism refers generally to an interaction of agents or conditions that produces a combined effect that is greater than the sum of the individual parts and effects. In this essay, we use the term as metaphor. Here, it signifies a heightened potential for social-justice change, which may be unleashed specifically through a conscious commitment to the dialogical project of linking subjugated spheres of knowledge with the established yet evolving scholarly practices of CRT. Synergism is a vitally important possibility for a project, such as CRT, that attempts to affect the political world through discursive intervention. Such a project is necessarily collective and collaborative, requiring analysis of information and exchange of insights gleaned from the experiences of movements to formulate discursive strategies that, in turn, ultimately must be tested in the context of actual, prospective struggle.

The intersubjective nature of the CRT project underscores its political-theoretical essence: The moment critical race theorizing loses its grounding in the political and the communal is the moment that CRT ceases to be an antisubordinationist project. The search for subjugated knowledge therefore is an attempt to preserve the history and the meaning of struggle as well as the context of movement politics. In this sense, such a search manifests a synergistic approach to critical theorizing, while the ahistorical pursuit of the "theoretical" represents an abdication of political engagement and the relinquishing of the full promise of antisubordinationist intellectual production.

We consequently envision a mode of synergistic theorizing grounded in movement history and knowledge that contains both substantive and methodological commitments. This envisioned mode of theorizing instantiates the contestation with power by racially conscious political movements by "doing" race-conscious theory whose "sci-

entism"—data, logic, verifiability, etc.—grows organically from political context. Under this vision of synergism, theory is judged against its ability to have coherence, relevance, and explanatory power vis-à-vis particular movement histories and actual power struggles; if a defining substantive commitment of CRT is understood to be "antisubordination" in favor of outsider groups, this method would entail not only "*looking* to the bottom" to inform CRT's focus, but also transcending the split between subject (theory) and object (outsider politics) by reconfiguring the relations of cognition. This much has been recognized since CRT's founding.

One of CRT's early critiques of CLS was that the latter's abstract theoretical trashing of "rights" did not capture community dynamics or the lived experience of people of color. CRT set out to remedy this approach by incorporating practice and experience from political struggle into the production of theory.[46] As outsider intellectuals, our goal and strategy articulation was—and is—to construct a dialogue that is intersubjective and genealogically wedded to the resistance discourses and practices that perform the movement.

Uniting grounded theory with informed practice through synergism perhaps is more urgent as we enter CRT's second decade than it was in its early years. The continuing and accelerating degeneration of equality jurisprudence, and the long-standing political–rhetorical attacks on the diversity ethic, cry out for a close, critical association between antisubordination theory and antisubordination practice through and within CRT. Right-wing political–rhetorical strategies such as the political-correctness attack on diversity activists, which in turn buttress judicial and scholarly retrenchment, underscore the need for CRT's oppositionalist intellectuals to be aware of movement dynamics in order to sustain and nurture progressive change. In addition, CRT scholars must remain cognizant of the "little histories" of resistance so that they can resist essentializing the "History" of social and jurisprudential change.

This heightened attention to movement needs and histories can ensure during the coming decade a healthy synergism between theory and praxis. It can also avoid the dangers of sublimation because, when they are successful, coalitional movements represent the practice of synergism—uniting grounded theory with informed practice. As we begin CRT's second decade, we must recall and recognize that the history and lessons of student resistance and other social-justice movements can help ground and animate antisubordinationist discourse projects in the realm of law and culture. Indeed, we may look to student and community organizing for examples of synergism from which CRT can learn.

In sum, CRT scholars must strive to become more accountable in our work to the people, goals, and ideas of movements. We must strive in the coming decade to overcome the tendency to construct with our work an intertextual universe that has, at best, a "virtual" relationship to social struggle. The intersubjectivity, not intertextuality, of the synergistic approach also can help ensure that our work will grow under ever more congenial "relations of production." And as *critical* academics, we must acknowledge the difficulty of maintaining the immediate connection to movement politics: To the extent that we perform as "disenchanted intellectuals," we should be mainly disenchanted with our collective first-decade failure to stay grounded at all times. The second decade thus presents CRT with a basic challenge: to remain audacious in our demands to power, and in speaking simple truths to power, but without the arrogance of telling communities in struggle how to dream, to imagine their empowerment, or to narrate

their political identity—especially insofar as we remain in the gilded cage of academe. We have to achieve a certain humility and accountability vis-à-vis those who not only confront power directly, but also bear the costs of that confrontation.[47] Synergism is "good" precisely because it helps us meet this basic challenge.

The Dangers of Sublimation: Before and After Postmodernism: Using activist understandings in one's work is often viewed within critical intellectual circles as the crude expression of selfish desire, a faux pas to be suppressed or forgiven—or, at best, to be appropriately cabined within a redeeming theoretical insight. But to us, this type of self-censorship is an example of sublimation. Sublimation, in its psychoanalytic use, has a structural form in which a primary realm (primitive desire) is subordinated to a secondary realm (socially acceptable behavior). To sublimate, in its metaphorical use here, thus means to divert the expression of an insight or an instinct to a form that is considered socially or culturally acceptable. In this context, sublimation may characterize a particular structuring of the historical and conceptual relationship between CRT and movement history, in which the primary realm (movement politics) is repressed or made harmless under the imagined imperatives of the secondary realm (theoretical discourse).[48] To illustrate, we offer the embrace and spread of antiessentialism within CRT as an example of sublimation.

Sublimation took shape in CRT through its "postmodern turn," especially its adoption of antiessentialism as a primary intellectual stance and dominant cultural norm. Antiessentialist theorists associated with CRT based their work in part on the experiences of the marginalized. In particular, they have recounted the experiences of African American women, who too often are absorbed, made invisible, and marginalized within predominantly white, straight, middle-class progressive movements. Similar moves also highlighted parallel issues regarding lesbians in feminist movements and of gay people of color in predominantly white-dominated gay/lesbian/bisexual/transgendered (GLBT) movements. These interventions were important and necessary. Indeed, insofar as antiessentialist theory is built on a foundation of movement experiences, it is consistent with our synergistic approach: At its best, antiessentialism sets the stage for the deconstruction of falsely universalistic group identities that obscure significant group particularities. But what starts as a bold critique of racism, or of other forms of exclusion within a larger progressive movement, *may* generate a troubling call to reject "shared victimization" in favor of more "positive," relational, and contingent identities.[49] The antiessentialist critique may yield such troubling calls because it questions the viability of identity-based communities, valorizing instead shifting "coalitions" composed simply of individuals and based on perceptions of common interest.

The grounding of such a coalition of "individuals" purports in antiessentialist theorizing to offer a more advanced and accurate account of both the political subject and politics, but the Boalt case study discussed earlier suggests that this proposition deserves to be approached with some skepticism. Recall, for example, that when the BCDF shifted from a group-based coalition of identity-based groups to an individual-membership organization, it fell into disarray and decline. When it lost its essentialist, race-plus, group-based structure, the coalition dissolved into an organization of leaders who lacked a base. Unfortunately, CRT's first decade of "unmodified antiessentialism" has included few limiting principles to prevent minority collectivities from being utterly

deconstructed into disunited and atomized individuals, themselves understood as unstable constructs who attain "identities" only through a process of perpetual cultural reperformance.

Consequently—and ironically—critical antiessentialist theorists may end up underestimating the power and force of racism and other forms of supremacy as *formidable and concrete political structures*. Focusing primarily on the realms of ideologies and cultures of racism, antiessentialists seek to combat racial oppression with conceptual reframings, counter-discourses, paradigmatic shifts, creative performances, and cultural contestations. But on the whole, they do not emphasize direct confrontation with entrenched political institutions and structures of racism that require strategic thinking, disciplined organization, and coordinated tactics. In this way, unmodified antiessentialism potentially underestimates the need for political unity and group-based, even "essentialist," structures of political organization to respond to the existing structures of oppression.[50]

Of course, CRT's postmodernism was motivated by the hope that antiessentialism would help to empower people of color, securing for racial out-groups an autonomy of self-definition that historically has been denied. In this way, race and gender essentialisms would be overturned. Incoherent group classifications would be unmasked as a stratagem of oppressive power that reinforced the invisibility of marginalized groups. Implicit in this turn was the valorization of syncretic methods of analysis and, ironically, a humanist ideal of intellectual and social exchange. Despite its imperfections, the postmodern turn's promise was both deconstructive and restorative: It would reveal the discursive and actual violence of modernist racial practices and open genuine space for the flourishing of the diverse, the multicultural. Antiessentialism invited coalitional possibilities for autonomously defined identities, but its danger would arise from the politics of timing and immediate context.[51]

The postmodern turn of the early 1990s took place across disciplines, including, but by no means primarily, within the legal academy. And although postmodernism seemed mainly to affect the scholarly and methodological approaches of left-leaning academics, its antiessentialism lent itself to furthering certain aspects of the right's attack on race-consciousness. Concurrently with CRT's embrace of antiessentialism, sociopolitical critics on the right and left questioned at the same time, but for different reasons, the coherence of the race concept, the assumption of its immutability, and the fiction of its transparency. Within and beyond CRT, race was being retooled variously as a social construction, a dangerous trope, or a performance, in contrast to outdated and discredited notions of race as a biological fact of difference among groups. Thus, one of the most significant outcomes of the postmodern turn for Race-Crits was that "race," as a basis of antiracist consciousness and group identity, was put under pressure, even erasure.[52] The political-correctness rhetoric, coupled with the erasure of race facilitated by antiessentialism, was synergistic in its racist effects.[53] In this political context, the postmodern turn in academe did not help diversity-movement politics that faced formidable administrative aggression (targeting student leaders for disciplinary action, arrest, and prosecution) and political and judicial retrenchment on race and rights.[54]

Today, in the aftermath of that unfortunate convergence, the unmet challenge for CRT, and especially for antiessentialists, is to propose political-organizing structures that can be an alternative to "essentialist" group-based political formations. How are such organizations to be built under the formulation of a contingent, temporary, and relational identity? On what foundation can difference and creativity be used to "will" political formations into existence? How will such a program be effective in challenging established structures of subordination that are powerful and organizationally structured—the reality of Euroheteropatriarchy?[55]

In our view, then, one of the main dangers to theory and movements posed by sublimationist forms of antiessentialism is its potential to promote an abstract and endless expedition into the celebration of individual particularity. We believe that an autonomous theory of antiessentialism with no limiting principles plays too easily into the hands of the enemies of progressive politics. Unmodified devotion to antiessentialism simply is beside the point in a political arena in which those opposed to inclusive change are themselves virulently essentialist.

What should be the limiting principles on antiessentialism discourse for a progressive scholarly organization seeking to implement antisubordination principles through movement politics? Limiting principles should reflect a commitment to activist struggle within and among communities of color for social justice. In recognition of the reality that social-justice aims often cannot be achieved in the absence of coalitional efforts, limiting principles on antiessentialism discourse must satisfy the rule of relevance to the possibility of effective coalitions for justice. In other words, the only reason to engage in antiessentialist discourse from an activist standpoint is to reckon with patterns of thought or action within progressive politics that inhibit coalitional efforts to implement antisubordination principles or achieve social justice.

Another danger of the sublimationist treatment of movements within CRT is the overestimation of both the extent and scope of regressiveness within race-plus organizational models to justify the antiessentialist turn.[56] To be sure, antiessentialist rhetoric and analysis will remain a useful method when the categories within which progressive politics takes place have become too rigid to ground useful coalitions. But respect for difference in activist politics represents at this point a platitude already evident to, and internalized by, conscientious essentialists in student resistance efforts. For only by recognizing, addressing, and transforming differences into political solidarities could student and other activists hope to go forward with a successful diversity movement. To be candid, race-plus organizers who effectively operated during the 1980s under the principle of "conscientious essentialism" already had learned and applied the lessons of antiessentialism, which CRT laboriously has struggled over, and without losing political focus—as suggested by the movement slogan, "Unified, but Not Uniform." In light of timing and context, the fascination with antiessentialism during CRT's first decade was a luxury available only to those who did not have to face the increasing difficulties of race-plus political organizing and coalition-building in the face of a growing anti-diversity backlash.

Thus, critical-race antiessentialists from the outset could have learned from student and other activist movements to distinguish between *conscientiously* essentialist political groupings that formed precisely as a response to antiessentialist critiques of existing movements (i.e., organizing among students of color that resulted from their feeling excluded from colorblind individual-membership organizations) and *crudely* essentialist political groupings whose narrow nationalisms or (hetero)sexisms subverted progressive political formations. Through greater attention and interaction, CRT scholars might have recognized, and possibly learned from, those vibrant diversity movements led largely by students of color, gays and lesbians, and women's

groups that were performing of necessity, and from the outset, a modified form of antiessentialism. Those missed original lessons cry out for recognition today, after ten years not only of CRT but also of backlash.

By excavating and sharing subjugated knowledge and repressed movement histories, CRT in its second decade may come to understand better how even imperfect movements have pushed forward the struggle we inherit today, just as our flawed efforts will nevertheless provide a basis for future resistance. Understanding through synergism our fragility and ability to prevail against overwhelming odds might inculcate a greater appreciation for intergroup justice as a key CRT goal, and help to stimulate intersubjective method that will promote greater expression of the "political" in our search for the "theoretical" through a modified form of antiessentialism. CRT in its second decade can help revive key lessons to be drawn from historical memory, which are so vital to the regeneration of community formation, to the advancement of race-based resistance, and to the grounding of antisubordination legal scholarship.[57]

Closing Thoughts on CRT's Organizational Structure

In closing, we raise some questions for the future of CRT as an organization. We see CRT in its current form of annual workshops and occasional conferences as an individual-membership organization of progressives of color, not a race-plus group-based coalition. In the future, the current formation may be replaced by other forms of organization. How will leadership development, agenda-setting, and strategic decision-making by people of color be respected under various models we might consider? Should CRT open its membership to all sympathetic parties? Is a race-plus coalitional structure in order? And if so, what are the implications for the current status of CRT under such a new structure? Would CRT "dissolve" into such a coalition? Or would it become an organizational member of the coalition?

CRT should heed the historical social-movement lessons noted earlier regarding the substantive and strategic significance of political structure. CRT should approach calls to open itself to becoming a membership organization composed of individuals with caution. Based on our case study, the ongoing centrality of race, as well as the ongoing salience of racial paternalism in progressive movements, demands that a race-conscious approach and leadership structure be built into progressive political organizations. It seems rather curious to us that some who acknowledge the importance of CRT's race-consciousness in legal scholarship seem to suggest simultaneously that we get "beyond identity" and, therefore, beyond the race-conscious organizational structure of CRT's historic workshops in favor of structureless gatherings open to all comers.

We see an increasing, rather than decreasing, necessity for progressive intellectuals of color to convene and form an identity-conscious community. For this reason, we believe that intellectuals of color can be a vital component in radically resisting contemporary race-based and race-coded subordination, from "three strikes you're out," to Propositions 187, 209, and 227, to *Hopwood*, and so forth. We also predict that if, instead, a "colorblind" formation prevails, organized around the (ironically) modernist basis of "politics, not identity," it will have a deleterious impact on the development of leadership among people of color—particularly of women of color, les/bi/gay people of color, and immigrants of color—in the larger intellectual-activist community. Indeed, colorblind political structures proposed in the name of more "progressive" politics ignore the very dynamics that historically gave rise to CRT and to other racial political forma-

tions—that is, the disaffection and alienation from the "left," which, in its "non-race-consciousness," produced default norms, agendas, theories, strategies, decision-making processes, and leadership that reflected white perspectivalism and dominance.

We should clarify that we are not suggesting a pre-Mecca Malcolm X rejection of progressive whites in the movement. Rather, we recognize the continuing force of racism even in progressive political communities, and the legacy of white supremacy in its suppression of leadership development among people of color, particularly those that are multiply identified. Until these larger forces are tamed, we believe, membership organizations of people of color will be needed. However, once such organizations or communities have been established, meaningful coalitions may be built with other organized constituencies. To develop this project further, we should encourage the further development of LatCrit, APACrit, and other racial sub-groupings, such as American Indian legal scholars, that will interact with CRT's constituency on an egalitarian basis. CRT might serve as the convener of a race-plus coalition with these groups, which might also include other LawCrits with established bases, such as FemCrits, GLBTCrits, CLS, SALT members, and New Approaches to International Law (NAIL) members, to name a few. If we take seriously the challenge of collective political engagement, synergistic theorizing, and intersubjective methodology, CRT in its next decade will need to address and resolve these questions of organizational structure. And to do so, it should heed the lessons of movement histories outlined earlier.

Conclusion

Antiracist organizing, we have shown, shares some of the complexities encountered in antiracist theorizing, but the strengths and weaknesses of the former are different from those of the latter. One of the great strengths of antiracist organizing within the student-diversity movement at Boalt was its adoption of organizational methods forged in the practical, everyday concerns of political struggle. In particular, the innovative approaches of prior successful student-of-color movements led to an organizational-coalition model linked to membership organizations made up of individuals from a range of people of color, les/bi/gay, and women's groups. This structure of race-plus organizing enabled students of color to contend with the entrenched power structure of legal education for significant institutional changes.

Our goal in this essay therefore has been to ground CRT in the history of student resistance movements both to reveal the political context of CRT's emergence and to raise for further reflection the strengths and weaknesses of the historical cross-pollination between praxis and theory. We have sought to do this not simply to add one more legend to the genesis stories that are told about a successful and powerful institutional innovation. Instead, our chief aim has been to suggest ways in which CRT-identified scholars might act collectively to contend with the continuing and coming storms of backlash and retrenchment against racial and social justice, which already engulf us.

Looking forward to the next decade of CRT, our synergistic, intersubjective approach links theory with the lived experience of subordination and political resistance thereto. Concretely, this approach may mean replacing or modifying the culture of antiessentialism in CRT, reclaiming the moral high ground for identity-based political organizing, and reaffirming the centrality of collective agency in the creation of political and counter-discursive space. In light of the sub-jugated, and now reclaimed, knowledge of the student-diversity struggles, the practical turn for CRT scholars in the coming decade could mean the employment of CRT to develop and mobilize egalitarian, race-plus coalitions to expand and advance transformative antisubordination strategies.

Appendix: Timeline Addendum: Race-Conscious Student Activism at UC Berkeley (1964–91)

Fall 1964: A new era of student activism is ushered in with the Free Speech Movement of 1964, which has its racial roots in the university's attempted suppression of antiracist organizing by members of CORE and other civil-rights organizations who had returned from Freedom Summer in Mississippi.

Fall 1968: Early race-conscious forms of political organizing on college campuses, beginning with the Third World Strikes at San Francisco State University, innovated a group-based coalitional model for shared decision-making and power-sharing that was successfully re-created in subsequent decades.

Winter 1969: TWLF forms and calls for Third World Strike

Spring 1969: Third World Strike ends with creation of ethnic-studies departments and adoption of affirmative-action recruitment and admissions policies.

Fall 1969: Entering class at Boalt comprises 12 percent students of color.

Fall 1970: Entering class at Boalt comprises 18 percent students of color.

Fall 1971: Entering class at Boalt comprises 31 percent students of color. Boalt faculty considers eliminating or significantly curtailing special admissions.

April–May 1972: Boalt Hall strike on admissions, led by Black, Chicano, and Asian American students and the school's lone Native American student, wins the law school's commitment to a 28 percent special-admissions goal.

March 1975: Alan Bakke is denied admission to the University of California, Davis, medical school at trial court. The school's special-admissions program is declared unconstitutional. Both sides appeal directly to the California Supreme Court.

1975: AALSA protests the removal of Japanese Americans from Boalt's special-admissions program and 50 percent cutback of Chinese Americans, absent any study.

September 1976: The California Supreme Court finds the special-admissions program in *Bakke* case to be unconstitutional.

1976: Soweto uprisings take place in South Africa.

1977–78: Anti-apartheid/divestment movement and activism/affirmative-action organizing around *Bakke* case. Issues involving international racism, such as South African apartheid and Central American solidarity work, attracted primarily white activists in the 1970s and early 1980s. Conversely, student-of-color activists tended to link racism overseas to racism closer to home, organizing actively around the *Bakke* decision on affirmative action in the late 1970s.

Fall 1977: The Coalition for a Diversified Faculty (CDF) forms at Boalt.

March 21, 1978: All-day CDF strike and teach-in is 75–90 percent successful.

June 28, 1978: The U.S. Supreme Court rejects quotas and affirms race as a "plus" factor in admissions.

Late 1970s: Formation of critical legal studies (CLS).

April 9, 1979: CDF files Title VI/IX complaints with U.S. Department of Housing, Education, and Welfare (HEW).

January 1980: HEW investigates the complaint but ultimately concludes that Boalt's faculty is no less diverse than that of other elite law schools.

1981: Harvard law students, led by Kimberlé Crenshaw, form the "Alternative Course" to replace Derrick Bell's "Race, Racism, and American Law" class, inviting many future critical-race scholars, including Richard Delgado, Neil Gotanda, Linda Greene, Charles Lawrence, and Mari Matsuda.

November 1982: Law Professor David Chambers publishes results of SALT Survey on Minority Group Persons in Law School Teaching.

1983: Chambers publishes results of SALT Survey on Women in Law School Teaching.

November 1983: Jesse Jackson announces his presidential candidacy and forms the Rainbow Coalition.

Fall 1984: Twenty-Year Commemoration of the Free Speech Movement. Veterans return and encourage anti-apartheid coalitions. UPC forms as a membership organization of progressives of color to address apartheid in South Africa and local issues of racism. Student-of-color and les/bi/gay students form the electoral coalition Cal-SERVE, which remains the oldest active political party in UC Berkeley student electoral politics.

November 1984: Randall Robinson of Transafrica; Civil Rights Commissioner Mary Frances Berry; and Washington, D.C., Representative Walter Fauntroy are arrested for their symbolic demonstration against apartheid in front of South African embassy. Within weeks, their arrests spark similar protests at embassies in a dozen cities, including Salt Lake City, Boston, Chicago, and Houston.

1985: Boalt faculty deny tenure to Marjorie Shultz, the first woman to come up for tenure at Boalt since 1972. Shultz appeals the decision within the university. The campuswide administration grants her an unusual lifetime security of employment as a lecturer.

November 1985: Law students active in UPC form United Law Students of Color (ULSC) to discuss issues of hostile environment, faculty diversity, and admissions at the law school.

April 7, 1986: Boalt students strike to protest the University of California's support of apartheid in South Africa and at home.

1986: Over President Reagan's strong objections, Congress imposes strict economic sanctions against South Africa.

Spring 1986: Strategic differences mount among students of color and whites who are organizing against apartheid across the country and lead to a public split at UC Berkeley. Efforts to build and grow the movement by UPC are criticized as "not radical enough" by the mostly white Campaign Against Apartheid (CAA) members, while CAA tactics designed to defy authority are seen by UPC as self-indulgent and far removed from the stated target of the movement—that is, the South African apartheid regime.

Summer 1986: UC Regents vote to divest funds from South Africa. Having won divestment of UC funds from South Africa in 1986, anti-apartheid activists of color focus on issues of racism at the faculty, student body, and curricular levels of the university. With the organizational structures and political momentum of the anti-apartheid movement, the diversity movements of the late 1980s and early 1990s begin to take shape.

Fall 1986: The faculty-diversity committee of ULSC expands its membership to the larger law-school community and adopts the name Boalt Coalition for a Diversified Faculty (BCDF).

1986: Feminists and scholars of color begin to organize at the annual CLS conference. The critical race scholar Charles Lawrence calls for voluntary quotas for minority hiring in member law schools of the Association of American Law Schools (AALS).

1986–87: The BCDF engages in an intensive lobbying and consciousness-raising efforts.

Fall 1987: The BCDF adopts a "race-plus" coalitional structure, with members from AALSA, BLSA, LRLSA, and the Boalt Hall Women's Association on the steering committee and continues base-building, education, and organizing efforts.

June 1987: Boalt faculty deny Eleanor Swift tenure. At the time of Swift's denial, Boalt has only two tenured female faculty out of forty-five total faculty. Swift files a grievance with the Committee on Privilege and Tenure.

1987: Scholars of color issue racial critiques of CLS and annual conference on the theme "The Sounds of Silence." Papers at this gathering are published as "Minority Critiques of Legal Academe" by *Harvard Civil Rights–Civil Liberties Law Review.*

March 1988: The BCDF calls for law-school strike, which is 80 percent effective. Twenty-eight students are arrested for trespassing after a six-hour sit-in to protest Boalt's hiring and tenuring record.

Fall 1988: Out of five hires, four are "diversity hires," including the first critical race theorist, Angela Harris; the first Latino, Dan Rodriguez; the feminist scholar Reva Siegel;

and Bryan Ford, an African American. These hires more than double the number of faculty of color at Boalt and increase the female faculty on the tenure track by approximately 50 percent.

October 1988: Eleanor Swift and her attorney, Mary Dunlap, announce a prima facie finding of sex discrimination by UC Berkeley's Committee on Privilege and Tenure. Two weeks later, Boalt faculty reconsider Marge Shultz's case and vote to grant her tenure.

1988: Law professor and SALT member Richard Chused conducts follow-up report to Chambers' surveys on the hiring and retention of women and minorities on American law-school faculties.

April 1989: The BCDF organizes the first Nationwide Law Student Strike for Diversity, which is highly successful. The National Lawyers Guild compiles the activities across the country into information packets.

August 1989: UC Berkeley Chancellor Heyman grants tenure to Eleanor Swift.

1989: The U.S. Supreme Court decides the *Croson* case, requiring strict-scrutiny standard of review for local affirmative-action plans.

1989–90: The proportion of full-time law faculty of color increases by 61 percent in one year.

April 1990: A campuswide strike for diversity at UC Berkeley is 80–90 percent effective and lends support to the second Nationwide Law Student Strike for Diversity.

Fall 1990: Richard Bernstein publishes "The Rising Hegemony of the Politically Correct," an influential article decrying "political correctness," in the *New York Times Magazine.* The *Croson* decision, tactical missteps by the BCDF, an emphasis on direct action and away from education and base-building, and the perception of success and institutional reforms lead to a decline in BCDF organizing, until California voters pass Proposition 209 in 1995, which eliminates affirmative action in public education. In response, Boalt student activism again becomes national news through the report "New Directions for Diversity," the Boalt Coalition for a Diversified Faculty/Student Body, and Students for Equal Opportunity.

Notes

1. Richard Delgado, editor of one of the first two leading anthologies on Critical Race Theory, begins his genesis story in the mid-1970s with an acknowledgment of the "early work of Derrick Bell and Alan Freeman"—both legal scholars writing on race. Professor Delgado notably identifies the American Civil Rights Movement and other nationalist movements as providing "inspiration" to CRT. He further acknowledges CRT's intellectual debt to critical legal studies, feminism, and continental social and political philosophy. See Richard Delgado, ed., *Critical Race Theory: The Cutting Edge* (Philadelphia: Temple University Press, 1995), xiii–xiv. See also Angela P. Harris, "Foreword—The Jurisprudence of Reconstruction," *California Law Review* 82 (1994): 741, 741 (1994), identifying July 1989 at the first Annual CRT Workshop as the birth date and birthplace of CRT.

Indeed, Richard Delgado was one of a handful of early faculty supporters of the 1980s–90s student movement for diversity. He supported the BCDF by speaking at our educational events and rejecting forcefully the standard rationalizations offered by the administration for its failure to diversify. Most recently, he performed the same function for a national group of students organizing to maintain diversity in legal education in the wake of *Hopwood* and Proposition 209.

2. Kimberlé W. Crenshaw, Neil Gotanda, Gary Peller, and Kendall Thomas, eds., *Critical Race Theory: The Key Writings That Formed the Movement* (New York: New Press, 1995), xiv, xix.

3. We also should avoid overstating the Harvard-centricity of CRT by focusing perhaps too much attention on Harvard's 1981 Alternative Course protest and the Harvard-based CLS movement generally. One first-wave RaceCrit provides a useful counterpoint in this context. Acknowledging that the material gains won by student-led diversity movements had a direct impact on CRT's rise, Mari Matsuda identifies as part of CRT's genesis the "resurgence of student activism," including "sit-ins, rallies, and guerrilla actions" at Boalt, Stanford, Harvard, and Columbia that resulted in "affirmative action hiring" and race-themed conferences: Mari J. Matsuda, *Where Is Your Body?* (Boston: Beacon Press, 1996), 50.

4. Eric K. Yamamoto, "Critical Race Praxis: Race Theory and Political Lawyering Practice in Post-Civil Rights America," *Michigan Law Review* 95 (1997): 821, 869, 874, observing that the disjuncture between "high theory" generated by critical race theorists and "frontline practice" exercised by progressive lawyers tends to result in abstracted theories that are untested and untestable through either practical experience or material gain for those who are racially subordinated. Although Yamamoto does integrate the role of community activists into his formulation of critical race praxis, throughout the article and in the title he emphasizes the interaction between legal race theory and political lawyering: ibid., 830-9.

5. We use the term "race-plus" to designate the centrality and historicity of race-based organizing that recognized a network of oppressions and embraces coalitional consciousness and solidarity with other outsider groups. Other potential bases for coalition include axes of antisubordination resistance, specifically feminist projects, GLBT liberation, and progressive white identity formation.

6. Mario Savio, "Berkeley Fall: The Berkeley Student Rebellion of 1964," in Mario Savio, Eugene Walker, and Raya Dunayevskaya, *The Free Speech Movement and the Negro Revolution* (Detroit: News & Letters, 1965), 15.

7. Farmer addressing a Free Speech Movement rally of more than 1,500 students and faculty members at UC Berkeley, December 20, 1964, quoted in ibid., 7.

8. Arguably, one could begin this tracing with the House of Un-American Activities Committee (HUAC) hearings conducting in San Francisco in 1960 that were protested by UC Berkeley students. However, the racial origins of that protest were more nebulous. Although there was chronological overlap between the HUAC protest and Civil Rights struggles in the South, the linkages among participants were much more tenuous: see Raya Dunayevskaya, "FSM and the Negro Revolution," in Savio et al., *Free Speech Movement*, 21-2. We start with the Free Speech Movement as one of the earliest, defining moments of mass antiracist student protest. Upon their return from Mississippi Freedom Summer of 1964, Berkeley civil-rights activist-students were confronted with a University of California administration ruling on September 14, 1964, that curtailed not only the substance and manner of speech on university grounds, but also the solicitation of funds and recruitment by civil-rights and other political organizations: ibid., 23-4.

See Eugene Walker, "Mississippi Freedom Summer," in Savio et al., *Free Speech Movement*, 12, noting that the leadership of the Free Speech Movement "were those who had been part of the Mississippi Freedom Summer Project." It is interesting to note that the abstraction of the racial focus of the Free Speech Movement was foreseen and resisted by its leaders, who, like later critical race theorists, had a power-based critique of liberals' understanding of free speech. "The liberal University of California administration would have relished the opportunity to show off in the national academic community a public university enjoying complete political and academic freedom and academic excellence. And if student politics had been restricted either to precinct work for the Democrats and Republicans, or to advocacy (by public meetings and distribution of literature) of various forms of wholesale societal change, then I don't believe there would have been the crisis there was. . . . The corporations represented on the Board of Regents welcome Young Democrats and Young Republicans as eager apprentices, and sectarian 'revolutionary' talk can be tolerated because it is harmless. The radical student activists, however, are a mean threat to privilege. Because the students were advocating consequential actions (because their advocacy was consequential): the changing of hiring practices of particular establishments, the ending of certain forms of discrimination by concrete acts—because of these radical acts, the administration's restrictive ruling was necessary": Savio, "Berkeley Fall," 16. Savio observed that the Free Speech Movement "gained its initial impetus from the very different involvements of what are mostly middle-class students in the struggles of Negro people": ibid., 18.

9. San Francisco State University's Third World Strike triggered similar protests across the country. See "Campus Protests Rock California, Nation," *Daily Californian*, January 10, 1969, 1, reporting on Black and Third World student unrest at Brandeis University in Massachusetts and at San Jose State College and San Fernando Valley State College in California; "Unresolved Demands Spark U.S. Protests: One Week of Student Strike—Student Strikes, Protests Trouble Nation's Schools," *Daily Californian*, January 13, 1969, 1, 4, updating reports on the Brandeis and San Fernando Valley student strikes and reporting on further actions taken by students of color at Swarthmore College in Pennsylvania, Queens College in New York, and Northwestern University in Illinois. In response to this and similar challenges by students of color nationwide, institutions of higher education across the country would undergo dramatic changes in admissions, hiring, and curricular development policies during the next decades.

To illustrate the need for such demands, prior to the strike a 1966 survey of the racial composition of the undergraduate student body at UC Berkeley revealed that African Americans, Chicanos, and Native Americans together amounted to a mere 1.5 percent of the student population while constituting 24 percent of the California state population: Matthew Dennis, "Defeat in Victory, Victory in Defeat: The Third World Liberation Front Strike of 1969," (unpublished ms., June 1987), 1–2, on file with Sumi Cho, noting that of more than 26,000 students, 1 percent, or 226, were Black; 0.36 percent, or 76, were Chicano; and 0.28 percent, or 61, were Native American.

10. San Francisco State's Third World Strike began in the fall of 1968, prompted in part by the firing of an African American professor and Black Panther, George Murray. A coalition of African American, Asian American, Chicano, and Native American student organizations made up the Third World Liberation Front, which organized the strike. San Francisco State strikers challenged their Berkeley counterparts to demand similar changes in higher education.

See notes 12 and 19 (citing news coverage of the agreement by San Fernando Valley State College to establish two ethnic-studies departments and to make greater efforts to hire faculty of color), which describe the adoption of a similar structure by both Cal-SERVE and the 1978 formation of the Coalition for a Diversified Faculty; Phil Semas, "San Francisco State Strike Dies; White Strikers Return to Class," *Daily Californian*, March 14, 1969, 1, 8, reporting on the partial victories of the strike, including the establishment of a Black Studies department and a school of Ethnic Studies and increased minority student admissions.

The TWLF's leadership structure featured a steering committee with equal numbers of voting representatives from each of the member groups. Decisions were taken by consensus whenever possible, and by majority vote when not possible. On replication of the TWLF model, see discussion at notes 12 and 19 and accompanying text.

11. The two issues of anti-apartheid and affirmative-action work were linked in student protests by organizers from each movement. For example, one May 18, 1977, *Daily Californian* newspaper ad for an anti-apartheid rally read:

Victory to the People of South Africa!
US, UC Out Now
Defeat the Bakke Decision

Similarly, at a 1977 sit-in at which fifty-six members of Campuses United Against Apartheid were arrested, the two demands of protesters were: 1) University of California and the United States out of South Africa; and 2) defeat *Bakke:* "Cops Arrest 56 at Sproul Sit-in," *Daily Californian,* June 3, 1977.

While students organizing for divestment of UC funds from South Africa were predominantly white, students of color were more active in organizing resistance to racism on issues closer to home, particularly around the *Bakke* case and the denial of tenure to Harry Edwards, an African American professor and founder of sports sociology. The 1970s anti-apartheid coalition included primarily the white student left (i.e., Campuses United Against Apartheid, Students for Economic and Racial Justice, the Revolutionary Student Brigade, the Council for Economic Democracy, and the Young Socialists Alliance), and secondarily organizations of students of color (United Students Against the Bakke Decision, the Third World Coalition, the Pan-Africanist Student Board, and the Ethnic Studies Fee Committee). See Sumi Cho, "A History and Analysis of the Anti-Apartheid Movement at UC Berkeley" (unpublished paper, December 1986, 4–11, on file with the authors. See also "Blacks Lack Campus Unity," *Daily Californian,* May 3, 1978, quoting Erica Huggins of the Black Panther Party stating, "I am ashamed white students are organizing a movement which should be full of blacks." The article later quotes the president of the BLSA, who explained that Black students had to combat the paternalistic assumption that they were at UC Berkeley simply out the generosity of liberals, and thus had to work harder to "prove" themselves and therefore did not have extra time to invest in outside activities.

12. For information on the South African embassy protests, see Manning Marable, *Race, Reform and Rebellion: The Second Reconstruction in Black America, 1945–1990* (London: Verso, 1991), 214. For Jesse Jackson's first presidential bid, see idem, *Black American Politics, From the Washington Marches to Jesse Jackson* (Jackson: University Press of Mississippi, 1985), 247–305.

We use the term "race-plus" to designate the centrality and historicity of race-based organizing that recognizes a network of oppressions and embraces coalitional consciousness and solidarity with other outsider groups. As such, other axes of anti-subordination resistance—such as feminist projects, gay/lesbian/bisexual/transgendered liberation, progressive white-identity formation, etc.—are potential bases for coalition. The race-plus electoral coalition known as Cal-Students for Equal Rights and Valid Education (Cal-SERVE) included the African Students Association, Asian Student Union, Inter-Tribal Council, Lesbian Gay Bisexual Alliance, and Movimiento Estudianti Chicano de Aztlán (MEChA). The UPC organized the key events in the 1980s anti-apartheid movement, including a ten-hour sit-in and the "largest number of students arrested at any one protest since the 'early 1970s'"; the student-faculty meetings with the UC Regents; and Bishop Tutu's visit to the Greek Theater: Chris Krueger, "UC Police Make 138 Arrests at Sproul Divestment Protest," *Daily Californian,* November 7, 1985, 1, 5.

13. For a thorough summary of CRT's contestation with CLS, see Crenshaw et al., *Key Writings,* xxii–xxvii. The formality–informality debate is perhaps best captured by the mini-story told by Race-Crit Patricia Williams recounting the experience of looking for a New York apartment with Peter Gabel, a CLS scholar. Gabel quickly located an apartment and sealed the deal with a "$900 dollar deposit, in cash, with no lease, no exchange of keys, and no receipt." In contrast, Williams singed a detailed, lengthily negotiated, finely printed lease: Patricia Williams, "Reconstructing Ideals from Deconstructed Rights," in Delgado, *Cutting Edge,* 86–7. Commenting on their vastly differing approaches to apartment-hunting, Williams observed:

> Peter, I speculate, would say that a lease or any other formal mechanism would introduce distrust into his relationships and that he would suffer alienation, leading to the commodification of his being and the degradation of his person to property. In contrast, the lack of a formal relation to the other would leave me estranged. . . .
>
> Peter's language of . . . informality, of solidarity, of overcoming distance—sounded dangerously like the language of oppression to someone like me who was looking for freedom through the establishment of identity, the *form*-ation of an autonomous social self. To Peter, I am sure, my insistence on the protective distance which rights provide seemed abstract and alienated. (Ibid., 87–8)

For a discussion of differing approaches and strategies of the UPC and CAA, see Melissa Crabbe, "Anti-Apartheid Forces Join, but Cultures, Tactics Differ," *Daily Californian,* April 29, 1986, 11, chronicling the different decision-making processes of the UPC and CAA.

14. On the open split between the UPC and CAA, see Crabbe, "Anti-Apartheid Forces," 1, 6, 11. Crabbe also quotes a University of California official stating his opinion that CAA believed that it had to "create a situation where confrontation will occur so they can get media attention.... The feeling is that legitimate protest, which does not disrupt, will not get sufficient attention, therefore it is not effective": ibid., 11. Crabbe also discusses the CAA's lack of direct-action principles, quoting the CAA's leader, Andrea Pritchett as saying, "The fact that we don't have a rigid program is good because it allows us to be influenced by other political views, but it's also a problem because in dealing with a situation like a riot, we don't have a unified position," and the increased vulnerability of men of color during protests, reflecting agreement among organizational leaders that "Third World students receive the brunt of police violence in any demonstration": ibid.

In rebuttal to the CAA charge of conservatism, UPC member Patricia Vattuone suggested the differing agendas and perspectives of the two groups: "We've been labeled less militant, and that's a problem.... We're not about rebelling against our parents and the institutions—those aren't the issues": ibid. See also "Statement of Purpose by UPC," *Daily Californian*, April 29, 1986, 6: "We do not view this movement as a struggle against authority. For us, the anti-apartheid movement, like the ... tutorial program run by students in the Berkeley elementary schools or our efforts to improve affirmative action on the campus, are all related to the overall purpose of our organization: to work for and support the liberation of our people and all people"; Pedro Noguera, "Fighting Racism Doesn't End with Your Diplomas," *Daily Californian*, May 15, 1986, 4–5: "We're trying to win our people over not just to struggle for divestment. We're trying to win them over for life, because we want them to be in this struggle after they graduate from school.... For those of you who would say that we are conservative for taking this on as our task, I challenge you. I ask what will you be doing in 10 years?"

15. On the established linkage between international and domestic racism, see Crabbe, "Anti-Apartheid Forces," 6, 11, noting that UPC agenda items and demands for improved graduate affirmative action and the institution of an ethnic-studies graduation requirement were adopted by other anti-apartheid groups for the sake of unity. On the unfinished business of the Third World Strike, see Keith Palchikoff, "Celebration and Rally: Activists Laud Divestment, Call for Action," *Daily Californian*, Sep-

tember 4, 1986: "Besides celebrating the July divestment vote, the [anti-apartheid] activists also called upon the crowd to support the institution of a required ethnic studies course." And see "After Divestment, What's Next? Ethnic Studies!!!!?" UPC flyer (undated), on file with Sumi Cho, and n. 21 later.

16. A 1969 *Daily Californian* article reported on an illegal rally staged by Boalt students to protest the administration's ban on rallies during the Third World Strike and observing that "law students are becoming actively involved in campus politics for the first time": Mathis Chazanov, "Boalt Students Stage Rally, Protest Administration Ban," *Daily Californian*, February 29, 1969, 1, 16. For coverage of the 1972 Boalt strike, see generally Hazel Harper, "Third World Cutbacks at Boalt Hall, Black Law Student Association Protests," *Daily Californian*, April 19, 1972, 1, 16; idem, "Black Students Strike at Boalt," *Daily Californian*, April 20, 1972, 1, 16; "Open Challenge to Boalt Faculty" (editorial page), April 20, 1972, 7; "Negotiations at Boalt," *Daily Californian*, April 21, 1972, 12; Ed Coyne, "Chicano Law Students End Boalt Hall Sit-In," *Daily Californian*, April 21, 1972, 1, 16; Hazel Harper, "Black Students Confront Faculty," *Daily Californian*, April 25, 1972, 1, 12; idem, "Boalt Decision," *Daily Californian*, April 25, 1972, 1, 16; "Boalt Faculty Response," *Daily Californian*, April 27, 1972, 1; "Black Students OK Boalt Offer," *Daily Californian*, April 28, 1972, 1; Jeanette Harrison and Robert Joffee, "Boalt Hall Blacks, Asians Vote to End Strike," *Daily Californian*, May 1, 1972, 1, 12; Hazel Harper, "Boycott Continues at Boalt," *Daily Californian*, May 2, 1972, 12. Information on the 1972 Boalt strike is supplemented by two interviews by Sumi Cho with participants at the time—Linda Greene, former president of the BLSA and a founding member of the Critical Race Theory Workshop who is now a professor of law at the University of Wisconsin, and Gerald Horne, a BLSA member and director of African American Studies at the University of North Carolina: Linda Greene, telephone interview by Sumi Cho, November 1997; Gerald Horne, interview by Sumi Cho, Flushing, N.Y., October 11, 1997.

17. Coyne, "Chicano Law Students"; "Boalt Hall Blacks, Asians"; Jaime Gallardo and Gonzalo Rucobo, "Chicano Response to the Sullivan Memorandum," *Daily Californian*, May 5, 1972, 7; "Chicano Boycott Still on at Boalt," *Daily Californian*, May 5, 1972, 12. On the AALSA protest, see Sandra Epstein, *Law at Berkeley: The History of Boalt Hall* (Berkeley: University of California at Berkeley, Institute of Governmental Studies, 1997), 278. On declining student

input into admissions decisions, see Epstein, *Law at Berkeley,* 278, 281.

18. As quoted in Grant Mercer, "Boalt Hall Students Plan Strike, Teach-In for Today," *Daily Californian,* March 21, 1978, 1.

19. The seven organizations that made up the coalition included the AALSA, the BLSA, the Boalt Hall Students Association, LRLSA, the National Lawyers Guild, the Native American Law Students Association, and the Boalt Hall Women's Association: "Diversified Faculty Issue Intensifies," *Suspended Sentence,* April 1979, 1, 3, on file with Sumi Cho. See also Tom Pecoraro, "Boalt's Minority Recruitment Effort Lagging," *Daily Californian,* February 28, 1978, 3. For coverage of the 1978 strike, see Mercer, "Strike, Teach-In"; "Diversified Faculty Issue"; Barbara Franklin and Grant Mercer, "Boalt Hall Hit by Sit-In, Strike," *Daily Californian,* March 22, 1978, 1, 12. For Dean Kadish's refusal, see "Diversified Faculty Issue," describing how Dean Kadish refused to begin the "official" February 1978 faculty meeting before CDF members spoke in order to avoid "setting a precedent" for student participation and input. The article also records the CDF's activities for 1977-78, closing the year with the March 21, 1978 strike: ibid., 3, 8.

20. The HEW investigation was discredited when the Boalt administration discovered that a department investigator had monitored three law classes without its knowledge or permission. Seriously undermined by the controversy, the investigation failed to confirm the students' charges: see Sue Feldman, "Boalt Hiring to be Probed by HEW," *Daily Californian,* September 26, 1979, 1; idem, "Agent Secretly Attends Boalt," *Daily Californian,* January 25, 1980, 1, 22; Epstein, *Law at Berkeley,* 282-3. On internal divisions within the Berkeley left, see Mike Casey, "Groups Seek to Unify Berkeley Left," *Daily Californian,* December 4, 1979, 1.

21. See ULSC, "Founding Meeting", flyer, November 19, 1985,on file with Sumi Cho, advertising the first meeting of United Law Students of Color to discuss "minority and women faculty, divestment, racism in the classroom, and affirmative action." As a result of the formation of the ULSC and its connection to the campuswide anti-apartheid movement, Boalt students sponsored a strike on April 7, 1986, to "protest UC support of apartheid in South Africa and at home," noting the "fruits of UC philosophy" to include "$2.5 billion in UC investments in South Africa, exactly 2 tenured Boalt minority faculty, and only 9.7% graduate students of color at UC Berkeley": see "Boalt April 7, 1986 Strike Flyer,"

on file with Sumi Cho. Neither of the co-authors recalls any consciousness of a previous CDF at the re-formation of BCDF in the 1980s.

22. On the Shultz denial, see Dan Ashby, "Marjorie Shultz: First Woman Granted Tenure at Boalt in the 1980s," *Berkeley Graduate,* October 1989, 18-20. For information on Swift's denial, see idem, "Eleanor Swift Becomes the Second Woman in the 1980s to Be Granted Tenure at Boalt," *Berkeley Graduate,* October 1989, 14-7. The information for the 1967 and 1987 faculty data were provided by the Boalt administration. For information on the Swift press conference, see Terry Link, "Ex-Professor Says Boalt Hall Is Sex Biased," *Oakland Tribune,* October 11, 1988, A7-8. For Shultz's grant of tenure, see Ashby, "Marjorie Shultz," 18-9. See also Marge Shultz to Sumi Cho, correspondence, September 1989, on file with Sumi Cho.

23. As two of the few students of color still involved with the BCDF, the authors intervened to propose a race-plus coalitional structure to the BCDF, which was passed by the membership. Cho and Westley served as two of the four original steering-committee members of the newly structured BCDF—as members of the Asian American Law Students Association and the Black Law Students Association, respectively–along with Renée Saucedo of La Raza Law Students Association, and Juliet Davison of the Boalt Hall Women's Association.

24. See generally *Harvard Civil Rights–Civil Liberties Law Review* 22 (1987): 301

25. For a report on the 1988 strike, see Ellen Goodwin, "28 Cited in Six-Hour Sit-In Protesting Bias in Hiring," *San Jose Mercury News,* March 23, 1988, 1B; Roland De Wolk, "Students Protest Shortage of Minorities and Women on Boalt Hall Faculty; 28 arrests," *Oakland Tribune,* March 23, 1988, B1. The authors credit Renee Saucédo, co-chair of the BCDF, for conceiving and coordinating the Nationwide Law Student Strike of 1989. There was some concern among the BCDF leadership that expanding the movement to a national level was premature and threatened to destabilize the local movement. One of the authors (Sumi Cho) felt that the BCDF should solidify its base and ally more closely with the campuswide movement for diversity before "going national." In retrospect, both positions seemed legitimate. For coverage of the 1989 Nationwide Law Student Strike, see National Lawyers Guild, "A Report from the National Lawyers Guild: Unequal Treatment under the Law–Racism, Sexism, Classism, Homophobia in America's Law Schools," *National Lawyers Guild,* April 1989. See also

"Law School Faculties Protested," *New York Times,* April 7, 1989; "Law School Students Protest Scarcity of Female and Minority Professors," *Chronicle of Higher Education,* April 19, 1989; Tom Rogers, "University of Miami Law Students Want More Blacks, Women on Faculty," *Ann Arbor (Mich.) News,* April 7, 1989; Debra Levi Holtz, "Law Students Arrested in Protest at Berkeley," *San Francisco Chronicle,* April 7, 1989; "Law School Students Protest Bias," *San Francisco Examiner,* April 7, 1989; Robert Westley, "Boalt Hall Students Strike for Diversity," *Daily California,* April 6, 1989; Pamela Coyle, "Students Strike for Diversity," *New Haven (Conn.) Register,* April 7, 1989; Patricia Barnes, "Dissatisfied Students Boycott Classes at Yale," *Connecticut Law Tribune,* April 10, 1989. The nationwide strike forced a sea-change in law schools' hiring culture. See nn. 33–8 and accompanying text. However, the very next year, the second nationwide strike threatened to be a failure at Boalt were it not for the strength of the campuswide diversity movement through the United Front. Whether the BCDF could have withstood the conservative onslaught of the early 1990s through a more focused local campaign is unclear.

In the summer after the nationwide strike, the campuswide administration awarded tenure to Eleanor Swift. On the campuswide administration's reversal of the Swift denial, see Sandy Louey, "Boalt Professor Wins Discrimination Fight," *Daily Californian,* August 28, 1989, reporting on an independent panel's unanimous finding of sex discrimination and UC Berkeley Chancellor Heyman's subsequent offer of tenure to Professor Swift. See also Ashby, "Eleanor Swift," 14. In exchange for the chance to have her case reviewed by an independent committee outside the law school, Professor Swift agreed to drop her gender-discrimination lawsuit against the university.

26. One of these missteps involved a letter from BCDF leaders to an academic couple being hastily recruited by the Boalt faculty for tenure-track positions. The BCDF charged that the waiver of standard search procedures was designed to eliminate student input in the name of affirmative-action recruitment (of a white female candidate and her white husband). Further, students felt that the "target of opportunity" (TOP) affirmative-action positions being used to convey additional funds to departments fielding diversity candidates were being misused, as TOP funds were benefiting the white male spouse of the white female candidate. In light of this history, the BCDF leadership and other law-student groups wrote to the candidates who

had been extended offers and asked them not to accept based on the need for greater racial diversity and for the process-based failures in their hiring. The letter to the candidates created an uproar from Boalt faculty and from a considerable segment of the student body. The BCDF's strategy seemed to emphasize increasingly ill-conceived direct actions, with no clear link to attainable demands and commensurate defense of those arrested. Ironically, the BCDF's major successes (in reversing two tenure denials and winning four of five diversity hires in one year) led to a perception among many students that the administration was now in good faith willing to diversify the faculty, or that the faculty had been adequately diversified.

27. For the rapid proliferation of the discourse of political correctness, see Sumi Cho, "Essential Politics," *Harvard Latino Law Review* 2 (1997): 450–1, nn. 33–7.

28. The conservative "political correctness" campaign proliferated rapidly after a *New York Times Magazine* article appeared in the winter of 1990–91: Richard Bernstein, "The Rising Hegemony of the Politically Correct," *New York Times Magazine,* October 28, 1990, sec. 4, 1. Nexis citations in "arcnews/curnews" reveal only seventy total citations in articles to "political correctness" for all of 1990. One year later, after the Bernstein article, Nexis records more than 1,500 citations, with a steady increase to more than 7,000 citations by 1994. See also Cho, "Essential Politics," 433, nn. 33, 36.

City of Richmond v. J. A. Croson, 488 U.S. 469 (1989), requiring strict scrutiny review of local affirmative-action plans. Prior to 1989, it could be said by diversity activists that no controlling legal authority had determined that publicly sponsored race-conscious remedies were illegal in an educational or academic setting. In 1989, *Croson* held that local racial set-asides in public construction contracts were subject to strict scrutiny. The narrative of *Croson,* which viewed the case as one about a majority-minority Black–white coalition seeking to ensure relatively modest but meaningful minority participation in a lucrative publicly funded enterprise saw the light of day only in Justice Thurgood Marshall's exasperated dissenting opinion. The majority, by contrast, saw only "reverse discrimination." What *Croson* seemed to say to diversity activists in particular was that our generation could not rely on the high court to support our politics in the way that a previous generation of Civil Rights activists could. In the language of Justice Sandra Day O'Connor's opinion, our politics would be viewed as "racial politics," and that was a bad thing as well as constitutionally forbidden to the state. For BCDF members, the message of *Croson* was even clearer: Time had run out on judicial tolerance of result-oriented diversity politics" *Croson*, 488 U.S., 469.

29. *Adarand Constructors, Inc v. Pena*, 515 U.S. 200 (1995), holding that all racial classifications imposed by government actors are subject to strict scrutiny analysis.

Podberesky v. Kirwin, 38 F. 3d 147 (4th Cir. 1994), amended and rehearing denied, 46 F. 3d 5 (4th Cir. 1994), cert. denied, 514 U.S. 1128 (1995), holding that a Black-only scholarship program was not narrowly tailored to asserted the goal of remedying present effects of past discrimination.

Hopwood v. University of Texas, 78 F. 3d 932 (5th Cir. 1996), rehearing denied, 84 F. 3d 720 (5th Cir. 1996), cert. denied sub nom. *Texas v. Hopwood*, 116 S. Ct. 2581 (1996), holding that racial preferences in a state university law school's admissions program violates equal protection.

Coalition for Economic Equity v. Wilson, 122 F. 3d 718 (9th Cir. 1997), cert. denied, 118 S. Ct. 17 (1997), denying motion for a stay of mandate.

On June 26, 1997, it was revealed that not one of the fourteen Black students admitted to Boalt Hall under the new policies adopted after passage of the anti-affirmative-action measure had decided to enroll.

Brown v. Board of Education of Topeka, 349 U.S. 294 (1955).

On resegregation, see Amy Wallace, "UC Law School Class May Have Only 1 Black," *Los Angeles Times*, June 27, 1997, A1.

On massive resistance, see Derrick A. Bell, Jr., *Race, Racism and American Law*, 2d ed.(New York: Little, Brown, 1980), 381-9, chronicling the varieties of resistance pursued by Southerners opposed to desegregation facilitated by the court's "all deliberate speed" order.

30. We use the term "institutional-cultural" to emphasize the importance of social institutions as both constrainers of action and constitutors of actors and interests. Institutional-cultural struggle by CRT and student activists was thus at once struggle *against* the institutional constraints of deracialized modes of pedagogy and legal analysis and *for* a constituting culture wherein radical subjects of color could flourish.

31. See, for example, Matsuda, *Where Is Your Body?* 74: "In April 1988, law students across the country held a national day of protest. They sat in to demand changes in hiring practices.... That same year, I got a call inviting me to teach as a visitor at Stanford Law School." Although Matsuda had the wrong year for the first nationwide strike—which was held in 1989, not 1988—the first (Boalt-only) law-student strike called by the BCDF did occur in April 1988 and received considerable local, regional, and national publicity.

32. As merely a partial listing, some of these actors include the Society of American Law Teachers and their members' surveys and reports that provided a wealth of information on the exclusionary effects of the closed system of hiring. In particular, the work of David Chambers, Charles Lawrence, and Richard Chused deserve special mention. Michael Olivas's "dirty-dozen" list, annual data compilation and resource base, and patient prodding/scolding prompted Latino/a hiring at many schools. The AALS Minority section, formed in the early 1970s, turned its attention early and often to the issue of minority hiring, issuing reports and sponsoring recruitment conferences for prospective candidates. We believe that a serious study of these diversity efforts by faculty would complement our study of student diversity activism.

33. David Chambers, "SALT Survey: Minority Group Persons in Law School Teaching," *SALT Newsletter*, Society of American Law Teachers, Washington, D.C., November 1982, 5. See also idem, "SALT Survey: Women in Law School Teaching," *SALT Newsletter*, Society of American Law Teachers, Washington, D.C., July 1983, 1, 3. The research of the liberal-progressive SALT, the largest membership organization of law faculty, produced some of the most useful research for the diversity movement, beginning with the Chambers survey. Charles Lawrence analyzed the Chambers survey in a law-review article calling for voluntary affirmative-action hiring in light of the dismal statistics unearthed: Charles Lawrence, "Minority Hiring in AALS Law Schools: The Need for Voluntary Quotas," *University of San Francisco Law Review* 20 (1986): 429, 439-9. In 1988, Richard Chused conducted a follow-up report to Chambers's on hiring and retention of women and minority law faculty: Richard Chused, "The Hiring and Retention of Minorities and Women on American Law School Faculties," *University of Pennsylvania Law Review* 137 (1988): 537.

34. Chambers, "Women in Law School Teaching," 6.

35. Data provided by Richard White, statistician for the AALS, telephone interview by Sumi Cho, November 14, 1997.

36. American Bar Association, *Approved Law Schools, 1998 Edition: Statistical Information on American Bar Association Approved Law Schools* (Old Tappan, N.J.: Macmillan, 1997), 451

37. For faculty data, see Sumi K. Cho, "Multiple Consciousness and the Diversity Dilemma," *University of Colorado Law Review* 68 (Fall 1997): 1035, 1052, n. 63, citing memo confirming statistics from Nola Yee, coordinator of publications and communications, Boalt Hall School of Law.

38. Data for this paragraph provided by White, interview.

39. Epstein, *Law at Berkeley*, 276, 322: "Written under the aegis of Boalt Hall Dean Herma Hill Kay and Dean Emeritus Sanford Kadish." For "under the aegis," see the back-cover summary. Epstein's sources for this period of heated contestation never cite a student but are confirmed by "faculty interviews," "one emeritus professor," and various deans: ibid.

40. Cecilia V. Estolano et al., "New Directions for Diversity: Charting Law School Admissions Policy in a Post-Affirmative Action Era" (unpublished report, 1997), 7–8, on file with the *Colorado Law Review* and Boalt Hall Law School Library.

41. V. Dion Haynes, "Lone Black in Law Class Fights End of Preferences," *Chicago Tribune*, September 29, 1997, C1., quoting a co-author of the "New Directions for Diversity" report.

42. See Michel Foucault, "Two Lectures," in Colin Gordon, ed., *Power/Knowledge: Selected Interviews and Other Writings, 1972–1977* (New York: Pantheon, 1980), 82–3.

43. Epstein, *Law at Berkeley*, 283 ("Angry students"), 322–3 ("law school agenda"). Epstein does note that the class boycott strategy was developed at Boalt and followed elsewhere, but the context is not one of ringing endorsement of the movement.

44. For "New Directions in Diversity" authors' erasure and disparagement of Boalt student activism, see nn. 51–2.

45. We use the term "counter-discourse" in the sense suggested by Nancy Fraser: "Members of subordinated social groups have found it advantageous to constitute alternative publics . . . parallel discursive arenas where members of subordinated social groups invent and circulate counterdiscourses." A counter-discourse, then, interprets social reality in a manner opposed to subordination: see Nancy Fraser, "Politics, Culture, and the Public Sphere: Toward a Postmodern Conception," in *Social Postmodernism: Beyond Identity Politics*, ed. Linda Nicholson and Steven Seidman (New York: Cambridge University Press, 1995), 287, 291.

46. Indeed, much of the first wave of CRT scholarship represents the synergistic approach in its relationship to antiracist organizing. In fact, many CRT founders wrote about movements or with movements in mind, attempting to intervene through their writings to produce new understandings of old problems in order to generate better theory. To name just a few examples, Derrick Bell's work directly confronted civil-rights lawyers' conflict of interest in representing their clients in the movement for school desegregation. Mari Matsuda grounded her call for a jurisprudential methodology that would "look to the bottom" by analyzing the Japanese American redress and reparations movement. Matsuda, Charles Lawrence, Richard Delgado, and Kimberlé Crenshaw collaborated to address the problem of "balancing" hate speech against First Amendment rights in their anthology, *Words That Wound*, a work that addressed the hostility that students of color often faced in campus environments. Based on his years of organizing, especially in the Chicano community, Gerald López developed a new orientation toward "rebellious" community lawyering that emphasized collaboration and empowerment, rather than the paternalistic, *noblesse oblige* model that civil-rights lawyers too often brought to the table. See generally Derrick A. Bell, Jr., "Serving Two Masters: Integration Ideals and Client Interests in School Desegregation Litigation," *Yale Law Journal* 85 (1976): 470; Gerald López, *Rebellious Lawyering: One Chicano's Vision of Progressive Law Practice* (Boulder, Colo.: Westview Press, 1992); Mari Matsuda, "Looking to the Bottom: Critical Legal Studies and Reparations," *Harvard Civil Rights–Civil Liberties Law Review* 22 (1987): 323; Mari J. Matsuda et al., *Words that Wound: Critical Race Theory, Assaultive Speech, and the First Amendment* (Boulder, Colo.: Westview Press, 1993).

Angela Harris contributed an important critique of feminist legal theory as falsely universal in "Race and Essentialism," based in part on experiences of women of color. In her subsequent "Foreword—Jurisprudence of Reconstruction," Harris realizes the synergistic potential of CRT's ability to provide analysis and direction for activist intellectuals to interact with intellectual activists. Most recently, Eric Yamamoto has called for a more "practical turn" in theorizing that would emphasize the relationship between progressive lawyering and critical theorizing through "critical race praxis." Yamamoto speaks to the Lowell high-school admissions controversy and the Hawaiian sovereignty movement in his production of knowledge. These are but a few of the early works that explicitly foregrounded power relations and collective community struggle as an empirical foundation for their theorizing. It is interesting to note that, with the exception of Yamamoto, all these works are clearly within the early foundational period of CRT, an observation we will revisit and expand on later. We believe that Harris's critical insights in "Race and Essentialism" were based on contestation of racism within the women's movement and certainly had potential to be synergistic, but ultimately ignored the larger political dynamic and danger of the right and segments of the left essentializing race-based movements. See generally Angela P. Harris, "Race and Essentialism in Feminist Legal Theory," *Stanford Law Review* 42 (1990): 581. We view much of Harris's later work as an eloquent corrective to her earlier work on antiessentialism. See generally Angela P. Harris, "Foreword: The Jurisprudence of Reconstruction," *California Law Review* 82 (1994): 741, 778. On critical race praxis, see Yamamoto, "Critical Race Praxis," 821.

47. Radical economists refer to the set of mutually reinforcing social and economic institutions as the "social structure of accumulation" (SSA). See John Miller and Chris Tilly, "The U.S. Economy: Post-Prosperity Capitalism?" *Crossroads* 23 (July–August 1992): 1, 2: "Successful accumulation requires a set of mutually reinforcing . . . institutions—rules of the economic game, implicit and explicit agreements, and the organizations that carry them out, including government agencies, business groupings, and popular organizations"). Such structures are fluid, have a limited lifetime, and are constantly being disassembled and reconstructed. For example, the post-World War II SSA involved three main components: 1) a "capital-labor accord," which offered labor stability to key economic sectors by offering "productivity-plus" pay formulas in exchange for "no-strike" provisions in bargaining agreements; 2) a "capital–citizen" accord that provided the safety net of New Deal programs in exchange for social stability; and 3) a Pax Americana accord, which relegated the United States to the dominant role in the world (capitalist) economy, with its attendant role as global policeman. These three "pillars" permitting smooth accumulation of capital remained solidly in place until the early 1970s. Each pillar began to "crack" at this time, leading to the disruption in the social structures of accumulation and economic instability: ibid., 2–3. See also David M. Gordon, Thomas E. Weisskopf, and Samuel Bowles, "Power, Accumulation, and Crisis: The Rise and Demise of the Postwar Social Structure of Accumulation," in *Radical Political Economy: Explorations in Alter-*

native Economic Analysis, ed. Victor D. Lippit (Armonk, N.Y.: M. E. Sharpe, 1996), 226.

The professional intelligentsia, especially in a field such as law, may have their own particular labor-capital/capital-citizen accords. Because of their generous remuneration (relative to other academics) and elevated social status, law professors—even antisubordinationist law professors—may feel obliged to honor the implicit agreement of "collegial discourse," at times a euphemism for the normalization of non-resistance to oppressive forces. The corporate academic institution, in exchange for its inclusion of the subaltern, can head off attacks of exclusionary practices from outside critics and thus guarantee its smooth accumulation process.

Angela Harris coined the term "disenchanted intellectual," in "Foreword," 741, 778.

48. The definition for "sublimation" is derived from Merriam-Webster's Collegiate Dictionary, 10th ed. (Springfield, Mass.: Merriam-Webster, 1993). On sublimation in its psychoanalytic use, Freud developed the controversial sublimation thesis, and we should point out that our appropriation of the term in no way is an endorsement of its application of psychoanalytic theory. Rather, as the text states, our use is a kind of structural analogy. See Sigmund Freud, *Introductory Lectures on Psychoanalysis* (New York: Norton, 1966), 23, 345-6.

49. For a sampling of antiessentialist critiques of allegedly universalistic movements, see generally Angela P. Harris, "Race and Essentialism"; Elvia Arriola, "Gendered Inequality: Lesbians, Gay Men, and Feminist Legal Theory," *Berkeley Women's Law Journal* 9 (1994): 103; Pat Cain, "Feminist Jurisprudence: Grounding the Theories," *Berkeley Women's Law Journal* 4 (1989-90): 191; Darren Hutchinson, "Out Yet Unseen: A Racial Critique of Gay and Lesbian Legal Theory and Political Discourse," *Connecticut Law Review* 29 (1997): 561; Francisco Valdes, "Queer Margins, Queer Ethics: A Call to Account for Race and Ethnicity in the Law, Theory and Politics of 'Sexual Orientation,'" *Hastings Law Journal* 48 (1997): 1293. For the rejection of "shared victimization," see Harris, "Race and Essentialism," 612, asserting that Black women can help the feminist movement "move beyond the fascination with essentialism" through "creative action," not "shared victimization."

50. This thought is counterintuitive for some feminists who have found the basis of a political community built around women to be the common situation of women. On the incompatibility

between anti-foundationalism and feminist politics, see Kate Soper, "Feminism, Humanism and Postmodernism", *Radical Philosophy* 55 (1990): 11, asserting that feminist politics implies a movement based on the solidarity and sisterhood of women and doubting whether there can be specifically feminist politics under the anti-foundationalist assumptions of postmodernism. Also left nonplused are racialized group members who experience race as belonging to a racially defined community with common interests and perspectives.

51. On erasure, see Diana Fuss, "'Race' under Erasure? Poststructuralist Afro-American Literary Theory," in *Essentially Speaking* (New York: Routledge, 1989), 73. For race concept, see Ian F. Haney López, *White by Law: The Legal Construction of Race* (New York: New York University Press, 1996). On the pitfalls of essentialism, see Harris, "Race and Essentialism," and Cheryl Harris, "Whiteness as Property," in Crenshaw et al., *Key Writings*, 276. The deconstructive and restorative promise of postmodernism is elaborated in Harris, "Foreword."

52. For an example of postmodernist leftist "trashing" in law, see Mark Tushnet, "An Essay on Rights," *Texas Law Review* 62 (1984): 1363. But cf. Kimberlé Crenshaw, "Race, Reform, and Retrenchment: Transformation and Legitimation in AntiDiscrimination Law," in Crenshaw et al., *Key Writings*, 110, for an early critique of CLS trashing of ideology "as the only path that might lead to a liberated future" for those who are racially oppressed. For race as social construction, see Michael Omi and Howard Winant, *Racial Formation in the United States* (New York: Routledge, 1986). At least since the publication of this seminal work on racial formation, race has increasingly been viewed in intellectual academic circles as a social construction that is neither biological nor static but, rather, in the process of change over time and subject to certain hegemonic paradigms of analysis. See Anthony Appiah, "The Uncompleted Argument: Du Bois and the Illusion of Race," in *"Race," Writing, and Difference*, ed. Henry Louis Gates, Jr. (Chicago: University of Chicago Press, 1985), 21. The usurpation of the social-construction thesis to serve the ends of white supremacy through colorblind jurisprudence is explored in Robert Westley, "White Normativity and the Racial Rhetoric of Equal Protection," in *Existence in Black: An Anthology of Black Existential Philosophy*, ed. Lewis R. Gordon (New York: Routledge, 1997), 91.

53. Of course, the charge of PC-repression was incendiary, unfair, and utterly effective—with no semblance of "equal time" given to student activists accused of engineering "hegemony" to respond through the mass media to the outlandish accusations leveled at them by the press and pundits. Unfortunately, it was conservative intellectuals, not critical theorists, who were practicing synergistic theorizing at this time—combining theory and action to assist right-wing movements in recapturing the moral high ground on race politics. Aided by the crusading disparagement of "identity politics" by academics on the left, conservatives generally made it difficult and unpopular—worse yet, unfashionable—to respond to charges of "political correctness" with a forthright defense of race-conscious politics and law.

For a discussion of the rise of right-wing think tanks and their role in constructing a regressive civil-rights discourse, see Richard Delgado and Jean Stefancic, *No Mercy: How Conservative Think Tanks and Foundations Changed America's Social Agenda* (Philadelphia: Temple University Press, 1996). For an analysis of the simultaneous rise and popularization of the attacks on "identity politics" and "political correctness" by the academic left and the political right, see Cho, "Essential Politics," 443–53.

54. To be sure, the postmodern turn opened up progressive space, at least within the academy, for alternative approaches to analysis beyond dualistic paradigms. In particular, the postmodern turn has opened racial discourses beyond the white-over-Black dichotomy, with the establishment of "LatCrit" theory and the proliferation of Asian Pacific American and Native American scholarship. For a sampling of the LatCrit literature, see Colloquium, "International Law, Human Rights, and LatCrit Theory," *University of Miami Inter-American Law Review* 28 (1997): 177; Symposium, "LatCrit Theory: Naming and Launching a New Discourse of Critical Legal Scholarship," *Harvard Latino Law Review* 2 (1997): 1; Symposium, "LatCrit Theory: Latinas/os and the Law," *California Law Review* 85 (1997): 1143; Colloquium, "Representing Latina/o Communities: Critical Race Theory and Practice," *La Raza Law Journal* 9 (1996): 1; and Symposium, "Difference, Solidarity and Law: Building Latina/o Communities Through LatCrit Theory," *UCLA Chicano–Latino Law Review* 19 (1997): 1. Race and gender antiessentialism, supported by the radical anti-foundationalism of the postmodern turn, has had the welcome effect of disarming those on the left who believed that coalition or movement politics necessarily took account of race and gender identity. Indeed, the failure to take account of identity had fatally flawed earlier student diversity movements.

It is more than ironic that, at the historical moment that people of color began entering the halls of higher learning in appreciable numbers and making demands for greater inclusion, we are asked to check our identities at the door, when our identities were the excuse for denying us entrance in the first place. Up to this moment, it was the almost exclusive prerogative of white power to both subordinate and exclude people of color and women and then tell us in a basically white communication how it was done. See, for example, Richard Delgado, "The Imperial Scholar: Reflections on a Review of Civil Rights Literature," in Crenshaw et al., *Key Writings*, 46, decrying the dominance of white male authors in leading law reviews writing about civil rights and only citing one another.

55. Though our responses to these questions are beyond the scope of this essay, we take up these issues in a forthcoming work. Preliminarily, we suggest that the essentialism–antiessentialism debate represents a false dichotomy that reflects not so much a theoretical problem as a political one. This problem is correctly identified by Angela Harris in her critique of feminist jurisprudence: "In feminist legal theory, as in the dominant culture, it is mostly white, straight, and socioeconomically privileged people who claim to speak for all of us" (Angela P. Harris, "Race and Essentialism in Feminist Legal Thought," in *Critical Race Feminism: A Reader*, ed. Adrien K. Wing [New York: New York University Press, 1993], 11). Given that the problem is distorted representation of group unity due to white, straight, or class privilege, we should challenge the illegitimate exercise of power and demand accountability while continuing to place a premium on political solidarity of viable group formations. Rather than championing creative individualism and attacking group-based political formations that have produced some relief from hegemony, we should insist on political accountability from the unrepresentative group that is speaking for all of us. Such an approach can challenge, rather than capitulate to, the continuing attack on group identities through the right's political-correctness campaign and the left's critique of identity (read: race, feminist, and gay) politics.

In our view, then, the crux of the problem is that the antiessentialist critique may misdiagnose the classic tension within progressive movements—that is, that of solidarity versus accountability. Antiessen-

tialists remain wary of inter-group political solidarity, equating it with a dangerous flattening of relevant difference. But the sublimation of the political problem of accountability into the more socially acceptable theoretical expression of antiessentialism within legal academe does a disservice to solidarity.

56. To address this problem, we suggest that activist RaceCrits provide the example to disenchanted RaceCrits that radical, race-based movements were not somehow *more* sexist, elitist, and homophobic than society at large. Many CRT scholars, especially those of the first wave, participated in race-based political formations, internalizing the various positive lessons and ethics of the movement, such as unity, solidarity, audaciousness, self-determination, critique and self-critique, and coalition. However, activist intellectuals also experienced the movement's negative excesses and weaknesses—its sexism, ethnocentrism, homophobia, fratricide, sectarianism, vanguardism, etc. In addition, the power of social institutions (media, entertainment industry, universities, law enforcement, courts) to disparage, defame, and make invisible such movements, combined with antiessentialist skepticism toward racial formations, resulted in a one-sided, negative characterization of such movements that even its former participants are hesitant to rebut publicly. This self-censorship by movement participants, combined with the distantiation of the antiessentialist wing of CRT, tends, ironically, to foster an essentialized notion of all racial political formations as crudely nationalistic, sexist, and homophobic. Detachment from such movements prevents theorists from appreciating the wide range of race-based political organizing, from progressive-coalitional to chauvinist-nationalist forms.

57. We borrow the term intergroup justice, closely related to "interracial justice," from Eric Yamamoto, who defines interracial justice as follows: "Interracial justice . . . reflects a commitment to anti-subordination among nonwhite racial groups. It entails in substance a hard acknowledgment of ways in which racial groups have harmed and continue to harm one another, sometimes through forms of oppression, along with affirmative efforts to redress past harms with continuing effects" (Eric K. Yamamoto, "Rethinking Alliances: Agency, Responsibility and Interracial Justice," *UCLA Asian Pacific American Law Journal* 3 [1995]: 3).

CHAPTER THREE

Keeping It Real:
On Anti-"Essentialism"

Catharine A. MacKinnon

THEORIZING THIS MOMENT[1] could begin with tracing the contributions of critical race feminism to feminism historically. Considering just African American women would begin with their resistance to slavery, proceed through their formative participation in and critique of the Black Civil Rights Movement, encompass groundbreaking initiatives such as the National Black Feminist Organization and Combahee River Collective, and observe their backbone role in the contemporary women's movement today. In these and many other ways, women of color—African American women, Latinas, Asian American women, Native women—have created feminism in their own image, a feminism of the real world largely obscured in academic feminism. The theoretical contributions of critical race legal feminists could also be analyzed—their foundational concepts, such as multiple consciousness, outsider jurisprudence, and intersectionality—as contributions to feminism. To the work of scholars like Kimberlé Crenshaw and Mari Matsuda, no secondary treatment can add or do justice. They make legal and social theory look and sound like

women, and you can't get more feminist than that.[2]

The travels of central ideas of Critical Race Theory and their effects on women could be traced. CRT's critique of racism has yet to be twisted into a defense of dominance and has had a major impact on equality and liberation thinking and practice around the world. CRT's rights theory has moved toward reconstructing the shape of the container: toward making rights non-individualistic, non-atomistic, contextual, substantive entitlements, challenging and changing the abstract, status-quo preserving, state-power-based concept of rights that we inherited. As articulated by Patricia Williams in her *Alchemy of Race and Rights,* for example, this concept of rights remains unrebutted by the right and uncorroded by the left (for no lack of trying).[3] As CRT, with the feminism that has been part of it from inception, becomes part of transforming human rights, human rights begin to be claimed as women's rights everywhere.

Storytelling, a key contribution of CRT to method, could also be retold. Widely appropriated, it may have lost some edge. But in the hands of its authentic practitioners, flowing together with feminism's consciousness-raising, storytelling remains a powerful direct means of grasping and exposing dominant realities and sharing subordinated ones. CRT also could be located in the larger world of theory by exploring propositions like "Critical Race Theory without race plus feminism without sex with a dash of Marxism without class gives you (presto) postmodernism!" Under current historical conditions, appropriating the approach while abstracting away the content is one of power's adaptations to challenge by transformative theory.

As one way into some of these questions, asked to explore the interface between feminism and CRT, I will consider the origins and consequences of one criticism of feminism by some critical race theorists during CRT's first decade: the notion that feminism is "essentialist." In my view, this notion is often wrong and, when wrong, has created a false antagonism with regressive consequences, one of which has been to surround analysis of gender with an aura of suspicion and stigma. "Women," I will argue, is not a racist term. Most critical race thinkers see straight through the charge that feminism is essentialist to feminism's analysis of the reality of male dominance as a social system. But, having become something of a reflex and fixture in postmodernist litanies,[4] the misrepresentation of feminism as intrinsically "essentialist" has been going on for a decade now, is often repeated, and has been attached regardless of accuracy.

In philosophy, essentialism refers to a core essence inherent in something—a word, a person, a group—defining what that thing is.[5] Historically, being essentialist on sex or race has meant being biologically determinist: as if people are the way they are, act and think and feel the way they do, have the abilities and resources and occupy the social status they have because of their sex- or race-specific biology. What is deemed the essence of race or sex—hence, the people who are raced or sexed—are biological facts like hormones, body type, and skin color. These so-called natural traits, in the essentialist view, determine social outcomes and individual qualities. Essentialism in this sense has long been central to the ideology of racism and sexism in its most vicious forms.

Contemporary thinkers have used the term in a variety of ways, its pliability and chameleon properties proving adaptive. I will focus on its use to claim feminism is racist. "Essentialism" in this sense means taking white women as the model of "woman," taking white women's status and treatment as paradigmatic of women as such. In this criticism, white solipsism produces a category, "sex," in which white women are mistaken for all women, in which women who are white define what gender means for all women. As to particular work, this characterization either is or is not accurate; it has been both. What it has become is something more: the claim that it is racist to speak of "women" at all.

Elizabeth Spelman criticizes the white template for women she finds in feminism by criticizing its "essentialism" as finding that "some 'woman' substance ... is the same in each of us and interchangeable between us."[6] In her view, feminism assumes and imposes a unit of analysis called "women" that is presupposed, internally uniform, fixed in nature, and rigid, by distinction with the diverse, heterogenous, and fluid reality women are said to inhabit. Here, feminism is implicitly biologist and racist. While treating women as if they are a biological group is not necessarily easy to avoid,[7] to say that a biologically determinist theory of gender is not very feminist is not very controversial. Contemporary feminism began by resisting biology as destiny.

If women's bodies determine women's inferior social status, the possibilities for sex equality are pretty limited. On this simplest level, one cannot be essentialist and feminist at the same time.

Angela Harris's widely cited critique of feminism defines "essentialism" as "the notion that a unitary 'essential' woman's experience can be isolated and described independently of race, class, sexual orientation, and other realities of experience."[8] Professor Harris's use of this term is predicated on Elizabeth Spelman's enumerated "assumptions of feminism."[9] These assumptions include "that women can be talked about 'as women,' ... are oppressed 'as women,' ... that women's situation can be contrasted to men's" and so on.[10] Professor Spelman is wrong to call these assumptions. They have been hard-won discoveries. Calling feminism "essentialist" in this sense thus misses the point. Analyzing women "as women" says nothing about whether an analysis is essentialist. It all depends on *how* you analyze them "as women": on whether what makes a woman be a woman, analytically, is deemed inherent in their bodies or is produced through their socially lived conditions.

An analysis of women that is predicated on women's experience is based on observed social conditions, hence can assume no uniformity of gender, biological or otherwise, because women's concrete social experience is not uniform. Any regularities the analysis finds it finds, which findings are then subject to examination by others. Discerning commonalities in experience is not the same as searching for an "essence." The socially constructed "woman" has no "essence." If women "as women" are social and concrete, they must encompass all of women's experiences of social hierarchy, because race, class, and sexual orientation (for instance) contribute to making women's concrete situation and status as women be what it is. A

genuinely feminist method is thus open to real women in the social world and builds its category, "women," from them.

If, by contrast, an analysis of women proceeds from an abstract idea—a category that is not predicated on and built of women's social reality but is a priori or biological or otherwise pre-fixed in asocial space (here Woman makes her appearance)—it is likely to be factually inaccurate as well as to impose a false sameness on women and to obscure power divisions within the group. Elizabeth Spelman asks, "Is it really possible for us to think of a woman's 'womanness' in abstraction from the fact that she is a particular woman?"[11] I don't know who her "us" is, but she writes as if to analyze women "as women" requires abstracting from women's particularities. But analyzing women "as women" can also require encompassing women's particularities. Professor Spelman assumes that feminist method is abstract in the sense of beginning with an idea of women rather than with women's material realities. Philosophers often do. But "sex" can be an abstract category or it can be a concrete reality. It is concrete in feminist work. "Essentialism," by contrast, has become an abstraction.

Further, it is not the view of feminism that gender is all there is—just that gender is never not there. Feminism does not claim that all women are affected the same by male power or are similarly situated under it—just that no woman is unaffected by it. Feminism does not see all women as the same; it criticizes this view. It does claim that all women are seen and treated as women in some way under male supremacy. This is not to say that feminism is always practiced, even by feminists. It certainly is not to say that feminism does not need to be more race-conscious; it does. Nor is it to say that some work, claiming feminism, has not been racist; it has. It is to say that some of the feminist analysis that has been dismissively tagged with what has become the academic epithet of "essentialism," as exemplary of the "straight, white, and economically privileged,"[12] including mine, is not.

My work, for example,[13] is socially based to the ground and built on women's realities, including those of women of color, from the ground up. It pioneered the theory that sexuality is socially constructed, for example. Its theory of gender is explicitly non-unitary and non-homogenous. While facing the fact that gender affects all women, it is clear that not all women are affected by male dominance in the same way or to the same degree. For example, it argues that: "feminism seeks the truth of women's commonality out of the lie that all women are the same."[14] It systematically addresses racism and makes point after point that it is said to miss.[15] The least privileged women, not the most, are its center and foundation.[16] It is not, as Professor Harris claims, a "color-blind"[17] theory. It does not employ or embody a "nuance" theory of women of color.[18] The fact that women of color in the United States are the worst-off women, due to racism, and are in fact hit harder by virtually every social problem that also afflicts white women, problems like poverty and sexual assault, is hardly an invidious white observation, although its reality reflects plenty of invidious white practices.[19] I do not relegate women of color to footnotes and brackets.[20] I do not assume that all women are white. I do not require women to choose between their ethnic identification and their gender, and then to choose gender.[21] I do not say or think that sex is more fundamental than race, more important than race, worse than race; that gender is primary and race is not; or any of a host of related assertions about my work that shouldn't have survived a cite check.[22] The misrepresentations in Professor Harris's Stanford article[23] are particularly hard to explain in light of her nearly contempora-

neous draft of a review of my *Toward a Feminist Theory of the State*, in which she observes that the book "tellingly points to the contradictions, paradoxes, and multiplicities hidden in every seeming unity."[24]

The "essentialism" charge has become a sneer, a tool of woman-bashing, with consequences that far outrun its merits. The widespread acceptance of the claim seems due more to its choice of target than its accuracy in hitting it. Male power is ecstatic; its defenders love the accusation that feminism is "essentialist," even though they don't really know what it means. They do know that it has divided women, which sure takes a lot of heat off.[25] The charge brings the moral authority of opposition to racism to the support of male dominance. "Essentialist" name-calling has become a weapon of choice against those who oppose pornography, prostitution, clitoridectomy, dowry burning, and other misogynst cultural practices, practices that target and harm women as women across cultures. Avoiding "essentialism" has become a politically and intellectually respectable pretext for dismissing and ignoring gender and the realities of sexual politics.

One deep project of anti-"essentialism" appears to be to undercut resistance to sexual oppression. First it is implied that the feminist protest against women's sexual definition and mistreatment is a protest against nature. In fact, it is the avatars of anti-"essentialism" who, when they read "sexuality," so deeply think biology that no amount of social, relational, and political analysis and observation deters them from the view that the biological is what is being analyzed and observed.[26] Then, it is more than suggested that political resistance to sexual abuse is a white thing. The idea here is that only white women (having no more significant problems to worry about) have the luxury of minding sexual objectification and sexual atrocities enough to make a big deal of them, so a feminism of resistance to sexual use and abuse is a white women's feminism.

What I want to say here is this: Sexual abuse is a real problem in the real world, not a move in an ideological or academic parlor game. Women of color are severely, pervasively sexually abused, including in racist ways worldwide. They are violated by it, resent it, resist it, want justice for it, and they want it to stop. Sexually abused women tend to know with real clarity that sexual abuse has everything to do with their being women. It is mainly academics and perpetrators who deny it.

Fear of being labeled "essentialist" for identifying the role of gender in sexual abuse has far-reaching consequences. Those within and outside the academy who know that male power in all its forms remains entrenched also know they face defamatory attacks and potential threats to their economic survival if they say so. As "essentialism" has become a brand, a contagious disease that you have to avoid feminism to avoid catching, it has become one more way that the connections and coherence of the ways women are oppressed as members of the group women can be covered up. It is silencing when women cannot tell the truth of what they know and survive; Professor christi cunningham is among the few who explore the dilemmas of discussing these subjects in public.

The defenders of dominance know, even if its postmodernist pretenders don't, that you can't change a reality you can't name. There is an ever-growing, largely unwritten, almost entirely unpublished literature on the sexual subordination of women of color. Women send it to me. When it takes a lot of courage to look at crucial intersectional issues—for example, the racist treatment of women of color in pornography, including its place in hate crimes, ground well prepared by Richard Delgado and others[27]—

when one risks being shunned in one's own critical community for raising issues of the sexual subordination of women of color, we need to ask who is doing this and why.

The "essentialism" charge, which has become a vehicle for misogyny, has also undermined the contributions that dominance theory, as developed in feminism, could make to antiracist work. Feminist dominance theory is a theory of social and political inequality as such. It builds on antiracism and builds it in. It is time for it to come home. Instead, in strenuous attempt to avoid the hated label of "essentialism," the revulsion at the "sameness" of all women falsely said to be inherent in gender analysis has produced a reflexive affirmation of "difference" in much critical race theorizing during the past decade or so. During this time, there seems to have been little or no awareness that sameness and difference are the two roads to nowhere that mainstream equality theory confines the unequal to walking.[28] In my opinion, failure to see this has crippled much antiracist legal work, including the fight for affirmative action, miring it in the sameness/difference equality trap that can only maintain white male power as is and fail to confront white male supremacy as such.[29]

Anti-"essentialism," as practiced, thus corrodes group identification and solidarity and leaves us with one-at-a-time personhood: liberal individualism. What a coincidence. With the inability to assert a group reality—an ability that only the subordinated need—comes the shift away from realities of power in the world and toward the search for "identity," excuse me, "identities."[30] It changes the subject, as it were, or tries to. But who wins? Can a postmodern humanism be far behind? "Identity" in its currently psychologically shrunk sense is not women's problem. Reality is: a reality of group oppression that exists whether we identify with our group or not.

It is not really necessary to say most of this to most of the critical race community. I therefore hope, and dare to believe, that CRT will avoid being diverted—as so much of academic feminism has been—into careerism, posturing, and seductive elite agendas. We need to theorize the place of the academy in the movement, to resist the forces that have created an elite that is accountable to power and principally responsive to its demands to de-realize reality. It would sound a lot less academic to call racism "racism" than to obscure it under "essentialism." It wouldn't be as high-sounding. But a lot more people would be involved in much larger discussion; the focus would be kept on dominance where it belongs; and none of the regressive consequences of the "essentialism" slur would result. This, then, seems a good moment to reaffirm the injunction to keep it real.

Notes

1. This talk was originally delivered as a short comment on the opening panel of the Critical Race Theory Conference held at Yale Law School, November 14, 1997, at which Professor Kimberlé Crenshaw and Professor Mari Matsuda delivered papers. It is dedicated to christi cunningham, who made it possible for me to say it.

2. Please see their articles in this volume.

3. Patricia J. Williams, *Alchemy of Race and Rights* (Cambridge, Mass.: Harvard University Press, 1991).

4. For an analysis of postmodernism that documents and expands on this point, see Catharine A. MacKinnon, "Points Against Postmodernism," *Chicago–Kent Law Review* 75 (2000): 687.

5. Aristotle's term that is translated "essence" is the Greek phrase "what it is to be." Thus, the essence of a house would be what it is to be a house—say, providing shelter or a place to live. So some characteristics would be central to a thing being what it is; others would be more peripheral. But, through changes, the "essence" of a thing is what inheres in it that makes it be what it is. See Aristotle, *Metaphysics VII, VIII*. See generally Martha Nussbaum, "Aristotle," in *Ancient Writers Greece and*

Rome, ed. T. James Luce (New York: Scribner, 1982), 377–416, and Martha Nussbaum, "Aristotle on Human Nature and the Foundations of Ethics," in J.E.J. Altham and Ross Harrison, *World, Mind, and Ethics: Essays on the Ethical Philosophy of Bernard Williams*, (Cambridge and London: Cambridge University Press, 1995), 86–131. Of relevance to the contemporary discussion is Aristotle's rejection of the idea that a universal, such as a Platonic form, is the essence of a thing. See *Metaphysics VII*, 13. Wittgenstein's treatment of the notion of "essential" focuses on the notion of what things have in common that are called by a common name, and the difficulties of doing so. See L. Wittgenstein, *Philosophical Investigations*, 2nd ed., trans. G.E.M. Anscombe (New York: Macmillan, 1972), ¶ 66, ¶ 67. Thus, in challenging readers to exhaustively define "games," he said, "What is common to them all? . . . If you look at them you will not see something that is common to all, but similarities, relationships, and a whole series of them at that. To repeat: don't think, but look! . . . And the result of this examination is: we see a complicated network of similarities overlapping and criss-crossing; sometimes overall similarities, sometimes similarities of detail": ibid., ¶ 66.

6. Elizabeth Spelman, *Inessential Woman* (Boston: Beacon Press, 1988), 158.

7. For further discussion, see Catharine A. MacKinnon, "From Practice to Theory, or What Is a White Woman Anyway?" *Yale Journal of Law and Feminism* 4 (1991): 113, discussing Susan Brownmiller and Simone de Beauvoir.

8. Angela P. Harris, "Race and Essentialism in Feminist Legal Theory," *Stanford Law Review* 42 (1990): 581, 585. As of 1995, this article was the most widely cited article in law published in 1990. Fred R. Shapiro, "The Most-Cited Law Review Articles Revisited," *Chicago–Kent Law Review* 71 (1995): 751, 777 (142 citations). Using the same method as Shapiro, I found that as of January 2, 1998, the Harris article had been referenced in 191 articles, 180 of them law journals.

9. For analysis, see e. christi cunningham, "Unmaddening: A Response to Angela Harris," *Yale Journal of Law and Feminism* 4 (1991): 155, 158.

10. See Spelman, *Inessential Woman*, 165.

11. Ibid., 13

12. See Harris, "Race and Essentialism," 588.

13. The issues discussed here are not confined to individuals, nor are they personal. However, research in 1999 disclosed more than one hundred law-review articles falsely referring to my work as "essentialist," usually based solely on citation to

Professor Harris's 1990 article. Only a handful even hesitantly questioned the label, and fewer still discussed my work itself. Representative examples from this flood of defamation include Katharine T. Bartlett, "Feminist Legal Methods," *Harvard Law Review* 103 (1990): 829, 874 ("A theory that purports to isolate gender as a basis for oppression obscures [factors other than gender that victimize women] and even reinforces other forms of oppression," citing Angela Harris for "mak[ing] this point specifically about MacKinnon"); Kathryn Abrams, "Title VII and the Complex Female Subject," *Michigan Law Review* 92 (1994): 2479, 2485 ("My use of the term *antiessentialism*. . . is more consistent with that of Angela Harris, who targets from the standpoint of black feminists what she described as the 'essentialism' of Catharine MacKinnon"); Linda C. McClain, "'Atomistic Man' Revisited: Liberalism, Connection, and Feminist Jurisprudence," *Southern California Law Review* 1171 (1992): 1171, 1186, but cf. Linda C. McClain, "Toward a Formative Project of Security, Freedom, and Equality," *Cornell Law Review* 85 (2000): 1221 (using MacKinnon's work itself to respond to Harris's charges); Thomas Ross, "Despair and Redemption in the Feminist Nomos," *Indiana Law Review* 69 (1993): 101, 105; Eric Blumenson, "Mapping the Limits of Skepticism in Law and Morals," *Texas Law Review* 74 (1996): 523, 557; Note, "The Myth of Context in Politics and Law," *Harvard Law Review* 110 (1997): 1292, 1295 ("As Harris argues, . . . essentialism may be identified in the writings of Catharine MacKinnon"); Kathryn Abrams, "Sex Wars Redux: Agency and Coercion in Feminist Legal Theory," *Columbia Law Review* 95 (1995): 304, 335, 336 (noting "Catharine MacKinnon is frequently taken to be the paradigmatic dominance feminist" and stating that "Dominance theory shares a central flaw of the 'essentialist' feminisms Harris critiques"); Nancy C. Staudt, "Taxing Housework," *Georgetown Law Journal* 84 (1996): 1571, 1573 ("Commentators who take an essentialist approach to women's subordination tend to make sex based generalizations about all women, regardless of the race, class, and sexuality differences among women," citing Harris's article for "discussing the marginalizing effects of Catharine MacKinnon's . . . theories of sexual difference"); Susan H. Williams, "A Feminist Reassessment of Civil Society," *Indiana Law Journal* 72 (1997): 417, 428 ("Feminists of color have been pointing out with increasing frequency that the view of women as simply the victims of society, shaped rather than shaping, has the effect of systematically excluding

them," citing only Harris "discussing the work of Catharine MacKinnon"); Daniel R. Ortiz, "Categorical Community," *Stanford Law Review* 51 (1999): 769, 801; Zanita E. Fenton, "Domestic Violence in Black and White: Racialized Gender Stereotypes in Gender Violence," *Columbia Journal of Gender and Law* 8 (1998): 1, 17, 52; Peter A. Alces and Cynthia V. Ward, "Defending Truth Beyond All Reason: The Radical Assault on Truth in American Law" (book review), *Texas Law Review* 78 (1999): 493, 528 (citing Harris's article as a "widely respected example" of Critical Race Theory and a "well-known critique of feminist essentialism" that "focuses specifically on 'gender essentialism' in the work of Catharine MacKinnon"); Jody Armour, "Critical Race Feminism: Old Wine in a New Bottle or New Legal Genre?" (book review), *Southern California Review of Law and Women's Studies* 7 (1998): 431, 434 (quoting Professor Adrien Wing's book criticizing "prominent white feminist Catharine MacKinnon . . . for using white women as the epitome of all women" and citing the Harris article); Kathryn Abrams, "The New Jurisprudence of Sexual Harassment," *Cornell Law Review* 83 (1998): 1169, 1192, 1201 (referring to "MacKinnonesque essentialism," citing Harris's article), 1214; Jane Wong, "The Anti-Essentialism v. Essentialism Debate in Feminist Legal Theory: The Debate and Beyond," *William and Mary Journal of Women and the Law* 5 (1999): 273, 284.

14. Catharine A. MacKinnon, "Feminism, Marxism, Method, and the State: Toward Feminist Jurisprudence," *Signs* 8 (1983): 635, 639. This passage is quoted in Harris, "Race and Essentialism," 592. Another example is: "The particularities become facets of the collective understanding within which differences constitute rather than undermine collectivity" (Catharine A. MacKinnon, *Toward a Feminist Theory of the State* [Cambridge, Mass.: Harvard University Press, 1990], 86).

15. See cunningham, "Unmaddening," 164-7. Professor cunningham documents how "Harris often repeats MacKinnon's ideas when she describes Black women's experiences of dominance."

16. After this talk was delivered, Professor Sallyanne Payton, as part of an online discussion that followed, said:

I was not at the CRT meeting. . . . I do happen to know what MacKinnon thinks, however, and I would be greatly surprised if she did not say what she thinks. Here is what she thinks, filtered through my way of talking.

The charge of "essentialism" as leveled against much of feminist writing is fair and accurate. That is, many white feminists seem to think there is something inherent about being female that accounts for women's attitudes and behaviors, crossculturally, and lots of them take Western white women as the normative representatives of true womanhood in the sense of true-to-nature womanhood, the rest of us being deficient or substandard or odd or whatever. The racist dimension of this stems from the fact that a great many white feminists seem to regard Western white male–female relations as prototypical of male–female relations, which conveniently reinforces the Western white male as the representative of the most advanced manhood: if male–female relations in non-Western cultures don't look like those in (middle-class) Western society, it is only because the non-Western men are not as advanced as the Western men.

It has been a long time since I have participated in feminist discourse, but I seem to remember that in the early days (1970s into early 1980s) this is how almost all the white feminists thought: they were interested in their relationships with their men, who were the powerful men. If the rest of us were not having their experience, it was because our men, being inferior, had not achieved power. So we had nothing to say: if our men ever achieved power in the sense in which white men had power, we would have the same kinds of experiences the white women were having. The actual experiences of women of color were therefore material for footnotes and asides: they were not central, not emblematic. White women controlled the discussion, which was about themselves. We spent years fighting this kind of thinking, with only mixed success.

The refreshing aspect of MacKinnon's approach is that she does not think this way. She did not start with the situation of the privileged white woman even though she was one; she started with the situation of the most powerless women in the system, and built her theory on what she saw as the relationship between male desire and opportunity where women were unprotected. The situation of the more privileged she then saw as the consequence of their relative sheltering from the full force of male domination. In MacKinnon's world the least privileged woman (frequently a

woman of color) therefore becomes emblematic; the more privileged woman is revealed to be a beneficiary of protection, and the typical white feminist a victim of the delusion that the status of middle-class white women is something more than an artifact of male protection for some specially favored women, a protection that is strenuously maintained. This line of thought ... moves the middle-class white women off of center stage and it forces the middle-class white men to look at the sexually gritty sides of themselves and the society that they have built. It moves the experience of women of color to center stage and it accounts for our experience in a way that is theoretically coherent. In MacKinnon's work, the experience of women of color is in the text, not in the footnotes.

No one's work is above criticism, but I think it cannot plausibly be argued that MacKinnon's feminism is essentialist. It actually comes closest to being essentialist in its treatment of men, not women, whose situation depends centrally on context and the particular cultural ways in which protections and vulnerabilities are constructed. I think that MacKinnon is sensitive on this point, not only because unexamined racism is a sin of which she is unwilling to stand accused inaccurately, but also because she thinks that people who believe that her feminism is essentialist and therefore racist do not avail themselves of the powerful critique of male dominance that might be analytically useful to them in anti-racist thinking.

This text is on file with the author.
17. See Harris, "Race and Essentialism," 598.
18. Ibid., 592, 595, 596. Cf. cunningham, "Unmaddening," 163–4: "MacKinnon's inclusive definition of women is evident.... Black women cannot be a nuance of women because Black women are women [in her work;] we are often the model. MacKinnon does not marginalize Black women, nor does she make us into something more than women, because MacKinnon considers Black women to be women."
19. Saying this is not to say that women of color's only problems are worse versions of white women's problems. Nor do I "define" Black women as "different": see Harris, "Race and Essentialism," 595. I reject "differences" definitions explicitly and implicitly. And Professor Harris is incorrect to suggest that "feminism unmodified" refers to women without particularities. It clearly refers to a politics of

women unmodified by pre-existing politics, like liberalism or socialism.

20. See Harris, "Race and Essentialism," 592-4, 603. See cunningham, "Unmaddening," 160-1: "MacKinnon does not relegate Black women to footnotes and brackets. Her theory is explicitly about us." How footnotes that document, credit, and elaborate, become "guilty" is unclear. See Harris, "Race and Essentialism," 603.

21. See Harris, "Race and Essentialism," 594. Cf. cunningham, "Unmaddening," 161-3.

22. See, for example, Martha Minow, "The Supreme Court 1986 Term Forward: Justice Engendered," *Harvard Law Review 101* (1987): 10, 63: "Some, for example, have expressly argued that sexism is more fundamental than racism," citing as the first of three sources Catharine A. MacKinnon, *Feminism Unmodified: Discourses on Life and Law* (Cambridge, Mass.: Harvard University Press, 1987), 166-8. I never made any such statement or adopted any such approach. Moreover, extensive evidence that this is not my view—including drawing on African American women's experiences and writings, discussions of racism throughout, a central focus on class, and a pervasive combined analysis of race and ethnicity with sex, much of which is accessible through the indices of my published books—had to be ignored. It is a lot to overlook.

Published in 1979, *Sexual Harassment of Working Women: A Case of Sex Discrimination* (New Haven, Conn.: Yale University Press), for example, explicitly builds the concept of sexual harassment itself on the experiences of Black women in particular. See, for example, pp. 33, 65 (Paulette Barnes); pp. 30, 73-4 (Maxine Munford); p. 60 (Diane Williams); p. 61 (Margaret Miller); p. 34 (referring to Pamela Price); see also pp. 42, 48, 52, 78-80, 84 (Carmita Wood). Nor is these women's ethnicity submerged in their gender. Why it was Black women who had what it took to bring all the early sexual-harassment cases is analyzed in terms of their race, sex, and class particularities: p. 53 ("Of all women, [black women] are most vulnerable to sexual harassment, both because of the image of black women as the most sexually accessible and because they are the most economically at risk"). Other Black women's voices analyzing women's condition are either quoted—see, for example, p. 176 (an anonymous Black woman); p. 273 (Pauli Murray); and p. 23 (Ntozake Shange)—or their insights are otherwise drawn on (see p. 275 [Toni Morrison]). Race and racism are discussed throughout, legally and socially, as a parallel to or contrast with sex and sexism: p. 129 ("The

analogy [between the histories of sex and race distinctions] should not be allowed to obscure the distinctive content and dynamics of sex and race"); specified within sex and outside of it: p. 176 ("The generality of 'women' and 'men' must be qualified by recognizing the distinctive effect of race"); and in interaction with and overlapping with sex: p. 30 ("Sexual harassment can be both a sexist way to express racism and a racist way to express sexism"). For additional examples, see p. 14 ("Black women are much more likely to be poor than white women"); pp. 17-8, 23, 30-1, 88-90, 97-8, 118-9, 127-41, 169, 173, 176-7, 189-90, 203, 210, 215 (Helen Hacker's work on black people as a group and women as a group); p. 247 ("Presumably, black women are doubly burdened"); p. 257 (noting that the filing of an amicus brief in a case by Organization of Black Activist Women "is of special interest since both the perpetrator and victim were black"); p. 267 (noting the history of scientific racism); p. 273 (noting scholarship in Black women's feminism); pp. 273-4 (noting scholarship on the parallel between race and sex); p. 274 (noting cases that point to the parallel between race and sex); and p. 274 (analyzing an article comparing racism and sexism). These are just some selected instances.

Feminism Unmodified, published in 1987, follows the same pattern. It criticizes non-reporting of the race of rape victims: pp. 81-2 ("The invisibility of women of color is such that if you do not say that a woman is of color, it is assumed that her race is nonexistent—therefore, oddly, white"). It locates women of color as active agents in their own cultures and in resisting white male domination: p. 69 ("What women like Julia Martinez might make equality mean, no white man invented"). It speaks of women of color's specific rates of rape (p. 82), death from illegal abortion (p. 25), and abuse in pornography (pp. 199-200). It refers to voices, work, insights, and experiences of women including LaDoris Cordell, Pamela Price, Michelle Vinson, Vanessa Williams, Gayatri Spivak, Beth Brant, and many others. It speaks about race in relation to sex (p. 2 ["We urgently need to comprehend the emerging pattern in which gender, while a distinct inequality, also contributes to the social embodiment and expression of race and class inequalities, at the same time as race and class are deeply imbedded in gender. For example, the sexualization of racial and ethnic attributes like skin color or stereotypes is no less a dynamic within racism for being done through gender"]) and on its own terms; about women of color as women and as women of color throughout. See, for example, pp. 7, 9, 25, 42, 44, 56, 63-7, 76, 81-2, 89, 101, 164-8, 178, 193-4, 199-200, 202, 208-9, 211, 220, 238 (explaining why "Black" is capitalized in the book and "white" is not), 248, 256, 302-3, 305.

The same is true of *Toward a Feminist Theory of the State* (Cambridge, Mass.: Harvard University Press), published in 1989. The introduction states: "All women possess ethnic (and other definitive) particularities that mark their femaleness; at the same time their femaleness marks their particularities and constitutes one. Such a recognition, far from undermining the feminist project, comprises, defines, and sets standards for it. It also does not reduce race to sex. Rather, it suggests that comprehension and change in racial inequality are essential to comprehension and change in sex inequality, with implications that link comprehending and changing sexism to comprehending and changing racism" (p. xii). Again, race and racism and its impact on men and women and theorizing their condition are discussed throughout (see, for example, pp. xi-xiii, 6, 26, 55, 63, 110, 125, 136, 138, 154, 172-3, 181, 204, 245, 288). In addition, the words and work, among others, of Johnnie Tillmon, Zora Neale Hurston, Harriet Jacobs, Alice Walker, and Audre Lorde are used to define the condition of women as such.

At the conference at which the remarks in the text above were delivered, the paragraph preceding this endnote (minus its footnotes) was spoken virtually as it appears here. After the panel, Professor Harris thanked me for the critique of her work, said it was fair and right, and expressed her appreciation for the attention to what she had said back then because my work had been important to her. Professor Crenshaw (who was sitting next to me when Professor Harris said this) and I both admired the courage and forthrightness of this statement.

23. On April 7, 1990, shortly after Professor Harris's article was published, Karen E. Davis wrote to her, analyzing many of the issues raised in the foregoing paragraphs:

I have always read Catharine MacKinnon's work as deeply anti-essentialist. It is deconstructive in the Derridean sense, except that she considers power while he doesn't. It is genealogical in the Foucauldian sense, except that she considers gender while he doesn't. MacKinnon's analysis of male power includes an analysis of its "essentialism" or "phallogicentrism," although she does not use these terms in her critiques of metaphysics, objectivity, liberalism, and "theory." . . . I believe you introduce essentialism into Catharine MacKinnon's work that isn't there.

In fact, I see in your writing a pervasive use of moral essentialism typical of that which pervades feminist theory. Throughout your article, power and powerlessness are understood in terms of guilt and innocence, good and bad. The most obvious example of this is where you attribute to MacKinnon the view that Black men are not as bad as white men, "although they are still bad, being men" [Harris, "Race and Essentialism," 596, n. 17]. The quote you cite, however, supports only MacKinnon's point that Black men are not as powerful as white men. Nowhere in her work does MacKinnon conflate powerful = bad, and powerless = good, as many strains of feminism are wont to do. Rather, she explicitly rejects the moralism and naturalism contained in the views that men abuse women because they are bad or naturally rapacious, and that "women might be congenitally nicer" [MacKinnon, *Feminism Unmodified*, 219].

While you say MacKinnon violates the particularities of the experiences of women of color, the standard against which you measure her work is not embodied experience but a formulation of five attributes of gender essentialism as abstracted from Elizabeth Spelman, a white feminist. You define gender essentialism as "The notion that there is a monolithic 'women's experience' that can be described independent of other facets of experience like race, class, and sexual orientation" [Harris, "Race and Essentialism," 588]. But nothing you quote in MacKinnon's writings in any way supports your premise that MacKinnon does this. In fact, the things you quote directly support the opposite reading. Your idea that she "postpones the demands of black women until the arrival of a 'general theory of social inequality'" [Harris, "Race and Essentialism," 593] is based incongruously on her statement that such a theory is prefigured in connections between race, sex and class: "gender in this country appears partly to comprise the meaning of, as well as bisect, race and class, even as race and class specificities make up, as well as cross-cut gender" [quoted in Harris, "Race and Essentialism," 593]. To accuse MacKinnon of a "colorblind" approach here is to miss her critiques of objectivity, of abstraction, and of the principles of neutrality in law. The whole point of her *Signs* articles is that a commitment in feminism to not submerging particularity into universals is a methodological departure from all previous theories.

You go on here to suggest parenthetically that MacKinnon is not committed to the effort such a theory will take, "(presumably that is someone else's work)." This not only belies her work but is gratuitously insulting. MacKinnon does not claim to present a finished thing but rather a contribution to a larger project which she sees as necessarily collaborative. To this end, her footnotes are not just lists, but an engaged intertextuality with shared and ongoing concerns.

The point where you come close to having to acknowledge her engagement with issues of race and class, you provide MacKinnon's theory with the appellation "nuanced," suggesting that nuance is essentialism's empty gesture toward engaging particularity. While this critique may be true of liberal feminism, it is not true of MacKinnon's radicalism. In her preface to *Toward A Feminist Theory of the State*, MacKinnon is herself quite critical of liberal feminism's response to the challenge of diversity: "to proliferate 'feminisms' (a white racist feminism?) in the face of women's diversity is the latest attempt of liberal pluralism to evade the challenge women's reality poses to theory, simply because the theoretical forms those realities demand have yet to be created" [MacKinnon, *Feminist Theory*, xii]. And yes, MacKinnon counts herself among the feminists who will be creating such a theory.

The other times you are close to being forced to acknowledge MacKinnon's attention to race and class, you castigate her for relegating these concerns to footnotes. You mention MacKinnon's use of footnotes about ten times without analyzing their function in her text. Do you have a meta-theory of footnotes in the same way you have a meta-theory of nuance or of essentialism? You seem to be banking on a tacit universal agreement ("we") that footnotes are always marginal and dismissive. Instead of outlining a textual examination of the structure of footnotes in MacKinnon's writing, you rely on the convention that footnotes are the place of empty gestures. Yet even a cursory textual analysis of MacKinnon's style would suggest

that her footnotes are an essential element of a multi-tiered structure of argument....

Toward a Feminist Theory of the State appeared last August, shortly after you presented your paper, but well in advance of the time you published it. In the preface to this book, MacKinnon specifically addresses methodological questions of essentialism and totalization that you and others have raised about her work (see especially, pp. xi-xii on racial particularity). It may well be that the bulk of your criticisms were preempted by MacKinnon's attention to them, so that all that was left of the substance of your critique is nuance and footnotes.

Your article speculates about why essentialism is so appealing to feminists and so easy to fall into, but does not consider essentialism as a strategy of hegemony, as MacKinnon does. MacKinnon's analysis of male power casts essentialism as a deliberate strategy of consolidating and authorizing political power. Essentialism is built into our language, our metaphysics, and our jurisprudence so that social inequality appears based on natural differences. Neutrality principles in discrimination law, for instance, systematically reinforce existing social inequalities. MacKinnon's insight forces a reexamination of Aristotle, from whom the doctrine derives that equality means treating likes alike and unlikes unalike [see MacKinnon, *Feminism Unmodified*, 37].

In your section "Beyond Essentialism" you credit to Martha Minow the realization that difference and identity are not inherent but are always relational [Harris, "Race and Essentialism", 610]. This echoes MacKinnon's analysis in the first Signs article that both women and men are socially constructed through political relations of sexual objectification. You attribute to Joan Williams the idea that "sameness" and "difference" must be supplanted by "a deeper understanding of gender as a system of power relations" [quoted in Harris, "Race and Essentialism," 612]. This insight is precisely MacKinnon's argument in "Difference and Dominance: On Sex Discrimination" [*Feminism Unmodified*, 32]. In fact, MacKinnon articulates these ideas as early as 1979 in *Sexual Harassment of Working Women*, particularly in the sections "What is Sex?" (pp. 149-157), and "Two Theories of Sex Discrimination" (pp. 106-126). Only the effacement of MacKinnon's contribution to feminist jurisprudence makes possible this truly puzzling circularity in your article in which her text is measured up against the substance of her theories and found wanting. (On file with the author)

After delivering the talk printed here, I learned that Professor Ann Scales had written the following in a draft of her article, "Disappearing Medusa: The Fate of Feminist Legal Theory," *Harvard Women's Law Journal* 20 (1997): 34, but decided not to publish this passage in that format on that occasion:

The anti-essentialism literature asserted three primary criticisms, directed primarily (and too generally) at feminism. First, that feminism, in describing the metaphenomenon of gender, treats the experience of privileged white women as if it were the experience of all women. Thus, feminism engages in false universalization. Second, feminism assumes gender as a metaphenomenon, as the primary oppression, to which all other oppressive situations endured by women are merely "additive." Thus, feminism is reductionist. Third, feminism, in its definition of gender as a condition of systematic sexual oppression, cannot adequately explain the survival of women, particularly women of color. Thus, feminism denigrates the creativity and agency of women, forever relegating women to the category of "victim" and actually impeding progress. Though I proudly identify myself as a radical feminist, I have no theoretical problem, by and large, with the anti-essentialism critique. I think it was initially overbroad, and initially misdirected, insofar as it targeted Professor MacKinnon. She has never posited a necessarily universal anything, never asserted that gender was the beginning or end of the story, and always celebrated the infinite forms of women's resistance, particularly by putting in context the dangers thereof. The overbreadth was in not distinguishing very carefully between radical feminism and "cultural" feminism, which relies on some inherent female point of view as a result of biology or otherwise. ("Disappearing Medusa: The Fate of Feminist Legal Theory" [draft], January 25, 1997, 14–6, on file with the author)

Another account of these issues is provided by Elizabeth Rapaport, "Generalizing Gender: Reason and Essence in the Thought of Catharine MacKinnon," in *A Mind of One's Own*, ed. Louise Antony and Charlotte Witt (Boulder, Colo.: Westview Press, 1993), 127.

24. See Angela Harris, "Categorical Rhetoric and Critical Social Theory: Review of Catharine A. MacKinnon, *Toward a Feminist Theory of the State*" (unpublished draft circulated on February 23, 1990), 26–7. The published version of the review does not include this passage. It says that the book "seems in tension with itself" because it sometimes "seems to want to transcend categorical discourse" and "repeatedly calls for a feminist analysis that is historical, contextual, and concerned with contradiction and paradox." Angela Harris, "Categorical Discourse and Dominance Theory," *Berkeley Women's Law Journal* 5 (1990): 181–3. In fact, my book never "calls for" analysis "concerned with contradiction and paradox." It does engage in an analysis that is historical, contextual, and attentive to the diverse realities of power.

25. See Anne C. Dailey, "Feminism's Return to Liberalism," *Yale Law Journal* 102 (1993): 1265, 1271: "As a result of the anti-essentialism critique, 'asking the woman question' assumes a new meaning; the focus of feminist inquiry shifts from the difference between men and women to the differences among women themselves." That is, divide and conquer.

26. See, for example, Nancy Fraser and Linda J. Nicholson, "Social Criticism Without Philosophy," in *Feminism/Postmodernism*, ed. Linda J. Nicholson (New York and London: Routledge, 1990), 31, who claim that Catharine MacKinnon has "constructed a quasi-metanarrative" around sexuality, which itself is said to be "associated with a biological or quasibiological need and is construed as functionally necessary to the reproduction of society" and "is not the sort of thing, then, whose historical origins need be investigated." The conflation of the sexuality I analyze with biology is in the minds of these writers. See also Catharine A. MacKinnon, "Does Sexuality Have a History?" *30 Michigan Quarterly Review* 1 (1991), delivered on September 12, 1990, considering sexuality's history.

27. See generally Mari J. Matsuda, Charles R. Lawrence III, Richard Delgado, and Kimberlé W. Crenshaw, *Words That Wound: Critical Race Theory, Assaultive Speech, and the First Amendment* (Boulder, Colo.: Westview Press, 1993), and in particular the lucid analysis by Kim Crenshaw. See also Sumi K. Cho, "Converging Stereotypes in Racialized Sexual Harassment: Where the Model Minority Meets Suzie Wong," in *Critical Race Feminism*, ed. Adrien K. Wing (New York and London: New York University Press, 1997), 203. By contrast with these works, it is my impression that most of those who adopt the anti-"essentialism" line criticized in this

paper defend pornography and oppose measures to address the harms to civil rights done through it.

28. See MacKinnon, *Toward a Feminist Theory of the State,* 215-34.

29. This analysis is developed more fully in Catharine A. MacKinnon, *Sex Equality* (New York: Foundation Press, 2001).

30. See, for example, Judith Butler, *Gender Trouble: Feminism and the Subversion of Identity* (New York: Routledge, 1990). The concept of "gender identity" in such work appears to derive from Dr. Robert Stoller's 1964 article on transsexuality. See Robert J. Stoller, "A Contribution to the Study of Gender Identity," *International Journal Psycho-analysis* 45 (1964): 220.

PART II

Crossroads

Section A: Race

Critiquing "Race" and Its Uses: Critical Race Theory's Uncompleted Argument

Robert S. Chang

IN "THE UNCOMPLETED ARGUMENT," Anthony Appiah tells us that W.E.B. Du Bois "came gradually, though never completely, to assimilate the unbiological nature of the races."[1] Du Bois, who "thought longer, more engagedly, and more publicly about race than any other social theorist of our century,"[2] wrote about race during a period characterized by a popular scientific racism, which attributed intellectual, cultural, and moral capacities on the basis of biological race. He argued against this notion of biological determinism or biological destiny that was used to justify the unequal treatment or unequal position of Blacks. But rather than deny the salience of race because of its dubious scientific basis, Du Bois argued for the importance of race, understood properly as a sociohistorical concept.[3] Appiah argues, though, that a sociohistorical concept of race is inextricably moored to its biological foundations in such a way that Du Bois set for himself an impossible project and "was unable to escape the notion of race he had explicitly rejected."[4]

Although it may be true that Du Bois never completely assimilated the unbiological nature of race, his argument has been taken up by critical race scholars, who seem fairly unified in regarding race to be a social construct.[5] There has, however, been disagreement as to its implications. The chapters in this section on race present different maps of this contested terrain. Before engaging with each chapter, I will provide context to show what is at stake.

A Little Context

"Race is a social construct." This statement has become a mantra in Critical Race Theory. It is a mantra in my course on race, racism, and U.S. law. Sometimes, for fun, I have my students say it out loud. Most of them are compliant and play along. "Race is a social construct. Race is a social construct. Race is a social construct." Nothing happens. They are not enlightened, and the world has not changed. The mantra does not appear to be working. So why the mantra?

Du Bois was writing against the grain of scientific racialism, which was used to justify the superior position of Whites and the inferior position of Blacks.[6] Science had created a racial logic where race referred not just to physical appearances but also to traits such as intelligence and moral capacity. Under this view, Blacks were deemed unintelligent, ineducable, lazy, sexually licentious, and so on. This lack of intelligence and inability to recognize and conform to moral rules resulted in the degraded condition of the Blacks and the elevated position of Whites. According to scientific racialism, this was the natural order of the world, not the result of specific and diffuse enactments of power. Du Bois, as part of his quest for racial justice, rejected the science that created this racial logic.

When critical race scholars declare race to be a social construct, what are we writing against? While scientific racialism is generally not a defensible position, there remains what might be described as a social or cultural racialism that attributes certain characteristics to racial groups and explains racial differences as the natural outcome of meritocracy and the free play of the market. This new racialism, which may not be so different from the old racialism, is necessary to maintain the widely held belief among Whites that race has little if any effect on one's life chances[7] in a country where the average wealth of a White household in 1993 was more than $45,740 and the average wealth of a Black household was $4,418.[8] The new racialism blames Blacks themselves for this disparity: "If blacks really wanted to, and were willing to work hard, ... their problems could be solved."[9] The new racialism allows Justice Sandra Day O'Connor, when confronted with the fact that 99.33 percent of a city's construction contracts were awarded to White contractors in a city whose population was evenly split between Blacks and Whites, to speculate that "Blacks may be disproportionately attracted to industries other than construction."[10] One might wonder, as does Anthony P. Farley in his chapter, "The Poetics of Colorlined Space," in this volume, what sort of explanation Chief Justice William Rehnquist might provide if asked why, of eighty-two law clerks he has hired over the years, none was Black. How does one account for the inexorable zero? Similar questions could be asked of all of the justices on the Supreme Court with regard to their racial hiring practices. Perhaps Black, Hispanic, and Asian American law students and recent law grads are disproportionately attracted to pursuits other than prestigious Supreme Court clerkships. Perhaps.

The new racialism differs from the scientific racialism Du Bois was writing against, but both operate to explain racial differences with regard to material conditions, justifying them as the natural order of things; both turn a blind eye to the way these racial disparities were consciously (intentionally) and unconsciously (negligently, recklessly) constructed by individuals and institutions. It is against the new racialism that CRT takes up the social construction argument. At stake is whether racism and its effects can be named and redressed.

Each of the chapters in this section begins from the premise that race, rather than being a biological phenomenon, is a social construct. From here, the chapters explore different ways in which "race" becomes constructed and inflected by color, nation, class, gender, and sexuality. These constructions are authorized by the law and operate to regulate the bodies we inhabit.

In their chapter, "Un-Natural Things: The Construction of Race, Gender, and Disability," Robert L. Hayman, Jr., and Nancy Levit explore the disjuncture between contemporary theorists who seem to accept social construction theory and the general public, legislators, and the judiciary who have largely escaped the influence of social construction theory. They draw important insights and analogies from the way law treats gender and disability. The chapters by Kevin R. Johnson and Sherene H. Razack are in some ways companion pieces. In "Race, the Immigration Laws, and Domestic Race Relations: A Critique," Johnson identifies and explores what he perceives to be a gap in coverage within CRT, which has not paid sufficient attention to the interplay of immigration and nationality laws with the construction and maintenance of race and citizenship. His chapter is a call for further inquiry within CRT. This call is, in some ways, answered in Razack's chapter, "'Simple Logic': Race, the Identity Documents Rule, and the Story of a Nation Besieged and Betrayed," which details a troubling Canadian national narrative that fits within a broader racial project to consolidate white supremacy globally. Its lessons for those interested in U.S. race relations are obvious, and it presents a model for the kind of work called for by Johnson.

The two remaining chapters in this section examine the body as it is mapped specifically and abstractly in social space. In "Straight Out of the Closet: Race, Gender, and Sexual Orientation," Devon W. Carbado reminds us that the body exists within lived space where race, gender, and sexuality (among other things) overdetermine our identities. He argues that there can be no racial project that does not consider the operation of gender and sexuality. Within this matrix of interlocking social constructions, he challenges us to examine and work to undermine our relative privileges if we are to avoid complicity in the very structures of subordination we claim to reject. And Anthony Farley's chapter presents a radical vision of why race

remains so entrenched in the fabric of our nation (and the West). It argues that race is a form of pleasure, with the Black body as fetish object. Racial subordination is to be understood or experienced as a form of sexualized pleasure, a pleasure that is not easily abandoned but which must be recognized if it is to be subverted.

Each of the chapters attempts to complete the arguments begun within Critical Race Theory. The chapters describe different ways to fulfill the premise and promise of Critical Race Theory. Next, I will examine each chapter in greater detail. I discuss the chapters in a sequence different from their order in this collection

Why Hasn't Social Construction Caught On?

Those unfamiliar with the development of racial thinking might start with Hayman and Levit's chapter. The authors provide a brief history of "race" along with a brief history of critiques of "race." They identify four important stages in the development of racial thinking in America. The first period, 1619-62 (dates are approximate), is characterized by the awareness of European colonists of a difference in color between themselves and Africans, but without the language of race, the differences did not manifest themselves in rigid hierarchies with exclusive domains. For example, free Blacks were integrated into the social and political communities in the colonies. The second period, 1662-1776, is characterized by the formalization of race, with the institution of slave codes and the surfacing of restrictions on free Blacks based on racial difference and not based on condition of servitude. Hierarchical structure shifts from servitude (which includes both free Whites and free Blacks over White indentured servants and Black slaves) to race (Whites over

Blacks). The third period, 1776–1835, is marked by the tremendous efforts to rationalize the ideal of equality of all men with the fact of slavery. The fourth period, 1835–?, is marked by the scientization of race, where a scientific language provided the much-needed rationale to justify the enslavement of Blacks in the South and the unequal treatment of Blacks in the North.

Hayman and Levit then provide an account of critiques of "race" along with the general consensus among anthropologists that "racial classifications have no discernable scientific value." They also observe that the extent of "interracial" sex in the United States has produced "multiracial" individuals and a "multiracial" America.[11] With such a history and current-day reality, to talk of "race" as biological is to participate in a fiction. Hence the turn to race as social construct.

From there, Hayman and Levit wonder why, given the consensus among contemporary thinkers that race is socially constructed, the general public, legislators, and the judiciary have yet to incorporate this insight into their worldview. In asking this question, they raise the important point that it is not enough for critical race scholars to have this conversation among themselves. If critical race scholars want social change to occur, they must think creatively about how to translate social construction theory to be meaningful to these target audiences. Hayman and Levit compare the relative success social construction theory has had in the areas of gender and disability, where courts seem more willing to accept the idea of social construction in recognizing discrimination and providing a judicial remedy.

For example, sex is sometimes understood as biological difference, whether at the physical or genetic level, whereas gender is usually understood as constructed by social forces. Hayman and Levit note that the Supreme Court began acknowledging the role institutions had in constructing gender through the use of stereotypical thinking: "that exclusion of men from a publicly funded nursing school ... risked reinforcing stereotypes of nursing as women's work";[12] that requiring spousal notification for abortion reinforced notions about women's roles and limited the "ability of women to participate equally in the economic and social life of the Nation";[13] that the publicly funded Virginia Military Institute "may not exclude qualified individuals based on 'fixed notions concerning the roles and abilities of males and females.'"[14] Hayman and Levit note that the Supreme Court seems cognizant of its "own role in shaping gender," and "for women the Court seemed close to a Field of Dreams theory of educational and occupational channeling: if we build the opportunities, they will come."

Hayman and Levit also draw on the area of disability. For example, one could understand someone in a wheelchair as being physically unable to enter a building unaided. Such a person might be described as disabled. But is the disability an innate characteristic of the person, or has the physical world been structured in such a way that the disability to enter the building might be thought of as socially constructed? Rather than simply accept the world as it is as inevitable, our society is beginning to understand that we need not have constructed the world in this way and that the appropriate remedy is accommodation.

The Supreme Court appears willing to accept that gender roles and disability are contingent, created and maintained by sociohistorical forces, and as such are capable of being dismantled or constructed differently. With this understanding, the court has been willing to intervene to equalize opportunities for women and people with disabilities.

Hayman and Levit wonder, though, why the Supreme Court has yet to assimilate the contingent nature of race. They explore three possible explanations: 1) empathetic identification and interest convergence; 2) attitudes and demographics; and 3) litigation strategies and concepts of identity. The third is the most relevant with regard to social construction and is the real payoff of their chapter. They examine the strategies used by litigants in important civil-rights cases involving women and racial minorities to see whether "feminist or civil rights lawyers talk explicitly about the social or political construction of gender or race" and "whether lawyers told the litigants' stories in narrative form, to demonstrate the effect of social policies on the lived experiences of individuals." Hayman and Levit note that the social construction argument has been repeatedly urged by litigants in gender cases, especially in the 1980s and 1990s, whereas it has not been argued in the same way in race cases. Also, with regard to narratives, it appears that individualized stories appear more frequently in the gender cases than the race cases. This might indicate one reason for the relative success of the social construction argument with regard to gender but not to race. Or it might indicate strategic choices, where empathetic identification in the gender cases and empathetic disidentification in the race cases led to different approaches. The authors admit that this is an initial exploration and that they can draw only tentative speculations from their analysis. But this is a rich area that has yet to be fully mined, and I encourage scholars to develop more fully what Hayman and Levit have begun.

Constructing Race Through Immigration Law

In "Race, the Immigration Laws, and Domestic Race Relations," Johnson explores an aspect of law that CRT has not suffi-

ciently analyzed. Although he recognizes that some recent LatCrit and Asian American legal scholarship has begun to focus on the immigration and nationality laws, Johnson makes a call for much-needed work. He ascribes the omission as stemming "in part from the longstanding assumption that race relations in the United States exclusively concerns African Americans and whites." Johnson's chapter is located within the growing body of work that is pushing CRT to recognize the histories and experiences of other racialized groups and to develop more sophisticated models of oppression that extend beyond bipolar models of domination.

Johnson pays particular attention to the connection between racism and nativism. While it may seem intuitive that there is a relationship between foreign and domestic racial subordination, figuring out how it works is the tricky part. While acknowledging the importance of economic, historical, and other social forces, Johnson draws in this chapter on psychology to understand how aggression directed at domestic minorities is transferred and displaced upon immigrants of color:

> Transference, often an unconscious event, occurs when "feelings toward one person are refocused on another." . . . [Displacement is] "a defense mechanism in which a drive or feeling is shifted upon a substitute object, one that is psychologically more available. For example, aggressive impulses may be displaced, as in 'scapegoating,' upon people . . . *who are not sources of frustration but are safer to attack.*"[15]

These ideas help him to understand how, at the end of the twentieth century, society, constrained by law and "modern sensibilities, cannot directly attack minority citizens [but] can . . . lash out with virtual impunity at noncitizens of color, claiming that the attacks are justified because 'aliens' lack rights under the law." Johnson warns against those who "dubiously assert that only substantial reductions in immigration levels will improve the economic well-being of African Americans and Latinas/os in the United States." Tempting as it may be for domestic subordinated groups to ignore racially exclusionary immigration laws, giving in to this temptation would actually reinforce the subordination of domestic minority citizens.

Johnson develops his argument by looking at two periods in U.S. history. The first involves Reconstruction and Chinese Exclusion. The second involves the World War II period. Transference and displacement have a certain persuasive force in explaining this country's complicated racial history. Instead of looking at just White–Black relations or White–Asian relations or White–Latina/o relations, Johnson provides a model that deals with multiple groups simultaneously. He notes that after the Civil War, "with the harshest treatment previously directed at African Americans declared unlawful, the nation in effect transferred animosity to another discrete and insular minority [the Chinese], whose status as racially different 'aliens' rationalized their discriminatory treatment under the law." This same dynamic took place during the World War II period, when "formal legal improvements [were] achieved by African Americans in combination with notorious attacks—sanctioned by law—on persons of Japanese and Mexican ancestry." Johnson rejects coincidence and calls for further critical inquiry into differential minority-group treatment.

Johnson's chapter is important because it highlights an area that CRT has not fully mined. His examination of the connection between immigration laws and domestic civil rights is only the beginning of the kind of analysis that will help us understand how race and nation are constructed where multiple groups are involved.

Race and Inter/National Narratives

Although the analysis in Razack's chapter, "'Simple Logic,'" is located in the specificity of Canada, it draws not just a Canadian national narrative but a narrative of a globalized white supremacy. Part of the power of the piece comes from the way it works through different levels: the particular, the national, and the global.

The particular begins with Bill C-86, which created "a class of people neatly labeled the 'undocumented,' people marked as less deserving of juridical and social rights by virtue of their lack of passports or 'proper' travel documents." Unlike the U.S. context, in which "undocumented" refers generally to those who entered the country through improper means or who overstayed their visas, "undocumented" in Canada can refer to those who are in fact granted asylum by Canada but who did not arrive in Canada with proper identity documents. These people, once granted asylum, are legally present in Canada but exist in a state of legal limbo because they must wait a long time (at first five, now three, years) before they are able to petition for permanent resident status. During this waiting period, they have limited access to education, credit, and employment, among other things. These provisions have had the greatest detrimental impact on 13,000 Somali refugees who were granted asylum but had to undergo the lengthy waiting period before becoming eligible for permanent resident status. Many families were kept separated because these "undocumented" but legally present Somali refugees could "not sponsor dependents outside Canada, or leave its borders. In some cases, this meant that children left behind in refugee camps could not be reunited with their parents."

The treatment of Somali refugees can be critiqued at the level of the particular. The insistence on proper identity documents of refugees seems to defy "simple logic":

The relationship is [tenuous] between the objectives of such provisions (to catch criminals) and the demand for proper identity documents. The possession of proper identity documents may reflect nothing more than the power and resources of an individual able to procure them. Refugees are seldom able to procure official documents without considerable risk, and those who flee states whose bureaucracies have collapsed have very limited options in this regard.

Although there is a pending case that challenges the identity provision as effectively discriminating on the basis of national origin, the illogic of the provision has yet to sway the general public, legislators, or the judiciary.

The illogic of the identity provision at the level of the particular is masked by the narrative constructed at the national level. Razack, through a careful examination of legislative committee hearings, pieces together "a national story of a Canada besieged and betrayed by bodies of color, . . . a story about a sovereign nation, overwhelmed by the large numbers of refugees coming to its borders, refugees attracted by rumors of Canadian generosity." Identity documents and other border-policing mechanisms become necessary then to protect innocent (White) Canadians from "the duplicity and cunning of people of color."

From the particularity of Bill C-86, which finds its meaning in the national mythology of Canada, Razack shifts to the global. The Canadian story is simply an example of the consequences when "globalization of markets continues to destroy the livelihoods of Third World producers, and Western arms sales prop up repression."[16] Parallel examples from Britain, the United States, Sweden, and Belgium show the importance of broadening the analysis of race beyond the particular, and even the national, to consider carefully the inter/national. The story that unfolds is the legacy of colonialism and imperialism (in their traditional, neo-, and post- forms). "Developed" countries use porous borders to extract resources from the rest of the world, disrupting the economies and cultures of the "developing" world. These disruptions push people out of their native lands and into "developed" nations in the form of migrants. While "developed" nations are happy to extract resources, the influx of migrants precipitates national identity crises that lead to renewed policing of borders, both literal and figurative. The irony is that "the issue of the 'undocumented' may well be the heart of today's political economy [where] Western nations thrive on the unequal structure of citizenship that is created when some workers have fewer rights than others."

Razack's chapter, like Johnson's, highlights the lessons to be learned by paying attention to the way borders are policed to construct and maintain racial privilege and subordination.

The Body as Constructed by Race, Gender, and Desire

Devon Carbado, in "Straight Out of the Closet," recognizes that the body exists within lived space where race, gender, and sexuality (among other things) overdetermine our identities. But recognizing this and setting forth a positive program for social change are two different things. Carbado makes two important moves in his chapter. The first is to reconceptualize the way we think about discrimination to include complicity. The second is to develop a notion of male feminism that acts on this knowledge without reinscribing (hetero)patriarchy.

At present, antidiscrimination law is dominated by what Alan Freeman has called the perpetrator perspective.[17] Under this view, "a perpetrator of discrimination [is] someone who acts intentionally to bring about some discriminatory result." Carbado seeks to recast perpetrators to include "those of us who unquestionably accept the racial, gender, and heterosexual privileges we have, and those of us who fail to acknowledge our victimless status vis-à-vis racism, sexism, and homophobia." The first step is to acknowledge the various forms of privilege that we have based on our race, gender, and sexual orientation. Carbado provides a model by setting forth lists of gender and heterosexual privileges. Through this, he invites us to create our own lists of the various privileges all of us have based on our various identity positions. The second, more difficult step is to accept accountability such that passivity in the face of such privilege is no excuse. He rejects claims of innocence. Those who do not actively and intentionally discriminate on the basis of race, gender, or sexuality but who passively accept privileges based on racism, sexism, and heterosexism are complicit in discrimination. Carbado would call such people perpetrators of discrimination.

Carbado's point, though, is not to call people names. Instead, he seeks to goad people into action. He warns that awareness and acknowledgment of privilege are not enough. One must also resist. Although Carbado does not develop fully a plan of resistance in his chapter, he proposes the intermediate step of "'critical acquiescence': criticizing, if not rejecting, aspects of our life that are directly linked to our privilege." Carbado helps to develop a positive program of antiracist male feminism, an area that requires further work within Critical Race Theory.

Centering the Body

Farley's chapter, "The Poetics of Colorlined Space," defies brief characterization. It is a wild, often brilliant journey through a dis-cursive space populated by discordant texts, narratives, and interpretations. It begins with the notion that race is a form of pleasure—bodily pleasure. Racialized bodies are constructed to serve, and are experienced as, the pleasure that accompanies both domination and submission. Race, then, is maintained not just through the exercise of power by the oppressor but also through the acquiescence (itself an act of power) of the subjugated. Unless this is understood, and perhaps even with this understanding, we are doomed by the colorline even as we dream of its demise.

Farley's chapter can best be characterized as a situationist text, employing the strategy of "détournement (turnaround, diversion, subversion, or hijacking), the reuse of old concepts in a new formation." Situationists characterized "modern capitalist society as an accumulation of spectacles in which '[a]ll that once was directly lived has become mere representation' [such that] all social relationships are mediated by images." This infiltration is such that "our very identities and desires have been transformed into spectacle." As a result,

> our bodies are spectacles. The racial body, the foreign body, the gendered body, the sexed body, the sexually oriented body; all are spectacles. Our relationships to one another and to ourselves are all mediated by the spectacle. We see one another, and ourselves, through the spectacle of race, nation, gender, sex, and sexual orientation. These spectacles come with imperatives that, being hidden within, remain beyond critique....
>
> The spectacle replicates itself in "a ceaseless manufacture of pseudo-needs" ... reduc[ing] us to passive spectators and bit actors in Situations not of our own making. The spectacles becomes hyper-real as we gaze upon it to find ourselves and one another. We try to gain acceptance and find our exclusion to be a desired thing. Black exclusion is a commodity. The spectacle of Black inferiority,

which justifies Black exclusion, is a commodity. We, in our excluded bodies, our inferior bodies, our bodies-without-buoyancy, our bodies-without-the-necessities, our bodies-without-respect, our colorlined bodies, our Black bodies, our bodies-in-pain, are commodities. Whites become and stay White by consuming the spectacle of our pain.

And why do Blacks participate in this spectacle? Why do Blacks submit? Farley answers that submission, itself, is experienced as pleasure. By believing in a future where one will not be judged by the color of one's skin, by having faith in this dream located always in the future, Blacks have accepted the pleasurescape that is known as the racialized body. Farley concludes apocalyptically:

> Everything is possible and nothing is forbidden once we have left the Civil Rights Movement dream behind and exchanged the pleasures of submission for the pleasures of disruption. Civil Rights will never bring about the raceless society. There are no responsible solutions. There are no safe words.

I realize that I have not done justice to Farley's chapter. It is not something that can be described. It must be read—or, rather, experienced. It is well worth the ride.

Conclusion

Despite the standard mantra within Critical Race Theory that race is a social construct, it remains an open question whether CRT has completely assimilated the unbiological nature of race. The chapters in this section represent different attempts to complete the argument, but insofar as race continues to affect one's life chances, it remains an uncompleted argument.

For those who would complete the argument, care must be taken to differentiate

between pre-1964 and post-1964 strategies. In the earlier era, social construction was argued to counter the old or scientific racialism. The goal was to end de jure discrimination against racial minorities and to secure, at the very least, equal treatment at a formal level, to not be excluded from restaurants, schools, neighborhoods, polling booths, and jobs on the basis of race. The social construction in the earlier era tried to establish the basic sameness of human beings so that racially discriminatory treatment could no longer be justified or sanctioned by law. But after formal equal treatment has been secured, the terrain shifts, with the major race cases today being about so-called reverse discrimination. Today, in the era of colorblind jurisprudence and the new racialism, social construction must be argued to establish that individuals and institutions have acted in concert to create differences in the material conditions of racial minorities and that this requires or justifies remedies that necessarily entail racially different treatment. As the chapters in this section set forth, this requires careful attention to the way race is inflected by color, nation, class, gender, and sexuality. They chart different ways to complete the argument begun by Du Bois.

Notes

1. Anthony Appiah, "The Uncompleted Argument: Du Bois and the Illusion of Race," "Race," Writing and Difference, ed. Henry Louis Gates, Jr. (Chicago: Chicago University Press, 1986), 21-2.
2. Ibid.
3. W.E.B. Du Bois, "The Conservation of Race," W.E.B. Du Bois Speaks: Speeches and Addresses 1890–1919, ed. Philip Foner (New York: Pathfinder Press, 1988), 75-6.
4. Ibid., 36.
5. All of the chapters in this section agree that there appears to be consensus on this matter. See also, John O. Calmore, "Critical Race Theory, Archie Shepp, and Fire Music: Securing an Authentic

Intellectual Life in a Multicultural World," *Southern California Law Review*, (1992): 2129; Ian F. Haney López, "The Social Construction of Race: Some Observations on Illusion, Fabrication, and Choice," *Harvard Civil Rights–Civil Liberties Law Review*, 29 (1994): 1.

6. Robert L. Hayman, Jr., and Nancy Levit provide an excellent overview of the development of racial thinking in their chapter in this volume. For more extended treatments, see Thomas F. Gossett, *Race: The History of an Idea in America*, 2nd ed. (New York: Schoken Books, 1997); Reginald Horsman, *Race and Manifest Destiny: The Origins of American Racial Anglo-Saxonism* (Cambridge, Mass.: Harvard University Press, 1981); and Winthrop Jordan, *White over Black: American Attitudes Toward the Negro* (Chapel Hill: University of North Carolina Press, 1968).

7. Howard Schuman, Charlotte Steeh, Lawrence Bobo, and Maria Krysan, eds., *Racial Attitudes in America: Trends and Interpretations*, rev. ed. (Cambridge, Mass.: Harvard University Press, 1997), 169.

8. U.S. Bureau of the Census, "Median Net Worth by Race and Hispanic Origin of Householder and Monthly Household Income Quintile: 1993 and 1991," *Asset Ownership of Households: 1993*, Web site, available from <http://www.census.gov/hhes/www/wealth/1993/wlth93f.html> (visited January 29, 1999), Table F. The average wealth of a Hispanic household was $4,656; Asians were not mentioned in the report.

9. Schuman et al., *Racial Attitudes*, 169.

10. See O'Connor, *City of Richmond v. Croson*, 488 U.S. 469, 503 (1989).

11. See also Shirlee Taylor Haizlip, *The Sweeter the Juice: A Family Memoir in Black and White* (New York: Simon and Schuster, 1994).

12. See Hayman and Levit's discussion of *Mississippi University for Women v. Hogan*, 458 U.S. 718 (1982), in this volume.

13. See Hayman and Levit's discussion of *Planned Parenthood v. Casey*, 505 U.S. 833, 856 (1992).

14. See Hayman and Levit's discussion of *United States v. Virginia (VMI)*, 116 Sup. Ct. 2264, 2279 (1996).

15. See Johnson's chapter in this volume (some alteration in original; citations omitted).

16. L. Fekete and F. Webber, "The Human Trade," *Race and Class* 39 (1997): 73.

17. Alan D. Freeman, "Legitimizing Racial Discrimination Through Antidiscrimination Law: A Critical Review of Supreme Court Doctrine," *Minnesota Law Review*, 62 (1978): 1049.

CHAPTER FOUR

The Poetics of Colorlined Space

Anthony Paul Farley

And as I sat there, brooding on the old unknown world, I thought of Gatsby's wonder when he first picked out the green light at the end of Daisy's dock. He had come a long way to this blue lawn and his dream must have seemed so close that he could hardly fail to grasp it. He did not know that it was already behind him, somewhere back in that vast obscurity beyond the city, where the dark fields of the republic rolled on into the night.

Gatsby believed in the green light, the orgastic future that year by year recedes before us. It eluded us then, but that's no matter—tomorrow we will run faster, stretch out our arms farther. . . . And one fine morning—.

So we beat on, boats against the current, borne back ceaselessly into the past.

—F. Scott Fitzgerald

Ceaselessly into the Past

The spectacle known as the Civil Rights Movement, like F. Scott Fitzgerald's green

light, remains an object of wonder. They "had come a long way" to reach the Supreme Court of the United States of America. They had come a long way to argue the great cases, such as *Brown v. Board of Education of Topeka* (1954) and *Loving v. Virginia* (1967).[1] They had come a long way to argue the cases that together were, "one fine morning—," supposed to form a new union between the master race and its excluded Others. As the marchers stood with the Reverend Dr. Martin Luther King, Jr., before the Lincoln Memorial, the unrequited "dream must have seemed so close that [they] could hardly fail to grasp it." It was one hundred years after the signing of the Emancipation Proclamation; they were not yet free, but they were still young and in love with the future. The terrifying sweetness of their old love songs to the white establishment is at once familiar and strange:

> At S&W one day, we will all buy a Coke
> and the waitress will serve us
> we'll know its no joke,
> hallelujah I'm a-travelin',
> hallelujah ain't it fine,
> hallelujah I'm a-travelin'
> down freedom's main line.[2]

The marchers "believed in the green light, the orgastic future that year by year recedes

Some parts of this chapter appeared as Anthony Paul Farley, "The Black Body as Fetish Object," *Oregon Law Review* 76 (1997): 457. An earlier version of this chapter was presented as part of a panel on "Race, Space and Place" at the 1997 Critical Race Theory Conference at Yale University.

before us." They "did not know that it was already behind [them], somewhere back in that vast obscurity" of revolutionary paths not taken.

The marchers were like Gatsby in so many ways. Gatsby's desire for the green light, for Daisy Buchanan, for the dream, for integration, for acceptance was his undoing. Gatsby "sprang from his Platonic conception of himself," not from wealthy parents, so in the end his perfection did not matter. Gatsby failed to understand that exclusion alone made the green light possible. Today's colorlined situation is the offspring of a similar unrequitable desire.

"Rich girls don't marry poor boys."[3] Fitzgerald's "East Egg" elites tell us what we already know but refuse to believe. What could be more direct than this message of class and gender? Perhaps only the message about the colorline that emerges in a conversation between two of those elites, Daisy Buchanan and her husband, Tom:

> "It's up to us who are the dominant race to watch out or these other races will have control of things." "We've got to beat them down," whispered Daisy, winking ferociously at the fervent sun.[4]

We cannot *all* get along. Good "race" relations are not possible. They have "got to beat [us] down" or cease to be white. What we call "race" is itself the act of oppression and the moment of surrender. Once branded with "race," we have been assaulted. Once we accept the brand, we have submitted.

We have not Overcome. We have been Overcome. We have been Overcome by our own belief in the "green light, the orgastic future that year by year recedes before us. It eluded us then, but that's no matter—tomorrow we will run faster." Gatsby believed in the American Dream, "the orgastic future" represented by Daisy Buchanan and the "green light," and he was ultimately destroyed by his belief. Gatsby had to be excluded for the green light to keep shining.

The marchers believed in the orgastic future and the green light. The word "orgastic" captures perfectly the erotic tangle of dreams and desires that causes masters and their slaves, owning classes and their working classes, and whites and their blacks to cleave to one another. The union of oppressor and oppressed begets the non-revolutionary situation.[5] Power is seductive. Put another way: Seduction is a strategy of power.

The green light is a way of organizing, of understanding, the space between "East Egg" and "West Egg." It is the space of longing and the space of refusal. It is the space that begets the elite and, necessarily, those Others whose exclusion renders elitism possible. It is a way of seducing us into the space of white-over-black. That space, the colorline, is a space of longing and refusal.[6] In it the *excluded* long for inclusion, the *included* enjoy their exclusivity, and each party pretends that it does not find in the other the necessary condition of its own possibility. Put another way, each is the other's bastard child. Domination and submission—each finds itself, its history and its genealogy, in the other. There are no whites without blacks, men without women, straights without lesbians and gays, rich without poor, or high caste without low. There is no hierarchy without pretense. We pretend that the space marked by the line is not filled with poetic significance. Strangely, even as we pretend, we become adept at navigating the emotional, the sensual, terrain of colorlined space. We become masters of submission—white and black.

We *pretend* because it is easier to dream of the green light and the orgastic future than to face the cruel inevitability of the current situation. Again, Fitzgerald is instructive: "There are only the pursued, the pursuing, the busy and the tired."[7] The green light, the orgastic future, is the form of pleasure that links the pursued with their pursuers and the busy with the tired. Both parties to the pseudo-conflict are linked by an erotic of mastery and slavery.

Race is a form of pleasure.[8] For whites, it is a *sadistic* pleasure in decorating black bodies with disdain. For blacks—in today's non-revolutionary situation—it has become a *masochistic* pleasure in being so decorated. Oppressors require an Other in order to imagine themselves as elite. The system acquires its stability from the desires it cultivates in its perpetually excluded Others. The green light over the bay, like the Civil Rights Movement longing for equal rights and inclusion ("diversity") within this oppressive order of things, is a form of longing that links oppressed to oppressor at levels too deep for the mind to touch.

This chapter is a postmodern reply to Critical Race Theory and critical legal studies. Both movements have traced, with breathtaking creativity, the myriad ways in which segregation has adapted itself to its post-civil-rights institutional environment. Both movements have relied on maps of the political economy of colorlined space to reach their powerful conclusions. I am following a new map, a map of the senses. The sensual contours of colorlined space must be heeded if we are to understand how the colorline operates and, more important, break free of its confines. CRT presents racism as permanent, but it does not explain why. CLS presents law as politics, but it does not explain why the politics that finds itself expressed as law is inevitably the politics of the colorline. CRT and CLS have failed to map an important aspect of colorlined space because they have both privileged the mind over the body. This article may be used as a map of colorlined space from the perspective of the body. It is a map of colorlined space—the pleasure-scape—that reveals the S/M nature of the current order of things.

Race is a form of bodily pleasure, akin to sexuality. "Look, A Nigger!" is a sensation that both the tormentors and the tormented feel within their bodies. Frantz Fanon writes:

"Look at the Nigger!" ... My body was given back to me sprawled out, distorted, recolored, clad in mourning in that white winter day. The Negro is an animal, the Negro is bad, the Negro is mean, the Negro is ugly.[9]

The legal expressions of the colorline are, similarly, sensations that people have both in and about their bodies. The master and his slave may both come to see and feel themselves through the law that defines, commands, and is the expression of their situation. Jean-Paul Sartre wrote:

Oppression based on slavery was not at first recognized by the law, but it soon becomes institutional. Thus a son of a slaveholder, born amidst a regime based on oppression, not only considers the fact of possessing slaves as natural but also as legitimate since this fact is one part of the institutions of his homeland. And the more he is raised to respect the authority of the State and to recognize his duties toward it, the more the right of possessing slaves appears sacred to him and the more it will remain beyond discussion. There is an underlying tie between the way of accepting and assuming different legal prescriptions (matrimonial, civic, military duties, etc.) and the way of accepting the right to possess slaves. It is the *ensemble* that is respected and recognized.[10]

Whether race finds its expression as slavery, segregation, or neo-segregation, the legal song remains the same. The pleasure of whiteness is spread throughout the entire ensemble. The law is an organ of perception—a great ephemeral skin—and through it we come to feel ourselves as masters and slaves, segregators and segregated, neo-segregators and neo-segregated, white and black, subject and object, and S/M.

Language is a skin: I rub my language against the other. It is as if I had words instead of fingers, or fingers at the tip of my words. My language trembles with desire. The emotion derives from a double contact: on the one hand, a whole activity of discourse discreetly, indirectly focuses upon a single signified, which is "I desire you," and releases, nourishes, ramifies it to the point of explosion (language experiences orgasm upon touching itself); on the other hand, I enwrap the other in my words, I caress, brush against, talk up this contact, I extend myself to make the commentary to which I submit the relation endure.[11]

The relationship of white-over-black endures because people have learned to take pleasure in it. We ignore the sensual aspects of color-lined space at our peril. We would do well to recall the warning and the prophecy of the Great American Novel: "So we beat on, boats against the current, borne back ceaselessly into the past."

Space

Inhabited space transcends geometrical space.
  —Gaston Bachelard[12]

We do not experience our surroundings as a series of cold architectural forms. Everything, for us as human beings, has an emotional surface, a sensual topology, from which it derives its significance. It is this sensual aspect of our physical environment that makes all of the difference for us. The bright, shining sled ("Rosebud" of *Citizen Kane*) we might have received one white winter's day was not only or primarily a wooden platform with metal runners attached. It was something else, something magical, a moment in which we basked in the green light of belonging and acceptance. In that moment—and it is a space as well as a time—our disparate thoughts about many things came together to form our personality.

To begin a study of the topography of colorlined space, I turn first to Gaston Bachelard's classic examination of the way we experience intimate places. The home,

for Bachelard, is the most important site for phenomenological investigation, because

without it, man would be a dispersed being. It maintains him through the storms of the heavens and through those of life. It is body and soul. It is the human being's first world. Before he is "cast into the world," . . . man is laid in the cradle of the house. And always in our daydreams, the house is a large cradle. A concrete metaphysics cannot neglect this fact, this simple fact, all the more since the fact is a value, an important value, to which we return in our daydreaming. . . . Life begins well, it begins enclosed, protected, all warm in the bosom of the house.[13]

After such a beginning in the protected environment of a home, "All really inhabited space bears the essence of the notion of home." This is so because "we live fixations, fixations of happiness. We comfort ourselves by reliving memories of protection."[14]

Bachelard writes, of course, of his universe. There are others, however, in which the home does not play the same role. Susanna Kaysen writes of movement between parallel universes:

People ask, How did you get in there? What they really want to know is if they are likely to end up in there as well. I can't answer the real question. All I can tell them is, It's easy. And it is easy to slip into a parallel universe. There are so many of them: worlds of the insane, the criminal, the crippled, the dying, perhaps of the dead as well. These worlds exist alongside this world and resemble it, but are not in it. My roommate Georgina came in swiftly and totally, during her junior year at Vassar. She was in a theater watching a movie when a tidal wave of blackness broke over her head. The entire world was obliterated—for a few minutes. She knew she had gone crazy. She looked around to the theater to see if it had happened to everyone, but all the other people were engrossed in the movie. She rushed out, because the darkness in the theatre was too much when combined with the darkness in her head. And after that? I asked her. A lot of darkness, she said. But most people pass over incrementally, making a series of perforations in the membrane between here and there until an opening exists. And who can resist an opening?[15]

The musician Gil Scott-Heron sings of the notion of home that emerges in the universe on the other side of the colorline: "Home is where the hatred is."[16] Both Bachelard and Scott-Heron are correct, depending on one's side of the colorline.

In the short story "Way in the Middle of the Air," Ray Bradbury explores the notion of home as the subaltern experiences it.[17] Home, in this case, is the United States of America, "one nation under God" for some and something entirely different for Others. The story is set in the year 2003; however, the town depicted resembles the South of the year 1946, when Bradbury first published *The Martian Chronicles*. "Did you hear about it?" the story begins. "'About what?' 'The niggers, the niggers!' 'What about 'em?' 'Them leaving, pullin' out, going away; did you hear?'" The whites, as the Great Migration begins, are astonished, "They can't leave, they can't do that," and, later, desperate:

> Samuel Teece wouldn't believe it. "Why, hell, where'd they get the transportation? How they goin' to get to Mars?" "Rockets," said Grandpa Quartermain.
> "All the damn-fool things. Where'd they get rockets?"
> "Saved their money and built them."
> "I never heard about it."
> "Seems these niggers kept it secret, worked on the rockets all themselves, don't know where—in Africa, maybe."
> "Could they do that?" demanded Samuel Teece, pacing about the porch. "*Ain't there a law?*"[18]

The law is invoked to stem the tide. "'Telephone the governor, call out the militia,' cried Teece. 'They should've given *notice!*'"[19] The departure of the blacks reveals the emptiness of the whites' lives. The emptiness is noted through the invocation of the legal concept of "notice."

When "Lucinda," the Teeces' maid, leaves to join the "black river" of refugees to Mars, Mrs. Clara Teece is overwhelmed:

> "It's Lucinda, Pa; you got to come home!"
> "I'm not coming home for no damn darkie!"
> "She's leaving. What'll I do without her?"[20]

Mrs. Teece's fantasies of sisterhood-without-equality are shattered when Lucinda says, "Good-by, Mrs. Teece." Mr. Teece, unable to silence his wife's unseemly tears, runs inside the store to fetch his "silver pistol." Their peaceful coexistence as white man and white wife is ended with the departure of the black maid from their formerly happy home. When Mr. Teece emerges from the inside of his home bearing a silver pistol (a white phallus) and harboring thoughts of homicide, Mrs. Teece is gone.

Silver pistol still in hand, Mr. Teece stops "Belter," a "tall negro man," to demand the payment of a fifty-dollar debt:

> "You recollect you owe me fifty dollars, Belter?"
> "Yes, sir."
> "You tryin' to sneak out? By God, I'll horsewhip you!"[21]

The sign of legal debt ("You recollect you owe me fifty dollars"), the sign of submission ("Yes, sir"), the sign of violence ("silver pistol"), the sign of divine sanction ("By God"), and the threatened humiliation ritual—the carving of the entire *ensemble* of signs into Belter's flesh ("I'll horsewhip you!")—all merge into Mr. Teece's identity and Belter's subalternation: "You're staying here to work out that fifty bucks, or my name ain't Samuel W. Teece." Mr. Teece's name could be written only *with* the aforementioned signs, and it could be written only *on* black flesh and it could be written only *through* violence. Of course, this is not a quarrel about the money. It is a quarrel about the colorline masquerading as a quarrel about money:

> "But if I work it out, I'll miss the rocket, sir!"
> "Ain't that a shame now?" Teece tried to look sad.
> "I'll give you my horse, sir."
> "Horse ain't legal tender. You don't move until I get my money." Teece laughed inside. He felt very warm and good. A small crowd of dark people had gathered to hear all this. Now as Belter stood, head down, trembling, an old man stepped forward.
> "Mister?"
> Teece flashed him a quick look. "Well?"
> "None of your damn business!"
> The old man looked at Belter. "How much, son?"
> "Fifty dollars."
> The old man put out his black hands at the people around him. "There's twenty-five of you. Each give two dollars; quick now, this no time for argument."
> "Here, now!" cried Teece, stiffening up, tall, tall.
> The money appeared. The old man fingered it into his hat and gave the hat to Belter. "Son," he said, "you ain't missin' no rocket."[22]

Mr. Teece uses law ("A horse ain't legal tender") to keep his black in his place and prevent him from leaving for space ("You don't move until I get my money"). This legal spacialization of people according to race is a form of ecstasy for Mr. Teece ("Teece laughed inside. He felt very warm and good"). The moment is short-lived. Mr. Teece is enraged at the thwarting of his race-pleasure and the threatened reorganization of race, space, and place.[23] All of the whites are amazed at the new emancipatory communism among their former chattel:

> It was happening all along the way. Little white boys, barefoot, dashed up with

the news. "Them that has helps them that hasn't! And that way they all get free!" ... The white men sat with sour water in their mouths. Their eyes were almost puffed shut, as if they had been struck in their faces by wind and sand and heat.[24]

The total transformation of the blacks from possessive individualists to beloved community transforms the blacks from possessions to persons. The white cries for Law grow more shrill:

> "I can't figure why they left now. With things lookin' up. I mean, every day they got more rights. What they want, anyway? Here's the poll tax gone, and more and more states passin' anti-lynchin' bills, and all kinds of equal rights. What more they want? They make almost as good money as a white man, but there they go."[25]

This is the familiar neo-segregationist invocation of the perpetual near-arrival of nearly equal rights. The blacks, in leaving for space, have rejected the entire ensemble.

Suddenly, "Silly," Mr. Teece's seventeen-year-old black employee, appears. Silly is late because he has taken the time to return Mr. Teece's bicycle. Mr. Teece orders Silly to work by invoking a contractual agreement:

> "Remember this?"
> "Sir?"
> "It's your workin' paper. You signed it, there's your X right there, ain't it? Answer me."
> "I didn't sign that, Mr. Teece." The boy trembled. "Anyone can make an X."
> "Listen to this Silly. Contract: 'I will work for Mr. Samuel Teece two years, starting July 15, 2001, and if intending to leave will give four weeks' notice and continue working until my position is filled.' There." Teece slapped the paper, his eyes glittering. "You cause trouble, we'll take it to court."
> "I can't do that," wailed the boy, tears starting to roll down his face. "If I don't go today, I don't go."[26]

The Law here emerges as the colorline that keeps one group white and another black and, more important, keeps Silly a slave and Mr. Teece a master ("You cause trouble, we'll take it to court"). The X represents every black person's signature—in this way, the X is the signature on the social contract. Across the colorline, the social contract is a fraud ("Anyone can make an X"). The social contract was, interestingly, "signed" on "July 15, 2001," the day after Bastille Day, and its terms seem a rejection of liberty, equality and fraternity. Malcolm X understood the relationship between the legal system and the social contract:

> [*Brown v. Board of Education*] was one of the greatest magical feats ever performed in America. Do you mean to tell me that nine Supreme Court judges, who are past masters of legal phraseology, couldn't have worked their decision to make it stick as law? No! It was trickery and magic that told Negroes they were deseg-regated—Hooray! Hooray!—and at the same time it told whites, "Here are your loopholes."[27]

Malcolm X and Silly arrive at the same conclusion regarding the fraudulent nature of the cross-colorline contract ("I didn't sign that").

Mr. Teece's "glittering" eyes show the law to be the organ of perception through which he feels his whiteness and with which he imposes Silly's blackness. The spell is broken when "Grampa Quartermain" inter-venes saying, "I'll take Silly's job," and is supported by the other white men on the porch. The first is last. At last, Silly departs for the rockets. Free at last.

The pivotal moment of whiteness recog-nizing its own artificiality (its dependence on blackness) comes when the departing Silly shouts, "one last time at Teece":

> "Mr. Teece, Mr. Teece, what you goin' to do nights from now on? What you goin' to do nights, Mr. Teece?"[28]

This moment of recognition, of being seen by his former object, produces an existen-tial crisis for the now objectified Mr. Teece. It is also painfully clear that the blacks have exchanged the pleasures of law and order or gradual change or patience or sub-mission for the pleasures of defiance and self-assertion:

> "What in hell did he mean?" mused Teece. "What am I goin' to do nights?"[29]

Memories of white race-pleasure, of volup-tuous white pleasure-in-cruelty, flood back to Mr. Teece's consciousness, just as the flood of blacks had departed from his town:

> He remembered nights when men drove to his house, their knees sticking up sharp and their shotguns sticking up sharper, like a carful of cranes under the night trees of summer, their eyes mean. Honking the horn and him slamming his door, a gun in his hand, laughing to him-self, his heart racing like a ten-year-old's, driving off down the summer-night road, a ring of hemp rope coiled on the car floor, fresh shell boxes making every man's coat look bunchy. How many nights over the years, how many nights of the wind rushing in the car, flopping their hair over their mean eyes, roaring, as they picked a tree, a good strong tree, and rapped on a shanty door![30]

The rap on the door was the Truth of the everyday humiliation rituals of Law. Too late, Mr. Teece realizes that

> it was a good question. He sickened and was empty. Yes. What will we do nights? he thought. Now they're gone, what? He was absolutely empty and numb.[31]

Mr. Teece is left with only sad memories of whiteness ("Did you notice? Right up to the very last, by God, he said, 'Mister'!"). Mem-ories and pathos and absolute fleshlessness are all that he has left ("He was absolutely empty and numb"). The blacks vanish into the starry void, the space they had occupied in the United States of America is empty, and the space they had filled in Mr. Teece's life becomes a void. Mr. Teece is left with only the memory of the now meaningless appellation, "Mister," Sartrean nausea, and an absolutely numbing emptiness ("He sickened and was empty"). Mr. Teece refuses to look at the departing rockets. "'Look!' 'I'll be damned if I will,' said Teece." Mr. Teece is damned. He is damned by his own need for race-pleasure. The blacks have exited the S/M scene of segregation, but for Mr. Teece there is *no exit*.

Spectacle

> The problem is to make space speak, to feed and furnish it; like mines laid in a wall of rock which all of a sudden turn to geysers and bouquets of stone.
> —Antonin Artaud[32]

Imagine the typical American family room, the center of the home that we carry with us everywhere, according to Bachelard, and the epicenter of hatred, according to Scott-Heron. Both theorists are correct, depending on one's side of the colorline. The chairs and tables in the American family room are arranged around the television, the window to the world. Our television, our opening to the world, was set against a large window that framed the backyard. Against the limits of the yard we gazed into the seemingly infinite depths of the brighter and smaller screen. The sun itself was eclipsed by the television. One day my youngest brother called out, "Hey, come here quick, this is my favorite part!" He was being ironic. I was sixteen, he was eight. I ran downstairs. He explained that this was his favorite scene in his favorite Tarzan film. We watched together, illuminated by the darkness, to see what the masters of the spectacle paradise were going to do to us.

An intrepid white explorer trudged up from the jungle along a steep, narrow mountain path. A mistake at such a height meant certain death. His love interest, just as white and almost as brave, followed three paces behind. Behind her followed a long line of native bearers, a Million Man March of anonymous black men, each carrying an unbelievably large box or bag or weird lumpy package on his head. Their naked arms, chests, and legs made them indistinguishable one from the other as they toiled for the two pith-helmeted, khaki-clothed subjects of the film—the white male explorer and his female satellite. Racism and sexism were paired on the screen, as in life. It was a moment pregnant with cinematic possibilities. My brother and I waited for the quickening.

Suddenly, one of the native bearers slipped and fell. We saw him spiral into the distance. He grew smaller and smaller as he spun downward through the air. Finally, he disappeared into the abyss. He made no visible impact on the river valley below. The critical moment came when the intrepid white explorer turned and exclaimed with horror, "The supplies!"

Living in a colorlined society, one experiences this moment of birth a million times—the colorline that cuts us loose from our humanity with the cry, "The supplies!" is an umbilical cord for white America. Just as there are no masters without slaves, there are no whites without blacks. The white identity is created and maintained by decorating black bodies with disdain, over and over again. The ritual scarification of Saturday morning TV negritude is the least of it.

The image makes itself real. We gaze on the spectacle, and the spectacle gazes back into us. Imagine now not my living room, but millions of living rooms. Millions and millions of bodies unfolding like flowers in the substitute sun of the cathode ray tube and growing into the "sprawled out, distorted, recolored" form assigned them by the masters of the spectacle paradise. Those bodies come to understand themselves as native bearers, as lost in the infinite depth of the abyss, as black. The television set in the family room of the home, the "first cradle of man," is an opening—"And who can resist an opening?" as Kaysen says. All within view fall through the screen, through the floors, through all the horrors of color-lined space to arrive as themselves: as subaltern black bodies. There is, then, no safe place for the subaltern, and, in Scott-Heron's words, "Home is where the hatred is." Even there, we are *made* to serve.

The colorline serves as the medium of communication between whiteness and itself. We are the colorline. The political is personal. Flannery O'Connor, in her short story "Everything That Rises Must Converge," shows the power of this aphorism. The story begins with a white mother–son conflict that takes place on the symbolic terrain of a newly purchased hat and, later, across the colorline:

> NARRATOR: "It was a hideous hat. A purple velvet flap came down on one side of it and stood up on the other; the rest of it was green and looked like a cushion with the stuffing out."
>
> SHE: "Maybe I shouldn't have paid that for it. No, I shouldn't have. I'll take it off and return it tomorrow. I shouldn't even have bought it."
>
> HE: "It was less comical than jaunty and pathetic. Everything that gave her pleasure was small and depressed him."[33]

Julian's mother laments the state of the world:

> SHE: "I tell you, the bottom rail is on the top" and "Your great-grandfather had a plantation and two hundred slaves."
>
> HE: "There are no more slaves."
>
> SHE: "They were better off when they were."[34]

Julian resents his mother for her striving after the former race glory of their family name as much as for his own failures ("He could not forgive her that she had enjoyed the struggle and that she thought she had won"[35]). As the pair walk to the bus stop, their conversation shifts to the colorline, her favorite topic:

> He groaned to see that she was off on that topic. She rolled onto it every few days like a train on an open track. He knew every stop, every junction, every swamp along the way, and knew the exact point at which her conclusion would roll majestically into the station: They should rise, yes, but on their own side of the fence.[36]

Julian, we learn, fantasizes about using the colorline as a method of hurting his mother. He knows that he can hurt her by subverting the race-pleasure on which she depends. The depth of Julian's fantasies ironically reveal the extent to which he is also dependent on race-pleasure:

> When he got on the bus . . . he made it a point to sit down beside a Negro, in reparation as it were for his mother's sins.
>
> He would have liked to get in conversation with the Negro.
>
> He might make friends with some distinguished Negro Professor or Lawyer and bring him to spend the evening.
>
> He imagined his mother lying desperately ill and his being only able to secure a Negro doctor for her. He toyed with that idea for a few minutes and then dropped it for a momentary vision of himself as a sympathizer in a sit-in demonstration. This was possible but he did not linger on it. Instead, he approached the ultimate horror. He brought home a beautiful suspiciously Negroid woman.[37]

The story reaches its apogee when a black woman wearing an identical hat sits down on the bus next to Julian's mother:

> His eyes widened. The vision of the two hats, identical, broke upon him with the radiance of a brilliant sunrise. His face was suddenly lit with joy. He could not believe that fate had thrust upon his mother such a lesson.[38]

The lesson, however, is utterly lost on Julian's mother: "A smile came over her face as if the woman were a monkey that had stolen her hat."[39] Only after Julian's mother has persisted in offering "a bright new penny" to the black woman's young son does she learn her final, perhaps fatal, lesson:

"Oh little boy!" Julian's mother called. . . . "Here's a bright new penny for you," and she held out the coin which shone bronze in the dim light. The huge woman turned and for a moment stood, her shoulders lifted and her face frozen with frustrated rage, and stared at Julian's mother. Then all at once she seemed to explode like a piece of machinery that had been given one ounce of pressure too much. Julian saw the black fist swing out with the red pocketbook. He shut his eyes as heard the woman shout, "He don't take nobody's pennies!" When he opened his eyes, the woman was disappearing down the street with the little boy staring wide-eyed over her shoulder. Julian's mother was sitting on the sidewalk.[40]

Like "Mr. Teece," Julian averts his eyes from the spectacle of the Old World's undoing ("He shut his eyes as he heard the woman shout"). Julian cruelly explains:

"Don't think that was just an uppity Negro woman," he said, "That was the whole colored race which will no longer take your condescending pennies. That was your black double. She can wear the same hat as you, and to be sure," he added gratuitously (because he thought it was funny), "it looked better on her than it did on you. What all this means," he said, "is that the old world is gone . . . You aren't who you think you are."[41]

The black fetish object rejects her role, the slave says "no," and the entire system—in that moment—is destroyed. The "black double" remakes herself through violence and in so doing unmakes Julian's mother ("You aren't who you think you are"). The

"black fist" is a moment of anti-spectacle. "He don't take nobody's pennies!" creates an anti-spectacle. It does not fit with, and so must shatter, everything that has gone before, "the old world is gone," but Julian's world also dissolves. Julian and his mother are bound umbilically by the colorline. Julian's world dissolves because his mother cannot live without her race-pleasure, and he cannot live without his mother:

"Home," she muttered. "Home," she said thickly. "Tell Grampa to come get me." "Tell Caroline to come get me." A tide of darkness seemed to be sweeping her from him. He turned her over. Her face was fiercely distorted. One eye, large and staring, moved slightly to the left as if it had become unmoored. The other remained fixed on him, raked his face again, found nothing and closed. "Help, Help!" he shouted, but his voice was thin, scarcely a thread of sound.[42]

One eye "unmoored" and the other "fixed" on her son, Julian's mother is swept away without the colorline to sustain her ("A tide of darkness seemed to be sweeping her from him"). The race-pleasure system, in political terms, appears as the colorline. Threats to the colorline are threats to personal identity and, more important, to the endless supply of pleasure produced by the colorline. She and he are alone at last—the umbilical cord connecting them to their whiteness and each other has been severed ("scarcely a thread of sound"). The Tunisian anticolonialist Albert Memmi wrote, "Racism is a pleasure within everyone's reach."[43] To be someone, in America, is to partake of race-pleasure. When race-pleasure is out of reach, it presents whites who enjoy the colorline with an existential crisis similar to Kaysen's description of madness: "She was in a theatre watching a movie when a tidal wave of blackness broke over her head. The entire world was obliterated—for a minutes."

The image of the black is ubiquitous. Whites return and return and return again to this fetish in order to satisfy a self-created urge to be white. The satisfaction of this will-to-whiteness is a form of pleasure in and about one's body. It is a pleasure that is satisfied through the production, circulation, consumption, reproduction, recirculation, and consumption of images of the not-white. The body is contested territory in the conflict over symbolic representation. Whiteness is a pleasure that has woven itself into all aspects of our culture and our identities. Visions of black subalterns dance through our dreams, our literature, our arts, our sciences, and our films like Shirley Temple and Mr. Bojangles.

Eros

The zipless fuck was more than a fuck. It was a platonic ideal. Zipless because when you came together zippers fell away like rose petals, underwear blew off in one breath like dandelion fluff. Tongues intertwined and turned liquid. Your whole soul flowed out through your tongue and into the mouth of your lover.
—Erica Jong[44]

Everytime I tell about it, I hurt in a new place.
—Anonymous victim of sexual abuse[45]

To be black is to possess a million stories of the abyss. For whites, these stories take the form of intense physical pleasure-in-whiteness. Race is an erotic encounter between two or more bodies. Race is akin to rape.[46] The zipless encounter that Jong describes is akin to the experience of bodily pleasure that whites obtain by enmeshing their Others in the colorline. It is important to remember that whiteness and blackness are nothing more than their relative positions in this violent encounter.

One spring day in 1976, on a bus chartered for a junior-high-school trip to Washington, D.C., one of my schoolmates stood and began to comb her long, brown hair. We were on a class trip to learn how laws were made and to witness the sites and monuments that make up the Republic to which we had been ordered to pledge allegiance every day of our elementary- and junior-high-school lives. She was tall and cool and pretty. She combed her long, brown hair slowly and deliberately. After a long while, she turned and addressed us all: "Whose comb was this? Thanks, I'm all done." No one responded. It seemed as though the unknown owner of the comb must not have been listening. Just then, one of our classmates answered in a mirthful voice: "It's Farley's comb." I, Farley, was the only black person on this otherwise all-white school trip to the nation's capitol. My classmates burst into laughter. The girl with the long brown hair turned crimson and began to cry in loud, long sobs. The sobs quickly turned into the sounds of retching, which were accompanied by shudders running through her now hunched form. She may have vomited. While her personal trauma unfolded, accompanied by squeals of laughter from all of her white classmates, I said nothing.

Those few minutes of mirth, sobs, laughter, and silence showed the colorline at work. The boy with the mirthful voice who falsely declared that the comb belonged to me knew the dance, and so the jest worked as he intended. The girl with the long, brown hair knew the dance, and so she wept and became nauseated at the public revelation of such improper intimacy with the Other. Our classmates knew the dance, and so the spectacle of such an untoward, albeit unintended, boundary crossing caused great amusement. I was silent. All of us experienced our connection through the colorline as a physical sensation, not as an abstract idea. We were all breathing to the same beat. One nation, indivisible, tightly bound by the colorline.

Erica Jong's words regarding the zipless encounter applied completely to my white classmates' actions on that school bus ("Tongues intertwined and turned liquid. Your whole soul flowed out through your tongue and into the mouth of your lover"). I was the soul of my white classmates. They transformed me with their jests, tears, and laughter. I could feel myself extruded as vomit, as sweat, as spit, as abjection itself. Their souls flowed out through their tongues, and I was filled with the nobodyness they desired of me.

The adrenaline rush of the wanton invocation of the colorline, the nausea and shame brought on by the ritual uncleanness of forbidden contact, the peals of cathartic laughter by those whitened by the ritual, and the abject silence of the "raced" were all part of the meaning of race. The year was 1976, it was the Bicentennial—the entire nation was celebrating white freedom and black slavery. What, to me, was their Bicentennial? The nation animated our bodies. To be black is to be available for humiliation, to be white is to partake of race-pleasure, and to be colorblind is to repress one's awareness of the entire enterprise. The colorline depends on all three aspects—humiliation, pleasure, and denial—for its power.

What is to be done when your subalternation, your pain, is the source of a pleasure that supports a political order that, in turn, ensures your subalternation? The colorline is intertwined with all the other large and small acts of dominance and submission that fragment and frame our collective imagination. I could feel the gaze of the stone-eyed statues of slavemasters such as George Washington and Thomas Jefferson that surrounded our trip to Washington, D.C. I understood my own surrender of self every moment that I caressed the slavemas-

ter iconography that we call "legal tender." Capital, like the capitol, is white: in God and slavery we trust. This was the belly of the beast—I lived, as I live now, in a nation that places statues of slavemasters in public spaces and pictures of slavemasters on its currency.

He felt as though he were wandering in the forests of the sea bottom, lost in a monstrous world where he himself was the monster. He was alone. And what of knowing that the dominion of the party would not endure *for ever*? Like an answer, the three slogans on the white face of the Ministry of Truth came back at him:

WAR IS PEACE
FREEDOM IS SLAVERY
IGNORANCE IS STRENGTH

He took a twenty-five-cent piece from his pocket. There too, in tiny clear lettering, the same slogans were inscribed, and on the other face of the coin the head of Big Brother. Even from the coin the eyes pursued you. On coins, on stamps, on the covers of books, on banners, on posters, and on the wrapping of a cigarette packet—everywhere. Always the eyes watching you and the voice enveloping you. Asleep or awake, working or eating, indoors or out of doors, in the bath or in the bed—no escape. Nothing was your own except the few cubic centimeters inside your skull.[47]

The colorline was not and is not a matter of politics or money or thought alone. It is also a matter of the flesh.

James Baldwin asked:

How can one be prepared for the spittle in the face, all the tireless ingenuity which goes into the spite and fear of small, unutterably miserable people, whose greatest terror is the singular identity, whose joy, whose safety, is entirely dependent on the humiliation of others?[48]

Baldwin's question has no answer. The "spittle in the face" is the victim's identity, just as it is the identity of the victimizer. The enemy is the face in the mirror, the spectacularized face, the face covered in spit. In George Orwell's *Nineteen Eighty-Four,* his protagonist Winston Smith reflects:

> "They can't get inside you," she had said. But they could get inside you. "What happens to you here is forever," O'Brien had said. That was a true word. There were things, your own acts, from which you could not recover. Something was killed in your breast; burnt out, cauterized out.[49]

I was silent. Silence, like crying and vomiting, is an act ("There were things, your own acts, from which you could not recover. Something was killed"):

> On that day, completely dislocated, unable to be abroad with the other, the white man, who unmercifully imprisoned me, I took myself far off from my own presence, far indeed, and made myself an object. What else could it be for me but an amputation, an excision, a hemorrage that spattered my body with black blood?[50]

I was silent during my moment of Bicentennial humiliation on the class trip to the nation's capital, and my classmate who was tall and cool and pretty played an active role to protect herself. My silence, her crying, the native bearer's ostentatiously disregarded plunge into the abyss of the Tarzan movie, and the hideous repetition of it all were the colorline. What could we say to each other?

> "I betrayed you," she said blandly. "I betrayed you," he said. She gave him another quick look of dislike. "Sometimes," she said, "they threaten you with something—something you can't stand up to, can't even think about. And then you say, 'Don't do it to me, do it to somebody else, do it to so-and-so.' And perhaps you might pretend, afterwards, that it was only a trick and that you just said it to make them stop and didn't really mean it. But that isn't true. At the time

when it happens you do mean it. You think there's no other way of saving yourself and you're quite ready to save yourself that way. You want it to happen to the other person. You don't give a damn what they suffer. All you care about is yourself." "All you care about is yourself," he echoed. "And after that, you don't feel the same toward the other person any longer." "No," he said, "you don't feel the same."[51]

You do not feel the same.

Jurisprudence of the Spectacle

> The command of the old despotisms was "Thou shalt not." The command of the totalitarians was "Thou shalt." Our command is "Thou art."
> —George Orwell[52]

> As for the Negro voting in my primary, we'll fight him at the precinct meeting, we'll fight him at the county convention, we'll fight him at the enrollment books, and, by God, we'll fight him at the polls if I have to bite the dust as did my ancestors!
> —John D. Long[53]

Segregation

The naive hope of the civil-rights era that more information about subaltern suffering would change the hearts and minds of a colorlined nation fades even further if we think of race as a form of pleasure. The suggestion that racism in today's post–civil-rights era is unconscious is beside the point if we think of race as a practice people enjoy, as a form of pleasure.[54]

What then must we do? The power effects of the myriad pleasure forms enjoyed under the rubric of race give rise to the colorline. The body is a social structure. The body is a form of connection, a way of knowing pleasure and humiliation, of experiencing the self in Others. Power masks itself.

Michel Foucault writes, "Power is tolerable only on condition that it mask a substantial part of itself. Its success is proportional to its ability to hide its own mechanisms."[55] Power, for Foucault, does not exist solely in the "negative and emaciated form of prohibition."[56] Rather, power is "the name that one attributes to a complex strategical situation in a particular society."[57] There is nothing about race that is separate from this complex strategic situation. What Foucault says of power in his discussion of sexuality is also applicable to the colorline:

> If sexuality was constituted as an area of investigation, this was only because relations of power had established it as a possible object; and conversely, if power was able to take it as a target, this was only because techniques of knowledge and procedures of discourse were capable of investing it. Between techniques of knowledge and strategies of power, there is no exteriority, even if they have specific roles and are linked together by their difference.[58]

The racialized body and its pleasures constitute one of the myriad masks of power.

Edmund White, writing in a different context, captured a notion that can be applied to life governed by the colorline: "People were bodies, I thought; the only valuable people have beautiful bodies; since my body isn't beautiful, I'm worthless. That was the humble feed I pecked at night and day."[59] Black is not beautiful in a world governed by the colorline.

Nobodying is a sensual experience that envelops everything. It does not limit itself to the body. It cannot, for the body is the lens through which we encounter the world: "More than a symbol, more than the bread and wine of Christ, the body is a knowing connection, it is the telling thing, the medium of experience, expression, being, and knowing."[60] People, neighborhoods, jobs, schools, style, language, religion, art— are all viewed and sensualized through the coloring lens of the racialized body. The entire world of the social is submitted to the pleasure economy of the colorline. The racialized body is a eulogized space; it is given a poetic significance by the colorline. But the body is not the only eulogized space. Its poetry spills out on the universe it both creates and inhabits. Blackness can come to color even such things as work. Consider the observation of Paul Goodman:

> Consider the current social imputation of many jobs as "menial." When I was young, driving a bus or a trailer-truck was manly, difficult, and responsible; now when there are many black drivers, it is ordinary. Construction work used to be skilled; but a black or Spanish bricklayer or mason tends to be unskilled. White road-workers in Vermont have a decent job; black roadworkers with the same equipment have a menial job. Postman, a job requiring unusual tact and judgement, has always been a dignified occupation; now that, like other Federal employment, it is open to many blacks, my guess is that it will be considered drab. A German or Jewish waiter is a mentor or kibitzer, a black waiter has a servile job. This social imputation of worth is made, of course, by both whites and blacks. Whites, however, usually don't give it a second thought, as their young move into other jobs. The question is why the blacks go along with the same imputation. The dismaying thing is the objective criteria like the kind of work, the worth of the product or service, and often the wages count for very little. In this frame of mind, it is impossible to be free and independent.[61]

You cannot run away from that which is always with you.

Follow the wake of a beautiful woman— that is, a woman who is socially constructed as beautiful—as she walks down a crowded street. The normal eddies and currents of human feeling are changed by her movements. Her walk down the street is experienced by the crowd as a physical sensation. "The girl can't help it!" sang Little Richard in his 1956 homage to female beauty in general, and the white actress Jayne Mansfield in particular. She seems to be felicity itself:

If she walks by the men-folks get
    engrossed,
THE GIRL CAN'T HELP IT!
If she winks an eye and bread slices to
    toast
THE GIRL CAN'T HELP IT!
If she's got a lot of what they call the
    most,
THE GIRL CAN'T HELP IT!
If she was born to please,
THE GIRL CAN'T HELP IT!
And if she's got a figure made to
    squeeze.
Won't you kindly be aware,
THE GIRL CAN'T HELP IT!⁶²

In the film of the same name, we see Mansfield, improbably blond, busty, and slim-waisted, walk down the street in full color. We also see the men seeing her. A prepubescent paperboy whistles at her like an adult wolf; an iceman's supply melts under his hands and pours from the bed of his truck onto the front of his trousers before spilling on the street; milk spurts forth from a milkman's bottle and runs all over his hand; finally, the spectacles of a too-curious neighbor shatter as he gazes on her body. She is trapped by the male gaze. The scene has all the gender subtlety of a hand grenade.

Follow the wake of a black person on that same street. The space he occupies is also a sensual space. White boys pull their white girlfriends closer. White women's knuckles whiten as they tug their purses closer. A symphony of automatic doorlocks and cold Venus-in-furs smiles accompany him down the sidewalk. Stepping indoors, he is harried by a flock of store detectives, security guards, and salespeople. The store detectives and security guards are silent, but the sales-people crow, "Can I help you find something?" until he quits the store. He is infelicity itself. He is trapped by the white gaze. The scene has all the race subtlety of a hand grenade.

Our images of felicitous space are produced by our images of infelicitous space, and vice versa. When the native bearer falls into the abyss, he plunges out of felicitous space in two senses. First, he falls to his death. Second, the native is a "Fallen" man. To be regarded as a native bearer, a black, is already to have Fallen. The scene compresses the natural and the social by pairing both falls, thereby doubly highlighting the Fallen nature of the native bearer. It thus seems quite natural that the intrepid white explorer would turn and shout, "The supplies!" on seeing the native bearer plunge out of sight. The practice of turning and shouting, "The supplies!" is the practice of nobodying the other. That is, the native bearer disappears into the abyss because we shout, "The supplies!"

The supplies! We watch these white mythologies over and over. They give a natural-seemingness to the colorline. They are a way to take pleasure in one's body through the body of the Other. Whites cannot think of themselves without the Negro. We are the "bright and morning star" in their navigation of existential space. In order to be, they must legislate us into being. Whites cannot feel themselves without the Negro. We are the "bright and morning star" in their navigation of sensual space, as well.

Consider the spectacle of the segregated bus. The image is ubiquitous. We can see the segregated bus in pre-Technicolor, grainy, black-and-white 1950s newsreel footage of utterly abject blacks in the back of the bus and utterly triumphant whites in the front of the bus. The back of the bus is a sensation of sweat, adrenaline, furrowed brows, and metallic tastes. Minstrelization is a thing one feels in one's body. It is what happens when you are ordered to "Jump Jim Crow!" Each act of submission is a spectacular leap into the abyss.

The whites, audience to this spectacular presentation, gaze voraciously on the anathematized black bodies by placing them behind their eyes in the non-space of the abyss, the disfavored and ritually unclean rear seats. The excrementalization of the bodies marked as black produces a corollary feeling of blessedness, an ecstasy of belonging and belovedness, in the bodies marked as white. Whiteness, emerging from sadistic insistence on the illusion of race through the painful application of blackness to the bodies of the innocent, produces pleasure. Whiteness emerges out of this Situation as a political orgasm. "Try arguing with an orgasm sometimes. You will find you are no match for the sexual access and power the materials provide," writes Catharine MacKinnon of pornography and the subordination of women.[63] The *ensemble* of law that creates and maintains the colorline is a form of racial pornography. Words are no match for the racial access and power the colorline provides. Indeed, the colorline is a place where debate does little more than provide the titillation of easily Overcome resistance.

The entire ensemble, the body of law that maintains the distance between colonizer and colonized or between black and white or between men and women or between here and there, is reified in the bodies it both constitutes and circumscribes. Individuals reify this fundamental contradiction in their hearts and minds. It imbues their behavior with the same bad faith and frenzy exhibited by the entire ensemble.

The state, and hence the law, emerge as constitutive parts of whiteness and the race-pleasure needed to create and maintain whiteness. The body of law is both flesh and discourse, because the state, through segregation, arranges both the public forum and the intimate choreography for the race-pleasure tryst. The time and place of this erotic experience between bodies made black and white are themselves the result of a complicated dance of private capital within a vast regulatory web, but the erotic experience is more than the political economy that sets the stage. The bodies come together again and again in a dance called segregation—de jure or de facto—and beget the colorline. Our society's economic and political structures stand in relation to race-pleasure in the way that the beehive's honeycombs stand in relation to honey. The sweetness, the race-pleasure, is the thing that supports the entire enterprise.

Indeed, segregation statutes can be read as a Kamasutra of race-pleasure. Elleke Boehmer, writing on the texts of Imperialism makes a point that is helpful in understanding the legal texts of the colorline:

> Readers ... experience Empire textually, through the medium of nineteenth- and twentieth-century novels and periodicals, travel writings, scraps of doggerel. Yet Empire was itself, at least in part, a textual exercise. The colonial officer filing a report on affairs in his district, British readers of newspapers and advertisements of the day, administrators who consulted Islamic and Hindu sacred texts to establish a legal system for British India: they too understood colonization by way of text. The Empire in its heyday was conceived and maintained in an array of writings—political treatises, diaries, acts and edicts, administrative records and gazetteers, missionaries' reports, notebooks, memoirs, popular verse, government briefs, letters "home" and letters back to settlers. The triple-decker novel and the best-selling adventure tale ... were both infused with imperial ideas of race pride and national prowess.[64]

The racial contours of the legislatively colorlined bodies stand out from the statute books like lovingly carved temple dancers. The judiciary, too, has its role in the orgastic reification of "race." Finally, we must not forget the role of popular justice and injustice in this festival of lawmaking. As with the Marquis de Sade's primers on lovemaking, bodies are typed and arranged in every possible permutation. The erotic plays over the now-black and now-white bodies with boundless enthusiasm for variety. One sees a detailed racial choreography of everyday life. Proximities, angles, activities, incentives, and punishments all were feverishly written into law. And, conversely, the law was a fever that both the segregators and the segregated came to feel within their bodies.

There was no social space that could not be colorlined by state legislators. For example, by 1949, the same year Orwell's *Nineteen Eighty-Four* was published, schools for the blind were racially segregated by state law in Arkansas, Florida, Kentucky, Louisiana, Mississippi, North Carolina, Oklahoma, Tennessee, Texas, Virginia, and West Virginia. Thus, even blindness could be made to see color through the peculiar miracle of segregation.

De jure segregation had expanded into every conceivable site by 1949. Consider the following actions by states. Madness was segregated: Mental patients were segregated in Alabama, Georgia, Kentucky, Louisiana, Maryland, Mississippi, Montana, North Carolina, Oklahoma, South Carolina, Tennessee, Virginia, and West Virginia. Disease was segregated: Alabama, Delaware, Kentucky, Maryland, Oklahoma, Texas,and West Virginia forbade race mixing of tuberculosis patients. Sports were segregated: Boxing, the "sweet science," was segregated by Texas law since the white power riots that followed Jack Johnson's victory over a white hope to become the first black heavyweight champion of the world. Parental love was segregated: Interracial adoptions were forbidden in Louisiana, Montana, South Carolina, and Utah. Belief was segregated: It was a crime to publish anything advocating social equality in Mississippi. Communication was segregated: Telephone booths were segregated in Oklahoma. Poverty was segregated: Paupers were to be segregated in Alabama and West Virginia. Fantasy was segregated: Tennessee and Virginia segregated movie theaters. Punishment was segregated: Black and white prisoners could not be chained together in Alabama, Arkansas, Florida, Georgia, North Carolina, and South Carolina. Thus, even the chains that linked the actors Tony Curtis and Sidney Poitier together in the 1958 Hollywood integration film *The Defiant Ones* were forbidden. Texts were segregated: Florida and North Carolina required separate textbooks for black and white schoolchildren. Happiness was segregated. Innumerable joys were segregated and thus made into sites for racialized joy: Billiard and pool rooms, parks, playgrounds, beaches and boating, racetracks, and circuses were all segregated by race in various states.[65]

State legislators were neither the beginning nor the end of sorrows; segregation was very much a creature of county and municipal ordinances. Within states, local governments refined and multiplied methods of segregation to satisfy their particular needs for race-pleasure. The City Code of Houston (1942), with its bold contradictions, is typical:

> Sec. 1387. Use of Public Building for Promotion of Religious or Racial Antagonism.—The rental or use of Sam Houston Coliseum, the City Auditorium or any other city-owned building, park or property used as a place of public assembly, for any purpose which will tend, by speech or otherwise, to engender racial or religious antagonism. The manager of the coliseum, with respect to the coliseum, the auditorium or other city-owned building, and the superintendent of parks, with respect to the use of park property, are authorized and directed to investigate all applicants for the proposed

use thereof by way of lectures, speech, debates and otherwise, and to deny the use thereof, if, in their opinion, the use will tend to engender religious or racial antagonism.

Sec. 1434. Emancipation Park to be used Exclusively by Colored People.—There is hereby set aside for the exclusive use of the colored people of the city, the park known as Emancipation Park, which park shall be under the jurisdiction and control of the department of public parks of the city. All other parks of the city now or hereafter existing and not set aside exclusively for the use of colored people shall be used exclusively by white people.

Art. III—Segregation of Races in Buses.

Sec. 2212. Penalty for Riding in Compartment After Having Been Forbidden to Do So.—If any passenger on any motor bus provided with separate compartments within the meaning of this article shall ride in any separate compartment not designated for his race after having been forbidden to do so by the conductor or other person in charge of said motor bus, he shall be guilty of a misdemeanor and shall be fined, upon conviction, not less than five dollars nor more than twenty-five dollars.

Sec. 2213. Article Inapplicable to Nurses and Officers.—The provisions of this article shall not be so construed as to prohibit nurses from riding in the same separate compartment of any motor bus with their employer, even though of a different race, and shall not prohibit officers from riding with prisoners of their charge.

In the segregated world of the colorline, pleasure soothes all contradictions, and so Houston was able to realize itself through a single municipal code that forbade the use of public spaces for lectures, speech, debates, and otherwise that "tend to engender religious or racial antagonism" and banned blacks from all parks save the perversely named Emancipation Park. Orwell wrote of this perverse integration of opposites:

Don't you see that the whole aim of Newspeak is to narrow the range of thought? In the end we shall make thoughtcrime literally impossible, because there will be no words to express it. Every concept that will be needed will be expressed by exactly one word, with its meaning rigidly defined and all its subsidiary meanings rubbed out and forgotten.[66]

To enjoy the experience of domination, one must create a situation of domination and then blind one's eyes to the evidence of one's own handiwork (Emancipation Park). In this way, caste becomes a bodily attribute—whiteness becomes superiority and blackness becomes inferiority. This process of becoming also means that superiority becomes whiteness and inferiority becomes blackness.

The lawyers, judges, legislators, and law professors mistook their own echoes for the voice of Nature and Nature's God. The system's minor contradictions, such as the exception for nurses, were easy to smooth over once the major contradiction of segregation was resolved. Is segregation an insult? One might even ask whether the order banning blacks from all parks save Emancipation Park does not itself violate the order banning any use of any public park that would "tend to engender religious or racial antagonism." The answer would be "no": "No, because it is God's plan, not ours." "No, because it is for peace and good order and thus the best for both races." "No, because it is a time-honored tradition."

The terrifying banality of the municipal code, the repetitive dichromatic world of the segregators, the fetishistic pursuit of the black body with an ardor-unto-boredom, an ardor that expanded itself to infinity and hence to invisibility as it fused with Nature and Nature's God, all made "race" synonymous with "segregation." And all of it made segregation a part of that-which-could-not-be-questioned. In the collective imagination of its Creators, in their hearts' conceit, seg-regation was not *created* at all. Confusing their hands with God's, they felt:

Almighty God created the races white, black, yellow, malay and red, and he placed them on separate continents. And but for the interference with his arrange-ment there would be no cause for such [interracial] marriages. The fact that he separated the races shows that he did not intend for the races to mix.[67]

And yet, this confusion was a confusion that contained yet another confusion that mas-queraded as clarity. The segregators, appar-ently recognizing that "here on Earth, God's work must truly be our own," did not allow their signifiers to shift:

Sec. 2215. Shifting Signs That Separate Compartments.—It shall be the duty of the person in charge of any motor bus, in his discretion, to shift the signs that sep-arate the two compartments for the white and for the black races, and any person other than said person in charge of said motor bus who shall shift or change from one place to another the signs separating the two separate com-partments of any motor bus shall be guilty of an offense and, upon conviction thereof in the corporation court, shall be fined not less than five dollars nor more than two hundred dollars.

It is hereby made the duty of the per-son in charge of any motor bus, where-upon or in which any person other than himself shall shift or change from one position to another any signs separating the two separate compartments of said motor bus, to report said person so offending to the corporation court and to file complaint against the said offender, and any conductor who shall fail to refuse to report such violation shall be guilty of offense and, upon conviction of the same in corporation court, shall be fined not more than fifty dollars.[68]

The writerly and readerly pleasures of col-orlining flesh in the pages of a text, legal or otherwise, are the same pleasures enjoyed on the colorlined "motor bus." Racial writ-ing and reading, like colonial writing and reading, is part of the sensual process of nobodying the Other.

The site and cite of colorlined pleasure merge when we reflect on the literarily defined, or spectacularized, nature of our bodies. Our bodies are parchment, and "race" has been a bold inscription on the leaves rep-resenting the contributions of the twentieth century. The racial pornographer, the legisla-tor, both carves his accusation into the black body and makes it true in the act of legislat-ing. That act is an act of race-pleasure. That Act is also an Act of race-pleasure. The leg-islative drafting, the executive enforcement, the judicial interpretation, the academic analysis, the jurisprudential theorizing, the regular police violence, the supplementary mob violence, the democratic legitimation, and the public awareness of these Acts are all acts of race-pleasure. Sade is helpful in under-standing the project on which these legal actors toiled so furiously:

After having immured themselves within everything that was best able to satisfy the senses through lust, after having established this situation, the plan was to have described to them, in the great-est detail and in due order, every one of debauchery's extravagances, all its diva-gations, all its ramifications, all its con-tingencies, all of what is termed in liber-tine language its passions.[69]

The four libertines of Sade's *The 120 Days of Sodom*, like the segregators, form a "society" for the purpose of torture and murder. Not content with the mere direct enjoyment of cruelty, the libertines establish a method of memorializing and systematizing their deeds, of translating their passions into texts. This transformation of passions to texts is itself a form of pleasure:

He who should succeed in isolating and categorizing and detailing these follies would perhaps perform one of the most splendid labors which might be undertaken in the study of manners, and perhaps one of the most interesting. It would thus be a question of finding some individuals capable of providing an account of all these excesses, then of analyzing them, of extending them, of itemizing them, of graduating them, and of running a story through it all, to provide coherence and amusement.[70]

The legislators of the pre-Civil Rights Movement era were engaged in the production of just such an accounting, analysis, extension, itemization, graduation, and narration of the colorline. Sade's libertines, like the segregators of the pre-Civil Rights Movement era or the neo-segregators of our own, "enclose themselves inside their retreat as within a besieged citadel, without leaving the least entrance to an enemy, the least egress to a deserter" and labor "over a code of laws."[71] Sade warns, "it is essential that these articles of government be known to the reader who, after the exact description we have given him of everything, will now have no more to do than follow the story, lightly and voluptuously."[72] Sade's statutes, like the statutes of the segregators, do not simply command humiliation; they are complicated texts of pleasure. That is, the statutes themselves are, textually, forms of race-pleasure.

In addition to being forms of pleasure and humiliation in themselves, the statutes serve to structure the pleasures and humiliations of our lives. Our personal narratives are both constituted and circumscribed by the colorline. Sade writes:

We have, moreover, blended these six hundred passions into the storytellers' narratives. That is one more thing whereof the reader were well to have foreknowledge; it would have been too monotonous to catalogue them one by one outside the body of the story. But as some reader not much learned in these

matters might perhaps confuse the designated passions with the adventure or simple event in the narrator's life, each of these passions has been carefully distinguished by a marginal notation: a line, above which is the title that may be given the passion. The mark indicates where the account of the passions begins, and the end of the paragraph always indicates where it finishes.[73]

In this passage, "the care taken to preserve the effectiveness and the framework of a dictionary within the 'body of the narrative' entails a painful didacticism, to the point of suggesting how the work should be used."[74] Like the segregator's statutes, Sade's *120 Days of Sodom* is easy to use, "as with a dictionary we can begin and end anywhere." Like the segregation statutes, Sade's statutes say everything:

We know who's who, what each person is capable of, what each person desires, etc. Everything is circumscribed from the outset, and nothing remains ambiguous.[75]

The subaltern world of the Sadean victim resembles the subaltern world of the native as described by Fanon and the segregated world of the colorline. It is:

A world divided into compartments, a motionless, Manicheistic world, a world of statues . . . a world which is sure of itself, which crushes with its stones the backs flayed by whips. . . . The native is a being hemmed in; apartheid is simply one form of the division into compartments of the colonial world. The first thing which the native learns is to stay in his place.[76]

Sade's statutes, like those of the pre-Civil Rights Movement world, constitute what Marcel Henaff calls an "encyclopedia of excess."[77] The encyclopedia of excess says too much in two distinct and contradictory ways: The encyclopedia of excess is a collision of impulses of totality ("saying too much" in the encyclopedic sense) and excess ("saying too much" in the sense of a demand that everything be revealed and the claim that "I'm going to tell all"). The encyclopedia of excess can be seen in Sade's "statutes" and in the statutes of the segregationist legislators.

The legislators aspire to totality and tell us every detail of the black body. They also embrace excess, for in telling all regarding the black body, they necessarily add supplemental information about themselves. This supplemental information is excess—that is, the legislators' aspiration for totality reveals their need to tell all about the black body. The legislators' need to tell all, which produces excess, also serves to undermine the tale they tell. The legislators describe blacks encyclopedically over and over again. The repetitive encyclopedic iterations of the same old story of natural inferiority belie the dispassionate objectivity on which the project of encyclopedic repetition depends. The production of the truth of black subalternation, then, is both dependent on and undermined by the legislators' pleasure in the production of the truth of black subalternation. The black body is produced as truth because of the legislators' passion for race-pleasure. The black body is undermined as truth because of the legislators' passion for race-pleasure. Or so it seems from outside of the pleasuredome.

Violence and pleasure was the truth of these statutes. The five-dollar or two-hundred-dollar fines of a typical municipal segregation ordinance or the prison terms of state segregation statutes were supported by the dangerous supplement of violence. Law needed lawlessness to function properly as law. The lawlessness required was not that of the outlaw; rather, it was that of the insider. That is, the law of segregation was given meaning not solely by those who defied the colorline but also by those who upheld the law of segregation by breaking all other laws, including the law of segregation, by supple-

menting the law with extralegal punishments. A typical report comes from the *New York Tribune* of February 8, 1904:

> Luther Holbert, a Doddsville [Mississippi] Negro, and his wife were burned at the stake for the murder of James Eastland, a white planter, and John Carr, a Negro. The planter was killed in a quarrel.... Holbert and his wife left the plantation but were brought back and burned at the stake in the presence of a thousand people. Two innocent Negroes had been shot previous to this by a posse looking for Holbert.... There is nothing in the story to indicate that Holbert's wife had any part in the crime.[78]

The Vicksburg, Mississippi, *Evening Post*, had a more elaborate account of the incident:

> When the two Negroes were captured, they were tied to trees and while the funeral pyres were being prepared they were forced to suffer the most fiendish tortures. The blacks were forced to hold out their hands while one finger at a time was chopped off. The fingers were distributed as souvenirs. The ears of the murderers were cut off. Holbert was beaten severely, his skull was fractured, and one of his eyes, knocked out with a stick, hung by a shred from the socket.... The most excruciating form of punishment consisted in the use of a large corkscrew in the hands of some of the mob. This instrument was bored into the flesh of the man and woman, in the arms legs and body, and then pulled out, the spirals tearing out big pieces of raw, quivering flesh every time it was withdrawn.[79]

These punishments were frequent: "On the average, a black man, woman or child was murdered, nearly once a week, every week, between 1882 and 1930 by a hate-driven white mob."[80] The strange fruits of lynching were the truth of all of the segregation statutes. We ought to think of these celebrations of white supremacy as trees of knowledge. After consuming the strange fruit, the celebrants clothed their bodies in whiteness. The segregationists' strange fruit gave the people the knowledge that the result of violation might be a "legal" punishment, but it might also be "corkscrews." The ritualistic nature of the preparation of the black bodies showed the pleasure that it gave the preparers.

Together, lynching and law produced the dramatic tension on which the production of race-pleasure depended. The black body, spectacularized by lynching as by segregation statutes, caught between the "good Negro's" humiliating imitation of life and the "bad Negro's" humiliating death by lynching, was overdetermined from without. The spectacle was, of course, taken in by white and black alike. For example, the following author, and the pair he writes about, all act as both the product and producer of the spectacle:

> To the White Citizens of Jackson County [Florida]:
>
> Just a few lines to let you all know that we good colored citizens of Jackson County don't feel no sympathy toward the nigger that —— the white lady and killed her. No! We haven't felt he did right because he should stay in his place, and since he did such as he did, we are not feeling we have a right to plead to you all for mercy.
> ***
> Your Faithful Servant,
> John Curry[81]

The "White Citizens" did indeed find "the nigger" alleged to have committed the act so horrifying to their sense of themselves that even their "Faithful Servant" could mention it only in code ("the nigger that —— the white lady and killed her"). The "Faithful Servant" of the "White Citizens" had no such difficulty using the word "nigger" and thus openly naming the act of racialization. An investigator for the NAACP reported:

> After taking the nigger [Claude Neal] to the woods about four miles from Green-

wood, they cut off his penis. He was made to eat it. Then they cut off his testicles and made him eat them and say he liked it. . . . Then they sliced his sides and stomach with knives and every now and then somebody would cut off a finger or toe. Red hot irons were used on the nigger to burn him from top to bottom.[82]

Subaltern flesh, like that ritualistically stripped from Claude Neal's bones, was transformed into and created by law, both state and federal, both legislative and judge-made. Robert Cover wrote of the connection between legal interpretation and pain and death:

> Legal interpretation takes place in the field of pain and death. . . . Legal interpretive acts signal and occasion the imposition of violence upon others. . . . Neither legal interpretation nor the violence it occasions may be properly understood apart from one another.[83]

What Cover writes of "pain and death" is also true of pleasure.

The case of *United States v. Cruikshank* (1875) illustrates how race-pleasure rituals such as the killing of Claude Neal were transformed into the textualized race-pleasure rituals of constitutional jurisprudence.[84] In *Cruikshank*, the Supreme Court held that the duty of protecting all its citizens in the enjoyment of equal rights was originally assumed by and remained with the states. Thus, the enforcement of the Fourteenth Amendment, which had been adopted for "the protection of the newly-made freemen and citizen from the oppression of those who had formerly exercised unlimited dominion over him," would be left to the very same authorities that had formerly exercised unlimited dominion over him.[85] It was this same "unlimited dominion" that had given rise to *Cruikshank* in the first place. In April 1873, whites in Grant and other surrounding Louisiana parishes organized themselves into the "White League"

ANTHONY PAUL FARLEY 119

and other Reconstruction resistance groups and declared their intention to rid their "white man's country" of its newly enfranchised "Black Devils."[86] When the whites sought a military solution to the problem of racially integrated Republican officeholders, armed blacks occupied the courthouse, the sole brick building in Califax, the parish seat, and took a stand.[87]

The blacks were defeated. Dozens were burned alive within the courthouse. Many of those who tried to flee the surrounded building were shot while others "were ridden down without mercy."[88] Estimates of the total number of blacks killed ranged from sixty-nine to more than one hundred; some estimates were as high as four hundred. Not all the murders occurred in the courthouse confrontation. Several blacks were shot or bayoneted long after their capture. Some were killed with the deliberate speed of the classic lynching. One of the whites recalled:

> Captain Dave Paul and Mr. Yawn came walking by me and says, "We got most of them, but the man which we want. We don't see him among the dead." I says, "Examine them carefully, maybe you can find him in there [the garden]." We walked down the line and there was a negro with his hat pulled down over his eyes. Jim Yawn was laying for the man who killed Jeff [in 1871]. Yawn lifted his hat up and grabbed him by the coat and says, "I got you," and took him about twenty steps away and shot him.[89]

Reconstruction was doomed but not quite dead, and so federal officials actually managed to obtain convictions of William Cruikshank and two others under the Enforcement Act of 1870 for violating the civil rights of black citizens. In overturning these convictions and returning blacks to the hands of their former masters, the Law—and the justices of the Supreme Court of the United States of America—textually par-

ticipated in the very race-pleasure ritual that had placed the case, and the strange fruit of Southern trees, at their table. The death of Reconstruction, the redemption of the pre-Civil War status quo, and the body of Law implicated in that death, that redemption, and that return to things past were all ways of spreading skin across territories and spaces.

The black body is a vast writing project. It is a twice-haunted, twice-scripted body. The good Negro and the bad Negro are animating spirits that emerge, like the Madonna and the Whore, depending on the performance desired. White pre-Civil Rights Movement desire for abject black bodies required, at times, the good Negro of minstrelsy and, at other times, the bad Negro of lynching. Pity and contempt were the twin emotions that accompanied the race-pleasure rituals: pity for the good Negro and contempt for the bad Negro. White power was both the product of the ritual and the condition of the ritual's possibility. The law produced absolute power in whites by reducing blacks, once again, to creatures dispossessed of any rights the "white man was bound to respect."[90] Absolute power produced dependency; dependency produced sycophancy; and sycophancy produced the race-pleasure that supported the entire enterprise of the colorline. Absolute power also produced desperation; desperation produced audacity; audacity produced rebellion; and rebellion, particularly its small-scale incarnations in crime and insolence, was used as the centerpiece of the lynching. In the pre-Civil Rights Movement world, the colorline frequently broke the surface of the race-pleasure documents produced by lawyers, judges and legislators. In the documents of the post-Civil Rights Movement world, however, the colorline is often found lurking at deeper, subtextual, levels.

To search is to desire. Whether we write or read, we enter a text looking—*cruising*—for the obscure object of our desire. The figure in the text, it seems, desires us.[91] Enter, it seems to say. It beckons and it hides. We think that the text is trying to tell us something. We seek and find the obscure object of our desire in even the most unlikely textual terrain. In fact, we always find the obscure object of our desire, no matter how the textual terrain is configured. In legal interpretation, to desire is already to have found. The writers and readers of the segregation era's laws found the black bodies they desired, just as the writers and readers of the neo-segregation era's laws find the black bodies they desire.

The post-Civil Rights Movement authors and readers of law have also stalked and captured the black bodies they desired. Critical legal studies and Critical Race Theory have painstakingly demonstrated the myriad ways in which the post-Civil Rights Movement rhetoric of antidiscrimination can and has been used to reify the old arrangements of the pre-Civil Rights Movement era. The basic colorlined order of things has not changed since *Loving v. Virginia*. Blackness today remains blackness, and whiteness today remains whiteness, although the sites and cites of the race-pleasure tryst have changed. Neo-segregationist rule fetishists continue to *cruise* texts for black bodies. Although the name given to the space of these twilight textual encounters may have changed, "You must remember this, a kiss is still a kiss, the fundamental things apply," however much time may have gone by.

Neo-segregation

As a case in point of this sort of sensitization through interaction, I take what can be described as a composite pattern of social sadism and social euphemism. "Social sadism" is more than a metaphor. The term refers to social structures which are so organized as to systematically inflict pain, humiliation, suffering and deep frustration on particular groups and

strata. This need have nothing at all to do with the psychic propensities of individuals to find pleasure in cruelty. It is an objective, socially organized, and recurrent set of situations that has these cruel consequences, however diverse its historical sources and whatever the social processes that maintain it. This type of sadistic social structure is readily overlooked by a perspective that can be described as that of the sociological euphemism. The term does not refer to the obvious cases in which ideological support of the structure is couched in sociological language. Rather, it refers to the kind of conceptual apparatus that, once adopted, requires us to ignore such intense human experiences such as pain, suffering, humiliation, and so on.
—Robert K. Merton[92]

Blacks and Mexican Americans are not academically competitive with whites in selective institutions. It is the result primarily of cultural effects. Various studies seem to show that blacks and Mexican-Americans spend much less time in school. They have a culture that seems not to encourage achievement.
—Lino A. Graglia[93]

Law creates the black body through minstrelization and criminalization. These are two sides of the same pre-Civil Rights Movement, good Negro–bad Negro coin. The good Negro today is either the less-than-competent "African American" who "needs affirmative action" or the fantasy "African American" who "would have made it even without affirmative action." The good Negro of fantasy never actually applies for any particular job or mortgage or lease; rather, he exists entirely in the Spectacle Paradise of television, the mythmaking world of Colin Powell or O. J. Simpson (before his ex-wife Nicole Brown's "wrongful death"). The bad Negro today is the criminal. The bad Negro is every black person until he proves himself a good Negro. The bad Negro of fantasy also exists in the Spectacle

Paradise to warn us that all Angels, even the black Angels of a lesser God, can Fall, like O. J. Simpson, and become Willie Horton, Bigger Thomas, or even the doubly fantasized child-kidnapping bad Negro of Susan Smith's and South Carolina's imagination. Law creates the conditions under which blacks will be deemed either minstrels or criminals. Minstrelsy, of course, leads to criminality, and vice versa.

Today's civil-rights statutes serve the same race-pleasure function as did yesterday's segregation statutes. The segregation statutes announced to the world that blacks were inferior. The attendant black pain was integral to the pleasure of whiteness. Our civil-rights statutes today serve to legitimate, not prevent, discrimination. Discrimination has continued, more or less unabated, despite the presence of these civil-rights statutes. Our civil-rights statutes serve mainly to delegitimize any claims that discrimination continues. This last task they do well—so well that discrimination today is spoken of only as a vestigial remnant of yesterday, not as the very pulse of morning. Thus, today's civil-rights statutes, like yesterday's segregation statutes, announce to the world that blacks are inferior.

Race works in mysterious ways. Our civil-rights statutes are designed from a "perpetrator perspective," not from a "victim perspective":

> From the victim's perspective, racial discrimination describes those conditions of actual social existence as a member of a perpetual underclass. . . . The perpetrator perspective sees racial discrimination not as conditions but as actions, or a series of actions, inflicted on the victim by the perpetrator.[94]

The victim perspective focuses on the problem of inequality, while the perpetrator perspective focuses on the problems of fault and causation. The victim lives in a toxic ocean of discrimination, but the perpetrator sees only the nets as problematic. By focusing on the problems of fault and causation, the perpetrator perspective guarantees that discrimination that is not located, litigated, and proved in a court of law will be protected and legitimated as non-discrimination. Thus, most anti-black behavior is legitimated as non-discrimination by today's civil-rights statutes. The statutes purport to do that which they do not do—namely, protect people of color from discrimination.

This legitimation of discrimination through antidiscrimination law has two effects, each of which is bound to the other. First, it has the effect of minstrelizing blacks in the white imagination, for

> the failure of the oppressed successfully to use such powerful, privileging legal means thus confirms their essential inadequacy. Reform, in the guise of a succession of Race Relations Acts, like so much reform becomes part of the problematic, creating and sustaining that which it purports to counter.[95]

While the pre-Civil Rights Movement segregation statutes merely served to accuse blacks of inferiority, civil-rights statutes serve to prove black inferiority, over and over again, with fetishistic intensity every time the civil-rights era is invoked. What is the Reverend Dr. Martin Luther King, Jr., today but a living, or perhaps undead, spectacularized symbol of white Supremacy? If there are no blacks today who seem competent to claim the victory that King is said to have won, what then? What is to be done? We use the phrase "affirmative action" instead of "race" and call that progress. The state of "black" America is a disaster:

- The median white family income in the United States is 136 percent of the median black family income.[96]
- The median net worth of white households in the United States is ten times

the median net worth of black households.[97]

- The average black family has no net financial assets.[98]
- Nearly three-quarters of all black children grow up in households possessing no net financial assets.[99]

The minstrelization of blacks is almost complete.

Minstrelization leads to pity and pity to charity and charity to dependence and dependence to subalternation. It can also lead to criminality. And that is the second effect of the post-Civil Rights Movement legitimization of discrimination through anti-discrimination laws. If the oppressed cannot make it through their own efforts, if only white charity can keep the iron spur of competition from piercing their black bodies, and if charity is not inexhaustible, then criminality must appear as a limit to and exorcism of white guilt. Criminality is the device for transforming pity into contempt and the good Negro into the bad Negro. Criminality is the other race-pleasure experience, and law manufactures it for its white consumers just as surely as law manufactures the minstrelsy that is its other face. Today, the spectacle of subaltern criminality has, to a large degree, replaced the "Whites Only" signs as the primary marker of race. According to the January 1997 report of the Sentencing Project:

- Twelve states and the District of Columbia incarcerate blacks at a rate more than ten times that of whites.
- From 1988 to 1994, 38 states and the District of Columbia experienced an increase in the racial disparity in their rates of incarceration. Nationally, the black rate of incarceration in state prisons during this period increased from 6.88 times the rate of whites to 7.66.
- In comparison to a similar increase in the number of imprisoned violent offenders

for blacks and whites from 1986 to 1991 (31,000 and 33,000, respectively) the increase in the number of black drug offenders in prison far outpaced that for whites, by 66,000 to 15,000. The black increase represented a 465 percent change between 1986 and 1991.

- The ongoing consequences of high rates of incarceration have impacts that may seriously erode the black community's participation in civic life, such as voting rights. Nationally, an estimated 1.4 million African American men are currently or permanently disfranchised from voting as a result of a felony conviction. This represents 14 percent, or one in seven, of the adult black male population of 10.4 million. In total, about 4.2 million persons of all races are currently disfranchised as a result of a felony conviction.[100]

Indeed, on any given day, one out of three black men between the ages of twenty and twenty-nine are either in prison or on parole.[101] Prison, as we all know, produces recidivism. Whites manufacture black criminality in order to enjoy the spectacle. It is the spectacle that makes whites white. It is the spectacle that explains the peculiar neo-colonial relationship between suburb and inner city today. The city is organized and maintained as a plantation. The plantation produces the spectacle of black subalternation. The plantation produces criminality in black. This crop is reaped for the six o'clock news, woven into fantasy during the movie hour, and recycled as news at eleven o'clock. A colorlined nation gazes into the Spectacle Paradise of television and finds itself whitened by the ritual and convinced of the truth of its pleasure.

We use the word "crime" instead of "race" and call it progress. The spectacle of subaltern criminality produces the imaginary distance between the neo-colony and the suburb, between blacks and whites. The spectacle of crime serves to divide the rainbow—blacks from whites and blacks from themselves and Others.

Washington v. Davis as Spectacle

While lamented by commentators and the bar, the relative paucity of African American judges has rarely been challenged as illegal and never as unconstitutional. Efforts to promote racial diversity on the bench are often couched in the soft language of inclusiveness, public confidence and promoting the appearance of justice. Racial diversity in the courts is almost never discussed in the more forceful language of rights and representation. The tentativeness of the judicial diversity discourse is a product in large part of continued resistance to the very idea that judges are representatives. Indeed, to describe judges as representatives is to invite hostility from both the bench and the bar. Diversity efforts are countered with the argument that judges are impartial and thus need not be representative of particular racial groups. Impartiality, as currently understood, stands as a barrier to achieving racial diversity on the bench.
    —Sherrilyn A. Ifill[102]

The picture was bleak. Employees in the lower-echelon jobs were virtually all staffed with blacks, the upper-echelon jobs were nearly all white. Laborers and messengers were commonly asked to perform menial work for the Justices.... Cleaning women lived in fear of being summarily dismissed for breaking something. They had to pay for all china and crystal broken while cleaning up for private dinners hosted at the Court by the Justices.
    —Bob Woodward and Scott Armstrong[103]

If a master is known best by his slaves, it is possible that a judge is known best by his clerks. It is possible that the impartiality of judges is belied by the presence of the colorline in their racially partial decisions regarding the employment of clerks. It is possible that judges judge cases in ways that preserve the myth of judicial impartiality. It is possible that judges strategically create blind spots in order to cloak their preference for whiteness in a cover of darkness. It is possible that justice is strategically blind.

The clerks make the work of the Supreme Court possible. Each year, more that seven thousand people and organizations take their cases all the way to the Supreme Court. The thirty-five or thirty-six clerks aid the Supreme Court in the following ways:

1. Clerks do the initial screening of petitions. The clerks participate in a "pool" in which they divide up the cases and write a single memorandum about each case that is sent to the justices.
2. The pool memoranda summarize the facts and the issues and often recommend whether the case should be accepted by the court for review.
3. All nine justices meet to decide whether to accept or deny a petition for review. If four of the nine say a case warrants review, it is docketed for oral arguments. Fewer than one hundred cases are accepted each term.
4. Some justices have clerks write a bench memo that summarizes the case and may also suggest questions the justice could ask during oral arguments.
5. The justices meet after oral arguments to take an initial vote and to assign the writing of the majority and dissenting opinions. Clerks usually write the first drafts.
6. Drafts are circulated to other justices for editing and revision. Clerks are often the lines of communication between the justices as they negotiate their finished opinion.
7. Opinions are handed down in the names of the justices. Clerks are never mentioned.[104]

Numbers: How does an entire race come to be represented by the spectacle of the grinning, white-gloved, being-for-others figure of the minstrel? Law is a production site for the spectacle of the minstrel. Consider the habit that all nine of the justices of the U.S. Supreme Court have made of not hiring black clerks:

Chief Justice William H. Rehnquist: 82 hires and 0 blacks

Justice John Paul Stevens: 61 hires and 3 blacks

Justice Sandra Day O'Connor: 72 hires and 1 black

Justice Antonin Scalia: 52 hires and 0 blacks

Justice Anthony McLeod Kennedy: 49 hires and 0 blacks

Justice David Souter: 35 hires and 0 blacks

Justice Clarence Thomas: 33 hires and 1 black

Justice Ruth Bader Ginsburg: 24 hires and 1 black

Justice Stephen Breyer: 20 hires and 1 black

Their statistics regarding Latina/o ("hispanic") clerks are even worse:

Rehnquist: 82 hires and 1 hispanic
Stevens: 61 hires and 0 hispanics
O'Connor: 72 hires and 1 hispanic
Scalia: 52 hires and 0 hispanics
Kennedy: 49 hires and 1 hispanic
Souter: 35 hires and 1 hispanic
Thomas: 33 hires and 0 hispanics
Ginsburg: 24 hires and 0 hispanics
Breyer: 20 hires and 1 hispanic

Nor are the numbers for Asian Pacific Americans cause for celebration:

Rehnquist: 82 hires and 0 Asian Pacific Americans

Stevens: 61 hires and 5 Asian Pacific Americans

O'Connor: 72 hires and 4 Asian Pacific Americans

Scalia: 52 hires and 0 Asian Pacific Americans

Kennedy: 49 hires and 3 Asian Pacific Americans

Souter: 35 hires and 1 Asian Pacific American

Thomas: 33 hires and 3 Asian Pacific Americans

Ginsburg: 24 hires and 1 Asian Pacific American

Breyer: 20 hires and 1 Asian Pacific American

The justices' hiring practices show a gender disparity as well as a race disparity. Only Breyer hires men and women at a 1:1 ratio (10:10). The rest, including O'Connor (40:32) and Ginsburg (14:10), all hire more men than women.[105]

In addition to an examination of the flesh, there seems to be an examination of ideology. Michael Luttig, a judge of the U.S. Court of Appeals for the Fourth Circuit, made the "Minstrelsy" test very clear: Judge Luttig, who, like Clarence Thomas, was appointed by the former President Bush, recently stated that he relies on word of mouth from his current clerks about up-and-coming students, because "the professors don't really know the students." Thus, per Luttig, many former clerks are implicated in the production of this spectacle. Luttig said that likely candidates are brought in for lengthy interviews aimed at making sure that "they take the law deadly seriously, and not as an engine for social change."[106] Luttig's rule, of course, would eliminate virtually all candidates of color. Luttig, one of the top "feeder" judges for the U.S. Supreme Court, has sent sixteen of his former clerks on to clerk for justices of the U.S. Supreme Court since 1991.

Who are these clerks? What or who do they represent? Are they products of what Fitzgerald's Daisy Buchanan called her "*beautiful white girlhood* [or boyhood]?"[107] Is black beautiful in their eyes or in the eyes of their employers? Is either question fair? Where might I begin a fair-minded inquiry? Luttig would not be able to hire a young

Charles Hamilton Houston, for example, and that hardly seems fair. Houston was the first black member of the *Harvard Law Review* (1921); he had a brilliant career as the resident vice-dean of Howard Law School (1930–34); he was the first special counsel to the NAACP (1935); he was the chief architect of the legal battle against segregation; and, finally, he was professor and mentor to the young Thurgood Marshall.[108] We know all these things about Houston, but we also know that he was black and not fair in color and that he was famous for insisting that a lawyer was either a "social engineer or a parasite on society."[109] As an admitted "social engineer" he would not pass Luttig's Minstrelsy test. Indeed, Luttig's test seems clearly designed to eliminate those who follow in Houston's wake.

Given the fact that there would be virtually no students of color at elite law schools but for Houston's belief that lawyers should *not* take the law seriously as law and should instead view themselves as "social engineers," Luttig's test is an interesting one. What could a "deadly serious" lawyer do with a case such as *Plessy v. Ferguson* (1896) and the weight of white precedent, lifestyle, hope, and expectation behind the doctrine of "separate but equal"?[110] The "deadly serious" lawyers of that era were parasites on received tradition. Those who "take law seriously as law" have never made a contribution worth noting. The "social engineers" have given us what little law has been worthwhile.

Recall that when the doctrine of "separate but equal" was first announced in *Roberts v. City of Boston* (1849), the lawyers representing five-year-old Sarah Roberts against the forces of school segregation were forced to cite a continental source—Rousseau—for the proposition that the tendency towards inequality ought to be resisted with law: "It is precisely because the force of things tends always to destroy equality, that the force of legislation ought

always to maintain it."[111] The lawyers argued, "[Segregation] tends to create a feeling of degradation in the blacks, and of prejudice and uncharitableness in the whites," to no avail.[112] The Supreme Judicial Court of Massachusetts, speaking through Chief Justice Lemuel Shaw, announced: "The increased distance, to which plaintiff was obliged to go to school from her father's house, is not such, in our opinion, as to render the regulation in question unreasonable, still less illegal."[113] The "fifth of a mile or seventy rods" Sarah Roberts had to walk to attend the colored school was, in phenomenological terms, as far as the distance from freedom to slavery or as far as a fall from grace.

The losing argument by Robert Morris, Jr., and Charles Sumner was the first civil-rights appellate brief ever filed by a black lawyer and a white lawyer in any case in America. Their journey, like that of Queequeg and Ishmael, was doomed from the start. Shaw wrote for insiders:

> The committee, apparently upon great deliberation, have come to the conclusion that the good of both classes of schools will best be promoted, by maintaining separate primary schools for colored and white children, and we can perceive no reason to doubt, that this is the honest result of their experience and judgement.[114]

It did not have to be this way. Shaw's own son-in-law, Herman Melville, began the epilogue of *Moby Dick* with words from Job, "And I only am escaped alone to tell thee," that reflected a deeper understanding of exclusion than that dreamed of in his father-in-law's jurisprudence.[115] Melville had a sense of the poetics of space and the cruelties of abandonment that seemed to have escaped his father-in-law. Consider Melville's description of the separation between Pip, a black sailor, and Stubb, a white sailor:

In three minutes, a whole mile of shore-less ocean was between Pip and Stubb. Out from the centre of the sea, poor Pip turned his crisp, curling, black head to the sun, another lonely castaway, though the loftiest and the brightest. Now, in calm weather, to swim in the open ocean is as easy to the practiced swimmer as to ride in a spring-carriage ashore, but the awful lonesomeness is intolerable. The intense concentration of self in the mid-dle of such a heartless immensity, my God! who can tell it? Mark, how when sailors in a dead calm bathe in the open sea—mark how closely they hug their ship and only coast along her sides. But had Stubb really abandoned the poor lit-tle negro to his fate? No; he did not mean to, at least.[116]

Pip is maddened by the abandonment: "The sea had jeeringly kept his finite body up, but drowned the infinite of his soul."[117] The doctrine of "separate but equal" meant rit-ualizing both abandonment and its denial ("The increased distance, to which plaintiff was obliged to go to school from her father's house, is not such, in our opinion, as to render the regulation in question unreasonable, still less illegal").

The Supreme Court lived this two-stranded lesson to its limit: Even its toilets were segregated, "separately and equally," until the year before *Brown v. Board of Edu-cation* (1954).[118] Surely, desegregating toilets would be an engineering task and not a way of "taking the law seriously as law." I imag-ine the excrementalized Others abandoned in the vortex. I imagine the disappearance of the Pequod in those swirling waters. I imag-ine the abyss. Call *me* Ishmael:

So floating on the waters of the ensuing scene, and in full sight of it, when the half spent suction of the sunk ship reached me, I was then, but slowly drawn towards the closing vortex. When I reached it, it had subsided to a creamy pool. Round and round, then, and ever contracting towards the button-like

black bubble at the axis of that slowly wheeling circle, like another Ixion I did revolve. Till, gaining that vital centre, the black bubble upward burst; and now, lib-erated by reason of its cunning spring, and, owing to its great *buoyancy*, rising with great force, the coffin life-buoy shot lengthwise from the sea, fell over, and floated by my side. Buoyed up by that coffin, for almost one whole day and night, I floated on a soft and dirge-like main. On the second day, a sail drew near, nearer, and picked me up at last.[119]

But perhaps water is the wrong metaphor. God already gave Noah the rainbow sign. There are no white sails on the horizon. And Ishmael is not my name, although I some-times find myself floating, "round and round ... on a soft and dirge-like main" in Houston's wake, *buoyed* up by that coffin. Sometimes, but not this time, I think of this timeless turning:

Weel a-bout and turn a-bout
And do just so
Every time I weel a-bout
I jump Jim Crow[120]

Do the clerks and their justices think of the whiteness of their workspace as they work and play? In the temple of wisdom regarding the law and justice, "Not under man but under God and Law," the priests and their acolytes are, virtually, all white. Is it a blinding whiteness, or is it a whiteness that is sometimes able to see itself as white? Perhaps in play, in moments of communal playfulness, the clerks and their justices find that their workspace-segregation lines come into focus. This play occurs on the court within the Court. The highest court in the land, "our" Supreme Court, contains a bas-ketball court within its walls. The clerks play basketball with one another in moments of unstructured, informal time. Do they see an absence among the players on the court that mirrors an absence among the workers, the clerks, of the court?

In the game of basketball, virtually all of the "heroes" whom young children—even, or especially, young white children—dream of becoming are black. There are white basketball heroes; however, the players that children most often pretend to be when they imagine themselves as professionals are black: Julius Erving (Dr. J.), Earvin Johnson (Magic), Michael Jordan (Mike). Indeed, global corporations such as Nike encourage everyone, "black and white together," to "be like Mike" on the basketball court. When the young clerks *play* at being black, when they strive to be black "like Mike," do they think about the whiteness of their bodies or their basketball court or their Supreme Court? Or does it just seem natural that their *workspace*, like their bodies and their basketball court, is so white?

The dearth of Supreme Court clerks of color is important as spectacle and as jurisprudence. As spectacle, it is either read as a statement that the justices follow the colorline or as a statement that people of color are racially inferior to whites. Both readings are the same reading. Neither of these readings may be an accurate reading of the hearts and minds of the justices. At the level of spectacle, the intent behind the numbers does not matter.[121] Nor does intent matter at the level of jurisprudence. As I will show, at the level of jurisprudence, the numbers become the jurisprudence. That is, the dearth of clerks of color becomes jurisprudence.

Numbers as Spectacle: Numbers tell us a lot. One says a lot, and zero says a lot more. One is the total number of black clerks that four of the justices—Breyer, Ginsburg, O'Connor, and Thomas—have ever hired. Zero is the total number of black clerks that four other justices—Kennedy, Rehnquist, Scalia, and Souter—have ever hired. The remaining justice—Stevens—has hired only three blacks since his career began in 1975.

It is worth examining the mind of this last, most ecumenical, of the justices. In *Texas v. Johnson* (1989), a case involving the public burning of an American flag in violation of a Texas statute forbidding the desecration of a venerated object, Justice Stevens, in an emotional dissent in defense of the Texas statute, listed a number of great Americans:

> The ideas of liberty and equality have been an irresistible force in motivating leaders like Patrick Henry, Susan B. Anthony, and Abraham Lincoln, schoolteachers like Nathan Hale and Booker T. Washington, the Philippine Scouts who fought at Bataan, and the soldiers who scaled the bluff at Omaha Beach.[122]

The lone black that made the list is, of course, most known for his compromise with segregation. Booker T. Washington burst on the national scene after giving his famous "Atlanta Compromise" speech at the 1895 Atlanta Exposition: "In all matters that are purely social we can be as separate as the fingers, yet one as the hand in all things essential to mutual progress."[123] At that time, to "take law seriously as law" was to understand that segregation was the law of the land. It was the year Frederick Douglass died. It was the year my grandfather, Richard Gustavus Adolphus Alexander Morris, was born in Jamaica. It was the year the uncompromising W.E.B. Du Bois become the first black person to *earn* a doctorate at Harvard University. It was the year before *Plessy v. Ferguson,* and it was a year before the compromised Booker T. Washington would become the first black person to be *given* an honorary degree from Harvard University. Washington's Atlanta Compromise was the original contract presented to the subaltern body: "All these things I will give you."[124] But what profit a man? The year 1895 was one of horror; it was a year of promise; it was a year like the first year; it was a year like the present.

Washington's compromise with segregation made him a national star with the white establishment. For most whites, he was a welcome relief from blacks such as Du Bois, founder of the NAACP. Washington's place as the lone black in Stevens's *Texas v. Johnson* dissent speaks volumes regarding the hearts and minds on the Supreme Court, just as Washington's place as the first black on the white establishment's list of most-favored subaltern spokespeople spoke volumes regarding the hearts and minds of the people of pre-Civil Rights Movement America.

These hiring records produce a spectacle. It is a spectacular accusation that blacks are inferior. Perhaps the justices do not intend to send such a message; nevertheless, the message is sent and read as either-or. The American public gazes on the spectacle, and the spectacle gazes back into them. One comes away "either" convinced that blacks are inferior "or" that the justices are anti-black: 0 in 82, 3 in 61, 1 in 72, 0 in 52, 0 in 49, 0 in 35, 1 in 33, 1 in 24, and 1 in 20 are ways to say that blacks are beyond the pale. This is said also of Latinas/os and Asian Pacific Americans.

At the level of spectacle, the numbers matter a great deal. The justices are not fools, and so they know that numbers matter. When the chief justice of the Supreme Court of the United States of America has a 0 in 82 hiring record against blacks, it says something about the law and the colorline: It says that they are the very same thing.

The numbers do not operate solely at the level of spectacle. They also operate at the level of actual lawmaking. The justices create a world that justifies the spectacle. Why? Because they enjoy the spectacle; they have power, and power means never having to say you're sorry. The Supreme Court would establish this principle during the nation's Bicentennial in *Washington v. Davis* (1976), the same year I took my junior-high-school trip to Washington, D.C.[125]

Numbers as Jurisprudence: In *Washington v. Davis,* the justices were explicit about the need to protect white intuitions regarding quality from equal-protection scrutiny. White hunches about quality produce the spectacle of the colorline. The justices could not have ruled for the plaintiffs in *Washington v. Davis* without ruling against themselves and thus undermining the very spectacle that they had worked so hard to create. Remember that Rehnquist did not create the inexorable zero in one day; he did it in hiring decision after hiring decision after hiring decision.

Perhaps the Supreme Court does not follow the colorline. Perhaps it is the case that writers such as Dinesh D'Souza, Richard Herrnstein, and Charles Murray are right about black inferiority. They have to be right about black inferiority in order for the numbers to be *just.* They have to be right for the numbers to be *just* numbers. D'Souza argues in *The End of Racism* that blacks are *culturally* inferior to whites, while Herrnstein and Murray argue in *The Bell Curve* that blacks are *biologically* inferior to whites.[126] Culture and biology represent the two claims of modern white-supremacist thought. Both claims end in social exile for blacks. Together, they constitute a biocultural territorial claim. This territorial claim, examined legally, is the same claim made by the Supreme Court. It is the same claim made by Al Campanis, then the vice-president of the Dodgers baseball team, on the fortieth anniversary of the desegregation of Major League Baseball. Campanis made his claim on ABC's national television-news program *Nightline:*

> TED KOPPEL: I mean, there are a lot of black players, a lot of great black baseball men who would dearly love to be in managerial positions. And I guess what I'm really asking you is ... why do you think it is? Is there still that much prejudice in baseball today?

CAMPANIS: No, I don't believe it's prejudice. I truly believe that they may not have some of the *necessities* to be, let's say, a field manager or perhaps a general manager.

KOPPEL: You really believe that?

CAMPANIS: Well, I don't say that all of them, but they certainly are short. How many quarterbacks do you have? How many pitchers do you have that are black? The same thing applies.

KOPPEL: Yes, but I mean . . . you know, I got to tell you, that sounds like the same kind of garbage we were hearing forty years ago about players when they were saying. . . .

CAMPANIS: Well.

KOPPEL: You remember the days, you know, hit a black player in the knees, and you know. . . . No—that really sounds like garbage, if you forgive my saying so.

CAMPANIS: No, it's not garbage, Mr. Koppel, because I played on a college team, and the centerfielder was black, and in the backfield at [New York University] with a fullback who was black, never knew the difference in whether he was black or white. We were teammates. So it might be that they . . . why are black people not good swimmers? Because they don't have the buoyancy.

KOPPEL: Oh, I don't—it may just be that they don't have access to all the country clubs and the pools. But I'll tell you what, let's take a break and we'll continue our discussion in a moment.[127]

Campanis argued the numbers did not matter. He explained that just as blacks cannot swim because they have no "buoyancy," they cannot coach baseball because they lack the "necessities." What are the "necessities"? What is it to be the truly qualified? Who knows what evil lurks in the hearts of men? I do not know. Perhaps no one knows. Does "buoyancy," like race, matter? Call *me* Ishmael.

Ironically, Jackie Robinson, the first black person permitted to play in "major league" baseball, and Al Campanis were once teammates. Indeed, Campanis made clear on *Nightline* that *some of his best friends were black.* ("I played on a college team, and the centerfielder was black, and in the backfield at NYU with a fullback who was black, never knew the difference in whether he was black or white. We were teammates"). Campanis's suggestion that blacks lack "buoyancy" seems implausible. It also seems implausible that blacks lack the "necessities" to coach baseball or to be Supreme Court clerks. Finally, it seems implausible that Chief Justice Rehnquist's intellect is simply out of every black person's league. Something else must be at play.

Quality: In *Washington v. Davis* we learn that "Test 21," a test of standard English, had the effect of eliminating a disproportionate number of black test-takers from consideration for employment as police officers in the District of Columbia's Metropolitan Police Department.[128] The eliminated would-be police officers, "Negroes" in the Supreme Court's Bicentennial parlance, filed a lawsuit claiming that they had been denied equal protection. They argued that the use of Test 21 was a violation of equal protection because it bore no relationship to job performance and it had a highly discriminatory impact on black candidates. The District Court sustained Test 21 but agreed that the evidence presented warranted three conclusions: First, the number of black police officers was not proportionate to the population mix of the city; second, a higher percentage of blacks failed Test 21 than whites; third, Test 21 had not been validated to establish its reliability as a measure of subsequent job performance. The Court of Appeals invalidated Test 21, endorsing by its actions the argument that the analysis set forth by the Supreme Court in *Griggs v. Duke*

Power Company (1971) for judging violations of Title VII of the Civil Rights Act of 1964 could be used to analyze violations of equal protection, whether under the Fifth Amendment or the Fourteenth Amendment.[129] In *Griggs v. Duke Power*, the Supreme Court determined that employers were free to use standards of hiring and promotion that had disproportionate effects based on race, provided that they could prove that their standards were a job-related business necessity. In *Washington v. Davis*, the Supreme Court rejected the *Griggs v. Duke Power* Title VII analysis as a method of judging violations of equal protection:

> It is untenable that the Constitution prevents the Government from seeking modestly to upgrade the communicative abilities of its employees rather than to be satisfied with some lower level of competence, particularly where the job requires special ability to communicate orally and in writing.[130]

Thus, the Supreme Court answered the "Negroes" with the very question to be decided. The "Negroes" had sought to force the "Government" to explain why it used Test 21, despite the fact that "four times as many" blacks failed the test than did whites. The court responded by saying that the fairness of the test—and, by implication, the biocultural inferiority of the black test-takers—were self-evident ("it is untenable that . . ."). It is only that which is self-evident that need not be proved or explained. The truth of black inequality was self-evident to the court.

In the history of struggles for land and freedom, explanation of secession has been regarded as a common courtesy. Our own Declaration of Independence (1776), as quoted in *Dred Scott v. Sandford* (1856), informs us that:

> When in the course of human events it becomes necessary for one people to dissolve the political bands that have connected with another, and to assume among the powers of the earth the separate and equal station to which the laws of nature and nature's God entitle them, a decent respect for the opinions of mankind requires that they should declare the causes which impel them to separation.[131]

It then proceeds to say: "We hold these truths to be self-evident: that all men are created equal." The notion that "a decent respect for the opinions of mankind" requires secessionists to explain "the causes which impel them to separation" runs deep in the United States culture. As does the notion that "all men [and women] are created equal."[132] To refuse to explain one's reasons for separation is to show profound disrespect to others. In *Washington v. Davis*, the Supreme Court upheld the right of whites to exclude blacks without explanation.

Washington v. Davis was a case about secession, explanation, and respect. Test 21 effected a separation—secession—of whites from blacks when a disproportionate number of whites passed and a disproportionate number of blacks failed. This secession was a challenge to the idea that "all men [and women] are created equal." The "Negroes," therefore, followed the United States' tradition and asked for an explanation—a declaration of the causes impelling the government towards separation. If the government could "declare the causes which impel them to separation"—that is, if the government could explain that Test 21 was a valid, job-related business necessity—then all parties could feel reconciled to the separation. The "Negroes" asked the Supreme Court to rule that a refusal to "declare the causes" was a violation of equal protection of the laws. The Supreme Court disagreed.

Washington v. Davis seems at odds with the principle of "respect" announced by the Founding Fathers in the Declaration of

Independence and quoted by Justice Roger Brooke Taney in *Dred Scott.* If a test or law or regulation has the effect of excluding those whom the Civil War Amendments were designed to protect, then the principle of "respect" would seem to demand an explanation—a declaration of causes. And an explanation in the form of a validation study was all that the "Negroes" requested. The response that "it is untenable that the Constitution prevents the Government from seeking modestly to upgrade the communicative abilities of its employees" is not a declaration of causes. It is a refusal to declare causes. The history of science is a history of how, once we try to move beyond our hunches, intuitions, and suspicions, the landscape of the "untenable" shifts, and that which we once thought we saw clearly now appears though a lens, darkly. If we return to the Dark Ages, many things become clear again. If we return to Justice Taney's opinion, things become very clear:

> It is too clear for dispute, that the enslaved African race were not intended to be included and formed no part of the people who framed and adopted this Declaration [of Independence].[133]

Then, as now, blacks were not regarded as people to whom "a decent respect" was due. Thus, in *Washington v. Davis* no explanation was provided to the "Negroes," because, per *Dred Scott,* "Negroes" are not people to whom "a decent respect" was due. Justice Taney wrote for the ages, in a language that survived the Civil War and the Civil War Amendments, when he declared of blacks that

> they had for more than a century before [the Declaration of Independence] been regarded as beings of an inferior order, and altogether unfit to associate with the white race, either in social or political relations; and so far inferior, that they had no rights which the white man was bound to respect.[134]

One must, therefore, read *Washington v. Davis* in tandem with the Declaration of Independence and *Dred Scott* in order to understand the ways of the colorline.

Washington v. Davis evokes Sartre's notion that each aspect of the legal order is bound to every other aspect of the legal order and that the law is an ensemble: "There is an underlying tie between the way of accepting and assuming different legal prescriptions (matrimonial, civic, military duties, etc.) and the way of accepting the right to possess slaves. It is the *ensemble* that is respected and recognized."[135] In *Washington v. Davis,* the Supreme Court, in the end, based its opinion on its respect for the ensemble:

> A rule that a statute designed to serve neutral ends is nevertheless invalid, absent compelling justification, if in practice it benefits or burdens one race more than another would be far reaching and would raise serious questions about, and perhaps invalidate, a whole range of tax, welfare, public service, regulatory, and licensing statutes that may be more burdensome to the poor and average black than to the more affluent white.[136]

The spectacle of black exclusion is its own justification: Because blacks are silently excluded from every opportunity ("a whole range of tax, welfare, public service, regulatory and licensing statutes"), they may also be excluded from the police department by an untested test. To require an explanation of the secession effect of Test 21 out of "a decent respect" for the excluded blacks would threaten the entire ensemble ("the whole range"). Seriously questioning the untested tests would threaten the heart of whiteness itself, the Supreme Court.

So the "Negroes" lose their bid to force the "Government" officials to "state causes" and thereby explain whether the disparate impact of Test 21 is a job-related business necessity. The justices all know that their own hiring practices regarding clerks would likely fail to meet their own *Griggs v. Duke Power* standard. Certainly, the spectacle of such whites-only hiring creates the appearance of impropriety. How might Chief Justice Rehnquist explain the inexorable zero?

The ability of white insiders to rely on untested tests is key to the maintenance of the colorline. An untested test is, in the end, a mere hunch, intuition, or suspicion regarding the "necessities." The hunches, intuitions, and suspicions of white insiders regarding the "necessities" or regarding the constitutive elements of quality form the basis for the tests used to determine who gets to become an insider. Most hunches regarding quality are somewhat self-referential. We believe quality to be that which makes us feel well qualified. Given that whites are disproportionately on the inside, white hunches intuitions and suspicions regarding quality will disproportionately become the untested tests. Thus, the whiteness of the workspace tends to replicate itself.

The colorline separates the inside from the outside. The insiders are white, and the outsiders are not. The insiders see themselves as qualified, truly qualified, to be inside. They see themselves as superior. The insiders see blacks as inferior. The insiders enjoy seeing blacks as inferior. They admire their whiteness in the mirror of black inferiority. Through the looking glass of race, whiteness and superiority become the same, and blackness and inferiority become the same. The looking glass—the colorline—cannot be examined, and so it all looks natural. And it is everywhere you look.

The Supreme Court, by protecting white hunches, intuitions, and suspicions from constitutional scrutiny, simultaneously protects its own white hunches, intuitions, and suspicions from constitutional scrutiny. Untested white hunches, intuitions, and suspicions are constitutionally protected from equal-protection challenges.

That is the result of *Washington v. Davis*. Suspicion proves itself: The justices create a world in which numbers cannot be examined and do not have to be explained, and then we blacks, strangers in a strange land, are told to treat this narrow, judicially created landscape of inquiry as "natural." It is only within the narrow confines of this Supreme Court-created space that it makes any sense to be confused about the meaning of *zero*. In any other space, the fact that the chief justice has never hired a black clerk would speak volumes. If the justices had ruled the other way in *Washington v. Davis*, then we would have an understanding that the zero would need to be explained and that the justices would all have some explaining to do.

If the *Griggs v. Duke Power* standard of Title VII disparate-impact analysis were the standard of constitutional equal-protection analysis, then "zero" would be read as "segregation" until and unless the justices explained themselves. The justices chose to close the landscape of inquiry in *Washington v. Davis* in 1976. We cannot ask, and they will not tell.

The justices are not the only ones hard at work in the business of spectacle production. The zeros are everywhere. The justices were aware that they were granting constitutional protection to the production of the spectacle even as they were hiding the production process from judicial (and public) scrutiny. The spectacle, then, is its own justification.

Production Values, or the Situationists Foreshadowed: Blackness is a necessity for whites. Without the spectacle of black inferiority, whites cannot maintain their whiteness. The colorline can be examined as marking the production site for the "necessities" of white existence.

The native bearers of the Tarzan film were burdened with the burdens of classic colonialism: The supplies! We can produce image after image of black bodies swaying under heavy supplies from our collective memory of the colonial moment. The lesions of memory, mystic chords for some, pain us still. Indeed, they pain us most when they throb to the pulse of morning. Today's moment is characterized by nothing so much as the realization that the days of the future are past. Our traditional methods have reaped only the traditional reward of the abyss. Today's native bearers march in a long Lacanian line, bearing on their backs the image of themselves as native bearers. It is the age of the image: The spectacle is the commodity. Perhaps it was always so. Consider the narrative of a black slave who eventually escaped to become a successful businessman by day and a death-defying conductor of the Underground Railroad by night:

> When he saw my work [he] flew into a rage, [and] beat me with a lath with a nail in it, until I had to go to a hospital for slaves. It was kept by a white woman who was inexperienced, and a heartless creature, as she not only neglected her patients, but would beat them unmercifully at the least provocation. I stood by helplessly and watched her beat the helpless. She was beating a woman with a rawhide whip when I protested. Instantly, [she] struck me across the face. Without a thought of what I was doing, I seized the whip and gave the white woman a sound beating, then ran out of the house, knowing full well what would happen to me if I was caught.... I stole on board the New Orleans steamer, and launched myself on an adventure that carried [me] into strange places and stranger incidents.[137]

Parker broke with his master and with the spectacle by taking a leap of faith. Dietrich Bonhoeffer, a German theologian who was martyred for violent resistance to the Third Reich, wrote of such faith:

> They must burn their boats and plunge into absolute insecurity in order to learn the demand and the gift of Christ.... The new *situation* must be created, in which it is possible to believe in Jesus as God incarnation; that is the impossible situation in which everything is staked solely on the word of Jesus.... Unless a definite step is demanded, the call vanishes into thin air, and if men imagine that they can follow Jesus without taking this step, they are deluding themselves like fanatics.[138]

Parker followed the call and understood the cost of discipleship. Parker had an understanding. He understood that for whites, his black body was both a product and a passion. He took his definite step to interrupt the economy of the spectacle. Consider his remarks on recapture:

> I was worth $1,800. For one to run away meant a loss of that much money, and anyone who aided me was a thief, worse than a thief, because he was an enemy to the institution of slavery. So the hand of the law, the anger of the people, and the consolidated fear of the south were all in a hot cry after anyone who helped to break down their institutions.[139]

And break them down we must. All of them—the entire ensemble. Like Bonhoeffer, Parker had a decidedly Situationist bent:

> Being of an active mind, I occupied myself by working out imaginary plans of escape. For the ten months I was in jail, I worked out these problems until formulating certain theories which were of great use to me later on. For instance, I soon demonstrated that a man with a plan always had the advantage of an unsuspecting person. Second, timing of execution was even more important than a plan. There were certain positions which were blind spots to my captors. If I occupied one of these blind spots, if I timed my next movement correctly, I could do anything up to murder without my victim knowing of my presence. It

became a sort of a play with me, which I enjoyed, because I made the white man helpless against me.[140]

The Society of the Spectacle holds us fast.

Black exclusion is a product. The race-pleasure whites derive from this product is the key to understanding the economy of the Spectacle. Black pain under neo-segregation is as *desired* a product under neo-segregation as it was under classic segregation and as under slavery. The neo-colony is designed to produce the spectacle of well-deserved black subalternation. In the green light of this spectacle, whites feel themselves as white. It is, for them, an ecstatic moment of belonging both to and in their spectacle-beatified bodies. It is, as they know, an ecstasy that can be achieved only through the black body in pain. It is a sadistic pleasure. They shout, "The supplies!" to herald the orgasmic disappearance of black bodies into the swirling vortex of colorlined need.

"The supplies!" The ensemble repeats the number of our name in the statistics it presses deep into our bodies. They use us for their pleasure and leave us with violence, narcotics, illiteracy, illegitimacy, and disease. We are blamed for the results of their abuse. And, marked with these numbers like the surplus population of the Third Reich, we work to make ourselves free. The freedom we are allowed is freedom only to manufacture ourselves as available bodies—as bodies available for humiliation. White America needs black suffering to maintain its whiteness. The legal system arranges the choreography of this dance. Law and order means that they lead and we follow. We follow the colorline all the way to the abyss.

The nation—the ensemble of law—animates our bodies. Our bodies have a legal structure: To be black is to be available for humiliation, to be white is to partake of race-pleasure, and to be colorblind is to repress all awareness of the entire. The colorline depends on all three aspects—humil-iation, pleasure and denial—for its power. We are "The supplies!" The ensemble creates the spectacle. Jurisprudence, as we have seen with *Washington v. Davis,* is one aspect of the spectacle's eternal hymn of self-praise. How and when do we stop singing for the master? Is there an end to this song and dance?

Toward a Situationist Jurisprudence

Introducing the Situationists

> Sartre begins *Orphee Noir* thus: "What did you expect when you unbound the gag that had muted those black mouths? That they would chant your praises? Did you think that when those heads that our fathers had forcibly bowed to the ground were raised again, you would find adoration in their eyes?" I do not know; but I say that he who looks into my eyes for anything but a question will have to lose his sight; neither recognition nor hate.
> —Frantz Fanon[141]

Our break with the spectacle must be total. We have failed to advance beyond the failure of the Civil Rights Movement for the same reason that the Civil Rights Movement failed: We have been mesmerized by the spectacle: "So we beat on, boats against the current, borne back ceaselessly into the past." The spectacle, like Gatsby's green light, has been our downfall. It is time for something completely different. The Situationists emerged in 1957 and published a journal, *Internationnale Situationiste,* until 1969. Borrowing from Marxist thought and from art movements such as Dada and Surrealism, they were angry at everything:

> A new spirit is rising. Like the streets of Watts we burn with revolution. We assault your Gods. We sing of your death. DESTROY THE MUSEUMS.... Our struggle cannot be hung on walls. Let the past fall under the blows of revolt. The guerrilla, the blacks, the men of the

future, we are all at your heels. Goddamn your culture, your science, your art.[142]

The Situationists made no claims to originality; in fact, they celebrated plagiarism. Everything, every societal given, could be subverted. *Détournement* (turnaround, diversion, subversion or hijacking), the reuse of old concepts in a new formation, was their watchword. For the Situationists, nothing was inevitable because everything could be hijacked:

> A new dynamism exists. One which has followed Futurism, Dadaism and Surrealism to a point where they must be left behind. Where they attempted to revolutionize "art" we must change life. We seek a form of action which transcends the separation between art and politics: it is the act of revolution. Each culture determines those forms its art will take and we seek nothing less than the destruction of this culture. We have an art which is a substitute for living, a culture which is an excuse for the utter poverty of life. The call for revolution can be no less than "total." To change the wielders of power is not enough, we must finally change life itself.[143]

They explained *détournement*, as "a game made possible by the capacity of devaluation."[144] Their revolution aimed at a complete *détournement* of the order of things symbolic and real—"all the elements of the cultural past must be reinvested or disappear."[145] Sadie Plant writes: "The notion of *détournement* was first developed by the Belgian surrealist Marcel Mariën ... [who] described *détournement* as a sort of embezzlement of convention."[146] The Situationists were convinced that

> the poetry and desire revealed by the détournement of the language of information, bureaucracy, and functional control was vital to the success of the revolutionary project, the situationist proposed a situationist dictionary as "a sort of codebook enabling one to deci-

pher information and rend the ideological veils that cover reality," and considered it "essential that we forge our own language, the language of real life."[147]

Because every convention could be turned around, "real life," for the Situationists, was a canvas on which anything could be painted. The Situationists endeavored to change life itself through a total assault on culture.

The chief theoretical contribution of the Situationists was their characterization of modern capitalist society as an accumulation of spectacles in which "all that once was directly lived has become mere representation."[148] In modern society, they proclaimed, all social relationships are mediated by images. Guy Debord writes: "The spectacle is not a collection of images; rather, it is a social relationship between people that is mediated by images."[149] It was this phenomenon of mediation that they labeled as the spectacle:

> Used from the very first as a term to designate contemporary culture—French: *spectacle*, a circus, a show, an exhibition— a one-way transmission of experience; a form of "communication" to which one side, the audience, can never reply; a culture based on the reduction of almost everyone to a state of abject non-creativity: of receptivity, passivity and isolation.[150]

The Situationists borrowed Marx's idea of commodity fetishism, the idea that relations of capital are reproduced in all social relations, and went further. They investigated the way in which our very identities and desires have been transformed into spectacle. We are seduced by the representations of our lives; we view ourselves through representations of ourselves, which, not surprisingly, vindicate the social order, the Society of the Spectacle, which bore them:

> The spectator's alienation from and submission to the contemplated object

(which is the outcome of his unthinking activity) works like this: the more he contemplates, the less he lives; the more readily he recognizes his own needs in the images of need proposed by the dominant system, the less he understands his own existence and his own desires. The spectacle's externality with respect to the acting subject is demonstrated by the fact that the individual's own gestures are no longer his own, but rather those of someone else who represents them to him. The spectator feels at home nowhere, for the spectacle is everywhere.[151]

We gaze on the spectacle, and the spectacle gazes back. The spectacle becomes a mirror as we constitute ourselves out of that which it presents us.[152]

Resistance is futile.[153] Even as we fight against control, "we" fight as subaltern, spectacularized identity groups. We are all, to a large degree, composed of the very hegemonic structures against which we battle. We thus end up performing our alienation, and thus internalizing the spectacle, even during our attempts at dis-alienation.[154]

Debord argued that, just as capitalism's domination of social life entailed a downgrading of being into having, so, too, has the present age of the spectacle entailed a shift from having to appearing:

> The spectacle corresponds to the historical moment at which the commodity completes its colonization of social life. It is not just that the relationship to commodities is now plain to see—commodities are now all that there is to see; the world we see is the world of the commodity.[155]

The spectacle is neither a distortion nor a decorative element. Rather,

> it is the very heart of society's real unreality. In all its specific manifestations—news or propaganda, advertising or the actual consumption of entertainment—the spectacle epitomizes the prevailing mode of social life. It is the omnipresent celebration of a choice already made in the sphere of production, and the consummate result of that choice. In form as in content the spectacle serves as total justification for the conditions and aims of the existing system.[156]

Everything in the Society of the Spectacle is an instance of the system representing itself. Our bodies are spectacles. The racial body, the foreign body, the gendered body, the sexed body, the sexually oriented body—all are spectacles. Our relationships to one another and to ourselves are all mediated by the spectacle. We see one another, and ourselves, through the spectacle of race, nation, gender, sex, and sexual orientation. These spectacles come with imperatives that, being hidden within, remain beyond critique, as with *Washington v. Davis*. Our identities are desires inculcated in us by the spectacle.

Our identities—that is, the desires around which we form our identities—are alien desires. The spectacle replicates itself in "a ceaseless manufacture of pseudo-needs," like Gatsby's green light.[157] The spectacle thus reduces us to passive spectators and bit actors in situations not of our own making. The spectacle becomes hyper-real as we gaze on it to find ourselves and one another. We try to gain acceptance and find our exclusion to be a desired thing. Black exclusion is a commodity. The spectacle of black inferiority, which justifies black exclusion, is a commodity. We, in our excluded bodies, our inferior bodies, our bodies-without-buoyancy, our bodies-without-the-necessities, our bodies-without-respect, our colorlined bodies, our black bodies, our bodies-in-pain, are commodities. Whites become and stay white by consuming the spectacle of our pain.

The spectacle is not limited. The spectacle is the entire field of vision, and the field is the world. We see one another only through the lens of desires, such as race, inculcated in us by the spectacle. Why do we not tear the whole thing down? Because we have come to believe in the green light. Like an addiction, the "orgastic future" becomes our identity. We think we can Overcome the obstacles in the path selected for us by the spectacle if only, if only, if only.... We believe that our work will make us free, but the reality is that

> the pusher always gets it all back. The addict needs more and more junk to maintain a human form ... to buy off the Monkey. Junk is the mold of monopoly and possession. Junk is the ideal product ... the ultimate merchandise. No sales talk necessary.... The junk merchant does not sell his product to the consumer, he sells the consumer to his product.[158]

The spectacle, like the pusher, always wins. The green light is the way the system "sells the consumer to [its] product." In thinking about the spectacle, the Situationists anticipated the postmodern view that

> we live in the midst of codes, messages, and images which produce and reproduce our lives. These may have had their origins in commodity production, but have since won their independence and usurped its role in the maintenance of social relations. All that remains is the pleasure of playing in the fragments, the disruption and resistance of the codes in which we live, the jouissance of realizing that the search for meaning is endlessly deferred and has no point of arrival and in the absence of new movements, styles, or genres, the continual reiteration of those of the past.[159]

The Situationist project was optimistic. Even the inevitability of defeat was transformed into the perpetual opportunity for revolution. The graffiti of Paris 1968, when Situationist and Situationist-inspired students (enragés) and workers united to capture the universities, the city, and the attention of the world, shows their joy:[160]

- All power to the imagination.
- Be realistic, demand the impossible.
- No replastering, the structure is rotten.
- Forget everything you've been taught. Start by Dream.
- Masochism today takes the form of reformism.
- All power to the worker's councils (an enragé).
- All power to the enraged (a worker).[161]

Total revolt was their goal as they endeavored to create an oppositionist culture that revolved around the pleasure of disruption. Seven aphorisms to create a new world.

A New Cathedral

> So man's insanity is heaven's sense; and wandering from all mortal reason, man comes at last to that celestial thought, which, to reason, is absurd and frantic; and weal or woe, feels then uncompromised, indifferent as his God.
> —Herman Melville[162]

Power, in the form of "codes, messages, and images which produce and reproduce our lives," as Plant writes, exists everywhere. The Foucauldean vision of relationships of power being immanent in every relationship is important in understanding what is meant by the Situationist notion of total critique. Foucault writes:

> There is no single locus of great Refusal, no soul of revolt, source of all rebellions, or pure law of the revolutionary. Instead there is a plurality of resistances, each of them a special case: resistances that are possible, necessary, improbable; others that are spontaneous, savage, solitary, concerted, rampant, or violent; still others that are quick to compromise, interested, or sacrificial; by definition, they can only exist in the strategic field of power relations. But this does not mean that they are only a reaction or rebound, forming with respect to the basic domination an underside that is in the end

always passive, doomed to perpetual defeat. Resistances do not derive from a few heterogeneous principles; but neither are they a lure or a promise that is of necessity betrayed. They are the odd term in relations of power; they are inscribed in the latter as an irreducible opposite. Hence they too are distributed in irregular fashion: the points, knots, or focuses of resistance are spread over time and space at varying densities, at times mobilizing groups or individuals in a definitive way, inflaming certain points of the body, certain moments in life, certain types of behavior.[163]

The Situationists' total critique was not a "great refusal" so much as it was an attitude of polymorphic resistance, as shown by a Columbia University flyer that read:

UNTIL OUR MOST FANTASTIC DEMANDS ARE MET, FANTASY WILL BE AT WAR WITH SOCIETY. SOCIETY WILL ATTEMPT THE SUPPRESSION OF FANTASY, BUT FANTASY WILL SPRING UP AGAIN AND AGAIN, INFECTING THE YOUTH, WAGING URBAN GUERRILLA WARFARE, SABOTAGING THE SMOOTH FUNCTIONING OF BUREAUCRACIES, WAYLAYING THE TYPIST ON HER WAY TO THE WATER-COOLER, KIDNAPPING THE EXECUTIVE BETWEEN OFFICE AND HOME, CREEPING INTO THE BEDROOMS OF RESPECTABLE FAMILIES, HIDING IN THE CHAMBERS OF HIGH OFFICE, GRADUALLY TIGHTENING ITS CONTROL, EVENTUALLY EMERGING INTO THE STREETS, WAGING PITCHED BATTLES AND WINNING (ITS VICTORY IS INEVITABLE).

WE ARE THE VANGUARD OF FANTASY.

WHERE WE LIVE IS LIBERATED TERRITORY IN WHICH FANTASY MOVES ABOUT FREELY AT ALL HOURS OF THE DAY, FROM WHICH IT MOUNTS ITS ATTACKS ON OCCUPIED TERRITORY.[164]

Disruption is always possible, "détournement ... confirms the thesis, long demonstrated by modern art, of the insubordination of words, of the impossibility for power to totally recuperate created meanings, to fix an existing meaning once and for all; in

a word, the objective impossibility of a 'Newspeak.'"[165]

This chapter has focused on the sensual aspects of colorlined encounters, in textual and other spaces, in an endeavor to explore the power-knowledge-pleasure spiral at the heart of what we call "race relations." The Situationist concept of *détournement* shows us that no one, no group, can be permanently "orientalized."[166] There are always what Duncan Kennedy calls "gaps, conflicts and ambiguities" in the spectacle that can be turned around, diverted, subverted, or hijacked and used as anti-spectacle.[167] The Situationists were determined to create a culture based on opposition to the spectacle. A Situationist jurisprudence could be the most radical gesture of all. We need to demand everything and to demand it everywhere and to demand it at once:

We need to work toward flooding the market—even if for the moment merely the intellectual market—with a mass of desires whose realization is not beyond the capacity of man's present means of action on the material world, but only beyond the capacity of the old social organization.[168]

Theory is valuable only insofar as it constitutes such a propaganda of desire:

We know with what blind fury so many unprivileged people are ready to defend their mediocre advantages. Such pathetic illusions of privilege are linked to a general idea of happiness prevalent among the bourgeoisie and maintained by a system of publicity that includes Malraux's aesthetics as well as the imperatives of Coca-Cola—an idea of happiness whose crisis must be provoked on every occasion by every means.[169]

Situationist jurisprudence ought always to provoke a crisis in any system of desire that leaves us blinded by the green light. We may, at this juncture, recall the sweet songs of the Civil Rights Movement that introduced this chapter:

> At S&W one day, we will all buy a coke and the waitress will serve us we'll know its no joke, hallelujah I'm a-travelin', hallelujah ain't it fine, hallelujah I'm a-travelin' down freedom's main line.

We must provoke a crisis in the system of desire constituted by the "imperatives of Coca-Cola" that so moved the motionless movement for civil fights.

Two ideas were key to the Situationists' oppositionist culture—psychogeography and the *dérive* (drift). Situationist jurisprudence would be a jurisprudence of psychogeography and drift. Drift was "a mode of experimental behavior linked to the conditions of urban society: a technique of transient passage through varied ambiences."[170] The Situationists proposed a culture based on continuous drift. The term "psychogeography" was proposed as a general term for the phenomena being investigated by drifting. Psychogeography was to set for itself the study of the "effects of the geographical environment, consciously organized or not, on the emotions and behavior of individuals."[171]

In 1953, Ivan Chtcheglov, then nineteen years old, completed a manifesto entitled, "Formula for a New Urbanism." Chtcheglov's work, written under the pseudonym Gilles Ivain, remained unpublished until it appeared in the very first issue of the journal *Internationnalle Situationiste* in 1957, just a few years before its author would be confined to a mental hospital.[172] Chtcheglov proclaimed that once the Hacienda, the new experimental city, had been built,

> everyone will live in [her] own cathedral. There will be rooms awakening more vivid fantasies than any drug. There will be houses where it will be impossible not to fall in love.[173]

Architecture was described as "the simplest means of articulating time and space, of mod-

ulating reality, of engendering dreams."[174] Architecture in the Hacienda was to become a way of "constructing situations" that would bring to light "forgotten desires" and create "entirely new ones."[175] The construction of Situations was the movement's defining activity:

> What does the word "situationist" mean?
> It denotes an activity that aims at making situations, as opposed to passively recognizing them in academic or other separate terms. This at all levels of social practice or individual history. We replace existential passivity with the construction of moments in life, and doubt with playful affirmation. So far philosophers and artists have only interpreted situations; the point now is to transform them. Since man is the product of the situation he goes through, it is essential to create human situations. Since the individual is defined by his situation, he wants the power to create situations worthy of his desires.[176]

The principal activity of the Hacienda's inhabitants was to be continuous drift. Drifting was to be their work and their play. Their continuous drift would be aided by the fact that the "changing of landscapes from one hour to the next [would] result in complete disorientation."[177]

The Hacienda was to be a city of games. Consider the following tract from the anarchist Black Mask group:

> LET US AVOID ALL THE LEADS TO NIGGERHOOD

> Stay on the right side of the TV set: watch them little black mothers running their ass off, undignified but athletic, knocking things over, getting clubbed stupid. They have a nigger fate in store for them. Getting beat is good for niggers. It confirms their niggerhood. It fits in with ghettoes, junk, filthy ugly tenements. Niggers get beat all the time. Look at that one, running, caught, sullen, not saying anything.... We could never be sullen like that. We know what his fate is.

He will become more and more nigger until he either kills himself, or is killed: both fates amounting essentially to the same.

WE WANT TO PLAY GAMES

Games are liberating.
Games are Utopian.
We become embodied in doing. But doing is a trap. One is forced to choose between a doing which is not a doing, a doing which does not have the feel of doing, a doing which does on their level of unreality; and, on the other hand a doing which is a breaking away from that level, a doing which is liberating ... and for which you get your head busted. No other alternatives: trapped in a nigger trap in spite of ourselves.[178]

The black body is shown as spectacle in this tract. One cannot escape "good Negro" ("a doing which is not a doing ... which does not have the feel of doing ... which does on their level of unreality") or the bad Negro ("a doing which is liberating ... and for which you get your head busted"). The spectacle of the black body recasts the body's struggle against oppression as "black" struggles against oppression. This transformation guarantees the colorline's survival, whatever the outcome of the struggle ("He will become more and more nigger until he either kills himself, or is killed: both fates amounting essentially to the same"). Even in struggle, one either plays the role of the crossover "good Negro" and fails, or one plays the "bad Negro" role of barbarian at the gate and fails—one fails to destroy the spectacle. In a lyrical essay that appeared in a 1963 volume titled, *White on Black: The Views of Twenty-two White Americans on the Negro*, Sarah Patton Boyle writes:

I personally think that the Good Negro is a wish-fulfillment image—an ideal, a longing made flesh. Everything about him comforts white Southerners, even his faults, which give them a feeling of moral status, a pleasant awareness of

their own high standards. As truly as the Southern white loves his Good Negro image, he hates his Bad Negro image. Again, anybody would. The Bad Negro is not really a man, but a repulsive, dangerous, sub-human creature with no feelings or standards of decency. He wallows in degradation, lives in burning lust for "pure, white" bodies.[179]

Both roles are identity traps. The racialized identity, the font of oppression, survives even in the bodies and souls of the enemies of the colorline. Undoing this trap requires an imaginative leap beyond the rules. This is what the Situationists meant by games. Such games or disorientations are necessary, for it is only when the word "black" cannot be understood that oppression by "race" will be fatally undermined.[180]

Debord describes one such game: "The production of psychogeographic maps, or even the introduction of alterations such as more or less arbitrarily transposing maps of different regions, can contribute to clarifying certain wanderings that express not subordination to randomness but complete insubordination to habitual influences."[181] The Situationists wanted to play games, such as wandering down a London street using a map of Paris, that would expose new possibilities hidden within once-familiar-sights-made-strange by our willed disorientation.[182] With the Situationists, Dada and surrealism moved to the broader canvas of life itself. In Debord's words: "That which changes our way of seeing the streets is more important than [that which] changes our way of seeing a painting."[183]

Chtcheglov's Hacienda was not a Utopia.

Utopias afford consolation: although they have no real locality there is nevertheless a fantastic, untroubled region in which they are able to unfold; they open up cities with vast avenues, superbly planted gardens, countries where life is easy, even though the road to them is chimerical.[184]

The Hacienda was to be what Foucault describes as a "heterotopia":

> Heterotopias are disturbing, probably because they secretly undermine language, because they make it impossible to name this and that, because they shatter or tangle common names, because they destroy "syntax" in advance, and not only the syntax with which we construct sentences but also that less apparent syntax which causes words and things (next to and also opposite one another) to "hold together." That is why utopias permit fables and discourse: they run with the very grain of language ... heterotopias ... desiccate speech, stop words in their tracks, contest the very possibility of grammar at its source; they dissolve our myths and sterilize the lyricism of our sentences.[185]

Chtcheglov's Hacienda was less a building plan than an architectural metaphor for a political idea: "the application of this will to playful creation ... to all known forms of human relationships."[186]

The Hacienda was a new form of human existence based on the embrace of a disorder

> worse than that of the incongruous, the linking together of things that are inappropriate; I mean the disorder in which fragments of a large number of possible orders glitter separately in the dimension, without law or geometry, of the heteroclite; and that word should be taken in its most literal, etymological sense; in such a state, things are "laid", "placed", "arranged" in sites so very different from one another that it is impossible to find a place of residence for them, to define a common locus between them all.[187]

The Situationists' Hacienda was an architectural metaphor for the celebration of what Foucault would later call the "insurrection of subjugated knowledges."[188] Subjugated knowledges take two forms. First are the historical contents of discourse that are masked by the dominant paradigm. This includes the resistances, struggles, and dominations in events and practices that have been subsumed in theoretical frameworks or universalist theories. This type of subjugated knowledge comprises the hidden histories of conflict that preceded the emergence of the dominant paradigm—for example, the history of violent, as opposed to non-violent, struggles against slavery, segregation, and neo-segregation.[189]

Second are the "naive" or "unruly" knowledges. These are forms of knowledge that have been disqualified, taken less than seriously, taken as irrelevant, or deemed inadequate by official histories. For example, the science fiction, short stories, personal reflections of a subaltern author. The discourses of the abyss—the mentally ill, the physically ill, the delinquent, the pervert, and other people, such as the native bearer, who hold knowledge that deviates from the established categories. The celebration of such counter-memories is a celebration of the Hacienda. The Hacienda was the Situationist dream of a permanent insurrection of subjugated knowledges. In sum, the constant pursuit of revolutionary paths not taken was given an imaginary architectural form in the Hacienda.

Nobodyness

"When I was a young man full of wildness and ideas, I read all the books from France by a man named Jules Verne. I see you know his name. But at night I many times thought I must be an inventor. That is all gone by; I never did what I thought I might do. But I remember clearly that one of the machines I wished to put together was a machine that would help every man, for an hour, to be like any other man. The machine was full of colors and smells and it had film in it, like a theater, and the machine was like a coffin. You lay in it. And you touched a button. And for an hour you could be one of those Eskimos in the cold wind up there, or you could be an Arab gentleman on a horse. Everything a New York man felt, you could feel. Everything a man from China tasted, your tongue knew. The machine was like another man—do you see what I was after? And by touching many of the buttons, each time you got into my machine, you could be a white man or a yellow man or a Negrito. You could be a child or a woman, even, if you wished to be very funny.'" The husband and wife climbed from the car. "Did you ever try to invent that machine?" "It was so very long ago. I had forgotten until today. And today I was thinking, we could make use of it, we are in need of it. What a shame I never tried to put it all together. Someday some other man will do it." "Some day," said John Webb. "It has been a pleasure talking with you," said the old man. "God go with you." "Adios, Señor Garcia," they said.

    —Ray Bradbury[190]

This chapter takes the form of the Hacienda. I celebrate "the insurrection of subjugated knowledges" by drifting, in a Situationist style, through the imaginary walls that separate the various discourses of nobodyness. This drift begins with the colorline. The experience of being cast/e down is not limited to the experience of being raced. I begin with the experience of colonialism. Memmi, in his introduction to the 1963 French edition of James Baldwin's *The Fire Next Time*, wrote:

> We have now learned that oppressed people resemble each other. Their own peculiar features and individual history aside, colonized peoples, Jews, women, the poor show a kind of family likeness; all bear a burden which leaves the same bruises on their soul, and similarly distorts their behavior. A like suffering often produces similar gestures, similar expressions of pain, the same inner paroxysms, the same agony or the same revolt.[191]

Each form of nobodyness sheds light on the others, if only by showing that none is a naturally occurring category and things could, therefore, be otherwise. The idea of "natural" differences is one of the masks of

power. Hierarchies created by society are insulated from criticism by a natural-seemingness born of myths, stories, science, rules of propriety and decorum, notions of personal identity, ideas of virtue, and forms of pleasure.

Hegemony is the ability to contain class antagonisms on a terrain in which one's legitimacy cannot be dangerously questioned.[192] "Natural difference" and the untested tests by which it is said to be discovered is such a terrain for white power because the "natural" marks the boundary of that which may not be dangerously questioned. Just as a Situationist *dérive* through London via a map of Paris liberates us from our usual ways of seeing architecture, an examination of the colorline through a different lens liberates us from our usual ways of seeing ourselves and one another. Such drifts often free us to make "the most radical gesture." The most radical gesture is that which transgresses against the idea of the natural or given or obvious. The response of the Zapatista Army of National Liberation to a reporter's query as to whether Subcommandante Marcos was gay demonstrated a strategic deployment of this transgressive notion:

> Marcos is gay in San Francisco, black in South Africa, an Asian in Europe, a Chicano in San Ysidro, an anarchist in Spain, a Palestinian in Israel, a Mayan Indian in the streets of San Cristobal, a gang member in Neza, a rocker in the National University, a Jew in Germany, an ombudsman in the Defense Ministry, a Communist in the post-Cold War era, an artist without gallery or portfolio, a pacifist in Bosnia, a housewife alone on a Saturday night in any neighborhood in any city in Mexico, a reporter writing filler stories for the back pages, a single woman on the subway at ten P.M., a peasant without land, an unemployed worker, a dissident amid free-market economists, a writer without books or readers, and, of course, a Zapatista in the mountains of southeast Mexico.[193]

The Zapatista parable mocks the idea of hierarchy itself. It avoids narrow nationalism and instead deploys the idea of family likeness to show twenty-one disparate masks of power. In each of the twenty-one antagonisms, power wears the mask of false necessity. The particular rituals of exclusion that produced each of the twenty-one forms of nobodyness have their own histories, as do the forms of resistance raised up against them, but each contest sheds light on other contests by showing their social, as opposed to natural, origins. The Zapatista uprising is a poetic embrace of "the insurrection of subjugated knowledges" and a celebration, like this chapter, of "the linking together of things that are inappropriate."[194] This "family likeness" of which Memmi writes stems from the common struggle to remove the idea of the natural from the flesh of the subaltern body.

The struggle, then, is not merely against one's masters, but against oneself. The struggle is to eliminate the existence of the subaltern as a social role or character structure. The roles or character structures noted in the Zapatista parable as gay, black, Asian, Chicano, anarchist, Palestinian, Mayan, gang member, rocker, Jew, ombudsman, Communist, artist, pacifist, housewife, reporter, woman, peasant, unemployed, dissident, and writer are all identity formations through which we struggle. Foucault discusses this idea of struggling through a subaltern identity formation in relation to the social construction of homosexuality. He notes that when sexuality was subjected to the medical and jurisprudential gaze, the "homosexual" emerged as a form of "perversity."[195] But that very label also made possible a "reverse discourse," or, to use the language of the Situationists, a *détournement*, whereby the "homosexuals" could speak for themselves:

> [We see homosexuals] taking such discourses literally, and thereby turning them about; we see responses arising in

the form of defiance: "All right, we are what you say we are—by nature, disease or perversion, as you like. Well, if that's what we are, let's be it, and if you want to know what we are, we can tell you ourselves better than you can." . . . It is the strategic turnabout of one and the "same" will to truth.[196]

The sexually oriented body, like each of the identities listed in the Zapatista quote, can be turned about and used against its manufacturers. A turn-about can also take the form of presenting the Supreme Court with its own statistical profile on the matter of race. Finally, a turn-about can take the form of using legal discourse to show the futility of legal discourse. This final turn-about is a way of delegitimizing the notion of gradual, orderly, and peaceful change. It is also a form of legitimating the radical actions of those who cannot wait any longer.

And, perhaps, the "will to truth" itself may be turned about.

If These Teardrops Had Wings

Angel of mercy whisk me away.
Sweep me into tomorrow so that this
    day is done.
We'd be finished with goodbye hearts
    already broken not
used to the lonely but one day along.
    —Vance Gilbert[197]

A full month after August 6, people said, corpses lay wherever you went in the city, skeletons were everywhere, and a nauseating smell blanketed the city. Flies were all over the place, as if someone had scattered red beans; the flies were so dense in the burned streetcars running in some parts of the city that they turned the passengers' skin pitch black; big black flies swarmed hideously, particularly on the faces of babies. Flies even got inside those aluminum lunch boxes with the tight lids and expired atop the rice.
    —Ota Yoko[198]

Some harms are irreparable. Sometimes we cannot "finish with goodbye," as in the song by Vance Gilbert. The colorline is such a harm. Our desire for the green light is a way of averting our eyes from the horrifying irreparability of it all. We want to believe that it is possible to mend our broken hearts. What if one bright day we suddenly Overcame? What would our world look like without the colorline? The question itself is incoherent because it assumes that we are somehow separate from the world. It assumes that the world could be the world without the colorline. It assumes that the world of the colorline is any less broken than our hearts.

Bradbury's short story "The Other Foot" illustrates the ways in which our notions of the everyday world are bounded by its irreparability and its unthinkability. It is set in the future:

> When they heard the news they came out of the restaurants and cafes and hotels and looked at the sky. They lifted their dark hands over their upturned white eyes. Their mouths hung wide. In the hot noon for thousands of miles there were little towns where the dark people stood with their shadows under them, looking up.[199]

The blacks of "Way in the Middle of the Air" are now residents of Mars: "'They say a rocket's coming, first one in twenty years, with a white man in it?' 'What's a white man? I never seen one." The young children are excited at the prospect of a stranger in the village, but the elders remember:

> "What right they got coming up here this late? Why don't they leave us in peace? Why didn't they blow themselves up on that old world and let us be?" "Willie, that ain't no Christian way to talk." "I'm not feeling Christian," he said savagely, gripping the wheel. "I'm just feeling mean. After all them years of doing what they did to our folks—my mom and dad, and your mom and dad—You remember?"[200]

Willie Johnson remembers, as do others, and they plan as they go to meet the white man:

> "The Shoe's on the other foot now. We'll see who gets laws passed against him, who gets lynched, who rides in the back of streetcars, who gets segregated in shows. We'll just wait and see."[201]

He remembers home, he remembers that "Home is where the hatred is:

> "Have you thought, Willie?" "That's all I done for twenty years. I was sixteen when I left Earth, and I was glad to leave," he said. "There wasn't anything there for me or you or anybody like us. I've never been sorry I left. We've had peace here, the first time we ever drew a *solid* breath."[202]

Willie Johnson's talk of land and freedom and the solidity of breath evokes Fanon's discussion of French Colonialism in Algeria:

> It is not the soil that is occupied. It is not the ports or the airdromes. French colonialism has settled itself in the very center of the Algerian individual and has undertaken a sustained work of cleanup, of expulsion of self, of rationally pursued mutilation. There is not an occupation of territory, on the one hand, and independence of persons on the other. It is the country as a whole, its history, its daily pulsation that are contested, disfigured, in the hope of final destruction. Under these conditions, the individual's breathing is an observed, an occupied breathing. It is combat breathing.[203]

A "delegation" is formed to "paint every streetcar," and volunteers come forward to make their new desire for segregation a reality with "the fresh glinting yellow words: For Whites: Rear Section." Delegations segregate theaters and stores: "Limited Clientele: Right to serve customer revocable at any time." The people feel themselves becoming masters through the erection of more and more legal signs of mastery:

> "Oh yes. We got to pass a law this afternoon; no intermarriages!" "That's right," said a lot of people. "All shoeshine boys quit their jobs today." "Quittin' right

now!" Some men threw down the rags they carried, in their excitement, all across town. "Got to pass a minimum wage law, don't we?" "Sure!" "Pay them white folks at least ten cents an hour."[204]

When the mayor accuses him of forming a "mob," Willie Johnson answers, "We'll have an election and get a new mayor."[205] The law's desires and the mob's desires are the same. They will elect a new government, and they will enact a complex racial choreography for everyday life. People will have their legal roles branded into their flesh by the various punishments and rewards of law. The law will be its own justification as it merges with our flesh. We become the legal roles we are assigned. The entire ensemble will sing the praises of the Spectacle. Those who worship the Rule of Law are those whose desires have already been textualized as the rule of law.

The moment arrives.[206] "Across the sky, very high and beautiful, a rocket burned on a sweep of orange fire. A white man emerges from the rocket, and his voice was very tired and old and pale:

> After you left the War came. We bombed all of the cities of the world. We destroyed New York and London and Moscow and Paris and Shanghai and Bombay and Alexandria. We ruined it all. And when we finished with the big cities we went to the little cities and atom-bombed and burned them.[207]

All the sites of their humiliation have been destroyed: "So we destroyed everything and ruined everything, like fools that we were and the fools that we are. We killed millions."[208]

The entire Earth, the former home of the blacks-when-they-were-blacks, is a city of corpses. The whites have been defeated by their own lives and by their own internal contradictions. In "And the Rock Cried Out," another Bradbury story on this theme, we read:

OCTOBER 4TH, 1963: UNITED STATES, EUROPE SILENT?

> The radios of the U.S.A. and Europe are dead. There is a great silence. The War has spent itself. It is believed that most of the populations of the United States is dead. It is believed that most of Europe, Russia, and Siberia, are equally decimated.
> The day of the white people of the earth is over and finished.[209]

The old white man from the rocket speaks of an utterly abject homeworld; moreover, he speaks from the subject position of utter abjection:

> We deserve anything you want to do to us, but don't shut us out. We can't force you to act now. If you want I'll get into my ship and go back and that will be all there is to it. We won't bother you again. But we'll come here and we'll work for you and do the things you did for us—clean your houses, cook your meals, shine your shoes, and humble ourselves in the sight of God for the things we have done over the centuries to ourselves, to others, to you.[210]

Groveling does not save the whites. Nothing can save them. Whether one stays or departs from the city of corpses, from the place of the inconsolable, matters little. The damage has already been done. The few survivors left on Earth are, says the old white man, "of all kinds and types." But it cannot be the happy rainbow of the flood. To see this white man, we must imagine ourselves as the ethnographers "discovering" this new race, *homo atomicus*:

> What stunned me was the indescribably eerie color of his skin. The skin all over his body was like someone in the last stages of tuberculosis, and that color had been painted over wit a more hopeless color, opaque like that of roasted eggplant. The skin around his eyes was tinted lightly, as if tattooed blue; his lips were ashen and dry. His hair was as thin as that of an eighty-year-old and had

turned the color of ash. His body was encrusted all over with spots—pale blue, purple, dark blue—the size of beans.[211]

Whites are now the color of inconsolability. Willie Johnson concludes, "Now the white man's as lonely as we've always been."[212] All the sites of humiliation are gone:

> Now he began to name cities and places, and streets. And as he named them a murmur rose up in his audience.
> "We destroyed Natchez . . ."
> A murmur.
> "And Columbus, Georgia . . ."
> Another murmur
> "We burned New Orleans . . ."
> A sigh.
> "And Atlanta . . ."
> Still another.
> "And there was nothing left of Greenwater, Alabama."[213]

The place of Willie Johnson's birth, Greenwater, is gone:

> Willie stood with the rope in his hands. He was remembering Earth, the green Earth and the town where he was born and raised, and he was thinking now of that town, gone to pieces, to ruin, blown up and scattered, all of the landmarks with it, all of the supposed or certain evil scattered with it, all of the hard men gone, the stables, the ironsmiths, the curio shops the soda founts, the gin mills, the river bridges, the lynching trees, the buckshot-covered hills, the roads, the cows, the mimosas, and his own house as well as those big-pillared houses down near the long river.[214]

The white man is saved because the White Man is dead. There are no more whites:

> Gone, all gone; gone and never coming back. Now, for certain, all that civilization ripped into confetti and strewn at their feet. Nothing, nothing of it left to hate—not an empty brass gunshell, or a twisted hemp, or a tree, or even a hill of it to hate. Nothing but some alien people in a rocket, people who might shine his shoes and ride in the back of trolleys or sit far up in movie theatres.[215]

All those lesions of memory were cauterized when "all that civilization [was] ripped into confetti and strewn at their feet." Willie Johnson drops his lynching rope, his lynching identity, and realizes that he has "seen the white man" for the "first time." Everyone agrees that "the Lord's let us come through, a few here and a few there. And what happens next is up to all of us."[216] The obliteration of these hated sites provides an opening, a way clear to a new order of things—and, in Kaysen's words, "Who can resist an opening?"

The entire ensemble, the physical spaces and the order of things, the laws through which people perceived their races, spaces and places, all had to be "ripped into confetti" in order to reach a new starting point. When the system is utterly destroyed, then and only then will we walk with dignity. "Equal Justice under Law" will happen when the stones into which that message has been carved, like the texts on which it has been scripted and the flesh which has embodied it, are "strewn at our feet." Or perhaps when the hearts of stone have been melted. At least, that seemed to be the prophecy of those who realized that the colorline concedes nothing on request.

The "necessities" of survival are produced, distributed, and legitimated by the spectacle of the colorline. Campanis's notion of the "necessities" is useful in understanding how the spectacle of exclusion constitutes its own vindication. For Campanis, the exclusion of blacks from the quarterback position in football and from the pitching position in baseball legitimates the exclusion of blacks from managerial positions in baseball ("How many quarterbacks do you have? How many pitchers do you have that are black? The same thing applies"). Exclusion is an ensemble. And the exclusion of blacks from swimming proves only that blacks lack the "necessities" ("So it might be that they—why are black people not good swimmers? Because they don't have the buoyancy"). We are left excluded from the necessities for life, and our exclusion is based on the idea that we lack the necessities to earn the necessities. And the spectacle of our exclusion itself becomes a commodity. Exclusion validates itself. The colorline validates itself. The spectacle is its own validation.

The absence of blacks and other Others from clerkship positions may not mean much in a macroeconomic sense; however, at the level of spectacle, it means a great deal. First, the numbers show that the justices of the U.S. Supreme Court have reached Campanis-like conclusions about black buoyancy in the applicant pool. Second, the reverence for that particular credential—the Supreme Court clerkship—in the legal academy and in the legal profession shows that Campanis's notions hold water with lawyers everywhere. Third, the centrality of law in public discussions of right and wrong shows that notions of "buoyancy" and "necessity" are submerged in our feelings and desires and thoughts at levels too deep to be removed. The baby is the bathwater when it comes to the colorline. The entire ensemble validates itself by creating the mechanism for its own examination. The entire ensemble animates the bodies of those who live within its borders. Same as it ever was.

The dearth of black Supreme Court clerks creates a spectacle of black inferiority. If there are no blacks with the "necessities" to be clerks, then, according to the peculiar logic of the colorline, blacks are inferior. The elimination of blacks from other positions seems natural. It seems to reflect the general spectacle of black exclusion. No black clerks, no black justices, no black doctors, no black academics, no black police officers, no blacks anywhere save as menial laborers. And this does have an economic effect, as Sartre noted:

These wretched people pay as much for these miserable living quarters as a white worker pays for clean and ventilated rooms. The merchants—black and white—who set up their businesses in these reserved quarters sell their foodstuffs and

basic necessities at higher prices than elsewhere. The housekeeper of a well-to-do woman in Chicago does her shopping in the rich quarters at the same time she does her patron's because the prices are significantly less for those same products sold in the Negro quarter. Thus, even at an equal salary, the money does not have the same value for blacks and whites. All this takes place as if blacks receive dollars which are devalued.[217]

And it all seems to just happen naturally. It happens naturally because the rules of exclusion are hidden from view. To demand an examination of the rules would, as we saw with *Washington v. Davis,* expose the great fraud of the entire ensemble. The Supreme Court itself would not be able to declare the causes that compel them to separate themselves from blacks. Neither Chief Justice Rehnquist nor his eighty-two white clerks would be able to explain the separation. The horror is that they do not have to explain, as we saw with *Dred Scott.*

One can, like Billy Pilgrim, the protagonist of Kurt Vonnegut's novel *Slaughterhouse Five,* get unstuck in time thinking about the sheer inhumanity of it all. Vonnegut's Pilgrim is kidnapped to the planet Tralfalmadore, where he learns:

All moments, past, present, and future, always have existed, always will exist. The Tralfamadorians can look at all the different moments just the way we can look at a stretch of the Rocky Mountains, for instance. They can see how permanent all the moments are, and they can look at any moment that interests them. It is just an illusion we have here on Earth that one moment follows another one, like beads on a string, and that once a moment is gone it is gone forever.[218]

In 1776, a Republic of Slavery is imagined in a document—the Declaration of Independence that declares "all men are created equal." Nearly one hundred years later, the almost-free-and-now-segregated slaves are handed back to their captors for lynching, dismemberment, and disfranchisement in a document—*Cruikshank* in 1875—that declares Reconstruction ended. A little more than one hundred years later, the almost-free-and-now-neo-segregated slaves are recaptured in a document—*Washington v. Davis* in 1976—that declares:

> A rule that a statute designed to serve neutral ends is nevertheless invalid, absent compelling justification, if in practice it benefits or burdens one race more than another would be far reaching and would raise serious questions about, and perhaps invalidate, a whole range of tax, welfare, public service, regulatory, and licensing statutes that may be more burdensome to the poor and average black than to the more affluent white.[219]

And on a school bus trip that same Bicentennial year, I learn a lesson that might have been obvious had I read *Dred Scott:*

> They had for more than a century before [the Declaration of Independence] been regarded as beings of an inferior order, and altogether unfit to associate with the white race, either in social or political relations; and so far inferior, that they had no rights which the white man was bound to respect.[220]

Since before 1676, "altogether unfit to associate with the white race":

> —"Look, A Negro!" I was responsible at the same time for my body, for my race, for my ancestors. I subjected myself to an objective examination, I discovered my blackness, my ethnic characteristics; and I was battered down by tom-toms, cannibalism, intellectual deficiency, fetishism, racial defects, slave ships, and above all else, above all: "Sho' good eatin."[221]

> —All round me the white man, above the sky tears at its navel, the earth rasps under my feet, and there is a white song, a white song. All this whiteness that burns me.... I sit down at the fire and I become aware of my uniform. I had not seen it. It is indeed ugly. I stop there, for who can tell me what beauty is? And

where shall I find shelter from now on? I felt an easily identifiable flood mounting out of the countless facets of my being. I was about to be angry. The fire was long since out, and once more the nigger was trembling.[222]

> —The evidence was there, unalterable. My blackness was there, dark and unarguable. And it tormented me, pursued me, disturbed me, angered me. Negroes are savages, brutes, illiterates. But in my own case I knew that these statements were false. There was a myth of the Negro that had to be destroyed at all costs.[223]

> —I tell you, I was walled in: No exception was made for my refined manners, or my knowledge of literature, or my understanding of the quantum theory. I requested, I demanded explanations. Gently, in the tone that one uses with a child, they introduced me to the existence of a certain view that was held by certain people, but, I was always told, "We must hope that it will very soon disappear." What was it? Color prejudice.[224]

And so I am brought back to myself across nearly four centuries, across a sea of time.

Our task seems less daunting when we remember that it is easy to destroy an illusion. The green light is an illusion. Time is an illusion. All we need to do is let go of our longing for the green light, and the entire physical universe can be melted like the clocks in Salvador Dali's *The Persistence of Memory.* Our ideas about the "necessities" are illusions—illusions of the colorline and illusions that the current order of things is the permanent order of things. Like Gatsby, we are prisoners of love, but nothing needs to be the way it is.

"The Other Foot" shows us the hatred that is woven into the fabric of our hopes and dreams. By rearranging our settled expectations with violence of interplanetary exodus, nuclear holocaust, and the end of the colorline, Bradbury exposes the false necessity of the status quo. He also shows us just how invested our dreams are with law, and vice versa. In understanding the green light to be the spectacle of our own undo-ing, we also come to understand that any-thing is possible. And recall that Hacienda must be *built.*

A Situationist jurisprudence is one that exchanges the pleasures of submission for the pleasures of disruption. It is a jurisprudence that takes the form of a "propaganda of desire"[225] for things that the system, as now constituted, cannot and will not pro-vide. It seeks that ecstatic moment, and it is a place as well as a time, in which the slave says "no":

> We need to create our own minds, to behave as if the revolution has already taken place. Paint all the paintings black and celebrate the dead art. We have been living at a masqued ball: what we think of as our identity is a schooled set of notions, preconceptions that are impris-oning us in history. From our own belief in our own identity flows ceaseless mis-ery—our isolation, our alienation and our belief that another man's life is more interesting than our own. It is only through valuing all the world equally that any of us will find liberation. An end to history is our rightful demand. To continue to produce art is to addict our-selves to our own repression. The refusal to create is the only alternative left to those who wish to change the world. Give up art. Save the starving.[226]

Conclusion: Everything Must Go

> The reactionary suicide is "wise," and the revolutionary suicide is a "fool," a fool for the revolution in the way that Paul meant when he spoke of being "a fool for Christ." That foolishness can move the mountain of oppression; it is our great leap and our commitment to the dead and the unborn. We will touch God's heart; we will touch the people's hearts, and together we will move the mountain.
> —Huey P. Newton[227]

Everything must go. A mid-1960s flyer from the International Werewolf Conspiracy regard-ing the student movement spoke in terms ap-plicable to other oppressive situations:

> The function of the student movement is not to make demands on the university, but to destroy the existence of the "stu-dent" as a social role and as a character structure. YOU MUST DESTROY THE STU-DENT WITHIN YOU. For only then can the struggle begin against the institutions and masters which have trained us for the submission and the slavery in which we now participate. Our goal is not to win concessions, but to kill our masters and create a life which is worth living … and IN AMERIKA LIFE IS THE ONE DEMAND THAT CAN'T BE FILLED.[228]

Hegemony works by insinuating itself into the hearts and minds of the subaltern as an identity formation. The racialized body is one such identity formation:

> The American blacks are the product of modern industry, just like electronics or advertising or the cyclotron. And they embody its contradictions. They are the people that the spectacle paradise must simultaneously integrate and reject, with the result that the antagonism between the spectacle and human activity is totally revealed through them. The spec-tacle is universal, it pervades the globe just as the commodity does. But since the world of the commodity is based on class conflict, the commodity itself is hierarchical. The necessity for the com-modity (and hence for the spectacle, whose role is to inform the commodity world) is to be both universal and hier-archical leads to a universal hierarchiza-tion. But because this hierachization must remain unavowed, it is expressed in the form of unavowable, because irra-tional, hierarchical value judgments in a world of irrational rationalization. It is this hierarchization that creates racisms everywhere.[229]

Liberation requires a casting aside of every-thing, including one's subaltern identity. It requires a casting aside of the entire ensemble.

I have tried to show the law as inextricably bound to the colorline. Indeed, the law emerges from these pages as one of the ways in which the race-pleasure sensation is experienced. Law is a way of touching—of enjoying—the abjection of the Other. Law creates the space, the subjects, the choreography, the words, the incentives, and the pleasures of the everyday practices of domination and submission I have described. To show the law as a theater of cruelty, as a source of S/M pleasure, as spectacle is to highlight the defeat of the Civil Rights Movement. The race-pleasure imperative of our masters makes it necessary for them to "beat us down." And we have been transfixed by the spectacle of our own undoing, like Gatsby before the green light. It does not have to be this way. Everything is possible, and nothing is forbidden once, we have left the Civil Rights Movement dream behind and exchanged the pleasures of submission for the pleasures of disruption. Civil rights will never bring about the raceless society. There are no responsible solutions. There are no safe words.

Octavia Butler's novel *Kindred* is about the literal and involuntary transportation, back and forth, between the present and the past:

> I could literally smell his sweat, hear every ragged breath, every cry, every cut of the whip. I could see his body jerking, convulsing, straining against the rope as his screaming went on and on. My stomach heaved, and I had to force myself to stay where I as and keep quiet. Why didn't they stop!
> "Please, Master," the man begged. "For Godsake, Master, please. . . .
> I shut my eyes and tensed my muscles against an urge to vomit.
> I had seen people beaten on television and in the movies. I had seen the too-red blood substitute streaked across their back and heard their well-rehearsed screams. But I hadn't lain nearby and smelled their sweat or heard them pleading and praying, shamed before their families and themselves. I was probably less prepared for the reality than the child crying not far from me.[230]

I hear Chief Justice Rehnquist singing in praise of an earlier time, a time of white-over-black, a time like the present:

FIRST VERSE:
I wish I was in the land of cotton,
Old times there are not forgotten,
Look away, look away,
Look away, Dixieland.

SECOND VERSE:
In Dixieland where I was born in,
early on a frosty mornin',
Look away, look away,
Look away, Dixieland.

CHORUS:
I wish I was in Dixie,
Horray! Hooray!
In Dixieland I'll take my stand,
To live and die in Dixie,
Away, away, away down south in Dixie.
Away, away, away down south in Dixie.[231]

Butler's protagonist (see boxed text) reflects on the "perforations in the membrane between here and there":[232]

"Most of the time, I'm still an observer. It's protection. It's nineteen seventy-six shielding and cushioning eighteen nineteen for me. But now and then . . . I can't maintain the distance. I'm drawn all the way into eighteen nineteen, and I don't what to do. I ought to be doing something though. I know that."[233]

Chief Justice Rehnquist sang *Dixie* at the 1999 Fourth circuit Judicial Conference, Judge Luttig's Circuit, as had apparently been his custom. The words of this song, like bombs bursting in the air; like inexorable zero; like Luttig's requiem for social engineering; like sweat, toil, tears, or blood in the face gave proof of the perforations between here and there, between the past and the present, between the right and left columns above: "And who can resist an opening?"[234] We know, and the Chief Justice's pro-slavery song reminds us that

> it is easy to slip into a parallel universe. There are so many of them: worlds of the insane, the criminalized, the crippled, the dying, perhaps of the dead as well. These worlds exist along side this world and resemble it, but are not in it.[235]

After seeing slave children playing a game of "auction," Butler's protagonist, a black women, shares her thoughts with her husband, a white man:

> I closed my eyes and saw the children playing their game again. "The ease seemed so frightening," I said. "Now I see why."
> "What?"
> "The ease. Us, the children. . . . I never realized how easily people could be trained to accept slavery."[236]

The pair, wife and husband, black and white together, manage to resist slavery, then and now, as "kindred spirits." Identities are orientations. Some of us develop orientations that support the spectacle, and some of us develop other orientations that cannot be made spectacle. These latter orientations I call anti-spectacular orientations.

Suspended in an ocean of spit, buoyed by the wet results of a centuries-old crying game, motionlessly moving like water in water, the words of my late countryman Bob Marley reach my ears. He is singing a song made famous by Bob Dylan, but the words have changed: "Time like a scorpion stings without warning."[237] The poison streams through my blood, "a tidal wave of blackness" breaks above my head and I roll, like a stone, to the bottom.[238] I am without "buoyancy," and the "necessities" are all above the surface, somewhere before we "first picked out the green light at the end of Daisy's dock ... somewhere in that vast obscurity ... where the dark fields of the republic [roll] on into the night."[239] There is no "West Egg," no "East Egg";[240] there is "just a monstrous world where [I find that I myself am] the monster."[241] "Away, away, away down south in Dixie," a Confederate song sung by the Supreme Court in its Bicentennial moment:

> A rule that a statute designed to serve neutral ends is nevertheless invalid, absent compelling justification, if in practice it benefits or burdens one race more than another would be far reaching and would raise serious questions about, and perhaps invalidate, a whole range of tax, welfare, public service, regulatory, and licensing statutes that may be more burdensome to the average black than to the more affluent white.[242]

"Look, A Negro!" The song remains the same.

Notes

Acknowledgments: I thank my co-panelists Keith Aoki, John O. Calmore, Richard Thompson Ford, and Elizabeth M. Iglesias for their insights. I thank David Kennedy, Duncan Kennedy, Stella Rosanski, the Harvard University Center for Literary and Cultural Studies, and the Harvard European Law Research Institute for inviting me to present these ideas to a multidisciplinary audience in 1997. I thank the editors of this volume, especially Jerome McCristal Culp, Jr., for their time and generosity with this article and the larger project of which it is a part. I thank my Boston College colleagues, especially Ruth Arlene W. Howe and Phyllis Goldfarb, for our constant conversation. Finally, I thank my wife, Maria Grahn-Farley, for her always brilliant comments and her constant support.

Epigraph: F. Scott Fitzgerald, *The Great Gatsby* (New York: Scribner, 1995), 189.

1. *Brown v. Board of Education*, 347 U.S. 483 (1954); *Brown v. Board of Education*, 349 U.S. 294 (1955); *Loving v. Virginia*, 388 U.S. 1 (1967).

2. The Carolina Freedom Fighters, "Hallelujah (I'm A-Travelin')," *Everybody Wants Freedom* (Battle Records, 1963). The words on the album cover shed a revealing light on the idealism of the Civil Rights Movement: "The Carolina Freedom Fighters were all jailed in the spring of 1963, during the massive freedom marches in Greensboro. None of the singers can be named—their status in southern schools is too delicately balanced to be endangered in this way. The names that matter are in the songs." The singers truly believed that formal equality, "the green light," would be their salvation.

3. *The Great Gatsby*, dir. Jack Clayton (Paramount Pictures, 1974), motion picture.

4. Fitzgerald, *Great Gatsby*.

5. There are many chapters written and yet to be written in the history of white supremacy. I do not use the term "black" to dismiss any of those chapters. Indeed, a reading of the black–white dynamic is not possible without a reading of those whom whites have branded with other subaltern labels: See Anthony Paul Farley, "All Flesh Shall See It Together," *Chicano–Latino Law Review* 19 (1998): 163. Arab American, Native American, Asian Pacific American, and Latina/o are just a few of the other labels. I hope that this writing will be read as an invitation to read and write the histories of other Others who struggle against white supremacy, just as I have read those histories as an invitation to do this writing. "Let us now emulate each other," said an anonymous Viet Cong woman a long time ago in an anti-colonial moment. I borrow her words from a pamphlet that I can no longer find, save in memory, for our current situation: Let us now emulate each other.

6. I use the term "colorline" throughout this chapter, but what follows will concern the myriad, interrelated boundaries of race, gender, sexuality, spirituality, physical ability, mental health, class, language, immigration status, nationality, and neighborhood that both fragment and frame our collective imagination. I do not suggest that these boundaries and their intersections can all be subsumed within a discussion of race. Rather, I make the more modest claim that an examination of the colorline shows its production and maintenance to be deeply implicated in the production and maintenance of the other boundaries of our society, and vice versa. This is an attempt to establish what Mary Ann Tolbert has called "a poetics of location"—that is, one that recognizes "the importance of self-consciously adopting different perspectives on a text at different times": Mary Ann Tolbert, "When Resistance Becomes Repression: Mark 13:9–27," in *Readings from this Place, Volume 2: Social Location and Biblical Interpretation*, ed. Fernando F. Segovia and Mary Ann Tolbert (Minneapolis: Fortress Press, 1995), 331–3. Such a poetics "eschews claims for universal readings in favor of local readings that are careful to indicate their context and limits." Finally, it "openly acknowledges its allegiance to the postmodern claim that language is constitutive of reality, rather than simply reflective of it": ibid. I use the term "colorline" to refer to scripts for and performances of racial identity.

7. Fitzgerald, *Great Gatsby*.

8. See Anthony Paul Farley, "The Black Body as Fetish Object," *Oregon Law Review* 76 (1997): 457

9. Frantz Fanon, *Black Skin, White Masks*, trans. Charles Lam Markmann (New York: Grove Press, 1967), 113.

10. Jean-Paul Sartre, "Appendix II: Revolutionary Violence," in *Notebook for an Ethics*, trans. David Pellauer (Chicago: University of Chicago Press, 1992), 561.

11. Roland Barthes, "Talking," in *A Lover's Discourse: Fragments*, trans. Richard Howard (New York: Hill and Wang, 1996 [1978]), 73.

12. Gaston Bachelard, *The Poetics of Space*, trans. Maria Jolas (Boston: Beacon Press, 1994), 7.

13. Ibid.

14. Ibid., 5–6.

15. Susanna Kaysen, *Girl, Interrupted* (New York: Vintage Books, 1993), 5.

16. Gil Scott-Heron, "Home is Where the Hatred Is," *The Revolution Will Not be Televised* (Flying Dutchman Records, 1974).

17. Ray Bradbury, "Way in the Middle of the Air," in *The Martian Chronicles* (New York: Bantam, 1979), 89.

18. Ibid., 91.

19. Ibid.

20. Ibid., 92.

21. Ibid., 93.

22. Ibid., 94.

23. See Keith Aoki, "Race, Space and Place: The Relation Between Architectural Modernism, Postmodernism, Urban Planning, and Gentrification," *Fordham Urban Law Journal* 20 (1993): 699.

24. Bradbury, "Way in the Middle," 95.

25. Ibid., 96.

26. Ibid.

27. Malcolm X with Alex Haley, *The Autobiography of Malcolm X* (New York: Ballantine Books, 1992), 242-3.

28. Bradbury, "Way in the Middle," 99.

29. Ibid., 100.

30. Ibid.

31. Ibid., 100.

32. Antonin Artaud, *The Theater and Its Double,* trans. Mary Caroline Richards (New York: Grove Press, 1958), 99.

33. Flannery O'Connor, "Everything That Rises Must Converge," in Flannery O'Connor, *Collected Works* (New York: Library of America, 1988), 485.

34. Ibid., 487.

35. Ibid., 491.

36. Ibid., 487-8.

37. Ibid., 494.

38. Ibid., 496.

39. Ibid.

40. Ibid., 498.

41. Ibid., 499.

42. Ibid., 499-500.

43. Albert Memmi, *Dominated Man: Notes Toward a Portrait* (New York: Orion Press, 1968), 201.

44. Erica Jong, *Fear of Flying* (New York: Holt Rinehart, 1988 [1973]), 11.

45. Judith Jarvis Herman and Lisa Hirschman, *Father–Daughter Incest* (Cambridge, Mass. Harvard University Press, 1981), 69.

46. I do not mean to suggest that rape is not a devastating blow against one's sense of self. Rather, I suggest that just as rape plays a role in the construction of gender and the gender line, so, too, does race play a role in the construction and the preservation of the colorline. Race itself, like gender itself, should be thought of as a product of force. The racialized body, no less than the gendered body, is the product of a forced thematization that is similar to rape.

47. George Orwell, *Nineteen Eighty-Four* (New York: Signet Classics, 1981), 25-6.

48. James Baldwin, "This Morning, This Evening, So Soon," in James Baldwin, *Going to Meet the Man* (New York: Dial Press, 1965), 123, 149.

49. Orwell, *Nineteen Eighty-Four,* 239.

50. Fanon, *Black Skin,* 112.

51. Orwell, *Nineteen Eighty-Four,* 239.

52. Ibid., 210-1.

53. South Carolina State Legislator John D. Long, as quoted in Stetson Kennedy, *The Jim Crow Guide: The Way It Was* (Boca Raton: Florida Atlantic University Press, 1990), 152.

54. But see Charles Lawrence, "The Id, the Ego and Equal Protection: Reckoning with Unconscious Racism,: *Stanford Law Review* 39 (1987): 317.

55. Michel Foucault, *The History of Sexuality,* vol. 1, trans. Robert Hurley (New York: Vintage Books, 1990), 86.

56. Ibid.

57. Ibid., 93.

58. Ibid., 98.

59. Edmund White, *The Beautiful Room Is Empty* (New York: Alfred A. Knopf, 1988), 85.

60. Linda Hogan, "Department of the Interior," in *Minding the Body: Women Writers on Body and Soul,* ed. Patricia Foster (New York: Doubleday, 1994), 159, 167.

61. Paul Goodman, "Racism, Spite, Guilt and Non-Violence," in *Decentralizing Power: Paul Goodman's Social Criticism,* ed. Taylor Stoehr (Montreal: Black Rose Books, 1994), 121, 129-30.

62. Bobby Troup, "The Girl Can't Help It" (1956), recorded by Little Richard on Speciality Records.

63. Catharine MacKinnon, *Only Words* (Cambridge, Mass.: Harvard University Press, 1993), 17.

64. Elleke Boehmer, *Colonial and Postcolonial Literature: Migrant Metaphors* (Oxford: Oxford Uniersity Press, 1995), 13.

65. "Chart III," in *States' Laws on Race and Color,* ed. Pauli Murray (Athens: University of Georgia Press, 1997 [1950]).

66. Orwell, *Nineteen Eighty-Four,* 46.

67. *Loving v. Virginia,* 388 U.S. 1, 3 (1967), quoting the trial judge from the Circuit Court of Caroline County.

68. These were large fines. This can be seen in the fact that the University of Texas Law School, a whites-only institution, charged only $25 per semester in tuition during 1942-43: See University of Texas Publication, no. 4316, April 22, 1943, and no. 4229, August 1, 1942.

69. Austryn Wainhous and Richard Seaver, comp. and trans., *The Marquis de Sade: The 120 Days of Sodom and Other Writings,* introductions by Simone de Beauvoir and Pierre Kossowski (New York: Grove Press, 1966).

70. Ibid.

71. Ibid., 240-1.

72. Ibid., 241.

73. Ibid., 254.

74. Marcel Henaff, "The Encyclopedia of Excess," in *Sade and the Narrative of Transgression,* ed. David Allison, Mark S. Roberts, and Allen S. Weiss (Cambridge: Cambridge University Press, 1995), 144-5.

75. Ibid., 145.

76. Frantz Fanon, *The Wretched of the Earth*, trans. Constance Farrington (New York: Grove Press, 1963), 51-2.

77. Henaff, "Encyclopedia," 145.

78. Walter White, *Rope and Faggot* (New York: Arno Press, 1969), 35.

79. Ibid., 36.

80. Stewart E. Tolnay and E. M. Beck, *A Festival of Violence: An Analysis of Southern Lynchings, 1882-1930* (Urbana: University of Illinois Press, 1992), xi.

81. James R. McGovern, *Anatomy of a Lynching: The Killing of Claude Neal* (Baton Rouge: Louisiana State University Press, 1992), 72.

82. Comments of NAACP Investigator Howard Kester, as quoted in ibid., 80.

83. Robert Cover, "Violence and the Word," in *Narrative, Violence and the Law: The Essays of Robert Cover*, ed. Martha Minow, Michael Ryan, and Austin Sarat (Ann Arbor: University of Michigan Press, 1992), 203.

84. *United States v. Cruikshank*, 92 U.S. 542 (1875).

85. *The Slaughterhouse Cases*, 83 U.S. 36 (1873).

86. Aviam Soifer, *Law and the Company We Keep* (Cambridge, Mass.: Harvard University Press, 1995), 120.

87. Ibid.

88. Ibid.

89. Ibid., 120-1.

90. *Dred Scott v. Sandford* 60 U.S. 393 (1856).

91. See generally Roland Barthes, *The Pleasure of the Text*, trans. Richard Miller (London: Cape, 1980 [1976]).

92. Robert K. Merton, "Insiders and Outsiders: A Chapter in the Sociology of Knowledge," in *Theories of Ethnicity: A Classical Reader*, ed. Werner Sollors (New York: New York University Press, 1996), 353.

93. Lino A. Graglia, Dalton Cross Professor of Law at the University of Texas Law School, as quoted in "University Professor Blasts Efforts for Diversity on Campus, Austin, Texas," *Houston Chronicle*, September 11, 1997, A25.

94. Alan David Freeman, "Legitimating Racial Discrimination Through Antidiscrimination Law: A Critical Review of Supreme Court Doctrine," *Minnesota Law Review* 62 (1978): 1049.

95. Peter Fitzpatrick, "Racism and the Innocence of Law," in *Critical Legal Studies*, ed. Peter Fitzpatrick and Alan Hunt (Indianapolis: Dartmouth, 1987), 130.

96. U.S. Bureau of the Census, *Number of African Americans in Poverty Declines: While Income Rises*, Census Bureau Reports, (Washington, D.C.: U.S. Government Printing Office, 1998). In 1997, "African American" households had a median income of $25,050. "White" households, however, had a median income of $38,972: ibid. The median income is defined as the annual income received in a regular or periodic manner and excluding lump-sum or one-time payments, such as inheritances and insurance settlements: T. J. Eiler and Wallace Frasier, *Asset Ownership of Households: 1993*, Bureau of the Census Current Population Reports no. 70-74 (Washington, D.C.: U.S. Government Printing Office, 1995), 18.

97. U.S. Bureau of the Census, *What We're Worth—Asset Ownership of Households: 1993*, Statistical Brief (Washington, D.C.: U.S. Government Printing Office, 1995). Median net worth is the amount of financial resources, equaling the value of your assets, minus any debts. Assets can include rental property; other real estate; motor vehicles; business or profession; U.S. savings bonds; IRA or KEOGH accounts; other financial investments, including mortgages held from sale of business; unit trusts; interest-earning assets at financial institutions and other interest-earning assets; homes; stocks and mutual-fund shares; and checking accounts: ibid.

98. Melvin L. Olivier and Thomas M. Shapiro, *Black Wealth, White Wealth: A New Perspective on Racial Inequality* (1995), 86. Financial assets include real estate, businesses, assets in banks and financial institutions, stocks, IRA and KEOGH accounts, bonds and mortgages, and stocks, and they exclude home and vehicle equity: ibid., 105.

99. Ibid., 90.

100. Marc Mauer, "Intended and Unintended Consequences: State Racial Disparities in Imprisonment," Sentencing Project (January 1997), 1-2.

101. Marc Mauer and Tracy Huling, "Young Black Americans and the Criminal Justice System: Five Years Later," Sentencing Project (October 1995).

102. Sherrilyn A. Ifill, "Judging the Judges: Racial Diversity, Impartiality and Representation on State Trial Courts," *Boston College Law Review* 39 (December 1997): 95, 97 (citations omitted).

103. Bob Woodward and Scott Armstrong, *The Brethren: Inside the Supreme Court* (New York: Simon and Schuster, 1979), 288.

104. Tony Mauro, "For Lawyers, Clerkship Is Ultimate Job. Year of Work in Top Court Brings Unrivaled Access," *USA Today*, March 13, 1998, 13A.

105. "Talking Points on the Supreme Court and Minority and Women Law Clerks," Washington Bureau of the National Association for the Advancement of Colored People, updated September 9, 1998.

106. Luttig, as quoted in Mauro, "For Lawyers."

107. Fitzgerald, *Great Gatsby*, 24.

108. J. Clay Smith, Jr., *Emancipation: The Making of the Black Lawyer 1844–1944* (Philadelphia: University of Pennsylvania Press, 1993).

109. Genna R. McNeil, *Groundwork: Charles Hamilton Houston and the Struggle for Civil Rights* (Philadelphia: University of Pennsylvania Press, 1983), 218.

110. *Plessy v. Ferguson*, 163 U.S. 537 (1896).

111. *Roberts v. City of Boston*, 5 Cush. 198, 59 Mass. 198, 204 (1849).

112. Ibid.

113. Ibid., 210.

114. *Roberts v. City of Boston*, 5 Cush. 198, 59 Mass. 198 (1849).

115. Herman Melville, *Moby-Dick* (Harper & Brothers, 1851), 521.

116. Ibid., 383.

117. Ibid.

118. Bernard Schwartz, *Decision: How the Supreme Court Decides Cases* (New York: Oxford University Press, 1996), 66.

119. Melville, *Moby-Dick*, 521.

120. Harold Beaver, in his commentary to *Moby-Dick*, sees this Jim Crow metaphor in Melville's descriptions of several events: See Harold Beaver, introduction and commentary to Herman Melville, *Moby-Dick* (New York: W. W. Norton, 1967 [1851]), 885, 966.

121. "Despite growing racial diversity within law schools and law reviews, white Justices of the U.S. Supreme Court have not included African-Americans within their ranks of law clerks. Consider that the majority of Justices—Justices Rehnquist, O'Connor (she has retained 1 as of late), Scalia, Kennedy, and Souter—have never hired an African-American law clerk. Indeed, even a liberal Justice like William Brennan never employed an African-American law clerk (on active duty in his chambers). It is hard to explain this all-white hiring. . . . Certainly, the all-white hiring of these white Justices conflicts with the record of Justice Thurgood Marshall. Justice Marshall hired seven (African-Americans) which equals the number hired by all other (white) Justices in the entire history of the Court": Winkfield Franklin Twyman, Jr., "A Critique of the California Civil Rights Initiative," *National Black Law Journal* 14 (1997): 192.

122. *Texas v. Johnson*, 491 U.S. 397 (1989) (Stevens, J., dissent.).

123. Booker T. Washington, *Up from Slavery* (New York: Penguin Classics, 1986), 221-2.

124. "Again the devil taketh him up into an exceedingly high mountain, and sheweth him all the kingdoms of the world, and the glory of them;

And saith onto him, All these things I will give thee, if thou wild fall down and worship me": Matthew 4:8-10 KJV.

125. *Washington v. Davis*, 426 U.S. 229 (1976).

126. For an argument that blacks are culturally inferior to whites, see generally Dinesh D'Souza, *The End of Racism* (New York: Free Press, 1995). For an argument that blacks are genetically inferior to whites, see generally Richard J. Herrnstein and Charles Murray, *The Bell Curve* (New York: Free Press, 1995). For an argument that biocultural inferiority theories are a tactic of colonialism, see generally Fanon, *Wretched of the Earth*.

127. *Nightline*, ABC, broadcast, April 6, 1987.

128. *Washington v. Davis*.

129. *Griggs v. Duke Power Company*, 401 U.S. 424 (1971).

130. Ibid.

131. *Dred Scott v. Sandford*.

132. Ibid.

133. Ibid.

134. Ibid.

135. Sartre, "Appendix II: Revolutionary Violence," 561.

136. *Washington v. Davis*, 248.

137. Stuart Seely Sprague, ed., *His Promised Land: The Autobiography of John P. Parker, Former Slave and Conductor on the Underground Railroad* (New York: Norton, 1996), 35.

138. Dietrich Bonhoeffer, *The Cost of Discipleship* (New York: Collier Books, 1963), 68

139. Sprague, *His Promised Land*, 53-4.

140. Ibid., 61.

141. Fanon, *Black Skin*, 29.

142. "Black Mask No. 1—November 1966," in *Black Mask and Up Against the Wall Motherfucker: The Incomplete Works of Ron Hahne, Ben Morea and the Black Mask Group*, ed. Jacques Vache (London: Unpopular Books and Sabotage Editions, 1993), 7.

143. Ibid., 43.

144. "Détournement as Negation and Prelude—Internationale Situationniste No. 3 (December 1959)," in *Situationist International Anthology*, ed. and trans. Ken Knabb (Berkeley, Calif.: Bureau of Public Secrets, 1995 [1981]), 55.

145. Sadie Plant, *The Most Radical Gesture: The Situationist International in a Postmodern Age* (London: Routledge, 1992).

146. Ibid., 86.

147. Ibid., 87.

148. Guy Debord, *The Society of the Spectacle*, trans. Donald Nicholson-Smith (New York: Zone Books, 1995), 12.

149. Ibid.

150. Christopher Gray, "Essays from Leaving the 20th Century," in *What Is Situationism? A Reader,* ed. Stewart Home (San Francisco: AK Press, 1996).

151. Debord, *Society of the Spectacle,* 2333.

152. See Jacques Lacan, "The Mirror Stage as Formative of the Function of the I as Revealed in Psychoanalytic Experience," in Jacques Lacan, *Ecrits: A Selection* (New York: W. W. Norton, 1977), 1–7.

153. This is the dilemma, writes George Orwell in another context. "To overthow the Party: Resistance is necessary, though hopeless": George Orwell, *Nineteen Eighty-Four* (London: Secker & Warburg, 1987), 177. Orwell recognized that "we all rail against class-distinctions, but very few people seriously want to abolish them": George Orwell, *The Road to Wigan Pier* (New York: HarBrac, 1958), 157. Orwell continues, "The fact that has got to be faced is that to abolish class-distinctions means abolishing a part of yourself": Orwell, *Wigan Pier,* 161. What Orwell writes of class in *Wigan Pier* and what he writes of the party in *Nineteen Eighty-Four* can also be applied to the colorline.

154. It is difficult to tell grace from a fall when contemplating alienation and its opposite. Consider the "victory" at the end of *Nineteen Eighty-Four:*

> The voice from the telescreen was still pouring forth its tale of prisoners and booty and slaughter, but the shouting outside had died down a little.... Winston, sitting in a blissful dream, paid no attention as his glass was filled up. He was not running or cheering any longer. He was back in the Ministry of Love, with everything forgiven, his soul white as snow.... The long-hoped-for bullet was entering his brain. But it was all right, everything was all right, the struggle was finished. He had won the victory over himself.
>
> He loved Big Brother. (Orwell, *Nineteen Eighty-Four,* 245)

Or the beginning of *Invisible Man:*

> It's so long ago and far away that here in my invisibility I wonder if it happened at all. Then in my mind's eye I see the bronze statue of the college Founder, the cold Father symbol, his hands outstretched in the breathtaking gesture of lifting a veil that flutters in hard, metallic folds above the face of a kneeling slave; and I am standing puzzled, unable to decide whether the veil is really being lifted, or low-

ered more firmly in place; whether I am witnessing a revelation or a more efficient blinding. (Ralph Ellison, *Invisible Man* [New York: Modern Library, 1992], 36)

155. Debord, *Society of the Spectacle,* 29.

156. Ibid., 13.

157. Ibid., 33.

158. William Burroughs, *Naked Lunch* (New York: Grove Press, 1991), xxxviii–ix.

159. Plant, *The Most Radical Gesture.*

160. For more on the role of the Situationist International and the events of May 1968, see generally René Viénet, "*Enragés* and Situationists," in *The Occupation Movement, France, May '68* (New York: Grove Atlantic, 1992.

161. See Situationist International, "Review of the American Section of the SI," Situationist International, New York (1969), 8, 38.

162. Melville, *Moby-Dick,* 384.

163. Foucault, *History of Sexuality,* 95–6.

164. Vache, *Black Mask,* 101.

165. The Situationists mirrored Foucault's insight that "discourses are not once and for all subservient to power or raised up against it, any more than silences are. We must make allowance for the complex and unstable process whereby discourse can be both an instrument and effect of power, but also a hindrance, a stumbling-block, a point of resistance and a starting point for an opposing strategy. Discourse transmits and produces power; it reinforces it, but also undermines and exposes it, renders it fragile and makes it possible to thwart": Foucault, *History of Sexuality,* 100–1.

166. Edward W. Said writes, "To a certain extent modern and primitive societies seem ... to derive a sense of their identities negatively. A fifth-century Athenian was very likely to feel himself to be non-barbarian as much as he positively felt himself to be Athenian. The geographic boundaries accompany the social, ethnic and cultural ones in expected ways. Yet often the sense in which someone feels himself to be not-foreign is based on a very unrigorous idea of what is 'out there,' beyond one's own territory. All kinds of suppositions, associations, and fictions appear to crowd the unfamiliar space outside one's own": Edward W. Said, *Orientalism* (New York: Random House, 1979), 54.

167. See generally Duncan Kennedy, *A Critique of Adjudication* (Cambridge, Mass.: Harvard University Press, 1998).

168. Guy Debord, "Introduction to a Critique of Urban Geography," in Knabb, *Anthology*, 6.

169. Ibid.

170. "Definitions," in Knabb, *Anthology*, 45.

171. Ibid.

172. Plant, *The Most Radical Gesture*, 1.

173. Ivan Chtcheglov, "Formula for a New City," as quoted in Greg Robertson, "The Situationist International: Its Penetration into British Culture," in *What Is Situationism? A Reader*, ed. Steward Home (Edinburgh: AK Press, 1996), 77-8.

174. Ivan Chtcheglov, "Formula for a New Urbanism," in Knabb, *Anthology*, 2.

175. Ibid., 3.

176. "Questionnaire, Internationale Situationniste No. 9 (August 1964)," in Knabb, *Anthology*, 138.

177. Chtcheglov, "Formula," 4.

178. Vache, *Black Mask*, 57.

179. Sarah Patton Boyle, "Inside a Segregationist," in *White on Black: The Views of Twenty-two White Americans on the Negro*, ed. Era Bell Thompson and Herbert Nipson (Chicago: Johnson Publishing, 1963), 48-9.

180. I am, of course, paraphrasing the late Mary Joe Frug's statement about the category of woman. Frug writes, "Only when sex means more than male or female, only when the word 'woman' cannot be coherently understood, will oppression by sex be fatally undermined": Mary Joe Frug, "A Postmodern Feminist Legal Manifesto (An Unfinished Draft)," in Mary Joe Frug, *Postmodern Legal Feminism*, (New York: Routledge, 1992) 153. The article was originally published in *Harvard Law Review* 105 (1991): 1045, 1075. Frug was murdered on April 5, 1991, in Cambridge, Massachusetts, before she had a chance to complete her manifesto. On the first anniversary of her death, students on the editorial board of the *Harvard Law Review* chose to mock her death, her life, and her theories in a special "Law Revue" show.

181. Guy Debord, "Introduction," in Knabb, *Anthology*, 7.

182. Chtcheglov, "Formula," 4.

183. Guy Debord, "Toward a Situationist International (June 1957)," in Knabb, *Anthology*, 25.

184. Michel Foucault, "Preface," in Michel Foucault, *The Order of Things: An Archaeology of Human Sciences*, trans. Les Mots et les choses (New York: Vintage Books, 1994), xvii-xviii.

185. Ibid.

186. Guy Debord, "Toward a Situationist," in Knabb, *Anthology*, 24.

187. Foucault, "Preface," xvii-xviii.

188. Michel Foucault, "Two Lectures," in *Power/Knowledge: Selected Interviews and other Writings 1972-1977*, ed. and trans. Colin Gordon (New York: Pantheon, 1980), 78, 81.

189. On slavery, see Herbert Aptheker, *American Negro Slave Revolts* (New York: Columbia University Press, 1943); on segretation, see Robert F. Williams, *Negroes with Guns* (New York: Marzani & Munsell, 1963); and on neo-segretation, see Assata Shakur, *Assata: An Autobiography* (Chicago: L Hill Books, 1987).

190. Ray Bradbury, "And the Rock Cried Out," in *The Vintage Bradbury*, ed. Ray Bradbury (New York: Vintage Books, 1990), 127. The invention will never come. The conversation takes place between white tourists from the United States and their Mexican taxi driver after a nuclear holocaust has destroyed the white nations of the Earth. The tourists, stripped of their white power, see themselves as they have always been seen by their Others. They see themselves, for the first time, in the mirror of their own exclusions. Having stepped through the looking glass, they see that they cannot live amid the hate that they and their colorlined lifestyles created. The days of their future, they find out, are past.

191. Memmi, *Dominated Man*, 16.

192. Eugene D. Genovese, *Roll, Jordan, Roll: The World the Slaves Made* (New York: Vintage Books, 1976), 26.

193. Quoted in Lawrence Ferlinghetti, "Ends and Beginnings," *City Lights Review* 6 (1994): 10

194. Foucault, "Preface," xvii-xviii.

195. Foucault, *History of Sexuality*, 101.

196. See David M. Halperin, "Saint Foucault: Towards A Gay Hagiography," in Foucault, *The History of Sexuality 101* (New York: Oxford University Press, 1997), 57.

197. Vance Gilbert, "If These Teardrops Had Wings," *Edgewise* (Rounder Records, 1994), compact disc.

198. As quoted in William Haver, ed., *The Body of This Death: Historicity and Sociality in the Time of AIDS* (Stanford, Calif.: Stanford University Press, 1996), 196.

199. Bradbury, "The Other Foot," 43.

200. Ibid., 45-46.

201. Ibid.

202. Ibid., 48.

203. Frantz Fanon, "Algeria Unveiled," in *A Dying Colonialism*, trans. Haakon Chevalier (London: Writers and Readers, 1980 [1965]), 65.

204. Bradbury, "The Other Foot," 50.

205. Ibid.

206. In thinking of this "moment," it would be good to turn to the discussion by Jerome McCristal Culp, Jr's discussion of the black "moment" in legal theory: See Jerome McCristal Culp, Jr., "Toward a Black Legal Scholarship: Race and Original Understandings," *Duke Law Journal* (1991): 39. Culp argues that in legal scholarship, Critical Race Theory is the cutting edge.

207. Bradbury, "The Other Foot," 52.

208. Ibid., 53.

209. Bradbury, "And the Rock Cried Out," 114-5.

210. Bradbury, "The Other Foot," 57.

211. Ota Yoko, *City of Corpses*, quoted in William Haver, The Body of This Death: Historicity and Sociality in the Time of AIDS 196 (1996).

212. Ibid., 57.

213. Ibid., 52

214. Ibid., 56

215. Ibid.

216. Ibid.

217. Jean-Paul Sartre, *Return from the United States*, trans. T. Denean Sharpley-Whiting, in *Existence in Black: An Anthology of Black Existential Philosophy*, ed. Lewis Gordon (1997), 86. Sartre's essay was originally published as "Retour des Etats Unis: Ce qui j'ai appris du probleme noir," *Le Figaro*, June 16, 1945. Sarte arrived in the United States for the first time on January 12, 1945, in New York City, and stayed for about four months.

218. Kurt Vonnegut, *Slaughterhouse Five* (New York: Dell, 1991), 27.

219. *Washington v. Davis*.

220. *Dred Scott v. Sandford*.

221. Fanon, *Black Skin*, 112.

222. Ibid., 114.

223. Ibid., 117.

224. Ibid., 117-8.

225. Debord, "Introduction," in Knabb, *Anthology*, 6.

226. Tony Lowe, "Give Up Art/Save the Starving," quoted in Gray, *What Is Situationism?* 77-8

227. Huey P. Newton, *Revolutionary Suicide* (New York: Writers and Readers Publishing, 1995), 333.

228. Vache, *Black Mask*, 111.

229. Ken Knabb, "Situationist International," in *Public Secrets: Collected Skirmishes of Ken Knabb,* *1970-1997* (Berkeley, Calif.: Bureau of Public Secrets, 1997), 370. A similar comment was made by John O. Killens, who wrote, "The American Negro, then, is an Anglo-Saxon invention, a role the Anglo-Saxon gentlemen invented for the black man to play in this drama known euphemistically as the American Way of Life. It began as an economic expedient, frankly, because you wanted somebody to work for nothing. It is still that, but now it is much more than that. It has become a way of life, socially, economically, psychologically, [and] philosophically": John O. Killens, "Explanation of the 'Black Psyche,'" *New York Times,* June 1964, 37-8, 42, 47-8, as quoted in "We Refuse to Look at Ourselves Through the Eyes of White America," in *Black Protest Thought in the Twentieth Century*, ed. August Meier, Elliott Rudwick, and Francis L. Broderick (Indianapolis: Bobbs-Merrill, 1971), 426.

Killens continues and notes that the revolutionaries of the 1960s are refusing to examine themselves through the eviscerating gaze of white America. "But now, in the middle of the 20th century, I, the Negro, am refusing to be your 'nigrah' any longer. Even some of us 'favored,' 'talented,' 'unusual,' ones are refusing to be your educated, sophisticated, split-leveled 'nigrahs' any longer. We refuse to look at ourselves through the eyes of white America": ibid.

230. Octavia Butler, *Kindred* (Boston: Beacon Press, 1988), 36-7. Reprinted by permission of the author.

231. Chief Justice William Rehnquist actually sang this Confederate marching song at the fourth judicial conference in 1999: See "U.S. Chief Justice Criticized for Dixie Sing-Along," Reuters, July 22, 1999.

232. Butler, *Kindred,* 101.

233. Ibid.

234. Kaysen, *Girl, Interrupted,* 5.

235. Ibid.

236. Butler, *Kindred,* 101.

237. Bob Marley and the Wailers, "Rolling Stone," *One Love* (UNI/Heartbeat, 1991), CD.

238. Kaysen, *Girl, Interrupted,* 5.

239. Fitzgerald, *Great Gatsby*, 189.

240. See generally ibid.

241. Orwell, *Nineteen Eighty-Four,* 25-6.

242. *Washington v. Davis*, 248.

CHAPTER FIVE

Un-Natural Things: Constructions of Race, Gender, and Disability

Robert L. Hayman, Jr., and Nancy Levit

Prologue

A century ago, the Supreme Court of the United States explained that legislation "is powerless to eradicate racial instincts"; that the U.S. Constitution "could not have been intended to abolish distinctions based upon color"; that if "one race be inferior to the other socially, the Constitution of the United States cannot put them upon the same plane." Racial caste defied radical egalitarianism; the racial order subsisted, as the Supreme Court put it, "in the nature of things."

So little has changed. As if to celebrate the centennial of *Plessy v. Ferguson*, the Supreme Court now tells us that desegregation orders are powerless to combat "white flight," a phenomenon rooted in "natural, if unfortunate, demographic forces"; African American populations in electoral districts are characterized not by shared "political, social, or economic interests," but merely by "race," a somehow distinct phenomenon; and affirmative-action programs cannot presume the existence of social or economic advantages based on "race," because—the social and economic facts notwithstanding—"consistency" demands that all "races" be viewed as if they were the same, because "we are just one race here ... American," and because, in any event, "Government cannot make us equal." It remains, still today, just in the nature of things.[1]

A Comparative Analysis

It is a commonly observed maxim of contemporary thought that "race" is socially constructed. But try explaining this maxim—to colleagues or students, to friends or relatives, or, God help you, to judges or legislators—and what you get in return is the bewildered stare that is otherwise reserved for UFO chasers, neo-Marxists, and people who speak in tongues. Hardly anyone, truth be told, seems to understand what is meant by this social construction of "race," and among those who do understand, hardly any seem to believe it. These are not, in the main, very good properties for a maxim.

And that seems to us unfortunate. The social-construction thesis is, we think, a compelling one, and its failure to secure acceptance outside a limited cluster of academic circles both distorts the dialogue on "race" and frustrates the practical movement toward racial equality. The thesis deserves—indeed, demands—respect from a wider audience.

So what precisely is the "social-construction thesis"? The negative aspect of the thesis is well settled: that race is not only, or even primarily, a biological phenomenon. The affirmative aspect of the proposition has proved more elusive. Race has been variously described as a cultural, an ethical, a legal, a political, a rhetorical, and a social construct. Of course, race can be all of these things, and there is more consensus here than the terms might suggest, for what they share is a view that the corporeal reality of "race" is less important than the response to it. The most salient aspects of "race," that is to say, are the treatments of race, the ways in which "race" orders and constrains us. These, in turn, constructionists note, have re-constitutive effects and ensure that race becomes in social fact what it is supposed to be in naturalist theory: a differentiating trait that orders us in hierarchical terms as members of inferior or superior races. Thus, the distinction between material reality and perception itself becomes meaningful in most social contexts—in the terrain, that is, of experience.

We think that the force of the constructionist position is overwhelming. But the naturalistic conception of race remains the conventional one, both in popular discourse and in legal discourse. Even in scientific circles, where the constructionist theory supposedly predominates, the biological model has its passionate defenders: Psychology, to take the most notable example, still suffers the plague of racial psychometrics.[2]

Our project here is to determine whether there is something about "race" that makes the social-construction thesis particularly problematic. Is a socially constructed "race," we wonder, either particularly elusive or particularly objectionable? We thought this project might be advanced by comparing the construction of "race" with the constructions of "disability" and of "gender."

Lawmakers seem somewhat hospitable to the notion that certain facets of identity can be reconstructed in and through culture. The Supreme Court, to take one example, has made some modest progress in recognizing the role of law in shaping cultural expectations and, as a consequence, in shaping or perpetuating gender roles. And accommodation laws, to take another example, make the social world less disabling—at least, in some small ways—for people with disabilities. We occasionally require, then, affirmative accommodation—we sometimes change the culture—to adapt to gender and disability.

But not to race. We remain at something of an impasse in urging the accommodation—the reconstruction—of "race." Folks just don't get the "social construction" of race. They seem unable, or perhaps unwilling.

Why hasn't the social-construction thesis been more fully accepted? We believe, first of all, that constructionist perspectives face two basic hurdles: a commitment to political liberalism and to the idea of a natural order. Regarding the first, the construction thesis denies the central liberal premise: the autonomy of the individual. It contests, in fact, both terms of the premise. It confronts the constraints on the modern subject and observes that those constraints are group-based.[3]

The construction thesis also challenges the integrity of the natural order. Historically, that order enjoyed a privileged status in American political thought, uniting, as it did, both the naturalist and empiricist strains of eighteenth-century political thought. The order continues to benefit from the modern preferences for elegant, concrete, and stable phenomena; the social-construction thesis, by contrast, may be too complex, too epiphenomenal, and too contingent for the predominant Newtonian mind-set.

As all of this implies, race is not the only salient feature of identity plagued by these biases. Constructionist views of disability and gender face the same obstacles. But race seems uniquely handicapped, and we wondered why.

We seek here to compare the way we understand the concepts of race, disability, and gender. Our task is not principally to compare the forms of discrimination, though similarities in the processes of construction—in the histories of discrimination—clearly inform, or cloud, our understanding. Our focus instead is on the concepts *as* concepts and on the ways in which those conceptions might hinder the constructionist project. Accordingly, we disclaim any attempt to disaggregate the aspects of identity—of course, in lived experience, they overlap—or to rank the various forms of oppression (even a hierarchy of oppression is, after all, still a hierarchy). In doing this interphenomenal comparison, we may not get beyond speculation; our main contribution may be to raise issues rather than offer answers.

Finally, we chose disability and gender not because they seem to us the only or even most appropriate points of comparison, but principally because of our own working familiarity with the constructs.[4] Our approaches to the comparative project, we should note, manifest slightly different emphases: Professor Hayman has principally focused on the practical and theoretical dimensions of "race" and "disability" as political concepts; Professor Levit has focused somewhat more on the strategic representation of the constructs of "race" and "gender" in legal-advocacy contexts. We attach no particular significance to these differences. They represent, we think, complimentary aspects of the same project.

The second part of this article offers a brief history of "race," tracing the historical forces and cultural choices that turned "race" into a scientific and everyday concept. It also surveys the evidence showing that "race" is, in reality, *scientifically unimportant* and politically unstable—that "race" is, in short, a social creation. In the third part, we compare the constructs of "race" and "disability," focusing principally on differences in the constructs themselves. We ask why race retains its salience as a biological phenomenon, when academicians and jurists have increasingly accepted a provisional, contextual, and constructed notion of "disabilities." In this part, we compare the Supreme Court's treatment of the constructs of "race" and "gender," looking at the relatively greater acceptance of the social-construction thesis for "gender" than for "race." Here we begin to offer some possible explanations to account for the greater willingness on the part of jurists and theorists to see gender and disability as social constructs.

Maybe the answer is as simple as white self-interest or greater empathetic identification with women or the disabled. Perhaps, though, the answer is more complicated than unconscious affiliation. It may have to do with the demographics of race or the different textures of race, sex, and ability prejudices. Maybe the explanation has to do with strategic choices. Thus, part three also raises the question whether litigation strategies of feminists or disability lawyers have succeeded in informative ways. Have gender and disability advocates done something strategic and special to make courts appreciate the social-construction thesis?

In the fourth part, we ask whether the social-construction thesis matters. Why should critical race theorists spend time unearthing the intellectual history of "race," "gender," and "disability," and engaging in discourse about the ways in which facets of identity are created in culture? We believe that the social construction thesis is at the heart of the story of race. Until the maxim of social construction is both understood and widely accepted, it will be easy to caricature "identity politics" as some sort of postmodern parlor game, easier still to divorce "race" and "race"-ism, and impossible to refute the meritocratic and market defenses of inequality. We hope then that a comparative analysis of race with other attributes of identity will offer a way to spark the dialogue about social construction—and, necessarily, about equality.

The Construction of Race

A Brief History of Race

Race is a recent phenomenon. W.E.B. Du Bois wrote in 1920 that the "discovery of personal whiteness among the world's peoples is a very modern thing." Bernard Crick, in his Foreword to the late Ivan Hannaford's study of "race," echoes Du Bois, observing that "racial conditioning is not part of the human condition."

Race appears to be a modern invention in a quite literal sense. Frank Snowden's study of the ancient Egyptians, Greek, and Romans, and Jan Nederveen Pieterse's iconographic study of the period agree that "race"—as we now conceive it—was viewed by ancient cultures benignly, when it was noticed at all. The attitude persisted through the middle ages, gradually changing during the sixteenth and seventeenth centuries. Only then—in the period of European expansion and conquest—did denigrating images of Africa and African peo-

ples begin to dominate in Western Europe: the Western attitude was "progressing."

After the Enlightenment, that attitude became more ideological. Ivan Hannaford identifies the period from 1684 to 1815 as the first significant stage in the evolution of the modern concept of "race": the empiricist preoccupation with classification; the emerging concept of a "natural law"; and the concurrent rise of the idea of a *volk* or culture combined to make possible the idea of discrete "races" of people. Yet even throughout the eighteenth century, the idea of "race" remained tentative, ambiguous, and highly idiosyncratic: Montesquieu, for example, used the term to identify the stages in the development of a nation's law. But the modernist emphasis on progress gradually secured this vital point of agreement: there were "races," and some were more advanced than others. Increasingly, non-European worlds became the counterpoints to modernization; "race" became a part of the demarcation.

Ultimately, "race" achieved the highest status in post-Enlightenment ideology: it became "science." The science of race developed in Western Europe roughly between 1790 and 1840. Physical anthropologists identified discrete classes of people; biologists debated their origins and natural compatibilities; cultural anthropologists matched the peoples to distinct civilizations. These were not merely "racial differences" that were being discovered; the science of race, rather, was ordering races, defining them as "superior" and "inferior." At its climax, in 1840, the anatomist Robert Knox declared, "That race is everything, is simply a fact, the most remarkable, the most comprehensive which philosophy has ever announced. Race is everything: literature, science, art—in a word, civilization depends upon it."[5]

In the United States, "race" was formed at this critical juncture and was complicated by America's extraordinary political developments. Precisely what vision of "race" the Europeans brought to America,[6] and how it took root in American soil, has been the subject of considerable historical debate. In the end, the past half-century of historical scholarship seems to have generated more substantial agreement than the debates might suggest. The study of American race and racism and their relationship to American slavery has yielded something of a consensus on the following six vital points.[7]

First, the early bondsmen were not only Africans, but included Europeans and Native Americans, as well. Second, Africans did not become the bondsmen of choice until late in the seventeenth century, and the development seems substantially unrelated to "racial" ideology. Third, the legal status of Africans and African Americans was ambiguous until the last quarter of the seventeenth century, and perhaps beyond. Fourth, the racial laws and rhetoric were not constant throughout the colonies or, after independence, throughout the states. Fifth, the commitments to the divisions of "race" were never universal. Sixth, and finally, there was apparently a considerable evolution of racial thinking. The details remain controverted, but it probably does not strain the historical consensus to suggest that "race" in America evolved in four stages.

Color-Consciousness:
1619–c. 1662
The early European colonists were undoubtedly aware of the color of the African's skin, and it assumed at some level a certain importance as a defining characteristic. But the fluidity of the servile and free classes, the integration of free blacks into the social and political communities, and the as-yet impoverished conception of "race" all suggest that whatever "race"-ism may have characterized the early colonies was vague, incomplete, and far from universal.

The Formalization of Race:
c. 1662–c. 1776
The restrictions of servitude hardened in the late seventeenth century, culminating in the adoption of the first major slave codes in 1680–82. Servitude became both perpetual and inheritable, typically transferred from the mother. Race emerged in this time period as a determinant of legal status The law gradually embraced the presumption that the "negro" was a slave and the "white" person was free. Interestingly, there was no concerted effort to define either "negro" or "white" in this time frame. Only the Virginia legislature made the effort, as it struggled to give meaning to the term "mulatto." At the same time, restrictions on "free" blacks surfaced in this period, though the inconsistencies in and among the "black codes" reflected continuing ambiguity and ambivalence.

The Explication of Race:
c. 1776–c. 1835
There were three ways to resolve the contradiction between the ideology of the revolutionary generation and the fact of chattel slavery. One way was to cure it through the abolition of slavery. This indeed was the response of those states where slavery was not an economic imperative. A second way was to demur: concede the philosophical inconsistency, but tolerate the contradiction on practical grounds. This was the initial response, at least, in the upper South, where slavery was assumed to be but a passing phase. A third way was to modify the ideology to incorporate what was by then a racial slavery, to carve out, in effect, a racial exception to the rules of liberty and equality. This, of course, would be the response wherever slavery needed more than an embarrassed defense—and that would be, eventually, throughout the American South. It is in this sense that "race" was born with the new nation.

The Scientization of Race:
c. 1835–?

The nascent "science" of "race" found a receptive audience in the antebellum South, where a besieged practice was in desperate need of some ideological foundations. "Science," of course, furnished the very best kind of post-Enlightenment foundations: "truths" that were not merely "self-evident," but "proved." Samuel Morton's *Crania Americana,* an 1839 exercise in racial craniometry, helped launch a tradition that would persist through emancipation, two Reconstructions, and beyond. Throughout, whenever "race" has been really needed, some "science" has been at hand to provide it.

A Brief History of Critiques of "Race"

Nineteenth-century abolitionism was a temporary obstacle to the science of "race"; twentieth-century nationalism, a major boon. In the United States, the physical anthropology of "race" was largely dormant during Reconstruction and its immediate aftermath but revived by the early twentieth century. Xenophobia, eugenics, and America's peculiar racism were part of the backdrop. By the time they were done, taxonomists would have divided us into as many as thirty-seven different races, some, of course, more "advanced" than others.

The horrors of the European Holocaust made the idea of "advanced races" unpalatable, and the emerging science of genetics made it untenable. The English biologist Julian Huxley and the American zoologist Herbert Jennings were among those who opposed the eugenics movement. They focused on a new genetic approach to race that sought, in Ivan Hannaford's words, "to distinguish the rational boundaries of science from the lunatic." In 1936, as the Law for the Protection of German Blood and German Honour was taking effect, Huxley and A. C. Haddon published *We Europeans.*

Their text used genetics to demonstrate the fallacies of hereditarianism and to debunk the concept of a biological race. "The term race," they concluded, "as applied to human groups, should be dropped from the vocabulary of science."[8]

In fact, there had been a competing conception of "race" almost from the beginning, a conception that recognized the role of social forces in constructing "race" and "races." Initially, it focused on the role of society in shaping the "racial" being: abolitionists—and later the postbellum egalitarians—stressed the role of slavery and discrimination in suppressing the abilities of black Americans: If the black race was inferior, the argument went, it was because it had been made that way. Still others dared to invert the "natural order," as in the Romantic racialism and Ethiopianism of the mid- to late nineteenth century. The danger, of course, was that flipping the position of the races left in place the conception of "race." It remained something natural.

But even the founders of the science of race doubted this point. Johann Friedrich Blumenbach is often considered the founder of physical anthropology; his 1795 text introduced the term "caucasian" and substantially accelerated the process of scientizing "race." But Blumenbach asserted the unity of mankind; insisted that the racial categories he created were overlapping; observed that the defining characteristics were substantially mutable; maintained that individual Africans "differ from other Africans as much as Europeans differ from Europeans, or even more so"; and denied that physical differences could be interpreted as inferiority or superiority.[9]

Blumenbach's initial insights were often obscured by the politics of "race," but "race," in the end, proved too weak a concept to do what science demanded. In 1904, Oswald Garrison Villard summarized for American readers the work of German ethnologists. "Race," he concluded, "is merely a pseudo-scientific or political catchword." The great bulk of racial science was, in Villard's words, "ethnological claptrap"; it was "humbug pure and simple."[10] The anthropologist Franz Boas soon extended and popularized the critique in *Anthropology and Modern Life*: "Race" resonated, Boas contended, precisely because we had been socially conditioned to think, and act, in terms of "race": "The formation of the racial groups in our midst must be understood on a social basis. In a community comprising two distinct types which are socially clearly separated, the social grouping is reënforced by the outer appearance of the individuals and each is at once and automatically assigned to his own group."[11]

Boas's critique of race was carrying the day even before the Second World War. The postwar generation completed the task. The anthropologist Ashley Montagu was among those at the forefront. In 1959 he wrote that

> for two centuries anthropologists have been directing attention towards the task of establishing criteria by whose means races of man may be defined. All have taken for granted the one thing which required to be proven, namely that the concept of race corresponded with a reality which could actually be measured and verified and descriptively set out so that it could be seen to be a fact.[12]

Montagu was one among many who thought the "race" project had compromised the scientific method: "The process of averaging the characters of a given group, knocking the individuals together, giving them a good stirring, and then serving the resulting omelet as a 'race' is essentially the anthropological process of race making. It may be good cooking, but it is not science, since it serves to confuse rather than clarify."[13]

More recent work confirms the critique: "Race" is principally a human invention.[14] Consider:

- Analyses of race differences are instantly confounded by the obvious conflation of the "racial" gene pools. Americans are—individually and collectively—a "multiracial" people.[15]
- The smallest proportion of genetic variation—just 7 percent of the polymorphic genes, which are in turn just 25 percent of the overall pool—is found between groups that have conventionally been considered "races." Significantly, no polymorphic gene perfectly discriminates among the traditionally classified racial groups.[16]
- The anthropological case for racial classifications is weak. Stephen Jay Gould follows nearly a century's worth of anthropological tradition when he suggests that racial classifications have no discernable scientific value. "Human variation exists," Gould concludes; "the formal designation of races is passé."[17]
- Among the sciences, only psychology seems not to have rejected a naturalistic "race." And it may be following suit: A recent essay in *American Psychologist* calls on psychologists to follow the lead of other disciplines and to reassess the utility of the "race" construct.[18]

All of which is to say that where "race" differences are significant, it is as a consequence not of nature, but of social choices.

Race and Disability

Following is a brief comparison of the constructs of "race" and "disability." For reasons that will become apparent, the initial discussion of "disability" focuses primarily on physical disability. The discussion, however, does not differentiate within that construct, though we do not deny that such differentiations are possible and, for subsequent stages of this project, may prove valuable.

Some Parallels

The constructions of "race" and of "disability" appear to share at least these two features: They have similar intellectual histories (and are thus at comparable stages in their evolution); and they are both shaped—and perhaps distorted—by the conventional conception of equality as "similarity" or "sameness."

Intellectual History

The disability construct has evolved in ways that roughly parallel the history of race. According to the anthropologist Henri-Jacques Stiker, through the Middle Ages, disability was not a discrete construct at all. Impairments or "infirmities" were largely indistinguishable from other forms of misery and suffering: in this age, disability "is neither inventoried, nor excluded, nor organized, nor viewed in any special way: it is simply there, part of the great human lot of misery. It too deserves mercy."[19] As Stiker suggests, the social response to "infirmity" was—as with all forms of suffering—largely ethical or spiritual, consisting in the main of charity and care.[20]

Enlightenment brought a discrete model of disability—or, rather, of "disabilities." The modernist preoccupation with systems and orders was reflected in a new emphasis on describing and categorizing impairments. Disability was distinguished from other forms of suffering—poverty is a conspicuous example—and the practical consequence was the segregation of disabled individuals into hospitals and institutions. Distinctions were drawn *within* the evolving construct, and gradations were formulated within the distinctions. "Mental" disabilities came to be distinguished from "physical" ones, and a science of teratology (from the Greek word *teras* 'monster') emerged for severe congenital defects. The social response, as this suggests, was largely a medical one. It consisted in the main of confinement and reintegration where that was consistent with the health both of the individual and of society.

A variation on this model emerged after the First World War. The emphasis on "rehabilitation" produced disability's lingering paradox—a paradox rooted in the determination to deny the very differences that inhere in the disability construct. The rehabilitation model converted reintegration into a technical (as opposed to a metaphysical) issue; the social response centered largely on the need to secure appropriate adjustments of the disabled individual.[21]

The construction of disability that finally emerged in the latter half of this century—the social construction—is rooted in the recognition that the gap between ability and disability is a social one, and that it may be society rather than the individual that needs adjustment. Constructionism has brought a critique of disability that problematizes, in its weak form, the cultural determinations of salient and valuable capacities and, in its more radical form, the culture-bound ideas of individual capacity and disability.

The disability and race constructs seem to have evolved along parallel lines and seem now to be at similar points. Not surprisingly, their contemporary iterations confront similar conceptual dilemmas:

From Within: The Subjectivity Dilemma

Both constructs are now situated in what might be characterized as part of the postmodern dilemma: Is it possible to assert the coexistence in a single self of an expressive subject, or an autonomous self, and a constructed object, or a self constituted and constrained by rhetorical convention and social practice? In disability discourse, the tension is reflected in what Susan Reynolds Whyte has identified as two radically different approaches to the question of impairment and personhood: There is, on the one hand, the "sweeping cultural history of

French tradition," which examines the "changing discourse on difference through historical epochs" and focuses on "how persons are constructed in relation to biology, religion, ethics, and the institutional structure of society"; and, on the other hand, there is an approach that "begins with individuals and tries to comprehend the experience of being an impaired person through first-hand accounts."[22] The same tensions are reflected in the dialogue on the current racial paradigm, principally in debates over the relationship and value of ethnicity theory and the weight to be accorded to racial agency or autonomy.[23]

From Without: The Liminal State
Constructions of disability and race may be at comparable stages of evolution from another perspective: Both reflect a gradual move toward inclusivity—toward, that is, the full incorporation of all disabled and racial groups into the polity and society—but both also reflect substantial uncertainty as to the proper means for achieving this end. Both constructs, in short, manifest an ongoing ambivalence about the differences still demarcated by the construction.

The late Robert Murphy observed that people with disabilities "exist in partial isolation from society as undefined, ambiguous people." Relying on anthropological studies of initiation rituals, Murphy suggested that people with disabilities seem suspended in a state of "liminality": After the requisite periods of isolation and instruction, they were poised "at the threshold" of a ritual emergence, then to be reincorporated into the community in a fully realized capacity. The same, it seems, might be said of race. The significant achievement of the second Reconstruction was its apparent success in reintegrating black Americans into social and political life. But not quite. As Orlando Patterson notes, works such as *The Bell Curve* remind us that full citizen-

ship remains an elusive goal. Racial minorities, like people with disabilities, remain in that liminal state.[24]

The Constraints of Equality: Sameness and Blindness
Constructions of race and of disability share an ironic feature: They both have a certain invisible quality. Both constructs are handicapped by the conception of equality as sameness. Access to equality is thus conditioned on the denial of difference; the difference itself becomes sub- or abnormal, or, equally oppressive, nonexistent. In the former instance, the passion for similarity incites repression of difference; in the latter instance, it incites rejection of the very idea of difference and, inevitably, of the people differentiated by the construct. The pretext of ignorance is reflected, for race, in the ironic rule of colorblindness and, for disability, in the "don't stare" rule. Both perpetuate the paradox. As Robert Murphy wrote, "Nothing could better teach a child to be horrified by disability; that the condition is so terrible that one cannot speak about it or even look at it." For race, of course, colorblindness generates comparable dilemmas.[25]

Some Distinctions

The constructions of "race" and of "disability" apparently have much in common, enough that we are not unwilling to suggest that "race" is, in some meaningful sense, a form of "ability" or "disability." But there are also significant differences in the constructs, differences that would seem to make the social-constructionist conception of "race" more problematic—that is, either more elusive or more objectionable—than the constructionist conception of most forms of "disability." We have tentatively identified at least six such differences: 1) There is a discourse of disability that has no parallel in "race"; 2) there is an asymmetry to the "ability"/"disability" paradigm that has no parallel in "race"; 3) "disability" both connotes and is conventionally understood to signify a loss of ability, while "race" signifies inherent capacities; 4) "disability" is local and contingent, while "race" represents a global and immutable quality; 5) "disability" signifies a disadvantage suffered by all disabled individuals, while "race" signifies a group trait that does not necessarily disadvantage the racial individual; and finally, 6) the social incentives for rehabilitating both individuals with disabilities and the very disability construct itself may be significantly greater than are the incentives for recognizing "race" and dismantling racial caste.

The Discourse of Disability Versus the Silence of Race: The World Health Organization defines "impairment" as "an abnormality or loss of any physiological or anatomical structure or function"; "disability" as "the consequences of an impairment"; and "handicap" as "the social disadvantage that results from an impairment or disability." Impairments, then, may be products of creation, but they are not "disabilities" until we experience them as such, and even then, it is a sociopolitical decision to "handicap" people due to their impairments.[26]

There is nothing in the discourse of "race" to signify these distinctions. "Race" is the conflation of corporeal reality, its experiential consequence, and its attendant social advantage (or disadvantage). Worse, the forced poverty of discourse represented by the rule of "color-blindness" makes "race" itself a linguistic pariah, but without the fall-back of discursive substitutes.

The Asymmetry of Ability/Disability Versus the Symmetry of Race: For ability/disability, the rhetorical opposites apparently comport with material reality; the *dis*advantages that

accompany *dis*ability are thus too obvious to ignore. Race, meanwhile, is a monolithic construct with no simple dichotomous referent. The construct must thus simultaneously signify both advantage (for some people of "race") and disadvantage (for other people of "race"). Even disaggregated—as, for example, in racial "majority" and "minority"—the apparent reality of diverse racial experiences, including multiracial experiences, confound simple dichotomous representations and fail to correlate perfectly with advantage and disadvantage. Witness the malevolent attempts to contrast African American experiences with Asian American or, with a new and frightening vigor, Jewish American experiences.[27] The "voluntary"/"involuntary" minority distinction seeks to fill the void, but it simply is not a readily accessible "essential" difference that would justify asymmetry in our comprehension and treatment of "racial" groups; the "black"/"white" dichotomy, meanwhile, is incomplete, indeterminate, and without inherent signifiers of obvious disadvantage.[28]

Disability Versus Inability: Disability signifies a deprivation or loss of ability. The rhetorical construct itself, then, suggests that the disadvantage is not due to an inherent lack of capacity. "Race" does not afford the same benefit. On the contrary, "race" in fact denotes a hierarchy of inherent capacity. Thus, the discourse of race obscures the role of society in enabling or disabling racial groups.

Local and Contingent Disability Versus Global and Immutable Race: Disability is obviously contextual: the loss of ability is neither total nor unalterable. The contextual nature of "race" is simply not so obvious: people seem to be of "race" in every social situation and for all time. A trait that is apparently local and contingent, such as disability, is more obviously the product of social forces than a trait, such as race, that is apparently global and immutable.

Individual Disability Versus Racial Groups: For "disability," the constructionist thesis may not be terribly at odds with the political ethos. Disability is, after all, individualized, and it is universal among individuals with disabilities. Rehabilitation, remediation, and even accommodation are thus of and for the individual, each of whom has experienced the loss. The "People First" movement has emphasized the point: "The disabled" is an outmoded construct, replaced by "people with disabilities." "Race," meanwhile, remains a more essentialist construct. People *are* their race, or at best are *of* their race, but they are not people *with* a race. This racial essentialism not only contributes to the sense that race is something inherent and not something appended (and thus perhaps constructed), but, ironically, also militates against "race"-consciousness: People may be of a racial group, but *as individuals* they are not necessarily burdened *with* racial disadvantage. Of course, this result is possible only by divorcing "race" from racism, but that divorce is maddeningly self-perpetuating. The racial individual does not necessarily labor under racial disadvantage and hence does not need—or deserve—"race"-conscious relief. Consequently, the unrecognized racial disadvantage goes unremedied, and the persistent hierarchy reinforces the notion of a natural racial order.

Egalitarian Motives: Rehabilitating "Disability" Versus Erasing the Color Line: Constructions of "race" and of "disability" may continue to reflect lingering social and psychological pathologies. Citing evidence that the forms of prejudice often go hand-in-hand, Robert Murphy concluded that "bigotry observes no boundaries."[29] But there may be differences here, if only ones of degree, and they

may reflect a greater willingness to equalize opportunities for people with disabilities, a willingness manifest in acceptance of the social-construction thesis and its attendant sense of social responsibility. Three factors lead us to suggest this possibility.

First, the economic incentives appear to be different for "race" and "disability." As Murphy notes, racial minorities "have served for centuries as a pool of cheap labor ... it pays to keep them down. There are, however, no strong economic reasons for systematically excluding and abasing the physically handicapped."[30] "Race" is, in fact, a remarkably weak scientific concept, and it has required as a consequence a comparatively vigorous political defense. That it has received that defense may be the most eloquent testament to the scope and depth of the vested interest in "race."

Second, "race" and "disability" may produce different existential dilemmas. Disability, Murphy wrote, "represents a fearsome possibility":[31] The response has been a refusal to yield to disability, even—and perhaps especially—when the underlying impairment is the result of "natural" forces or fate. This is, in effect, a certain denial of disability, and it appears at times in the willful (if unconscious) avoidance of disability, and at other times in defiant attempts to "eliminate" disability through rehabilitation. The roots of racial disadvantage, meanwhile, are in some ways different and may produce a different kind of denial. Racial disadvantage is, after all, more obviously our own creation, and the fact that disadvantage may generate guilt more than fear is the result of an apparent unwillingness or inability to accept responsibility for the truths of racism. There is a certain superficial paradox here—we defiantly struggle to assert control over the uncontrollable while disclaiming responsibility for the eminently controllable. But there is also a certain coherence—disability and racism are simply maladies of different orders, and we cannot admit our vulnerability to either.

Third, and finally, people with disabilities may lay a greater claim to either the empathy or the sympathy of majority populations than do minorities of race. The relatively greater segregation of racial minorities means that their disadvantages are both less apparent and perhaps of less concern to the majority population. Moreover, race prejudice may be overtly socialized in the majority population in ways that prejudice against people with disabilities is not. In sum, the dominant attitude toward racial minorities may be characterized by somewhat greater ignorance and indifference, as well as hostility.

Race and Mental Retardation

In the course of comparing the "race" and "disability" constructs, it occurred to us that within the "disability" construct there is a near perfect analogy to "race": As a construct, "race" remarkably parallels "mental retardation." As the following discussion suggests, this is more than mere coincidence.

There are at least three significant parallels between "race" and "mental retardation": First, the history of the constructs are quite similar; second, both constructs signify a hierarchy of presumed inability, differentiating on the basis of inherent, global, and subnormal attributes; and third, both constructs are radically reductive, permitting no assertions of difference within the constructed groups.

Intellectual History: The conventional construct of mental retardation is the medical model, which locates mental retardation within the biological constitution of the disabled individual. The role of science in such a conception is to cure or eliminate mental retardation, and the role of the state is to limit the social costs of the disability. The social construction of mental retardation emerged in the mid-twentieth century, shifting the locus of disability from the biological makeup of the individual to the society that limits her opportunities. The social—or "cultural" or "political"—construction of mental retardation recognizes that individuals may appear to possess certain mental limitations for a wide variety of reasons, not many of which are "natural," but that it is society that uses those limitations to disable it. The role of science in such a conception is to understand the interplay between the individual's perceived limitations and the societal responses they evoke. The role of the state is to limit or eliminate the disabling societal restrictions that confront the disabled person.

Today, the prevailing standard defines mental retardation as "significantly subaverage general intellectual functioning existing concurrently with deficits in adaptive behavior and manifested during the developmental period." Mental retardation is thus a norm-referenced statistical creation. It reflects neither a diagnosis of an inherent condition nor an absolute judgment about "intelligence"; it merely reflects the judgments, first, that the labeled individual demonstrates lesser aptitudes and abilities than the norm on some standardized measure of those particular qualities, and second, that there is something to be gained by application of the label.

In an absolute sense, then, there is no such thing as a mentally retarded person. Only culture—in setting the norms, in creating the measures, and in applying the labels—can make someone mentally retarded. The label could be designed to help: to bring educational opportunities, vocational opportunities, and life choices that *should* come automatically to all people but do not. But it can also be used to harm: to limit opportunities based on the perception or presumption that the labeled person is incapable or unfit.

To be mentally retarded, in such cases, is to be inferior, and the label can make that inferiority increasingly "real." Through the complex interactions between the society and the labeled person, the "mentally retarded" person appears "retarded" and, increasingly, tailors her behavior to accommodate the expectations and constraints of her social environment. The opportunities afforded her in that environment become increasingly limited, and so, too, do her achievements, in a relentless, self-perpetuating cycle.

Mental retardation, in the end, is not so much a product of creation as it is a product of human re-creation. People are created as just people; they are made "mentally retarded" just because they need to be labeled that way for one political reason or another.[32]

It is the same, of course, with "race." And with "race," as with "mental retardation," we seem reluctant to believe it. We seem unable to escape the constraints of the conventional or biological model.

Presumptions of Inability: Mental retardation is in one significant respect not a disability at all: People with mental retardation are not disabled, they are *unable.* The condition is widely regarded as inherent and immutable. People with mental retardation never possessed average mental capacities, and they never will. Moreover, the inability is global. The construct is rooted in "general" intellectual deficiency, and that deficiency is itself generalized to signify a presumption of universal unfitness for social life. Thus, the Supreme Court—reflecting a truly staggering indifference to context—can insist that people with mental retardation "are different, immutably so, and in relevant respects," and mean by this last suggestion that mental retardation is relevant "as a general matter." Finally, the immutable "difference" is indeed a subnormality. Members of the group are generally presumed to lack

merit, and assistance to them is either an expression of sympathy or—in competitive contexts—an anti-meritocratic and unfair preference.[33]

On each score, again, it is the same with "race."

Reductionism and Difference: We recently celebrated the discovery that not all people with mental retardation are exactly the same. We celebrated it because it enabled us to deny, initially, the existence of a group identity, and, consequently, the rationale for group empowerment. Thus it was in *City of Cleburne v. Cleburne Living Center* that the petitioner city—which had denied a zoning permit to a group home for people with mental retardation based on concerns about and ostensibly for those residents—argued, without any apparent sense of irony, that the mentally retarded class was too varied, vague, and indeterminate to permit the conclusion that it comprised a "discrete" and "insular" minority for purposes of equal-protection review. The Supreme Court, with no greater sense of irony, accepted this absurd proposition.[34] But all this demonstrates, of course, is that the conventional construct of mental retardation is so radically reductive that it cannot tolerate either the notion of difference *within* the class or ambiguities *between* classes: assert those differences and ambiguities, and the construct magically disappears. But of course, the construct lingers, in the actions of the Cleburne city council, in the Supreme Court's assertion of "relevant" differences, and in all the other ways in which people with mental retardation suffer—as a class—discriminatory treatment rooted in their presumed differences. That, of course, *is* the construct of mental retardation. Its most salient aspect is the discriminatory treatment rooted in stereotyped differences, treatment that forges a group identity in spite of differences within the group and uncertainty about the group's parameters.

Substitute "race" for "mental retardation" (and *Miller v. Johnson,* for example, for *City of Cleburne v. Cleburne Living Center*). Again, it is all the same.[35]

These similarities really ought not to be surprising. The histories of "race" and "mental retardation" are, after all, more than parallel. They have a common history: They were made similarly, and they were made together.

For people with mental retardation, that history has included compulsory segregation (in part due to the impracticability of sterilization and euthanasia, perhaps the functional equivalent of the aborted colonization schemes for the freedmen); exclusion from mainstream public education; peonage in almost every form; bans on marriage and voting; and systematized incarceration or confinement based on the fiction of innate dangerousness.[36] This is, of course, very much like the history of "race."

Or, perhaps, it *is* the history of race. The intellectual inferiority of racial groups was, after all, a vital part—perhaps *the* vital part—of American race formation. Conversely, race was a vital ingredient—again, perhaps *the* vital ingredient—in the development of the modern concepts of formal intelligence and mental deficiency. Part of the correlation was rhetorical. To take one example, a British physician first identified Down's syndrome in 1866, and because the condition reminded him of Central Asian faces, it would be known for the next hundred years as "mongoloid idiocy." But part of the correlation was alleged to be empirical. Binet's intelligence tests were corrupted by a generation's worth of American eugenicists and psychometricians determined to establish an intellectual racial order. Their studies were at times overtly racist, and always—as a large number of them belatedly recognized, either contestable or simply in error. But they

defined the field. Thus, Ales Hrdlicka could unequivocally assert, in a 1921 lecture at American University, that "there is no question that there are today already retarded peoples, retarded races, and that there are advanced and more advanced races, and that the differences between them tend rather to increase than to decrease." Hrdlicka was demonstrably wrong on one score: The differences between the "retarded" and "advanced" races have tended—over the past half-century—to decrease rather than increase. But this is so because we stopped making those differences increase—for a while.[37]

Race as Disability

We are not at all reluctant to suggest that "race" may be understood as a form of "ability" or "disability." We are somewhat less certain about the implications of a tentative conclusion that "race" is constructed like, more particularly, a mental disability.

We are certain that it is important to look hard at the *processes* of construction, not just at the constructions that result. It seems clear that for some races, the attribution of "race" has been principally an attribution of intellectual inferiority or superiority. There is a link, after all, between the commercial success of *The Bell Curve* and the recent spate of attacks on Critical Race Theory that target, above all, race theorists' alleged deficiencies in "reason." "Race" obviously has been constructed, for some, as a mental deficiency.

But in the process of constructing "race" that way, a different condition emerges. Here are the symptoms: first, the delusional beliefs that only one set of traditions is worth preserving, only one set of cognitive processes constitutes intellect, and that only one set of perceptions comports with material reality. Second, a disorientation to place and time, characterized by an unawareness of context and an inability to appreciate the lived experience of systemic advantage and disadvantage. And finally, a not-too-subtle form of paranoia, manifest in fears that Critical Race Theory portends the end of Western civilization, coupled with the odd notion that it somehow takes great courage for white people to confront minority groups. All of which is to say that the process of constructing "race" may reflect, at least in part, not so much a mental deficiency as a mental illness.

That, of course, is too glib. But we think it is important to note that "race" can be a disability for all of us.

Race and Gender

Legal Treatment of the Constructs

The Supreme Court is responsible for a long line of cases holding essentially that women's biological capacities should determine their legal rights. In 1873, the Supreme Court denied Myra Bradwell the right to practice law because the "natural and proper timidity and delicacy which belongs to the female sex evidently unfits it for many of the occupations of civil life."[38] In the following century, the Supreme Court supported various forms of restrictive labor legislation for women and laws limiting women's participation in the nation's civic life. Even after it settled on intermediate scrutiny for gender classifications in 1976, the court said solemnly that real biological differences between men and women could justify differences in treatment. The court gave salience to physical differences between men and women in cases ranging from *Rostker v. Goldberg*, supporting Congress's determination that women were biologically unsuitable for combat positions, to *Michael M. v. Superior Court of Sonoma County*, in which the court located potential criminal responsibility for statutory rape in biologi-

cal differences between young men and women.[39]

Despite its history of vesting biological differences between men and women with social significance, in the mid-1980s the Supreme Court began to acknowledge the social processes by which gender is created. In *Mississippi University for Women v. Hogan*, the court held that the exclusion of men from a publicly funded nursing school violated equal protection. The court recognized the role of stereotypical thinking in *creating gender* when it held that the university's policy risked reinforcing stereotypes of nursing as women's work. In *International Union, UAW v. Johnson Controls*, the court again noted the institutional role in constructing gender. The court struck down an employer's fetal-protection policy, which kept fertile women out of the company's higher-risk—and higher-paying—lead-exposure areas. This gender grouping, the Supreme Court acknowledged, was not natural or inevitable; it was a social choice about the significance of possible pregnancy: whether women should be allowed to risk their own health and the health of their unborn children. The court's use of stereotyping analysis in *Hogan* and *Johnson Controls* is an explicit recognition of some aspects of the social construction of gender. It demonstrates the court's willingness to question the institutional use of gender norms in assessing job performance.[40]

Recently, the court went further than acknowledging the gender-constructive process of stereotyping in major social institutions. It began to recognize its own role in reconstructing gender. In *Planned Parenthood v. Casey*, the court examined the burdens that restrictive abortion laws place on the social roles of women. The court struck the state's spousal-notification provision for abortion as unconstitutional. In doing so, it considered a wealth of social-science evidence showing that notifying husbands of their wives' intent to seek an abortion created not only an actual physical risk of spousal battery, but also a fear of that risk, which was "likely to prevent a significant number of women from obtaining an abortion." The court recognized the proactive effect of laws in constructing the social and economic roles of women: "The ability of women to participate equally in the economic and social life of the Nation has been facilitated by their ability to control their reproductive lives."[41]

While it is difficult to find precise factual parallels between the sex and race cases, some cases are thematically comparable. Consider a comparison of two cases, one about sex segregation in educational institutions, *United States v. Virginia (VMI)*, and one about racial segregation in educational institutions, *Missouri v. Jenkins*. This may be an unfair comparison in one sense, given the different postures of the cases, but the comparison offers an illustration about the Supreme Court's views regarding institutional responsibility for constructing identity. The court held that the publicly supported Virginia Military Institute's all-male admissions policy was unconstitutional. As it traced professional and military schools' history of resistance to the inclusion of women, the majority was alert to the power of institutions to shape beliefs. "State actors controlling gates to opportunity," Justice Ruth Bader Ginsburg wrote for the Supreme Court, "may not exclude qualified individuals based on 'fixed notions concerning the roles and abilities of males and females.'"[42] Implicit in its holding is a glimmer of recognition of the court's own role in shaping gender. More than that, for women the court seemed close to a Field of Dreams theory of educational and occupational channeling: If we build the opportunities, they will come.

For racial minorities, there was no Field of Dreams. In *Jenkins* the magnet concept of attracting white students from sur-rounding suburban districts to an urban area that was 68 percent non-white was an unconstitutional remedy. Despite allegations that Kansas did not have any "black" high schools and therefore exported its blacks to Missouri schools, the trial court ruled during the liability phase that the Kansas suburbs were not part of the segregation problem in the two-state region. In the remedy phase, the Supreme Court held that "this interdistrict [magnet] goal is beyond the scope of the intradistrict violation."[43] Social institutions, in short, have no responsibility for constructing race or for reconstructing it.

Possible Explanations for the Court's Acceptance of the Constructions of "Gender" and "Disability"

Empathetic Identification and the Interest-Convergence Thesis

The most obvious explanation for the relative successes of the social-construction thesis may have to do with empathetic identification or its more malignant sibling, white self-interest. (White) people can see themselves as someday becoming disabled: developing a disease, losing a limb, or simply aging. And all white people have mothers. Many also have sisters or wives or daughters. The majority of people *are* female. Most whites do not have any relatives of color that they know about. How many whites have more than one or two good friends of color? So whites may have greater empathetic capacity for the situations of women and the disabled.

Derrick Bell argues that racial reforms succeed when they comport with whites' interests. Members of the dominant race permit minority successes only when whites perceive that those reforms would be in their own self-interest.[44] Applying the interest-convergence thesis to the relative situations of women and people of color, we can see different outcomes. It benefits men to have women as breadwinners in the family; they also benefit when tasks such as lawn-mowing, money-managing, or car repair cross the gender line. On the contrary, many of the successes of racial minorities—at least, in the perception of many whites—threaten to usurp or replace jobs or positions in school. It is no accident that the case that could have sounded the death knell for affirmative action in employment had it not been settled. *Piscataway Township Board of Education v. Taxman*[45] was framed as a one-to-one replacement case. Acknowledgment of the cultural construction of gender may work to the advantage of whites (or their relatives or friends), while any admission that race is a social and political creation is disadvantageous.

Attitudes and Demographics

Perhaps the answer lies in part in a slightly different direction: the demographics of race and sex in this country or the different workings of race and sex prejudices. Of course, racism and sexism are intertwined and "mutually reinforcing" oppressions,[46] but sexism, on an institutional level, is increasingly unacceptable. For example, witness the public attention to issues of rape, sexual harassment, women's economic empowerment, and gender violence, and the passage of favorable legislation such as the Violence Against Women Act and the Family and Medical Leave Act. Systemic racism, on the other hand, has acquired increasingly complex justificatory mechanisms—the new racism of reverse-discrimination suits, calls for colorblind and "free" market constitutionalism, and denial of the significance (and even the fact) of racial segregation in America.

Demographically, women constitute half of America, while racial and ethnic minorities are numerically much more isolated. Blacks make up approximately 12 percent

of the population; Latinos, 10 percent; and Asians, 3 percent. In terms of daily interaction and contact, the lives of men and women are largely integrated. Women and men live together side by side and participate in the same important life events: births, schooling, marrying, and burying. This integration makes the rise of women, some of men's most intimate partners and relatives, easier to handle, and sometimes even economically beneficial. People of color and whites are less likely to be exposed to each other and do not interact on a daily basis. By all sociological measures of assimilation, whites and racial minorities are both segregated and spatially isolated. Racial minorities are unevenly distributed in a community; neighborhoods are racially concentrated; those enclaves are isolated from neighborhoods of different racial composition; and neighborhoods of racial minorities, particularly blacks, are often clustered near urban areas.[47] We can ignore race in ways we cannot ignore gender because we do not have to live with people of different races.

Maybe we are more ashamed of the social construction of race, and perhaps that shame translates into denial. It is acceptable to admit publicly that one gave one's daughter Barbie dolls and one's son G.I. Joes, but one cannot publicly admit to race prejudice. Maybe the shame about racism prevents us from talking about race? The level of collective denial is shown by the furor over the recent resolution introduced in Congress requiring the government to apologize officially for slavery. Whether one believes that the gesture is empty without an understanding of white supremacy and accompanying reparations is not the point. The point is the number of Americans who, in letters to the editor or polls or radio talk shows, deny that they or their relatives ever participated in slavery or any of its continuing accompaniments.[48]

And instead of directly confronting our shame about, and our responsibility for, racism, whites come up with ways to avoid talking about talking about it. We pretend to be raceless; we aspire, according to the Supreme Court, to be "colorblind"; and when well-meaning people raise the issue of racism, they are accused of "playing the race card." "The not-so-subtle implication," Margaret Russell says, "is that talking about race has turned into a matter of sophistry, gamesmanship, and hyperbole."[49]

Even etymologically, we do not have the words to capsulize the social construction of race. Gender is the social construction of sex; no parallel term exists for the social construction of race. Although in academic literature we speak of the inscription of race or "racializing," these concepts are not sound bites that have sifted into the public consciousness the way "gender" has. The concept of gender was created to show the role of patriarchy in manufacturing certain aspects of sex. Similarly, the idea of disability was created to demonstrate how society has constructed impairments. It is social power that turns impairments into disabilities. The idea of racism was supposed to do the same thing, but it hasn't worked out that way.

Litigation Strategies and Concepts of Identity

One avenue of explanation we investigated is the extent to which feminist and critical race lawyers have succeeded in bringing the social-construction thesis to the attention of judges. Here we concentrated not on the facets of identity as constructs, but on their strategic re-presentations by litigants. We searched for evidence of the social-construction argument in two dimensions. The first was direct evidence of the theoretical argument: Did feminist or civil-rights lawyers talk explicitly about the social or political construction of gender or race? The

second was more indirect evidence: whether lawyers told the litigants' stories in narrative form to demonstrate the effect of social policies on the lived experiences of individuals. Our research was not exhaustive—we principally examined Supreme Court parties briefs and amicus briefs—and has omitted the narrative dimensions of lobbying and publishing stories in the press, which may be some of the most effective forms of storytelling. We also recognize that neither feminist nor critical race lawyers form a united band of adherents with a single litigation strategy, so our conclusions are little more than tentative speculations.

Briefing the Concept of Social Construction for the Court

We first looked to see whether the parties or amici explicitly briefed the issues of the social construction or the biological importance of race or sex. In several sex-discrimination cases, litigators and amici carefully pointed out to the court that no social consequences follow inescapably from biological differences. Differences between men and women were important in certain settings because institutional actors chose to vest them with social meaning. In *Johnson Controls*, for example, amici sharply distinguished between biological differences and women's social roles, arguing that the biological capacity to become pregnant should not dictate women's employment prospects. This theme—that government makes people unequal when it creates classifications purportedly based on biology—is repeated throughout several of the most prominent gender cases in the 1980s and 1990s.[50]

In *United States v. Virginia (VMI)*, the government argued that the military institute *chose* to deem biological differences between men and women important when those differences had very little to do with VMI's purposes or pedagogy. The petitioners in *VMI* did not stop with the argument that gender differences were being created by the school's policy. They took the argument one step further and urged the court to recognize the reconstructive possibilities, reminding the Supreme Court that the trial court had "found that VMI had substantial transformative potential." The school was able to take average young men and turn them into citizen soldiers; there was no reason that the school could not do the same with young women.[51]

But the briefs in a number of race cases also attempted to start a dialogue about the social construction of race. In redistricting cases, for example, amici attempted to show the political consequences of stating that race is unimportant. The NAACP Legal Defense and Education Fund argued in *Abrams v. Johnson* that race-consciousness in drawing district lines is vital to the political voice and, thus, the identity of minority race groups. An amicus brief in *City of Richmond v. J. A. Croson,* argued for the constitutionality of a city's minority set-aside plan as a remedy for past discrimination by others. The brief tied segregative practices and governmental politics of exclusion—the social creation of categories of people unworthy of receiving government contracts—to contemporary statistics. In various ways, critical race briefs attempted to show the ways institutions manufacture racial disparities.[52]

When litigants expressly raise the social-construction issue, how does the Supreme Court respond? Just a century ago, the court explicitly biologized race, holding that it was not unconstitutional for Louisiana to require Homer Plessy, who was one-eighth black and seven-eighths white, to ride in a separate railway car from white passengers. In his brief to the Supreme Court, Plessy explicitly raised the idea that races were socially constructed in several ways—noting that the states did not share a definition of "colored" and that the reputation of racial-belonging was a socially created property

interest. Justice Henry Billings Brown accepted Plessy's argument about the varying definitions of "race" but used it only to refute Plessy's suggestion that he was actually "white," the definition, Brown noted, being purely a matter of state law. Brown, however, ignored the implications of this legal and social construction of races, except to blame racial minorities for attaching any pernicious construction to the government-enforced separation of the races. "We consider the underlying fallacy of the plaintiff's argument to consist in the assumption that the enforced separation of the two races stamps the colored race with a badge of inferiority. If this be so, it is not by reason of anything found in the act, but solely because the colored race chooses to put that construction upon it." The irony of acknowledging varied state definitions of "race" while holding tenaciously to ideas about the "natural"-ness of race escaped the court as it repaired to naturalistic conceptions of both race and racism: "If the two races are to meet upon terms of social equality, it must be the result of natural affinities, a mutual appreciation of each other's merits, and a voluntary consent of individuals.... Legislation is powerless to eradicate racial instincts, or to abolish distinctions based upon physical differences."[53]

The modern court's epistemology of race has not departed from these foundations. In voter-redistricting cases, the court views racial communities as connected by no more than skin color or ancestry, as having no commonalities of political interest. In affirmative-action and desegregation decisions, the court is unwilling to consider this country's segregative past.[54] Race, for the court, is not a community of interest; it is not lived experiences. Race has no culture, no history. It is not a social category at all. It is formal, legal, and natural.

There was one pair of cases in which the court was willing to entertain the idea that race is socially constructed. In *Shaare Tefila Congregation v. Cobb,* Jews whose synagogue was desecrated sued under Section 1982, claiming that although Jews were not a racially distinct group, they were so perceived and subjected to racial or ethnic discrimination. In the companion case, *Saint Francis College v. Al-Khazraji,* a professor alleged that he was denied tenure because of his Arab ancestry. The briefs in these cases cited historians and anthropologists for the proposition that racial classifications were scientifically unstable and biologically unimportant.[55]

The Supreme Court held that although currently Jews and Arabs are considered Caucasian, when Section 1982 was passed in the nineteenth century, these groups were considered to be members of separate, nonwhite races. While the court used nineteenth-century encyclopedic and dictionary definitions to ascertain the historical view of race at the time the statute was passed, the decisions evince some recognition that definitions of races are cultural and alterable over time. The acknowledgment in *Al-Khazraji* of social-science evidence that race is a sociopolitical creation, however, is tucked into a single footnote. The case is also filled with qualifiers—about the constructivist views regarding race of "some, but not all, scientists"—which kept the court from a more welcoming embrace of the social-construction thesis. Perhaps it is no coincidence, though, that in *Shaare Tefila* and *Al-Khazraji* the court was willing to acknowledge the social-construction thesis when both plaintiffs were members of racial groups today considered to be Caucasian.

Narrative Descriptions: The Lived Experiences of Social Construction

Consider a second method of conveying social construction to the court: presenting evidence of the experiential effect of institutional policies on creating attributes or accompaniments of race or gender. In other words, telling the stories in human terms of the ways in which laws create and shape facets of identity. At first glance, particularly in amicus briefing, it seemed that feminist lawyers were somewhat more willing to tell the stories of their individual clients than critical race lawyers were to tell the stories of individuals of color.

Women's stories were told in cases ranging from reproductive rights to employment discrimination and sexual harassment. Sometimes, as with the efforts of women to compel the State of Illinois to seek child support on their behalf, the stories seemed not to have mattered at all. Other times, the stories may have made a difference. In 1986, the National Abortion Rights Action League and the NOW Legal Defense and Education Fund developed a litigation strategy of presenting the Supreme Court with amicus briefs in abortion cases that contain first-person stories of women's experiences with both legal and illegal abortions.[56]

Known as the "Voices Briefs," these narratives of reasons for having abortions and horrifying experiences when laws restrict access to abortion are intended to convey through personal accounts to seven older men and two older women—none of whom presumably has ever had an abortion—what the abstract right of reproductive choice means on an experiential level.[57] The strategy was intended to focus the court's attention not on the theoretical or moral justifications for or against abortion regulations, but on the experiences of those most affected by them: to make the *law reflect women's concrete, lived experiences.*

Although it is unclear whether members of the court ever read the Voices Briefs or were persuaded by them, language in *Thornburgh v. American College of Obstetricians and Gynecologists* and some of the subsequent reproductive-rights cases indicates that the stories may have created some empathetic understanding among members of the court. The court began to recognize the concrete experiences and situations of particular women: women who might live in fear of domestic violence if spousal notification were required; teenagers who might have been prevented from obtaining an abortion if the state required notification of both parents; and women entering clinics providing pregnancy-related services who were intimidated by "sidewalk counselors," who surrounded them, "crowding, jostling, grabbing, pushing, shoving, yelling and spitting."[58]

It seemed, at first, that in many of the amicus race briefs, the lawyers stuck closely to the legal arguments, offering less personal revelation. In cases regarding the constitutionality of an at-large voting plan for election of county municipal judges and set-asides for minority-owned business, for example, the briefing principally consisted of the formal application of legal precedents to the facts at hand.[59]

Is it possible that critical race lawyers were reluctant to tell stories, to reveal and expose themselves or their clients in court? Could the very widespread nature of the problems (the sweep and impact of the voting-rights cases, for example) discourage personal stories on the race side? This wanders into speculation, but perhaps sexism is more amenable to individualized personal stories than racism is. Or perhaps civil-rights lawyers found more power in talking about rights than in telling stories?[60] Or maybe storytelling itself is gendered. Perhaps it is easier for women (or their lawyers) to talk about their situations on a personal level—although the storyteller who pioneered the tactic as a litigation strategy was Thurgood Marshall.

On closer inspection, though, the strategies of critical race lawyers seem to adapt most closely to the context of the cases. In employment-discrimination cases, even though many were class actions in which

the proof is often statistical in nature, the amicus briefs attempted to put flesh on the bare bones of the arguments.[61] In death-penalty or selective criminal prosecution cases, the empirical evidence—of the comparative numbers of blacks and whites accused, convicted, and on death row—which often *is* the story is contained in the briefs.[62] The briefs in *Wisconsin v. Mitchell* recounted hate-crimes stories:

> In Tampa, Florida, three white men abducted a black tourist, robbed him, doused him with gasoline, and burned him on New Year's Day, 1993. Investigators found a note signed "KKK," which read "One less nigger and one more to go." ... Just a year ago in the Bronx, a fourteen-year-old black adolescent and his twelve-year-old sister were beaten, robbed, and smeared with white shoe polish by four white teenagers while being told it was "their day to be white."[63]

Some of the widest instances of institutional wrongdoing, such as desegregation remedies, voting rights, and employment-preference cases, are told not in terms of first-person stories but in terms of the collective harms they worked on a race of people.[64]

Are there better ways to tell the stories of race? How do you tell the first-person stories of sweeping denials of rights, in voting, education, and employment? There may be room to think about how to make more vivid and evocative the effects of collective denials of voter participation or representational opportunities on the daily lived experiences of individuals: to tell the story of the person who was not elected or the community that could have been.[65] As Steve Ralston of the NAACP Legal Defense and Education Fund says, "We've always felt that an important part of getting certiorari or a particular outcome in a race case is giving the Court the sense than an injustice was done, and the best way to get that across is usually through a person's story."[66]

But the answer to the different successes of the social-construction thesis does not seem to lie with different strategies. Possibly, perhaps much more likely, the breakdown in communication has less to do with the people who aren't saying things and more to do with the people who aren't hearing them.

Consider the media airplay given to race cases. White plaintiffs have recently brought constitutional cases seeking retrenchment of gains made during the Civil Rights Movement. These "reverse-discrimination" cases do not make up a large portion of the federal docket: One survey from 1990-94 estimated that between 1 and 3 percent of discrimination cases were brought by white plaintiffs. Neither are they successful: In three-quarters of the cases, the white plaintiffs lost. But these cases are prominently celebrated in the popular media.[67]

Whites are depicted as the innocent victims of affirmative action, and people of color are demonized for benefiting at their expense. Compared with collective harms to a people—such as enslavement and lynching and "Black Codes" and oppression, which sound like words from history—individual whites, such as Allan Bakke, Cheryl Hopwood, and Sharon Taxman are portrayed as contemporary sympathetic plaintiffs who have recently lost educational opportunities or jobs.[68] Whites have so effectively co-opted the role of victim—and, indeed, created a whole complex discourse of victimization—that any time people of color point out instances of racist behavior, they are whining. This strategy for denying the existence of racism means, as Jerome McCristal Culp has pointed out, "means that whenever we begin to discuss racial issues, we switch and talk instead about injuries to white Americans."[69]

And there is an odd and unfortunate detachment of the concepts of race and racism, which allows white people to make themselves into victims, allows the concept of reverse discrimination to be equivalent to the centuries and the deep horrors of racism, keeps the idea of biological race intact, and completely elides ideas of power. There is a vital need to reconnect race and racism and a need for retelling the stories of the real victims of race so that race ceases to be the white person's story.

Re-creating Race

One final question demands our attention: Is the social-construction thesis worth the intellectual effort? Aside from a commitment to intellectual honesty, is there any practical reason to press the point that race is socially constructed? We think there are at least four such reasons:

Explicating "Race"-consciousness: Race and "Race"-ism

The constructionist thesis reconnects "race" with "race"-ism. It was a "race"-ist culture that created the meaning of "race"—that seized on random human attributes, generated categories from them, ranked those categories on a hierarchical scale, and defended the whole sorry enterprise as "science." It is a "race"-ist culture still that embraces the outmoded conception of "race" as something biological, inherent, innate, and immutable, and simultaneously refuses to acknowledge the real meanings of "race"—the lived and living history of "race," its social, economic, and political consequences. It is "race"-ism, then, that compels the denial of its own paradox: There is no such thing as "race," but "race" matters all the same. And it is "race"-ism that denies this truth. There is nothing natural about any of it.

The constructionist thesis thus provides an epistemic basis for the metaphysical distinctions typically used to justify race-conscious remediation. Those metaphysical distinctions are not without merit. The differences between inclusion and exclusion, tolerance and oppression, and benign and invidious distinctions are, we think, real ones. But in this context, the opponents of real equality abandon their longstanding insensitivity to differences in perspective. White people, they insist, may perceive benign discrimination as invidious (and inclusion as exclusion, tolerance as oppression, and so on). But the social-construction thesis makes plain that the racial differences here are not merely ones of perspective. The different perspectives merely reflect the different situations made for the races, and responses to those situations—including the responses to constructed advantage and disadvantage—are qualitatively different from the initial determination to regard some races as inherently inferior or superior.

Recognizing the social dimension of race thus provides one useful answer to the tired and facile arguments of symmetry and colorblindness. There is an obvious epistemic basis for race-conscious remediation: The remedial response is to the treatment of race and its continuing effects, not a response to the deficiencies of the biological being. The precise contours of the contemporary racial construct—the current constraints of race—are subject to debate, but that debate, we think, would be a useful one.

Reconciling Realism and Originalism: Race and Reconstruction

The struggle for a genuine equality under law has been hindered by an understandable ambivalence toward the record of Reconstruction. Progressives have been hesitant to rely on originalist understandings, because many of those specific understandings—regarding school segregation, for example, or miscegenation—do not seem to be partic-

ularly progressive. The constructionist view might help resolve some of that ambivalence. It is possible to view the Reconstruction framers as politically progressive but merely unable to transcend the epistemology of their day. That epistemology, of course, included a biological conception of race. We can accept the framers' principles, then, and reject the limitations imposed by their outmoded epistemology. Our equality becomes, as a consequence, more real.

Such an approach not only liberates the record of the Reconstruction debates—and there is much there for advocates of equality to celebrate—but it also removes the absurd cloud of impropriety that still lingers over decisions such as *Brown I* and *Loving v. Virginia*. Justice Antonin Scalia notwithstanding, *Plessy v. Ferguson* was not correctly decided. *Plessy*, we now can see, was wrong not only in its conception of a self-imposed stigma of inferiority, but also in its related—and, in fact, foundational—conception of race. Chief Justice Earl Warren, on the other hand, was correct when he concluded in *Brown I* that the framers' thoughts on school segregation were "inconclusive" and when he insisted in *Loving* that their specific intent regarding "miscegenation" must yield to the "clear and central purpose" of the Reconstruction amendments. The recognition that specific practices and claims were rooted in an outmoded epistemology makes indifference to these views proper, both morally and methodologically. Indeed, it is itself a form of originalism. Many of Reconstruction's framers explicitly sought to bequeath to future generations both language and moral principles that transcended their specific practices and understandings.[70]

Avoiding the Formalist Conundrum: Race and Reality

Even under a formalist conception of equality—of equality as sameness and symmetry—

the social-construction thesis reveals prospects for a fuller equality, one "rooted in the gritty realism of social context."[71] Longstanding fictions such as the requirement of an anthropomorphic intent and the public–private dichotomy are invariably problematized by an appreciation of the role of social forces in constructing racial reality. Social construction, in short, illuminates social responsibility.

De-bunking Meritocracy: Race and Reason

Market and meritocratic defenses of inequality are difficult to sustain under the social-construction thesis. Any honest review of the history reveals that race and merit—including concepts of intellectual merit—were constructed together. If they continue to correlate today, this is so only because they were made to correlate initially, and because the correlations are permitted to endure.

Conclusion

One of our favorite stories about the construction of "race" is told by Judge Richard Posner, who unwittingly, we think, proves both that race is socially constructed and that some folks have an inexplicable inability to see their own role in its construction. Judge Posner's most recent critique of Critical Race Theory focuses on the works of Professor Richard Delgado, who, in Judge Posner's words, "claims to be a member of . . . a group that he calls 'people of color.'" But the judge is puzzled by the membership qualifications for the group. The group, he complains, "seems to be more a state of mind than a race." And "race," of course, is more than the professor's "state of mind." The judge tells this story to prove it:

I have met Professor Delgado. He is as pale as I am, has sharply etched features in a long face, speaks unaccented English, and, for all that appears upon casual acquaintance, could be a direct descendant of Ferdinand and Isabella.

All of this provides evidence of what Judge Posner calls "Delgado's whiteness."[72] It is as shameless an exercise in amateur ethnology as anything offered by the opponents of the First Reconstruction and lacks, for conclusiveness, only the judge's report on the length of Professor Delgado's shinbones. Of course, it is blind to the experience of "race," to the life that is lived in "race," either in spite of—or because of—not only our physical appearance but also the "race" of our families, the "race" suggested by our name, and, yes, the "racial" communities with which we choose to identify. But there are constraints on that choice, and what Judge Posner ultimately succeeds in proving is that "race" is indeed "a state of mind"—the judge's, and that is the only one that matters.

But that conceit, of course, is the real problem with "race." And it is why we need, perhaps more than ever, a richer discourse: one that engenders a fuller appreciation of the real meanings of "race," one that helps us confront the ways in which "race" continues to disable us all.

Notes

Acknowledgments: Our thanks to Michelle Johnson for her research assistance; David Achtenberg, Anthony Alfieri, Robert Chang, Joan Mahoney, and Steve Ralston for the inspiration of their ideas; Ian Haney López and D. Marvin Jones for their kind and helpful comments before, during, and after the panel on "The Social Construction of Race"; and Angela Harris for her thoughtful editorial insights.

1. *Plessy v. Ferguson,* 163 U.S. 537 (1896); *Missouri v. Jenkins,* 515 U.S. 70 (1995); *Jenkins* (O'Connor, J., concurring); *Miller v. Johnson,* 515 U.S. 900 (1995); *Adarand Constructors, Inc. v. Pena,* 515 U.S. 200 (1995);

Adarand (Scalia, J., concurring); *Adarand* (Thomas, J., concurring).

2. See, for example, Richard J. Herrnstein and Charles Murray, *The Bell Curve: Intelligence and Class Structure in American Life* (New York: Free Press, 1994).

3. Cf. Frank I. Michelman, "Foreword—Symposium: Representing Race," *Michigan Law Review* 95 (1997): 723, 724, recounting the bases for liberal opposition to "the contentious crt race proposition."

4. See Robert L. Hayman, Jr., *The Smart Culture: Society, Intelligence, and Law* (New York: New York University Press, 1998); idem, "Presumptions of Justice: Law, Politics, and the Mentally Retarded Parent," *Harvard Law Review* 103 (1990): 1201; Nancy Levit, *The Gender Line: Men, Women, and the Law* (New York: New York University Press, 1998); idem, "Feminism for Men: Legal Ideology and the Construction of Maleness," *UCLA Law Review* 43 (1996): 1037.

5. W.E.B. Du Bois, "The Souls of White Folk," in *W.E.B. Du Bois: Writings 923,* ed. Nathan Huggins (New York: Literary Classics of the United States,Viking Press, 1986); Bernard Crick, "Foreword," in *Race: The History of an Idea in the West,* ed. Ivan Hannaford (Baltimore: Johns Hopkins University Press, 1996), xiii; Frank M. Snowden, Jr., *Before Color Prejudice: The Ancient View of Blacks* (Cambridge, Mass.: Harvard University Press, 1983), 63; Jan Nederveen Pieterse, *White on Black: Images of Africa and Blacks in Western Popular Culture* (New Haven, Conn.: Yale University Press, 1992), 23.

6. And the American version of "race" was apparently inherited from Europe: The indigenous peoples did not develop a comparable construct: M. Annette Jaimes, "American Racism: The Impact on American-Indian Identity and Survival," in *Race,* ed. Steven Gregory and Roger Sanjek (New Brunswick, N.J.: Rutgers University Press, 1994), 41.

7. For a general historiography, see Hayman, *Smart Culture,* 134-42. See also Alden T. Vaughn, *Roots of American Racism: Essays on the Colonial Experience* (New York: Oxford University Press, 1995), 136-74; James Campbell and James Oakes, eds., "The Invention of Race: Rereading White over Black," *Reviews of American History* 21 (March 1993): 172.

8. Julian S. Huxley and A. C. Haddon, *We Europeans* (London: Jonathan Cape, 1936), 107-8.

9. Hannaford, *Race,* 205-13

10. James M. McPherson, *The Abolitionist Legacy: From Reconstruction to the NAACP* (Princeton, N.J.: Princeton University Press, 1975), 352.

11. Franz Boas, *Anthropology and Modern Life* (New York: W. W. Norton, 1962), 71.

12. Ashley Montagu, "Introduction," in *The Concept of Race,* ed. Ashley Montagu (London: Collier Macmillan, 1964), 5.

13. Ashley Montagu, *Race, Society and Humanity* (Princeton, N.J.: Van Nostrand, 1963), 6.

14. See, for example, Hayman, *The Smart Culture,* 115-58; Michael Omi and Howard Winant, *Racial Formation in the United States* (New York: Routledge, 1994), 53-76.

15. F. James Davis, *Who Is Black? One Nation's Definition* (University Park: Pennsylvania State University Press, 1991), 21.

16. R. C. Lewontin, Steven Rose, and Leon J. Kamin, *Not in Our Genes: Biology, Identity, and Human Nature* (New York: Pantheon, 1984), 121-7.

17. Stephen Jay Gould, *The Flamingo's Smile: Reflections in Natural History* (New York: W. W. Norton, 1985), 193-5.

18. Albert H. Yee et al., "Addressing Psychology's Problems with Race," *American Psychologist* 48 (November 1993): 1132. For a fuller account of the history of "race"—and the critiques of "race"—see Hayman, *The Smart Culture,* 99-166.

19. Henri-Jacques Stiker, *A History of Disability* (Ann Arbor: University of Michigan Press, 1999), 79.

20. Ibid., 65-89.

21. Ibid., 121-89.

22. Susan Reynolds Whyte, "Disability Between Discourse and Experience," in *Disability and Culture,* ed. Susan Reynolds Whyte and Benedicte Ingstad (Berkeley: Unviersity of California press, 1995), 267.

23. See, for example, Eric K. Yamamoto, "Rethinking Alliances: Agency, Responsibility and Interracial Justice," *UCLA Asian Pacific American Law Journal* 3 (1995): 33, 53-6.

24. Robert Murphy, "Encounters: The Body Silent in America," in Ingstad and Whyte, *Disability,* 140, 153-5; Orlando Patterson, "For Whom the Bell Curves," in *The Bell Curve Wars: Race, Intelligence, and the Future of America,* ed. Steven Fraser (New York: Basic Books, 1995), 187, 203.

25. Ingstad and Whyte, *Disability,* 8; Murphy, "Encounters," 153.

26. Hayman, "Presumptions of Justice," 1248.

27. See, for example, Richard A. Posner, "The Skin Trade" (book review), *New Republic,* October 13, 1997, 40, 42, asserting that "Jews, like east Asians, have a very strong ethic of success through education," as distinct from, apparently, "blacks and Hispanics."

28. On the "voluntary"/"involuntary" minority distinction, see John U. Ogbu, "Overcoming Racial Barriers to Equal Access," in *Access to Knowledge: An Agenda for Our Nation's Schools*, ed. John I. Goodlad and Pamela Keating (New York: Henry Holt, 1990), 59, 61-4.

29. Murphy, "Encounters."

30. Ibid.

31. Ibid., 143.

32. Hayman, "Presumptions of Justice," 1213-6, 1248-52.

33. *City of Cleburne v. Cleburne Living Center,* 473 U.S. 432 (1985); Brief for the United States as Amicus Curiae Supporting Reversal in *City of Cleburne v. Cleburne Living Center,* 473 U.S. 432 (1985) (No. 84-468), 18 ("Persons who are mentally retarded have special needs and abilities, which quite properly elicit our sympathies. . . . The legislative response to mental retardation often has been to accommodate the special needs of class members while allowing for the limitations on their abilities."); Amicus Curiae Brief by the Federation of Greater Baton Rouge Civic Associations, Inc., in *City of Cleburne v. Cleburne Living Center,* 473 U.S. 432 (1985) (No. 84-468), 7 ("In attempting to assign a 'suspect' or 'quasi-suspect' classification to the mentally retarded, there seems to be an underlying current or motivation to grant thereby greater rights than are possessed by the ordinary, normal citizen. Such reasoning is contrary to the very concept of the Equal Protection Clause of the United States Constitution."), 19 ("no basis exists for granting to the mentally retarded a 'suspect' or 'quasi-suspect' classification and thereby a uniquely superior right with which to shatter 'The American Dream' [for residential homeowners]").

34. Brief for Petitioner, *City of Cleburne v. Cleburne Living Center,* 473 U.S. 432 (1985) (No. 84-468), 15-6; *City of Cleburne.*

35. *Miller v. Johnson.*

36. Motion and Brief Amici Curiae of Association for Retarded Citizens/USA et al., *City of Cleburne v. Cleburne Living Center,* 473 U.S. 432 (1985) (No. 84-468), 12-20; see also Robert L. Hayman, Jr., "Beyond Penry: 'The Remedial Use of the Mentally Retarded Label in Death Penalty Sentencing,'" *University Missouri at Kansas City Law Review* 59 (1990): 17.

37. Michael Bérubé, *Life as We Know It: A Father, a Family, and an Exceptional Child* (New York: Random House, 1996), 25-7; Hayman, *The Smart Culture,* 118.

38. *Bradwell v. Illinois,* 83 U.S. 130, 141 (1873) (Bradley, J., concurring).

39. See *Hoyt v. Florida,* 368 U.S. 57 (1961); *Goesaert v. Cleary,* 335 U.S. 464-6 (1948); *Muller v. Oregon,* 208

U.S. 412 (1908); *Rostker v. Goldberg,* 453 U.S. 57 (1981); *Michael M. v. Superior Court of Sonoma County,* 450 U.S. 464 (1981).

40. *Mississippi University for Women v. Hogan,* 458 U.S. 718 (1982); *International Union, UAW v. Johnson Controls,* 499 U.S. 187 (1991).

41. *Planned Parenthood v. Casey,* 505 U.S. 833, 893, 856 (1992).

42. *United States v. Virginia (VMI),* 116 518 U.S. 515, 541 (1996).

43. *Missouri v. Jenkins,* 515 U.S. 70, 92 (1995).

44. Derrick A. Bell, Jr., "Brown v. Board of Education and the Interest-Convergence Dilemma," *Harvard Law Review* 93 (1980): 518, 523.

45. *Piscataway Township Board of Education v. Taxman,* 521 U.S. 1117 (1997).

46. Paulette M. Caldwell, "A Hair Piece: Perspectives on the Intersection of Race and Gender," *Duke Law Journal* (1991): 365, 371.

47. See "Latinos, Asians Are Expected to Fuel U.S. Population Growth," *Baltimore Sun,* March 14, 1996, 3A; Douglas S. Massey and Nancy A. Denton, *American Apartheid: Segregation and the Making of the Underclass* (Cambridge, Mass.: Harvard University Press, 1993), 77.

48. See, for example, Julie Brennan, "Time to Put Slavery Behind Us and Move into 20th Century," *Dayton Daily News,* June 24, 1997, 15A: "I don't feel that I need to apologize to anyone for slavery. My family had no slaves"; Mona Charen, "Apology to Blacks Is Empty Symbolism," *St. Louis Post-Dispatch,* June 19, 1997, 07B: "To apologize for slavery now somehow unearths it as a live moral question. We might as well start apologizing for the Crusades and the Spanish Inquisition."

49. Margaret M. Russell, "Beyond 'Sellouts' and 'Race-Cards': Black Attorneys and the Straitjacket of Legal Practice," *Michigan Law Review* 95 (1997): 766, 792.

50. See Brief Amicus Curiae in Support of Petitioners by Trial Lawyers for Public Justice, *International Union, UAW v. Johnson Controls,* 499 U.S. 187 (1991) (No. 89-1215); Brief of Amici the American Civil Liberties Union et al., *California Federal Savings & Loan v. Guerra,* 479 U.S. 272 (1987) (No. 85-494).

51. Petitioner's Brief, *United States v. Virginia (VMI),* 518 U.S. 515 (1996) (No. 94-1941).

52. See Appellants' Brief, *Abrams v. Johnson,* 521 U.S. 74 (1997) (No. 95-1425); Brief of Amici the Lawyers' Committee for Civil Rights under Law et al., *City of Richmond v. J. A. Croson,* 488 U.S. 469 (1989) (No. 87-998).

53. Brief for Plaintiff in Error, pp. 8, 10–1, *Plessy v. Ferguson* (No. 210), reprinted in1 *13 Landmark Briefs and Arguments of the Supreme Court of the United States: Constitutional Law*, ed. Philip B. Kurland and Gerhard Casper (Washington, D.C.: University Publications of America, 1975), 28, 35, 37–38. *Plessy v. Ferguson*, 163 U.S. 537, 550 (1896).

54. See Robert L. Hayman, Jr., and Nancy Levit, "The Tales of White Folk: Doctrine, Narrative, and the Reconstruction of Racial Reality," *California Law Review* 84 (1996): 377.

55. *Shaare Tefila Congregation v. Cobb*, 481 U.S. 615, 617–8 (1987); *Saint Francis College v. Al-Khazraji*, 481 U.S. 604 (1987).

56. See, for example, Brief for Petitioner, *Harris v. Forklift*, 510 U.S. 17 (1993) (No. 92-1168); Brief Amici Curiae in Support of Petitioners by the American Civil Liberties Union and the American Civil Liberties Union–Wisconsin, *International Union, UAW v. Johnson Controls*, 494 U.S. 1055 (1990) (No. 89-1215). Compare Amicus Brief of the Anti-Poverty Project of the Edwin F. Mandel Legal Aid Clinic of the University of Chicago Law School in Support of Respondent, *Blessing v. Freestone*, 520 U.S. 329 (1997) (No. 95-1441), telling clients' stories of their repeated efforts to get the Illinois State Attorney's Office to take steps to enforce child-support orders, and the state's failure to communicate with clients, causing delays ranging from four to thirteen years, with *Blessing v. Freestone*, 520 U.S. 329, 348 (1997), holding that individuals have no private right to force state agencies to comply with federal Social Security Act provisions because the federal statute "was not intended to benefit individual children and custodial parents, but is simply a yardstick for the Secretary" to assess a state's performance. See, for example, Brief for the Amici Curiae Women Who Have Had Abortions and Friends of Amici Curiae in Support of Appellees, *Webster v. Reproductive Health Services.*, 492 U.S. 490 (1989) (No. 88-605); Brief of Amici Curiae National Abortion Rights Action League et al., *Thornburgh v. American College of Obstetricians and Gynecologists*, 476 U.S. 747 (1986) (Nos. 84-495, 84-1379).

57. See Robin L. West, "The Constitution of Reasons," *Michigan Law Review* 92 (1994): 1409, 1435–6.

58. *Thornburgh v. American College of Obstetricians and Gynecologists*, 476 U.S. 747, 763 (1986); *Planned Parenthood v. Casey*, 505 U.S. 833, 888–92 (1992); *Hodgson v. Minnesota*, 497 U.S. 417 (1990); *Schenck v. Pro-Choice Network of Western New York*, 519 U.S. 357, 362 (1997).

59. Amicus Brief for the American Civil Liberties Union, the Lawyers' Committee for Civil Rights under Law, and the NAACP Legal Defense and Education Fund, Inc., *Lopez v. Monterey County*, 519 U.S. 9 (1996) (No. 95-1201); Amicus Brief for the NAACP Legal Defense and Education Fund, Inc., *City of Richmond v. J. A. Croson*, 488 U.S. 469 (1989) (No. 87-998), offering statistical evidence of the fate of minority-owned businesses, but no stories from minority business owners.

60. Cf. Patricia J. Williams, "Alchemical Notes: Reconstructing Ideals from Deconstructed Rights," *Harvard Civil Rights–Civil Liberties Law Review* 22 (1987): 401, 405.

61. Petitioner's Brief, *Watson v. Fort Worth Bank and Trust Co.*, 487 U.S. 977 (1988) (No. 86-6139): "The summer of 1973, Fort Worth Bank and Trust hired Clara Watson, Petitioner, a black, to the job of proof operator, and put her in a back room, not visible to the bank's customers. She joined only four other black employees: the porter, the kitchen attendant, and two others who printed checks in the basement. Years passed and Clara Watson approached the bank's senior vice-president for personnel, Gray Shipp, with her interest in becoming a teller. Mr. Shipp put her off: a teller, after all, had to handle too much money 'for blacks.'"

62. See, for example, Amicus Brief of the NAACP Legal Defense and Education Fund, Inc., and the American Civil Liberties Union in Support of Respondents, *United States v. Armstrong*, 517 U.S. 456 (1996) (No. 95-157).

63. Brief of the Cities of Atlanta et al. in Support of Petitioner, *Wisconsin v. Mitchell*, 508 U.S. 476 (1993) (No. 92-515).

64. Amicus Brief of the NAACP Legal Defense and Education Fund, Inc., in Support of Appellees, *Shaw v. Reno*, 509 U.S. 630 (1993) (No. 92-357): "For nearly one hundred years, African American voters had no opportunity to participate equally in the political process and no African American was elected to Congress from the State of North Carolina." But see Brief of Amici the NAACP Legal Defense and Education Fund, Inc., et al. in Support of Petitioners, *United States v. Fordice*, 505 U.S. 717 (1992) (No. 90-6588), telling stories of how Medgar Evers's application to attend the University of Mississippi Law School and James Meredith's application to attend the University of Mississippi were rejected, and the history of white resistance to educational integration in Mississippi.

65. The Congressional Black Caucus tried to tell just such a story in its amicus brief in *Miller v.*

Johnson, arguing that minority-majority districts are crucial to obtaining adequate political representation for African Americans. "By 1901 (the end of the First Reconstruction), the massive disfranchisement of African-American voters through fraud, intimidation, and a variety of invidiously discriminatory devices (such as poll taxes and literacy tests) had entirely purged Congress of African-American members. From 1901 to 1928, there were no African-Americans in Congress; from 1929 to 1944 there was but one. And the voice of Congress's sole African-American representative from 1935 to 1943, Arthur Mitchell of Illinois, was all but silenced by the antagonistic posturing of his white colleagues—some of whom were members of his own party": Brief of the Congressional Black Caucus as Amicus Curiae in Support of Appellants, *Miller v. Johnson,* 515 U.S. 900 (1995) (Nos. 94-631, 94-797, 94-929).

66. Interview with Steve Ralston, counsel for the NAACP Legal Defense and Education Fund, July 2, 1997.

67. Alfred W. Blumrosen, "Draft Report on Reverse Discrimination Commissioned by Labor Department: How the Courts Are Handling Reverse Discrimination Claims," *Daily Labor Report* (BNA), no. 56, at D-22 (March 23, 1995), surveying more than 3,000 reported opinions. Robert S. Chang, "Reverse Racism! Affirmative Action, the Family, and the Dream That Is America," *Hastings Constitutional Law Quarterly* 23 (1996): 1115, 1117.

68. See, for example, Elliot E. Slotnick, "Television News and the Supreme Court: A Case Study," *Judicature* 77 (1993): 21, 33.

69. See Jerome McCristal Culp, Jr., "Water Buffalo and Diversity: Naming Names and Reclaiming the Racial Discourse," *Connecticut Law Review* 26 (1993): 209, 217.

70. *Brown v. Board of Education of Topeka (Brown I),* 347 U.S. 483 (1954); *Loving v. Virginia,* 388 U.S. 1 (1967). For accounts of the Reconstruction debates, including the competing visions of "race" and "equality," see Hayman, *The Smart Culture,* 56-72, 103-13, 171-80, 221-9, 325-49.

71. D. Marvin Jones, "The Death of the Emperor: Image, Text, and Title VI," *Vanderbilt Law Review* 45 (1992): 349.

72. Posner, "The Skin Trade," 41.

CHAPTER SIX

Race and the Immigration Laws: The Need for Critical Inquiry

Kevin R. Johnson

DURING ITS FIRST FULL DECADE, Critical Race Theory has failed to explore fully the relationship between race and immigration law. This material omission results in part from the longstanding assumption that race relations in the United States exclusively concern African Americans and whites.[1] Such a binary perspective, however, obscures the relationship between the subordination of various minority communities. It is simply not possible to appreciate fully the treatment of any particular racial group without understanding the deeply interrelated and intertwined oppression of all racial minorities in the United States.[2] Because immigration law unquestionably is central to Asian and Latina/o subordination, a complete picture of racism requires study of how the immigration laws have adversely affected those communities.

In expanding the breadth of CRT's inquiry, we must take care not to "dilute or obscure [the] claims and interests of African Americans"[3] or to blame them for the mistreatment of "foreign" minorities. Nevertheless, CRT must come to grips with the challenges posed by the international com-plexities of racial subordination. As emergent critical Latina/o, or LatCrit, and Asian American legal scholarship have made clear, immigration law, which implicates such global linkages, is fertile for critical examination.[4] For CRT to achieve its full potential, race scholars must begin a careful examination of immigration law and policy, extracting its teachings about race and racism in the United States. If it does not, CRT faces diminishing influence, if not irrelevance.

Analysis of the connection between domestic and foreign racisms flows naturally from previous critical studies. CRT, for example, demonstrated the linkage between U.S. foreign policy and domestic civil rights by considering how the desegregation efforts in the 1950s advanced this nation's Cold War against communism.[5] LatCrit theorists also have begun to explore the transnational effects of domestic subordination.[6]

The first part of this chapter postulates that the exclusions found in the immigration laws effectuate and reinforce racial subordination in the United States. The second part identifies areas of immigration law that, although facially neutral, have racial effects and deserve concentrated critical inquiry. This analysis demonstrates how the racial implications of the immigration laws must be fully understood before CRT can begin to master the complexities of racial subordination in the United States.

In sum, this essay identifies possible relationships between domestic racial subordination and the laws regulating immigration to the United States. Although these laws often are dismissed as racist, precious little time has been spent on analyzing how they are part and parcel of subordination in the United States. Such linkages deserve CRT's attention.

A Deeper Understanding of the History of Racial Exclusion in the U.S. Immigration Laws

Racism, in combination with economic and other powerful social forces, unquestionably has shaped immigration law and policy in the United States. Historically, the people of this country have racialized foreign peoples, even those commonly classified today as white, and treated them as being of distinct and inferior "races."[7] Consequently, nativism, and antipathy for the foreign, is intertwined with racism in immigration history. The anti-Latin American and Asian immigrant sentiment in the modern United States is particularly virulent because of physical difference and the perception that the immigrants are racially different from the Anglo-Saxon core. This has contributed to the reference to today's anti-immigrant sentiment as "racist nativism" or "nativist racism."[8]

Because racial animosity does not exist in a vacuum, one would expect to find a relationship between foreign and domestic racial subordination. Commentators from across the political spectrum have recognized this

connection, including some who dubiously assert that only substantial reductions in immigration levels will improve the economic well-being of African Americans and Latinas/os in the United States.[9]

The Relationship Between Hatred of Domestic and Foreign Minorities

Critical theorists long have found psychological theory useful for analyzing racism and its legal implications.[10] The U.S. government's harsh treatment of immigrants of color at times of improvements for African Americans—such as the combination of the ratification of the Fourteenth Amendment with the Chinese exclusion laws in the nineteenth century, along with the mass deportations of people of Mexican ancestry and the demise of the "separate-but-equal" doctrine for African Americans in the public schools in 1954—may be explained in part by the psychological constructs of "transference" and "displacement." Transference, often an unconscious event, occurs when "feelings toward one person are refocused on another."[11] A related phenomenon, "displacement," is "[a] defense mechanism in which a drive or feeling is shifted upon a substitute object, one that is psychologically more available. For example, aggressive impulses may be displaced, as in 'scapegoating,' upon people ... *who are not sources of frustration but are safer to attack.*"[12]

As the twentieth century closed, public officials and government in the United States, in light of the country's constitutional heritage and modern sensibilities, cannot directly attack minority citizens on account of race without being challenged as "racist." Society can, however, lash out with virtual impunity at non-citizens of color, claiming that the attacks are justified because "aliens" lack rights under the law. Such outbursts may be understood as the displacement of frustration from domestic minorities to immigrants of color. Two pivotal periods in U.S. history illustrate the explanatory power of transference and displacement. They also show the relationship between the treatment of domestic and the treatment of foreign minorities.

Chinese Exclusion and Reconstruction: Transference and displacement help us understand how formal legal advances for African Americans in the nineteenth century came at a time of escalating Chinese misfortune. With the harshest treatment previously directed at African Americans declared unlawful, the nation in effect transferred animosity to another discrete and insular minority, whose status as racially different "aliens" rationalized discriminatory treatment under the law.

The horrible mistreatment of Chinese immigrants by federal, state, and local governments, as well as by the public at large, in the 1800s represents a bitter underside to U.S. history. Using as a model the pre-Civil War fugitive slave laws that regulated the movement of African American slaves among the states,[13] Congress passed the infamous Chinese exclusion laws prohibiting the immigration of people of Chinese ancestry. At the same time, discrimination and violence against people of Chinese ancestry was rampant, particularly in California. Efforts to exclude Chinese immigrants from U.S. shores were inextricably linked to the subordination of Chinese people within the country's borders.

The timing of the backlash in U.S. history against the Chinese is critically important. Congress passed the first wave of anti-Chinese immigration laws not long after the Fourteenth Amendment, which barred states from denying "any person ... the equal protection of the laws," became the law of the land. A member of Congress justified the less favorable treatment of Chi-

nese people compared with African Americans "because [the Chinese] are foreigners and the Negro is a native."[14] During this era, anti-Chinese agitators in California enjoyed the support of Southerners interested in rejuvenating the racial caste system that had been formally dismantled by the Civil War and Reconstruction. As one historian observed, "With Negro slavery a dead issue after 1865, greater attention was focused" on Chinese immigration.[15]

A constitutional landmark of the era offers insight into the dominant mind-set about the relationship between the nation's treatment of African Americans and its treatment of Chinese immigrants. In his dissent in *Plessy v. Ferguson,*[16] often lauded for its grand pronouncement that "Our Constitution is color-blind," Justice Harlan noted the irony that the "separate-but-equal" doctrine applied to blacks but not Chinese immigrants, "a race so different from our own that we do not permit those belonging to it to become citizens of the United States." At the same time, Justice Harlan left no doubt about his fundamental belief in white supremacy; in his words, "the white race deems itself to be the dominant race in the country. And so it is, in prestige, in achievements, in education, in wealth, and in power. So, I doubt not, it will continue to be for all time." Thus, even those willing aggressively to defend the rights of African Americans felt justified in denigrating Chinese people. Legal punishment of the Chinese replaced that previously reserved for African Americans.

Transference and displacement obviously cannot explain everything about racial subordination during this, or any, period. Complex social, economic, historical, and psychological forces combined to create the complex race relations of the late nineteenth century. To fulfill its mission of racial justice, however, CRT should offer its insights to explore and uncover the intricate relationships among these various influences. Only then will critical theorists be in a position to appreciate fully the multifaceted complexities of racial subordination in the United States.

Japanese Internment, Brown v. Board of Education, *and Operation "Wetback":* Transference and displacement also help us understand another pivotal era in U.S. history. The World War II period saw formal legal improvements achieved by African Americans in combination with notorious attacks—sanctioned by law—on people of Japanese and Mexican ancestry. This sequence of events, like the first, suggests the operation of transference and displacement in confluence with other factors.

In *Korematsu v. United States,*[17] the Supreme Court rejected constitutional challenges to the U.S. government's internment of people of Japanese ancestry. In attacking the "Japanese threat" to national security, the government did not distinguish between non-citizens who had immigrated from Japan and U.S. citizens of Japanese ancestry. The internment order expressly applied to "all persons of Japanese ancestry [on the West Coast], both alien and non-alien."[18] Stripped from their homes and communities, all were jailed in desolate locations.

As the Japanese endured internment during World War II, African Americans, due to increased labor demand fueled by the military effort, experienced dramatic improvements in employment opportunities and civil-rights protections. For example, the U.S. government promoted integration of workers and prohibited discrimination against African Americans. Thus, the status of African Americans improved at the same time that the status of Japanese Americans greatly deteriorated. This combination reflects displaced animosity and a shifting of racism from African Americans to people of Japanese ancestry, capitalizing on animosities inflamed by the nationalist fervor that accompanied the war with Japan.

Compare two landmark Supreme Court decisions of this era—*Korematsu* (1944), one of the most horrible equal-protection cases of the twentieth century, and *Brown v. Board of Education of Topeka,*[19] perhaps the most venerated Supreme Court decision in U.S. history. *Korematsu* upheld the government's lawful denial of the rights of all people of Japanese ancestry. *Brown,* in contrast, declared unequivocally that the "separate-but-equal" interpretation of the Equal Protection Clause was a dead letter, thereby vindicating the legal rights of African American citizens.

The post-World War II era also saw a crackdown by the U.S. government on Mexican immigrants, as well on as citizens of Mexican ancestry. In 1954, the very same year that the Supreme Court handed down *Brown v. Board of Education,* the U.S. government commenced Operation "Wetback," a mass-deportation campaign in the Southwest. "The Mexican American community was affected because the campaign was aimed at only one racial group, which meant that the burden of proving one's citizenship fell totally upon people of Mexican descent. Those unable to present such proof were arrested and returned to Mexico."[20]

Bracketing the first postwar decade, two famous Supreme Court opinions, along with a government-sanctioned anti-Mexican crusade, capture the transference and displacement of animosity for African Americans. The law formally barred segregation of African Americans while it subjected despised "foreigners" to internment and deportation.

The sequence of events strongly suggests a relationship in the treatment of domestic and "foreign" minority groups, and thus in domestic and international subordination. How could the starkly different treatment of African Americans and Asians and

Latina/os be mere coincidence? Racisms in the United States are deeply intertwined and interrelated, as shown by the frequent efforts to pit minority against minority. At a minimum, the differential treatment of minority groups at the same historical moments deserve critical attention.

Transference and displacement also help us understand the anti-immigrant sentiment of the 1990s, which is discussed in the next section. In the wake of the civil-rights revolution, antipathy against African Americans in large part has been driven underground. In the 1990s, hate could be unleashed against Latin American and Asian immigrants, who could be attacked as legally suspect "aliens" with few rights. Consequently, racism shifted to some extent from African Americans to Latino/as and Asians.

Racial Exclusions in the Immigration Laws Reinforce the Subordination of Minority Citizens

A peculiarity of U.S. immigration law sheds additional light on the linkage between immigration law and the United States' domestic racial sensibilities. Although the Equal Protection Clause generally requires strict scrutiny of racial- and national-origin classifications, the Supreme Court in 1889—in a decision followed to this day—upheld a federal law barring immigration to the United States by people of Chinese ancestry and emphasized that Congress's "determination is conclusive upon the judiciary."[21] This pronouncement encapsulates what became known as the "plenary power" doctrine; it puts near-complete authority, or "plenary power," over immigration matters in the hands of the political branches of government. Consequently, the majority may use the political process to attack non-citizens in direct and express ways that it cannot with respect to citizens.[22] The differential legal protection of citizens and non-citizens

strongly suggests how society might treat citizens who share the race of non-citizens if the existing legal safeguards were diluted or removed. This fear is real. As we have seen, attacks on "aliens" often prove overly inclusive and result in attacks on domestic minorities who are viewed as "foreign."

Racial exclusions in the immigration laws, which often are obscured through a variety of means, tangibly injure U.S. citizens who share the ancestry of the excluded groups. "When Congress declares that aliens of Chinese or Irish or Polish origin are excludable on the grounds of ancestry alone, it fixes a badge of opprobrium on citizens of the same ancestry.... [Such exclusions have] *the effect of labeling some group of citizens as inferior to others because of their race or national origin.*"[23] President Harry Truman unsuccessfully vetoed the Immigration and Nationality Act of 1952 for precisely this reason: The law carried forward the national-origins–quota system favoring immigration from northern Europe, which Truman found indefensible because of its premise that "Americans with English or Irish names were better people and better citizens than Americans with Italian or Greek or Polish names."[24]

Recognizing such dangers, Mexican American activists consistently have resisted the harsh attacks on immigration and immigrants that adversely affect people of Mexican ancestry. Similarly, African American leaders protested when the U.S. government callously denied entry to black refugees facing death from the political and economic turmoil gripping Haiti. Asian advocacy organizations likewise objected to restrictionist and welfare "reform" measures that adversely affected the Asian immigrant community in the 1990s. These groups understand the link between discrimination under the immigration laws and the respect (or lack thereof) of their domestic civil rights.[25]

Exclusionary immigration laws also have an impact *within* minority communities. Such laws find support among some Mexican Americans, for example, because they are led to believe that their relatively low economic status results from Mexican immigrants who "unfairly" compete with them in the job market.[26] Race and class function in tandem to create this intra-group tension. However, the commonality of treatment (and unified interest in combating this treatment) by dominant society based on race often outweighs any differences. As *Korematsu* exemplifies, people generally classify all people of a particular ancestry as the same and fail to make fine distinctions among them based on abstract legal classifications about immigration status.

In sum, racially exclusionary immigration laws reinforce the subordination of domestic minority groups in complex ways. They stigmatize existing minority communities and limit their growth and development. The exclusion of outsider groups who are subordinated domestically helps maintain white privilege in the United States. It is imperative that CRT begin to examine the relationship between immigration law and race. By clearing the underbrush, CRT can establish the relationship in the subordination of different minority groups in the United States. Only then will we be in a position to articulate a complete agenda for lasting change.

The Need for Critical Analysis of the Immigration Laws

As this account suggests, CRT must begin to analyze the significance of the exclusionary immigration laws to its racial-justice project. To aid this analysis, this section identifies areas in which race and racism have shaped contemporary immigration law and policy, and in which further inquiry is

essential. Most important, this sketch illustrates how the influence of race on immigration law is not just a historical artifact but remains a living part of the law. We should better appreciate how the formal legal lines between "alien" and citizen mean little for those seeking full membership and true cultural citizenship in the United States.[27] At this time, critical theorists have the opportunity to investigate how racially neutral legal doctrine obscures the racism embedded in the immigration laws.

Immigration Law 101: The Racial Impact of "Neutral" Laws

In passing the Immigration Act of 1965, Congress abolished the national-origins-quota system, a formulaic device created in 1924 to favor northern European immigration. The 1965 law, however, for the first time in U.S. history, imposed an annual limit (120,000 persons) on migration from nations in the Western Hemisphere.[28] Supporters of this unprecedented limitation sought to put a lid on Latin American immigration. In the words of a blue-ribbon immigration commission: "In the years after World War II, as the proportion of Spanish-speaking residents increased, much of the lingering nativism in the United States was directed against those from Mexico and Central and South America. . . . Giving in to . . . pressures as a price to be paid for abolishing the national origins system, Congress put into the 1965 amendments" the Western Hemisphere ceiling.[29] Despite the anti-Latina/o plank, the 1965 Immigration Act often is trumpeted as a glowing civil-rights achievement.[30]

After 1965, the racial demographics of the immigrant stream changed significantly. Due to a number of exceptions to the Western Hemisphere ceiling, the 1965 act failed significantly to curtail migration from Latin America. Increasing numbers of Latin

Americans, as well as Asians, have immigrated to the United States since 1965. Their racial difference, combined with other social forces, contributed to the groundswell of restrictionist sentiment in the 1990s.[31]

The Immigration Act of 1965 also imposed an annual numerical limit on immigrants from each nation.[32] Today, this per-country quota of fewer than 26,000 creates lengthy lines for immigrants from developing nations, such as Mexico, the Philippines, and India, and relatively short, or no, lines for people from most other nations. In April 1999, for example, the U.S. government was granting fourth-preference immigrant visas (brothers and sisters of adult citizens) to citizens of the Philippines who had applied in November 1978, compared with June 1988 for all but a few nations. For third-preference immigrant visas (married sons and daughters of citizens), applications of Mexican citizens filed in September 1990 were being processed in March 1998, compared with July 1995 for applicants from most other nations.[33] Thus, because of the per-country cap, similarly situated people may wait radically different amounts of time for admission simply because of their country of origin. Given the overlap between national origin and race, this system has racial effects.

Similarly, the immigration laws historically have allowed the exclusion of any non-citizen who is "likely at any time to become a public charge," an inadmissibility ground that Congress made more stringent in 1996.[34] Under this provision, poor people can be denied entry into this country for no other reason than that they are poor. The law makes it more difficult for working-class and poor citizens and immigrants to bring family members to the United States and for low-income people to immigrate to this nation. This exclusion, which by far is the most frequently invoked substantive ground for denying a non-citizen entry into

the United States, has a disproportionate effect on non-citizens of color from developing nations; it has long served as an important device in limiting immigration from Mexico.

In serving as a proxy for race, the public-charge–inadmissibility ground also shows the intersection of race and class in the immigration laws. Efforts are made to exclude poor Latin American migrants from joining the poor (in the aggregate) Latina/o community in this country. The poor from Asia are also denied entry. Although poor people from white nations are also excluded, the number affected is not nearly as great (because many white nations are economically developed and because people of color constitute a large majority of the world's population) as it is for potential immigrants of color. Class-based exclusions thus have racial effects.[35]

Besides excluding racial and ethnic minorities through a number of devices, the immigration laws include a special built-in preference for white immigrants. In the Immigration Act of 1990, Congress responded to the shift in the racial demographics of immigration after 1965 by creating a "diversity" visa program that operates as an affirmative-action program for white immigrants.[36] Although facially neutral, this complicated scheme in operation prefers immigrants from nations populated primarily by white people. It reserves visas for nationals from low-immigration countries, which includes most European nations, and denies visas to citizens of high-immigration nations such as Mexico, the Philippines, India, and China.[37] Although it ostensibly seeks to promote "diversity" in the immigrant stream, the diversity-visa program is "an 'anti-diversity' program; it causes the resulting population mix to be *less* [racially] diverse than it would otherwise be."[38]

In sum, the modern immigration laws have adversely affected non-citizens of color.

Although facially neutral, these laws limit the immigration of non-white people and detrimentally affect the ability of non-white U.S. citizens and immigrants to reunite families. They give positive preferences to prospective immigrants from "white" countries. None of the requirements, however, has been the subject of in-depth CRT analysis and commentary. Their discriminatory impact has been observed by immigration specialists, but without a thorough investigation of how they fit into the larger pattern of white privilege in the United States. These and many other features of the immigration laws deserve comprehensive critical inquiry.

Responses to Migration Flows from Developing Nations: Turning Our Backs on People of Color

Race is critically important to a full understanding of the United States' response to emergent migrant flows from developing nations. Although many have lauded the Refugee Act of 1980[39] for creating an ideologically neutral right to apply for asylum, the law was motivated in part by the hope of limiting the number of Vietnamese refugees coming to the United States, whom the president had admitted liberally after the fall of Saigon in 1975.[40] Consequently, the act included various provisions designed to prevent a repeat of a Vietnamese-style influx from other non-white countries or regions.

Since 1980, the U.S. government has gone to extraordinary lengths to halt other refugee flows. For example, fearing a mass-migration of poor Latino/as in the 1980s, the United States engaged in the practice of mass detention of Central American asylum-seekers, unlawfully encouraging them to forgo their legal right to apply for asylum.[41] Many were detained in remote locations far from family, friends, and community and often unable to obtain legal counsel. Told by the Immigration and Naturalization Service that they could never obtain relief, hundreds of Central Americans waived the right to a hearing on their asylum claims and "voluntarily" returned to face possible political persecution in their native countries.

The United States' policy toward Haitian asylum-seekers achieved a new level of callousness. As the result of a military coup in September 1991, "hundreds of Haitians [were] killed, tortured, detained without a warrant, or subjected to violence and the destruction of their property because of their political beliefs. Thousands [were] forced into hiding."[42] Fleeing the political violence, many Haitians began the desperate journey by boat to the United States. To halt the flow of refugees, President George Bush, in a policy later continued and aggressively defended by President Bill Clinton, began repatriating all Haitians in May 1992 without any attempt to determine (as required by international law) whether they might in fact be fleeing political persecution, which would make them eligible to remain in the United States. The Supreme Court upheld the executive branch's unprecedented Haitian-repatriation policy, without addressing the claim in the amici curiae brief submitted by the NAACP, TransAfrica, and the Congressional Black Caucus that the policy was racially discriminatory and that the Haitians were being subjected to "separate-and-unequal" treatment.

Evidence supported the claim of racial discrimination against the Haitians. People of color from Haiti apparently were the first refugees *ever* singled out for interdiction on the high seas by U.S. armed forces. (Later, after the much-publicized *Golden Venture* ran aground off the coast of New York in 1993, the United States extended interdiction to ships carrying Chinese migrants.) During roughly the same time, the United

States continued to receive the relatively "whiter" Cubans, often embracing them with open arms as a way to condemn the government of Fidel Castro.[43]

Similarly, the United States has steadfastly resisted migration flows from Mexico. Despite the fact that undocumented people come to the United States from all over the world, the near-exclusive focus of governmental and public attention has fallen on illegal immigration from Mexico. In the 1990s, well-publicized border-enforcement operations, little different from military sweeps, were aimed at sealing the U.S.–Mexican border and keeping undocumented Mexican citizens out of this country.[44] The death toll of Mexican migrants has risen substantially. The efforts to exclude Mexican immigrants stigmatizes people of Mexican ancestry in the United States, who are in effect told that the nation has enough of "them."

The unprecedented militarization of the United States' southern border followed an anti-immigrant outburst in California, which (as with the Chinese exclusion laws a century before) became a leader in the anti-Mexican backlash. California voters in 1994 passed Proposition 187, an initiative designed, among other things, to kick undocumented children out of the public schools. This law "force[d] the immigration issue onto the national agenda in a way that had not occurred since the passage of the National Origins Quota Acts in 1924."[45] The bitter initiative campaign revealed more generalized anti-Mexican American animus as well as anti-immigrant sentiment.[46]

Although U.S. immigration policy is chock-full of race lessons, CRT theorists have missed the opportunity to consider carefully the U.S. government's harsh treatment of Central American, Haitian, Mexican, and other non-white migrants.[47] During its second decade, CRT stands to gain much from the exploration of the racial underpinnings and operation of immigration measures. Indeed, in order to incorporate Latina/o and Asian American perspectives fully into the analysis of racial subordination, CRT must embark on the study of how immigration law and policy reinforces the racial status quo in the United States.

Conclusion

The U.S. immigration laws reveal volumes about domestic racial subordination. Historically, those laws have been designed to keep out non-white "foreigners" who share or personify the ancestry of disfavored domestic minorities. Racial exclusion remains part and parcel of the immigration laws, although it generally operates more subtly than in the heyday of Chinese exclusion. To fully understand and dismantle white privilege, CRT therefore must analyze carefully the relationship between the external and the internal exhibitions of racism, which requires a thorough analysis of how immigration law operates to exclude non-white racial minorities.

To advance such analysis, this chapter sketches ideas about how the complexities of the immigration puzzle fit together. The psychological constructs of transference and displacement help us reconcile some seemingly inconsistent episodes of U.S. history, such as Reconstruction and Chinese exclusion in the 1800s and *Korematsu*, Operation "Wetback," and *Brown v. Board of Education* in the World War II era. By legitimizing legislative violence against "aliens" and citizens of particular national origins, the plenary-power doctrine serves as a red flag suggesting how minority citizens might be harshly treated absent the constraints of law. To unpack this intricate webbing, we must begin to consider how the daily operation of immigration law—and its elaborate system of ceilings, quotas, exclusions, and removal grounds—disparately affect immigrants and communities of color and how this impact relates to domestic racial subordination. This expansion is necessary to move CRT forward into a second decade of struggle for racial justice.

Notes

Acknowledgment: Thanks to Frank Valdes for his enthusiasm for this project, thoughtful editing, and moral support.

1. See Richard Delgado, "Rodrigo's Fifteenth Chronicle: Racial Mixture, Latino-Critical Scholarship, and the Black–White Binary," *Texas Law Review* 75 (1997): 1181, for a discussion of the prevalence of the Black–White paradigm in the modern analysis of civil rights.

2. See Kevin R. Johnson, "Racial Hierarchy, Asian Americans and Latinos as 'Foreigners,' and Social Change: Is Law the Way to Go?" *Oregon Law Review* 76 (1997): 347; George A. Martínez, "African-Americans, Latinos, and the Construction of Race: Toward an Epistemic Coalition," *UCLA Chicano–Latino Law Review* 19 (1998): 213. Similarly, racial subordination and gender oppression are inextricably related. See Adrien K. Wing, ed., *Critical Race Feminism: A Reader* (New York: New York University Press, 1997); Celina Romany, "Women as Aliens: A Feminist Critique of the Public/Private Distinction in International Human Rights Law," *Harvard Human Rights Journal* 6 (1993): 87.

3. John O. Calmore, "Our Private Obsession, Our Public Sin: Exploring Michael Omi's 'Messy Real' World of Race: An Essay for 'Naked People Longing to Swim Free,'" *Law and Inequality Journal* 15 (1997): 25, 61.

4. See, for example, Elvia R. Arriola, "LatCrit Theory, International Human Rights, Popular Culture, and the Faces of Despair in INS Raids," *University of Miami Inter-American Law Review* 28 (1996–97): 245, analyzing the impact of border enforcement on lives of people of Mexican ancestry; Robert S. Chang and Keith Aoki, "Centering the Immigrant in the Inter/National Imagination," *California Law Review* 85 (1997): 1395, analyzing domestic immigration effects of international developments; George A. Martínez, "Latinos, Assimilation and the Law: A Philosophical Perspective," *UCLA Chicano–Latino Law*

Review 20 (1999), studying why Latinas/os cannot morally be forced to assimilate into a society that will not accept them; Berta Esperanza Hernández-Truyol, "Natives, Newcomers and Nativism: A Human Rights Model for the Twenty-First Century," *Fordham Urban Law Journal* 23 (1996): 1075, analyzing impact of nativism on immigration laws.

5. See Mary L. Dudziak, "Desegregation as a Cold War Imperative," *Stanford Law Review* 41 (1988): 61.

6. See, for example, Elizabeth M. Iglesias, "Human Rights in International Law: Locating Latina/os in the Linkage Debates," *University of Miami Inter-American Law Review* 28 (1996–97): 361.

7. See generally Matthew Frye Jacobson, *Whiteness of a Different Color: European Immigrants and the Alchemy of Race* (Cambridge, Mass.: Harvard University Press, 1998), for a discussion of this racialization process.

8. See Rodolfo F. Acuña, *Anything but Mexican: Chicanos in Contemporary Los Angeles* (London and New York: Verso, 1996), ix; Robert S. Chang, "Toward an Asian American Legal Scholarship: Critical Race Theory, Post-Structuralism, and Narrative Space," *California Law Review* 81 (1993): 1241, 1255–8.

9. See, for example, Peter Brimelow, *Alien Nation* (New York: Random House, 1995), 173–5.

10. See, for example, Charles R. Lawrence III, "The Id, the Ego, and Equal Protection: Reckoning with Unconscious Racism," *Stanford Law Review* 39 (1987): 317, analyzing the psychological dynamics of unconscious nature of racism and demonstrating how it requires change in Supreme Court's equal-protection analysis; Peggy C. Davis, "Law as Microaggression," *Yale Law Journal* 98 (1989): 1559, considering the adverse psychological effects of microaggressions, subtle put-downs, and slighting of racial minorities.

11. Thomas L. Shaffer, "Undue Influence, Confidential Relationship, and the Psychology of Transference," *Notre Dame Lawyer* 45 (1970): 187, 205. See generally C. G. Jung, *The Psychology of the Transference* (Princeton, N.J.: Princeton University Press, 1966), articulating a general theory of transference.

12. David Krech, Richard S. Crutchfield, and Norman Livson, *Elements of Psychology* (New York: Alfred A. Knopf, 1970): 354 (emphasis added).

13. See Gerald L. Neuman, *Strangers to the Constitution* (Princeton, N.J.: Princeton University Press, 1996), 39–40.

14. *Congressional Globe,* 39th Cong., 1st Sess. 1056 (February 27, 1866) (comments of Representative Higby). For a succinct history of the treatment of

the Chinese in the United States, see Ronald Takaki, *Strangers from a Different Shore: A History of Asian Americans* (Boston: Little, Brown, 1989), 79–130.

15. Stuart C. Miller, *The Unwelcome Immigrant: The American Image of the Chinese, 1785–1882* (Berkeley: University of California Press, 1969), 151; see also Alexander Saxton, *The Indispensable Enemy: Labor and the Anti-Chinese Movement in California* (Berkeley: University of California Press, 1995), 260, stating that, in 1867, the California Democratic Party "launched their offensive against the Chinese ... a new issue, uncontaminated by the sad history of the civil war, yet evocative of that entire syndrome of hatreds and loyalties which still could not quite openly be declared" (emphasis added). Of course, racism against African Americans did not end with the ratification of the Reconstruction amendments. Rather, Blacks continued to suffer with the rise of Jim Crow and the horrible violence directed at them.

16. *Plessy v. Ferguson*, 163 U.S. 537, 559, 561 (1896) (Harlan, J., dissenting).

17. *Korematsu v. United States*, 323 U.S. 214 (1944).

18. Civilian Exclusion Order No. 57 of May 10, 1942, 7 Fed. Reg. 3725, quoted in Natsu Taylor Saito, "Alien and Non-Alien Alike: Citizenship, 'Foreignness,' and Racial Hierarchy in American Law," *Oregon Law Review* 76 (1997): 261, 274.

19. *Brown v. Board of Education of Topeka*, 347 U.S. 483 (1954).

20. Juan Ramon García, *Operation Wetback: The Mass Deportation of Mexican Undocumented Workers in 1954* (Westport, Conn: Greenwood Press, 1980), 230–1.

21. *The Chinese Exclusion Case (Chae Chan Ping v. United States)*, 130 U.S. 581, 606 (1889) (emphasis added).

22. See generally Kevin R. Johnson, "*Los Olvidados*: Images of the Immigrant, Political Power of Noncitizens, and Immigration Law and Enforcement," *Brigham Young University Law Review* (1993): 1139, analyzing the political powerlessness of non-citizens and the ability of vocal minority of restrictionists to dominate immigration law and policymaking.

23. Gerald M. Rosberg, "The Protection of Aliens from Discriminatory Treatment by the National Government," *Supreme Court Review* (1977): 275, 327 (emphasis added).

24. *Public Papers of the Presidents of the United States: Harry S. Truman* (Washington, D.C.: U.S. Government Printing Office, 1952–53), 443.

25. See, for example, David G. Gutiérrez, *Walls and Mirrors: Mexican Americans, Immigrants, and the Politics of Ethnicity* (Berkeley: University of California Press, 1995), 209–10, discussing the staunch resistance of Mexican American activist groups to restrictionist immigration measures; Brief of the NAACP, TransAfrica, and the Congressional Black Caucus as Amici Curiae in Support of Respondents, *Sale v. Haitian Centers Council, Inc.*, 509 U.S. 155 (1993) (No. 92-344), claiming that the Haitian interdiction and repatriation policy was racially discriminatory; Steven A. Holmes, "Anti-Immigrant Mood Moves Asians to Organize," *New York Times*, January 3, 1996, A1, analyzing Asian protests over new immigration laws and welfare "reform."

26. See generally Gutiérrez, *Walls and Mirrors*, studying the history of tensions between Mexican immigrants and the established Mexican American community in the United States.

27. For an exploration of this concept for Latino/as, see William V. Flores and Rina Benmayor, eds., *Latino Cultural Citizenship: Claiming Identity, Space, and Rights* (Boston: Beacon, 1997).

28. See *Immigration Act of 1965*, Public Law No. 89-236, §§ 2-3, 21(e), 79 Statutes 911, 911-5, 921.

29. U.S. Select Commission on Immigration and Refugee Policy, *Staff Report* (Washington, D.C.: U.S. Government Printing Office, 1981), 208 (footnote omitted).

30. See Gabriel J. Chin, "The Civil Rights Revolution Comes to Immigration Law: A New Look at the Immigration and Nationality Act of 1965," *North Carolina Law Review* 75 (1996): 273, 300-2, collecting sources supporting the "racial egalitarian motivation" behind the 1965 act.

31. See, for example, Brimelow, *Alien Nation*, arguing for drastic restrictions in the levels of immigration because of mass immigration of non-assimilable racial minorities.

32. *Immigration and Nationality Act* (INA) § 202(a), 8 U.S.C. § 1152(a); see Stephen H. Legomsky, "Immigration, Equality and Diversity," *Columbia Journal of Transnational Law* 31 (1993): 319, 333, noting the disparate impact of per-country ceilings; Jan C. Ting, "'Other Than a Chinaman': How U.S. Immigration Law Resulted from and Still Reflects a Policy of Excluding and Restricting Asian Immigration," *Temple Political and Civil Rights Law Review* 4 (1995): 301, 308, noting the negative impact of ceilings on Asian immigration. Not until 1976, however, did Congress apply the per-country limit to nations in the Western Hemisphere.

33. See U.S. Department of State, Bureau of Consular Affairs, "Immigrant Numbers for April 1999," *Visa Bulletin* (Washington, D.C.: U.S. Government Printing Office, March 1999), 1, 2.

34. See INA § 212(a)(4)(A), 8 U.S.C. § 1182(a)(4)(A).

35. Employment-based visas in the immigration laws, conditioned on the perceived value added by the immigrant to the U.S. economy, see INA § 203(b), 8 U.S.C. § 1153(b), implicate race and class concerns similar to those raised by the public-charge–inadmissibility ground.

36. See INA § 203(c), 8 U.S.C. § 1153(c).

37. In fiscal year 1995, Poland was the leading source country for immigrants under the permanent diversity-visa program. Under the transitional program that ended that year, the leading source countries were Ireland, Poland, and the United Kingdom. See U.S. Department of Justice, *1995 Statistical Yearbook of the Immigration and Naturalization Service* (Washington, D.C.: U.S. Government Printing Office, 1997), 21.

38. Stephen H. Legomsky, *Immigration and Refugee Law and Policy*, 2nd ed. (Westbury, N.Y.: Foundation Press, 1997), 210 (emphasis in original).

39. See *Refugee Act of 1980*, Public Law No. 96-212, 94 Statutes 102 (1980).

40. See Bill Ong Hing, *Making and Remaking Asian America Through Immigration Policy* (Stanford, Calif.: Stanford University Press, 1993), 123–9.

41. See, for example, *Orantes-Hernandez v. Thornburgh*, 919 F. 2d 549 (9th Cir. 1990), enjoining the Immigration and Naturalization Service from engaging in a variety of practices that discouraged Salvadorans from seeking asylum.

42. *Sale v. Haitian Centers*, quoting the District Court's "uncontested finding of fact."

43. For a nuanced study of the complexities of Cuban immigration to the United States, see María Cristina García, *Havana USA* (Berkeley: University of California Press, 1996).

44. See generally Timothy J. Dunn, *The Militarization of the U.S.–Mexico Border, 1978–1992* (Austin: CMAS Books, University of Texas at Austin, 1996), analyzing greatly enhanced border enforcement.

45. Louis DeSipio and Rodolfo O. de la Garza, *Making Americans, Remaking America: Immigration and Immigrant Policy* (Boulder, Colo.: Westview Press, 1998), 112.

46. See generally Kevin R. Johnson, "An Essay on Immigration Politics, Popular Democracy, and California's Proposition 187: The Political Relevance and Legal Irrelevance of Race," *Washington Law Review* 70 (1995): 629, analyzing the anti-Mexican element to the Proposition 187 campaign.

47. One CRT book does focus on the racial requirements for naturalization: see Ian F. Haney López, *White by Law: The Legal Construction of Race* (New York: New York University Press, 1996).

CHAPTER SEVEN

"Simple Logic": Race, the Identity Documents Rule, and the Story of a Nation Besieged and Betrayed

Sherene H. Razack

Simple logic dictates that Canada should protect itself against any Tom, Dick, or Harry wanting to enter the country—and you realize that some of these people are false claimants, don't you?

—Fernand Jourdenais, Member of Parliament (Progressive Conservative), 1992

Because they have no ID, we will not grant these people permanent resident status until they have had time to demonstrate respect for the laws of Canada and for us to detect those who may be guilty of crimes against humanity or acts of terrorism. . . . The message is clear—fraud will not be tolerated.

—Lucienne Robillard, Minister of Employment and Immigration (Liberal), 1996

NATIONAL STORIES, narratives, or narrations enable members of nations to think of themselves as part of a community. Stories

This chapter was originally published in a slightly expanded form in *Canadian Journal of Law and Social Policy* 15 (2000): 183–211.

make it possible for individuals who are unknown to one another to imagine that they share a common bond. It is in this sense that Benedict Anderson writes that nations are imagined.[1] However, national stories, including a story about the nation's origins and its history told over time, are contested stories. As Edward Said reminds us, in imperialism, where the battle is over land—"who owned the land, who had the right to settle and work on it, who kept it going, who won it back, and who now plans its future"—national narratives are those of the dominant group: "The power to narrate, or to block other narratives from forming and emerging, is very important to culture and imperialism, and constitutes one of the main connections between them."[2]

As a white settler society founded on the basis of the theft of Aboriginal lands, the Canadian national story, told in the nation's literature, artistic, and cultural production, as well as in its parliaments, newspapers, and educational institutions, has largely rested on the idea that peoples of European origin are the country's original citizens and the ones who are largely responsible for its development. Cast as the "original" citizens in a story requiring the disavowal of both Aboriginal peoples and people of color whose labor also built the country, European Canadians come to represent the idea of the citizen. This official story is manifestly a racial story, producing European Canadians as entitled to the fruits of citizenship and all others as external to the nation. In this chapter examining political rhetoric and discourse, I first trace the national story that underpins immigration reform in Canada; specifically, I turn to reforms limiting the rights of refugees who have been granted asylum. The racial underpinnings of the Canadian national story in immigration reform are also evident in American and European political contexts. I then discuss the outlines of this racial story as it is told in countries of the North to consolidate white supremacy globally.

In immigration, the Canadian national story of the 1990s is a simple one. Canada is besieged. Every Tom, Dick, and Harry wants to get in. They will stop at nothing. They do not respect us. They will return our generosity with betrayal. We have no choice but to become strict and to monitor more closely who is coming in. This is "simple logic," a story told to justify tighter border controls. In the 1990s, Canada, like so many other Western nations, embarked on a series of immigration reforms intended not only to tightly regulate who could get in but also who was entitled to the full benefits of citizenship. Identity documents became a useful tool in this project of nation-building. Stricter requirements for "proper" identity documents at the point of entry, stiffer penalties for those who either did not possess them or used false documents, and special measures to curb smuggling rings that provided false documents were proposed in most Northern countries. Most of these measures

have remained in place throughout the 1990s. For example, the Canadian measures that are the focus of this essay are matched by those in the American Personal Responsibility and Work Opportunity Act of 1996, which includes provisions aimed at increased patrols at the border, greater detention and deportation operations, greater penalties for human smuggling and document fraud, and measures intended to curb fraudulent access to social services. A number of European states have adopted measures similar to the Canadian ones, as well, targeting both refugees and illegal immigrants.[3]

Beginning with Bill C-86 (amending the Immigration Act[4]), introduced into the House of Commons under a Conservative Party government in June 1992 and passed into law six months later, and continuing with the creation of the Undocumented Convention Refugee[5] in Canada Class in 1997 under a Liberal Party government, Canada joined other Western nations in the creation of a class of people neatly labeled the "undocumented," people marked as less deserving of juridical and social rights by virtue of their lack of passports or "proper" travel documents. Under the amendments to the Immigration Act introduced in Bill C-86, a refugee who arrives at the border without appropriate identity documents has a greater burden of proving that he or she is a Convention Refugee, a condition of obtaining asylum. Once granted asylum, under Section 46.04(8) of the Immigration Act, she does not have the right that other refugees have to apply for permanent resident status.[6] The anomalous situation arises that a refugee can satisfy one arm of the immigration department, the Immigration and Refugee Board, that she is a legitimate asylum-seeker in need of protection (in spite of the heavier burden of proof) and still not win the approval of another arm to become a permanent resident of Canada. Convention Refugees caught in what is almost literally a no-man's-land (most of the refugees caught in this way are women and children) between asylum and permanent resident status are mostly of Somali origin. By most accounts, there are 13,000 persons in this state of legal limbo in which they possess only some of the rights and benefits of citizenship.[7]

As the decade of the '90s wore on, the full impact of Section 46.04(8) began to be felt. For example, without permanent resident status, Somali Canadians could not sponsor dependents outside Canada or leave its borders. In some cases, this meant that children left behind in refugee camps could not be reunited with their parents. Treated as foreign nationals, they paid higher university fees and encountered a number of credit and employment roadblocks owing to their irregular citizenship status.[8] Under pressure by refugee advocates and communities to do something, the federal government (then Liberal) responded in late 1996 with the proposal of a special class of Convention Refugee who could be landed without fulfilling the identity-document requirement. The class, known as the Undocumented Convention Refugee in Canada Class (UCRCC), applies only to those citizens of countries listed in Schedule XII of the Immigration Regulations.[9] Currently, only Somalia and Afghanistan are listed. People without satisfactory identity documents from these two countries become eligible for membership in this class, and thus for landing, five years from the date they are granted asylum. Although a five-year wait for permanent resident status seems preferable to legal limbo, the UCRCC nevertheless further entrenched the idea, first given legal expression in Bill C-86, that Convention Refugees without identity documents remain socially suspect and entitled to fewer rights in law than other Convention Refugees. In December 1999, Minister of Citizenship and Immigration Elinor Caplan announced that the five-year waiting period would be reduced to three years.[10] Observers have continued to point out the consequences of delayed landing for Somalis (three years is a long time to wait for family reunification) and to note that one year after the UCRCC regulation, only 748 Convention Refugees had been landed under the new regulation.[11]

Perhaps the most remarkable thing about these identity-documents provisions concerning refugee claimants is that very few people have trouble seeing either their illogic or their discriminatory impact. It is relatively easy, for instance, to see how tenuous the relationship is between the objectives of such provisions (to catch criminals) and the demand for proper identity documents. The possession of proper identity documents may reflect nothing more than the power and resources of an individual to procure them. Refugees are seldom able to procure official documents without considerable risk, and those who flee states whose bureaucracies have collapsed have very limited options in this regard. However, over the past decade, these obvious shortcomings have not led to the demise of identity provisions, and they are currently the subject of a constitutional challenge.[12] The plaintiffs allege that the identity provision of the Immigration Act has the effect of discriminating on the basis of national origin, contrary to Section 15 of the Canadian Charter of Rights and Freedoms. They argue that because Somali nationals are unable to obtain existing documents from Somalia owing to the collapse of that country's bureaucracy, their inability to satisfy the requirement arises because of their country of origin. The subsection thus creates a distinction between Somalis and other Convention Refugees. Further, the UCRCC does not fully remove the penalty.

In this chapter, I explore why the identity-document provisions have continued to stand and why they may even survive a constitutional challenge in spite of the compelling legal arguments against them. In effect, I explore what gives vitality to laws that are so evidently discriminatory. In different ways, both Conservative and Liberal governments have remained faithful to "simple logic" and to the penalizing of Convention Refugees who do not possess "suitable" documents, although it is clear that Conservative regimes are more attached to such policies than are Liberal ones. It seems fruitless, then, to search for an explanation in political ideology per se. Clearly, the story that Conservative and Liberal political elites tell around the identity provisions strikes deep chords in the national psyche, as these politicians well know. That is to say, it is a story that makes sense to the public even when the facts speak otherwise. It possesses an *internal* coherence that is not undermined by the many counter-arguments that are offered.

With the objective in mind of tracing the internal coherence of the storyline of identity documents—why it makes sense to lawmakers and, indeed, to many Canadian, American, and European people—I propose to explore political discussions of the identity-documents provisions in 1991 and in 1996. First, I examine the hearings of the legislative committee that examined Bill C-86 in 1991-92, one of the first occasions for an intensive public discussion over identity provisions and a rich source for the tracing of the structures of parliamentary thinking. I then follow the story through to 1996, when the same committee, by then under the Liberals, conducted hearings on the UCRCC regulations. I argue that "simple logic," as it is talked about in these discussions, relies for its coherence on a national story of a Canada besieged and betrayed by bodies of color. "Proper" identity documents become defensible in this vision of Canada as a way of separating the deserving

from the undeserving and as a way of dealing with the inevitable duplicity of people of color. The storyline is hard to pin down as one that is explicitly about race, because its racist structure is not overt. Instead, "Canada besieged and betrayed" is told as a story about a sovereign nation that is overwhelmed by large numbers of refugees coming to its borders—refugees who are attracted by rumors of Canadian generosity. Immigration scholars often accept this story uncritically and refer to the "grapevine" that enables asylum-seekers to learn of Canadian affluence and sends them flocking to our borders.[13]

Underpinned by the image of crowds at the border who simply want what we have, the story of a nation besieged and betrayed is, I contend, a modern version of an old racist narrative. When refugee analysts report that the number of claimants jumped dramatically from 400 a year in the late 1970s to 5,200 annually between 1982 and 1984, and confirm that the numbers increased even more in the 1990s,[14] the threat posed by hordes of color seems self-evident; the increases over this twenty-year period would seem to support the contention that Canada is indeed besieged. It becomes hard to discern the racial ideas that animate the reporting of the increases, ideas about the "original" citizens of Canada whose superior civilization so attracts the "crowds" of color at the border. Faced with the numbers only, it is also difficult to see that the increases may not in fact represent a siege but a necessary flow of labor to a country that deeply relies on it.

I suggest that white citizens come to *believe* that they are overrun, and that their generosity is being abused, because of the underlying notion that the crowds at the border are simply greedy Third World peoples out to take advantage of unsuspecting white Canadians who are entitled to live in a calm, ordered space. White citizens also come to believe that as the "original" inhabitants, they are both obliged and entitled to discipline the non-white Others who come to their borders. The relationship between white citizens and refugees is deeply colonial and is revealed in the unselfconscious talk about teaching refugees to be truthful and to learn respect. Non-white citizens sometimes come to share in these beliefs, too, understanding their own presence in the country as more legitimate in comparison with those seeking entry now. Without the racial component, the story of siege and betrayal and the stern measures required to protect the "original" citizens would be less than convincing. The national story works because it is able to draw on colonial notions of a superior white civilization encountering the barbarism of (in this case) Africa and (in an earlier time) Aboriginal peoples. So appealing is the story's underlying racist logic that it cannot be easily undermined by alternative stories.

Belief in the story *secures* a racial hierarchy of citizenship as much as it relies on it. That is to say, white citizens come to believe in their entitlement to the full benefits of citizenship (and the lesser entitlement of others) and at the same time, that entitlement becomes real. While only some people of color are rendered juridically unequal by the laws born of "simple logic," all people of color are marked by the stories of race, immigrants, welfare fraud, and criminality that abound in the identity-documents discussions. The "undocumented" become stand-ins for the race, and no one of color is free from the possibility that he or she will be considered illegitimate, fraudulent, and out to get more than is her due, passports notwithstanding.

My argument focuses on the deployment of the rhetoric of betrayal in the demand for "proper" identity documents of refugees at the point of entry. In liberal democracies, overtly racist acts cannot be tolerated. But

if the story of an overtly racist act is transformed into the story of a state forced to defend itself from bodies bent on betraying its trust, then such acts become acceptable and even laudable. They become self-defense, our rage justifiable in view of the extent to which we, extraordinarily generous but gullible, have been tricked. Citizens learn through such stories who they are. It is in this way that we can speak of the identity-documents provisions as a pedagogy of citizenship, one that is required in the building of an unequal *structure* of citizenship. We cannot counter "simple logic" merely by revealing its underlying incoherence, as most critics of the identity-document provision have done. The identity-documents rule *has* coherence in the context of the national story of white innocence and the duplicity and cunning of people of color. It has coherence in a fantasy in which dominant subjects come to know themselves as morally superior, as simply doing what has to be done to preserve home and nation. This is where we must begin. To contest "simple logic," we must ask what the fantasy *does* to bodies as it winds its way through Parliament, the media, and Canadian homes. It constitutes bodies of color as illegitimate, and white bodies as entitled; its lifeblood as a story is the notion of the innocence of this white settler society. I show the operation of the fantasy in the following political discussions.

"Simple Logic"

Bill C-86: "Simple Logic" 1992

In more than 121 pages, Bill C-86[15] laboriously spells out the measures Canadians are forced to take when confronted by an epidemic of welfare fraud and crowds at the border. For example, Bill C-86 includes a safe-country provision denying refugees who have passed through a "safe" country en route to Canada the right to make a claim. Immigration officers are given greater powers to determine who has in fact done this. Family reunification is encouraged, but only a restrictive definition of family prevails. An assortment of security measures, including the identity-documents provisions and the fingerprinting of all refugees, is included. In examining the discourse around identity documents in Bill C-86, it is possible to trace how linguistic and narrative strategies allow racist ideas to be communicated in ways that are difficult to pin down as racism.

For example, the minister of immigration in 1992, Bernard Valcourt, uses a language of betrayal and conjures up images of innocent Canadians and duplicitous migrants when he articulates the underlying rationale for Bill C-86. Canadians, he notes, are characteristically kind and generous but *we don't want to be taken for a ride.*[16] Two kinds of people "take Canadians for a ride": fraudulent claimants of welfare and fraudulent refugee claimants. This conflation of internal and external enemies is evident throughout Bill C-86 and particularly in the discussion of identity documents at the border. We must insist on proper documents at the border (and not only during the asylum hearing) because if we don't know who people are when they come in, they can go on to defraud welfare by using a variety of fake names.

To give these assertions a context in which they might be understood, Conservative politicians deliberately pursued a linguistic strategy of conflating the illegal migrant and the Convention Refugee through the use of the term "undocumented." Convention Refugees are not in fact "undocumented" as the phrase is commonly used in the United States—that is, to describe someone who has sneaked into the country without applying for entry. Convention Refugees do apply for entry and undergo a rigorous hearing procedure in which the establishment of identity is an

important part. Confronted with the issue of Somalis and Afghanis without documents, for example, the Immigration and Refugee Board developed procedures in asylum hearings that would enable it to assess identity, the lack of legitimate passports or travel documents notwithstanding.[17] Further, many refugees are "documented," but the documents they possess have been assessed by officials at the border as insufficient for the purposes of establishing identity. The difference in legal status between a Convention Refugee and an individual who has not gone through any official channels, however, did not stop Canadian politicians from using the rhetoric of "undocumented." In adopting this term, the Canadian government made sure that an aura of criminality would cling to people whose claims have in fact been accepted and who are thus legally present in Canada.

I do not want simply to contribute to the analysis of Bill C-86 by demonstrating, with respect to the identity provisions, the narrative and linguistic moves that enable the communication of racist ideas, although they bear noting when the task is to decode "simple logic." Instead, I want to move from the disembodied realm of linguistic devices to the speakers themselves. That is, how do the speakers of the dominant narratives understand themselves; from what place do they "live the nation"? Fantasy is a useful notion when trying to capture how individuals imagine the landscape in which they are living and in which *their own identities* take shape. Utilizing fantasy in her work, Lauren Berlant writes that the concept designates "how national culture becomes local—through the images, narratives, monuments and sites that circulate through personal/collective consciousness." Through these images and narratives, citizens are taught personally and collectively to imagine who they are and "to perceive the nation as an intimate quality of identity."[18]

The national fantasy—the images and narratives that animate Bill C-86—has a very simple structure: who We are versus who They are, and the laws we require to protect ourselves from this difference. In 1992, the bill's framers insisted that we are a nation besieged. The country faced a huge backlog of applications from people seeking to enter Canada either as immigrants or refugees. Making the case for greater vigilance, Minister of Immigration Bernard Valcourt asked reasonably, "Who could refute that in a country like Canada, facing all of these pressures of these mass movements of people, our immigration officers don't have the power to do their jobs?" Such powers as the bill intended to give to immigration officials could be defended by relying on a long-standing national narrative: We attract more than our share of immigrants and refugees because we are known to be fair-minded, democratic, and generous. As Valcourt put it simply, "We are a trusted country in the world." In a country where "citizenship means something," we are naturally overrun by those who want what we have. As a result, against our nature, we are forced to impose harsh measures such as the fingerprinting of all asylum-seekers but only until we are sure of the identities of those who come to our door. At such time, the fingerprint records will be erased, the interminable wait for full citizenship will be over, and the new Canadian will become equal to "the baby who is born Canadian" with all its rights intact.[19] It would all be worthwhile. (By the end of the decade, of course, this image could no longer be used, because babies born on Canadian soil but of refugee parents no longer had access to national health care in the province of Ontario.)

The government offered few facts and figures in support of its narrative of siege and betrayal. In place of specifics, two stories circulated to give content to the threat. The first was a story about smuggling rings, and the second was one of welfare fraud. The two stories came together, such as when Brian Grant, director of control policy for the Department of Employment and Immigration, told the committee that "undocumented" arrivals were unheard of in 1976, whereas in 1992 smuggling and counterfeiting had become sophisticated, and many more people had come to realize that Canada is a land of opportunity, a land worth getting to for its social benefits.[20] Here the siege narrative is bolstered by the idea that Canada is a popular destination because it is so generous to its citizens. Significantly, if people are "undocumented," it is only because they are smuggled in. "Undocumented" is conflated in this logic with criminality.

Identity documents enter this story as the bridge between our reputation and the proposed harsh measures. The problem facing Canada is presented as a simple one. In the words of the minister: "It is absolutely impossible to board any plane in the world without documents, yet they come here and land at our airports without the trace of a document. That is impossible." He continued with an analysis of the problem and its solution:

> We know one thing. There is this multi-million-dollar business of smuggling, and of consultants abusing people out there, and they are being encouraged to do that because those poor people are being exploited. We understand that. But if that person came along and said, listen, this is not a proper document, this is a forged document, I had to do this to flee persecution, that will never be held against that person in Canada. But the person who comes here and then plays with I don't know who.... There are smugglers in airplanes who collect all the papers of the people. It creates problems. That is why we have created this disincentive to people by saying that if they come to Canada, they had better have their documents, because with this guaranteed legislated benefit of the doubt,

they will not get like the others who follow the rules and come here honestly, saying I had to have these documents— they are not mine—because I wanted in. That is why we did that.[21]

A figure emerges, shadowed by another: People who "follow the rules" (and confess that their documents are false) highlight for us the treachery of those who do not follow the rules, rely on smugglers, and destroy their documents. Our rules will benefit the former and catch the latter. Holders of fraudulent documents will not be penalized. A torturous distinction must then be made between the moral characters of those who commit fraud and those who destroy their documents.

The logic of the identity-documents provisions is fragile from the start. Fake documents are preferable to destroyed documents. Refugees are the hapless victims of smugglers, yet they must be punished for destroying their documents. Intended as a disincentive for people who destroy their documents, and ultimately as a barrier against smuggling rings, the identity provisions rely on the notion that people who use smuggling rings probably are not bona fide Convention Refugees. Yet given the number of roadblocks in the way of refugees from Africa (many of whom are women and children) making their way to Canada (few Canadian immigration offices in the region, no direct flights to Canada, the vigilance of airline companies, and so on), it is difficult to arrive at the Canadian border without recourse to such smuggling rings.

"Simple logic" soon began to move beyond the story of smuggling rings. The goal, it turned out, was not only to stop smuggling rings, as became apparent in the discussion of fingerprinting and identity documents. This was only where it began. If we fingerprint refugees, we will be able to detect which I.D. belongs to whom, and thus stop the smuggling rings. "The issue is

not criminality; the issue is identity," the minister insisted, but the two were in fact shown to be indivisible when he added, "and you get the added benefit that on the domestic scene you can exchange this information with provincial governments who have to cope with not many, but too many, who abuse the welfare system because of their position as refugee claimants."

Having to produce identity documents at the outset, then, will encourage refugees not to abuse the welfare system. Responding to a question about the relationship between the identity provisions and welfare fraud, the minister offered his welfare story: "You must remember the case in Montreal where a person made 14 different claims under 14 different names and was getting 14 welfare checks." The bill will help, he assured Harry Chadwick, the Conservative Member of Parliament for Bramalea-Gore-Malton, in dealing with welfare, unemployment, and credit-card fraud. We learned that in "one city alone, 60 people are alleged to have collected about $2 million through fraudulent welfare claims."[22]

Identity documents, then, protect us from the enemy outside our borders and the enemy within. They even reduce stereotyping of immigrants, as Brian Grant of the Department of Immigration argued to the committee when he contrasted the nice side of immigration, "bringing families together," with its "dark side" of criminality. Since identity documents in and of themselves cannot specifically tell us who is a genuine Convention Refugee and who is not, however, or who will abuse our systems and who will not, their true value lies elsewhere. They tell us more *generally* about an individual's intrinsic moral character. They tell us, in the words of Grant, who is "truthful":

We expect truthfulness in response to our questions. We expect the appropriate documentation from anyone coming forward, seeking to enter Canada. Once they are in Canada, we ask that they renew their documents as required. Finally, we ask that they respect Canadian law. That's essentially what the control is based on.[23]

Refugees who admit that they have forged documents are at least being truthful in the moment of interrogation, and will not therefore be penalized, confirmed John Butt, director of protection policy for the Department of Employment and Immigration.[24] (In fact, the law makes no distinction between those without documents and those with fake documents. Butt's statement was part of the government's own duplicity.) The rhetoric of truth-seeking strikes a chord in listeners, not only because of its superficial logic (of course, people should be truthful and *trusting* of the Canadian government), but also, as I suggest later, because of who the unnamed liars are: refugees of color whose duplicity and criminality are easily believed in. The demand for documents also has a pedagogic purpose: It teaches refugees who Canadians are, and Canadians in this scenario are simply reasonable people who demand honesty. One wonders whether the logic here turns on the view that refugees are not likely to be people who value honesty as do Canadians.

Immigration officials admitted to committee members that documents can be lost during the conditions of flight and that refugees might be reluctant to admit possessing forged documents at the border for fear of being turned back and for fear of implicating others still left at home. They acknowledged, too, that complicated identity issues are better dealt with during the formal asylum hearing. These acknowledgements, however, did not disturb "simple logic." As the chairman of the committee simply reaffirmed at the end of the day, if refugees do not have identity documents, it is likely because a smuggler made them get rid of them.[25] In this story, a refugee who

gets to our borders without identity documents is someone we do not know, and someone who is likely to defraud us, as well as someone who is duped by smugglers. Her character and history are fixed for us in the moment of the encounter at the border. She is not someone with a past, although she is someone with a guessed-at future—that of welfare abuser.

When we examine more closely the encounters between Conservative committee members and critics of the identity-documents provisions, the figure that gives "simple logic" its coherence is further revealed. For example, when Lucya Spencer of the National Organization of Immigrant and Visible Minority Women of Canada described at length the difficult conditions of flight for women and the necessity of using forged documents, and when she noted that of 30,000 refugee welfare claims in 1991, only 43 were of a fraudulent nature, Fernand Jourdenais, a member of the government, replied contemptuously and patriarchally that these facts amount to a claim that we should simply take refugees at their word when we first encounter them: "Should we accept a person who states 'Mon nom est Lucya Spencer, and I am an honest girl?' How do I know who you are if I cannot really prove that you are?"[26] Ignoring her reply that identity can surely be established in an asylum hearing and that fraud is rare, he simply reasserted "one bad one is one bad one." The figure of the refugee who is likely to deceive generous and unsuspecting Canadians is held as trump, introduced time and again by Conservative politicians to win the rounds.

A similar encounter transpired between Pascual Delgado of the Canadian Hispanic Council when he offered details as to why Latin American refugees are unlikely to have documents. His counter-story elicited the following emotion-laden response from Ross Reid, parliamentary secretary to the minister of Indian affairs and northern development and the representative for St. John's East:

> God forbid that I would defend the bureaucrats in this particular area, but my experience, I have to tell you, is that their obsession is not so much to keep people out. *Their obsession is to know who it is that they are dealing with.* My experience—and it tends to be limited to the Horn of Africa, Central America, the Eastern European situation, and Newfoundland—has been very much one where they say, "If I know who you are, I do not have a big problem with you being in Canada, as long as you are dealing with me straight. Don't try to rip me off as the immigration officer. Don't, at least in my sight, try to rip off the system." That is more the obsession I see. It is not to keep people out. Even the toughest immigration officers that I know in Newfoundland, who would be just as happy to line people up against the wall, are the first ones to call the Association for New Canadians and say, "This person is dealing with the system in an honest and direct way; help him." That is what I tend to see. I tend to see much more an obsession with the idea that, I would really like to know who you are, and if you are going to be straight with me I am going to help you. It is not to keep people out.[27]

Here the speaker repeats three times that it is honesty he wants, an honesty that can be revealed only in the production of identity documents at the border. In effect, Reid details the script that refugees must learn and perform. They must learn that Canadians are straightforward people who want only the truth. If the obsessive need to "know who we are dealing with," repeated like a talisman to ward off any complicating details, is convincing, it is because the unknown native is a powerful and historical symbol for white people.

Speakers who contested the main story of a kind, truth-loving, and generous nation were met with a defensiveness that verged on hysteria. Few witnesses brought up the subject of racism, but when they did, an immediate and vehement denial and censure emerged from certain members of the committee. For example, Dan Philip of the Black Coalition of Quebec opened his presentation with a reminder to the committee that the minister of immigration had recently remarked in the House that the majority of Somalis were nomads who did not want to come to Canada anyway. Philip described the minister's statement as "one of the most punishing statements made by a minister in recent times, because the people of Somalia, some of whom are here, have been trying to get their families here." By tying in such statements to the privileged treatment accorded to the white-skinned refugees from Yugoslavia, and noting the unequal treatment of Haitian refugees, however, Philip was immediately seen to have crossed the line of civilized communication. Douglas Fee took him to task:

> I do have a problem with some of your language.... You described the refugee determination system as hell, and yet the UN High Commissioner for Refugees, a representative from the Carnegie Foundation, and other credible groups have all told us our program is an example for the world and one of the best. Our acceptance rate is extremely high. There are actually very few people rejected. So I find it difficult to accept your argument that our determination system is all that bad.[28]

When Philip clarified that he was speaking of responses to specific groups, and notably to Somalis, he received another defensive explosion from Fee: The entire world was caught unaware by Somalia, and nobody was able to respond quickly. Canada should not be singled out for blame. As Fee put it: "We recognise that the situation is bad, but what would you have us do beyond what we are doing?" Philip patiently explained again what could be done, but Fee still replied: "We are a small nation; . . . there is a limit to what a small nation can do."[29]

Philip encountered here the moral outrage that follows the naming of racism; his points remained out of bounds, impolite, accusatory, and exaggerated accounts that committee members could only dismiss. Within the official narrative under construction in these exchanges, innocent Canadians who are doing all they can now confront people with whom they are deeply unfamiliar and whom they have reason to suspect. Members of the government note that some of the people seeking entry have "lived on the fringes of legitimacy" and may be people who are "simply not suitable for this particular country."[30] This is why Canada must insist on "knowing who people are."

The "chaos" of Africa makes the task of identifying people both imperative and difficult. As Gordon Fairweather, chair of the Immigration and Refugee Board, explained to the committee, Canadians face a special challenge in knowing who Somalis are (and thus in protecting themselves from being duped by them). Repeating the colonial story of Somalia as a land beset by warring tribes, a story that Catherine Besteman describes as a reformulation of the story "they are all so primitive in Africa,"[31] Fairweather suggested that when we (in the civilized North) find ourselves in the middle of this tribal mess, we can find our way out again only when we are able to confirm the tribal identity of the players.[32] If the demand for identity documents makes sense, it is largely because it is the only way in which order can be imposed on the alien masses at the border. How else can one deal with such an onslaught of foreignness?

The critics of Bill C-86 who appeared before the legislative committee had to struggle with the implacable fantasy of the envious and foreign hordes at the border.

Their counter-stories had little impact. Professor James Hathaway asked why Canada would penalize someone for destroying documents after one member of the Immigration and Refugee Board had already established that he or she is a bona fide Convention Refugee. Warren Allmand, a Liberal Member of Parliament, reminded the committee that the Geneva Convention makes clear that refugees must not be turned back because they lack suitable documents. He noted that refugees are afraid to admit they have forged documents because this could be used later to assess the truthfulness of their claim to persecution. In any event, as he and several others, including the Refugee Lawyers Association, noted, refugees must produce confirmation of their identity at the refugee hearing. When they fail to establish identity, their claims for asylum usually fail. In the refugee hearing, however, identity is not established solely through official documents such as passports and travel documents.[33]

Refugee advocates appearing before the legislative committee repeatedly confirmed that more often than not, refugees must resort to false documents and that, owing to their histories of state persecution, they will believe smugglers over the Canadian government when advised to destroy documents. Immigrant associations, such as the Multilingual Orientation Services Association for Immigrant Communities, went into considerable detail about the conditions of flight of the refugees they knew. For example, Fiona Begg, a community worker, described the political context of refugees who are native people from Guatemala (where the military deliberately burns records), whose histories of persecution are easily corroborated by means other than passports or birth certificates. Ted Walker of the Alberta Association of Immigrant Serving Agencies added that the Immigration and Refugee Board has been known to suspect the credibility of claimants who *have* documents, based on the inference that someone who possesses documents was probably not in a great deal of danger.[34] These arguments and narrative strategies, however, were no match for the figures that give coherence to "simple logic"— the duplicitous native, the tribal unknown. The bill passed in December 1992 and became law in February 1993.

The Undocumented Convention Refugee in Canada Class: "Simple Logic" 1996

Three years after the passage of Bill C-86, a Liberal government proposed to remedy the hardship that Section 46.04(8) imposes on Somalis and Afghanis. In the tone of someone granting special rights, the Regulatory Impact Analysis Statement published in the *Canada Gazette* (1996)[35] established the creation of a special class of refugees who can be landed despite their lack of documents. Convention Refugees from Somalia and Afghanistan are first described in the statement as innocent victims of regimes that have more or less collapsed. The hardships of not being landed are duly noted—in particular, the delay in the reunification of families. However, the government makes clear, the plight of such refugees must be balanced against Canada's need to protect itself from a small minority of individuals who conceal their country of origin and identity in order to receive protection. Requiring refugees to wait five years before earning the right to permanent residency gives the government time to establish who is criminal and who is not. The regulations are vague about how this might be done, other than to work with the communities in question and to assess "conduct" (in lieu of the background checks done with other applicants) during the five years. The lengthy waiting period is acknowledged but firmly endorsed as necessary in order "to test, over time, the ongoing willingness of those refugees to

respect the laws and norms of Canadian society."

"Simple logic" remains intact, although slightly muted, in the Regulatory Impact Analysis Statement. The country has a right to protect itself from those who seek to defraud it, and it must teach Convention Refugees to respect the laws of Canada, according to the new Minister of Immigration Lucienne Robillard. Reminiscent of the earlier discussions about teaching refugees to be honest, the figure of the alien migrant who is unlikely to know about honesty and respect for the rule of law highlights the civility and moral superiority of Canadians. Less punitive than Section 46.04(8), the creation of the UCRCC nevertheless establishes a penalty—and one that is quite substantial: a five-year wait for equal citizenship. The penalty is justified for those who have not yet demonstrated their qualifications to receive the full benefits of citizenship.

In the hearings of the legislative committee, a committee by then made up of fewer Conservatives,[36] fidelity to "simple logic" was once again most evident in the responses of officials from the Department of Immigration and from Conservative members of Parliament. Both simply reiterated that it is reasonable for Canada to know who it is dealing with, and that five years allows us to tell who is a criminal and who is not. Val Meredith, the Reform Party Member for Surrey–White Rock–South Langley, illustrated the narrative conventions of "simple logic" best when she asked, no fewer than ten times in a ten-minute exchange with two witnesses appearing before the committee: "Is it unfair of Canada as a country to expect to receive, at the point of entry, some documentation of identity, some travel documentation?" The question, rephrased only slightly each time and asked of the two witnesses who attempted to explain alternative means of establishing identity,[37] turns on an abstraction: the right of Canada to know who it is dealing with through identity documents given at the point of entry. No context was allowed, such as why it might be that a legitimate Convention Refugee would not be able to respect this right.

This is perhaps the outstanding feature of "simple logic": its reliance on "simple referentiality," a bounded system of logic that ruthlessly excludes anything outside its own limited parameters. Further, as the literary-studies theorist Homi Bhabha points out, drawing on Edward Said, the realist features of this kind of logic are structurally similar to colonial logic: The Other can be only known only on the colonizer's terms. As Said elaborates, "Anyone employing orientalism, which is the habit for dealing with questions, objects, qualities and regions deemed Oriental, will designate, name, point to, fix, what he is talking or thinking about with a word or phrase, which then is considered either to have acquired, or more simply to be, reality.... The tense they employ is the timeless eternal; they convey an impression of repetition and strength."[38] Within this bounded system of logic, the colonizer can insist on knowing the colonized in ways that are impossible for the latter to fulfill. The Other cannot win under these terms and conditions, described here as fairness and straight dealing.

If the right to police the border is paramount and excludes all other considerations, then the other features of "simple logic" become defensible. Meredith insisted repeatedly that to grant any exceptions to the documents rule would be to reward people who destroy their documents and to send the message that Canada's borders are wide open. Here, as in the Bill C-86 discussions, these arguments appeal to those who believe that the "crowds" at the border, the "hundreds of millions of mobile individuals seeking a different life worldwide—people in movement [who are] looking for a better life" simply want what we have. Clearly, then, "Canada cannot possibly take all the people who would like a better life economically." Within "simple logic," refugees are often bogus. To create the UCRCC will simply invite more fraud. Refugees will simply claim to be Somali in order to get in.[39]

Witnesses who appeared before the Standing Committee on Immigration attempted to expand the boundaries of "simple logic," as was done in the C-86 discussions. Unlike the 1992 Standing Committee, the Standing Committee of 1996 was somewhat moved by some of these arguments and stories. In its final report, it recommended a two-year waiting period and the eligibility of children of refugees for sponsorship as soon as an application for permanent resident status is made. It also recommended that guidelines be developed as to what constitute suitable documents, a recommendation that even the dissenting Conservative members supported.

Surprisingly, in spite of the committee's recommendations, "simple logic" survived relatively intact once again. Even though the Conservative members of the committee were a distinct minority and the government was a Liberal one, the government rejected the committee's recommendations. On January 19, 1997, the regulations were passed, and the five-year wait remained in place. The regulations' inconsistencies and impracticalities were swept aside on the strength of an impregnable internal logic: Canada is besieged and betrayed on every turn and must adopt stern measures to police its borders. We can only surmise that most members of the House of Commons agreed with (or saw the political advantage of) this narrative and believed, on the one hand, in the existence of highly suspect people of color who need to be watched and, on the other, "original citizens" who must patiently teach these "Others" the deceptively "simple" terms of Canadian respect and decency.

Finding Racism in "Simple Logic" 2000

Faced with the immovability of "simple logic," and the seeming rationality of a country protecting its borders from the unscrupulous, only a few critics have suggested that racism is what enables the identity-documents rule applied to refugees to find support over the past decade. In 1999, when Canada accepted 5,000 refugees from Kosovo and exempted them from the identity-documents provisions, racism surfaced briefly as a plausible explanation for the differential treatment meted out to Somalis and Afghanis. Refugees from Kosovo were fast-tracked, granted permanent residence status, and assisted with family reunification; all such benefits were denied to Somalis.[40] Because the refugees from Kosovo are white and the Somalis are black, one newspaper columnist has suggested that racism is the most obvious explanation for the imposition of a five-year wait on Somalis and Afghanis.[41] These few moments aside, however, critics of the identity-documents provisions have mainly stayed in the less confrontational realm of "disproportionate impact" and "systemic discrimination," concepts that do not produce the defensiveness that a charge of racism does. Thus, the Somali community, immigration lawyers, human-rights analysts, scholars, and activists point out the rule's disproportionate impact on Somalis and Afghanis, whose countries of origin remain in a state of collapse. They note once again that many refugees are forced to flee without documents, are often endangered if they do carry them, and, in any event, can usually prove who they are in an adjudication hearing once safely inside Canadian borders. Legal scholars add that the identity-documents provisions contravene various international conventions to which Canada is a signatory.

These scholars demonstrate how slight the relationship is between the rule and its declared objective of catching war criminals and welfare abusers. It seems clear, Julia Dryer concludes, that the war criminals who are the object of the bill are likely to be individuals in the best position to obtain identity documents, given that many would have been officials in the former Somali government of Sayed Barre. More to the point, because 80 percent of those without documents are women and children, who are highly unlikely to have been government officials, Dryer reasonably concludes that the Undocumented Convention Refugee in Canada Class regulation is intended to work on a symbolic rather than on a practical level.[42]

It is in the realm of the symbolic that it becomes difficult to steer clear of the issue of racism. The figures who inhabit the land of "simple logic"—the refugee bent on deceiving us, the alien who must be taught, and the citizen who is envied for all the good things his or her country offers—is eerily reminiscent of Franz Fanon's description of the colonizer and the colonized. The colonized man is an envious man, Fanon writes, "and this the settler knows very well; when their glances meet he ascertains bitterly, always on the defensive, 'they want to take our place.'"[43]

How does it come to be that a complex situation—a refugee fleeing persecution and a nation assessing his or her story—can be reduced to the "simple logic" of knowing "who we are dealing with" at a single moment in time through a passport or a travel document, even a forged one? Such a determined decontextualization and an insistent return to the simple narrative that "we must know who they are" draws its strength from another underlying colonial notion. Fanon is instructive here:

> It is not enough for the settler to delimit physically, that is to say with the help of the army and the police force, the place of the native. As if to show the totalitarian character of colonial exploitation, the

settler paints the native as a quintessence of evil. Native society is not simply described as a society lacking in values. It is not enough for the colonist to affirm that those values have disappeared from, or still better never existed in, the colonial world. *The native is declared insensible to ethics.*[44]

The threat that the immoral native poses only subsides when we contain it: "In the colonial context, the settler only ends his work of breaking in the native when the latter admits loudly and intelligibly the supremacy of the white man's values."[45] The settler needs to be reassured that the native has left behind the vestiges of tribalism. Five years' wait is not too long a time to tell whether the mud of the native town still clings to him or her. The race shadow behind the insistence on identity documents and on the five-year wait helps us to understand why the very logical counter-arguments proposed by critics of the identity provisions carry so little weight. As Toni Morrison writes, "Contradiction, incoherence and emotional disorder 'fit' when the subject is black." No logic need be given "the general miasma of black incoherence."[46] The figure of the refugee in these discussions is simultaneously the hapless victim of smugglers, the persecuted, and the wily and cunning traitor who will turn around the first chance he gets and abuse our generosity (although the majority of refugees without documents are women). These shadows circulate in the text, giving substance to the story of our need to know "who they are" and our need to make them wait for the full benefits of citizenship. The story thus acquires a kind of coherence and logic it would not otherwise have. If we believe that refugees can lose their documents and *are* at risk when they carry them, how can we penalize those who cannot immediately confirm their identities with documents? We can do so if we are equally convinced that the refugee bodies of today

are capable of—and, indeed, bent on—deceiving us, and if we see ourselves as having the right and the obligation to teach them about our unquestionably "superior" values.

Who is the subject who might believe so easily that she or he is besieged and likely to be deceived, the subject who believes she or he must teach Others about values? Writing of the social construction of whiteness, Richard Dyer describes the ways in which whites have constructed themselves in a story of origins as moral and virtuous, capacities that have enabled them to tell the story of having "developed" (rather than colonized) lands occupied by others. The Canadian national story, Dyer writes, relying on the work of Carl Berger, is a characteristic one in this respect, with its rhetoric and imagery of enterprising and hardy citizens of a cold land who, through their hard work, have forged a nation out of nothing.[47] In this compressed narrative, white people become the original inhabitants, because it is only they who are cast as capable of making the country what it is. They bring order and civilization where previously there was none—a logic that survives intact in the responses of Canadian courts to Aboriginal land claims.[48]

A story of origins thus told depends on the erasure of non-white inhabitants and on their inferiority. Either the land was empty or it was filled by those too lacking in enterprise to develop it. To be white is to be honorable, square-dealing, and enterprising, while to be non-white is to be dissolute and dishonest, a national mythology that has considerable historical and contemporary appeal for both elite and non-elite white citizen subjects. As Carl Berger has traced historically, Canadian nationalist thinkers have relied on the myth that stronger and superior Northern peoples also have a superior capacity for governing themselves and a correspondingly greater commitment to liberty. As Berger comments, to "the equation of 'northern' with strength and the strenuous virtues, against 'southern' with degeneration and effeminacy, was added the identification of the former with liberty and the latter with tyranny."[49] Thus, when Southern peoples migrate to Canada, they are assumed to come with values that undermine the nation.

The sheer intransigence of "simple logic" and its capacity to withstand its critics are indicators that it relies on the same kind of racial story of origins to which Dyer refers. When we are confronted by the grip that national mythologies have on ordinary people, Gail Ching-Liang Low suggests, it is useful to turn to concepts such as fantasy, focusing on the desires revealed in how individuals imagine their nations.[50] What, then, is revealed in the insistent refrain that "we must know who they are" through passports and travel documents? Does the notion of Somalis as people who need to be taught respect and honesty help to convince Canadians that they are indeed civilized?

Iain Chambers describes how national fantasies work when he explores the hold that the extremely right-wing politician Enoch Powell had in Britain and the wide support he won for his anti-immigration platforms. Powell, who rose to prominence in the 1970s with images of the English "race" overwhelmed by hordes of immigrants, manipulated a limited set of images (Oxford and Cambridge, Queen Victoria and Churchill, and the storming of Dunkirk) that called to mind a British story of origins, one of white enterprise and superiority. To be British was to be "spiritually and morally the 'centre' of the world," a worldview that lay at the heart of Powell's contention that Britain was in danger of losing its hold due to immigration. Critics who contested his anti-immigration story appeared to be "desecrating the national heritage," and indeed both sides of the House of Commons and the media appeared to believe in these powerful images as much as Powell did.[51] In the same way, to

contest that Canadians are a generous and fair-minded people is to "desecrate" the national heritage. A powerful rage and censure descends on those who would do so, particularly on those who ought to be grateful for being accepted into the country in the first place.

The key contention of "simple logic"—that the "original" Canada is imperiled owing to the arrival of refugees and immigrants (who are coincidentally dark-skinned and from the South)—easily draws on an older storyline evident in American racist thinkers of the early twentieth century, a process that Joseph Bendersky traces in his article "The Disappearance of Blonds: Immigration, Race and the Reemergence of 'Thinking White.'" Informed by a man who was visiting New York that the man's family had been told that they were particularly at risk of theft and assault in New York because of their blond hair, Bendersky explores how this storyline of blonds in peril from the alien darker masses should come to be so easily believed by the tourist. He traces the genealogy of this idea in racial thinkers at the turn of the twentieth century, from prominent American Social Darwinists who worried that white blood would become tainted through miscegenation to influential scholars who lamented the passing of the great Nordic race. Bendersky shows how the storyline depends on the idea that the inferior non-white races "motivated by pure race envy and jealousy" want all the good things that whites have made for themselves.[52]

The racial epic of a higher civilization threatened by a rising tide of color has sustained several anti-immigration campaigns throughout the century. As morally superior "truth tellers" who possess "innate ethical endowment," whites are naturally besieged by Jews and the darker races, as Edward Ross, a prominent racial thinker, put it in 1914. The emotional intensity of the racial epic was such that even those who had never seen Jews and immigrants subscribed to it, and politicians were able to count on it when courting electoral support. By the late 1930s, when overt mention of the imperiled Nordic race was no longer socially acceptable, the racial epic was told as a story of a democratic land overwhelmed by "a wide influx of people who know nothing about our institutions and care less for them." Ultimately, in the 1990s, the racial epic comes to rely on the figure of the illegal immigrant, the immoral man intent on taking what is not his, a man whose culture and morality is the very opposite of the American way of life.[53]

Immigration as a story of a sovereign nation forced to protect itself from the unscrupulous and envious hordes remains the contemporary racial epic, a feature noted by scholars working in other contexts, as well. Allan Pred, discussing Swedish moves to control its borders tightly in the 1990s, describes the narratives of Swedish politicians who argue that alien migrant cultures threaten the Swedish way of life. Remarkably similar to Canadian political talk about testing to see whether refugees have learned respect for the Canadian way of life, Swedish narratives are underpinned by the idea that Sweden is overwhelmed by immigrants and refugees who know little of Swedish values and customs and who often are not capable of respecting them. As the Swedish Social Democrat Averker Astrom put it:

It is neither amoral nor against the law to investigate whether he or she [the potential immigrant or asylum-seeker] has a criminal past, maybe as a terrorist; nor to ask oneself whether the individual in question appears willing or is capable of becoming a loyal member of Swedish society and whether he has what it takes to thrive; nor to try to judge whether he or she comes from a country or culture whose customs and usages are so extremely different that a reasonably

harmonious adaptation is difficult or impossible.[54]

The position that alien migrants threaten the original way of life relies on what Pred calls "a particular geographical imagination," a remembering of Sweden prior to the arrival of migrants. When racist Swedish youth beat a Somali man in the city of Göteborg, their defense counsel argued that his clients were not racist: "They only consider Sweden to be packed to the limit."[55] The social space is thus reimagined to support the idea of the threatening immigrant whom we must control. For the idea of difference as threat to work, Marc Swyngedouw writes for the Belgian context, a prior idea of an original family of people must be in place. Thus, an idea of racial descent underpins the notion that the hordes are at the gate and are unlikely to share our values.[56] It underpins as well the notion that we must know who they are, a knowledge that does not include knowing about their histories or about our own complicity in the events that brought them to our borders. Instead, we must know their essence— whether or not they are like us.

The racial story of identity documents, our insistence on knowing who refugees are *outside* of history, derives strong support from the liberal notion of a sovereign state that has a right to control entry and to maintain a distinction between the rights of those inside and those outside its borders. The notion of a sovereign state standing outside of its history is eminently compatible with the narratives of whiteness described by Dyer. How the state has come to be, the bodies on which it has relied, and the historical and contemporary relationships that sustain it (for example, Northern exploitation of the South through trade policies) do not typically enter the discussion of rights. Insistently told as an a-historical and national rather than an international story, liberal terms of reference that turn on abstractions make it difficult to consider how it comes to be that there is a flow of bodies from the North to the South and how the North is itself implicated in the production of these migrations and refugee flows. For most people, it is difficult to cut through the rhetoric about tribal warfare in Africa, and the "crisis" produced by 37,000 refugees at the door, in order to find the Canadian economic and foreign policies that directly contribute to the crises in Africa. Arguing that the creation of an impregnable border serves only to increase the smuggling of immigrants, and thus revenues to crime syndicates, Liz Fekete and Frances Webber put the issue of complicity baldly:

> So long as globalization of markets continues to destroy the livelihoods of Third World producers, and western arms sales prop up repression, people will try to escape; and so long as their legal means of escape are blocked, whether by protectionist labour policies or by slamming the doors on refugees, they will be forced to use dangerous and illegal means.[57]

The argument that the acceptance of 37,000 refugees marks a national crisis thrives, in spite of the knowledge that the Canadian economy depends on immigration to survive. Such details sink under the weight of the rhetoric of an entitled, de-historicized, and autonomous citizenry and sovereign nation. It is sobering to consider the French academic Emmanual Terray's point that the issue of the "undocumented" may well be the heart of today's political economy.[58] Western nations thrive on the unequal structure of citizenship that is created when some workers have fewer rights than others. Indeed, these nations so depend on the labor of the juridically marginalized and their legally produced vulnerability that their economies would come to a standstill without such inequalities.

Beyond the measures discussed in this essay, which are aimed at refugees, "simple logic" is deployed to win support for a number of initiatives aimed at illegal immigrants. For example, the United States provides a stellar example of the drastic border-policing and internal-surveillance measures of the 1990s with California's Proposition 187, a measure aimed at illegal immigration.[59] The underlying logic of Proposition 187 was that if you cut state services to the "undocumented," they would stop coming, because services (welfare, health, and education) were why they came. Proposition 187 was followed by federal measures to improve border security and impose higher penalties for those caught smuggling in the "undocumented" and bills limiting the "undocumented" from gaining access to education and health care.[60] Even critics of these measures, Linda Bosniak shows, find it difficult to refute the underlying premise of such measures—namely, that states have a right to protect themselves from "border violators" who are "an assault on the integrity of sovereign statehood itself."[61] This simple assertion is easily harnessed to the racial story of the North deluged by the foreign, greedy, and unscrupulous hordes of the South. The power of the racial narrative *enables* the decontextualized notion of a sovereign state to stand, leaving little room for critically interrogating the idea of border violators and the complicity of the Northern states that have produced them. This is the central dynamic of "simple logic" and the engine that drives the continuing erosion of citizens' rights today.

Conclusion

Its economic value notwithstanding, if "simple logic" has thrived, it is because it is able to draw on a particular racial story of origins, a story about a kind and generous Northern nation overrun by refugees and immigrants who are simply out to abuse the country's generosity. Whether this story is articulated as openly as it is by the more Conservative politicians, it remains sufficiently in place and has an underlying emotional appeal such that the contrasting image of refugees who have specific histories and who are likely genuinely to be fleeing persecution, cannot take root. In the case of Convention Refugees, facts regarding the rarity of fraud, the existence of alternative strategies to identify who people are, counter-stories about the conditions under which most refugees flee, and descriptions of the hardships imposed mostly on women and children who must wait three years for equal citizenship do not suffice to dislodge "simple logic." Those who contest it are up against a powerful national mythology, a drama involving reasonable and civilized white people who only want honesty, and racial Others who are stubbornly bent on deceiving them. It is the simplest of storylines, and a very old colonial one. Today, when the storyline is again deployed to justify an unequal structure of citizenship, we would do well to remember Jonathan Benthall's point that human rights without citizens' rights are extremely limited rights.[62]

Postscript: Who Counts

"Simple Logic" was very much in evidence when a version of this chapter first went to press in a Canadian journal. The publishers of the journal initially stopped publication of the article, maintaining that some of the arguments potentially exposed them to the risk of a libel suit. Objecting (among other things) to my characterization of the political speech of several members of Parliament as racist, the publishers asked me to delete statements for which, in their view, there was no proof. As Said noted earlier of colonial logic, a true statement is one in which a word or a phrase simply connotes reality. For instance, when I claimed that a speaker spoke contemptuously and patriarchally, supporting my claim with a quotation in which the speaker addressed a woman as "girl" and over-simplified her position, this did not constitute a true statement because there was no direct evidence that these responses were contemptuous and patriarchal. The publishers called for quantitative evidence of various kinds, asking in several instances that I ensure that I had counted or quoted correctly. For example, they asked, Did the federal Member of Parliament Val Meredith literally ask the same question ten times in ten minutes, and were her interventions counted and timed? (They were.) Like "simple logic," these objections rely on a bounded system of logic in which proof that racism exists can be established only within a positivist framework. In such a framework, a comment is racist only if the speaker has said that Somalis are inferior. If the speaker has simply said over and over again that sovereign states have a right to protect themselves from unscrupulous individuals, this comment, standing all alone and without the social context that gives it meaning, does not offer evidence of racism. The publishers sought a legal opinion before eventually allowing the article to be printed. While the lawyer retained by the publishers declared the article to be within the realm of "fair comment," he nevertheless advised that the author check (among other things) that Meredith had in fact made the same statement ten times in ten minutes.[63] When the evidence of racism is challenged, it is usually challenged within the boundaries of "simple logic"—that is, within a framework that admits only abstractions and that excludes the social and the historical that give the words their meaning.

The attempt to stop some of the arguments made in this article from going to press also shows important features of how

218 "SIMPLE LOGIC"

racism is organized. The publishers' objections turned on the assumption that I had not correctly *counted*. Even though each of the dozen or so points that were challenged was footnoted, the publishers felt entirely secure in demanding that I count again. As Patricia Monture Angus suggests (in this volume), perhaps what is really being objected to is who is doing the counting. Finally, it is instructive that such demands proceed as far and as fast as they do. "Simple logic" relies on the power of the dominant group to assert its position. Although there were many individuals who saw through the ludicrousness of the publishers' position, it was nevertheless a position that received enough support that a costly libel lawyer was hired. Here is perhaps the most important feature of how "simple logic" works: Who can say that the emperor has no clothes and survive to tell the tale?

Notes

Acknowledgments: The author deeply appreciates the research assistance and critical feedback of Sheila Gill, Donna Jeffery, Teresa Macias, Jennifer Nelson, Hijin Park, and especially Leslie Thielen-Wilson, whose thoroughness and insight made this article stronger than it might otherwise have been.
Epigraphs: House of Commons, "Legislative Committee of the House of Commons on Bill C-86," *Minutes of Proceedings and Evidence*, 3rd Sess., 34th Parl., no. 4, 1991-92, 25 (hereafter, *Minutes*). "Minister Robillard Announces Measures for Refugees Lacking ID to Become Permanent Residents," News Release 96/27, November 13, 1996 (Citizenship and Immigration).

1. Benedict Anderson, *Imagined Communities* (London and New York: Verso Press, 1983).

2. Edward Said, *Culture and Imperialism* (New York: Alfred A. Knopf, 1993), xiii.

3. For example, German asylum laws were also amended in 1993 to deny asylum to anyone arriving via "a safe third country" and reclassified the number of countries in which political persecution by the state is recognized: Stephen Scheele, "The Politics of Western Immigration," *Indiana Journal of* *Global Legal Studies* 3, no. 1 (1995): 280. Boyd writes of asylum reforms in France for the same period, which grant broader police powers. In these reforms, asylum-seekers who commit deliberate fraud are not granted asylum. Fraudulent identity documents presumably fall into this category: Michael Boyd, "Jaws of the Crocodile: 1993 Asylum Reforms in France," *Georgetown Immigration Law Journal* 10 (1996): 262. Penalties are imposed on transport carriers who transport (from one European country to another) an "alien" who does not possess the necessary travel documents: Boyd, "Jaws," 272.

4. House of Commons, *Bill C-86, An Act to Amend the Immigration Act and Other Acts in Consequence Thereof,* 3rd Sess., 34th Parl., 1991-92 (first reading June 16, 1992); *Immigration Act,* RSC 1985, c. I-2.

5. According to Canada's *An Act to Amend the Immigration Act, 1976 and to Amend Other Acts in Consequence Thereof* (R.S.C. 1985, c. 1-2 2[1]), a "convention refugee" is one who "by reason of a well-founded fear of persecution for reasons of race, religion, nationality, membership in a particular social group or political opinion,

(i) is outside the country of the person's nationality and is unable or, by reason of that fear, is unwilling to avail [her]self of the protection of that country, or
(ii) not having a country of nationality, is outside the country of the person's former habitual residence and is unable, or by reason of that fear, is unwilling to return to that country."

6. *Immigration Act,* sec. 46.04(8), states as follows: "An Immigration officer shall not grant landing either to an applicant under subsection (1) or to any dependant of the applicant until the applicant is in possession of a valid and subsisting passport or travel document or a satisfactory identity document."

7. Andrew Brouwer, *What's In a Name? Identity Documents and Convention Refugees* (Ottawa: Caledon Institute for Social Policy, 1999), available from: <http://wwwmaytree.com/publications_name.html>; Julia Dryer, "The Undocumented Convention Refugees in Canada Class: Creating a Refugee Underclass," *Journal of Law and Society* 13 (1998): 167.

8. Amended Amended Statement of Claim in *Hussein Jama Aden et al and Her Majesty the Queen,* Court File No. IMM500/501-96 (FCTD).

9. Citizenship and Immigration, "Regulations Amending the Immigration Regulations 1978, Regulatory Impact Analysis Statement," *Canada Gazette,* part I, vol. 130, no. 46, November 16, 1996.

10. Citizenship and Immigration, "Fact Sheet for Undocumented Convention Refugee in Canada Class (UCRCC)," December 30, 1999, available from: <http://wwwcic.gc.ca/english/refugee/ucrcc-e.html>.

11. Brouwer, *What's In a Name?* 11.

12. Amended Amended Statement of Claim in *Hussein Jama Aden.*

13. Freda Hawkins, "The Asylum Seekers," *Behind the Headlines* 52, no. 2 (1994–95): 1; Ninette Kelley and Michael Trebilcock, *Making of the Mosaic: A History of Canadian Immigration Policy* (Toronto: University of Toronto Press, 1998), 412.

14. Kelley and Trebilcock, *Making of the Mosaic,* 412.

15. Bill C-86 was debated in an all-party legislative committee made up of five members of the ruling party (the Progressive Conservatives) and three members of the opposition, including one member of the New Democratic Party and two members of the Liberal Party. The committee sat for four months and heard from fifty witnesses, including nineteen unions, corporations, and individuals; seven legal associations; and twenty-four non-governmental organizations. The minister and officials of the Department of Employment and Immigration also appeared to defend the bill and answer questions: Steven Dumas, "An Analysis of Bill C-86: Canada's Refugee Status Determination Process" (master's thesis, Department of Sociology, University of Manitoba, 1995), 57.

16. Quoted in Lisa Jacubowski, *Immigration and the Legalization of Racism* (Halifax: Fernwood Publishing, 1997), 71.

17. Immigration and Refugee Board, "Commentary on Undocumented and Improperly Documented Claimants: Assessing the Evidence, Enhancing the Procedures," March 11, 1997.

18. Lauren Berlant, *The Anatomy of National Fantasy: Hawthorne, Utopia and Everyday Life* (Chicago: University of Chicago Press, 1991), 3, 5, 20.

19. Ibid., 9–10, 5 (B. Valcourt).

20. *Minutes,* no. 3, 48–50.

21. Ibid., no. 2, 8.

22. Ibid., 9, 22, 28; ibid., no. 13, 12.

23. Ibid., no. 3, 46–7.

24. Ibid., 89.

25. Ibid., no. 12, 33.

26. Ibid., no. 5, 10.

27. Ibid., no. 7, 148 (emphasis added).

28. Ibid. (emphasis added) (Philip); ibid., 72; ibid., 50 (Fee).

29. Ibid., no. 12, 50, 52.

30. Ibid., no. 15, 27 (Friesen); ibid., 32 (Reid).

31. Catherine Besteman, "Representing Violence and 'Othering' Somalia," *Cultural Anthropology* 11, no. 1 (1996): 129–33.

32. *Minutes,* no. 5, 83.

33. Ibid., no.7, 115 (Hathaway); ibid., no. 3, 89 (Allmand); ibid., no. 5, 58 (Refugee Lawyer Association); ibid., no. 3, 100.

34. See *Minutes,* no. 4A, 8–10 (Amnesty International); *Minutes,* no. 4, 69 (Inter-Church Committee for Refugees); *Minutes,* no. 12, 29 (Inter-Church Committee for Refugees).

35. Citizenship and Immigration, "Regulations," 3258.

36. The House of Commons of Canada Standing Committee on Citizenship and Immigration met to discuss and hear witnesses regarding the landing of "undocumented" refugees in three separate meetings over the course of two days. Meetings 31 and 32 were held on December 3, 1996; meeting 33 was held on December 5, 1996. Among the eight committee members were (at least) five Liberal MPs and members of two right-leaning political parties (Reform and the Bloc Quebecois). The committee heard evidence from a total of twenty-three witnesses. The committee tabled its report to the House of Commons of Canada on December 12, 1996 (Hansard 7423).

37. House of Commons, Standing Committee on Citizenship and Immigration, *Minutes of Proceedings and Evidence,* no. 31, December 3–5, 1996, 1–4 (Jeff Lebane, director-general of refugees) (hereafter, Standing Committee); ibid., no. 33, 7–9 (V. Meredith).

38. Edward Said, *Orientalism* (London: Routledge and Kegan Paul, 1978), 72, as quoted in Homi Bhaba, *The Location of Culture* (London and New York: Routledge, 1994), 71. Bhaba's point is cited by Iain Chambers, "Narratives of Nationalism: Being 'British,'" in *Space and Place: Theories of Identity and Location,* ed. Erica Carter, James Donald, and Judith Squires (London: Lawrence and Wishart, 1993), 153.

39. Standing Committee, no. 31, 5, 6, 21; ibid., no. 33, 35 (V. Meredith); ibid., 41 (V. Meredith); ibid., 49 (V. Meredith); ibid., no. 32, 15 (V. Meredith).

40. Citizenship and Immigration, "Refugees from Kosovo," *News Update,* May 10, 1999, 1.

41. M. Landsberg, "Why Waive Unfair Rules Only for Kosovo Refugees?" *Toronto Star,* 17 April 1999, L1.

42. Dryer, "Undocumented Convention Refugees," 179.

43. Franz Fanon, *The Wretched of the Earth* (New York: Random House, 1963 [1961]), 39.

44. Ibid., 41 (emphasis added).

45. Ibid., 43.

46. Toni Morrison, "The Official Story: Dead Man Golfing," in *Birth of a Nation'hood: Gaze, Script, and Spectacle in the O.J. Simpson Case,* ed. Toni Morrison and Claudia Brodsky Lacour (New York: Pantheon Books, 1997), ix.

47. Richard Dyer, *White* (New York and London: Routledge, 1997), 21; Carl Berger, "The True North Strong and Free," in *Nationalism in Canada,* ed. Peter Russell (Toronto: McGraw-Hill, 1966), 3.

48. Dara Culhane, *The Pleasure of the Crown* (Vancouver: Talon Books, 1998).

49. See Berger, "The True North," 15.

50. Gail Ching-Liang Low, "His Stories? Narratives and Images of Imperialism," in Carter et al., *Space and Place,* 188.

51. Iain Chambers, "Narratives of Nationalism," in Crater et al., *Space and Place,* 147.

52. Joseph W. Bendersky, "The Disappearance of Blonds: Immigration, Race and the Reemergence of 'Thinking White,'" *Telos* 104 (1995): 135, 141.

53. Edward Ross, as quoted in ibid., 143; ibid., 150, citing discussions in Congress in 1935); ibid., 156.

54. Allan Pred, "Memory and the Cultural Reworking of Crisis: Racisms and the Current Moment of Danger in Sweden, or Wanting It Like Before," *Environment and Planning D: Society and Space* 16 (1998): 643-4.

55. Ibid., 654.

56. Marc Swyngedouw, "The 'Threatening Immigrant' in Flanders 1930-1980: Redrawing the Social Space," *New Community* 21, no. 3 (1995): 337.

57. Liz Fekete and Francis Webber, "The Human Trade," *Race and Class* 39, no. 1 (1997): 73.

58. Cited in Jonathan Benthall, "Repercussions from the Eglise Saint-Bernard," *Anthropology Today* 13, no. 4 (1997): 1-2.

59. California Education Code 48215(a) (West Supp. 1995); California Health and Safety Code 130(a) (West Supp. 1995); California Welfare and Institutional Code 10001.5 (West Supp. 1995). For an insightful critique of Proposition 187, see Linda Bosniak, "Opposing Prop. 187: Undocumented Immigrants and the National Imagination," *Connecticut Law Review* 28, no. 3 (1996): 555.

60. Linda Ocasio, "The Year of the Immigrant as Scapegoat," *Report on Immigration, North American Congress on Latin America (NACLA) Report on the Americas,* vol. 29, no. 3, November-December 1995, 14-7.

61. Bosniak, "Opposing Prop. 187," 67.

62. Benthall, "Repercussions," 2.

63. All letters containing the evidence for this account are in the author's possession.

CHAPTER EIGHT

Straight Out of the Closet: Race, Gender, and Sexual Orientation

Devon W. Carbado

Heterosexuality . . . needs to be recognized and studied as a political institution.
    —Adrienne Rich

Heterosexuality is a problem. Male heterosexuality is double trouble.
    —Bruce Ryder

It may be . . . that a damaging bias toward heterosocial or heterosexist assumptions inheres unavoidably in the very concept of gender. . . . The ultimate definitional appeal in any gender-based analysis must necessarily be to the diacritical frontier between different genders. This gives heterosocial and heterosexual relationships a conceptual privilege of incalculable consequence.
    —Eve K. Sedgwick

Heterosexuality [is] the grail, the ultimate in human maturity and happiness.
    —Gore Vidal

Other versions of this chapter appeared in Devon W. Carbado, ed., *Black Men on Race, Gender, and Sexuality: A Critical Reader* (New York: New York University Press, 1999) and *Berkeley Women's Law Journal* 76 (2000).

Privileged Perpetrators

TYPICALLY, we define a perpetrator of discrimination as someone who acts intentionally to bring about some discriminatory result. This is a narrow and politically palatable conception. Those of us who unquestionably accept the racial, gender, and heterosexual privileges we have, and those of us who fail to acknowledge our victimless status vis-à-vis racism, sexism, and homophobia, are also perpetrators of discrimination.[1]

Taking identity privileges for granted helps to legitimize certain problematic assumptions about identity and entitlement. These assumptions make it difficult for us to challenge the starting points of many of our most controversial conversations about equality. We simply assume, for example, that men should be able to fight for their country (the question is whether women should be entitled to this "honor"); that heterosexuals should be able to get married (the question is whether the "privilege" should be extended to gays and lesbians); that white men should be able to compete for all the slots in a university's entering class (the question is whether white women and people of color should be entitled to "preferential" treatment).

Admittedly, linking perpetrator status to identity privilege might prove too much. All of us enjoy at least some privilege. Are all of us perpetrators of discrimination? Perhaps. The answer may depend on what we do with, and to, our privileges. All of us, through the ways in which we negotiate our identities, play a role in entrenching a variety of social practices, institutional arrangements, and laws that disadvantage other(ed) people. All of us make choices every day that legitimize certain discriminatory practices. I chose to work at the UCLA Law School even as Proposition 209 has drastically reduced the number of certain students of color, and especially Black students, at the law school. Many of us get married or attend weddings even as lesbian and gay marriages are not legally recognized. Others of us have racially monolithic social encounters, live in de facto white-only (or predominantly white) neighborhoods, or send our kids to white-only (or predominantly white) schools. Still others of us have "straight-only" associations—that is, our friends are all heterosexuals, and our children's friends all have mommies and daddies. These choices are not just personal; they are political. And the cumulative effect of these micropolitical choices is the entrenchment of the very social practices—racism, sexism, classism, and homophobia—that we profess to abhor.

In other words, there is a link between privilege and discrimination. Our identities are both reflective and constitutive of certain systems of oppression. Racism requires white privilege. Sexism requires male privilege. Homophobia requires heterosexual privilege. Thus, all of us have an obligation to expose and to challenge our privileges.

We have to remake ourselves—our identities—if we are to remake our institutions. We cannot hope to institutionalize our political commitments unless we personalize our politics. Resistance to identity privileges may be futile; we cannot know for sure. But to the extent that we do nothing, this much is clear: We perpetuate the systems of discrimination that our identities reflect.

But precisely what constitutes a privilege? How do we identify our privileges? And what acts are sufficiently disruptive of our privileges to amount to resistance? Focusing on male and heterosexual privileges, this chapter addresses these questions in the context of a discussion about men and feminism. For as I will show, men can and should employ feminism to identify and resist male and heterosexual privileges.

This chapter advances an argument that many progressives might agree with—namely, that men should embrace and assert a feminist political identity. Yet the argument is certainly not uncontroversial. Men's assertions of feminist identity raise serious concerns about 1) political territory (whether feminism is women's political terrain); 2) safe space (whether feminism is a place for women to escape men's epistemological dominance); and 3) authenticity (whether feminism is constructed on, and intended to be a voice for, women's experiences). Significantly, in arguing that men should identify as feminists, I am not suggesting that men should endeavor to speak in a "different" (read, women's) voice. Moreover, men's feminism should not attempt to replicate women's feminism.

Nor do I mean to suggest that men, as feminists, should presume to speak for women. The last thing we need is more men—under the guise and ostensible legitimacy of feminism—presuming to define the nature of women's experiences. Women "do not want you (men) to mimic us, to become the same as us; we don't want your pathos or your guilt; and we don't even want your admiration (even if it's nice to get it once in a while). What we want—I would even say, what we need—is your work. And like all serious work, that involves struggle and pain."[2]

Part of the work of men's feminism should involve men coming to terms with, recognizing and challenging, men's intersectional privileges. This should be a fundamental component of any male feminist project. Thus, the political thrust of this chapter is the employment of feminist insights to expose and contest the male experiential side of heteropatriarchy.

Male Feminist or Oxymoron?

It might indeed be the case that "men's relation to feminism is an impossible one," that men cannot be feminists. This "impossibility thesis" is quite arresting. Here is a strong articulation of the argument:

> Women are the subjects of feminism, its initiators, its makers, its force; the move and the join from being a woman to being a feminist is the gasp of that subjecthood. Men are the objects, part of the analysis, agents of the structure to be transformed, representatives in, carriers of the patriarchal mode; and my desire to be a subject there too in feminism—to be a feminist—is then only also the last feint in the long history of *their* colonization.[3]

Even assuming that this male/object-female/subject dichotomy is accurate, the analysis avoids the central normative question: Conceding that women were the initiators of feminism, its makers, its force, should it remain so? Proponents of the "impossibility thesis" seem to suggest that, quite apart from what we might want, it must be so: The impossibility of men's relationship to feminism stems from the very different (unequal) social reality that

men and women live. Because "there is no equality, no symmetry ... there can be no reversing: it is for women now to reclaim and redefine the terrain of sexuality [and feminism], for us [men] to learn from them."[4]

Importantly, the claim that men cannot be feminists is not urging political abdication—that men should not attempt to transform hierarchical gendered arrangements. Rather, the argument is that the antipatriarchal work that men perform is not feminism. Men's feminism, the argument goes, is a contradiction in terms. Because women are the "natives" of feminism, men necessarily are the "colonists."[5] Alas, there is no male exit from patriarchy.

I am not persuaded that men's relationship to feminism is an impossible one. I advance two arguments to explain why. First, men's feminism need not reflect men's epistemological dominance (men speaking for or definitively about women's experiences). Second, feminism is more about ideology and political commitment than it is about male or female identity per se. I elaborate on these arguments below.

Men Are Not Where Women Are: A Starting Point for Men's Feminism

Few people would quarrel with the notion that men and women have different social realities. This realization is often invoked to support the argument that men cannot be feminists. Yet the fact that men and women live different social lives might be a starting point for men's feminism. Men's realization of gender difference and gender hierarchy can provide us with the opportunity to theorize about gender from the gender-privileged positions we occupy as men. Indeed, men's challenges to gender hierarchy should be grounded in men's and women's positional difference. Such challenges should expose the extent to which gender is socially constructed and contingent; make clear that gender is about power and marginalization; and highlight the fact that men, and not just women, live the gender difference. Men's feminism need not attempt to speak in a "different voice." Instead, men's feminism should be *explicitly* informed by men's experiential differences. These differences could be the basis for raising consciousness among and between men. I am not speaking about consciousness-raising "for the purpose of finding the 'hairy beast' or the 'wild man' within."[6] The consciousness-raising that I have in mind would help men identify and challenge the social practices in their lives that entrench and normalize their privileges.

It is not clear to me that men's feminism would merely reproduce "what has come before"—that is, patriarchy. Men's feminism could en-gender men, persuade men to examine their gender(ed) subjectivities. Part of the problem with discourses produced by men is their ungendered, purportedly neutral, substantive content. Men's discourses are carefully abstracted from men's experiential realities. Employing feminism, men could begin to examine the specific ways in which *their* gender identity structures and helps give meaning to *their* everyday social interactions and informs their epistemology.

The personal is political—one of feminism's first principles. This first principle *could* support a feminist project that centers the male subject as a problematic and privileged identity. It is easier for men to acknowledge the realities of gender subordination in women's lives than it is for us to acknowledge the realities of gender privilege in our own. Generally speaking, men do not perceive themselves to be en-gendered. Gender, for men, is a term that relates to women and women's experiences; it is synonymous with "female." Thus, men have not paid much attention to the ways in which the social constructions of gender shape and

define men's experiences as men. Indeed, men accept their identities as pre-political givens. The gender question, when it is addressed, is rarely about the nature and consequences of men's privilege. Rather, it is about the nature and consequences of women's disadvantage.

A men's feminist project could challenge men's tendency to conceptualize gender outside their own experiences as men. As Hélène Cixous has observed, "Men still have everything to say about their sexuality."[7] It remains the "dark continent."[8] Men's engagement *in* feminism (assuming that men can be feminists) or *with* feminism (assuming that they cannot) could generate self-criticism. Employing this self-criticism, men could expose the interpersonal ways in which they install patriarchy and identify the distributive consequences of that installation for men and women.

Significantly, patriarchy is not just "out there," external to our relationships and experiences. It is manifested in, and constituted by, how we choose to structure those relationships and experiences. Part of a men's feminist project, then, should be to persuade men to see themselves as body-coded (as distinct from naturally created) men. With this gender awareness, men are in a political position to challenge the ways in which they enact and naturalize the patriarchal codes of manhood in their everyday social encounters.

Gender Identity and Feminist Ideology

Another way to advance the claim that men's relationship to feminism is not necessarily impossible or even problematic is to distinguish between feminism (ideology) and women (identity). Although men can be feminists, they cannot experience women's social realities. An analogy to race is helpful. Whites can—and, indeed, should be encouraged to—be antiracist. However, they cannot experience Blackness. This identity-experi-ence-ideology dichotomy suggests that the men-and-feminism question need not be about political terrain or gender essential-ism; it can be about political vision. I develop this argument more fully later in the context of theorizing Black men's relationship to Black feminism. But to reiterate the general idea: Ideology and political commitment, not gender identity, defines (or should define) feminism.

Black Men and Black Feminism

What if the question becomes: What is Black men's relationship to Black feminist discourse? Does the preceding analysis change? The short answer is, not entirely. Yet there are some differences that relate to the ways in which gender is negotiated in antiracist politics.

Authenticity and Dominance

The problems relating to authenticity, epis-temological dominance, and safe space do not disappear when the men-and-feminism debate is racially rearticulated as the Black men and Black feminism debate. Let us begin with authenticity. Some Black feminists argue that the terms *feminist* or *feminism* should refer to female proponents of gender equality, and the terms *profeminism* or *pro-feminist* should refer to antipatriarchal men. They "biologize" feminism to support this feminism–profeminism dichotomy: Women can be feminists because they are women; men cannot be feminists because they are men. Sex is both qualifying and disqualify-ing—authenticating and "inauthenticating."[9]

The problem of epistemological domi-nance arises because knowledge production is always already gendered. This is true even when the intellectual location of this pro-duction is ideologically oriented to the left.

The question then becomes: Is this domi-nance reflected in Black antiracist discourse? More specifically, is there evidence of Black men's control of Black feminist discourse? Some Black feminists say "yes." They refer to the canonization of Black literary theory by Henry Louis Gates, Jr., as a concrete exam-ple. They argue that Gates is "single-hand-edly reshaping, codifying and consolidating the entire field of Afro-American studies, including black feminist studies." The results of Gates's intellectual monopoly "are inevitably patriarchal. Having established himself as the father of Afro-American Lit-erary Studies . . . he now proposes to become the phallic mother of the newly depolicit-ized, mainstreamed, and commodified black feminist literary criticism."[10]

The argument that Gates has monopo-lized our understanding of Black literary theory—including Black feminism—relates to a more general claim that Black feminists advance about the intellectual and political space Black men occupy in discourses about race: Black men have more authority than Black women to speak for the race. To the extent that Black men engage in feminism or define the content of Black feminism, they entrench and legitimize this authority. In this sense, the apprehension some Black feminists have about Black men's partici-pation in Black feminism reflects a deeper concern about the relationship between gender and racial authority within Black antiracist politics.

Identity Authenticity Versus Politics

Notwithstanding concerns about authen-ticity and dominance, Black men—like all men—can and should be feminists. This argument privileges politics over identity. A person's standing to claim a feminist sub-jectivity should depend on the person's political commitments. Central to this claim is the notion that all of us (men and women) have a stake in transforming gender relations. Feminism provides an ideological vehicle for all of us to do this work.

A "(Black) women's-only" conception of (Black) feminism is misguided for at least two reasons. First, it provides men with a political out, creating the impression that feminism is women's work. Surprisingly, "even as [feminists] were attacking sex role divisions of labor, the institutionalized sexism which assigns unpaid, devalued, 'dirty' work to women, they were assigning to women yet another sex role task: making a feminist revolution."[11] This sexual division of political labor is problematic. It authorizes men to opt out of the political struggle of dismantling gender hierarchy. The legitimation of this political exit means that the primary agents in perpetuating gender hierarchy avoid the patriarchal burden of eliminating it.

The second problem with the conceptualization of feminism as a "women-only" political movement is that the idea is often buttressed by a social construction of gender that posits all men as the enemy. This conceptualization ignores the fact that men are differently situated with respect to patriarchy and patriarchal agency; race, gender, class, and sexuality structure how men perform and thus experience their manhood. As bell hooks explains, "Assertions like 'all men are the enemy,' and 'all men hate women' lump all groups of men in one category, thereby suggesting that they share equally in all forms of male privilege."[12] Moreover, these assertions are based largely on white, upper- and middle-class women's relationships with white, upper- and middle-class men. Feminist discourses about men and feminism should not essentialize male identity.

One can agree with the claim that the men-and-feminism debate should be about political vision and action and still not be sanguine about Black men's participation in Black feminist discourse. For in addition to the concerns about dominance and authenticity, Black men's participation in Black feminism (like men's participation in feminism more generally) raises questions about safe spaces. The notion here is this: Black feminism constitutes "A Room of One's Own" for Black women—a place for Black women. Given men's tendency both to dominate and to control discourse, the argument might go: Black men's presence in Black feminism would violate or disrupt (the nature of) this "room."

Although the concerns about safe space are quite real, I do not believe that they require the conclusion that men cannot be feminists. Indeed, the men's feminist project that I have in mind encourages, supports, and respects the need for "women-only" associations. Men's feminism, as I imagine it, rejects the idea that men have a *right* to participate in or define the gender boundaries of women's social, political, and intellectual organizations.

I have argued that men can be feminists. Is this a controversial claim? Yes. I have discussed why the argument is controversial and revealed how the controversy is manifested in discourses about Black men and Black feminism. In the next section, I sketch out the ideological contours of a men's feminist project specifically to illustrate how men can employ this project both to identify and to challenge men's heterosexual privileges.

Rethinking Manhood to "Unbecome" Men

The argument that men can be feminists invites several queries. What does men's feminism look like? Is there a men's feminist methodology? How can men's feminism facilitate the dismantling of men's heterosexual privileges? This part explores these questions.

A fundamental goal of men's feminism should be to facilitate the process of men unbecoming men. In other words, men's feminism should help men unlearn and repudiate the patriarchal ways in which they have learned to *become* men. Ever since Simone de Beauvior articulated the idea that women are not born women but, rather, become women, feminists have been grappling with ways to strip the category "women" of its patriarchal trappings. The hope is to locate the pre-socially constructed, pre-patriarchal woman—the woman whose personal identity has not been overdetermined by her gender.

The feminist search for the pre-patriarchal woman is not based on the notion that, in the absence of patriarchy, there is some true female essence. (Indeed, it might not even be meaningful to refer to a person whose identity has not been overdetermined by female gender norms as a woman.) The point is that people who are body-coded as female cannot experience their personhood outside the social construction of their gender, which is agency-denying and subordinating.

Of course, gender for men is also socially constructed. One must learn to be a man in this society, because manhood is a socially produced category. Manhood is a performance. A script. It is accomplished and re-enacted in everyday relationships. Yet men have not been inclined to examine the sex/gender category we inhabit, reproduce, and legitimize. Nor have men developed a practice of exposing the contingency and "false necessity" of manhood. There is little effort within men's communities to locate, or even imagine, the pre-patriarchal man, the man whose personal identity has not been overdetermined by his gender. We (men) sometimes discuss gender inequality, but rarely do we discuss gender privilege. The assumption is that our privileges as men are not politically contingent but social givens—inevitable and unchangeable.

Men should challenge the social construction of gender employing our privileged gender(ed) experiences as starting points. We should detail and problematize the specific ways in which patriarchy structures and determines our social lives. This experiential information should not displace or replace victim-centered or bottom-up accounts of sexism. That is, men's articulation of the ways in which they are the beneficiaries of patriarchy should not be a substitute for women's articulations of the ways in which they are the victims of patriarchy. Both narratives are valuable and illuminating. The telling of both narratives helps to make clear that patriarchy is bidirectional: Patriarchy gives to men what it takes away from women; the disempowerment of women is achieved through the empowerment of men.[13] Patriarchy effectuates and maintains this relational difference. The social construction of women as the second sex requires the social construction of men as the first.

Heterosexism, too, effectuates and maintains a relational difference that is based on power. There is no disadvantage without a corresponding advantage, no marginalized group without the powerfully elite, no subordinate identity without a dominant identity. Power and privilege are relational; so, too, are our identities. "What heterosexism gives straight men and women, what it takes away from lesbians and gays, is heterosexual privilege."[14] The normalization of heterosexuality is achieved only through the "abnormalization" of homosexuality. Yet rarely do heterosexuals critically examine their identities as heterosexual, their sexual-identity privilege. Indeed, even pro-gay rights heterosexuals conceive of sexual identity as something that other(ed) people have, something that disadvantages other(ed) people, rather than something that heterosexuals have that gives them advantages.

Men's feminism should identify the privileges reflected in the relational constitution of the male identity. Moreover, it should offer some suggestions for how individual men can identify these privileges and relinquish them. Equality cannot be achieved unless privilege is relinquished. Andrea Dworkin and Catharine MacKinnon put the point this way: "Equality means someone loses power.... The mathematics are simple: taking power from the exploiters extends and multiplies the rights of those they have been exploiting."[15]

Such a zero-sum political framing of equality, however, may be damaging. The framework can be employed to fuel various conservative positions about rights. Consider, for example, the standard argument made by some conservatives that extending marriage rights to gays and lesbians would cheapen or harm heterosexual marriage. In some sense, this argument is accurate: To the extent that lesbian and gay marriages are legalized, the "value" of heterosexual marriage—its cultural, political, and social currency—is diminished. Part of the perceived value of marriage as an institution derives from its heterosexual exclusivity. Not everyone has a right to get married, and currently, no one has a right to gay marriage. The right to marriage must be heterosexually earned. In our present political and legal culture, the social meaning of marriage as the normal and most respectable way to express love and commitment requires heterosexuality. Thus, legalizing lesbian and gay marriages would change not only the social meaning of marriage, but also the social meaning of homo- and heterosexuality.[16] The reason for this is that the regulation of marriage has—at least, in part—always been about the regulation of morality, including sexual morality. Legalizing gay marriage would help to moralize—to render socio-sexually respectable—homosexuality. This is precisely why some

gay rights proponents continue to employ marriage as a site for a broader sexual-identity-equality struggle, and this is precisely why many conservatives police the borders of marriage so vigorously.

A Men's Feminist Method: Identifying Everyday Privilege

> It's up to him [man] to say where his masculinity and femininity are at.
> —Hélène Cixous[17]

I have argued that men's feminism should not attempt to replicate women's feminism in the sense of trying to articulate the nature of women's experiences. Instead, men's feminism should be male-centered, striving to render concrete the ways in which men—especially white, heterosexual men—benefit from patriarchy. This part provides a methodology for how men might do so.

Gender Privilege (and Race)

A white heterosexual man's engagement with feminism might begin by acknowledging that He (the white heterosexual man) is the norm. Mankind. The baseline. He is our reference. We are all defined with Him in mind. We are the same as or different from Him.

A clear, and now fairly uncontroversial, illustration of the male norm in operation is revealed in the debates about women's equality. Essentially, two competing paths exist to pursue women's equality in the United States: demonstrate that women are either the same as or different from men. "The main theme in the fugue is 'we're the same, we're the same, we're the same.' The counterpoint theme (in a higher register) is 'but we're different, but we're different, but we're different.'" Both of these conceptions of gender have man as their reference. "Under the sameness standard, women are measured according to our correspondence with man. . . . Under the difference standard, we are measured according to our lack of correspondence with him."[18]

Yet men are taught to be unaware of their en-gendered lives. We are taught to be unaware of the baseline privileges of gender. The "taboos against . . . male self-analysis"[19] compound the problem. As a consequence, men do not recognize men's privileges. We accept present-day social gender arrangements and ideologies about gender as necessary, pre-political, and inevitable.

Moreover, even when we perceive our gender privileges as privileges, rarely are we willing publicly to acknowledge them as such. Given a choice between analyzing how gender norms unfairly disadvantage women and exposing the ways in which these same norms privilege men, men prefer to analyze women. This is unfortunate. Considering that gender hierarchy requires gender privilege, men's intellectual inattentiveness to men's privilege entrenches the social and political differences of gender.

Broadly speaking, there are two categories of privileges men's feminism should attempt to identify. The first category can be described as "an invisible package of unearned assets that [men] can count on cashing in each day."[20] The second category includes a series of disadvantages that men do not experience precisely because they are men. The following list presents examples from both categories.

Gender Privileges: A List

1. I can walk in public, alone, without fear of being sexually violated.
2. Prospective employers will never ask me if I plan to have children.
3. I can be confident that my career path will never be tainted by accusations that I "slept my way to the top" (though it

could be "tainted" by the perception that I am a beneficiary of affirmative action).
4. I don't have to worry about whether I am being paid less than my female colleagues (though I do have to worry about whether I'm being paid less than my white male colleagues).
5. When I get dressed in the morning, I do not worry about whether my clothing "invites" sexual harassment.
6. I can be moody, irritable, or brusque without it being attributed to my sex, to biological changes in my life, or to menstruating or experiencing "PMS" (though it might be attributed to my "preoccupation" with race).
7. My career opportunities are not dependent on the extent to which I am perceived to be as good as a man (though they may be dependent on the extent to which I am perceived to be a "good black"—i.e., racially assimilable).
8. I do not have to choose between having a family or having a career.
9. I do not have to worry about being called selfish for having a career instead of having a family.
10. It will almost always be the case that my supervisor will be a man (though rarely will my supervisor be Black).
11. I can express outrage without being perceived as irrational, emotional, or too sensitive (except if I am expressing outrage about race).
12. I can fight for my country without controversy.
13. No one will qualify my intellectual or technical ability with the phrase "for a man" (though they may qualify my ability with the phrase "for a Black man").
14. I can be outspoken without being called a "bitch" (though I may be referred to as uppity).
15. I do not have to concern myself with finding the line between being assertive

and aggressive (except with respect to conversations about race).

16. I do not have to think about whether my race comes before my gender, about whether I am Black first and a man second.

17. The politics of dress—to wear or not to wear make-up, high heels, or trousers, to straighten or not to straighten, to braid or not to braid my hair—affect me less than they do women.

18. More is known about "men's" diseases and how medicine affects men's bodies than about "women's" diseases and women's bodies (though diseases that disproportionately affect Black people continue to be understudied).

19. I am not "supposed" to change my name on getting married.

20. I am rewarded for vigorously and aggressively pursuing my career.

21. I do not have to worry about opposite-sex strangers or close acquaintances committing gender violence against me (though I do have to worry about racial violence).

22. I am not less manly because I play sports (though I may be considered less Black and less manly if I do not play sports).

23. My reputation does not diminish with each additional person with whom I have sexual relations.

24. There is no societal pressure for me to marry before the age of thirty.

25. I can dominate a conversation without being perceived as domineering (unless the discussion is about race).

26. I am praised for spending time with my children, cooking, cleaning, or doing other household chores.

27. I will rarely have to worry whether compliments from my boss contain a sexual subtext (though I will worry that they may contain a racial subtext).

28. I am not expected to have a small appetite.

29. The responsibility for birth control is not placed on my shoulders, and men are not accused of getting pregnant.

30. There is a presumption that a person of my gender can run the country (though there is uncertainty about whether a person of my race can run the country).

31. White men don't have to worry about whether their gender will interfere with their ability effectively to bargain for a house, car, and so on.

32. If I kiss someone on a first date, I do not have to worry about whether I have provided that person with a defense to rape.

33. Men I know do not consistently address me by pet names such as "baby" or "sweetheart," nor do strangers employ such terms to refer to or greet me.

34. I do not have to worry about resisting chivalry—refusing to go through the door first, paying for myself, and so on to maintain my independence.

35. I do not have to think about the "female gaze" (though I do have to think about the racial gaze).

36. I do not have to worry about being heckled or harassed by strangers because of my gender (though I do have to worry about "drive-by" racial harassment).

37. I do not have to worry about leaving particular events early—such as sporting events—to avoid a ridiculous wait for the bathroom.

38. I do not have to worry about varicose veins, spinal malalignment, or disk injury from wearing high heels.

39. To the extent that I dry-clean my clothes, I do not have to worry about the gender-surcharge.

40. Every month is (White) Men's History Month.

This list does not reflect the privileges of all men. It is both under- and over-inclusive. Class, race, and sexual orientation affect men's identities, shaping the various dimensions of men's privilege. For example, the list does not include as a privilege the fact that men are automatically perceived as authority figures. Although this may be true of white men, it has not been my experience as a Black man. Moreover, the list clearly reveals my class privilege. My relationship to patriarchy is thus not the same as that of a working-class Black man. In constructing a list of men's privileges, then, one has to be careful not to universalize manhood, not to present it as a "cohesive identity" in ways that deny, obscure, or threaten the recognition of men's multiplicity.

However, even taking men's multiplicity into account, this list of men's advantages does not go far enough. These items do not directly address what might be referred to as "male patriarchal agency"—the extent to which men make choices that entrench men's advantages and women's disadvantages. Some of the privileges I have identified are the products of the cumulative choices men make every day in their personal and professional lives. The identification of privileges, then, is not enough. Resistance is also necessary.

Negative Identity Signification

Part of the reason men—especially white, heterosexual men—do not conceive of themselves as *(m)en*-gendered, and part of the reason men do not recognize their privileges, relates to negative identity signification. White, heterosexual men live on the white side of race, the male side of gender, and the straight side of sexual orientation. To put the point a little differently: White, heterosexual, male identity is socially construed to be normative.

Those of us on the "other" side of race, gender, or sexual orientation have to contend with and respond to negative identity signification. That is, we live with (even as

we fight against) the reality that our identities are not normative. We are "different." Thus, our identities have negative social meanings. Some of these meanings are more entrenched in the American psyche than others. Race, gender, and sexually oriented assumptions about personhood are especially difficult to dismantle.

For example, when I walk into a department store, my identity signifies not only that I am Black and male but also that I am a potential criminal. My individual identity is lost in the social construction of Black manhood. I can try to adopt race-negating strategies to challenge this dignity-destroying social meaning. That is, I can work my identity (to attempt) to repudiate the stereotype.[21] I might, for example, dress "respectable" when I go shopping. There is, after all, something to the politics of dress, particularly in social contexts in which race matters—that is, in every American social context. I can appear less "Black" in the sense of social meaning via my sartorial practices. Purchasing an item, especially something expensive, immediately on entering the store is another strategy I can employ to disabuse people of my "Blackness." This sort of signaling strategy will reveal to the department store's security personnel what might not otherwise be apparent because of my race and gender: that I am a shopper. If I am not in the mood to dress up, and I do not want to spend any money, there is a third strategy I can employ: Solicit the assistance of a white sales associate. This, too, must be done early in the shopping experience. A white salesperson would not be suspected of facilitating or contributing to Black shoplifting and can be trusted to keep an eye on me. Finally, I might simply whistle Vivaldi as I move among the merchandise. Only a good (safe, respectable) Black man would know Vivaldi or whistle classical music.[22]

White people do not have to worry about employing these strategies. White people do not have to work their identities to respond to these racial concerns. Nor should they have to. No one should. However, white people should recognize and grapple with the fact that they do not have to employ or think about employing these strategies. White people should recognize that they do not have to perform this work. This is a necessary first step for white people to come to terms with white privilege. Barbara Flagg and Peggy McIntosh—two white women—make similar arguments. Their self-referential examination of whiteness is the analytical analogue to my examination of male identity and heterosexuality (examined later).

According to Flagg, "There is a profound cognitive dimension to the material and social privilege that attaches to whiteness in this society, in that the white person has an everyday option not to think of herself in racial terms at all." This, reasons Flagg, is indeed what defines whiteness: "To be white is not to think about it." Flagg refers to the propensity of whites not to think in racial terms as the "transparency phenomenon."[23]

Importantly, Flagg does not suggest that white people are unmindful of the racial identities of other whites or the racial "difference" of non-whites: "Race is undeniably a powerful determinant of social status and so is always noticed, in a way that eye color, for example, may not be." Rather, her point is that, because whiteness operates as the racial norm, whites are able "to relegate their own racial specificity to the realm of the subconscious." As a result, racial distinctiveness is Black, Asian, Latina/o, Native American, but it is not white. To address transparency, Flagg suggests the "[reconceptualization of] white race consciousness [to develop] a positive white racial identity, one neither founded on the implicit acceptance of white racial domination nor productive of distributive effects that systematically advantage whites."[24]

McIntosh's work provides a specific indication of some of the everyday "distributive effects" of white racial privilege. Thinking about how men's privileges are normalized in everyday life but denied and protected by men, McIntosh "realized that since hierarchies in our society are interlocking, there was most likely a phenomenon of white privilege that was similarly denied and protected." To illustrate the extent to which white privilege structures and is implicated in day-to-day social encounters, McIntosh exposes the "unearned" advantages that she accrues on a daily basis because she is white. For example, precisely because she is white, McIntosh did not have to educate her children to be aware of systemic racism for their own daily physical protection. Nor, observes McIntosh, does she have to worry about whether negative encounters with certain governmental entities (e.g., the IRS, the police) reflect racial harassment.[25]

McIntosh is careful to point out that the term "privilege" is something of a misnomer: "We usually think of privilege as being a favored state, whether earned, or conferred by birth or luck. . . . The word 'privilege' carries the connotation of being something everyone must want. Yet some of the conditions I have described here work to systematically overempower certain groups." Accordingly, McIntosh distinguishes between "positive advantages that we can work to spread . . . and negative types of advantage that unless rejected will always reinforce our present hierarchies."[26]

Heterosexual Privilege (and Race)

> I am a Negro Faggot, if I believe what movies, TV, and rap music say of me. . . . Because of my sexuality, I cannot be black. A strong, proud, "Afrocentric" black man is resolutely heterosexual, not even bisexual. Hence I remain a Negro. My sexual difference is a testament to weakness, passivity, the absence of real guts—balls.

Hence I remain a sissy, punk, faggot. I cannot be a black gay man because, by the tenets of black macho, a black gay man is a triple negation.
 —Marlon T. Riggs[27]

Like whiteness, heterosexuality should be critically examined. Like whiteness, heterosexuality operates as an identity norm. Heterosexuality functions as the "what is" or "what is supposed to be" of sexuality. This is illustrated, for example, by the nature-versus-nurture debate. The question about the cause of sexuality is almost always formulated in terms of whether homosexuality is or is not biologically determined rather than whether sexual orientation, which includes heterosexuality, is or is not biologically determined. Scientists are searching for a gay, not a heterosexual or sexual-orientation, gene. Like non-whiteness, then, homosexuality signifies "difference"—more specifically, sexual-identity distinctiveness. The normativity of heterosexuality requires that homosexuality be specified, pointed out. Heterosexuality is always already presumed.

Men's feminism should challenge the normativity and normalization of heterosexuality. Male feminists should challenge the heterosexual presumption. But potential male feminists might be reluctant to do so. Such challenges (might be thought to) create homosexual suspicion. Moreover, even to the extent that heterosexuals are willing to destabilize heterosexual normativity by, for example, exposing their heterosexuality—"coming out" as heterosexuals—such strategies can function to reinforce heterosexual normalcy. I develop these arguments in the following section.

Heterosexual Anxieties about Homosexual Suspicion: Preserving the Heterosexual Presumption: Straight men, even progressive straight men, might be reluctant to challenge heterosexual privilege to the extent that such challenges call into question their (hetero)sexual orientation. As Lee Edelman observes in a related context, there "is a deeply rooted concern on the part of . . . heterosexual males about the possible meanings of [men subverting gender roles]." According to Edelman, heterosexual men consider certain gender-role inversions to be potentially dangerous because they portend not only a "[male] feminization that would destabilize or question gender" but also a "feminization that would challenge one's (hetero)sexuality."[28]

Edelman's observations suggest that straight men want to preserve what I am calling the "heterosexual presumption." Their investment in this presumption is less a function of what heterosexuality signifies in a positive sense than a function of what it signifies in the negative—*not* being homosexual.

And there are racial dimensions to men's investment in heterosexuality. For example, straight Black men's strategies to avoid homosexual suspicion could relate to the racial aspects of men's privileges: Heterosexual privilege is one of the few privileges some Black men have. These Black men may want to take comfort in the fact that, whatever else is going on in their lives, they are not, finally, "sissies," "punks," "faggots." By this surmise, I do not mean to suggest that Black men's heterosexuality has the normative standing of white men's heterosexuality. It does not. Straight Black men continue to be perceived as heterosexually deviant (overly sexual; potential rapists) and heterosexually irresponsible (jobless fathers of children out of wedlock). Still, Black male heterosexuality is closer to white male heterosexual normalcy and normativity than is Black gay sexuality. Consequently, some straight (or closeted) Black men will want to avoid the "black gay man . . . triple negation" to which Riggs refers.

Exposing Heterosexual Normalcy: "Coming Out" as Heterosexual: Perhaps heterosexuals should develop a practice of "pointing out" their heterosexuality to destabilize the notion of homosexual difference and to highlight male heterosexual privileges. Perhaps heterosexuals should be encouraged to "come out" as heterosexuals. One argument to support this practice would be that the more heterosexuals explicitly invoke their heterosexuality, the less it operates as an unstated norm. Although this argument has some force, I am uncomfortable with the idea of heterosexuals "coming out."

My uneasiness is unrelated to concerns about whether individual acts of heterosexual signification undermine political efforts to establish a privacy norm around (homo)sexuality. The privacy-norm argument would go something like this: To the extent that heterosexuals are "closeted" (i.e., private) about their (hetero)sexuality, they help to send a message that (homo)sexuality is a private matter and should be irrelevant to social and political decision-making.

I am not persuaded by this sexual-identity–privacy argument. It is analogous to race-neutrality arguments: Not invoking race, ignoring race, keeping race "private" helps to delegitimize the invidious employment of race as a relevant social category. However, keeping race private and removing race from public discourses further entrenches racism. The social realities of race derive in part from the fact that race is always already public—a status marker of difference. Race continues to matter. Therefore, we ought to talk about it—and publicly. Avoiding public discussions about sexuality is not a sensible way to address the social realities of homophobia. Sexuality matters. Thus, we ought to have public discussions about why and how it matters. We have to deal with sexuality before we can get beyond it.

My concerns about heterosexuals "coming out" relate to the social meaning of that act. Individual acts of heterosexual signification contribute to the growing tendency on the part of people who are not gay or les-

bian to employ the term "coming out" to reveal some usually uncontroversial or safe aspect of their personhood. Nowadays, people are "coming out" as chocolate addicts, as yuppies, as soap-opera viewers, and even as Trekkies. Sometimes the "outing" is more political. "I 'out' myself as a conservative," I heard someone say recently. This appropriation and redeployment of the term is problematic to the extent that it obscures the economic, psychological, and physical harm that potentially attends the gay and lesbian coming-out (or outing) process. Although context would clearly matter, there is usually little, if any, vulnerability to "coming out" as a conservative, as a yuppie, as a Trekkie, and so on. Nor is there usually any vulnerability to "coming out" as a heterosexual. The assertion of heterosexuality, without more, merely reauthenticates heterosexual normalcy.[29]

Yet more and more heterosexuals are "coming out," and often with good intentions. This "coming out" is performed explicitly and implicitly—affirmatively and by negation. Consider, for example, the way Houston Baker comes out in a panel discussion about gender, sexuality, and Black images: "I am not gay, but I have many gay friends." When asked about his decision to reveal his sexual identity in the negative (Baker did not say, "'I am a heterosexual,' but 'I am not gay'"), Baker responds that in thinking about our identities, "you decide what you are not, rather than leaping out of the womb saying, 'I am this.'"[30]

The questions about whether Baker should have "come out" as a heterosexual in the affirmative or the negative obscures the fact that it is the "coming out" itself that is potentially problematic. As Bruce Ryder points out, "Heterosexual men taking gay or lesbian positions must continually deal with the question of whether or not to reveal their heterosexuality."[31] On the one hand, self-identifying as a heterosexual is a way to position oneself within a discourse so as not to create the (mis)impression of gay authenticity. Moreover, revealing one's heterosexuality can help to convey the idea that "heterosexism should be as much an issue for straight people as racism should be for white people."[32] On the other hand, "coming out" as a heterosexual can be a heteronormative move to avoid stigmatization as gay or lesbian. It can function not simply as a denial of same-sex desire, but also to pre-empt the attribution of certain stereotypes to one's sexual identity. The assertion of heterosexuality, stated differently, is (functionally, if not intentionally) both an affirmative and a negative assertion about sexual preferences ("I sleep with persons of the opposite, not the same sex") and about the normalcy of one's sexual relationships ("therefore I am normal, not abnormal").

Keith Boykin, former director of the Black Gay and Lesbian Leadership Forum, maintains that "heterosexual sexual orientation has become so ingrained in our social custom, so destigmatized of our fears about sex, that we often fail to make any connection between heterosexuality and sex."[33] Boykin is only half right. The socially constructed normalcy of heterosexuality is not due solely to the desexualization of heterosexuality in mainstream political and popular culture. It is also due 1) to the sexualization of heterosexuality as normative; and 2) to the gender-norm presumptions about heterosexuality—that it is the normal way sexually to express one's gender.

Moreover, it is not simply that homosexuality is sexed that motivates or stimulates homophobic fears about gay and lesbian relationships. These fears also relate to the fact that homosexuality is 1) stigmatized and 2) perceived to be an abnormal way sexually to express one's gender.[34] The disparate social meanings that attach to gay and lesbian identities, on the one hand, and to straight identities, on the other, make individual acts of heterosexual signification cause for concern.

Recently, I participated in a workshop where one of the presenters "came out" as a heterosexual in the context of giving his talk. This sexual-identity disclosure engendered a certain amount of whispering in the back row. Until that moment, I think many people had assumed the presenter was gay. After all, he was sitting on a panel discussing sexual orientation and had participated in the Gay and Lesbian Section of the American Association of Law Schools. There were three other heterosexuals on the panel, but everyone knew they were not gay because everyone *knew* them; they had all been in teaching for a while, two were very senior, and everyone knew of their spouses or partners. Everyone also knew that there was a lesbian on the panel. She, too, had been in teaching for some time and had been out for many years. Apparently, few of the workshop participants knew very much about the presenter who "came out." Because "there is a widespread assumption in both gay and straight communities that any man who says something supportive about issues of concern to lesbian or gay communities must be gay himself,"[35] there was, at the very least, a question about his sexuality. Whatever his intentions were for "coming out," whatever his motivations, his assertion of heterosexuality removed the question.

It is the politics behind the removal of the question—the politics of sexual-identity signification—that we should be concerned about. Is it an act of resistance, or does it reflect an acquiescence to existing social meanings of sexual identity? Consider, for example, the television situation comedy *Spin City*, in which Michael Boatman plays the role of Carter Heywood, an openly gay Black male character. Boatman is clearly very comfortable with the role and is "believably gay"—perhaps, for some, "too believably gay." Thus, in a recent article in

Essence about Boatman, the author makes clear rather quickly that Boatman is not in fact gay—he just plays a gay man on television. The Author also reveals that it was not Heywood's sexuality that attracted Boatman to the role (he had not set out to play a gay man) but, rather, Heywood's career. The relevant text reads: "It was Heywood's job description (a civil rights attorney who joins the mayor's office) rather than his sexuality that attracted the 32-year-old actor to the groundbreaking sitcom. 'We've been exposed to the stereotype of swishy gay men,' explains the *happily married* acting veteran."[36] The text thus removes the question about Boatman's (homo)sexuality.

I became sensitized to the politics of heterosexuals "coming out" in the context of reading about James Baldwin. Try to find a piece written about Baldwin, and count the number of lines before the author comes out as heterosexual. Usually, it is not more than a couple of paragraphs, so the game ends fast. The following introduction from a recently published essay about Baldwin is one example of what I am talking about: "The last time I saw James Baldwin was late autumn of 1985, when my wife and I attended a sumptuous book party."[37] In this case, the game ends immediately. Independent of any question of intentionality on the author's part, his wife functions as an identity signifier to subtextually "out" his heterosexuality. We *read* "wife"; we *think* heterosexual. My point here is not to suggest that the essay's overall tone is heterosexually defensive. I simply find it suspicious when heterosexuals speak of their spouses so quickly (in this case, in the very first sentence of the essay) when a subject (a topic or a personality—here, James Baldwin) implicates homosexuality.

There is no point wondering what the author of the essay was "doing" with Baldwin in Paris. The game is over. The possibility of a gay subtextual reading of the text vis-à-vis the author's relationship with Baldwin or the author's sexual identity is rendered untenable by the rhetorical deployment of the "wife." Her presence in the text operates not only to signify and authenticate the author's heterosexual subject position but also to signify and functionally (if not intentionally) stigmatize Baldwin's gay subject position. The author engages in what I refer to as "the politics of the 3Ds"—disassociation, disidentification, and differentiation. The author is "different" from Baldwin (the author sleeps with women), and this difference, based as it is on sexual identity, compels the author to disassociate himself from and disidentify with that which makes Baldwin "different" (Baldwin sleeps with men).

Heterosexual significations need not always reflect the politics of the 3Ds. In other words, the possibility exists for heterosexuals to point out their heterosexuality without re-authenticating heterosexuality. Consider, for example, the heterosexual privilege list that follows. As a prelude to the list, I should be clear to point out that the list certainly is not complete. Nor do the privileges reflected in the list represent the experiences of all heterosexuals. My goal in presenting this list, then, is not to represent every heterosexual man. Instead, the purpose is to intervene in the normalization of heterosexual privileges. With this intervention, I hope to challenge the pervasive tendency of heterosexuals to see homophobia as something that puts others at a disadvantage and not something that actually gives them advantages.

Heterosexual Privileges: A List

1. Whether on television or in the movies, (white) heterosexuality is always affirmed as healthy or normal (Black heterosexuality and family arrangements are still, to some degree, perceived to be deviant).

2. Without making a special effort, heterosexuals are surrounded by other heterosexuals every day.

3. A husband and wife can comfortably express affection in any social setting, even a predominantly gay one.

4. The children of a heterosexual couple will not have to explain why their parents have different genders—why they have a mommy and a daddy.

5. (White) heterosexuals are not blamed for creating and spreading the AIDS virus (though Africans—as a collective group—are blamed).

6. Heterosexuals do not have to worry about people trying to "cure" their sexual orientation (though Black people have to worry about people trying to "cure" Black "racial pathologies").

7. Black heterosexual men did not have to worry about whether they would be accepted at the Million Man March.

8. Rarely, if ever, will a doctor, on learning that her patient is heterosexual, ask whether the patient has ever taken an AIDS test and, if so, how recently.

9. Medical service will never be denied to heterosexuals because they are heterosexuals (though medical services may not be recommended to Black people because they are Black).

10. Friends of heterosexuals generally do not refer to heterosexuals as their "straight friends" (though non-Black people often to refer to Black people as their "Black friends").

11. A heterosexual couple can enter a restaurant on their anniversary and be fairly confident that staff and fellow diners will warmly congratulate them if an announcement is made (though the extent of the congratulation and the nature of the welcome may depend on the racial identities of the couple).

12. White heterosexuals do not have to worry about whether a fictional film villain who is heterosexual will reflect negatively on their heterosexuality (though Blacks may always have to worry about their racial representation in films).

13. Heterosexuals are entitled to legal recognition of their marriages throughout the United States and the world.

14. Within the Black community, Black male heterosexuality does not engender comments such as "What a waste," "There goes another good Black man," or "If they're not in jail, they're faggots."

15. Heterosexuals can take jobs with most companies without worrying about whether their spouses will be included in the benefits package.

16. Child molestation by heterosexuals does not confirm the deviance of heterosexuality (though if the alleged molester is Black, the alleged molestation becomes evidence of the deviance of Black [hetero]sexuality).

17. Black rap artists do not make songs suggesting that heterosexuals should be shot or beaten up because they are heterosexuals.

18. Black male heterosexuality does not undermine a Black heterosexual man's ability to be a role model for Black boys.

19. Heterosexuals can join the military without concealing their sexual identity.

20. Children will be taught in school, explicitly or implicitly, about the naturalness of heterosexuality (they will also be taught to internalize the notion of white normativity).

21. Conversations about Black liberation will always include concerns about heterosexual men.

22. Heterosexuals can adopt children without being perceived as selfish and without anyone questioning their motives.

23. Heterosexuals are not denied custody or visitation rights of their children because they are heterosexuals.

24. Heterosexual men are welcomed as leaders of Boy Scout troops.
25. Heterosexuals can visit their parents and family as who they are and take their spouses, partners, or dates with them to family functions.
26. Heterosexuals can talk matter-of-factly about their relationships with their partners without people commenting that they are "flaunting" their sexuality.
27. A Black heterosexual couple would be welcomed as members of any Black church.
28. Heterosexual couples do not have to worry about whether kissing each other in public or holding hands in public will render them vulnerable to violence.
29. Heterosexuals do not have to struggle with "coming out" or worry about being "outed."
30. The parents of heterosexuals do not love them "in spite of" their sexual orientation, and parents do not blame themselves for their children's heterosexuality.
31. Heterosexuality is affirmed in most religious traditions.
32. Heterosexuals can introduce their spouses to colleagues and not worry about whether the decision will have a detrimental impact on their careers.
33. A Black heterosexual man does not have to choose between being Black and being heterosexual.
34. Heterosexuals can prominently display their spouses' photographs at work without causing office gossip or hostility.
35. (White) heterosexuals do not have to worry about "positively" representing heterosexuality.
36. Few will take pity on a heterosexual on hearing that she is straight, or feel the need to say, "That's okay" (though it is not uncommon for a Black person to hear, "It's okay that you're Black" or "We don't care that you're Black" or "When we look at you, we don't see a Black person").
37. (Male) heterosexuality is not considered to be symptomatic of the "pathology" of the Black family.
38. Heterosexuality is never mistaken as the only aspect of one's lifestyle; it is perceived instead as merely one more component of one's personal identity.
39. (White) heterosexuals do not have to worry about the impact their sexuality will have personally on their children's lives, particularly as it relates to their social lives (though Black families of all identity configurations do have to worry about how race and racism will affect their children's well-being).
40. Heterosexuals do not have to worry about being "bashed" after leaving a social event with other heterosexuals (though Black people of all sexual orientations do have to worry about being "racially bashed" on any given day).
41. Every day is (White) Heterosexual Pride Day.

Conclusion: Resisting Privileges

I have argued that men should employ feminism to expose and challenge men's privileges. In advancing this argument, I do not mean to suggest that the role of male feminists is to legitimize "untrustworthy" and "self-interested" victim-centered accounts of discrimination. There is a tendency on the part of dominant groups (e.g., men and heterosexuals) to discount the experiences of subordinate groups (e.g., straight women, lesbians, and gays) unless those experiences are authenticated or legitimized by a member of the dominant group. For example, it is one thing for me, a Black man, to say I experienced discrimination in a particular social setting; it is quite another for my white, male colleague to say he witnessed that discrimination. My telling of the story is suspect because I am Black (racially interested). My white colleague's telling of the story is not suspect because he is white (racially disinterested). The racial transparency of whiteness—its "perspectivelessness"—renders my colleague's account "objective."[38]

The problem of racial-status (in)credibility is quite real. Consider how Cornel West alludes to it in the following anecdote about his inability to get a cab in New York City:

> After the ninth taxi refused me, my blood began to boil. The tenth taxi refused me and stopped for a kind, well-dressed, smiling female fellow citizen of European descent. As she stepped in the cab, she said, "This is really ridiculous, is it not?"
>
> Ugly racial memories of the past flashed through my mind. Years ago, while driving from New York to teach at Williams College, I was stopped on fake charges of trafficking cocaine. When I told the police officer I was a professor of religion, he replied, "Yeh, and I'm the Flying Nun. Let's go, nigger!" I was stopped three times in my first ten days in Princeton for driving too slowly on a residential street with a speed limit of twenty-five miles per hour.... Needless to say, these incidents are dwarfed by those like Rodney King's beating.... Yet the memories cut like a merciless knife at my soul as I waited on that godforsaken corner. Finally I decided to take the subway. I walked three long avenues, arrived late, and had to catch my moral breath as I approached the white male photographer and white female cover designer. I chose not to dwell on this everyday experience of black New Yorkers. And we had a good time talking, posing, and taking pictures.[39]

West is connecting two problematic episodes. His racial representations of these episodes reflect concerns about his racial credibility. West's narrative suggests that he is worried about how his readers will read

him (is he a trustworthy witness?) and thus *read* the events he describes (do they reflect racism?). West understands that he is (or, rather, will be constructed as) an unreliable witness to his own racial victimization. That is, he is fully aware that, as a Black man, his racial story (like his racial identity) is suspect. Thus, he rhetorically deploys a "disinterested" witness to legitimize and authenticate his racial narrative—the woman "of European descent." She can be trusted. She is white and respectable—"well-dressed" and "smiling." To the extent that she confirms West's racial interpretation of the cab story—"This is really ridiculous, is it not?"— the notion is forwarded that West is not racially imagining things; in fact, his race is interfering with his ability to get a cab. The employment of whiteness to authenticate West's first story racially renders West's second story (in which West is called a "nigger") more believable.

Male feminists should be careful not to replicate the kind of authentication strategy reflected in West's anecdote. In other words, male feminists should not perform the legitimation function that the white woman's challenge to racism performs in West's text. To the extent that male heterosexuals participate in discourses on gender and sexuality, they should not create the (mis)impression that, because they do not experience the subordinating effects of patriarchy and heterosexism, their critiques of patriarchy or heterosexism are more valid and less suspect than the critiques propounded by lesbians, straight women, and gay men.

Assuming that the male-feminist method I have described avoids the problem of authentication, one still might wonder whether the project is sufficiently radical to dismantle gender and sexual-orientation hierarchies. Certainly, the lists I have presented do not go far enough. They represent the very early stages in a more complicated process to end gender and sexual-orientation discrimination.

The lists, nevertheless, are politically valuable. For one thing, the items on the lists reveal that men enforce and maintain their gender privileges through the personal actions that they take and do not take every day. For another, to the extent that the lists focus our attention on privileges, they invite men to think about the extent to which they are unjustly enriched because of certain aspects of their identities.

To be sure, men will not be eager to learn or quick to accept the notion that they are unjustly enriched. The realization and acknowledgment of unjust enrichment carries with it the possibility of disgorgement. However, to the extent that men actually come to see their privileges as forms of unjust enrichment (and the lists help men do precisely that), they are more likely to take notice of the ways in which unjust enrichment operates systemically.

None of this is to say that awareness and acknowledgement of privilege are enough. Resistance is needed, as well. But how does one resist? And what counts as resistance? With respect to marriage, for example, does resistance to heterosexual privilege require heterosexuals to refrain from getting married or attending weddings? It might mean both of those things. At the very least, resistance to identity privilege would seem to require "critical acquiescence": criticizing, if not rejecting, aspects of our life that are directly linked to our privilege. A heterosexual who gets married or attends weddings but who also openly challenges the idea that marriage is a heterosexual entitlement is engaging in critical acquiescence.

In the end, critical acquiescence might not go far enough. It might even be a cop out. Still, it is a useful and politically manageable place to begin.

Notes

Acknowledgments: For comments on earlier versions of this essay, I thank Daphne Bishop, Jennifer Gerarda Brown, Kimberlé Crenshaw, Adrienne Davis, Katherine Franke, Jody Freeman, Nanci Freeman, Jane Goldsmith, Laura Gomez, Mitu Gulati, Angela Harris, Darren Hutchinson, Kenneth Karst, Gillian Lester, Frances Olsen, Julie Ralston, David Sklansky, Lauren Teukolsky, Frank Valdes, Adrien Wing, and the participants at the Cornell Feminist Legal Theory Workshop (Summer 1999), the Fordham Critical Race Theory and Feminism Workshop (Spring 1998), and the Iowa Journal of Gender, Race, and Justice Symposium (Fall 1998). Peter Van Oosting and the Hugh and Hazel Darling Law Library at the UCLA School of Law provided invaluable research and editorial assistance. For administrative assistance, I thank Mina Quintos.

Epigraphs: Adrienne Rich, "Compulsory Heterosexuality and Lesbian Existence," in *Powers of Desire: The Politics of Sexuality*, ed. Ann Snitow, Christine Stansell, and Sharon Thompson (New York: Monthly Review Press, 1987), 177, 182. Bruce Ryder, "Straight Talk: Male Heterosexual Privilege," *Queen's Law Journal* 16 (1991): 287. Eve K. Sedgwick, *Epistemology of the Closet* (London: Harvester Wheatsheaf, 1990), 32. Gore Vidal, "Foreword," in Jonathan Ned Katz, *The Invention of Heterosexuality* (New York: E. P. Dutton, 1995), vii, viii.

1. See generally Stephanie Wildman, *Privilege Revealed: How Invisible Preference Undermines America* (New York: New York University Press, 1996).

2. Alice Jardine, *"Ordor di uomour compagnons de route,"* in Jardine and Smith, *Men in Feminism*, 54, 60.

3. Stephen Heath, "Male Feminism," in Alice Jardine and Paul Smith, *Men in Feminism* (New York: Routledge, 1987), 1.

4. Ibid., 14

5. See Joseph A. Boone and Michael Cadden, "Introduction," in *Engendering Men: The Question of Male Feminist Criticism*, ed. Joseph A. Boone and Michael Cadden (New York: Routledge, 1990), 3.

6. See Ryder, "Straight Talk": 300, critiquing the movement associated with Robert Bly that encourages men to come in contact with the wild, aggressive side of their personalities.

7. Hélène Cixous, "The Laugh of Medusa," trans. Keith Cohen and Paula Cohen, *Signs* 1 (1976): 875, 877, n. 1.

8. Rosalind Coward, *Female Desire* (London: Paladin, 1984), 227, explaining that Freud used this

expression to solve the mystery of women's sexuality at the turn of the century.

9. See generally Joy James, "Antiracist (Pro) Feminisms and Coalition Politics: 'No Justice, No Peace,'" in *Men Doing Feminism*, ed. Tom Digby (New York: Routledge, 1998), 237, 240.

10. See, for example, Michele Wallace, *Invisibility Blues: From Pop to Theory* (London and New York: Verso, 1990), 251; James, *Men Doing Feminism*, 282.

11. bell hooks, *Feminist Theory: From Margin to Center* (Boston: South End Press, 1984), 67.

12. Ibid.

13. Of course, not all men are empowered by patriarchy in the same way: Race, class, and sexual orientation shape the nature of men's relationships to patriarchal privilege. Perhaps it is more accurate to say, then, that patriarchy gives to (some) men (more than others) what it takes away from (some) women (more than others); the disempowerment of (some) women (more than others) is achieved through the empowerment of (some) men (more than others). See Karen D. Pyke, "Class-Based Masculinities: The Interdependence of Gender, Class, & Interpersonal Power," *Gender and Society* 10 (1996): 531 ("The effects *of* gender on interpersonal power relations are not one-dimensional. Hierarchies *of* social class, race, and sexuality provide additional layers of complication. They form the structural and cultural contexts in which gender is enacted in everyday life, thereby fragmenting gender into multiple masculinities and femininities"; the italics are mine).

14. Ryder, "Straight Talk": 290.

15. Andrea Dworkin and Catharine A. MacKinnon, *Pornography and Civil Rights: A New Day for Women's Equality* (Minneapolis: Organizing Against Pornography, 1988), 22-3.

16. Racializing the discussion of marriage adds further complications. Historically, Black people's relationship to marriage has been complicated by the fact that Black people, as an enslaved people, could not marry. See Adrienne D. Davis, "The Private Law of Race and Sex: An Antebellum Perspective," *Stanford Law Review* 51 (1999): 221, 245 ("Within the institution of slavery, as elsewhere, the use of marriage to distinguish the sexual family from the legal family had profound symbolic effects. It entailed ideological production as well as distributive consequences"). The racial regulation of marriage did not end with slavery. Within the context of Jim Crow, anti-miscegenation statutes regulated the extent to which Black people could marry interracially.

17. See Cixous, "Laugh of Medusa": 877.

18. Catherine A. MacKinnon, "Difference and Dominance: On Sex Discrimination," in *Feminism UnModified: Discourses on Life and Law* (Cambridge, Mass.: Harvard University Press, 1987), 33-4.

19. Elaine Showalter, ed., "Introduction: The Rise of Gender," in *Speaking of Gender* (New York: Routledge, 1989), 1, 6.

20. See generally Peggy McIntosh, "White Privilege and Male Privilege: A Personal Account of Coming to See Correspondences Through Work in Women's Studies," in *Power, Privilege and Law: A Civil Rights Reader*, ed. Leslie Bender and Daan Braveman (St. Paul, Minn.: West Publishing, 1995), 22-3.

21. See Devon W. Carbado and Mitu Gulati, "Working Identity," *Cornell Law Review* 85 (2000): 1254, describing the ways in which employees reveal their identities in the workplace and arguing that people work their identities to avoid discrimination.

22. See Brent Staples, "The Future of Black Men," in *Brotherman: The Odyssey of Black Men in America*, ed. Herb Boyd and Robert L. Allen (New York: One World, 1995), discussing the author's attempts to appear harmless while walking at night by whistling Vivaldi.

23. See Barbara Flagg, "Was Blind, But Now I See: White Race Consciousness and the Requirement of Discriminatory Intent," *Michigan Law Review* 91 (1994): 953, 957, 963.

24. Ibid., 957, 970-1.

25. McIntosh, "White Privilege," 25-6. See also hooks, *Feminist Theory*, 54-5, interrogating whiteness.

26. McIntosh, "White Privilege," 23.

27. Marlon T. Riggs, "Black Macho Revisited: Reflections of a Snap! Queen," in *Black Men on Race, Gender, and Sexuality: A Critical Reader*, ed. Devon W. Carbado (New York: New York University Press, 1999).

28. Lee Edelman, "Redeeming the Phallus: Wallace Stevens, Frank Lentricchia, and the Politics of (Hetero)sexuality," in *Engendering Men: The Question of Male Feminist Criticism*, ed. Joseph A. Boone and Michael Cadden (New York: Routledge, 1990), 50.

29. In some sense, heterosexuals are out all the time, kissing comfortably in public, sharing wedding pictures at work, announcing anniversaries, and so on. These are not the practices I am referring to when I suggest that heterosexuals should perhaps develop a practice of "coming out." For none of these heterosexual significations challenges the socially constructed normalcy of heterosexuality. Later in the article, I provide an indication of how

heterosexuals *might* be able to assert their heterosexuality without further entrenching heterosexual
normalcy.

30. Houston A. Baker, Jr., "'You Cain't Trus' It':
Experts Witnessing in the Case of Rap," in *Black
Popular Culture,* ed. Gina Dent (Seattle: Bay Press,
1992), 132, 139.

31. Ryder, "Straight Talk," 303.

32. Ibid.

33. Keith Boykin, *One More River to Cross: Black
and Gay in America* (New York: Doubleday/Anchor
Books, 1996), 42.

34. See Francisco Valdes, "Sex and Race in Queer
Legal Culture: Ruminations on Identities and Inter-
Connectivities," *Southern California Review of Law and
Women's Studies* 5 (1995): 25. See also Bender and
Braveman, *Power, Privilege and Law,* 187 ("Disappro-
bation of homosexual behavior is a reaction to the
violation of gender norms, rather than simply scorn
for the violation of norms of sexual behaviors"), and
Elvia R. Arriola, "Gendered Inequality: Lesbians,
Gays, and Feminist Legal Theory," *Berkeley Women's
Law Journal* 9 (1994): 103, 122, observing that gay iden-
tities are often theoretically connected to gender.

35. Ryder, "Straight Talk," 303.

36. See Michael Boatman, "Acting 'Out,'" *Essence,*
September 1997, 78.

37. Leon Forrest, "Evidences of Jimmy Baldwin,"
in *Relocations of the Spirit* (Wakefield, R.I.: Asphodel
Press/Moyer Bell, 1994), 267.

38. See Kimberlé W. Crenshaw, "Foreword—
Toward a Race-Conscious Pedagogy in Legal Education," *National Black Law Journal* 11 (1989): 1,
employing the term "perspectivelessness" to
describe the ostensibly race-neutral way in which
law is taught.

Peter Halewood comments on this problem from
a white, heterosexual, male perspective. According
to Halewood: "Because I am white and male, the
Article is more likely to be accepted (or ignored) by
colleagues as a scholarly application of scholarly
ideas than it would be if written by a black female
professor. A black female author of this piece would
probably encounter more skepticism about the
method, claims, and motives of the article [*sic*] and
would probably be viewed, at least by some, as being
oversensitive and making trouble for her mostly
white and male colleagues": Peter Halewood, "White
Men Can't Jump: Critical Epistemologies, Embodiment, and the Praxis of Legal Scholarship," *Yale
Journal of Law and Feminism* 7 (1995): 6.

To avoid contributing to this authentication of
whiteness and delegitimation of Blackness, Halewood argues: "Rather than approaching the subject of law and subordination as neutral, theoretical experts or as political vanguardists, white male
legal academics must recognize the legitimacy-
even the superiority-of certain 'outsider' perspectives on these issues, and assume the role of secondary contributors to the development of
scholarship in these areas": Halewood, "White
Men Can't Jump," 7.

39. See Cornel West, *Race Matters* (Boston: Beacon Press, 1993), xv–xvi.

Section B: Narrativity

Celebrating Racialized Legal Narratives

Margaret E. Montoya

Arguably, the most significant impact of critical theory has been the reformation of legal analytical practices through the use of stories.
—Leslie Espinoza and Angela P. Harris

WRITING AN INTRODUCTION for a group of articles dealing with narrative gives me a chance to offer public tribute to the many storytellers who have imprinted my memory with the accounts of their experiences. Like countless others, I have been privileged to read the autobiographies, self-portraits, allegories, fables, and fictive narratives that are now part of the oppositional legal canons being developed by Outsiders: people of color, feminists, Queers, the dis/abled. Allow me a momentary recollection: Patricia Williams finding comfort in her lease and her robe, Rodrigo "fractalizing" Richard Delgado, Mari Matsuda basking in the accents of Hawaii, Chuck Lawrence dreaming, Michael Olivas talking with his grandfather, and Trina Grillo conferencing with Stephanie Wildman and Elvia Arriola's more recent story of being the Outsiders' Outsider.[1] Such stories have reframed my understanding and worldview.

Writing this introduction also allows me to reflect on why RaceCrits and LatCrits and other Outsiders value narratives. Racialized stories provide new metaphors, nuances, linkages, and inspiration, creating a narrative economy of shared vocabularies and common images for those of us engaged with antisubordination projects. Raced stories also show the complexity of racial relations both within and among subgroups. This introduction discusses the value of narratives within three general aspects of the antisubordination project known as Critical Race Theory—namely, discursive subversions, identity formation, and healing and transformation.

Theorizing about Narratives

Discursive Subversions

The last half of the twentieth century witnessed the dismantling of the formal barriers excluding people of color, women, sexual and religious minorities, the dis/abled, the poor, and immigrants from participation in socioeconomic activities. One of the results of admitting significant numbers of Outsiders as faculty and students to universities and professional schools has been widespread changes in teaching and scholarship practices. Deemed the "culture wars" by the right and by the media, the challenge to the homogeneity of the traditional canons throughout the disciplines has been vehemently contested. Debates about the integration of feminist and critical social practices rage unabated in any number of disciplines.

The dispersion of racialized narratives, one of the tools developed by RaceCrits and LatCrits, into legal scholarship and pedagogy challenges and subverts the dominant discourse in various ways. Such stories displace conventional wisdom and disrupt official histories. Gerald López's description of a Mexican house cleaner seeking naturalization and the examination of white society's historical responses to assertions of tribal sovereignty by Robert A. Williams, Jr., are examples of stories told from the perspective of those at the bottom of power relations.[2] López directly challenges established notions of legal subjectivity; he challenges conventions about whose lives are worthy of reflection when considering issues of legal process and doctrinal complexity. Even as López inveigles us to consider those at the margin, he warns about their rational mistrust of lawyers, the inadequacy of lawyering skills and concepts, and the invisibility of class barriers. Both López and Williams displace the dominant legal narratives about people of color. López's client is resourceful, ambitious, and adept, giving the lie to stereotypes of illegal immigrants. Similarly, Williams unravels the dominant narratives that sustain the legal rationales for the dispossession and genocide of Indian peoples. By describing Indian justice systems and governance structures while interrogating the theories and justifications of the dominant culture, Williams reinscribes the meaning of legal stories by re-encoding and transposing images of savagery and civility.

Identity Formation

Stories by and about Outsiders resist the subordinating messages of the dominant culture by challenging stereotypes and presenting and representing people of color as complex and heterogeneous. A primary feature of white supremacy is the identification of positive attributes—virtue, intelligence, beauty, sobriety, creativity—with white folks. Non-whites, as their foil, are associated with irrationality, dirtiness, vice, ugliness, lasciviousness, and intoxication.[3] Even today, policing practices, folklore, high art, popular culture, and marketing campaigns operate synergistically to create and maintain racist images of non-whites.

Outsider stories also explore the manner in which identity borders and boundaries are controlled, sometimes formally by the legal system and sometimes informally through popular culture. Insider–Outsider relations depend on a high level of awareness of how race-linked markers and behaviors are coded and decoded. For example, Peggy Davis analyzes the daily micro-aggressions experienced by black people, describing an archetypal black woman whose simple question about whether the elevator is going up is answered with rolling eyes, disdainful looks, and snide responses.[4]

Autobiographical stories within legal discourse expose how the forces of domination are experienced at the individual level: how they are perceived from a given perspective, and how they make one feel. Jerome Culp writes about disclosing to his students that he holds advanced degrees from Harvard Law School and the University of Chicago along with the fact that he is a coal miner's son.[5] His story works because he reveals what it feels like to be at once the impeccably credentialed insider and the unassimilable Outsider through color and phenotype. These stories increase the understanding of the interpenetrations among the identities associated with race, color, gender, class, sexual orientation, nationality, and disability, and the interpenetrations of those identities with legal practices. These stories also increase our understanding of how identities are interlaced with legal discourse and legal practices.

RaceCrit and LatCrit narratives connect biography to history.[6] In a recent article titled "Border/ed Identities,"[7] I use the device of small-scale autobiographical narratives told alongside corresponding large-scale sociolegal narratives involving the Latina/o community. In one of three scaled narratives, I juxtapose my mother's story about riding the "Mexican schoolbus" in southern New Mexico with an analysis of school-discrimination cases in the Southwest, including *Westminster v. Mendez*,[8] a 1946 Ninth Circuit case outlawing de jure segregation of Mexican American children in Orange County, California.

Such narratives invoke the right of the subordinated person to narrate—to interpret events in opposition to the dominant narratives, and to reinvent one's self by bringing coherence to one's life stories. These counter-stories constitute social practices that reconstruct the storyteller's individual identities while expanding the possible life scripts available to Others. For this reason, narratives are also cultural tools: They are tools for teaching Others not only how to be and how to behave, but also how it is possible to be and to behave.

Outsider stories, often freighted with the emotions of marginality and the agony of the social pariah, have dialectical and epistemological features that distinguish them from the stock stories of the dominant cul-

ture. Arriola's accounts and enactments accept the risk implicit in autobiography, including the psychic and professional risks involved when one identifies as a Latina lesbian within racist and homophobic institutions. In breaking her silence, Arriola rejects anemic displays of academic diversity and insists instead on grounding legal analysis within transgressive life experiences, thereby pointing the way out of conventional formats for herself and for the rest of us.[9]

Healing and Transformation

Two of the effects of Outsider scholarship—subverting the dominant discourses on race and reinventing our individual and collective identities—focus on Outsiders' relations with the dominant culture. The third set of effects—healing and transformation—focuses more on our relations with ourselves and others, including whites, involved in our antisubordination projects.

It is a widespread notion that narrative has healing effects. Many indigenous peoples, as well as mainstream religions and modern psychiatry, believe in the curative power of narrative, or the notion that ideas can provoke physiological responses.[10] The following example demonstrates how institutionalized this notion has recently become. The U.S. Veterans Administration (VA) has agreed to pay partial costs of traditional healing ceremonies for Navajo veterans.[11] These healing ceremonies use storytelling as the starting point of the healing process. Their names are related to the traditional stories invoked in the healing. Some of the ceremonies covered by the VA include the Enemy Way (to readjust homecoming warriors to normal sociocultural system) and the Smoke Ceremony (to address and relieve emotional problems of the warrior and reestablish a good foundation, proper thinking, and strong emotions). Others are called the Flint Way, the

Blessing Way, the Shooting Way, the Evil Way, the Monster Way, the Night Way, and the Protection Prayer.[12] These healing rites "express the potential for curing physical and emotional illness through [Navajo] myths and rituals."[13]

Drawing on literature from the mental-health disciplines, Espinoza has prevailed on us to consider and to interrogate the healing powers of our stories.[14] She writes:

> The narrative potential of critical theory lies in its ability to free us to move backward and forward in time, to "re-story" the past and to "re-imagine" the future. Racial oppression is a disease of domination that has proved itself immune to accepted treatments. It is time for *curanderas,* healers who base their art on an oral tradition rooted in the community and attentive to the suffering of individuals.[15]

Stories alone, however, cannot heal us. They also cannot bridge the ruptures between and among Outsider communities or address the economic, educational, and environmental crises of segregated communities—the *barrios,* ghettos, reservations, and borderlands—wherever they are located. Stories must move us to action and inform our praxis. In the way storytelling has redirected our scholarship and transformed our conferences, storytelling and other critical tools must refashion our curricula and pedagogies in order to reinvent lawyering techniques.

RaceCrits and LatCrits such as John Calmore, Gerald López, john powell, and Eric Yamamoto; radical feminists such as Andrea Dworkin, Catherine MacKinnon, and Ann Scales; and critical white clinicians such as Peter Margulies have linked the representation of marginalized clients with critical theory. These linkages involve deepening the subversive potential of narrative by applying our storytelling techniques to hearing client stories, then translating them into innovative legal strategies, claims, and

remedies. These linkages also involve exploiting the identity-formation potential of narrative by using classrooms, courtrooms, legislative chambers, and, when necessary, the streets as sites for challenging master narratives. Finally, these linkages between narrative and client representation can create a bridge between the academy and the community where we can work collaboratively to transform these largely forgotten worlds and thereby heal ourselves.

My Readings of Four Racialized Narratives

The chapter "Dinner and Self-Determination" by Henry J. Richardson III enacts a conversation between an African president and an African American law professor. This chapter employs a dialogic format developed by Derrick Bell in his conversations with the fictitious Geneva Crenshaw[16] and Richard Delgado in his conversations with Geneva's brother Rodrigo.[17]

Conventional stereotypes of blacks (whether U.S. or African) are brushed aside from the start of this story. Here, at a dinner in the fictional Malawana, the Outsiders occupy the center of intellectual and political discourse. What Richardson's narrative quickly makes evident is that the political concerns at the center—maintaining power and containing dissent—may not change merely because the prior Outsiders are now the elites and the rulers. Richardson's dialogue uses the white–black master narrative about hegemony and exclusion through representative democracy as Alice's proverbial looking glass, because here tribal affiliation rather than "race" marks the borders of power to determine who is in and out.

Richardson's narrative prevails on RaceCrits and LatCrits to reflect on what happens once people of color have power. What does meaningful self-determination mean for Crits? This is not an irrelevant inquiry. Native and indigenous peoples, especially those with strong ties to traditional communities, are breaking their silence and reasserting the right to self-determination and self-definition.[18] In doing so, they are creating transnational alliances by telling stories that introduce different perspectives on race, identity, land ownership, citizenship, and governance. This inquiry is also pertinent given the current political challenges to native peoples' sovereignty, a legal right that distinguishes them from other racialized groups. Richardson's narrative helps us consider "color-on-color" stories, told from a globalized perspective but with local resonances.

This interplay between local and global perspectives is also evident in Patricia Monture-Angus's chapter, "On Being Homeless: One Aboriginal Woman's 'Conquest' of Canadian Universities, 1989–98." She links two fundamental Aboriginal conditions—being conquered and thereafter being dispossessed of land—with her survival within the university. She redefines Aboriginal homelessness to include the multiple experiences of exclusion, silence, and marginalization within her academic workplaces. Monture-Angus tells the "story" of her search for an intellectual home. But there is nothing fictive about this story; it is a story told while the emotions from the lived experiences still grip the storyteller.

Monture-Angus's accomplishment is to blur the boundaries between oral and written stories: We hear her voice as she talks to us. She is correct that in her hands, at least, "writing [does not] fundamentally [render] unrecognizable the oral form of the storytelling tradition [of Aboriginal peoples]."[19]

This article widens the window that has begun to open allowing RaceCrits and LatCrits to learn from and about indigenous and Native cultures.[20] Monture-Angus's discussion of indigenous and Aboriginal identity introduces a vocabulary that is unusual within U.S. RaceCrit and LatCrit circles but that nevertheless has parallels with the vocabulary of the Native peoples of the United States. For example, when she writes about "Halfbreeds" and "Métis," she urges us to understand that issues of blood quantum, community recognition of the individual, government-identification procedures, and "reserves"[21] and reservations, and creates an identity landscape that is very different from that of other people of color.

Monture-Angus breaks the traditional silence on academic politics and subverts the compact under which many of us are allowed into the academy. She forthrightly announces that she is in the academy as the eyes and voice of her people and will not be quieted or blinded to the many ways in which white supremacy, power, and privilege operate against her and, by extension, against others. Her rejection of the silence by which we are all rendered complicit is courageous because we know that further penalties or indignities can be imposed on her, even after tenure battles are won, for telling stories out of school. Monture-Angus demonstrates for us that our lens for analyzing, unmasking, and changing relations of subordination can effectively be turned on our immediate environments and our colleagues. In giving voice to her pain, she speaks for many of us who have not dared to put into print what she now does.

Victoria Ortiz and Jennifer Elrod begin their chapter, "Construction Project: Color Me Queer + Color Me Family = Camilo's Story," with an autobiographical story about raising their Latino son, Camilo, in a Lesbian family. The construction project involves articulating a theory that is broad enough to encompass the multiple strands of progressive political philosophies associated with multilayered identities (working-class, leftist, feminist, people of color, and "of white,"[22] dis/abled, and Queer). This project is also implicitly engaged in the construction and reconstruction of identities—the authors', their son's, and ours.

The narrative seeks to have us understand that the source of Camilo's pain in having his definition of family challenged and his universe denied is not only his friend Ramon's ignorance. More important, Camilo's pain and that of his mothers stems from collective biases—in this case homophobia, which often makes us complicit through the policing of the boundaries of the licit and illicit.

"Family" and "mom" define us all by their presence or their absence, and we have a huge stake in what they represent. In this story, Ramon, with the innocence and candor of youth, functions as our identity police with his confident assertions that mothers, especially Mexican mothers, cannot be lesbians. Camilo's story reveals that the signifiers "Mexican" and "mom" do not automatically define sexual orientation. Nor is "mom" defined in a binary coupling with "dad." Here, mom is coupled to mom. And family and Mexican family are reinvented and "re-storied," to use Espinoza's phrase.[23]

This recounting is not without risk, however. Ortiz and Elrod's narrative suggests difficult questions for those of us enthralled by stories. Whose stories are we "authorized" to tell? Those involving our children pose particularly difficult issues of consent and collaboration, and those involving clients implicate the ethical issues of confidentiality and privacy. Ortiz and Elrod's recollections avoid these pitfalls because the reader knows that Camilo is both subject and co-author of his two-part story that begins in pain and ends in quiet acceptance from Rachel, his high-school girlfriend.

Ortiz and Elrod demonstrate narrative's power to heal. By making their story public, by breaking silence, they revalidate for themselves, for their son, and for us the validity and integrity of their life stories.

Risk, remembered and re-enacted, is also a feature of Thomas Ross's chapter, "The Unbearable Whiteness of Being." Ross, an accomplished white scholar, describes his unease about going to the Critical Race Theory Conference at Yale. Interestingly, his discomfort is not theoretical or intellectual; it is social. He approaches the conference with considerable trepidation about the meals, the breaks, the Friday night musical extravaganza, and the Saturday night "cocktail party." Ross, with surprising openness, admits that he fears being unknown, ignored, thought uncool and without rhythm.

Ross's fears are engendered by racial stereotypes, as though all people of color, even geeky academics, have rhythm and know how to clap and dance. As if! Stereotypes are hardwired into all of our brains, and their effects are largely unconscious.[24] Actually, stereotypes can be really hard to live up to: What if one is black or brown and doesn't have rhythm to dance, sing, or clap? That is why I, too, arrived at that conference with similar fears. I arrive once more feeling the ill fit between me and the grandeur of the elite academies' cathedrals and the overly intellectualized and jargonized give-and-take of the panels. I experience the social events as parades, with their insider rituals, where the Spreading Grays envy the Horny Hardbodies while the Wannabes circle the OnceWeres who circle the Icons.

Ross is correct to see his fears as a window into privilege. Voicing his trepidation on arriving at a conference of color and his relief on leaving disturbs the ease and comfort that comes with skin privilege. Each such disruption helps others recognize the various sources of privilege which also bear disrupting. As we have learned, privilege and hierarchy continually reproduce and reassert themselves. We must, therefore, search out techniques for discovering and dismantling the structures and strictures of power. Narrative is one technique.

Notes

Acknowledgments: I thank the organizers of the Critical Race Theory Conference held at Yale University Law School and the editors of this anthology. Critical scholarship on "race" continues to be an individual and collective struggle for new languages, greater equity, and reformed aesthetics, a struggle that reinforces our complex commitments to our friends, families and communities. It is unbelievably wonderful to be part of this movimiento, esta lucha.

Epigraph: See Leslie Espinoza and Angela P. Harris, "Afterword: Embracing the TarBaby—LatCrit Theory and Sticky Mess of Race," *La Raza Law Journal* 10 (1998): 499, 544 and *California Law Review* 85 (1997): 1585, 1630. Espinoza and Harris's article uses a dialogic method to raise penetrating questions about the centrality of African Americans in the racial critiques of other groups of color and to critique LatCrits for replicating the paradigmatic, doctrinal, and academic myopia of other critical discourses, getting stuck on the "Tar Baby" of race.

1. See Patricia J. Williams, *The Alchemy of Race and Rights: Diary of a Law Professor* (Cambridge, Mass.: Harvard University Press, 1991); Richard Delgado, *The Rodrigo Chronicles: Conversations about America and Race* (New York: New York University Press, 1995) (Fractals, discovered by Benoit Mendelbrot, are a mathematical depiction of structures with repeating rhythms and periodicities, a feature called self-similarity. Ferns, broccoli, and tree bark are examples of naturally occurring fractals. A distinctive aspect of fractals is that the closer one looks at them, the more detail is revealed); J. Richard Eiser, *Attitudes, Chaos, and the Connectionist Mind* (Oxford: Blackwell Publisher, 1994); Mari J. Matsuda, "Voices of America: Accent, Antidiscrimination Law, and a Jurisprudence for the Last Reconstruction," *Yale Law Journal* 100 (1991): 1329; Charles R. Lawrence III, "The Word and the River: Pedagogy as Scholarship as Struggle," *Southern California Law Review* 65 (1992): 2231; Michael A. Olivas, "The Chronicles, My Grandfather's Stories, and Immigration Law: The Slave Traders as Racial History," *St. Louis University Law Journal* 34 (1990): 425; Trina Grillo and Stephanie Wildman, "Obscuring the Importance of Race: The Implication of Making Comparisions Between

Racism and Sexism (or Other -isms)," *Duke Law Journal* (1991): 397; and Elvia Arriola, "Welcoming the Outsider to an Outsider Conference: Law and the Multiplicities of Self," *Harvard Latino/a Law Review* 2 (1997): 397.

2. See Gerald P. López, "The Work We Know So Little About," *Stanford Law Review* 42 (1989), and Robert A. Williams, Jr., "Documents of Barbarism: The Contemporary Legacy of European Racism and Colonialism in the Narrative Traditions of Federal Indian Law," *Arizona Law Review* 31 (1989): 237.

3. See Tomás Almaguer, *Racial Fault Lines: The Historical Origins of White Supremacy in California* (Berkeley: University of California Press, 1994), 22, citing Ronald Takaki, *Iron Cages: Race and Culture in Nineteenth-Century America* (New York: Oxford University Press, 1979).

4. See Peggy C. Davis, "Law as Microaggression," *Yale Law Journal* 98 (1989): 1559.

5. See Jerome M. Culp, Jr., "Autobiography and Legal Scholarship and Teaching: Finding the Me in the Legal Academy," *Virginia Law Review* 77 (1991): 539.

6. See Patricia Ewick and Susan S. Silbey, "Subversive Stories and Hegemonic Tales: Towards a Sociology of Narrative," *Law and Society Review* 29 (1995): 197.

7. See Margaret E. Montoya, "Border/ed Identities: Narrative and Social Constructions of Personal and Collective Identities," in *Crossing Boundaries: Traditions and Transformations in Law and Society Research,* ed. Austin Sarat, Marianne Constable, David Engel, Valerie Hans, and Susan Lawrence (Evanston, Ill.: Northwestern University Press, 1998), 129-59.

8. *Westminster School District of Orange City v. Mendez,* 161 F. 2d 774 (1947) affirming *Mendez et al. v. Westminster School District of Orange City et al.,* 64 F. Supp. 544 (S.D. Cal. 1946).

9. Arriola, "Welcoming the Outsider."

10. See Stephen S. Pearce, *Flash of Insight: Metaphor and Narrative in Therapy* (Boston: Allyn and Bacon, 1996), 16.

11. See *Albuquerque Journal* (April 10, 1998), C8, col. 1, copy on file with the author.

12. Ibid.

13. Ibid.

14. Espinoza and Harris, "Afterword" (p. 544 in *La Raza Law Journal;* p. 1630 in *California Law Review*). Espinoza uses the subheading "'Therapeutic' Critical Theory?" to introduce the section.

15. Ibid. (p. 545 in *La Raza Law Journal;* p. 1631 in *California Law Review*).

16. Derrick A. Bell, Jr., *And We Are Not Saved* (New York: Basic Books, 1987).

17. Delgado, *Rodrigo Chronicles*.

18. See Christine Zuni-Cruz, "Strengthening What Remains," *Kansas Journal of Law and Policy* 7 (Winter 1997): 17.

19. See Chapter 11 ("On Being Homeless") in this volume. Professor Monture-Angus understands that she must train her readers and uses footnotes to provide explicit instructions. See also Ewick and Silbey, "Subversive Stories," and *Mendez v. Westminster*.

20. Christine Zuni-Cruz, Luz Guerra, and Estevan Rael y Galvez have made presentations at RaceCrit and LatCrit meetings on indigenous and Native perspectives on legal discourse. See, for example, Luz Guerra, "LatCrit y La Des-Colonización Nuestra: Taking Colón Out," *Chicano–Latino Law Review* 19 (1998): 351.

21. See Chapter 11 ("On Being Homeless"), n. 18, in this volume for Monture-Angus's explanation of this term.

22. "Of white" is the authors' neologism to acknowledge skin privilege.

23. See Espinoza and Harris, "Afterword" (p. 545 in *La Raza Law Journal;* p. 1631 in *California Law Review*).

24. See Charles R. Lawrence III, "The Id, Ego, and Equal Protection: Reckoning with Unconscious Racism," *Stanford Law Review* 39 (1987): 317.

CHAPTER NINE

The Unbearable Whiteness of Being

Thomas Ross

Prelude: Coming to New Haven

I REHEARSED THE EXCUSES I might offer to Jean. "It's a difficult time for me to be away.... My son has an important athletic event that weekend.... I have such a limited travel budget, and I am already committed." I could think of many things to say; none of them rang true.

When I promised Jean Stefancic that I would come to the Critical Race Theory Conference at Yale and be part of her panel, it had seemed like a great idea. It would be a historic event, everyone would be there, nothing could be more important, it seemed. But as the weekend rapidly approached and the discounted airline ticket had to be bought or lost, I hesitated.

I knew why. First, although I knew some of the people who would be there, I could count none of them as a close friend. In that sense, I would be alone. I imagined the social events, the lunches, the breaks between sessions, the dinners. With whom would I sit? With whom would I speak? Would I look foolish? I dreaded above all else the Friday evening dinner, an "*audience-participatory* musical extravaganza!" I imagined looking particularly idiotic, halfheart-edly clapping to the music, hopelessly out of rhythm. All things considered, the Critical Race Theory Conference began to look like an academically enticing yet socially dubious proposition.

But I discerned what appeared to be another reason for my hesitation, residing a little deeper in my consciousness. You see, I'm a White man. Although I knew that the conference would be multiracial, including other Whites, I also knew that this gathering would be importantly different from most of the other academic conferences I might attend. Scholars of color would dominate this conference, both in sheer numbers and, perhaps more important, in clout. The planners, the showcase speakers, the "big shots" were almost all scholars of color.[1] As a White man, in this place, for this time, I would be a racial minority. Some of those present might discount me and my ideas on race precisely and simply because of my racial status.

Put simply, as the Critical Race Theory Conference loomed on the horizon, I felt more and more uncomfortable about attending. Some of the reasons would have applied to almost any conference. But some of those reasons seemed uniquely a product of my own racial identity and the racial nature of this conference.

Quite obviously, I decided to attend the conference. Sitting in the plane on the way to New Haven, Connecticut, I rehearsed my talk silently and thought about my discomfort. I saw this discomfort as a window into what would be the theme of my talk and of this essay—the idea of White privilege. I knew, as we descended into New York, that I had actually been playing mind games all along. What I feared, really, was finding no friendly face at my dinner table or some other social disaster. I did not really fear that others would discount my ideas on race; I did not really worry that my race would be a liability. How could I truly think that my Whiteness could be a source of insecurity? As a White man, who had grown up outside the harrowing field of poverty, I had been taught that I presumptively belonged anywhere; that I was presumptively worthy in any respect and knew what I was talking about, on race or whatever. I would walk through this gathering as any other White, buoyed by White privilege, expecting the disfavor of some in the audience but not really very worried about it.[2]

And so I went to New Haven and, after finding some friendly strangers with whom I shared lunch, I dutifully reported to the assigned room and delivered a talk more or less along the lines of what follows under the heading, "Unbearable Whiteness."

Unbearable Whiteness

As we enter the new millennium, with the institutions of slavery and apartheid receding ever further in the wake of history, our society seems as riven as ever over race. Our contemporary flash points—affirmative action, illegal immigrants, O. J.—expose the great racial divide. How is it that, after so many years, so much blood, and in the midst of so many professions of good faith, race and racism remain social fixtures?

The fact that many Whites are unabashed racists is part, and a big part, of the answer. These are men and women who, without hesitation, will say that Blacks are lazier, less intelligent, less trustworthy, more violence-prone, dirtier, and more sexually wanton than Whites.[3] Armed with these prejudices, they resist any social, business, or personal contact with Blacks. They abhor affirmative action as an undeserved gift to unworthy Blacks. Such racist Whites can be found behind the wheel of a pickup truck with a Confederate-flag decal on the back window or seated in the leather chair of the corner office of a leading law firm or behind the wheel of a police cruiser. These Whites will deploy their power to act out and thus prop up, not dismantle, racism.

Other Whites say that they reject racism and do not see Blacks as an inherently inferior race, while at the same time they embrace the basic precepts of racism. For example, the suburban White mother, explaining her opposition to the racial integration of her neighborhood, might say, "I'm not against Blacks moving in; that's fine with me. But I am concerned about my family's security." If challenged, she would deny that she was a "racist," probably even resent the very suggestion. Nevertheless, she would hold to her position—namely, that although not every Black person is a criminal, as a generalization, Blacks are much more likely to present problems. Many Whites embrace this form of "non-racist racism."[4] These Whites are unlikely candidates for leadership roles in the effort to dismantle racism, the tenets of which they actually and consciously embrace.

This "non-racist racism" way of thinking is exemplified by the government's drug-courier profiles.[5] A Black man is detained at an airport security check because he fits the profile. The comparable White man glides on through. Henry Louis Gates, Jr., has coined the criminal offense "DWB," or "Driving While Black," to describe the phenomenon of police stopping Black motorists with no real provocation other than the race of the driver.[6] Any defense of this odious practice must come in one of two forms—crude racism or "race-consciousness" racism. It is often hard to discern which way of thinking is at work, at least in the absence of a racial epithet in the explanation.

Apart from the unabashed White racists and the "race-conscious" White racists, there are what I call the "right thinking Whites," the category in which I place myself. We reject the tenets of racism. We understand that race is a purely social construction, and a vicious one at that. The problem for us, we say, is that we are still racists at the unconscious level. Having been taught the precepts of racism for so long and from so many sources, we cannot slough off all that teaching. For us, it is something like a nasty habit or mannerism, something of which we are often unaware. When we catch ourselves acting in accordance with the racist teachings that lurk in our unconsciousness, we instantly amend our behavior or judgment accordingly. When we fail to catch ourselves, we act out the racism.

For example, several days before I departed for the conference, I drove my thirteen-year-old son to the junior high school. He was late and thus almost alone going into the building. Another student, apparently an older high-school student, was walking into the building several yards behind my son. The high-school student was Black. As I sat in the car, I watched the two boys all the way into the building. And, in the moment of doing so, I realized what had happened. Had the second boy been White, I probably would have simply driven away, without monitoring my son's journey into the building.

Thus, I live in the realm of Whites who reject racism yet hold it in our unconscious. We are the repentant ones and, at times, the self-righteous ones. Among Whites, we are the most likely candidates for leadership in the dismantling of racism. Yet most of us have a difficult time truly "choosing against our Whiteness," to use Ian Haney López's phrase.[7] Something holds us back, something other than our unconsciously held racism. The simple truth is that, to some significant degree, we do not really want to give up our Whiteness.

In a world where Whites hold most of the power—financial, legal, political, social—and where the tenets of racism remain firmly entrenched in the consciousness and unconsciousness of those Whites, being deemed White counts for a lot.[8] Most of the commentary on race has focused on the burden of racism on those deemed not White. However real and monstrous this burden, it is important to remember that the entire purpose of the social construction we call race is, and always has been, to serve the interests of those deemed White, to create the benefits that go along with being deemed White. Slavery gave Whites a labor force to which they owed nothing and from which they might demand anything. Apartheid provided Whites with a formal structure that facilitated the unequal distribution of the state's wealth and favor, all during a period of our history that still carries the ironic label "separate but equal." Contemporary racism, the legacy of our past, like apartheid and slavery before it, provides Whites with an intangible but powerful sense of racial superiority. When, for example, we entertain the assumption that Blacks, generally speaking, are not hard-working, we are always implicitly proclaiming the industriousness of Whites. Every place that excludes Blacks becomes a place where Whites are presumably welcome. The cumulative effect of all this racism is that Whites emerge with a presumptive sense of worthiness and belonging. This is the terrible and illicit gift of racism, a gift I receive every day of my life.

Right-thinking Whites of course know all this and reject the gift. They know that race is a purely social construction and renounce any claim to racial superiority. It is all terrible nonsense, we say.

Yet, it is not clear that right-thinking Whites truly believe it is all such nonsense. Many Whites, including right-thinking ones, have an essentially incoherent understanding of race. On the one hand, they do see the burdens of contemporary racism. The playing field is uneven, with Blacks facing an uphill run. These Whites support affirmative action because it offsets to some degree the burden of racism and because it promotes the racial diversity of the places where affirmative action operates. So far, so good. On the other hand, these Whites are unlikely to see themselves as especially benefited by their Whiteness. In fact, most Whites, even some right-thinking Whites, see themselves as burdened by their Whiteness in the contemporary world of "political correctness" and affirmative action. Consider, for example, the political and rhetorical forces that swept California's Proposition 209 into law.[9] The difference among these Whites is that the right-thinking ones are likely to accept their burden as an appropriate self-sacrifice, while the others whine on about the great victim of our time, the "innocent" White man.

Within this incoherent understanding of race, it is as though there are two playing fields, one uneven and unfair, reserved for Blacks, and one even and fair, on which Whites play the game called their lives. Whites suppose that, while Blacks have carried an unfair burden, they have simply lived their lives without hindrance or help on account of their racial identity. This is the great and critical myth of contemporary Whites, the myth of the racially unassisted life. Within the White consciousness, just as every achievement of a Black person is likely to be discounted by the idea of affirmative action, every achievement of theirs is supplemented by the myth of the unassisted, "by the sweat of their brow," life. Every White, in his own head, is Horatio Alger.

Fran Lebowitz has described the advantages of Whiteness through the example of the contemporary phenomenon of second- and third-generation movie stars.[10] She noted that whenever the sons and daughters, or grandchildren, of movie stars who themselves have joined the ranks of Hollywood fame—the Douglases, the Fondas, and so on—are interviewed and asked the inevitable question, "Has being the son/daughter of Mommy/Daddy movie star been an advantage?" they always respond more or less the same way. "Sure, it helped me get through the door, but after that, I was on my own and had to sink or swim on my own merit." This, says Lebowitz, is ludicrous. Getting through the door is pretty much all there is to it, and not just in movie acting. The hard part is getting admitted to the elite school, getting the competitively sought clerkship, and so on. Once you're through that door, you need only perform in the ordinary and simply competent manner and keep out of trouble, and you succeed. The offspring of movie stars enjoy two basic advantages. First, and most obviously, their mom or dad can pick up the phone and call the producer or director and ask a favor. Still, to actually become a movie star, the public has to accept you as a star. Here, the second advantage kicks in: We, the public, are more likely to accept them as movie stars because they literally look like movie stars. It somehow seems to make sense; the face is familiar, the name is familiar. This, says Lebowitz, is what it means to be White. We look like the people in charge—the bosses, the wealthy folk, the masters, the professors, the lawyers, and so on. In the eyes of other Whites, we look the part.

From the White perspective, there is a naturalness to the White vistas that centuries of racism have carved in our society. Our White senators, White lawyers, White movie stars all look the part. As we gaze upon the ranks of the powerful and privileged in this country, the sea of White faces looks right to us. This way of seeing and feeling is embedded in our law. In the classic 1989 affirmative-action case, *City of Richmond v. J. A. Croson*,[11] the majority of the Supreme Court gazed upon the city's record of construction contracting, saw virtually nothing but White contractors, and felt quite comfortable with that picture. Justice O'Connor even speculated that perhaps Blacks "may be disproportionately attracted to industries other than construction."[12] Richmond, Virginia? The construction industry? Nothing but Whites? What could be more natural, from the White perspective?

Whites and second-generation movie stars are alike in another way. Neither group wants to confront fully and honestly its illicit advantages, and for essentially the same reason. The movie star's sense of self is inextricably and powerfully tied to the status and accomplishments that make her a "movie star." To acknowledge that she achieved those accomplishments and that status through an illicit boost would shake the movie star's self-conception. It would be like playing and winning a game, only to discover that someone had bribed the officials to tilt the game your way. What would that do to the sense of accomplishment you would feel in winning? And how much of a sense of self-worth would survive once you faced the fact that deep down you really knew that the officials had been bribed, and yet you played on pretending that the game was fairly constructed? It is no wonder that the sons and daughters of movie stars hold

on to the myth of their essentially unassisted rise to stardom.

Similarly, it is no wonder that Whites hold the myth of the racially unassisted life. Without this myth, every achievement, every aspect of our lives—our social position, our wealth, our circle of friends, where we live, the quality of our educational experience, our conception of our physical beauty, whether we made partner, whether we got tenure, any sense of being elite—all of it, the whole thing, would be called into question. It is a door we do not want to open.

But, without opening this door, it is hard to imagine that Whites will be effective agents in the dismantling of racism. To be effective agents, right-thinking Whites must do more than they are now doing. It will not be enough to express their abhorrence of racism. It will not even be enough to throw their voice and influence to the cause of affirmative action or other social programs designed to mitigate the burdens of racism. This we already do, and it is too little. To have any hope of being effective participants in the assault on racism, Whites will have to rip away their own Whiteness. Every discernible advantage that might come our way by reference to our Whiteness should be spurned. We ought to boycott every institution that makes us welcome by making non-Whites unwelcome. Each of us should confess to the illicit advantages we have enjoyed and be prepared to alter our self-conception accordingly. We need to face a truth that is almost unbearable.

But will we?

Postlude: Going Home

The conference is over, and I'm traveling in my rental car to La Guardia Airport to catch a plane home. Most of my fears about social disaster were not realized. A few awkward moments standing alone at the perimeter of the crowd at the Saturday evening cocktail party, not seeing a single soul I knew, looking just like the forlorn loner I was in that moment. Yet, almost always I felt as though I belonged. Richard Delgado and Jean Stefancic sought me out at the dinner Saturday evening. Stephanie Wildman waved me over to join her at Saturday afternoon's plenary session. Gerald Torres dragged me across a crowded hallway to join his small group and to praise my book. And so on. I honestly had a great time, learned much, and left feeling as though my work had a point. I was on a definite high as I traveled the interstate Sunday morning, heading home.

At the dinner Saturday evening I met a young Black woman, Robin Magee, who asked for a ride to La Guardia. I was happy to oblige. As we rode along, we talked about the conference and mostly of some strange coincidental connections. It turned out that she taught at a law school that had interviewed me for its deanship years before. It was a pleasant trip.

As we unloaded our bags from the car at the car-rental place, I noticed a White businessman looking at us. Nothing sinister or angry in his look. Just a look. Yet like my experience watching my son into his school building, the eyes lingered, precisely because a Black person was in the picture, and the picture, through the eyes of the White man, looked suspicious.

All of these thoughts ran through my head on the plane ride home. I imagined writing this essay and composed pieces of it in my head. Vignettes of the conference popped into my consciousness. I recalled again the kindness and generous words. I was truly glad to have gone. But more than anything else, as the plane sailed above the clouds away from New York, I was glad to be heading home. I do not travel a great deal, perhaps a half-dozen trips a year. I always miss my family while I am away and almost never sleep well in a hotel room. Still, sitting in that plane seat, I wondered whether I was happy to be heading home for yet another reason. Whites generally possess a natural, transparent sense of their racial identity. During the time I spent in New Haven, I could not indulge myself in that luxury. The words of others, and the words spinning from my mouth and in my head, all reminded me of my Whiteness and my illicit gift. What I now wondered, heading home, was whether a part of me was glad to be returning to a world where I might once again sink into the comfort of inattention to my Whiteness. As the plane descended into Pittsburgh, I saw the familiar skyline of downtown, and my eyes looked across the river to the rolling hills of the southern suburbs, not quite able to make out the cluster of lights that would be my neighborhood, and I knew that what I feared was true and that hating this longing did nothing to make it less real and did nothing to make it less shameful.

Notes

1. By naming here the members of the Conference Organizing Committee, some of the "big shots"— Jerome Culp, Harlon Dalton, Leslie Espinoza, Angela Harris, Peter Kwan, Frank Valdes, and Eric Yamamoto—I am able to suggest some support for my textual assertion and, at the same time, express my great appreciation to them for their efforts to make this extraordinary gathering a reality.

2. The idea that no White person could ever feel insecurity on account of his racial status is long-standing. In the infamous late-nineteenth-century *Plessy* case (*Plessy v. Ferguson*, 163 U.S. 537, 544 [1896]), Justice Henry Billings Brown expressed the point. After declaring that any stigma that a Black person felt by the apartheid laws was a self-imposed one, he went on to say: "The [stigma] argument necessarily assumes that if . . . the colored race should become the dominant power in the state legislature, and should enact a law in precisely similar terms, it would thereby relegate the white race to an inferior position. We imagine that the white race, at least, would not acquiesce in this assumption." White

supremacy was, and remains, a powerful and, for many Whites, indelible piece of their self-conception. It is something that no racially drawn law, no censure from the Black critic, can shake.

3. In this essay, I write simply of White and Black. Racism is, of course, a larger beast. Whites also fear and despise Latinos, Asians, and Native Americans. By my use of the Black-White vocabulary, I do not wish to deny or minimize the breadth and nuance of contemporary racism. I choose the narrower focus in part because, from the White perspective, the poles of the racial spectrum are Black and White, with no race lower in esteem than the Black. Finally, I write of Blacks and Whites because I have more personal experience of White racism toward Blacks than I do of White racism directed at Latinos, Asians, or Native Americans.

4. This way of thinking about race has a long lineage. For example, the lawyers advocating the constitutionality of apartheid in *Brown v. Board of Education of Topeka*, 347 U.S. 483 (1954), repeatedly relied on this strange rhetoric. The attorney general of North Carolina argued: "We have more consciousness of race in North Carolina than is to be found in some of the border and northern states. That race consciousness is not race prejudice. It is not race hatred. It is not intolerance": Transcript of Oral Argument, 13-14, *Brown v. Board of Education*, reprinted in *Landmark Briefs and Arguments of the Supreme Court of the United States*, 49A (1975), 1227-8. Similarly, John W. Davis proclaimed: "You say that [segregation is a product of] racism. Well, it is not racism. [It is a matter of] race and race tension, not racism": Transcript of Oral Argument, 43, *Brown v. Board of Education*, reprinted in *Landmark Briefs and Arguments*, 491.

5. See Michael Higgins, "Looking the Part," *American Bar Association Journal* 83 (November 1997): 48; Mark Kadish, "The Drug Courier Profile: In

Planes, Trains, and Automobiles; and Now in Jury Boxes," *American University Law Review* 46 (1997): 747.

6. Henry Louis Gates, Jr., "Thirteen Ways of Looking at a Black Man," *New Yorker*, October 1995. The contemporary Supreme Court shows no interest in putting any constitutional roadblock in the way of the police practice of stopping people because they somehow look like criminals, at least as long as there is some pretextual trivial traffic violation involved: See *Whren v. U.S.*, 517 U.S. 806 (1996). See also Tracey Maclin, "The Decline of the Right of Locomotion: The Fourth Amendment on the Streets," *Cornell Law Review* 75 (1990): 1258.

7. See Ian Haney López, *White by Law—The Legal Construction of Race* (New York: New York University Press, 1997), detailing and critically analyzing the history of the federal law restricting naturalized citizenship to "white persons."

8. In this chapter, I again make a simplifying and potentially misleading move. I lump all Whites into a single category. Doing so risks a White version of the error of essentialism that Angela Harris and others have so tellingly criticized. See, for example, Angela P. Harris, "Race and Essentialism in Feminist Legal Theory," *Stanford Law Review* 42 (1990): 581. I know that the experience of being White is more complicated than my simple Black-White dichotomy suggests. Although all Whites receive the illicit gift of White privilege, many Whites—women, gays, lesbians, Jews, poor people, and others—are the subject of fear and hatred by other Whites.

9. See Derrick A. Bell, Jr., "Proposition 209: A Temporary Diversion on the Road to Racial Disaster," *Loyola Law Review* 30 (1997): 1447.

10. Fran Lebowitz, "Fran Lebowitz on Race," *Vanity Fair*, October 1997, 220.

11. *City of Richmond v. J. A. Croson*, 488 U.S. 469 (1989).

12. Ibid., 500.

CHAPTER TEN

Construction Project: Color Me Queer + Color Me Family = Camilo's Story

Victoria Ortiz and Jennifer Elrod

Prologue

OUR SON, CAMILO, was eight years old. He arrived home one day from his after-school program, his large brown eyes swollen and filled with tears. He broke into sobs, fighting for air. His shoulders heaved, and he wept as if his heart would at any moment burst from his small chest. We two were immediately overwhelmed with speculative visions of the kind of dire adult-type tragedies he might have witnessed: violence in the street, disaster at his school, the death of a beloved teacher, or a fatal accident observed.

"What is it, sweetie?" we asked, as we scooped him into our arms, hugging him tightly and trying to comfort him.

Through tearful gulps, his overflowing eyes sending streams down his bronze cheeks, Camilo gasped and hiccuped his story: Ramon, then his best friend, the only other Latino child in the class, had stubbornly challenged Camilo's assertion—made over milk and cookies at midafternoon—

that his mother was a lesbian and that he lived with her and his Other Mom.

"She *can't* be a lesbian! She's *not* a lesbian! She has you, so she *is not* a lesbian. My Mother said so. Anyway, you and your Mom are Mexican, so she can't be one of them," Ramon had insisted.

"Yes, she *is* a lesbian! I *know* she's a lesbian! She *told* me she *is*!" Camilo had declared, adamant in his conviction of the truth about his family, and outraged that his closest friend would challenge this incontrovertible fact.

We held Camilo in a three-way embrace as we sought to calm and reassure him.

Yes, his mom really was a lesbian. Yes, he really had two moms. Yes, he had been right to stand fast upon the truth that was his and ours. Yes, the reality of his life experience was that he was the son of two lesbians, and that we were a family.

And: Yes, there were always going to be people who would deny his and our existence, sometimes out of ignorance, sometimes out of fear, sometimes out of malice. But that didn't change the fact of our being three valuable individuals or our being a legitimate family.

And: Yes, our family would always face the possibility of being besieged, but we would hold together in mutual, three-way love, surrounding ourselves with friends and relatives who really loved us, those who were part of our extended family, our community.

And then the three of us named those special people who really cared and who always respected us as individuals and as a family: Bobbye, Jim and Amy, Kae Ming, Sarah, Johnny Wray, Sara and Al, Lucy, Valentina, Amilcar and Wanda, Betty and Pancho, David, Betsy, Bob, Barbara, Hassan, Tony and Richard, Bea and Sam, Dinah.

The list grew longer and longer and, as we almost chanted this litany of comforting and familiar names, Camilo finally fell asleep, and we two collapsed on the living-room couch, seeking comfort and guidance from each other.

Introduction

In this chapter, we present a critical account of our search for a functional, practical theory of Color Me Queer, Color Me Family, a theory that will work for us, for our family, for our future. Through the narrative of our family life and Camilo's growing from child to adult, we trace and reflect on the way we searched for ourselves, our son, and our family in a variety of traditional and non-traditional frameworks. Along the way, we examine and apply traditional legal studies, Marxism, Critical Legal Studies, feminism, Critical Race Theory and Critical Race Feminism (CRF), LatCrit, other outsider legal theories, Disability Theory, and Queer Theory and praxis. From these bodies of work we pull the basic building blocks of our theory. Using the mortar of dialectics, we construct a theory for ourselves and our family—three people, two lesbians and one boy, two

Latinas/os and a person of white[1]—as well as for our various and overlapping communities, including mothers of young children, lesbian mothers, women, Latinos and Latinas, whites, social activists for justice, public-interest lawyers, and many others.

At that moment more than eleven years ago, however, when we were just beginning our effort to construct a user-friendly, dykes-as-mothers, brown-and-white-couple-as-parents theory that might help us to locate the confluence and find the balance in our all-too-often segmented lives, we were unsure as to how to undertake this project. We were certain, though, that we wanted a theory that would help us to guide to healthy, loving adulthood our young Latino son, a theory that would recognize and value those important parts of our selves and our backgrounds—sexual orientation, race, gender, class, national origin, and physical ability—and integrate them into our daily lives in positive ways so that we might counter all the negative external forces (legal, social, and cultural) that impinged on us, our son, our family, and our society. Always uppermost in our minds were the questions we were forced to ask ourselves as we confronted the social challenges and the personal struggles that we faced every day:

Why *can't* lesbians be Moms? Why *can't* a Latina woman love a woman of white, and vice versa? Why *can't* a boy defend his family—even if it is configured in a way that may be different from the traditional nuclear family? Why *can't* a child be allowed to live in a fully congruent way without being shut down? Why is being Queer so queer, so different, so threatening, so unacceptable, even unbelievable to some? For out of the mouths of babes....

What Ramon said to Camilo so many years ago, and what Camilo insistently and persistently said back to him, still reverberates for the three of us today. Its poignancy demands that we reflect deeply on what homophobia and other forms of interlocking biases do to children and adults and how they cause fragmentation, confusion, and spirit murder, a condition that "produces a system of formalized distortions of thought [and] social structures centered on fear and hate."[2]

The opening story from Camilo's young life, one of so many small daily episodes that form a person as she or he grows, captures for us the intersections of the multiple and complex strands of all the "-isms" that we still confront as we live our lives.[3] It underscores the tension and interplay between the private and public spheres, and between the micro and macro realms, in which we live each day. We thus started our construction project: to craft a strong theoretical structure that would have a practical application to our three lives on a daily basis. As we advanced in the building of our new theoretical/practical construction, we incrementally brought to bear on the discourse we examined much of the progress produced by our earlier work.

Traditional Theories

Traditional Legal Theory

We were both law students and Camilo was in second grade when we began to look for the basic raw materials and additional analytic tools we needed for our construction project. We therefore turned to the most readily available resource for us: the law library. We examined legal theory wherever and whenever we thought we had encountered it. Much as Elvia Arriola, Margaret Montoya, and Patricia J. Williams searched desperately as law students for reflections of themselves in the cases and legal theories they studied at Boalt or Harvard,[4] we combed through legal and jurisprudential writings trying to find something that would be useful to us as Camilo's moms, as lesbians, as a biracial Queer family, as social activists, and as budding lawyers and legal scholars.

Not surprisingly, at that point in 1986, we found very little in the law library to guide or inspire us. On the one hand, legal history provided ample dramatic evidence of the interrelationships among people's struggles for justice and the occasional, all-too-slow, indeed reluctant, responses from the formal legal system.[5] On the other, there was too much uncritical reliance on the legal institutions and the "rule of law" as quasi-divine emanations, resistant to all change unless it furthered the goals and expanded the benefits of people who were affluent, male, white, heterosexual, young, able-bodied, educated, fully employed—in a word, those with access to power and to institutions that controlled and directed people's lives.

Over supper in the evenings, we would hear about Camilo's day: his fall in the playground or his class's field trip to a museum or his success on a math test. In turn, we would tell him the "stories" of the struggles for social and legal justice we had studied that day, stories such as those behind *Brown v. Board of Education* and *Bowers v. Hardwick*. As a family, we discussed the need for patience, stubbornness, courage, and discipline made evident by those micro events and macro struggles.[6] We saw that our small encounters, the micro-aggressions we suffered and the acts of personal resistance in response, were necessarily connected to the social dynamics, macro-oppressions, and historical struggles that came through to us from the pages of case books and legal treatises. Our family life was distinctly affected by this interplay of private and public existence, of personal and social history. We came to understand how much our own condition was often defined through daily acts of oppression and resistance—those small, everyday moments of standing up and saying you have two Moms, or coming out as lesbian mothers, or all the countless other ways in which people in families like ours respond to the constant challenges inherent in being something other than the "typical" family.

We thus gave heightened importance in our frequent discussions to the need for our family and our lives to be contextualized into a broader social struggle. And we saw, too, that justice and equality would be painfully slow and only painstakingly accomplished. In this way, Camilo saw that significant change comes about only through personal, sustained, and multidimensional struggle. These discussions established the foundational lesson for all of us: that we needed time, patience, and commitment to develop, and to live, a vision that was new, a bond that was likely to be met with opposition—our family. Traditional legal theory thereby became our point of departure for the journey that since then has brought us to CRT, its second decade, and perhaps even beyond.

Marxism

Our need to work and live within a theoretical and functional framework that would truly challenge—even threaten—the status quo led us initially to Marxism, because we both believed that class analysis and socioeconomic assessment of oppression are key components of any critical anti-subordination project. Economic inequities have a pervasive impact on everyone; they shape the material conditions of life. Our own experiences have exposed us in varying ways to the ravaging impact of unrestrained capitalist expansion on the majority of the world's people, and we have no doubt that much of what is wrong in today's world can be laid at the doorstep of advanced monopoly capitalism and of the contemporary version of imperialism it has spawned.[7]

But the greatest lesson for us from Marxism was dialectics. Dialectics provided us and Camilo with an approach to the exploration of our daily lives as non-linear, and to the examination of the tensions and contradictions of our individual and family experiences. This approach helped Camilo and the two of us understand that, although our family was not the traditional mother-father dyad, although it was not uniracial, it nevertheless was as legitimate and real a family as the normative model.

At that time, indeed still, one of our main concerns was how to teach Camilo about race within his own family. We wanted to show him that all white people are not bigots, that people of color and white people could and should be actively antiracist, individually and together. Dialectics, because it reinforces the theme of partnered as well as oppositional dualities—sometimes in harmony, sometimes in contradiction—enabled us to discuss with Camilo issues of race and racism as he confronted them in his own life and as our society confronted them daily: Camilo's confusion at hearing anti-Queer sentiments expressed by people of color, or racist sentiments expressed by white women, or misogynist comments by gay men was more easily rendered manageable and more readily resolved when he had learned about contradiction and the daily uses of dialectics. This technique made it less complicated (though never easy) to talk with Camilo about the contradictory examples of prejudice and bigotry of one kind or another within groups or from people who were themselves "different" in one way or another.

But all too often the most cogent leftist or Marxist thinkers have barely recognized the role of women, have downplayed or downright ignored the impact of racism, have provided not even an afterthought or footnote addressing homophobia and heterosexism, and have omitted disability and able-bodiedness as subjects worthy of critical analysis. This oversight has led to an impoverishment of Marxist or leftist theory, to an absence of diverse perspectives capable of revealing the interlock of various bigotries, and to an erasure of the experiences of all the Others whose lives are brutally molded by racist, sexist, or homophobic permutations of capitalism.[8] Because leftist class analysis did not acknowledge that race, gender, sexual orientation, and physical ability cut across and inform *all* class differences, even as they are dialectically informed *by* class differences, our construction project took us beyond Marxism.

Critical Legal Theories

Critical Legal Studies

Of course, others in legal culture at that time similarly found it useful to apply Marxist tools to the analysis and interpretation of legal discourse and institutions. The movement called Critical Legal Studies thus seemed initially promising to us, challenging as it did the formalism and traditionalism of mainstream legal studies. We found value in the CLS position that our legal institutions and theories serve primarily to maintain in power those who made and defended those very institutions and theories. And we certainly agreed with CLS scholars that the law is systemically and systematically mystified for outsiders for the purpose of legitimating existing distributions of power and privilege.[9]

However, CLS was lacking: It was a body of theory that was too elite, too andro-, hetero-, and Eurocentric, too removed from daily life. Like Patricia J. Williams, Richard Delgado, Mari Matsuda, and so many others, we found that CLS fell far short of providing the kind of comprehensive critical theory necessary to expose and dismantle the structures of power and privilege: "What is often missing from CLS works is the

acknowledgment that our experiences of the same circumstances may be very, very different, the same symbol may mean different things to each of us."[10] CLS as a critique of the legal system—without addressing the needs of the multiply diverse disempowered, without providing concrete, practical solutions—was, like Marxism, not sufficient.[11] Because we were not able to bring CLS into our home, into our everyday realities, into our dinnertime conversations and our storytelling with Camilo, we turned to other theories both within and outside the legal academy.

Feminism

As lesbians and feminists we returned over and over again—in our scholarly labors as well as in our family and personal endeavors—to historical and contemporary feminism, seeking both the materials and the tools for constructing our theory. And, of course, we found a number of useful, and indeed inspiring, contributions. We are both daughters of the "revolutionary" branch of the second feminist wave,[12] and we value the lessons that feminism teaches us about power and powerlessness, about woman-centeredness, and about sisterhood. In particular, we both long ago adopted as our own the notion that the personal is political and that "politics"—like theory—is lived in the flesh.

However, we view gender as a critical but not unitary issue. We readily see from our own experiences as women, and from those of our women friends, the myriad ways in which women are subaltern in relation to work, home, family, education, intimate relations, media, and the like. We thus embrace the concept of sisterhood primarily as a way to link women of white and women of color in their commonality, as well as in their different and discrete personal and social histories, in a Eurocentric, heteropatriarchal culture.

While much of feminism resonates with us as Women, a great deal of it also fails to interrogate the subordination faced simultaneously by lesbians; as an interracial lesbian couple, and as non-normative parents, we have concluded that feminism per se partially fails women like us because of its relative inattention to heterosexism both within itself and throughout society, and because of its similar inattention to racism and classism. Indeed, when we went to feminist meetings and rallies with Camilo, we were soon made aware of the position, explicit and implicit, that two lesbians of different colors and a boy child could not be a family. At these events we discovered there were no discussions of the ways in which lesbian moms could participate in policy-making around family issues, no discussions of the impact of race on women and our families. We found few connections between our lives as lesbian moms or as a biracial lesbian couple and the theoretical critiques of the mostly white, heterosexual feminists in whose midst we found ourselves at those events. We were heartened, then, by the work of feminist women of color who undertook the critique of essentialism in critical and feminist legal theory.

Critical Race Theory and Critical Race Feminism

As we advanced our construction project of lived theory, we finally came upon Critical Race Theory and Critical Race Feminism. The growing body of CRT and CRF connected our project to the work being produced by a growing number of thinkers, women and men of color, who challenged the status quo of legal culture, systematically dissecting it and thereby calling into question the deepest social and economic foundations upon which it was constructed. Again and again, CRT and CRF texts demonstrated the ways in which the law, as

a white-dominated institution, was (and is) used as an instrument of oppression, denial, and degradation against non-white communities, especially African Americans. CRT and CRF challenged the fabric of society through the examination and critique of the category of race as it plays out in the law and legal institutions and gave us both hopes and tools to nourish our project.[13]

Of special interest to us was the fact that women of color in the legal world, as well as in the academy, began injecting their own particular perspectives, *as women of color*, and began developing the CRF movement from within CRT. CRF was promising because it began addressing the tensions and connections between race and gender, the intersectionality of those two components, and the need to resist essentializing along race or gender lines. In their groundbreaking work, Angela Harris, Kimberlé Crenshaw, Mari Matsuda, and many other non-white women legal scholars prominent in the birth and development of CRT and CRF forced legal culture and critical theory to acknowledge the intersectionality, connectivity, and multiplicity of raced, gendered, and even classed experiences as they are played out in subordinated people's encounters with the dominant legal system.

The use of narrative by CRT and CRF was particularly helpful to us. Narrative counteracts traditional legal scholarship that places "the Law" and "holdings" above—and far removed from—human subjectivities and experiences. Such distance renders legal theory not only abstract but also effectively unassailable because it claims that it is objective, allowing no challenges. But narrative allows both teller and reader to understand and contest—assail—the legal system. Narrative, because of its frank subjectivity, is active resistance to traditional legal theories.

In practice, we already had been using storytelling as a technique to engage Camilo critically in his own personal and intellectual development. And we had consistently modeled the interaction of the first person (singular and plural) with the third: I and We were always in relation, back and forth, to Her, to Him, to Them. This methodology reinforced for us and for Camilo the interconnection between the micro and macro of our lives. The homophobic slight of Ramon's that had wounded Camilo at school became, through narrative, a manageable life experience as we were able together to connect it not only to pervasive social intolerance for Queers and Queer families but also to stories of historical acts of resistance by Queers as well as all other oppressed groups. Needless to say, we were gratified to find confirmation of our practice in the narrative techniques of CRT and CRF.

Yet, despite their many significant contributions, neither CRT nor CRF, nor the two combined, provided all the answers for us. Although we value highly CRT's and CRF's creative, insightful contributions, we are still concerned about the omission of Queers. Surely some people of color also are Queer; surely some people of color love and form families with people of white who are Queer. And we were troubled also by the absence of "other" people of color. Where were the stories about or the analyses of Native Americans? Where were the Latinas/os, the Asian Americans, and the other Others? Surely their experiences were valuable and necessary to a broader understanding of difference and its deployment in the structuring of social and legal subordination.

Having encountered and embraced CRT and CRF, we knew that we needed to continue crafting our theory, but now we were in possession of a number of valuable tools: narrative, antiessentialism, intersectionality. These discursive insights and techniques emboldened us to believe that we could craft our own sound theoretical structure, which would have practical application to the material realities of our lives as a Queer,

multiracial family. We now needed more tools to examine further how multiple axes of difference, otherness, and outsiderness are formed by and inform legal discourse and daily life.

Other Outsider Jurisprudence

As CRT and CRF grew, other outsiders raised new and important issues: Asian Americans, Pacific Islanders, Native Americans, Latinas/os, Mestizas/os, and other people of color began to offer their views about, their experiences of, their theories on, their solutions to a white-dominated legal discourse that systematically erased or devalued them by either omission or commission.[14] Robert Chang suggested that the binary of black–white is an incomplete tool for analyzing and understanding the experiences of discrimination endured by Asian Americans, who are labeled by the dominant society as both the model minority and the foreigner.[15] Using the history of the indigenous peoples of North America and storytelling, Robert A. Williams, Jr., unpackaged the challenges of building coalitions, of learning to cooperate, of forging alliances despite vast cultural differences.[16] This expanding discourse both strengthened and transcended our project's connection to CRT and CRF.

In particular, we are tremendously excited by the burgeoning LatCrit movement, which is providing progressive legal scholars with a virtual torrent of theoretical and practical insights about culture, language, religion, migration, and family life. As a contribution to our theory-building, LatCrit has given us in particular the validation of community and family as critically relevant to antisubordination legal discourse and praxis. But as our exposure to this ever-broadening body of theory advanced, we remained convinced that some key components of social and human experience were still missing from these developments. One of these is physical (and "mental") ability and disability.

Disability Theory

Our continuing exploration of outsider theory as lived experience expanded further when we examined Disability Theory. We found in it a wealth of concepts, foci, and approaches that resonate deeply. Disability Theory is firmly grounded in the material reality of the lives and experiences of people—in this instance, those deemed disabled—and in the increasing activism of a wide variety of groups and organizations. Disability Theory thus has much in common with the theories developed by other outsider groups, and many disability theorists acknowledge this debt. Disability discourse raises issues of acknowledgment and erasure and, from there, questions of "passing," of "closeting," and of "coming out" that are associated with medicalization and social demonization and that closely resemble the patterns and mechanisms of subordination that afflict other marginalized groups.

Two concepts from Disability Theory were particularly useful building blocks for our own project: the central element of physicality, and ableism in language and critical discourse. Disability Theory addresses society's contention, explicit and implicit, that people must be categorized according to what we are "able" to do or not do, and how or how "well" we are able to do it or not, with our bodies or parts of our bodies. This social classification interacts with and is integrated into the social constructs of race and gender (including genderized racial categories and racialized gender categories) in that "acceptable" images of disability are generally white, male heterosexuals in wheelchairs (Christopher Reeve) and "unacceptable" are women and people of color with other visible disabilities

or "deformities." Thus, the foundational premise of disability analysis is that the concept "disabled" also is a social construction that posits physical (and "mental") normality or normativity as an essential category against which all who do not conform are devalued.[17] As Rosemarie Garland Thomson observes, "Although much recent scholarship explores how difference and identity operate in such politicized constructions as gender, race, and sexuality, cultural and literary criticism has generally overlooked the related perceptions of corporeal otherness we think of variously as 'monstrosity,' 'mutilation,' 'deformation,' 'crippledness,' or 'physical disability.'"[18] It is precisely this new examination of corporeality, of physicality as social construction, that adds yet another key dimension to the expanding critical paradigm of our ongoing construction project. Disability Theory thereby provides our project with a tremendously promising point of entry into the critical study of difference and its use to construct interlocked power hierarchies.

As with racism, sexism, classism, and homophobia, we began increasingly to notice how our everyday experiences are rife with examples of ableism. In particular, we started noting with more critical awareness the recurrent, and often inadvertent, examples of ableism in the very language of critical discourse: Think of "the ways in which the terms 'visible' and 'invisible' are used as metaphors [in much outsider culture and jurisprudence]. Notice how these metaphors privilege *seeing*. [Notice, too, the] metaphors of 'voice' and 'silence.'"[19] The critique of disability theorists thus raises a broad range of matters pertinent to outsider jurisprudence as antisubordination method; disability theories, from many different vantage points, enhance social-justice scholarship and practice. The addition of Disability Theory to the expanding universe of outsider scholarship has enriched both our work and our lives.

It also has enriched our parenting. Because we value the power of the Word, we were, as mothers, always committed to teaching Camilo to avoid using dehumanizing and stigmatizing terms. Yet as parents of a growing child, we were always conscious of social atmosferes to which Camilo was exposed, which too often diminished, reviled, rejected, and mocked people because of so-called abilities or disabilities; which ranked people based on how they walk or move about, how they communicate and with which sense or body part, how they look, how many limbs or digits or other body parts they have (or do not have). Fortunately, Camilo's early schooling experiences had given him the opportunity to learn about and play with richly diverse groups of children, so that communicating through signing, moving about in a wheelchair, or having one leg or two arms of divergent size meant only difference to him, not better or worse. Many times when we were out with Camilo—at the movies, in a park, at political events—he would notice people using sign language and others in wheelchairs or on crutches. His earliest comments were likely to be, "Why are they all white?" rather than, "Why are they 'like that'?" Camilo was accepting of physical difference and took it to be the norm that any given gathering of people would include the full range of apparent human abilities. He was, at the same time, profoundly conscious of racial "differences" and of the frequent informal segregation or self-segregation of distinct racial-social groups in our society.

What Camilo was noticing without being able to name it was the impact of class and race within the communities of the disabled. The disabled poor, like all the poor, are less "visible," less organized into activist groups, less consciously present in our daily lives. And disabled people of color similarly are less likely to be included in the political and social groups of the disabled due to the prevalence of racism. Though reflective of prevalent social ills, Disability Theory significantly advanced our project and led us to its next stage.

Queer Theory

As with feminism and other encounters, our social identities made Queer Theory an obvious source in the crafting of our ongoing construction project. Furthermore, the spectacular proliferation during the past several years of books, articles, anthologies, conferences, and programs devoted not only to the study of the histories and lives of lesbians, gay men, bisexuals, transsexuals, and transgendered people, but also to the development of new theoretical perspectives based on minority sexual identities and orientations, stimulated us to delve more deeply into what was soon called (not without controversy) Queer Theory. This development has been felt within legal culture, which also has experienced the emergence of a Queer legal theory in recent years.

How useful Queer theorizing would have been to the three of us when Camilo was ten and came home with a note from his teacher, indicating that he had not taken seriously the assignment to draw his family tree. Specifically, Camilo had crossed out the line that said "Mother and Father" and had instead written, "Mother and Mother." He had constructed the rest of the "tree" with members of both our families, including his white cousins. The teacher berated Camilo for his insistence that this tree depicted his real family and suggested that a parent–teacher conference was needed.

We were thrilled that Camilo actively resisted the teacher's attempt to distort his family reality and to force it to fit into her definition of a "true" family. We reinforced for Camilo—and for ourselves—the importance of standing fast in the face of a denial and devaluation of his/our family. We were proud of his courage and determination to "educate" his teacher about the many types of family configurations that populate this society and the globe.

Since then, it has become clear to us that Queer Theory focuses on issues missing from many other frameworks that we had examined. Queer Theory centers the realities of Queers, of sexual outlaws; it foregrounds discussion not only of sexual orientation but also of its extra-sexual implications. By helping people to understand that sexual orientation is not "just" about sexuality, Queer Theory addresses power relations and material conditions that critical legal scholars, Marxists and leftists, feminists of all stripes, other outsiders, and critical race theorists and critical race feminists should be, and often are not, examining:

> In different ways queer politics [and theory] might therefore have implications for any area of social life. Following Marx's definition of critical theory as "the self-clarification of the struggles and wishes of the age," we might think of queer theory as the project of elaborating, in ways that cannot be predicted in advance, this question: What do queers want?[20]

We are encouraged, too, by the growing body of Queer scholarship being produced by critical legal scholars. Using many of the tools and approaches of other progressive legal movements—both activist and theoretical—Queer legal theorists provide new insights and valuable guidance for all of us. Their very presence in the field makes a continued marginalization of Queer issues more difficult for other legal scholars, both outsider and "mainstream."

However, in reading Queer Theory we have been disappointed to encounter a number of shortcomings similar to those of Marxism, (white) feminism, CRT and CRF, and other outsider theory. They include a tendency to limit the scope and reach of the

analysis to a single axis and to focus on issues of import to a relatively narrow segment of the Queer world—generally white (though not always), generally male (though increasingly less so), generally able-bodied (though with some significant exceptions), and generally in relatively affluent social and economic positions. Even so, Queer Theory today represents for us one of the most inviting of the theories to which we have recourse; in spite of its limitations, Queer Theory (like Disability Theory) generally is more intersectional and daring than other bodies of critical theory. We thus continue with our project.

Building Our Theory

What binds the three of us together and links us to CRT and CRF scholars, to LatCrit theorists, to feminists, to disability activists, to Queers, to people who are poor, and to other outsiders is a condition that we all share: our "otherness." But we do not seek to collapse these categories of race, age, gender, sexual orientation, able-bodiedness, and economic status. Our aim is to resist the blurring, the blending, the eliminating, the ignoring of categories. At the same time, we use the broader category of Otherness to suggest an analytical framework that allows us, that requires us (and other outsider theorists), to formulate antisubordination theory in ways that recognize, value, and affirm difference across multiple axes of identity and position.

Francisco Valdes suggests that "Queer" ought to be used as more than simply a label by which lesbians or gay men or other sexual minorities are categorized, either in a pejorative or a positive manner. He expands the word to include all those who are outsiders, those who are Other. We also adopt this definition of Queer.[21] It follows from this that Queer legal theory should accomplish most of what we seek to build, beginning with the very word "Queer":

> Substantively, "Queer" serves as a reminder and a challenge (to ourselves) to avoid replicating oppressive aspects of the past and present that we seek to discredit and displace with our critiques. This term challenges us to honor the inclusiveness and egalitarianism that the term, at its best, signifies. In doing so, this term specifically challenges us to avoid indulging and perpetuating the androsexism and racism that afflict sexual minorities as much as they afflict the sexual majority.[22]

Thus, to complete our construction project, Color Me Queer, Color Me Family, we must understand the discursive past in order not to repeat it; we must fight hard to remain connected to all others who are Other; we must consciously build for a future both linked to and distinguished from the present and the past. We must gain our strength and inspiration from our daily realities as a multiply Queer family.

Theorizing "Family" as a Unit of Resistance

Where did we start building our theory? We began, of course, with ourselves, with our family, with each other. I look at You, You look at Me, and we each see both an Other and a Self: a Latina sees a woman of white, a woman of white sees a Latina; a woman sees a woman, a lesbian sees a lesbian. Surely there is a powerful potential for human creativity in the simple contemplation of this apparent paradox: I am You are Me. . . . I am not You are not Me! What does this say about our ability to understand, to pull apart, to reconstruct the old realities within each of us in order to produce something that allows for a brand-new vision of them? We start with ourselves.

Having journeyed through various schools of jurisprudence and social theory, where are we? We can identify three overlapping but distinct themes in our thinking: the construction and celebration of Otherness and difference across multiple axes; the necessity for micro- and macro-resistance as a continuing act of survival; and the centrality of family as a unit of resistance. Because the first and second of these are relatively well established in outsider scholarship, we focus this concluding section on the third—the theme that also most closely comports with our construction project: Color Me Queer, Color Me Family.

Charlotte Bunch has urged that critical feminist analyses should commence with the differences among and between women (people), not as contrary to similarities or samenesses, but as a means of reaching an understanding of connectedness.[23] We agree strongly and use this admonition when we theorize "Family" as a potent unit of resistance to multiple and interlocking forms of subordination. The family as a social (and, indeed, economic) unit has been construed differently by different societies and cultures at different times in history and in different parts of the world. But due to the widely acknowledged socializing role of the family unit, dominant social and legal forces everywhere regulate, support, oversee, and—in a number of ways both positive and negative—control family development, including the place of each family member within the unit and in relation to the larger society. Thus, most societies allow, foster, or accommodate (often reluctantly or by default) a variety of units that are deemed families, though some may be valued more than others. Without doubt, all such units are in fact a part of the society that they inhabit and help to maintain.

In the process of constructing our theory, we have found that family structure—as with race, gender, class, physical (dis)ability, and sexual orientation—is simply a social construction, one that always is subject to contestation. Especially in the context of contemporary "culture wars," the family is a concept and reality that is at once claimed and construed by dominant ideological forces. It is also (and all too often) underestimated or ignored by those who in their theory or praxis seek to challenge prevailing oppressive structures. In particular, we have found too little attention given to expansive critical analysis that would illuminate the social and legal issues besetting a Queer, multiracial, multicultural family such as ours.

And yet in almost all societies, people often of necessity *create* their own family, or family-like unit, in the absence of a socially or legally sanctioned unit in which they have preordained membership. Distant relatives take in orphaned children; neighbors care for the childless elderly folks next door; young people on their own form many different kinds of communal living units; and groups of Others provide for one another the love, care, nurturing, and support that should come from traditional family units but for many reasons may not be forthcoming.[24] These alternative arrangements provide a rich well of potential antisubordination power because they implicate a complex but common set of interests among or across the many groups and persons who make up nontraditional families.

Given this backdrop, outsider theorists must begin to embrace, analyze, and value the political, not simply the personal, potential of "alternative" families. And when we observe the multiple forms of "family" affected profoundly by sociolegal constraints and restraints, it is clear that these theorists need to blend and borrow from the existing array of outsider theories to do so effectively. This multidimensionality is especially important when we train critical attention on the proliferation of family types that, by their diverse forms of overlapping Otherness, are targeted by social and legal forces for restructuring, co-optation, denial, or destruction.

Our own Queer, multicultural family, then, is not as much an anomaly in the broader, social, legal, and historical context as we might have thought that day, more than a decade ago, when we took the first steps toward theorizing our practical daily experiences—and our resistance to their debilitating effects. The presence of so many Others who, like us, daily challenge and resist the pressures to re-form and reconfigure family lives and relationships confirms the connectedness and interconnectedness among all Others. The differences among Others are mirrored in the differences among Other families. The varieties of subordination that converge on, or are activated through, the "family" may well be considered as "connectors" among those families.

In this way, family is recast as a unit of resistance, not simply or chiefly as a personal and social extension of the dominant society and its ideology. From our perspective, the family becomes a focal point of and incubator for antisubordination discourse and practice. The pressures withstood by our Queer family have enabled us to grow together—to understand with greater nuance the combined effects of interlocked oppression and the urgent need to meet each attack with smaller and greater acts of individual and familial resistance.

Praxis

In the years after Camilo confronted Ramon's undisguised disbelief about his lesbian mothers, Camilo had to contend again and again with establishing with his peers—at school, at work, in his community of friends—*who* he is and *who* we are, as three individuals and as a family.

Lesbians and gay men, as well as bisexual and transgendered people and many other Others, must "come out" in one way or another, often many times a day, and certainly on countless occasions in a lifetime.

That process of coming out is both affirming and frightening. The closeted individual is empowered by coming out, for telling the truth is a potent tonic. At the same time, it can be a traumatic process, entailing risks, rejection, censure, and loss of friendship because of the listener's fear, prejudice, or ignorance.

So, too, the children of these Others— who for the simple reason of association are themselves rendered Others. The children, too, must "come out" to everyone with whom they interact, or they must decide not to do so. One way or another, homophobia and similar social ills force these children to go through all the intense emotions (fear, anxiety, dread, exhilaration, empowerment) that their Other parents experience when they "come out" for themselves.[25]

While still in elementary school, Camilo continued to be open about the configuration of his family. He made two Valentine's Day cards every year, one for each of us. He argued strenuously with his friends about the legitimacy (he knew nothing about legalities, of course) of "women marrying women" and "men marrying men." He invited his classmates home for birthday parties or sleep-overs, caring little what they might think about the two women in the household sharing a bed.

When Camilo reached his early adolescent years, things began to change. He grew self-conscious about having to *be* self-conscious whenever the subject of Family came up, whenever the three of us were together at his school or in the neighborhood, whenever he invited someone home for a visit. Camilo's embarrassment made him suffer, because he felt he was being disloyal to us. And yet, quite relentlessly, the world he and we are living in made him strongly wish at times that his was a "normal" family, one with a Mom and a Dad. At the same

time, this period saw the development in Camilo of a strong sense of personal ethics, of right and wrong, of fairness and justice. He knew that the homophobia (and also the racism and all the other "-isms") he was beginning to recognize in the news, on television, in the movies, and from his friends was a dangerous, poisonous force. He was horrified and enraged when people whom he knew and respected resorted to insulting and biased joking, which he experienced as a direct attack on him and on us. And at times he felt fearful about responding, about "outing" himself as the son of lesbians, which he would have to risk to come to our defense as his mothers and as a family.

The beginning of the end of Camilo's struggle with "coming out" as the son of lesbians occurred when his feelings for Rachel, his first important girlfriend, became deep enough that he felt he must now share with her his most intimate secrets—chief among which was the Queerness of his family. He sweated and agonized over just how he was going to tell her, where he should begin the conversation, what awful responses she might utter. As it turned out, Camilo and Rachel went to a diner, neutral territory. He hemmed. He hawed. Finally, he blurted out his scary truth about our family. And Rachel responded calmly that she had known all along and did not find it peculiar or disturbing.

Camilo felt such empowerment at having been brave enough to tell Rachel and such relief at finding that he had not lost her love and respect because of who his mothers are or how his family is configured, that he embarked on an almost frenetic and repeated "coming out" with all his friends. At least once a week, we would hear from him that he had "told someone about us and our family." Even new friends became the recipients of this important confidence from Camilo virtually at the start of the relationship. For Camilo, the need to test his friends and companions by assessing their reactions to his "coming out" became, and continues to be, paramount. Happily, he has encountered very few turned-up noses or suddenly terminated friendships. Instead he has become a happier young person, more at ease *himself* with his family's configuration.

What this ongoing experience of Camilo's "coming out" for himself and for his mothers tells us is that humanity can be gained only by being able to be *who you are,* in all its complexity, with all its component identities. The essentializing of people based on a single trait, characteristic, or attribute has, we have found, seriously debilitating consequences on tranquil, healthy growing-up. Why should Camilo, or any other child, have to decide on a central identity as the son of lesbians? If he were forced to make such a decision, how could he then develop a sense of being Latino, or heterosexual, or male without bisecting his wholeness, and perhaps even separating himself from his family in order to assume a different core identity?

When we allow any aspect of ourselves to be erased as Others and in self-defense and protection lock ourselves into one compartment—only one of the many facets of who we each are—we lose our wholeness and our connectedness with all those who are not like us as far as that one component goes and limit ourselves to interrelating with only lesbians, or Latinas/os, or white people, or women. How impoverished our lives become. The strength we gain from being Others who are connected to similar Others is diminished in relation to the degree of our concomitant isolation from dissimilar Others—and, indeed, even from those whose race, class, gender, sexual orientation, or physical ability are privileged by society. We are empowered by finding and nurturing our shared Otherness with all Others, even though or especially because their differences are different from ours.

Conclusion

Although Camilo has grown to young manhood, our construction project continues, both as Theory and as Family. We, and he, have crafted a solid foundation, selecting those lessons—personal and practical—that we have gleaned from a variety of discourses and experiences. As we continue to build our theory, we select tools and materials from a broad range of insights that have come before and that themselves continue to develop. We find and make connections from one to the other and among all of them. Our theory must be like the lives we each live: made up of many parts, sometimes in apparent contradiction, most often striving for harmonious coexistence. Our own individual, familial, and community multiplicity is reflected in the variety of sources and positions that our theory reflects.

As we move into our second decade as a family, we look ahead to a bright future. As CRT and CRF move into their second decade, we are full of expectations for further groundbreaking and powerfully creative work. Unlike many traditional theories, CRT and CRF have a dynamic, organic quality. As they have grown from the work of the first wave of scholars, critical race theorists and critical race feminists have inspired other outsiders in our midst—LatCrits, Native Americans, Asian Americans, Pacific Islanders, and others. CRT and CRF are now in a position to embrace even more theoretical foci and contributions, and we look forward to incisive cross-pollination among and between CRT and CRF, LatCrit, Disability Theory, and Queer Theory. With each recognition of a new perspective, and with critical analysis of diversely "different" experiences, CRT and CRF have enriched us all, have increased the theoretical base for all scholars, and have contributed greatly to the creation of a growing community of outsider, different, non-normative, Other theorists and activists. In the second decade of this movement, as in the second decade of our family, we need and seek more and better of the same.

Notes

1. Jennifer Elrod describes herself using the term "person of white" in recognition that white is a racial category that carries with it the power of skin-color privilege in this society. However, she wants to avoid appearing to assume any normativity to the category of white. See generally Richard Delgado and Jean Stefancic, eds., *Critical White Studies: Looking Behind the Mirror* (New York and London: New York University Press, 1997).

2. Patricia J. Williams, *The Alchemy of Race and Rights* (Cambridge, Mass.: Harvard University Press, 1991), 73.

3. Kimberlé W. Crenshaw, "Race, Reform, and Retrenchment: Transformation and Legitimization in Antidiscrimination Law," *Harvard Law Review* 101 (1988): 1331; idem, "Demarginalizing the Intersection of Race and Sex: A Black Feminist Critique of Antidiscrimination Doctrine, Feminist Theory and Antiracist Politics," *University of Chicago Legal Forum* (1989): 139; Marlee Kline, "Race, Racism, and Feminist Legal Theory," *Harvard Women's Law Journal* 12 (1989): 115; Regina Austin, "Sapphire Bound!" *Wisconsin Law Review* (1989): 539; Angela P. Harris, "Race and Essentialism in Feminist Legal Theory," *Stanford Law Review* 42 (1990): 581; Adrien K. Wing, "Brief Reflections Toward a Multiplicative Theory and Praxis of Being," *Berkeley Women's Law Journal* 6 (1990-91): 181; Celina Romany, "Ain't I a Feminist?" *Yale Journal of Law and Feminism* 4 (1991): 23; Regina Austin, "Black Women, Sisterhood, and the Difference/Deviance Divide," *New England Law Review* 26 (1992): 877; Peggy Davis, "Contextual Legal Criticism: A Demonstration Exploring Hierarchy and 'Feminine' Style," *New York University Law Review* 66 (1991): 1635; Cheryl I. Harris, "Whiteness as Property," *Harvard Law Review* 106 (1993): 1707; Sumi K. Cho, "Korean Americans vs. African Americans: Conflict and Construction," in *Reading Rodney King, Reading Urban Uprising,* ed. Robert G. Williams (New York and London: Routledge, 1993), 196; Linda S. Greene, "Feminism, Law, and Social Change: Some Reflections on Unrealized Possibilities," *Northwestern University Law Review* 87 (1992): 1260; Elvia

Arriola, "Law and the Gendered Politics of Identity: Who Owns the Label 'Lesbian'?" *Hastings Women's Law Journal* 8 (1997): 1.

4. Elvia Arriola, "Welcoming the Outsider to an Outsider Conference: Law and the Multiplicities of Self," *Harvard Latino Law Review* 2 (1997): 1; Margaret E. Montoya, "*Máscaras, Trenzas, y Greñas:* Un/masking the Self While Un/braiding Latina Stories and Legal Discourse," *Harvard Women's Law Journal* 17 (1994): 185; Lani Guinier, "Becoming Gentlemen: Women's Experiences at One Ivy League Law School," *University of Pennsylvania Law Review* 143 (1994): 1; Williams, *Alchemy,* 55. Women and men of color who are law professors have expressed this same experience: Cheryl Harris, "Law Professors of Color and the Academy: Of Poets and Kings," *Chicago–Kent Law Review* 68 (1992): 331; Jennifer Russell, "On Being a Gorilla in Your Midst, or the Life of One Blackwoman in the Legal Academy," *Harvard Civil Rights–Civil Liberties Law Review* 28 (1993): 259. See also Richard Delgado, "Minority Law Professors' Lives: The Bell-Delgado Survey," *Harvard Civil Rights–Civil Liberties Law Review* 24 (1989): 349.

5. See, for example, *Brown v. Board of Education of Topeka,* 347 U.S. 483 (1954); *Heart of Atlanta Motel v. United States,* 379 U.S. 241 (1964); *Griggs v. Duke Power Company,* 401 U.S. 424 (1971); *Romer v. Evans,* 517 U.S. 620 (1996).

6. See, for example, Richard Kluger, *Simple Justice: The History of Brown v Board of Education and Black America's Struggle for Equality* (New York: Random House, 1977); *Bowers v. Hardwick,* 478 U.S. 186 (1986).

7. Bobbye S. Ortiz, ed., *History as It Happened* (New York: Monthly Review Press, 1990); Paul Buhle, *Marxism in the United States* (New York: Verso, 1987); Eduardo Galeano, *Open Veins of Latin America: Five Centuries of the Pillage of a Continent* (New York: Monthly Review Press, 1973); Bertell Ollman, *Alienation: Marx's Conception of Man in Capitalist Society* (Cambridge: Cambridge University Press, 1971).

8. Catharine A. MacKinnon, "Feminism, Marxism, Method, and the State: Toward a Feminist Jurisprudence," *Signs* 8 (1983): 635.

9. Mark Kelman, *A Guide to Critical Legal Studies* (Cambridge, Mass.: Harvard University Press, 1987).

10. Patricia J. Williams, "Alchemical Notes: Reconstructing Ideals from Deconstructed Rights," *Harvard Civil Rights–Civil Liberties Law Review* 22 (1987): 401, 409. See generally Kimberlé W. Crenshaw, Neil Gotanda, Gary Peller, and Kendall Thomas, eds., *Critical Race Theory: The Key Writings*

That Formed the Movement (New York: New Press, 1995), 63-121.

11. See, for example, Richard Delgado, ed., *Critical Race Theory: The Cutting Edge* (Philadelphia: Temple University Press, 1995), 85-94; Crenshaw et al., *Key Writings*, 60-122.

12. While the "second-wave" feminism that flourished in the 1960s and 1970s was better known for being liberal than radical, and radical feminism as such was often characterized as separatist and defiantly anti-organizational, "revolutionary" feminism brought an economic, if not Marxist, analysis to the examination of patriarchy. It called for a complete structural reordering of society and its economic and political and familial institutions as the only way poor women and women of color, as well as middle-class white women, could hope to achieve some semblance of equality: See, for example, Wilma Mankiller, Gwendolyn Mink, Marysa Navarro, and Gloria Steinem, eds., *The Reader's Companion to U.S. Women's History* (New York: Houghton Mifflin, 1998), 192-221.

13. See generally n. 4; see also Ian F. Haney López, *White by Law: The Legal Construction of Race* (New York and London: New York University Press, 1996).

14. See Robert S. Chang, "Toward an Asian American Legal Scholarship: Critical Race Theory, Post-Structuralism, and Narrative Space," *California Law Review* 81 (1993): 1244; Lisa C. Ikemoto, "Traces of the Master Narrative in the Story of African American/Korean American Conflict: How We Constructed 'Los Angeles,'" *Southern California Law Review* 66 (1993): 1581; Jenny Rivera, "Domestic Violence Against Latinas by Latino Males: An Analysis of Race, National Origin, and Gender Differentials," *Boston College Third World Law Journal* 14 (1994): 231.

15. See Chang, "Asian American Legal Scholarship."

16. Robert A. Williams, Jr., "Linking Arms Together: Multicultural Constitutionalism in a North American Indigenous Vision of Law and Peace," *California Law Review* 82 (1995): 981.

17. Rosemarie Garland Thomson, *Extraordinary Bodies: Figuring Physical Disability in American Culture and Literature* (New York: Columbia University Press, 1997); Shelley Tremain, ed., *Pushing the Limits: Disabled Dykes Produce Culture* (Toronto: Women's Press, 1996); Lois Keith, ed., *What Happened to You? Writings by Disabled Women* (New York: New Press, 1996); Deborah Root, *Cannibal Culture: Art, Appropriation, and the Commodification of Difference* (Boulder, Colo., and Oxford: Westview Press, 1996); Lennard J. Davis, *Enforcing Normalcy: Disability, Deafness, and the Body* (London and New York: Verso, 1995); Sara Halprin, *"Look at My Ugly Face!":Myths and Musings on Beauty and Other Perilous Obsessions with Women's Appearance* (New York: Penguin Books, 1995); Jennifer Terry and Jacqueline Urla, eds., *Deviant Bodies: Critical Perspectives on Difference in Science and Popular Culture* (Bloomington and Indianapolis: Indiana University Press, 1995); Raymond Luczak, ed., *Eyes of Desire: A Deaf Gay and Lesbian Reader* (Boston: Alyson Publications, 1993).

18. Thomson, *Extraordinary Bodies*, 5.

19. Tremain, *Pushing the Limits*, 18.

20. Michael Warner, ed., *Fear of a Queer Planet* (Minneapolis: University of Minnesota Press, 1993), vii.

21. Francisco Valdes, "Queers, Sissies, Dykes, Tomboys: Deconstructing the Conflation of 'Sex,' 'Gender,' and 'Sexual Orientation' in Euro-American Law and Society," *California Law Review* 83 (1995): 347.

22. Ibid., 349.

23. Charlotte Bunch, "Bringing the Global Home," in Charlotte Bunch, ed., *Passionate Politics* (New York: St. Martin's Press, 1987), 328-45.

24. Martha A. Fineman, *The Neutered Mother, the Sexual Family and Other Twentieth Century Tragedies* (New York and London: Routledge, 1995).

25. See, for example, Arriola, *Welcoming the Outsider*, 397; Judy Scales-Trent, *Notes of a White Black Woman: Race, Color, Community* (University Park: Pennsylvania State University Press, 1995), 73-8.

CHAPTER ELEVEN

On Being Homeless: One Aboriginal Woman's "Conquest" of Canadian Universities, 1989–98

Patricia Monture-Angus

I USE THE NOTION of "homelessness" with hesitation. I acknowledge that I exercise much privilege in my life (income, education, profession, and so on). I have a physical home. My quest, since I started teaching nine years ago at Dalhousie Law School in Halifax, Nova Scotia, is for an intellectual home. After the first two years of teaching on a term contract, I secured a tenure-track position at the University of Ottawa's law school. Restlessness, a feeling I now understand as "homelessness," set in before that first move from Halifax to Ottawa. This paper is both my story and a reflection on my "conquest" of the university since I began teaching in 1989.

This narrative is personal. Although some will think that I have chosen to break with academic tradition, this is false. As Himani Bannerji notes:

> It has been difficult to write about being a student and a teacher in Canada. I

would rather not have learnt or taught all the lessons that I did in these classrooms which mirror our everyday world. But there is no better point of entry into a critique or a reflection than one's own experience. It is not the end point, but the beginning of an exploration of the relationship between the personal and the social and therefore the political. *And this connecting process, which is also a discovery, is the real pedagogic process, the "science" of social science.*[1]

The method that I adopt comes from within the tradition of storytelling that is one of the foundations of Aboriginal[2] traditions, including what I understand to be an intellectual tradition.[3] The Aboriginal intellectual tradition is not really singular, as we are many diverse traditions and cultures. These traditions must not be minimized, as Aboriginal peoples also come from societies that have, and always have had, systems of knowledge. I am not convinced that writing fundamentally renders unrecognizable the oral form of the storytelling tradition.[4] In academic circles a parallel exists in the recognition of the "narrative" method.[5]

After a few years as a law professor, I felt[6] I existed in a cavern. At first it was a tiny, deep crack in the wall or floor of legal knowledge. Now and again I could peek over the side of that crack. Eventually, I began to hear an echo in this crack (probably my own spirit cries, trapped). I recognized that the shape of my experience and perhaps the shape of my oppression had changed now that I was no longer a student.

As a law teacher, I was forced to teach ideas that I found both unconscionable and often ridiculous to my Aboriginal way of knowing. The easiest example is teaching property law. I must digress for a moment and note that I did choose to teach property law because it allowed me to displace some of the standard curriculum in first-year law with a full semester on what might be inappropriately labeled "Aboriginal Title."[7] I thought that displacing mainstream curriculum in a required first-year course was an important strategy for transforming the perimeters of legal education—that is, I taught some students who would not otherwise have signed up for an upper-year "Aboriginal" course with "someone like me".[8]

The unconscionable edge in teaching property law was presenting the idea that "the crown owns all the land." This concept was difficult for me to present in a convincing fashion with due regard to the "knowledge" that the idea was and is the philosophical underpinning of the entire property-ownership system in Canada. Equally, in constitutional law or public law courses, I ran into the problematic notion of the "rule of law."[9] I taught a public law class during the "Oka occupation,"[10] where Minister of Justice Kim Campbell (a woman) used the "rule of law" to justify the military force against Mohawk people (men, women, and children), my peo-

ple. My class evaluations were critical that year of how often I mentioned "Mohawk stuff," even though I recall raising the topic once. Oddly, I had thought the "Oka occupation" was a national political and legal crisis and therefore was an appropriate topic for a public law class. The crack was then recognizable as a cavern, full of my spirit screams echoing.

I had been interested in law, perhaps dragged to it because of my life experiences (orphaned, adopted out, sexually abused as well as several other abuses, including the ones I self-inflicted).[11] As I recovered my life, these experiences turned into interests in social justice and the rights of Aboriginal people. Sadly, the list of course options at Canadian law schools did not give me much opportunity to develop these interests in the classroom. What I wrote about, thought about, and read about was separated from what I taught about. The result felt like an intellectual form of multiple personality.

As I indicated, my legal interests are probably best described as interests in social justice. I spent a lot of time while I was a law student going to jail. On Thursday nights I sat in the circle with the Native Brotherhood at Kingston Penitentiary (then a protective-custody maximum-security institution). On Monday nights, I sat in the circle with the Native Sisterhood at the Prison for Women. This was the only federal[12] prison for women at the time. It was through these prison experiences that I began to see law school as a total institution, with its goal being a particular kind of "timid" brainwashing (remember, "the crown owns all the land"). My volunteer "work" at the prisons allowed me a prism through which to see my own legal oppression, although I saw it as fundamentally less honest (there were no bars, no guards, and no guns) and gratefully less coercive. I do not think the law schools efforts to "rehabilitate" me into a "law-abiding citizen" were very effective.[13] This recognition is meant to be a comment not on any specific teacher but on the way I experienced the institution as an institution of constraint.

My interests might deceivingly look as if they would fit into "criminal law" courses. These courses, however, do not consider the systemic impact of the application of criminal law to "peoples" who are over-represented as "clients" in institutions of criminal justice. This is the situation for Aboriginal Peoples in Canada. Less recognized is the extreme under-representation of Aboriginal people in positions of power and authority in the criminal-justice system (judge, lawyer, police officer, prison guard, parole officer, and so on).[14] More important, these courses do not offer any opportunity to address solutions to the systemic problems Aboriginal people face in the existing system of Canadian criminal justice. This goal is in fact the central reason I went to law school. This is the work I remain committed to doing.

A further example of the constraints I experienced in course selection are the courses that carry the title "Aboriginal Rights." Most, if not all, Canadian law schools offer at least one course in "Aboriginal Rights." In the four Canadian law schools I experienced (two I was taught in; two I taught in), these courses were all taught by senior white, male faculty members. When Aboriginal faculty joined either of the two law schools in which I taught, we were never asked or given the opportunity to teach the "Aboriginal Rights" courses. Interestingly, the Aboriginal faculty I taught with were all women (one Cree and two Ojibwe). I also understand that this is not the experience of at least one of the Aboriginal men now teaching at a Canadian law school.[15] This is an interesting illumination of the way in which gender has an impact on my racialized experience of the law school. Even if I had been offered such a course to teach, I doubt very much that I would have been interested in the so-called opportunity. The truth of the matter is that there is not really anything

"Aboriginal" about these courses. The courses are about the application of Canadian law on or to Aboriginal peoples.

An obvious solution to the problem of "mainstream" curriculum would be to develop some of my own courses. Unfortunately, by the time I began teaching law, fiscal restraint was already the reality in Canadian law schools. Seminar offerings were being actively limited, if not reduced. Just before I left the University of Ottawa, the dean had advised me that I would be able to teach criminology only every second year. New courses, especially courses in "alternatives," were not being encouraged. As a result of both fiscal restraint and the very structure (and presumptions) of legal education, it became very difficult to hope that my future experience of law school as a law teacher would be something other than alienating.[16]

Reflection exposes to me that the precondition necessary to my participation in an institution of mainstream society is my ability to maintain hope that the institution is in a process of transformation. Generically, my frustration with law school resulted from the recognition that change that was systemic and structural was not forthcoming. Although Aboriginal professors were welcomed into the law school, our participation was silently conditional on our acceptance of the already entrenched pedagogical structure. Law schools' curricular visions are rigid, especially in the first year, when students take some combination of contract-, criminal-, constitutional-, tort-, and property-law courses. This structure is not generally critiqued or specifically critiqued (that is why no Aboriginal- or treaty-rights course is required in the first year). Through the course of my legal education I began to understand that law is the greatest fragmentation of knowledge that I have ever encountered. It is not just the substantive decisions of law and lawmakers that have negative consequences for Aboriginal people; it is the very process by which those decisions are made that is a problem. I began to see this as one of the problems that is central to the oppression of Aboriginal nations and their citizens.[17]

As a result, the longer I stayed in the law school, the more I began to feel like a "miss-fit." I use this concept because I did not *believe* I (that is, individually) was being willfully marginalized, isolated, or alienated by the institution or my colleagues. It was a feeling not about me but about the place. This, at least, allowed for some daily "comfort" in the sense that I knew the problem was not me. It is knowing the problem is systemic and located outside of self. Although I understood (or thought) this, it is not what I *felt*. What I felt, over the much longer term, was more insidious. What I felt was both individualized and personal. I was eventually left feeling "crazy" or "miss-fitted" (as in being the extra piece in a puzzle).

I do not remember when I first started thinking about Native Studies as an "alternative" (alternative meaning only as a discipline different from the one I had been trained/educated in). It is an alternative that is parallel to wanting to be back home on the "reserve,"[18] where my "cultural" safety is not threatened and assaulted daily. I suspect it began when I was still a law student. It was probably on one of those ever-too-many days when the only conscious thoughts I had were of quitting law school and going home. After all, for Indian people, committing to post-secondary education either as a teacher or as a student most often means living off the "reserve." This commitment means yearning for your people and your place. It means accepting that the spirit screams will be the steady and constant backdrop to your educational experiences.

In the fall of 1993, at an Aboriginal justice conference in Saskatoon where I was speaking, I was approached by a member of the Native Studies department at the University of Saskatchewan to apply for a newly created tenure-track job. This invitation forced me to confront the decision about leaving law-school teaching sooner that I was prepared to make it on my own. Later that academic year, I applied for and was offered that job.[19]

The fact that my partner is from Saskatchewan was significant in our decision-making about this job offer and move some 2,000 miles across the country. For some time we had been discussing our need to get out of the city (the urban mainstream) and move to a "reserve." I also admit that we had been fighting for some time about whether it would be his Cree community or my Mohawk one. I am not going into detail here, because I have a need to discuss my heterosexual union (and yes, I think it's important to name that privilege). There is another text going on here.

Once a decision is made to locate your residence on the "reserve" to be near the "good Indian stuff" (such as culture, language, and ceremony—the things that are more easily accessible on the "reserve"), your choices are severely restricted. Although there are some five hundred-odd "reserves" in Canada, you are entitled to live on the "reserve" on which you or your partner (not necessarily heterosexual partner) are registered. This severely limits economic, career, and professional choices. For example, no university is located on a "reserve" (let alone on my or my partner's "reserve").

When I was contemplating this move, I did not know any other Aboriginal professors who had made such a move. It was not until July 1, 1989, that any Aboriginal person was hired on a full-time basis by a Canadian law school (all three were women). Sadly and of note, none of us continues to teach law. I am the only one left teaching (granted, I also left the law school). The lack of role models and mentors has been a clear gap in my academic experiences as both student and teacher.

I joined the Faculty of Arts and Science, Department of Native Studies, on July 1, 1994. After much consideration, I had decided that I would not be satisfied with my place in a law school until I had some experience elsewhere in the university against which to compare that experience. It was clear that the department was interested in interviewing legal scholars, as two of the three people short-listed were lawyers. None of the applicants had a Ph.D. I do not accept that this means we were less well qualified. It has been four years since I left the law school. This is long enough to begin assessing the impact of leaving law and joining Native Studies.

There is no doubt that my classroom experience has significantly improved. As I indicated earlier in this chapter, the way law fragments knowledge moves Aboriginal understandings to the margins and sequesters them in upper-year elective courses. Native Studies does not marginalize Aboriginal people in this manner; instead, it has as its center of study Aboriginal people. This is not to suggest that the problem of fragmentation of knowledge does not exist in Native Studies. It does. It just does not exist in a way that marginalizes teachers and courses on Aboriginal peoples at the outset.

My teaching evaluations have been consistently above the department average. I no longer face the indignant assault of students who just cannot accept a Mohawk woman teaching them Canadian law. I no longer have to read comments such as "She wears too many beads and feathers to class" on teaching evaluations. This is one less assault I bear. It is not so much the evaluations in of themselves that I found so disturbing in law school. It was knowing that some of my students thought racist things about me as I stood at the front of the classroom on a daily basis.

The other advantage that the move to Native Studies allowed me was that I now teach solely in my area of interest, Aboriginal justice (which includes but is broader than mere criminal justice), including a class on First Nations[20] Women and the Law. Now what I read, write, and teach fits together in such a way that I do not feel as if my mind is divided into multiple personalities.

It is clear that I am a much more satisfied teacher as a result of the shifting of my university "home." It is also clear that my classroom is a safer place for me. I am afraid that this is the end of the "good news." On a bit of a tangent, I do recognize the contradiction in this analysis. I do believe that the law school would be enriched by the offering of the kinds of "social" justice/Aboriginal justice I now teach. It has to be recognized that law schools, at least Canadian ones, are currently incapable of preparing Aboriginal students for the practice of Aboriginal law (in Canada), particularly in Aboriginal communities. The addition of individual and isolated Aboriginal law professors to this conundrum is not a solution. It might address someone's "guilt," but it fixes little.[21]

Before sharing the rest of this story, it is important to describe the department in which I now teach. When I joined the department in 1994, there were four other full-time faculty members. There was one other woman, a Cree, who was educated as a historian.[22] It is important to understand that in seven years of university teaching, I was very careful not to be isolated as the only woman, or the only "Indian" woman, on the faculty. This is first demonstration of the degree to which survival in the university is instrumental. Second, I now find myself in the position of being the only tenure-track woman, although I was more than careful not to choose it.

When I joined the Department of Native Studies, the other three positions were held by white men,[23] including the professor who had solicited my application. One was a historian. One was a geographer. The other was an anthropologist. All three of the white men were tenured full professors. In a department of five, three is a majority.[24] Clearly, the majority of three can choose to be the gatekeepers of every decision in the department that requires a vote. This can happen, and has happened, no matter how many times they dress their power up in the róbes of consensus decision-making.[25]

The position held by the Cree woman was filled by a Métis man who had worked as a term appointment in the department for a number of years.[26] Only the three white men have Ph.D.s. The Métis man has a master's degree in sociology. My recollection of his hiring was that he was told by one of my colleagues that he would not be granted tenure without completing a Ph.D. I am opposed to this position. Possessing a doctoral degree is no guarantee that, as an Aboriginal person, you have the necessary community knowledge or "cultural" understanding to be a professor of Native Studies. The tenure processes at the University of Saskatchewan—and specifically, the departmental standards—do not recognize community knowledge or cultural understanding as a consideration (serious or otherwise) for tenure. The standards that are used elevate the importance of "purely" academic credentials, such as those signified by degrees granted. No process is articulated by which community knowledge and cultural understanding could be measured (and I am not convinced that my department or the university in general has the expertise available to create such a measure).

Interestingly enough, none of the five of us holds a degree in Native Studies. To date, I do not believe that any Canadian university has graduated a Ph.D. in Native Studies[27] (but I would gladly stand corrected). Speaking only for myself, I have never taken a single course in Native Studies. I can only assume, then,

that the fact that I was an Aboriginal person had something to do with my hiring. A Native Studies department staffed largely or exclusively by non-Aboriginal people has serious problems of legitimacy, especially in the Aboriginal community.

To complete this picture, the Department of Native Studies now has a Cree man (also a lawyer completing an LL.M.) on term contract.[28] This is his second year on a one-year term contract. I suspect, although I have not counted, that 50 percent[29] of our teaching is completed by sessionals.[30] I would approximate that 50 percent of the sessionals are women, and 50 percent would be Aboriginal. An external evaluation of the department completed in 1992 (*The Kirkness Report*) noted that

an additional observation is warranted. Only one of the permanent faculty is a Native person. She is also the only woman in the department. Given that a high proportion of the department's majors are Native women, this is an unfortunate imbalance. Apart from the gender issue, a low ratio of Native tenure stream faculty means that *the department is not living up to its original mandate by failing to provide an appropriate number of professional role models for Native students.* We realize that the present imbalance likely reflects past difficulties in recruiting a sufficient number of Aboriginal people with the necessary professional credentials. Nonetheless the current imbalance has an unfortunate result. It conveys the erroneous message that Native professionals are mostly second-class because they are the majority of the temporary appointments unlike non-Natives who have the majority of the permanent ones. This situation must be rectified.[31]

Many of you will already see the disturbing and all-too-familiar patterns present in the composition of this department. It is a disturbing pattern of systemic exclusion of Aboriginal people and women (including Aboriginal women) from positions of power and authority in the department. At the same time that I experience the department as one of exclusion, I can also see that my Aboriginal presence offers a necessary legitimacy to the department.

It is equally true and obvious to state that much of the work in the department is built on the backs of a sessional workforce. Given the over-representation of women and Aboriginal people (including women) in this group, this recognition is doubly reprehensible. In my opinion, marginalizing Aboriginal instructors to the sessional workforce dangerously mimics stereotypes of the intellectual inferiority of Aboriginal peoples. Likewise, it reinforces the negative stereotypes about the value of women's work.

The history and development of Native Studies might be interestingly compared to the development of programs and departments in Women's and Black Studies. The first Native Studies department appeared in Canada in the early 1980s. I wonder whether a Women's Studies department of five, run by three white men (or three men of any race[32]), could currently quietly exist? I do not think that this can be defended by pointing out that the number of women on campuses far outpaces that of Aboriginal scholars. What about Black Studies? How many departments of Black Studies would be "allowed" to be run by white men (or white women)? Why is this acceptable in Native Studies? I think the difference can be attributed to the colonial experience and the resulting (and remaining) colonial mind-set. It is still seen (albeit silently) as acceptable that the "Indian" needs the help and guidance of the white man. This is ridiculous, but it has not been seen as enough of a problem to cause the university to act in a way that would shift the representativeness and power dynamics in the Department of Native Studies at the University of Saskatchewan.

The notion of considering the degree of power of enclaves of "Others" on campus must be contextualized with some historical fact. Slavery was abolished in 1865 in the United States. In 1951, the bar against Indian people hiring lawyers was removed from Canada's Indian Act. In 1951, the criminalization of ceremonies was also removed from the Indian Act. In 1960, the federal franchise was extended to registered Indians. In 1968, the law that stripped university graduates of their Indian status was also repealed. In 1985, the last residential school was closed, with the majority of the schools being closed in the 1960s. That is, almost one hundred years passed after slavery was abolished in the United States before Canada formally removed the most offensive provisions from its statute books that accorded grave and unequal treatment to Indian people. This exposes a fact I have know for some time: I am at the cutting edge of the "first wave" of Aboriginal academics who are experiencing the university in "groups" rather than in absolute isolation. I do have some colleagues who are Aboriginal. There are, in some universities and some departments, critical masses of Aboriginal students.

In these times of fiscal cutback and faculty reduction, even if the university (as an institution) recognized the inappropriateness of the departmental composition, there is no process in place to remedy the situation (other than attrition). For example, the university has little, if any, power to reorganize professors across departments. The administration clearly has no power to force another department such as anthropology or history to take a professor from the Native Studies department. Even if a non-Aboriginal professor in Native Studies recognized the need to give up his (or her) tenured position in the department, there is no mechanism by which to accomplish this without personal and perhaps career hardship.

My experience of the composition of the department of Native Studies in which I teach, as well as of the university that houses us, is not merely conjecture or speculation. The composition of the department and the structure of the university has had a personal impact of some significance. Just a few days prior to my departure for the Critical Race Theory Conference at Yale University in November 1997, I received a telephone call from the acting associate dean in the College of Arts and Science notifying me that the College Review Committee had denied my application for tenure. The most devastating aspect of this denial was the charge that my writing was not up to university standards and that I had not published enough articles in refereed journals.[33]

The committee was also concerned that I did not have a graduate degree. When I was hired, I had completed an honors degree in sociology and held a law degree from Queen's University. Although I had started graduate work in law at Osgoode Hall Law School and completed my course work by May 1989, I had not completed the thesis requirement.[34] My letter of appointment when I was employed some five years later by the University of Saskatchewan was not conditional on the completion of this degree.[35] I am unaware whether the committee considered the fact that I had been educated as a lawyer and that my application to the university had actually been solicited on that basis.

On the plane on the way to the conference at Yale, I took the opportunity to reread the report of the President's Advisory Committee on the Status of Women at the University of Saskatchewan. With the news of the College Review Committee's denial[36] of my tenure only days before leaving for Yale, I was seeking solace in the university experiences of other women. At the same time, I was also trying to organize my thoughts around the presentation I was about to make. As I read, for the first time in my life I could see the experience of gender discrimination before I could identify the discrimination based on race or culture. This was an odd feeling and not one I was perfectly comfortable with, as I had never before experienced gender harassment. I would differentiate harassment based on sex and gender; however, the results are similar.

On the plane on the return trip from Yale, I read selected papers in a book I had purchased while in the United States. I read the paper by Sumi Cho in which she documents the sexualized racial harassment of two Asian women. I was horrified by what had happened to the women. At the same time, I was quite taken with the description of racialized sexual harassment that Professor Cho articulated.[37] However, I was not fully convinced that this term accurately described my experiences at the university. Despite my attraction to the term, I concluded that the harassment I experienced at the University of Saskatchewan was not racialized sexual harassment but sexualized racial harassment.

Professor Cho describes racialized sexual harassment as "a particular set of injuries resulting from the unique complex of power relations facing Asian Pacific American women and other women of colour in the workplace."[38] As she describes,

the process of objectification that affects women in general takes on a particular virulence with the overlay of race upon gender stereotypes. Generally, objectification diminishes the contributions of women, reducing their worth to male perceptions of female sexuality. In the workplace, objectification comes to mean that the material valuation of women's contributions will be based not on their professional accomplishments or work performance but on men's perceptions of their potential to be harassed.[39]

Although it may be only a difference of semantics, I believe that what has happened to me in the year surrounding my tenure application is not sexual harassment. The harassment is racial, but I have been singled out for this treatment because I am a woman. The racialized men in my department do not seem to have the same experience that I have, although I do see patterns and instances where they, too, are treated as "inferior" (or junior) solely because they are Aboriginal. It is for this reason that I have turned the phrase around, placing the emphasis on race. The harassment I have experienced is based on a gendered (or sexualized) construction of the "good Indian."

Professor Cho's work was also important to me, as it gave me the concepts of primary and secondary injury. She describes primary injury as "the offending conduct legally recognized as sexual harassment" and secondary injury as "the actions of employers and institutions that ally with the harrasser."[40] When I first read the article, these phrases did not carry the meaning with which I find them significant today.

In the fall of 1997, several months before the tenure decision, when I returned to the university, I indicated to some of my friends that I was feeling really out of sorts with my job in Native Studies. I was having a difficult time conjuring up the belief that there was hope for the respectful inclusion of Aboriginal systems of knowledge even within the university department that was dedicated to the study of my people. All too often I had experienced the knowledge base of Native Studies as one that objectified Aboriginal people (and peoples) because of the preoccupation with (social) scientific rigor. The tenure struggle interrupted this feeling of hopelessness, and I found myself in the middle of a battle to remain a member of an institution I was not convinced I really wanted to be part of in the first place.

At the first meeting with union representatives,[41] I remember stating that I was not sure whether I wanted to engage and participate in the tenure appeal. I felt very much that I had more power in the face of

the denial than I had ever had within that particular institution. I believed that, in the face of the denial, I had the power to humiliate the institution. I did not have the energy to be asked to fight for my personal survival when I saw so much wrong in the institution that hurt Aboriginal people. I was being asked to engage in a skirmish and ignore the larger war that was being waged around me. At the time, I predicted to several friends that, once the "tenure wars" were complete, I would find myself back in the very same place, hanging on to very little hope that the institution could accommodate Aboriginal aspirations.

Unfortunately, this prediction held true, and this is precisely the place that I returned to thinking of Professor Cho's description of primary and secondary injuries. I would add to this list of harms a third category of injury: the injury of false amelioration. By this I mean the remedy that is created by appearance only. The tenure denial was only a symptom or example of the problem in the way in which I am allowed to occupy space at the university. By fixing only the symptom, the structural and systemic problems continue unabated.

It was my prediction that if the tenure appeal was awarded in my favor, the university and its administrators would begin to treat me as though they had done something "for me." I was to celebrate and be indebted to the institution for being successful in "winning" the battle that should never have been waged. I find this construction of the events incredible. I should never have been subjected to the tenure denial, and even the dean described the committee's decision as "wrong-headed."[42] The tenure denial by the College Review Committee[43] was not about me. It was demonstration of the degree to which equity has been talked about in the institution but still means nothing in the day-to-day operation of the institution. No more was the appeal about me; it was merely an opportunity afforded to me to understand the university at a different level. I see now that I am surrounded by a superficial equity literacy. The institution can write eloquent things, but it does not act in a meaningful way on those very things. The paper on which equity is written does not protect me.

As I prepared for my plenary session at the Critical Race Theory Conference, I felt trapped. Perhaps I should not have gone to the conference, as I was not in a balanced place from which to speak. I was both in pain and terribly confused. The negative tenure decision had not only wounded me, but it had drastically shaken my confidence. I felt trapped because if I did not speak to what was happening in my own life, I would have felt dishonest. How could I stand before a roomful of academics (especially the people of color) on a panel of regard, as a "leading scholar," when I did not "own" that position at home? Yet I did not want to expose such a fresh wound.

On the morning of my session, as I walked to the law school, I knew that I had to tell my story as part of the story of Aboriginal people. I understood that it was a personal confrontation with trust and humility. Even though it was one of the most difficult talks I have ever given, I am glad that I spoke out, spoke up, and talked back. I carried from that room precisely what I had not had when I walked in: strength and courage. As I sat before the tenure-appeal committee, I conjured up all the strength and beauty of the faces, especially the faces of color, in the auditorium at Yale that morning in November. I conjured up the energy you sent me as you stood and put your hands together when my courage faded and my words were gone. That gift of energy came from a circle—a circle of friends and colleagues where I share both sameness and difference. It is the small corner of "home" I have in the academic world.

Yes, my tenure appeal was successful. On January 9, 1998, my appeal was heard before the University Review Committee. This committee, with little deliberation (as one member of the panel shared with me), unanimously supported the granting of my tenure. When I spoke to that committee, I began my comments by sharing that I knew the denial was not about me. Equally important to me was to share with the committee the reasons that this decision was devastating to me. Despite my "success" in the "white" world, I am nevertheless still an "Indian" woman. This means that I have been subjected to and am the object of a lifetime of oppression. Sometimes this oppression is direct and sometimes it is indirect as I sit and watch it unfold in the community around me. As a result, my immediate response to the tenure denial was to accept that I was not as good as a white person and that there was absolutely no sense in trying to prove that I was. I, too, even as professor and privileged, carry with me the kernels of internalized oppression. These kernels, once watered by the attacks on my accomplishments, germinate.

It was not easy to conclude this chapter with the first words I have shared publicly, in writing, on my tenure story. Most days I am not angry or bitter. It does remain difficult to know that the university, the institution of higher learning I once placed on a pedestal, is not a safe place for me. It is not "home" to my Aboriginal intellect. This story does not have a natural end. It is not yet final any more than it is resolved. Yet I am grateful to the small places we tease out of institutions that do not nurture, sustain, or encourage us. Instead, I carry the image of the proud faces of color standing. For now, that image is home.

Notes

Acknowledgments: I pay particular respects to the June 1997 Annual Critical Race Theory Workship in New Orleans and those who attended the bian-nual conference at Yale Law School in the fall of 1997. It is not that I agree with all of Critical Race Theory. I am an Aboriginal woman, and much of what I think and feel differs. But this is the first group of legal scholars with whom I feel safe enough to think out loud.

This paper was also presented at the first Native Studies conference hosted by Boise State University in February 1998 and at the Graduate Students' Conference, "Changing the Climate," at the University of Saskatchewan in March 1998. I thank the various people who provided comments after the three conference presentations. In addition, I pay respects to Professor Denise S. McConney for her helpful comments on an earlier draft.

This paper was concurrently written with two other papers, "Sharing University Experiences: A Preliminary Discussion of Equity Initiatives for Aboriginal Peoples," in *Conference Proceedings: Equity and Graduate Studies,* ed. Kay Armatage (Toronto: University of Toronto Press, 1998), and "Resisting the Boundaries of Academic Thought: Aboriginal Women, Justice and Decolonization," *Native Studies Review* 12 (1998). These three papers are part of a common mosaic.

1. Himani Bannerji et al., eds., *Unsettling Relations: The University as a Site of Feminist Struggles* (Toronto: Women's Press, 1991), 67 (emphasis added).

2. Despite the fact that this will be published in the United States, I defer to the Canadian terminology that refers to citizens of "Native American" nations as Aboriginal people or peoples. The Canadian constitution defines Aboriginal peoples as the "Indian, Inuit and Métis." The Canadian constitution does not further define these three terms.

3. Robert Allen Warrior, *Tribal Secrets: Recovering American Indian Intellectual Traditions* (Minneapolis: University of Minnesota Press, 1995).

4. For a further discussion of law, literature, and storytelling, see Patricia Monture-Angus, "Native America and the Literary Tradition," in *Native North America: Critical and Cultural Perspectives,* ed. Renee Hulan (Toronto: ECW Press, 1998).

5. Judith M. Newman, *Interwoven Conversations: Learning and Teaching Through Critical Reflection* (Toronto: OISE Press, 1991), 11.

6. I have chosen to use this "emotional" concept (feeling). It is not that I do not know. It is not that I have no knowledge or theory to ground this analysis. I do, and it is the knowledge and knowing that took me to the conclusion. And the conclusion is a feeling. In my way of understanding, feeling is a harder place to reach than thinking.

7. I must also acknowledge that I did not participate in this "mission" alone. Two talented and courageous law teachers had already begun this initiative when I arrived at the University of Ottawa. My regards to Darlene Johnston and Cynthia Peterson.

8. A note on my unconventional use of quotation marks seems appropriate here. I use quotation marks whenever the English word I am adopting to fit a Mohawk idea does not really fit. The quotation marks mean "kind of." In other places, they are pointed and used in the spirit of the contrary (a trickster spirit).

9. There are several ways in which the idea of a "rule of law" complicates my relationship to the law. The idea of equality that this rule embraces is one of utter sameness. I acknowledge, as has the Supreme Court of Canada in *O'Malley v. Simpsons-Sears,* 2 S.C.R. 536 (1985), that treating people who are unequal equally actually can result in inequality. I would go a little further than Canada's highest court and note that this perpetuates historic inequality and re-creates it in new forms.

10. It is interesting to note the ironic fact that this siege against Mohawk people carries the name of the "white" town whose local government was attempting to build a golf course over burial grounds. It does not bear the name of the oppressed or dispossessed (perhaps victims): Kahnestake.

11. I discussed this at length in "Self-Portrait: Flint Woman," in Patricia Monture-Angus, *Thunder in My Soul: A Mohawk Woman Speaks* (Halifax: Femwood Publishing, 1995), 44–52.

12. In Canada, federal prisoners are those serving sentences of two years and longer. Provincial prisoners are those serving sentences shorter than two years. This classification of prisoners depends solely on the length of sentence, not the classification of offense. On any given day, approximately 10,000 men are serving federal sentences, while only 500 women are doing so. Because of this drastic difference (one I hope never to see change, unless, of course, the number of federal male prisoners decreases to 500!), prior to 1994, there was only one federal women's prison in Kingston, Ontario. This created the unfortunate, and discriminatory, effect that women did not have the opportunity (as most men did) to serve their sentences in their province of origin (unless, of course, they were from Ontario). In 1990, the Correctional Service of Canada mandated a task force to examine the situation of women prisoners and make recommendation about what to do with the Prison for Women in Kingston. I was one of two Aboriginal members

of the working group of this task force: See Correctional Service of Canada, *Creating Choices: The Report of the Task Force on Federally Sentenced Women* (Ottawa: Correctional Service of Canada, 1990). Based on the recommendation of this task force, Corrections Canada now operates five regional facilities for women, including a healing lodge for Aboriginal women.

13. These phrases are borrowed from the Mission Statement of the Correctional Service of Canada. I borrow them with a sense of irony located in my Mohawk belief that the laws of Canada cannot and do not apply to Mohawk people until our consent is gained. Until then, it is inappropriate to suggest that I am a "law-abiding" Canadian citizen.

14. A. C. Hamilton and C. M. Sinclair, *Report of the Aboriginal Justice Inquiry of Manitoba: The Justice System and Aboriginal People* (Winnipeg: Queen's Printer, 1991), 85-8, 109-13, 658-9.

15. Professor Larry Chartrand, University of Ottawa, personal conversation with the author, October 1997.

16. I discuss my experience as a law student in "Ka-nin-geh-heh-gah-e-sanonh-yah-gah," in Monture, *Thunder in My Soul*, 11-25; my concerns about legal education in "Now That the Door Is Open: Aboriginal Peoples and the Law School Experience," in ibid., 90-118; and of the academy in general in "Flint Woman: Surviving the Contradictions in Academia," in ibid., 53-73.

17. Elsewhere (in Monture, "Flint Woman," 59) I noted: "When I enrolled in law school, I honestly believed that Canadian law would assist Aboriginal people in securing just and fair treatment. This is why I agreed to study law. Since then, I have learned that the Aboriginal experience of Canadian law can never be about justness and fairness for Aboriginal people. Every oppression that Aboriginal people have survived has been delivered up to us through Canadian law. This is true of the taking of our land and our children. Residential schools were established through law. The same is true for the outlawing of our sacred ceremonies and what is currently done to our people in the criminal courts of this land. What I learned long after my law school graduation was that Canadian law is about the oppression of Aboriginal people. My years in law school were so painful because oppression, even if only in study, is a painful experience."

18. I have been asked on more than one occasion by Elders and traditional people not to use this word. "Reserves" are places that were not created by the Indian imagination but thought up by the

"white man." It is a place of our confinement. To be true to who we are as "Indian" nations, we must think in terms of territory.

19. The job advertisement in the newspaper of the Canadian Association of University Teachers read: "Applications are invited for a tenure-track position at the Assistant Professor level in the Department of Native Studies, commencing July 1, 1994. *Consideration will be given to candidate with at least a Masters degree, or equivalent degree(s) or practice experience.* The department is especially interested in candidates with specialization in one or more of the following Native Studies subject areas: Contemporary Native Politics and Self-Government, Justice Systems and Law. Candidates must have an active interest in research. Candidates with other qualifications will be considered. Teaching duties include lecturing in introduction to Native Studies. The Department of Native Studies offers Bachelor of Arts, Bachelor of Arts (Honours) and Special Case Masters of Arts degrees. Candidates should submit a curriculum vitae and arrange for three letters of reference to be forwarded to.... The competition will close when the position is filled. This advertisement is especially directed to Native People in both Canada and the United States. In accordance with Canadian immigration requirements, this advertisement is directed to Canadian citizens and permanent residents. The University of Saskatchewan is committed *to the principles of employment equity*" (emphasis added).

20. I use this term as synonymous with "status Indian"—that is, someone who is entitled to be registered under the provisions of Canada's Indian Act.

21. Without apology after nine years of teaching, I am tired of these so-called university solutions that only absolve "white" guilt.

22. This woman left in June 1995 to take up the headship of Indian Studies at the Saskatchewan Indian Federated College.

23. I admit to my naivete. This should have been a significant warning.

24. During the six months in which this paper was being written, one of the three men resigned his position and accepted the headship at the University of Alberta's Department of Native Studies. The University of Saskatchewan administration has not given us permission to fill this vacancy, explaining that the college was undergoing a review of faculty positions due to fiscal cutbacks. The College of Arts and Sciences was required to eliminate ten such positions before 1999. In fairness to the college, the resignation did not take place until some months

after the university had announced the appointment, and the delay did make it very late in the academic year to secure the exemptions to hire or to conduct a hiring process.

Although I can understand the need for the university to be fiscally responsible, I do not understand why this responsibility is not balanced against the university's commitment to equity. In the 1998–99 academic year, the department comprised four tenured or tenure-stream people and two term positions. Whether we will be allowed to fill the vacant tenure-track position in the future and whether it will be filled by an Aboriginal person (woman) remains to be seen.

25. I understand that on more than one occasion I have offended my departmental colleagues (one threatened to sue me for libel) by doing or speaking this "math" (that is, the mere counting of heads and noting gender and race). I have been labeled a troublemaker and worse. Unfortunately, some members of the university community accept that I am an instigator. What they fail (or refuse) to acknowledge is that I am *responding* to a situation I did not create. That is not "instigating" (and I remain curious about why that is a negative label). It is an issue of "chilly climate" at which I am pointing my finger. My comments point to a structural barrier in how I experience the department. My comments are not personal comments about the three men.

26. The composition of the department discussed in this chapter reflects the situation in the academic year 1997–98.

27. In the fall of 1996, my department secured the approval for a "regular" (as opposed to a special-case) master's program. In September 1997, we admitted our first special-case Ph.D. candidate, a Halfbreed woman.

28. Several of my colleagues have expressed reservations at hiring another lawyer should we receive permission to hire. This idea frustrates me, as a significant number of Aboriginal people have chosen not to pursue graduate studies but have gone to law school instead. There are approximately 600 Aboriginal people in Canada with law degrees (and I presume that this is significantly greater than those who hold Ph.D.s). It seems to me that this desire of both Aboriginal individuals and our communities (as you do not commit to an undertaking as large as a law degree without community input and support) should be respected by the department. The fact that reservations about hiring another lawyer have been expressed also exposes an interesting comment on what the department sees

as interdisciplinarity (that is, that interdisciplinarity is gained by having differently trained scholars in the department).

In addition, I find that their construction of the Aboriginal lawyer is overly narrow. Aboriginal law is an immense field (at least equal in scope to the areas covered by the "mainstream" lawyer). It covers the area from contracts and torts through criminal to corporate law. It includes unique tax problems and unique ownership problems, as well as Aboriginal and treaty-rights questions. To expect a single Aboriginal lawyer to have expertise in all these areas is ridiculous. To construct Aboriginal law around some false and narrow construct of "Aboriginality"—that is, unique, small, and special— is nothing but racism.

29. In 1994, the department secured a new tenure-track position. Until then, the department's complement was four tenure-track positions. In 1992, the department was evaluated by two external reviewers. They noted that, "Indeed, one of the most striking aspects of the current programme is the extent to which it relies on sessional and term teachers; between 1989–90 and 1991–92 these faculty have accounted for almost seventy per cent of the department's annual course offerings": Verna J. Kirkness and Arthur J. Ray, "Evaluation of the Native Studies Department, University of Saskatchewan," *The Kirkness Report* (unpublished), April 15, 1992, 7, copy on file with the author.

30. In Canada, "sessional" is the word used to describe a professor hired and paid on a per-course basis.

31. Kirkness and Ray, "Evaluation," 10–1 (italics in original).

32. It is my suspicion (perhaps hope) that a man of color would not put himself in a position of control (or as part of a "coalition" of control) in a Native Studies department.

33. At the time of my tenure application, I had published one book (not an edited text; it was all my own writing) and had a signed contract for a second book; eight refereed papers; eleven chapters in books; six government-commissioned reports; and five other articles. This publishing record is significantly more substantial than that of the last person who received tenure in my department.

34. One of the pleasant outcomes of this story is that I was finally inspired to finish my LL.M. This degree was granted by Osgoode Hall Law School.

35. I was hired as an associate professor.

36. In October 1997, I secured the department's recommendation for tenure. The Collective Agree-

ment requires that the departmental committee for tenure and promotion decisions comprise five people (who have already been tenured). My department has only three tenured members, of whom one was on an unpaid leave. As a result, my tenure committee comprised two members of the department and three members recruited from other departments (Anthropology, English, and Women's Studies) in the college as selected by the acting dean.

37. See Sumi K. Cho, "Converging Stereotypes in Racialized Sexual Harassment: Where the Model Minority Meets Suzie Wong" in *Critical Race Feminism: A Reader*, ed. Adrien K. Wing (New York: New York University Press, 1997), 203-20, n. 204.

38. Ibid.

39. Ibid., 105.

40. Ibid., 204.

41. I attempted to file a grievance in May 1997 against the university for its failure to provide me with a work environment that was conducive to my work. I was told that the union is unwilling take a stand when the issue pits union members against each other. This position is also expressed in *"Reinventing Our Legacy:* The Chills Which Affect Women," a report by the President's Advisory Committee on the Status of Women at the University of Saskatchewan, which notes: "This [sexual harassment] poses a particular challenge to any union to which a complainant belongs. There are a number of reasons for this. Although in theory the complaint is against the employer because the employer is responsible for maintaining a workplace free of sexual harassment, in practice it can be seen as a dispute between two union members—*with the union caught fast in the middle.* Both the complainant and the alleged harasser have certain rights, including the right to be fairly represented by the bargaining unit. This requires the union to balance the competing interests of each party" (as quoted in *Break-*

ing Anonymity: The Chilly Climate for Women, ed. The Chilly Collective [Waterloo: Wilfrid Laurier University Press, 1995], 197; italics in original).

In reality, it is not the union that is caught squarely in the middle. The inability of unions to balance (perhaps, prioritize) the rights of employees who are being harassed because of their gender, race, or culture against the rights of more "traditional" scholars results in the complete failure of the union to provide remedies for employees who have been harassed.

One of the people I met with on the tenure-denial issue was the very individual who had told me I had no "chilly-climate" grievance against the university, as the conduct I complained about was initiated by a colleague who belonged to the same bargaining unit. This compromised my ability to believe that the union was acting (or could act) in my best interest in the tenure matter.

42. Personal correspondence on file with the author. I remain uncomfortable talking about the tenure decision. There are several layers to this discomfort. First, it is still too fresh a wound. Second, and more distressing for me in the present context, is that I still do not understand the limits of university convention—silent convention, I suspect—about what we professors ought and ought not to write about. The unwritten rule turns me inside-out as it asks me to conspire against my own interest. Sometimes the only power I have is to name the oppression.

43. The College Review Committee was composed of six natural scientists and two social scientists on the day my application was heard. I have considered that legal method, writing, and theory are in many ways unlike method, writing, and theory in both the natural and social sciences. I understand that probably operated against my interests. However, as I was hired as a legal scholar, I find the result not only unfortunate but ironic.

CHAPTER TWELVE

Dinner and Self-Determination

Henry J. Richardson III

Editors' note: This chapter takes the form of a fictional conversation over a private dinner in Malawana, southern Africa, between H. E. Chogwe Bandwere, president of Malawana, and Darnell Jones, professor of international law at First-Rate Law School in the United States.

PRESIDENT BANDWERE: I am pleased to meet you, after hearing the reports of your enthusiastic reception in speaking to our students and faculty at our National Law School. And I appreciate that your trip here from the United States was made possible through the American Embassy by the United States Information Agency and its Overseas Lecture Program.

PROFESSOR JONES: It is likewise good to finally meet you, Your Excellency. I am glad to be able to return to your country after having visited some years ago, shortly after your independence. As you know, I have concentrated in my work on international law on issues affecting African and African-heritage peoples, including my own African Americans. Your faculty and students at National Law School are quite knowledgeable and stimulating. They posed penetrating questions and concerns about interna-

tional law, human rights, and justice, both in Africa and globally. I might add also that some of the most penetrating of these concerns were about the future of this country, with all due respect to you, sir.

PRESIDENT BANDWERE: Yes, I am aware that National University students and faculty generally have problems with my government—whether it and I are sufficiently democratic and representative of the major tribes and other groups in Malawana and how their rights are being violated.[1] I am pleased that you shared your observations, because I invited you to dine privately with me so we could talk frankly and confidentially, and so I could solicit your expertise and insights about world events on matters such as democracy and self-determination. Not only Southern African governments but also many governments around the world face serious problems about governmental authority and demands for changes by dissidents. And I must include in this list several Western governments, including the United States.

PROFESSOR JONES: I have worked on some of these questions, and I am pleased to share what insights I have. I should say, however, in the interest of honesty between us, that you may not like some of the things I might say about the roles of governments and elites and how different approaches to issues of rights, self-determination, and sovereignty might be necessary for the near future. Present conventional wisdom about government leadership in relation to their citizens under international law has become inadequate for fashioning just solutions to these problems.

Further, let me confess that my academic work is part of my own personal process of understanding the relationship of African Americans to international law and global trends as we make our way in the United States. In this regard, I am in your country living through several identities. I am a citizen of the United States, and its land is my land. I am an African American steeped in the Civil Rights Movement, in the history of my people, committed to the best possible future for African peoples and to the enhancement of human dignity for all peoples and persons. I am also an international lawyer and legal scholar who sees international law as the law of the global community, and not least for African peoples.[2] I am a Black man who has understood some of it, but still has much to learn about the contributions of and conditions of women of color as their welfare and rights are affected.[3] And finally, I am all of these, and hopefully a little more, in a person who had it made financially possible to speak at your law school and for us to share this delicious dinner by a decision of an agency of the United States government. I believe the global policies of the United States to be of some use, sometimes, in pointing towards a better future. But American policies are equally part of the global difficulties that you and I are discussing this evening. As the world's remaining superpower, the US has implemented strategies of domination through legal forms that reflect the racism in its domestic policies.

PRESIDENT BANDWERE: Thank you for saying this, because it confirms my original feeling that you and I might share much by speaking freely, across our different but linked backgrounds, as African and African-heritage people who are committed to being as wise and just as possible about the fundamental questions. I was born in a village upcountry from here, before our liberation movement for national independence really got organized. Thanks to my parents and the elders in my village, as well as the help of foreign missionaries, I was pushed to finish secondary school here, and I was able to go to London for my university and law degrees. While there, I joined the overseas wing of our liberation movement, then returned to Malawana to become active in underground activities but also in open political organizing for independence, including undertaking overseas missions through the Malawana Congress Party to expel British colonialism. The party drew most of its membership, as it still does, from my tribe, the Timchewa, but we have reached out to the other two major tribes in Malawana, and after independence I have made that a major priority. The Timchewa still hold the majority of seats in Parliament, but both of the other tribes also have representatives. The judicial system, the armed forces, the national and local civil service, the business sector, and the private commercial sector all have become increasingly diverse among tribal affiliation, as have the legal and other professions.

There is a real sense of nationhood among all peoples in Malawana. I see and feel it as I move around the country, but I am aware that many people believe that the Timchewa dominate, and some do not like it. Some people attribute the free elections that brought me to the presidency four years ago, when the "Old Man"—the father of our Independence—died, to this domination, although I can assure you we did all we could to ensure fairness in voting. I am also aware that concerns about more political and economic participation and representation, such as those you heard at our law school, are not limited to elite groups in Malawana. Finally, you are well aware that we are a developing, middle-size African country, with some natural resources and many human resources within our borders. We are at peace with our neighbors, but we have large development problems and a history as a colonial territory, which still burdens us. We are friendly to the United States, but we watch its actions and those of its multinational corporations, a number of which are invested here, very carefully. We are as active as possible in the United Nations and otherwise in the international community to protect our interests.

PROFESSOR JONES: I was aware of some of this information, but I now understand more from your telling it. As you know, there is much international ferment in the post-Cold War era about critical questions. Issues of sovereignty, self-determination, and internal ethnic and communal conflict within states are challenging the stability of states. United Nations peacekeeping and the role and reform of the United Nations, including the role of the secretary-general, and the issue of how to handle the overweening leverage of the United States are critical to the legal authority of the world's universal international organization. Issues governing the equitable allocation of international trade, investment, and other wealth resources are driven by an enormous concentration on international business and economic reasoning. However, the enforcement of international human rights, and the global demand for increased democracy—or, at least, for more representative government—are being inserted into all these questions. The United States and all of the Northern Tier states, as well as

Malawana and the Southern Tier states, including in Africa, are caught up in these trends.[4]

Increasingly, international legal scholars and decision-makers are questioning the adequacy of the state to protect the rights of its citizens and reduce conflict among them. They are recommending that the international community intervene in more direct ways into states where there is open conflict. The U.S. government, in its self-absorbed role as the world's remaining superpower, has not shared with its own citizens how being a "superpower" has a different meaning in a different world from during the Cold War. Its current actions in the United Nations and other policies generally aim to enhance its own power. We are both aware that all of these issues have a history in the international community that stretches for each country back into the colonial era, and that any proposals of where to go from here cannot be divorced from that history.[5] Would you share with me, Your Excellency, your view of Malawana's position in all of this?

PRESIDENT BANDWERE: I have a great dilemma. The establishment of some international mechanism to defend, for example, human rights and democracy within states might be helpful to all emerging democracies. But what am I to do with my own, and my people's, distrust, and that of other developing peoples, of such mechanisms—a distrust that past interventions have created and with which we are all quite familiar? My own doubts are strong, and it will not be easy to convince our people that this time, this type of intervention with deep consequences for our collective lives, livelihood, and self-image is for a good cause and that it will benefit our right to choose freely who will govern us. It might be worthwhile, indeed, to start a campaign to restore trust among Northern and Southern Tier peoples throughout the world. The big countries, however, must demonstrate that things are now different and that the causes for this type of action are—this time—really just. My dilemma comes from my duty to my people and the trust they repose in me. How, and on what basis, can I consent, and urge my people to consent, to such outside interventions as the best way to help them exert their rights, and not fall into the believing ingenuously that justice or morals are the "normal" reasons for intervention, and thus betray my people's belief in my good judgment and wisdom?

PROFESSOR JONES: It is indeed a dilemma. There is no easy answer, and many groups are responding in many ways, including in the United States and other countries.[6] Not to respond to them is itself a response that may be unfortunate. Many legal scholars and leaders of color in the United States who are concerned with international affairs have long believed that we must introduce progressive concepts into U.S. jurisprudence better to empower peoples of color, and that this is an effective spur to a more just American foreign policy based on the rule of international law, interpreted to protect human dignity. Work toward this objective was begun during the Civil Rights Movement,[7] accelerated during the anti-apartheid and Free South Africa movement,[8] and should become more focused through Critical Race Theory, whose scholars are increasingly addressing these questions. Critical Race Theory and its growing, if contentious, acceptance have for the first time given people of color the opportunity to be jurisprudential producers and help decide which approaches to law will be authoritative, rather than our having to continue to settle for being jurisprudential consumers and working within approaches defined to protect European-directed interests.

PRESIDENT BANDWERE: I have heard of Critical Race Theory, and my ambassador has acquainted me with some of its writings. It seems to be connected to a wider multicultural movement. But I had the impression that these African American scholars and others of color were so buried in the urgency of domestic problems in the cities and the reversal of previously established rights that international questions were being ignored.

PROFESSOR JONES: There is something to what you say. However, there was an early thread of Critical Race Theory inquiry into comparative law questions, as their resolution affects the rights of peoples of color. For example, Richard Delgado used comparative law inquiry to demonstrate the communal as well as individual impact of "hate speech"; he pointed out that under many constitutions other than that of the United States, protection of minorities against hate speech was rightly administered as a justified exception to the right of free speech.[9] Patricia Williams has shown how "African apocalypse disaster" journalism, now so popular with right-wing conservatives, tortures American public discourse in ways that are dehumanizing to Blacks by destroying correct versions of African history in the international community, by laying a foundation for the return of colonialism, and by inviting the American media to compare African conditions negatively and thus remind African Americans that "you all have it so much better in the United States," with the implied threat from whites that this conveys.[10] I used a comparative analysis of international responses to the Los Angeles rebellion of 1992 to show the poverty of American discourse on race, such that it could not frame the question of the responsibility of policymakers in Washington for the conditions leading to that rebellion.[11]

PRESIDENT BANDWERE: What you report may in time have some effect on U.S. policies in ways related to my dilemma. But for the moment, these approaches seem somewhat indirect. Are there other developments that might be more immediately pertinent?

PROFESSOR JONES: Yes, in a sense there are. Recently, RaceCrits, as we are called, have shown a new urgency to address issues of international law directly regarding peoples of color within the United States and majority peoples of color in the international community. A few years ago, Isabelle Gunning addressed the question of female genital mutilation to propose new ways, based on a combination of women's rights and an appreciation of African history, to give such women standing to represent their own interests under international law.[12] Other recent calls have been for RaceCrits to take a hard look at notions of "globalization" and its relationship to international hierarchy, including economic apartheid, and to develop a concept of the "racial economy" of the post-Cold War international transition and its relationship to domestic social transformations.[13]

And in the late 1990s, I, along with other scholars such as Ruth Gordon,[14] challenged the new snappy conservative media label of "failed states," which many conservatives would apply to less-developed countries such as Malawana as a basis for reinstituting colonialism. We have tried to show how destructive such a doctrine would be to peoples of color internationally and in the United States if it were to pass into international law.[15] I have also shown how the divide-and-conquer co-optation strategies used by the U.S. government and France against the African countries, to force the resignation of U.N. Secretary-General Boutros Boutros-Ghali and his replacement by Kofi Annan, were a mirror image of historically and co-optation strategies frequently used against African Americans to prevent "undesirable" Black leaders from being installed.[16] Adrien Wing has given us new legal ground on which to stand through the notion of "spirit injury" as a basis for prosecuting rape as a war crime.[17] Other progressive scholars such as Richard Falk and Gernot Kohler have contributed helpful work, such as the notion of "global apartheid" and the importance of defining international law "as if people really mattered."[18]

Finally, the project of applying Critical Race Theory has received a large boost from our close brothers and sisters, the LatCrits, who in a symposium led by scholars such as Elizabeth Iglesias, Berta Hernández, and Jose Alvarez went beyond simply stating the need for widespread CRT inquiry into international law and actually began to lay out approaches in some detail to address the subordination of peoples of color, including Latina/o peoples in the American hemisphere, through North American legal interpretations.[19] RaceCrits must now profit from this work and push our more Afrocentric inquiries with greater speed.

PRESIDENT BANDWERE: What you are saying does bring me a little closer to my dilemma. But I feel we have not addressed its heart. The response to your talk this afternoon is not the first time that scholars and others among my people have denounced my government as violating their rights by not representing all of the tribal and communal traditions of the country. They and all other similar groups proclaim that they have rights of self-determination under international law against my government, which should be immediately enforced. I feel caught between those demands, which do not seem to have the welfare of the nation at heart, and my experience, which teaches me that giving in to such demands will tend to fragment the country and produce conditions that threaten the development we have achieved.

Further, I have other indications that pursuing such a path will make Malawana less attractive to outside foreign investors, and we need their capital, technology, and new jobs for our continued development. I am in favor of human rights, but they must be in proper balance with the duties of each citizen to the state.[20] We have many problems, many of which are caused by outside forces and Northern Tier policies that are beyond our control. Yet I am aware that, since the end of the Cold War, global demands for self-determination are very prevalent, and they affect what will happen in Malawana. I have already begun planning for elections within the next two years, as our constitution dictates, but my dilemma continues.

PROFESSOR JONES: I agree that the right of self-determination of peoples is key here, and I understand how claims to this right by groups within Malawana are troublesome to you and your government. In the post-Cold War period there have been many claims to this right by peoples within states around the world: in Africa, Eastern Europe, the former Soviet Union, and Mexico, to give only a partial list. The process of collective claim to this right has now become part of the constitutive structure of the international community; it is not simply isolated instances of local rebellions. Based in part on this pattern of facts, an international human right to representative government has also been confirmed through the clarifying work of Thomas Franck.[21] So the facts recognized as critical to legal interpretation have already begun to change. One question is whether international legal doctrine will adapt in equitable ways.

PRESIDENT BANDWERE: I think I understand your points about international law. But now I must ask how well Malawana's interests will be protected as that law develops in the way you describe.

Our self-determination is being threatened by several factors, both internal and external. For example, our labor unions played a large and valuable role in our independence struggle. But now their leadership has been taken over by people who are dedicated to elevating the immediate welfare of their members above any legitimate government policy, and they are opposing any measure that I, as president, propose. We believe that outside influences are playing a role here.

Also, we have recently organized a small stock market to make Malawana a regional capital-trading center in Africa and attract international equity capital. Until last month, we had retained a major economic consulting firm from London to advise our Central Bank and Treasury on establishing certain supportive domestic and monetary economic policies. We decided that we had learned all we could from them and that we had sufficient talent of our own to do that work. So we let them go and replaced their jobs with African economists and bank officials. I tell you that this was so negatively viewed in London, New York, and other European financial centers that our major stock-market index dropped by 50 percent in two days, and trading had to be halted. This is a direct strike on our economy by European and American financial interests based on their negative stereotypes about Africans' inability to administer modern national—especially economic and financial—policy.

PROFESSOR JONES: This sounds like international racism through economic strategies. Modern international law has always found it difficult—assuming that its decision-makers are operating in good faith—even to frame these problems you report as issues for a legal remedy. Many legal scholars and social scientists consider international economic racism to be the effect of the vagaries of an "international free market," and thus beyond appropriate legal regulation. And international law has been so state-centric that linked processes operating inside and outside a given state are usually defined in segmented ways, assigning responsibility according to the territory where such consequences—such as your labor union problems—occur. This jurisprudence is much too limited; indeed, it is being criticized not only by critical race theorists, but also by many other progressive scholars and officials.

PRESIDENT BANDWERE: I believe I understand. But I have to say that our sovereignty as a nation is threatened from yet another, more recent direction. I am sure you are aware of demands made by the United States and other rich countries to most developing countries, including more African countries, that we take equal steps to curb our greenhouse-gas emissions to any obligations in this regard on those rich countries. Your American ambassador has been to see me several times on this subject, both before and after the Kyoto Conference in 1988 on climate change. Malawana fought very hard in Kyoto against such a principle, because it is unjust and crippling for us to stifle our economic growth just when we are "taking off." And all the data show that the United States is the biggest polluter of all. Nevertheless, the American ambassador has threatened economic pressure against us if we do not go along, which we have refused to do. So we will see. Because the United States and other industrialized countries also did not offer to contribute any of the very high costs to us of the expensive technology for our factories to curb their emissions, we see no reason to cooperate. And I believe that even were such aid forthcoming, it would benefit only a small elite group of our people—and certain international investors.

You, Professor Jones, talk to me about international law. Yet it seems to me that your country, the United States, is trying to impose a principle of "false equality" among rich nations and developing nations as a means of controlling the entire system of international law. Such a situation works against Malawana's interests, and I cannot accept it. I have told you of several ways that recent international trends are affecting Malawana and other African states. I fear that opposition groups will take advantage of my government's difficulties in resolving these questions. Can you provide additional context to help me further understand how these trends affect African-heritage peoples?

PROFESSOR JONES: Perhaps I can do so by changing the focus somewhat. Implicit claims to the right of self-determination by African-heritage peoples as against Europeans go all the way back to the beginning of Afro-American history in the early seventeenth century, arising virtually throughout the New World. The notion of "claims to self-determination" could be extended to slave opposition and revolts against the international slave system during the same period and earlier. This includes those peoples in Africa who tried to oppose or opt out of the European-sponsored slave-supply system to feed the international slave trade. Their spiritual history incorporates the great African empires from the ninth century forward, such as Songhai.

Periodically, in slaveholding territories, these revolts resulted in "maroon communities," in which Blacks—sometimes with Latino/a and Indigenous peoples' help—organized themselves into functioning communities that were as independent as they could make them. These immediately became military targets for slaveholders who correctly perceived the threat they represented, in ideology and practice, to international slavery. The Republic of Palmares in

Brazil in the late sixteenth century was the capstone, remaining viable for more than sixty years. Those communities that were not quickly conquered were negotiated with, often with a degree of "sovereignty" conceded to them by slaveholders under "treaties." These concessions were part of wider interlocking strategies for healing breaks in the international slave system by using local techniques of co-optation and division. Maroon communities were thus a claim by Blacks to the right of a group enabling it to decide its own political destiny as freely as possible in the circumstances. Maroon communities were formed for Black people to escape from slavery but equally for *self-defense* against the inherent violence of the slave system and the inevitable deadly counterattacks of white European slaveholders and their governments.

PRESIDENT BANDWERE: Yes, I remember similar ideas coming out during the most intense times of our armed liberation struggle for Malawanan independence. We were organizing to *defend* ourselves against the colonial regime. But we were also organizing for a new future of freedom. We successfully made our revolution and assumed the heavy responsibilities of a modern African state. We have achieved sovereignty as a nation by fighting for self-determination as a people. All our people must now realize this and move forward. I fear that many still do not.

PROFESSOR JONES: I think you have just restated part of your dilemma. You believe that the right of self-determination was fulfilled on the achievement of statehood. But others among your people may disagree on this issue. This can raise complex issues.

Orlando Patterson has argued that modern self-determination claims by Blacks, African Americans, and Africans are founded primarily on "brotherhood," which, he in turn argues, must be a means

only to other substantive goals.[22] I believe that Patterson is only half correct, because the primary goal historically is self-defense against slaveholders' military aggression and, later in Africa, against colonial military aggression. It continues today as self-defense of Blacks and other peoples of color against cultural aggression, spirit injury, rights reversal, and economic aggression by whites and conservatives. I cannot readily separate "self-defense" from "brotherhood," because we have had to defend ourselves for so long.

The basic self-defense goal is already incorporated into international law as legal support for the use of force by liberation movements, including your own struggle in Malawana. And Patterson warns that "brotherhood" may well become a rationale for fascism.[23] This warning is, I believe, premature so long as the "brotherhood" objectives on the ground support self-defense and survival objectives, and as long as outside aggression promises harm in any meaningful way to that group. We can hope that, in the future, such organized self-defense will be unnecessary, but the burden will be heavy for the near future on all who assert this. Thus, with all respect, Your Excellency, groups among your citizens may be being harmed in ways that are quite damaging to them, but that are difficult to perceive from outside if your government officials are not open to new forms of communication and learning.

PRESIDENT BANDWERE: This is helpful. I believe my government can consider how to make new approaches to dissident groups.

PROFESSOR JONES: Yes, that might be a beginning. But I must emphasize that, just as the first major wave of self-determination claims for decolonization in the 1950s and '60s defined matters of fundamental rights, so does this second wave. This time, such rights are related to peoples who are internal to established states where there are problems and potential violence. Thus, this is not only a process question; it is also a question of substantive rights that forces governments to confront their claimed prerogatives of sovereignty in each situation.

PRESIDENT BANDWERE: I hear your point, but if I followed its logical implications in Malawana there would be other kinds of difficulties. However, I also understand you to say that self-determination is both an international movement, once again, and a legal right. Am I correct?

PROFESSOR JONES: Yes. W.E.B. Du Bois framed the essential self-determination question at the Versailles Peace Conference by demanding that it be applied not only to Southern European peoples *within* the colonial system, but also to peoples of color *subject to* colonialism around the world. His insight that the problem of this century is that of the colorline,[24] which has been reiterated for the next century by John Hope Franklin, posed the huge methodological question to white scholars, which they have largely ducked or denounced:[25] to prove or disprove the proposition when the accepted methodologies are not formulated to recognize racism in international relations. It also anticipated U.N. General Assembly findings seventy years later that the right of self-determination is seminal to protecting all other human rights. Finally, he correctly saw that protecting the right of self-determination (and other fundamental rights) for peoples of color throughout the world was essential to protecting them for African Americans.

PRESIDENT BANDWERE: But Du Bois was heavily criticized for his views in the United States, was he not, including by many Black Americans?

PROFESSOR JONES: Yes, he was. In fact, he was ejected from the NAACP in the late 1940s.[26] In part, this was a reflection of the volatility of the notion of self-determination for Black people in America in the face of pervasive racism, two world wars, and the rise of the decolonization movement. Blacks who argue for self-determination have been labeled "dangerous extremists" by most whites, and many Blacks have bought into this. Yet there has always been a continuing thread of such claims, which has sometimes resulted in action, such as by the Republic of New Africa in the early 1970s, which demanded a separate state in the South. White America reacted violently to this. In fact, most African Americans call America home, but within that framework they search for empowerment through a mixture of autonomy and assimilation that they can control. Thus, implicit claims for the right of self-determination for African Americans as an internal, or encapsulated, people remain alive in the United States, and they are symbiotic with the international trends we are discussing.

PRESIDENT BANDWERE: So you are saying that even if Malawana progresses in its national economic development over the years to attain levels of progress akin to Northern Tier states, internal claims for self-determination by various groups within our country may persist?

PROFESSOR JONES: Yes, I believe so, but it depends on how authentically and constitutively representative any Malawanan government is of its peoples. This is the core of today's global claims for self-determination. Equally important is how governments, including African governments, and Northern and Southern Tier elites interpret the right of self-determination. Part of the current problems with peoples and states is that the right under conventional—that is, state-driven—doctrine is interpreted to preserve the existing national state system and current governments in each state. With all due respect to you, Your Excellency, this fits nicely with alliances between African or other Southern Tier elites and elites in Group of Seven countries to perpetuate their own rule. Such alliances aim to preserve the status quo for, among other things, European-beneficial investment-protective stability in each state or arms-supply agreements to preserve developing country regimes that are friendly to Northern Tier elites.

The application of state-centric views on self-determination also supports the conventional legal interpretation of the "ability of national states to carry out their international obligations." It does so by heavily referring to states' capacity and willingness to honor their contracts with Northern Tier commercial interests, including not being too politically fragmented to do so with the degree of business efficiency demanded by those interests. Thus, the suppression of the right to representative government of the common folk in Africa, regarding either reforming their home state or in their international legal ability to form another state, is linked to postulated reciprocity among sovereign states' being maintained by a *limited* legal interpretation of self-determination.

In order to cure this use of international law and self-determination to maintain structures of domination, people of color might have to push to reaffirm the right of self-determination for internal peoples on the local level and push to get direct international assistance to empower them to enjoy this right on an ongoing basis. In order to do this, some jurisprudential standpoint is needed from which actions of sovereigns can be normatively assessed as a basis to, among other things, widen international scrutiny into uncovering and defining subtle forms of oppression against common Black folk.

PRESIDENT BANDWERE: I am getting somewhat disturbed by your position. My government, faced with serious problems, does

its best, as do I, to be honest and fair toward all our people. Yet you say not only that this is not enough, but that unless some impossible standard of representative government and internal self-determination is met, my government and numbers of other governments might be illegitimate under international law. I do not believe this to be a correct statement of international law. My government must ensure stability in Malawana in order to protect the general welfare of all its people.

PROFESSOR JONES: You are correct that conventional interpretations of self-determination put out by many foreign offices, based on state practice and excluding all other forms of international authority, do not agree with my analysis. But as long as state practice remains the primary approach to international law, the rights of peoples and groups within a state to be free of local oppression are very difficult to define, much less protect, particularly because under the same interpretations national governments have great leeway legally to use military force—and worse—to suppress such groups. Those groups then have two choices under conventional legal interpretations: either "shut up" or work toward an illegal secession from the country. Putting them in this kind of legal box only raises the potential for violence.

However, even under a positivistic territorial-sovereignty–based jurisprudence, there is precedent for international recognition of groups of internal peoples by outside states—namely, under the old doctrine of recognition of belligerency. That doctrine allowed outside neutral states to recognize internal groups in a second state who had militarily seized control of territory from the central government to allow international commerce to carry on in spite of the loss of part of its territory by the central government. But the major problem then was predictive of the continuing problem today: in order for such groups and peoples to protect themselves and enjoy a right of self-determination that was internationally recognized, they had to be militarily successful, with all the destruction and loss of life that entails. They had no other option in law. Blood was considered an appropriate price to maintain territorial sovereignty as the basis of international law.[27]

Even after the doctrine of recognition of belligerency was folded into the law of the U.N. Charter, you yourself were caught up in a similar situation during the time of decolonization: Liberation movements usually had to be militarily successful—at least, to the point of imposing heavy costs on the colonial regime. The right of self-determination had to be earned by violence and only by violence. Now there are expectations that these premises should change, especially regarding this second post-Cold War global demand by internal peoples to self-determination. This is my position.

PRESIDENT BANDWERE: You are being unrealistic. I will not simply turn the national government over to any dissident group that asks for it. Some of these people are only after power for their own corrupt ends.

PROFESSOR JONES: If you define the problem that way, you are correct that doing so will lead to more trouble. But, Your Excellency, please reflect on the fact that part of the price of your being a national president under current sovereignty-driven interpretations of international law is that you are forced to believe that 1) any "dissident" of any consequence must be suppressed or the entire state will unravel; and 2) it is the *sole* responsibility of your government and you as its president to "save" the state because you are the "sovereign," and that is the essence of sovereignty. This is why people coming from this vantage point view the right of self-determination as a threat and

are devoted to narrow interpretations of the right.

PRESIDENT BANDWERE: You are correct. That is what I believe, and that is my interpretation of my own experience.

PROFESSOR JONES: Your answer, as an African leader in a state that is having problems, underscores the importance of new approaches to international law, to give leaders such as you more options and to give people in Malawana who may be oppressed or feel themselves oppressed more options without either side reflexively resorting to violence. Let me make two further observations. First, the genie of global claims to self-determination cannot be put back in the bottle, including the claims of peoples of color wherever they are located. The right to self-determination is a fundamental one. Experience has shown that it cannot be abrogated, and attempts to interpret it out of existence have failed. Therefore, all governments must establish some new relationship with the identified peoples and groups among their citizens. Second, international legal process through the United Nations has begun to stir in response, and proposals are being made to institutionalize the United Nations' ability to carry out preventive diplomacy within states, even without their government's consent, if a situation of oppression and potential violence warrants it. Up to now, the competence of the secretary-general, for example, to do such fact-finding and mediation was limited to ad hoc informal measures, mostly dependent on government consent, and we still have those problems today.

PRESIDENT BANDWERE: I do not like or agree with your last point at all. I must retain the authority to consent to any mission from outside coming into this state, especially if it aims to deal with such sensitive problems.

PROFESSOR JONES: Your Excellency, with all due respect, you have just stated a core element of the problem. The fact that the law upholds sovereign consent for all governments has helped create the very difficulties that Malawana and other states are now having with internal groups and peoples. The present "wisdom" of trying to restrict the right of self-determination, instead of reaffirming it under U.N. Charter principles at the local level, is exhausted. You may withhold your consent to actions by the secretary-general that other tribes in Malawana will have directly requested, but it is a dynamic situation, and conventional legal interpretations, including interpretations of the authority of your consent in the face of a claim of self-determination, will not solve it. They will lead to more conservatives in European states yelling about "failed states" and demanding the recolonization of Africa. More international scrutiny of the right kind, not less, is needed, for internal groups being oppressed to have options under international law other than violence against your government. Some way must be found to extend to them international recognition of their right to self-determination without their having to resort to overthrowing your government.

But likewise, some way must be found so that national governments are truly representative of all peoples in the territory rather than functioning through strategies of domination and oppression, even subtle and sophisticated oppression. Otherwise, such governments should not continue to get the benefits of being recognized as "the government." I have elsewhere recommended that the U.N. secretary-general be authorized to establish Mediating Forums to evaluate which groups, including the government, are willing to abide by U.N. Charter's principles, and reach a new and more just constitutive accommodation in the country, then to extend international recognition to those groups.

PRESIDENT BANDWERE: I am unhappy, and indeed angry, at your implicit accusations of me and my government. We did not fight a liberation struggle to have a bunch of dissidents undermine the state. I believe this dinner is close to being over.

PROFESSOR JONES: If I could prevail on your patience and generous hospitality, Your Excellency, for one final observation: International law has done you and other leaders a disservice by putting the entire burden of saving the state on your shoulders and giving you only power-oriented, dominating strategies by which to do so as they relate to your people's desire to be truly represented. If what I have said tonight is at all correct, then trends are pushing the international community under its law into picking up part of that burden and sharing it so that it no longer rests on you alone. Thus, your highest responsibility will be not to repress those groups who are oppressed and claim greater autonomy, but to avail yourself of international assistance, under U.N. Charter principles, that will help bring about a new relationship between those internal groups willing to work with other groups to reach a new national accommodation with a national government of the same spirit.

PRESIDENT BANDWERE: I believe you have said enough. Thank you for coming and sharing your thoughts. Good night, Professor Jones.

PROFESSOR JONES: Good night, Your Excellency, and thank you for your hospitality.

Notes

Acknowledgment: This chapter was presented in preliminary form as a paper at the 1997 Critical Race Theory Conference at Yale University. I am grateful for the warm reception and helpful comments from that panel session. The notes below reflect the initial appearance of the cited concepts by either person in this fictional dialogue.

1. A. Peter Mutharika, "The Role of International Law in the Twenty-First Century: An African Perspective," *Fordham International Law Journal* 18 (1995): 1706.

2. Henry J. Richardson III, "The Gulf Crisis and African-American Interests under International Law," *American Journal of International Law* 87 (1993): 42.

3. Hope Lewis, "Women (Under) Development: The Relevance of 'The Right to Development' to Poor Women of Color in The United States," *Journal of Law and Policy* 18 (July–October 1996): 281.

4. See generally Henry J. Richardson III, "'Failed States,' Self Determination and Preventative Diplomacy: Colonialist Nostalgia and Democratic Expectations," *Temple International Comparative Law Journal* 10 (1996): 1, discussing patterns of dominance and discrimination among Northern and Southern Tier national states.

5. Makau wa Mutua, "The Banjul Charter and the African Cultural Fingerprint: An Evaluation of the Language of Duties," *Virginia Journal of International Law* 35 (1995): 339; idem, "Why Redraw the Map of Africa: A Moral and Legal Inquiry," *Michigan Journal of International Law* 16 (Summer 1995): 1113.

6. See generally Virginia Gambo, "Justified Intervention? A View from the South," in *Emerging Norms of Justified Intervention*, ed. Laura W. Reed and Carl Kaysen (Cambridge, Mass.: Committee on International Security Studies, American Academy of Arts and Sciences, 1993), 115, 121, referring to the "Delgado Dilemma." Briefly, the Delgado Dilemma, named for the scholar who first posed it, refers to the dilemma faced by many Third World leaders in trying to identify *constructive* Northern Tier-sponsored interventions into their countries in the name of "democracy" after so many bitter experiences with *destructive* interventions from the same sources: see Richardson, "Failed States," 12–13.

7. Henry J. Richardson III, "African-Americans and International Law: For Professor Goler Teal Butcher, with Appreciation," *Howard Law Journal* 37 (Winter 1994): 217.

8. Richardson, "Gulf Crisis," 50–1.

9. Richard Delgado, "Words That Wound: A Tort Action for Racial Insults, Epithets, and Name Calling," in *Critical Race Theory: The Cutting Edge*, ed. Richard Delgado (Philadelphia: Temple University Press, 1995), 159–68.

10. Patricia J. Williams, "Alchemical Notes: Reconstructing Ideals from Deconstructed Rights," in Delgado, *Cutting Edge*, 84.

11. Henry J. Richardson III, "The International Implications of the Los Angeles Riots," *Denver University Law Review* 70 (1993): 213.

12. Isabelle R. Gunning, "Arrogant Perception, World-Traveling and Multicultural Feminism: The Case of Female Genital Surgeries," in *Critical Race Feminism: A Reader*, ed. Adrien K. Wing (New York: McGraw-Hill, 1997), 352; see also Hope Lewis, "Between Irua and 'Female Genital Mutilation': Feminist Human Rights Discourse and the Cultural Divide," in Wing, *Critical Race Feminism*, 352.

13. Kimberlé W. Crenshaw, Neil Gotanda, Gary Peller, and Kendall Thomas, "Introduction," in *Critical Race Theory: The Key Writings That Framed the Movement*, ed. Kimberlé Crenshaw, Neil Gotanda, Gary Peller, and Kendall Thomas (New York: New Press, 1995), xxx.

14. Ruth E. Gordon, "United Nations Intervention in International Conflicts: Iraq, Somalia and Beyond," *Michigan Journal of International Law* 15 (1994): 519; see also idem, "Some Legal Problems with Trusteeship," *Cornell International Law Journal* 28 (Spring 1995): 301.

15. Richardson, "'Failed States.'"

16. Henry J. Richardson III, "Africa In-Depth, Ouster of Boutros-Ghali a Painful Loss to United Nations," *Philadelphia Sunday Sun*, January 12, 1997, 8.

17. Adrien K. Wing, "Brief Reflections Toward a Multiplicative Theory and Praxis of Being," in Wing, *Critical Race Feminism*, 27; Adrien K. Wing and Christine A. Willis, "Sisters in the Hood: Beyond Bloods and Crips," in Wing, *Critical Race Feminism*, 243; Adrien K. Wing and Eunice P. de Carvalho, "Black South African Women: Toward Equal Rights," in Wing, *Critical Race Feminism*, 387. See also Patricia J. Williams, "Spirit-Murdering the Messenger: The Discourse of Finger Pointing as the Law's Response to Racism," in Wing, *Critical Race Feminism*, 229.

18. Richard Falk, "Contending Approaches to the World Order," in *Toward a Just World Order*, ed. Richard Falk, Samuel S. Kim, and Saul H. Mondlovitz (New Brunswick, N.J.: Transaction Publishers, 1982), 146; Gernot Kohler, "Global Apartheid," in Falk et al., *Just World Order*, 315–25.

19. Elizabeth M. Iglesias, "International Law, Human Rights and LatCrit Theory," *University of Miami Inter-American Law Review* 28 (1996–97): 177.

20. See *African Charter on Human and Peoples' Rights* (Addis Ababa: Organization of African Unity (OAU) General Secretariat, Division of Press and Information, 1981).

21. See generally Thomas M. Franck, "The Democratic Entitlement," *University of Richmond*

Law Review 29 (Winter 1994): 1, discussing the growth in the international system of the expectation that those in power govern with the consent of the governed; idem, "The Emerging Right to Democratic Governance," *American Journal of International Law* 86 (1992): 46, discussing the international institutions involved in democratic governance and the complexities of the right to democracy in accordance with global public policy.

22. Orlando Patterson, *The Ordeal of Integration, Progress and Resentment in America's 'Racial Crisis'* (Washington, D.C.: Conterpt Publisher, 1997), 99-103.

23. Ibid.

24. Gerald Horne, *Black and Red: W.E.B. Du Bois and the Afro-American Response to the Cold War 1944–63* (New York: State University of New York Press, 1986). Cf. David Levering Lewis, *W.E.B. Du Bois: The Fight for Equality and the American Century, 1919–1963* (New York: Henry Holt, 2000), 59-60.

25. Richardson, "'Failed States.'"

26. Ibid.

27. Ibid., 75-6.

Section C: Globalization

Critical Race Theory in Global Context

Celina Romany

THE LONG ABSENCE of "critical" schools of thought in legal academia has paved the way for Critical Race Theory in this country. It is now clear that critical perspectives on racial and gender subordination—perspectives that reflected the experiences of subordinated people—were long overdue. As an alternative methodology and a source of theoretical and practical knowledge, CRT has shown in this past decade that critical perspectives on social, political, and economic subordination must give space to marginalized voices. This collage of voices has made CRT a significant critical force in legal theory.

With respect to international law, critical legal studies scholars have elaborated strong critiques of positivist and formalist thinking.[1] Yet these critiques fail to consider issues of race and ethnicity. Moreover, they often dwell too long on the theoretical plane and fail to move beyond negative critique. CRT's critique of race and gender subordination is therefore pivotal to any new approaches to international and comparative law. Nevertheless, the complexity of racial, gender, and economic subordination in the global landscape requires caution, particularly given that critical race theorists aim to transcend negative critique and create a jurisprudence of reconstruction.[2]

A history of Critical Race Theory is of particular importance in exploring its potential contribution to international law, international human rights and comparative law. The influence of colonial/post-colonial studies, fueling the force of CRT's critique in the international domain, must be acknowledged.[3] Colonial/post-colonial studies pioneered a critical view of internal colonial systems of law and of an international legal framework, indebted to a Western Enlightenment project, *passing* for universal.[4] As a multilayered analysis, an anti-colonial perspective proved to be a more encompassing critique than the one-dimensional class analysis that prevailed during the Cold War era. With the end of the Cold War, the constraints of a "class-only" analysis became more evident. Violent conflicts today are a bitter reminder of the failure to recognize the alleys of identity subordination within a stratified world.

The diversity of theoretical currents that shape CRT should not obscure its international potential. As Angela Harris has noted, CRT's modern/postmodern impulses are not crippling contradictions, but strengths to be celebrated. Particularly given its commitment to liberation politics,[5] CRT's internal diversity can only harden the spine of its critical scope.

CRT—Distant Encounters

As a scholar/activist residing in the United States[6] and in conversations with friends and colleagues from Latin America about the "politics of location," I become more aware of CRT's national specificity. Sometimes I engage my interlocutors with a fierce defense of its international potential. In my best attempts to become a theoretical translator, I become Andromeda.

Describing a jurisprudence of "reconstruction" that focuses on the social construction of race and that moves beyond more class-focused progressive critiques brings up a lot of questions. What do I mean by race? Race as a social construct, as culture?[7] What are the differences between race and ethnicity? Can such an analysis be nationally specific? Are there any regional common denominators? Does a U.S.-based CRT analysis properly deal with historical variables of slavery and of racial mixture, with multiple racial categories? How can the "minority" CRT approach—stemming from the demographic reality of African Americans and other ethnic groups in the United States—be extrapolated to predominantly black societies such as Brazil and to the rest of the Latin American and Caribbean countries, with their significant number of Mestizos?[7] What debt is owed to theory-of-liberation icons such as Frantz Fanon[8] and Aimé Césaire,[9] who emerged during the 1960s from this region?

Does "race-as-a-social-construct" adequately capture the multidimensionality of colonial/post-colonial exploitation? What about the rise of neo-liberal capitalism and, in turn, the impact of transnational capital on nation-states and on forms of racial and ethnic subordination?

As we enter the more specific world of international law and human rights, we swim in deeper waters. How do we reconcile an individual-rights paradigm with group rights and collective struggles for self-determination, such as those waged by indigenous peoples within this region? How do we extrapolate a politics of difference and resistance located in the United States that, when carried to the world of international politics, wears a homogeneous U.S. label?

These are some of the questions that should inspire dialogues between CRT scholars and their international counterparts. Some of these questions are addressed by the essays collected in this section, illustrating the complexity, yet potential strength, of the knowledge derived from such dialogues.

Racialization Maneuvers

Analyzed by CRT scholars, the study of how "racial categories are created, inhabited, transformed and destroyed"[10] offers layers of critique for international law and international relations. Likewise, the international human-rights scenario presents the opportunity to critique, against the background of racializing practices, national applications of a model of universal and individual rights that neglect social and economic forces of marginalization. In addressing different international legal scenarios, the diversely positioned authors in this group of essays seize on racialization maneuvers as a common theme in CRT's attempt to develop alternative notions of democracy and freedom.

Racialization maneuvers at both international and national levels appear in different forms in these chapters: in visions of liberal equality in international human-rights law that fail to recognize the absence of justice in the family (Hernández); in internal policies of nation-states that marginalize key ingredients of participatory democracy, such as economic rights (Iglesias); in the entrenchment of a "dominant gaze" in narratives of development (Carrasco); and in universalistic human-rights notions that, in assessing cultural practices, devalue difference (Gunning). The pervasive colonialist impulse of "Northern" values and practices in the articulation and enforcement of international human rights (in sync with the geopolitical hegemony of the "North") constitutes the face of a legitimation crisis in these fields. As "jurisprudential producers," CRT scholars center their critique in the positive and negative forces of this legitimation crisis.

Self-determination, Globalized Citizenship, and Economic and Social Rights

In her chapter, Berta Hernández-Truyol presents a refined version of the requisite two-way street. Using international human-rights discourse as a platform to pierce the veil of sovereignty, Hernández submits it to a CRT assessment in her effort to reconstruct its master narrative of equality. CRT becomes the deconstructive lens for exposing the hegemonic influences and controls in prevalent conceptualizations of equality. Gender omissions and hierarchical stratification of rights that leave the experiences of marginalized sectors outside codifications are to be corrected by "globalizing localism" and by "localizing a globalism."

After examining contradictions in conventions dealing with discrimination, especially the omission of "sex" in the Race Dis-

crimination Convention, Hernández urges the deployment of "local" critical race feminist accounts to revise international versions of equality and non-discrimination. Equally important is the use of CRT in deconstructing the hierarchies ingrained in "generational stories" of international human rights, stories loaded with liberal values that segregate the political from the "socioeconomic." The concept of "race" is also subject to critiques that expose the limits of the black–white paradigm. On the localizing-globalization front, Hernández views the possibilities of cross-fertilization in having international recognition of private family life subjected to local critiques of notions of family life that serve to perpetuate the subordination of women.

Furthermore, Hernández is engaged in a jurisprudence of reconstruction. In re-visioning equality at the levels of national and international human rights—a prerequisite for her concept of globalized citizenship—she suggests that we transcend the rigid boundaries that exist among political, social, cultural, and economic rights. The re-visioning is not about individuals as independent of immediate social or political conditions, she says. Rather, it is about individuals having and living within varied cultures and communities.

In the economic realm, Elizabeth Iglesias extends to the critical race theoretical model an invitation to venture into the deeper waters of a reconstructed class analysis. Reminding us of the centrality of law as a discursive and material producer of racial spaces, she takes us on a journey through the domestic and global alleys of poverty in order to show the implication and pervasive presence of law in perpetuating the frozen niches of dispossession. Iglesias unmasks the racialization maneuvers embedded in neoliberal economic policies that reify a color-blind free market, while offering a much needed reformulation of the relationship between *classical* and *class* analysis and the politics of identity. In doing so, Iglesias highlights the embeddedness of neo-colonial constructions in the creation of the racialized "closed borders that constrain the free-market flows" and inserts the identity politics model, absent in alternative progressive critiques of global neo-liberal constraints.

Hernando de Soto's institutional class approach serves as a "counterpoint"/departure for exposing the role of law in producing institutional arrangements that strip collective political identities of their transformative potential in the struggle for social justice. Through "interpretive spaces," law (legal doctrines such as the business-judgment rule and minority business set-asides) rhetorically manipulates the economic-political dichotomy and ultimately suppresses the democratization of power.

In examining the normalizing processes of two law regimes—the World Bank Inspection Panel (the "regulation" of development lending) and the provisions of the Community Reinvestment Act of 1977—Iglesias demonstrates the potential that Critical Race Theory has for delegitimating the political-economic dichotomy that frames critiques along the loaded categories of "efficient markets" and "inefficient special-interest political interventionism." The unpacking of the assumptions informing these constructions are key platforms for critiques of the compartmentalization that permeates institutional development policies and the international human-rights law framework. The Chixoy River Dam project in Guatemala is a tragic example of such compartmentalization, and the hierarchical and dichotomous relationship between social and economic and political and civil rights comes to mind, as well. Iglesias is on the right path when she reminds us that "to *do* critical theory is precisely to struggle over the way we should *understand* and hence *resist* the production of subordination."

Cultural Devaluation

The limitations of a race analysis that does not incorporate broader notions of culture—the zone of "occult instability where the people dwell"[11]—was noted in the early stages of CRT scholarship.[12] These early theorists were recognizing colonialism's oxygen: cultural inferiorization and devaluation. It is through the "strategy of disavowal ... where the trace of what is disavowed is not repressed but repeated as something different—a mutation, a hybrid"[13] that cultural devaluation makes its social entrance. Early colonial critiques had a clear understanding that without cultural imperialism—dispersed and normalized in everyday cultural practices—the colonial project was bound to fail.[14]

The degrees of sophistication of cultural imperialism have been amply documented.[15] Assimilation to the "normal other" via notions of universal equality that conceal white supremacist values, in the context of the U.S. "showcase of democracy of the world," is a complex phenomenon that requires equally complex critiques. CRT is steadily moving in the direction of providing those accounts[16] and has crafted its critiques in line with new experiences brought about by changes in the U.S. "minority" population and in light of an intensified awareness of the structural limits of the equal-opportunity model for African Americans.

The chapters by Enrique Carrasco and Isabelle Gunning employ a cultural lens to address the legitimation crisis inherent in a dominant gaze. Carrasco is particularly attracted by methodology. His interest in CRT methods focuses on their potential use in exposing the privileging of dominant voices in narratives of development. By exposing the components of mainstream notions of development, Carrasco highlights the presence of this gaze. Colonial and post-colonial studies inform his indictment of notions of development that speak of economic growth in terms of "control over nature" and of "neutral"/scientific economics that through their "engineering" conceal a normative analysis informed by very particular ethical considerations.

The colonialist impulse in liberal humanist values takes Carrasco to the exploration of nineteenth-century colonial narratives. Predominant accounts of Asian economic failures serve as a scenario of comparison with these narratives. The market is portrayed as objective, and, as Carrasco reminds us, the final indictment of disembodied portfolio investors and apolitical international capital flows is that Asian managers are corrupt and bad managers.

How do we begin to account for the connections among race, ethnicity, and development? How do we begin to reveal the racial and ethnic face of poverty in the North–South divide? How do we expose World Bank and International Monetary Fund policies for their sterilized rendition of poverty by way of the numbing qualities of statistics compiled by "objective" experts?

Maintaining his focus on methodology, Carrasco cautions us on being caught in mutually exclusive adherences to modern or postmodern influences in CRT. Along with Angela Harris, he suggests that it is best to select the best of two worlds, to appropriate the strengths of each influence.

Postmodern accounts, on the one hand, contribute to the unveiling of the social construction of law and post-colonial development and can provide needed language for the constitution of subjects and identities.[17] These accounts can shield us from overconfidence in emancipatory routes in the rule of law. Practical lessons of modernist accounts, on the other hand, are to be redeemed. Mindful of the "failures of neo-Marxist approaches," Carrasco shies away from frontal assaults on neoliberalism.

Rather, his task is to commit to modernism and retain a willingness to criticize, to seize the potential of the "sophistication and disenchantment mood" which recognizes the limits of rational reason.[18] In his view, the power of counter-narratives (of development from the "bottom") leads to more convincing answers.[19]

Isabelle Gunning is close to Hernández in challenging the legitimacy of liberal notions of human rights and equality that devalue cultural difference by virtue of colonizing/racializing maneuvers. Gunning also critiques national practices that re-create those values, thus creating hierarchies and structures that in turn create social and economic segregation. In examining the impact that a colonizing and patriarchal international law has on national and state laws criminalizing female genital circumcision, she demonstrates the compoundedness of cultural and gender devaluation suffered by African women who reside in the United States.

The landscape of U.S.-based lobbyists and legislators presented by Gunning, re-created in international-law spheres, reveals race and gender hierarchy. White feminists and white progressive voices don't quite "get it," according to Gunning. Women of color in the United States often suffer from this myopia, as well. The recent relocation of African women, coupled with the educational and class gaps between these women and their African American sisters,[20] offers Gunning a scenario for a critique of women-of-color "essentialism" and proves the need to monitor the "national–provincial" impulses of CRT, which are visible in its ties to a United States location.

Clearly distrusting law as a representative tool for women of color, Gunning reveals the results of the absence of African women in the process of policymaking on this issue. No serious discussion about the efficacy of criminalization versus a public-health approach has taken place, forcing many African feminists "to attack a part of their culture that they dislike by denouncing the entire culture that they love." Language labels have created huge camps of contention: Those in favor of the term "mutilation" are considered the true opponents of the practice, while those who favor the term "circumcision" are viewed as insufficiently critical and, consequently, rarely listened to.

Concluding that the failures of international law to address the concerns of women of color spill over into national and state legislation, Gunning reveals the symbolic order of law in generating cultural meanings that degrade the everyday practices of these African women.

Conclusion

The chapters in this section provide a panorama of insightful critiques and a rich variety of perspectives that signal the range of voices that a globalized and interconnected world demands. CRT methods, infused by prior positive and negative lessons, can enrich early critiques that, while challenging imperialistic practices and economic exploitation, concealed identity politics. The exposure of systems of governmentality, which create a symbolic and material order of devaluation and inferiorization, must travel new routes that can better articulate marginalized stories of groups who experience diverse forms of subordination. This section is a sample of the possibilities that lie ahead.

Notes

1. Martti Koskeniemi, *From Apology to Utopia: The Structure of International Legal Argument* (Helsinki: Finnish Lawyer's Publishing, 1989).

2. Angela P. Harris, "Foreword—The Jurisprudence of Reconstruction," *California Law Review* 82 (1994): 741.

3. Ibid., 774-777. See Eric Yamamoto, "Rethinking Alliances Agency, Responsibility and Interracial Justice," *University of California Asian Pacific American Law Journal* 1 (1995): 32. (Yamamoto, however, refers to the undetermination of racial-group agency in colonial/post-colonial critiques.)

4. Celina Romany, "State Responsibility Goes Private: A Feminist Critique of the Public/Private Distinction in International Human Rights Law," in *The Human Rights of Women: National and International Perspectives,* ed. Rebecca Cook (Philadelphia: University of Pennsylvania Press, 1994), 88-9.

5. Harris, "Foreword," 760. See "Latina/o Critical Theory Symposium Issue: International Law, Human Rights and LatCrit Theory," *University of Miami Inter-American Law Review* 28 (1996-97), on the need to assess international law from a critical perspective.

6. A more accurate description of my place of residence is "the floating island"—a direct allusion to a transnational identity that moves back and forth from two islands: Puerto Rico and Manhattan. See Celina Romany, "Neither Here nor There . . . Yet (Gender and Colonial Subordination)," *Callaloo* (Johns Hopkins University Press) (Fall 1992).

7. See generally Michael Omi and Howard Winant, *Racial Formation in the United States* (New York: Routledge, 1994).

8. Frantz Fanon, *The Wretched of the Earth* (New York: Grove-Atlantic Press, 1963).

9. Aimé Cesáire, *The Collected Poetry,* trans. Clayton Eshelman and Annette Smith (Berkeley: University of California Press, 1983).

10. According to Michael Omi and Howard Winant, "the concept of racialization signifies the extension of racial meaning to a previously racially unclassified relationship, social practice, or group": Omi and Winant, *Racial Formation,* 203. The quote is from ibid., 55.

11. Fanon, *The Wretched.*

12. Neil Gotanda, "A Critique of 'Our Constitution Is Color Blind,'" *Stanford Law Review* 44 (1991): 1; John Calmore, "Critical Race Theory, Archie Shepp, and Fire Music: Securing an Authentic Intellectual Life in a MultiCultural World," *California Law Review* 65 (1992): 2129.

13. Homi K. Bhabha, "Signs Taken for Wonders," in *The Post-Colonial Studies Reader,* ed. Bill Ashcroft, Gareth Griffiths, and Helen Tiffin (New York: Routledge, 1995).

14. Yet equally planted were the seeds of resistance. Roberto Fernández Retamar says it best: "The deformed Caliban-enslaved, robbed of his island,

and trained to speak for Prospero—rebukes him thus: 'you taught me language and my profit on't /Is, I know how to curse'" (Roberto Fernández Retamar, *Caliban and Other Essays*, trans. Edward Baker [Minneapolis: University of Minnesota Press, 1989], 14).

15. See Edward Said, *Culture and Imperialism* (New York: Alfred A. Knopf, 1993).

16. See Henry Richardson, "'Failed States' Self-determination, and Preventive Diplomacy: Colonialist Nostalgia and Democratic Expectations," *Temple International Comparative Law Journal* 10 (1996): 1.

17. Harris, "Foreword," 763.

18. Ibid.

19. Carrasco also notes that the task is to "produce counter-hegemonic development stories from the bottom to critically and radically monitor neoliberalism."

20. Gunning views as a "separate" group those African women who, participating at the international level, often adopt dominant views.

CHAPTER THIRTEEN

Global Markets, Racial Spaces, and the Role of Critical Race Theory in the Struggle for Community Control of Investments: An Institutional Class Analysis

Elizabeth M. Iglesias

All things and all circumstances must first be created on the mental plane.
—U. S. Anderson

The ruling ideas are nothing more than the ideal expression of the dominant material relationships grasped as ideas.
—Karl Marx

IN THIS CHAPTER, I examine the role of law in the production of racial spaces. An initial comment about the term "racial spaces" is a good place to start. Viewed through the lens of neo-liberal economic theory, the term "racial spaces" is a meaningless formulation, because in neo-liberal economics communities are conceptualized as net-

This essay first appeared in *Villanova L.Rev.* 45 (2000), 5. It appears here courtesy of the author and Villanova Law Review.

works of markets. Capital flows reflect the purportedly "colorblind" imperatives of profit maximization, and race-neutral laws of supply and demand work to allocate capital to the highest-value user across competing networks of markets according to their competitive and comparative advantages. Indeed, from this perspective, the redlining practices and disinvestment decisions through which minority communities in the United States have been converted into ghettos are not only inexplicable, but ultimately *immaterial,* because "it is difficult to see why communities *in general* suffer a net harm when funds are transferred between them (although some communities may be net importers of credit and others net exporters)."[1]

By contrast, the term "racial spaces" refers to a social reality created by and experienced through patterns of mobility and immobility that have been organized around the logic and historical practices of white supremacy— a logic in which neither people nor capital have ever circulated freely. In the United States, practices of racial segregation and discrimination have historically prevented, and continue today to prevent, the free movement of people.[2] The free markets of neo-liberal economic theory have yet to produce the unrestricted access to housing or employment or credit that would be necessary, though not sufficient, to render every community a fungible network of markets. In Latin America, racial spaces are the product of processes that are both analogous and, at the same time, unique to a region where white supremacy is mediated through the political apparatuses and economic structures of neo-colonial dependency, state corporatism, military bureaucratism, and authoritarian repression. One need only consider the involuntary resettlements where the many displaced are encamped, imprisoned by local disciplinary apparatuses—in some instances under military order,[3] in other instances under the auspices of World Bank project managers.[4] These resettlements are spatial artifacts of the relationships of power and powerlessness that entrap and immobilize the vast majority of the world's peoples: the lack of resources that would enable them to *move freely;* and the closed borders that constrain the free-market flows of neo-liberalism within the racial parameters delimited by First World nativism.

These patterns of mobility and immobility are a central element in the production of racial spaces. But the concept of "racial spaces" has additional value beyond foregrounding aspects of social reality that remain inexplicable or immaterial to neoliberal ideology. As a theoretical construct, the concept of racial spaces provides new ways of understanding the production of subordination—understandings that may

help resolve the supposed conflict between class-based and race-based emancipatory movements. Racial spaces are visible artifacts both of racial segregation and of the relations of investment, production, and exchange that are reflected in the export of capital, in monopolies of political and economic power, and in the restricted circulation of goods, services, and capital within racially subordinated communities. Conceptualized in this way, the very existence of racial spaces raises fundamental questions about the relationship between racial inequality and the political and economic structures and processes of the neo-liberal political economy, both in the United States and throughout Latin America. Can racial subordination be eliminated within the institutional arrangements of a neo-liberal political economy? And, perhaps more to the point, where and how is law implicated in the production of these spaces?

The rest of this chapter is divided into two parts. The first part illustrates the kinds of contributions Critical Race Theory can make, and should be making, to the struggle for social racial justice, generally, and to the transformation of racial spaces, in particular. In order to underscore the global dimensions of this project, I focus on the work conducted by the Institute for Liberty and Democracy in Peru (ILD) and reported on by the Peruvian economist Hernando De Soto in his now famous book *The Other Path.*[5] This work analyzes the plight of informal workers in Peru. According to De Soto, Peruvian poverty is not caused by the structures of capitalist accumulation, international dependency relations, or social discrimination. Instead, it is caused by a domestic legal system that condemns the vast majority of people to the instability, uncertainty, and vulnerability of illegality by making legality inaccessible to all but the wealthy. Since differential access to legality is more fundamental in structuring class hierarchies and antagonisms than differential ownership of the means of production, De Soto proposes an alternative analytical framework that replaces the Marxist notion of class with what he calls an "institutional-class paradigm." In this analytical framework, poverty is a function of the way the legal system divides "those who obtain advantages and privileges from the state from the competitive majority against whom an inadequate legal system discriminates."[6]

De Soto's call for a new theoretical approach and his efforts to articulate this new approach as an "institutional-class analysis" offer some important points and *counterpoints* of departure for understanding the role of law in producing the relations of poverty and marginalization that are mapped across the globe as racial spaces. In the second part of this essay, I develop these counterpoints by offering an alternative institutional-class analysis. This alternative framework locates the production of racial spaces, not per se in the differential access to legality enjoyed by rich and poor but, rather, in the way law, understood broadly to include its substantive norms, procedures, and institutions, operates in different ways to allocate differential power among competing groups across many institutional contexts. It is precisely by institutionalizing relations of differential power that law organizes institutional class structures. The degree to which these structures reproduce poverty and subordination depends, in turn, on the degree to which they enable or disable self-organization and mobilization among the multivariate collective political identities through which subordinated groups might seek to transform the political economy. To illustrate the elements of this kind of institutional-class analysis, I focus specifically on the institutional-class structures that are organized in and around two particular sociolegal contexts: the struggle for low-income community lending in the United States as mediated by the Community Reinvestment Act of 1977 and its various amendments, and the struggle over development lending as mediated by the World Bank's Inspection Panel.

These two legal regimes—one domestic, the other international—were both designed to combat the fact that, contrary to neo-liberal economic rhetoric, when economic decisions are sheltered from political oversight and regulation, capital does not flow efficiently or even rationally. Both legal regimes are efforts to institutionalize procedures that will increase the participation of affected communities in the decision-making processes through which capital is allocated. The Community Reinvestment Act is directed at federally regulated banks and savings-and-loan institutions, while the Inspection Panel accepts complaints arising out of World Bank loan practices and development projects.

My purpose is not to provide a comprehensive, technocratic account of these two sociolegal regimes but, rather, to use them as vehicles for illustrating some general observations about the nature of power, the role of law in configuring relations of power and marginalization through the organization of institutional-class structures, and the role of these institutional structures in the continued reproduction of racial spaces, both within and beyond the United States. These general observations, in turn, are directly relevant to ongoing debates over the contributions Critical Race Theory, *understood specifically as a practice in the production of legal theory,* can and should be making to the social-justice struggles of various and variously subordinated groups.

An increasingly popular *theory* is circulating in and about the legal academy that the production of Critical Race Theory is at best only marginally or indirectly relevant to the struggle for social justice, and at worst a self-serving desertion of the front line, a headlong plunge into the greener fields of the academy. In this essay, I engage this theory—by unabashedly mapping out a different theory. Most generally, I challenge the idea that there is some avenue of agency outside and beyond the theoretical constructs over which we struggle when we *do* critical theory. Indeed, to *do* critical theory is precisely to struggle over the way we should *understand* and hence *resist* the production of subordination. This is because strategies we pursue through direct political action, litigation, or lobbying are driven, at least in part, by the way we understand the meaning of subordination, the nature of power, and the conditions that enable solidarity and structure individual identities, as well as by our understandings of the role of law in producing the material dispossession and institutional marginalization that is experienced as subordination.

Making effective strategic decisions about how to or not use law in the struggle for social justice is hard, but it is even harder than we may realize as we plunge into frontline legal battles. Relations of domination and marginalization have survived even the most progressive legislative interventions and litigation victories, in part because the decentralization of legal decision-making power across many different judicial, quasi-judicial, political, and quasi-political forums makes it hard to see, and therefore harder to combat, the cumulative impact of liberal ideology on the legal distribution of power among different groups in different social spaces. Read through an institutional-class analysis, an apparent legal victory in one case can quickly be transformed into a politically regressive defeat in another—depending on the way the legal "victory" tends to structure institutional power among com-

peting groups.[7] As a result, the effective use of law requires strategies that can counteract the rhetorical maneuvers and procedural devices through which liberal legal interpretation systematically and repeatedly excludes the agency of the oppressed from the realm of the lawful. When this exclusion occurs, effective social transformation comes to depend on the assertion of illegal agency and the hyper-vulnerability it entails, while social justice and the hope of lasting change come to depend on the reconstruction of legal agency.[8] Whatever the response to institutionalized powerlessness and marginalization, law is clearly implicated in the production of both. This may make law of limited instrumental value as a tool in the struggle for social racial justice, but the role of law in the institutionalization of powerlessness makes it a fundamental "stake" in this struggle.

Put differently, although law won't change the world, any emancipatory movement must seek ultimately to change the law. And to do so, it will need theory. This is because all action is embedded in a theory—and, even more important, in a structure that is itself embedded in and organized by a theory. Just as neo-liberal institutional class structures are organized through the articulation of neo-liberal theories in legal doctrine, the institutionalization of a new order of power and knowledge will depend at least in part on further dissemination of the kinds of ideas RaceCrit scholars have only just begun to address. It will depend, above all, on a vision of social justice that engages, rather than ignores, the international dimensions of racial subordination, the centrality of poverty in the subordination of peoples of color throughout the world, and the role of law in organizing and disorganizing the intra- and intergroup solidarities that are so central to effective collective action in any institutional context.[9]

Between Structure and Agency: Institutionalized Power and Powerlessness and *The Other Path*

In *The Other Path,* Hernando De Soto provided a vivid, though fundamentally romanticized, account of the informal economy in Peru. While the dominant narratives of the 1980s represented the informal economy as a black market populated by tax-evading free-riders, De Soto introduced the idea that black-marketeers were among the most dynamic agents of economic and social development in Peru, at least in the four economic sectors studied by the ILD. Focusing on business, manufacturing, housing, and transportation, De Soto argued that the informal economy had evolved in large part because the Peruvian legal system was too complex, corrupt, and restricted to function as an effective framework for regulating the activities of Peru's impoverished majority. For many Peruvians, working, investing, and other forms of collective action organized outside the legal system have often been the only way to survive, but as De Soto emphasized, the costs of "informality"—the costs of having to operate illegally—are substantial. Informal trade, transportation businesses, manufacturing enterprises, and the illegal settlements—established both through violent and incremental land invasions—were then and still are profoundly vulnerable. This vulnerability condemns informals to a life of uncertainty, instability, and fear of extortion, imprisonment, and physical attacks, and, most significant, to the possibility that their operations will be shut down, they and their families evicted, and their life's work and investments lost.

De Soto's account of the plight of Peruvian informals provides a useful point of reference for achieving two different but related objectives. The first objective is to show how Critical Race Theory can best contribute to the struggle for social racial justice. De Soto's study of the informal economy in Peru illustrates the limitations of political strategies that dichotomize theory and praxis and glorify the mobilization of collective action as the model of transformative agency. The instances of collective action he depicts are compelling, transformative in certain respects, perhaps even heroic at times, but hardly emancipatory. Indeed, De Soto's study is a vivid illustration of the disjuncture between intention and effective agency that makes the *theoretical* analysis of power—its nature, structures, and modalities—a crucial prerequisite in designing effective strategies for direct collective action or in determining which of the many different litigation struggles or lobbying efforts should claim our energies and attention. De Soto's account also advances my second, more specific objective of analyzing how law participates in the production of racial spaces within and across the territorial boundaries of the nation-state.

The title of the book *The Other Path* is a play on *Sendero Luminoso* (the Shining Path), the Peruvian guerrilla movement founded in 1970 that, by the 1990s, was one of the most violent insurgencies still active in Latin America.[10] As its title suggests, De Soto's book, based on studies conducted in the early 1980s—before the disorganization and eventual demise of the Soviet "evil empire"—promised an alternative to the many different avenues through which the oppressed and impoverished of Peru might otherwise seek to improve their lives: an alternative to an Indian revolt to restore the Inca empire; to international communism; to export-driven development, particularly of the coca-plant variety; an alternative, even, to the community-based movements inspired by liberation theology.[11]

Perhaps for these reasons, De Soto's book on the survival strategies pursued by the poorest of the Peruvian poor was received with unusual interest and the enthusiastic endorsement of the neo-liberal conservatives of the world, who were even then uniting around an all-out campaign to tax the pampered poor and redistribute to the needy rich.[12] In those heady days of unrestricted corporate greed, *The Other Path* was so well received that it prompted praise from none other than then President Ronald Reagan, who, in his 1987 address to the United Nations General Assembly, had this to say:

> The scholar, Hernando De Soto, and his colleagues have ... described an economy of the poor that bypasses crushing taxation and stifling regulation.... By becoming underground entrepreneurs themselves, or by working for them, the poor have become less poor and the nation itself richer.... The free market is the other path to development and the one true path. It is the people's path. And unlike other paths, it leads somewhere. It works.[13]

The question, of course, is why a book about the coping strategies of the poorest of the Peruvian poor would generate such interest and inspire such a warm embrace from the high priest of U.S. imperialism and global capitalism. The answer is easy. The book has been popular among neo-liberal conservatives because it provided a simple analysis of the problem of poverty and a simple solution that just happened to coincide with what global capitalists still want to believe: that the best way to deal with the problems of the poor is to establish effective legal structures for the recognition and enforcement of property rights and contractual agreements and then to let the free market run its course.

I want to focus initially on one of the studies through which De Soto purports to demonstrate this point.[14] The purpose of the study was to "explain why some people prefer formality and others informality." This led the ILD researchers to conduct a

series of inquiries. First, they talked directly to informal workers, who complained that the legal procedures required to formalize their economic activities were prohibitively costly and complex. This in turn inspired the ILD to conduct a simulation in order to measure the costs of access to legality.

In the summer of 1983, a team of ILD researchers set up a small garment factory in an industrial area on the outskirts of Lima, organizing it as a sole proprietorship. To establish this business, they rented a factory building, installed garment machinery, and recruited four university students to go through the legal procedures required to formalize the business. The study was designed to be representative of the situation faced by ordinary Peruvians. Accordingly, formalizing the simulated garment factory required going through approximately 60 percent of the bureaucratic procedures common to all industries and 90 percent of the procedures required of non-incorporated sole proprietorships.[15] The students were also instructed to handle the bureaucratic "red tape" without the assistance of intermediaries and to pay bribes only when necessary to continue the simulation.

The results of the study are instructive. It took 289 days, working full time, for the four university students to acquire the eleven permits needed to complete the simulation. Two of the ten bribes solicited had to be paid. The total costs in actual expenses, wasted time, and lost profits were estimated at $1,231, or thirty-two times the minimum monthly wage in Peru at that time. Perhaps most interestingly, De Soto repeated the simulation in Tampa, Florida, where the procedures to achieve the same result reportedly took only three and a half hours.[16]

This study is interesting both on its own terms and in terms of the conclusions De Soto and other neo-liberal conservatives like to draw from it. On its own terms, the study has lessons for us about the nature of power, the role of law in producing and disorganizing power, and the relationship between structure and agency in the struggle for social justice. In fact, I want to focus more precisely on the nature of the agency Peruvian informals exercised in and around the social, legal, and political structures. This focus will underscore a point that many of us already know but too often forget in the debate over the relative priority of theory or praxis in the struggle for justice. Clearly, Peruvian informals expended enormous amounts of time, energy, and resources in pursuing their objectives. It is equally clear from De Soto's two simulations that legal structures determined whether those efforts would take 289 days or three and a half hours to achieve their objectives. The point is this: The more effort it takes, the less power one has. From this perspective, the fact that Peruvian peasants established their informal settlements in and around Lima through the direct collective action of both gradual and violent land invasions, or that the Community Reinvestment Movement negotiated a series of community-development loans after mobilizing massive protests in the credit-starved communities of the United States, is evidence more of the powerlessness and marginalization of these communities than of their power.

In order to understand this point, it is important to understand that agency is not the same thing as power. Effective power is best understood as a function of the routine relationships between human agency and the institutional structures in which it is exercised. Collective political mobilization—the demonstrations in the streets—can be represented and experienced both as occurring outside dominant institutional arrangements and as transforming inherited political identities. However, the raw power to achieve one's ends or protect one's interests through the extraordinary efforts involved

in mobilizing and maintaining broad-based social movements and political coalitions can hardly be equated with the power that rests on the legally sanctioned institutionalized *authority* to effectuate these objectives through the routine practices and procedures of existing institutions.[17]

It follows, therefore, that the struggle against subordination must be understood as a struggle for power within the institutional arrangements through which power is legally organized and deployed. This in turn means that the antisubordination objectives at the heart of Critical Race Theory depend as much on reorganizing these institutional structures, reforming the legal doctrines that construct them, and reconstructing the order of knowledge that informs and legitimates these doctrines, as on the mobilization of collective action. This is particularly true given the extent to which direct action is constrained by the structural contexts within which it is always already located—at least until "the revolution." Even then, the structural arrangements of the past tend to have an uncanny hold on the possibilities of the future. To the extent that the role of law in perpetuating these structures is neither immediately obvious nor easily confronted, combated, or transformed, Critical Race Theory can make a significant contribution by helping us understand how relations of power and powerlessness are institutionalized in and through different legal regimes; by helping us locate and assess the institutional positions subordinated people tend to occupy in these legal regimes; and by helping us determine how best to restructure these institutional arrangements in light of what we have learned about the way identity politics can enable or disable the solidarities and alliances needed to combat subordination.

More concretely, my point is this: Case studies of Peruvian land invasions are compelling reminders that direct collective action does not rewrite the laws or reorganize oppressive institutions. Although activists may cherish the notion that *others* will be inspired (or compelled) to rewrite the laws and reorganize these institutions, collective action does not guarantee that these others will have the political will to complete the task in the face of new and ever-evolving obstacles. Nor even less does it ensure that *anyone* will have the ability to conceptualize or the technical resources or "know-how" to effectuate *emancipatory* institutional transformation for the long run.[18]

Reports from South Africa offer another instructive example because they provide a window into the kind of reality collective mobilization has often confronted "after the revolution." Alan Mabin reports that when South African community-based organizations, otherwise known as "the civics," and government officials began negotiations in 1989 to dismantle the urban structures constructed over decades of apartheid and colonialism, "all the creative thinking seemed to come from the civic side." The negotiations began in the context of a state of emergency. The civics successfully organized massive boycotts of rents on public housing and service charges in the townships. When the civics succeeded in expanding the scope of negotiations from issues related to ending the boycotts to the nature, structure, and operation of local government, "it seemed that this emancipatory movement, which sought to represent the township masses, stood at the point of taking power at the local level from existing authorities."[19] By all accounts, they failed.

The first explanation is easy: The people who mobilized in the streets were completely unprepared—either for the vicious brutality their political achievements would unleash or for the routine processes, the endless meetings, and technocratic negotiations through which the struggle for antiracist democratic reform would move out of the streets and into the bureaucratic

offices of state power.[20] Thus, although grassroots mobilization did achieve significant political victories, by the 1990s, "the civics' ... are fragmented, weak and no longer have the same popular support. They have been weakened by the whole process of national negotiations and, above all, by the terror unleashed in the townships through Inkatha."[21]

The second explanation for the civics' failure to consolidate and institutionalize their power focuses on the crisis of political vision reflected in the news reports from South Africa: ANC PLEDGES FISCAL DISCIPLINE. In the new South Africa, the Freedom Charter gave way to supply-side economics, and the commitment to economic "Growth Through Redistribution" gave way to the political economy of structural adjustment: no significant new taxes, exchange controls to be phased out, and free trade to be phased in.[22]

The devolution of the emancipatory project in South Africa clearly illustrates the fact that the power to say "no" to oppression does not automatically translate into the power to create a reality to which we can say "yes."[23] Indeed, even the power to effect radical change does not automatically translate into the ability to conceptualize the institutional arrangements that can sustain the values and objectives of emancipation. Without institutional transformation, everything directly done can be directly or indirectly undone. Without conceptual evolution informed by a critical understanding of the way new processes such as flexible production, globalization, and the proliferation of political identities can affect relations of subordination, the struggle for emancipatory social transformation may end up solving the problems of the past and leaving the new processes of subordination intact. This is precisely because the problems of development are the problems of institutionalizing an alternative order of knowledge and power, and these problems, being both structural and conceptual, require the kind of structural and conceptual reforms that are generated only in and through the production of theory.

If the goal is to eliminate subordination, it is not enough to glorify the fact that human agency can transcend its context or that mass political coalitions can destablize a racist regime or block the merger of a banking institution that has failed to invest in low-income communities. At some point, the claims advocated and interests represented by any mass social-political movement must be translated into new institutional structures through which currently subordinated groups can effectively assert their interests on a routine basis, without having to engage forever in the extraordinary efforts of mass mobilization. However, the institutionalization of a new order of power and knowledge does not follow automatically from mass mobilization. Rather, it requires legal-reform interventions informed by the kind of theoretical work that enables critical analysis of the way legally constructed institutional arrangements organize authority and allocate power across the different economic classes and political identities that interact in and through these institutions.

When I think about the South African civics trying to dismantle apartheid under new conditions of increasing suburbanization and flexible production, or the Peruvian informal workers trying to eke out a minimal existence despite, and in the shadow of, the regulatory and bureaucratic legal obstacles that construct them as illegals, with all the vulnerabilities that creates for them, I am increasingly convinced that the struggle for social justice is profoundly in need of a theory about the way to do legal theory as much as it needs the mobilization of collective action or the production of legal scholarship aimed at generating new doctrinal

formulations for ongoing litigation. Critical analysis of the role of law in the organization and disorganization of institutional structures is all the more pressing because the call to agency under conditions of institutionalized powerlessness is a call to perpetual marginality in a war without end.

As the examples of the Peruvian informals and the South African civics illustrate, direct collective action may achieve, and has in the past achieved, some momentary advances; nevertheless, these examples also suggest the degree to which any emancipatory achievements will remain profoundly unstable until the legally constructed institutions of white supremacy and the anti-democratic institutions of the anti-political economy are replaced with a new order of knowledge and power.[24] In the theory about how to do theory that I am imagining and deploying in this essay, the most *critical* task for Critical Race Theory is to develop a compelling account of the way *law* constructs these institutional arrangements; the way these institutional structures demobilize and disorganize the collective political identities through which subordinated groups might seek to transform the political economy, for example, as community members, consumers, workers, racial minorities, or welfare recipients; and the kinds of institutional arrangements that should replace them.

Focusing more specifically on the role of law in the production of racial spaces, the first task is to identify the institutional arrangements through which racial spaces are produced. These spaces are artifacts of investment and disinvestment decisions made as much by private economic actors, such as banks and business corporations, as by government officials. Often these decisions have been made without the knowledge, and even over the violent objections, of affected communities. The ability, *the power,* to make these decisions, even in the face of sustained and organized community opposition, exists precisely because of the relations of power and powerlessness that are institutionalized through legal doctrines that effectuate and legitimize hierarchical, non-participatory, and exclusionary allocations of decisional authority. This includes legal doctrines such as the business-judgment rule and prohibitions on compulsory credit allocation, as well as restrictions on shareholder democracy, minority-business set-asides, and state regulations limiting corporate political expenditures. In each of these instances, the legal doctrines and constitutional interpretations through which these legal rules are articulated are the interpretive spaces in which the democratization of power—whether economic or political—is systematically suppressed through the rhetorical manipulation of the economic–political dichotomy.[25]

On its own terms, this is what De Soto's study of the obstacles informal workers confront in attempting to legalize their economic activities reminds me of: the need for critical theory that attacks the institutionalization of subordination and the conceptual order that sustains it, even as it engages the more difficult task of imagining and articulating an alternative institutional order. But De Soto's simulation has other lessons when we focus more specifically on the way this simulation has been used by neo-liberal conservatives to "name the problem" and "prescribe a solution."

Neo-liberal conservatives also draw a lesson about human agency from De Soto's simulation and the structural constraints it reveals. It is a lesson about the power of human agency to transcend and transform the conditions of subordination of a life of poverty. The lesson they draw is that the human spirit is cross-culturally driven by a desire to achieve, and that poor people would achieve if only the government would just get out of the way.[26] This is, of course, a meaningful conclusion to draw

when the problems of the poor are presented as a consequence of the regulatory bureaucracy that suppresses the entrepreneurial human spirit.[27] When the state oppresses the market, when political power interferes with economic freedom, what else is to be expected?

Clearly there is something wrong when compliance with the law makes effective agency functionally impossible for all but a few determined individuals with the resources and stamina to persevere. Clearly there is something wrong when non-compliance reduces the vast majority to a state of vulnerability and insecurity so profound that every operation becomes a fly-by-night endeavor. But this situation is not unique to Peru. On the contrary, in the United States the hyper-regulation of the poor has all but guaranteed that people in public housing will never start their own businesses. Lease provisions on public housing have routinely prohibited efforts to generate income at home, so that "residents must either covertly conduct business out of their apartments or forbear from doing business at all."[28]

The real puzzle is this: Why is it that the neo-liberal conservatives' response to De Soto's account of the plight of the Peruvian informals does not dismiss them as the ones who simply didn't try hard enough? After all, everyone confronts obstacles; every action has its costs, and some informal businesses have been relatively successful despite the obstacles. Since when have obstacles been anything but a reason to try harder? Could it be that neo-liberal conservatives have at last discovered that the ideology of the self-made, lift-himself-up-by-the-heman-bootstraps entrepreneur ignores fundamental aspects of the reality of poverty; the lack of resources and options that characterize racial spaces; the insecurity and immobility that condemn such a large majority to the repetition of redoing, over and over, that which they have already done? And why should anyone ever have to work that hard to survive? Could it be that the neo-liberal mind has at long last registered the claim that hard work is not the answer to the problems of people whose hard work only leaves them exhausted and (still) impoverished?

Not so fast. Certainly such conclusions go beyond anything the neo-liberal can or would endorse. For the neo-liberal, the conclusions to be drawn are much narrower and more targeted. De Soto's account earns their endorsement because it foregrounds government irrationality—free the market, and there will be no racial spaces. "Free-market" capitalism is the solution to, not the cause of, the informal economy. It is the solution to, not the cause of, racial subordination.

I want to offer a different account of the neo-liberal political economy—one that locates the production of racial spaces at the intersection of two apparently mutually incompatible "market" processes—and to suggest that the simple solution of deregulating the over-regulated would not even remotely begin to address the profound impact of these two processes on the reproduction of the poverty and racism that construct racial spaces. These two processes are the "rock and the hard place" of market globalization and segmentation, and minority communities are caught right between them in their struggle for access to and control over the distribution of finance capital.

First, the idea that deregulation will liberate the poor ignores the differential access to capital that is being accelerated through the process of financial integration and the globalization of capital markets. In a *deregulated* global capital market, every credit application competes with every other credit application.[29] This means that potential homeowners in the inner cities of the United States compete for loans with the Hunt brothers in their efforts to corner the silver market[30] and the speculative self-

enrichment schemes of the latest wave of (savings-and-loan) robber barons.[31] In a deregulated market, these competing credit applications are not assessed in terms of their contributions to community development or even to the establishment of profitable economic activity. Rather, they are compared in terms of their profit maximization *for finance capital*. Put differently, even profitable economic activity can be starved for capital, because investment in profitable activity is not the same as profit maximization. This is not new to the free-market system; what is new is that the globalization of capital markets enables the law of greed to go global. All the world's a portfolio. The de-territorialization of investment has accelerated the processes of investment and disinvestment that are producing racial spaces, as finance capital abandons economic development and redevelopment in search of hyper-profits in the hyper-spaces of finance capital beyond the territorial boundaries of any particular community or nation. And this applies as much to Third World capital. What's good for the First World gander is good for the Third World goose, as shown in Third World capital flight. If it's more profitable to invest in foreign-denominated financial instruments than in real economic activity, then who is to blame for underdevelopment?[32]

Ironically, however, poor and minority communities are also starved for capital because of market segmentation. Minority businesses operating in minority communities report that profitable business ventures are starved for capital, but not because the businesses cannot offer above-market interest rates. In fact, minority businesses routinely have to offer above-market rates to obtain the few loans they do get outside protected credit programs. The problem is not price per se but the fact that they often cannot get private commercial loans at *any* price.[33] If U.S. minority businesses have such a hard time getting the credit they need to gain access to the free market, why would anyone believe that Peruvian informals will have access to the credit they need once the solution of deregulation is implemented?[34] Indeed, market segmentation is at least as pervasive and more flagrantly institutionalized in Latin American capital markets, where domestic banks have gorged on enormous profits by manipulating differentials in international and domestic interest rates and by trading on the fact that small companies have much less access to foreign lenders and investment bankers than large companies in a few privileged sectors (such as the automobile and pharmaceuticals sectors). Like minority businesses in the United States, though for different reasons and through different mechanisms, small and medium-size businesses in Latin America have found domestic credit "exceptionally expensive" and foreign credit inaccessible at any price.[35]

But certainly capital markets cannot be *both* integrated and global and, at the same time, racially segmented and compartmentalized. This apparent contradiction is inexplicable in neo-liberal economic theory because it can be understood only if one is willing to consider the possibility that the flow of capital is embedded in a broader cultural phenomenon of racial discrimination and that institutions other than the state are implicated in the production of economic marginalization and poverty. That the "free market" operates in the shadow of racial discrimination, through the exercise of both individualized discretion and institutionalized decision-making criteria, is a notion neo-liberal ideology refuses to internalize in its theoretical constructs.

In the United States, discrimination in the flow of finance capital has been a primary factor in the production of racial spaces through the practice of redlining minority communities and the denial of

capital to minority entrepreneurs. Disinvestment, coupled with the containment practices of racial segregation, converts minority communities into ghettos. In the Third World, the production of racial spaces has been effected through development projects that rip people out of their traditional social relations of production and exchange—directly through the financing of involuntary resettlements and indirectly through finance practices that privilege major industries over micro-businesses and export sectors over domestic sectors.

From this perspective, to suggest that poverty will be eliminated simply by freeing the entrepreneurial human spirit from the regulatory squeeze is to ignore completely the role of so-called private institutions of capitalism, such as banks and corporations, in the production of racial spaces. It also ignores the role of law in enabling institutionally dominant classes to make decisions that produce these results, even over the many legal challenges and sometimes violent opposition of affected individuals and communities. Thus, while De Soto is most certainly on the right track in targeting law and legally constructed institutional arrangements as fundamental factors in the production of poverty, his institutional-class analysis is simplistic and incomplete in two critical and interrelated respects. First, it presupposes the points it purports to demonstrate—namely, the superiority of a neo-liberal social order organized around the strategically manipulated separation of economic and political social spaces and processes. Second, although De Soto makes a compelling case that differential access to legality produces a new class structure of institutionally mediated hierarchies and antagonisms, he fails to perform an institutional-class analysis of the private institutions that tend to dominate in deregulated economic spaces. This omission may be consistent with his neo-liberal biases, but not with his purported objective of revealing the causes and solutions to the problem of poverty.

In the next part of this chapter, I will illustrate how a more *critical* institutional-class analysis could enrich Critical Race Theory by 1) increasing our understanding of the role of law in the production of subordination; 2) enabling us to see the difference between legal reforms that create new causes of action and reforms that reorganize the distribution of institutional power;[36] and 3) contextualizing our analysis of identity politics and the formation of political identities within an analysis of the way the legal organization of institutional classes channels and constrains the political aspirations and collective solidarities needed for progressive change in particular institutional contexts.

Like De Soto's, my institutional-class analysis seeks to replace Marxist class categories with an analysis of the way relations of privilege and marginalization are legally constructed. However, I do not presuppose but, rather, critically analyze the separation of economics and politics—in fact and in fiction.[37] Moreover, my institutional-class analysis focuses more comprehensively on the way power is organized by legal institutions and legal institutions are organized by the interpretive manipulation of legal doctrines and categories. Thus, in analyzing how law participates in the production of poverty and the racialization of spaces, I focus specifically on 1) the way decision-making power over the allocation of capital is legally institutionalized; 2) the order of knowledge that rationalizes and legitimizes these institutional structures in legal discourse; and 3) the way these institutional structures, in turn, organize relations of power and powerlessness among the various groups affected by capital-allocation decisions emerging from these institutions.

Beyond the Other Path: An Institutional-Class Analysis of the Community Reinvestment Act and the World Bank Inspection Panel

The U.S. Community Reinvestment Act (CRA) of 1977 and the World Bank Inspection Panel are products of collective political and legal struggles to gain some control over the capital-allocation and investment decisions that have so seriously affected poor communities both in the United States and throughout the world. In the United States, the Community Reinvestment Act represents an early, but still controversial, victory against the redlining practices through which U.S. banking institutions converted low- and moderate-income communities into virtual wastelands, sucking them dry of the credit flows and investment capital they need to repair and improve physical infrastructures, enable economic growth, and maintain social stability, and exporting local deposits in the search for more profitable investment prospects elsewhere. Like the CRA, though through different procedures, the World Bank Inspection Panel is designed to make lending practices more accountable to the communities they affect. My objective in this section is to suggest how these two legal regimes should be analyzed in an institutional-class analysis.

Both the CRA and the Inspection Panel are legal interventions designed to reorganize pre-existing institutional arrangements. The CRA intervenes in the allocation of finance capital by targeting institutional arrangements that are themselves organized by a number of domestic legal regimes, including banking and consumer-protection laws, civil-rights statutes, and common-law doctrines such as the business-judgment rule. These domestic legal regimes construct institutional classes by organizing relations of power and powerlessness among the various groups that interact in and through these institutional structures, such as bank managers, regulators, depositors, borrowers, and community-reinvestment organizations—all of whom are interested in and affected by capital-allocation decisions. The Inspection Panel, on the other hand, targets institutional arrangements organized by international law and development practices. These are the institutional arrangements that both constitute and mediate relations of power and powerlessness among international organizations, sovereign states, and a growing number of internationally mobilized nongovernmental organizations (NGOs). In both instances, the important point is that law organizes classes by organizing the power relations that will operate in different institutional contexts.

The organization of power and powerlessness constructs institutional classes and determines the relative disjuncture different institutional classes will experience in the relationship between structure and agency. Institutional classes with significant institutional power will experience little disjuncture; others who are more marginalized within the power relations that organize the institution will confront significant disjuncture between their objectives and aspirations *for* the institution and their ability to effectuate these objectives *in and through* the institution. As a result, institutionally marginalized classes often have no alternative but to seek their objectives through external mobilization, thus incurring the costs and suffering the legal vulnerability that invariably accompanies such mobilization.[38]

Institutional-class analysis thus enables us to see similarities in the way power is structured across different institutional contexts and regulatory frameworks. Law is pervasively implicated in the organization of institutional classes. Racial spaces, defined by poverty, marginalization, and immobility, are produced through patterns of investment and disinvestment decisions that are themselves outcomes of differential power among institutional classes. Clearly, some classes profit from these patterns of investment and disinvestment; others have struggled hard to alter them. Yet the structures of institutional authority that law defines and enforces against internal and external challenge determine the interests that routinely prevail in any institutional class conflict.

In the struggle over the allocation of capital, for example, law determines who gets to decide who gets capital, using what decision criteria, to achieve what purpose, with what level of accountability to whom, and under what review procedures. The distribution of power within an institutional arrangement depends on where and how different groups are positioned in relation to each of these decision points. Accordingly, institutional-class analysis seeks to reveal the way power is legally distributed among the different groups within a specific institutional context in order to understand better the possibilities for reorganizing institutional-class structures. This analysis is both structural and discursive because it focuses on how different group interests are *positioned within* the institutional structures and how these interests are *represented in* dominant legal discourse. A brief review of the CRA and the World Bank Inspection Panel will help to illustrate these points more concretely.

The Community Reinvestment Act

The story of the CRA is a useful place to examine the role of law and legal theory in progressive social change, particularly given my earlier analysis of the way collective action is embedded in structural constraints that can fundamentally distort its ultimate social impact. These structural constraints on the agency of the oppressed are precisely the kinds of constraints that have most effectively withstood the impact of insurgent attacks or direct collective protests because they exist, operate, and stake out their longevity in the realm of ideas. The realm of ideas establishes the parameters of legal reform, and it is these parameters that must be redefined and replaced by a successful revolution in the same realm of ideas—a revolution whose major resource is critical theory.

The Community Reinvestment Act has been a controversial flash point ever since it was first enacted in 1977. Neo-liberal conservatives have attacked the statute as a special-interest political intervention that threatens the ultimate viability of the American banking system by distorting economic rules of supply and demand, requiring federally regulated banking institutions to make unprofitable loans in order to advance non-economic social and political objectives and superimposing an outdated model of community banking on an increasingly integrated global market to the detriment of all interested parties, including the low- and moderate-income communities it seeks to protect. Government allocation of credit is, to the neo-liberal conservative mind, an embryonic cancer embedded in the CRA, poised at any opportune political moment to escape the boundaries of the act and deliver the U.S. banking system to the inefficiencies of a state-managed economy or, worse yet, to socialism.

Looking at the statute, one might wonder at all the hysteria. The statute establishes no private right of action and, indeed, imposes no justiciable obligation whatsoever. It simply directs each of the four federal banking-regulatory agencies[39] "to assess" and "to take into consideration" an institution's record in "meeting the credit needs of its entire community, including low- and moderate-income neighborhoods, consistent with the safe and sound opera-

tion of each institution" when deciding whether to approve an application for a deposit facility by a banking institution under their supervision.[40] And yet this statute is credited by its supporters (and detractors) for redirecting the flow of significant amounts of capital into community-development projects, albeit for reasons that have nothing to do with the operation of the act's intended enforcement structure.[41] Indeed, the CRA has never operated as initially intended.

As legally structured, the substantive obligations of the CRA, requiring regulated institutions to refrain from geographic discrimination by meeting the credit needs of low- and moderate-income communities, were to be enforced by bank regulators at such time as regulated institutions might submit an application to acquire a depository facility.[42] An adverse CRA finding would provide a basis for the agency to withhold approval of the applicant's business plans. However, throughout the history of the act, bank regulators have rarely denied expansion applications on CRA grounds. Instead, the effectiveness of the CRA enforcement process has rested in the leverage it has provided to community groups in negotiating community-reinvestment agreements.[43] Prior to the CRA's enactment, anti-redlining community struggles had no avenue of effective agency other than public demonstrations and deposit-withdrawal campaigns, because requests to negotiate with bank management about bank investment practices were routinely ignored or affirmatively rebuffed. The CRA changed this dynamic by making bank-regulatory procedures a forum where community complaints about redlining practices would have to be heard.

From an institutional-class perspective, the CRA is a useful start in the right direction. A private right of action to enforce justiciable substantive obligations in a judicial forum arguably might have substantially depoliticized community organizations by shifting agency from community-group organizers to the lawyers who would then fight in the relatively inaccessible forums of judicial process. Instead, the CRA effected a significant redistribution of institutional power among bank managers, regulators, and communities by providing community groups with formal standing to intervene in the regulatory process through which banking institutions get their business-expansion plans approved. This standing has provided community groups with the leverage they needed to be heard. Bank managers started negotiating in earnest with community groups only after the CRA's intervention altered the institutional balance of power between management and communities. This redistribution of power occurred not because bank regulators have been particularly responsive to CRA protests, but because these protests can now trigger substantial, if not fatal, delays in implementing the business plans bank managers desire to pursue. This, in turn, has ensured that the "real action" remains at the negotiating table, where community groups and bank managers attempt to work out lending commitments that will avert CRA protests, rather than channeling the action into the regulatory process where community organizers and negotiators would most likely give way to legal advocates.

Of course, the redistribution of power effected through the CRA enforcement structure has made the act highly controversial, leading opponents to complain that it authorizes regulatory extortion and gives community groups the "extra-ordinary authority to hold up mergers and other obligations."[44] The CRA has been attacked more generally for introducing special-interest politics into, and subordinating the economic logic of the market in, the allocation of capital. In one of many legislative rounds, CRA opponents proposed to amend the statute to eliminate the original enforcement mechanism completely in favor of a "market solution" based on full disclosure. The idea behind this market-based solution was that bank customers would be free to enforce the CRA by taking their business elsewhere.

More recently, after years of political mobilization, CRA opponents have managed to strike a major blow at the democratizing elements of the CRA enforcement structure through various provisions of the Financial Services Modernization Act of 1999.[45] These provisions establish "safe harbors," which alter the examination schedule for banks that have assets of less than $250 million by providing that such banks shall not be examined more than once every four to five years, depending on the rating received during their last CRA examination. They also impose significant new burdens on community groups asserting CRA challenges by establishing a presumption of compliance absent substantial verifiable information to the contrary, thus increasing the community group's costs of even getting to the table. Finally, and perhaps most disturbing, the so-called sunshine provisions of the act affirmatively discriminate against CRA community groups by imposing differential regulatory burdens on CRA agreements. These new regulatory burdens require parties to such agreements to report annually on the terms of such agreements—but only when the agreements are between a depository institution and a nongovernmental entity or person who has commented on, testified about, discussed with, or otherwise contacted the bank concerning the CRA. Agreements made with developers and for-profit corporations are not covered; only agreements entered into in response to CRA inquiries or enforcement efforts.

These new provisions substantially alter the distribution of institutional power previously organized by the enforcement structure of the CRA. Community groups now face new barriers against participating effectively in CRA negotiations with regulated institutions. They not only bear substantial new costs in getting to the bargaining table, but the paper and accounting work associated with "sunshine" reporting may also increase the costs of administering negotiated agreements to degrees that make the struggle for such agreements pointless. The fact that these new provisions discriminate against low- and moderate-income community groups based on their exercise of basic First Amendment rights of freedom of expression, such as the right to testify and to petition government, suggests that the next major round in this struggle will be kicked back to the courts. This leads me to two final points—both of which are informed by an effort to imagine the kind of theory required by the continuing struggle over community participation in the allocation of financial capital.

The first point is that the CRA will remain a highly visible and vulnerable target until some significant victories are won in the realm of legal discourse. This is particularly true if the next round of challenges is to be waged in the courts, where the interpretation of constitutional doctrine has long been captive to the ideological and rhetorical manipulation of discursive constructs such as the economic–political dichotomy.[46] In this field of contestation, the most significant victory would be definitively to delegitimate the economic–political dichotomy, particularly as it is rhetorically manipulated and strategically deployed in neo-liberal discourses. This is because neo-liberal conservatives effortlessly translate the fundamental struggles reflected in the CRA—over the purposes and procedures that should guide the allocation of capital—into a struggle between "efficient markets" and "inefficient special-interest political interventionism." Unpacking the unjusti-

fied assumptions and affirmative misrepresentations embedded in such formulations would alter the discursive universe in which the CRA would be attacked and defended.

Second, and equally important, an institutional-class analysis informed by theoretical advances made in the study of social-movement formations and postmodern political identities suggests that the foregoing analysis of the institutional-class conflict between bank managers and community organizations explores only one dimension of the interclass dynamics that must be attended to in developing legal interventions that will produce more progressive institutional arrangements. For example, communities may be inadequately represented or some community representatives may be tempted to cut special deals for their particular constituents when negotiating community-reinvestment plans at the bargaining table with bank managers, thus raising many of the same issues raised by a Critical Race Feminist analysis of exclusive representation in the context of labor's collective bargaining with management.[47] Identifying these issues and designing institutional reforms that can address them is important theoretical work that will go a long way toward channeling reform energies into the kinds of structures that will make emancipatory agency more effective in struggling against the institutional processes that produce racial spaces.

The World Bank Inspection Panel

Like the earlier CRA analysis, an institutional-class analysis of the World Bank Inspection Panel begins by identifying the various institutional classes whose interactions are mediated by the legal regimes into which the Inspection Panel intervenes. These include the sovereign borrowers, bank project managers, NGOs representing affected communities, the affected communities as self-conscious and mobilized agents, and project contractors such as suppliers, engineers, and planners, among others. The second step is to identify the power bases of each institutional class, the way their interactions are legally mediated, and the way these institutionalized relations of power and powerlessness are implicated in the decisional outcomes through which World Bank development projects have contributed to the production of poverty and the proliferation of racial spaces throughout the Third World.

The Inspection Panel was established by the executive directors of the World Bank in 1993 in response to heavy criticism that the bank's lending practices were irrational; that its financing of large-scale energy projects had resulted in the involuntary resettlement of numerous viable communities; and that its policies promoted environmental destruction in the areas purportedly under development. The quality of the bank's portfolio was judged low, and its lending practices increasingly unprofitable.[48]

The Inspection Panel establishes a potentially significant precedent that may open the way for more fundamental institutional reforms in the field of international law and development. It is the first time that an international forum has been created to deal specifically with the claims of non-state, non-business groups affected by the decisions of an international organization. These same communities were formerly prisoners of impunity, locked behind the legal fiction of state sovereignty. I call it a fiction because the doctrine of sovereignty has not served to shield Third World governments from the intrusive and coercive conditions attached to many World Bank loans, particularly structural-adjustment loans. Nevertheless, this doctrine has routinely been invoked to make the state's internal political process—that is, its treatment of its

own citizens—unreviewable and, ultimately, irrelevant to the negotiation of World Bank development loans. Indeed, the World Bank routinely has dismissed allegations of project-related human-rights violations by borrower governments on the grounds that its Articles of Agreement prohibit the bank from interfering in the domestic "political affairs" of its member states.[49]

The case of the Chixoy River Dam project in Guatemala is one notorious example of how bad these project-related human-rights violations can get.[50] In 1978, the World Bank lent Guatemala $72 million to build a dam on the Chixoy River. When the local population, mostly indigenous Achi Indians, began to organize to resist their eviction from the area, the state responded: Three soldiers assigned to guard the project site fired on a group of citizens who had gathered in a nearby church to rally against the project. Seven people were killed. Terrorized but determined, the people continued to condemn the government's relocation plan, particularly its failure to provide for fair compensation. The villagers were then ordered to report to a civil-defense meeting at a nearby village. Seventy-two of the seventy-three men who went to the meeting were assassinated. A month later, a group of soldiers attacked the village, which at that point was populated almost entirely by women and children because the men had gone into hiding after the earlier massacre. The women and children were raped and killed, and their bodies were thrown into the ravines.

Four months after the massacre, the village disappeared into the rising waters of the Chixoy reservoir, but when the dam was completed, it did not work. As it turned out, the dam was built in a geologically unstable area known for seismic faults. There were so many engineering errors that the dam stopped producing electricity after five months of operation. The World Bank's response was to lend the government of Guatemala $47 million more for repairs. Due to corruption, mismanagement, and incompetence, the initially projected $340 million dam ended up costing $1 billion, not to mention the destruction of an entire village and the murder of its inhabitants.[51]

Although these events occurred twenty years ago, instances of project-related human-rights violations continue. Indeed, of the ten formal Requests for Inspection processed by the World Bank's Inspection Panel during its first three years, at least one case involves allegations of grievous violations directed specifically at communities attempting to resist the destructive impact of a World Bank-financed project.[52] This Request for Inspection concerns the bank's failure to comply with many of its internal policies and operational directives in connection with the World Bank's National Thermal Power Corporation Project (NTPC) in India. According to Probe International, Indian project authorities have resorted to a range of repressive tactics designed to force the local population to move from the project area. State officials have reportedly engaged in beatings, arrests, surveillance, imprisonment, and destruction of property, even as NTPC contractors have been forcibly bulldozing the land of families who have not agreed to move.[53] Almost 200,000 people have been removed from expropriated farmland and forced into crowded resettlement colonies, where they have been relegated to small subsistence plots and short-term contract work. Not only have they been denied the supposed benefits of the project (e.g., electricity), but the basic infrastructure of the settlements has not been maintained, resulting in lack of water, clogged drains, broken water pumps, and lack of medical supplies or services.

The fact that perhaps until now, affected communities have lacked any effective avenue of agency within the state's political or administrative structure for resisting the harmful impact of development projects has been a fundamental and constitutive element of their powerlessness. Standing to invoke the Inspection Panel may change the relations of power and powerlessness between communities and state officials by giving communities an alternative avenue of recourse: direct access to the World Bank's executive directors, by way of the Inspection Panel and its mandate to ensure that World Bank projects are implemented in a manner consistent with the bank's internal policies and operational directives. These directives cover an array of issues, ranging from public participation at all stages of a project to the appropriate procedures for conducting environmental assessments. The Request for Inspection in the NTPC case cited violations of no fewer than six of the World Bank's internal policies and operational directives: 1) Economic Evaluation of Investment Operations; 2) Environmental Assessments; 3) Involuntary Resettlements; 4) Indigenous Peoples; 5) Project Supervision; and 6) Community Participation.

As with both the CRA and the continuing controversy that surrounds it, however, the ability to generate an institutional regime that internalizes the claims and interests, and routinizes the participation, of impoverished communities in the decision-making processes through which World Bank investment capital is allocated depends, at least in part, on our ability to redefine the way the economic–political dichotomy is mapped across the discursive fields of law—in this case, international economic law. It is precisely this dichotomy that underpins and legitimates the substantial limitations imposed on the Inspection Panel's jurisdiction to conduct inspections and make recommendations that address allegations of project-related human-rights violations. The panel's jurisdiction is narrowly restricted to determining whether the bank's staff has failed to comply with the bank's own internal policies and directives. The panel is *not* authorized to assess the legality of state action under international human-rights law, for this might too quickly produce substantial interventions in the domestic political affairs of the borrower state. Its limited jurisdiction keeps the panel within the boundaries of economic concerns because it ensures that the panel will function only to make bank staff accountable to bank policies, which are themselves designed to promote the economic viability of the bank's projects, as defined by the bank's management. Proposals to expand the panel's jurisdiction to address human-rights violations by officials of the borrower would quickly confront the fiction of state sovereignty as inscribed in the political prohibition of the bank's Articles of Agreement.

Equally significant, the Inspection Panel has no jurisdiction to conduct investigations or make recommendations in cases where the alleged harms suffered are caused not by the bank staff's failure to follow internal policies or directives but, rather, by the bank's policies themselves. From an institutional-class perspective, the implications of this jurisdictional limitation are profound. The fact that a panel inspection may lead the executive board of directors to pull the plug on projects where the state's actions are inconsistent with bank policies may certainly empower communities in their interactions with state officials eager for the bank's financial assistance, but it does nothing to empower communities vis-à-vis the bank's executive board or its policies. The panel's recommendations are merely advisory to the executive board, which is itself constituted through a governance structure of weighted voting. Under the bank's Articles of Agreement, voting rights are allocated among member states according to the state's contributions to the

bank's callable capital, thus ensuring greater influence over bank policies and activities to capital exporters over debtor states and, in particular, to the United States. Thus, the Inspection Panel may simply end up encouraging communities to place their hopes and channel their energies into appeals to a highly political and ultimately unresponsive, if not positively hostile, forum, dominated at best by the assumptions of neo-liberal economic ideology and at worst by the strategic self-interested policies of the richest countries.

From this perspective, it is important to note that none of the ten Requests for Inspection formally reported in the Inspection Panel's first two annual reports deals with any claim arising out of a World Bank structural-adjustment loan. With just two exceptions,[54] each of the requests has focused exclusively on claims arising out of World Bank project loans. This is curious, because the bank has, since the 1980s, increasingly focused on policy-based lending. Its structural-adjustment loans have been disbursed throughout the Third World, and particularly in Latin America, to induce Third World governments to implement domestic policies that are more consistent with neo-liberal economic ideology. This has meant a standard recipe of cuts in public services, privatization of state-controlled enterprises, elimination of subsidies for domestic consumption, export-promotion policies that channel resources away from production for the domestic market in order to earn the foreign exchange needed to repay the World Bank and other international creditors, elimination of exchange controls, and currency devaluations that raise the domestic price of imports.

These conditions so routinely attached to World Bank structural-adjustment loans constitute major incursions into the domestic policymaking prerogatives of the state. By triggering substantial opposition from affected communities, these loan-conditioned policies have also escalated the political instability of numerous governments in Latin America.[55] In Nicaragua, to give just one example, government "stabilization" policies aimed at meeting the conditions of a World Bank structural-adjustment loan provoked a remobilization of former combatants—with ex-contras and ex-Sandinistas even joining together in 1992 to protest the government's failure to keep its promises of access to land, credit. and employment. Again, in 1994, Nicaraguans responded to the economic crisis generated by the government's structural-adjustment policies with a series of public strikes, including a transportation strike that effectively stopped the distribution of goods within the country for eight days in protest against hikes in the price of fuel.

Although a number of Latin American governments have tried to address popular concerns through a constructive national dialogue and to resist the conditions imposed by World Bank structural-adjustment loans,[56] neither dialogue nor resistance has been very effective, in large part because the terms of World Bank structural-adjustment loans are, in effect, non-negotiable.[57] They are driven by the self-serving ideology of the rich, which proclaims, like opponents of the CRA in the United States, that unregulated private markets will produce higher standards of living in the long run, despite abundant evidence that the "long run" has come and gone, leaving only an increasing concentration of wealth among elites across the globe, the further immiseration of the poor, and the degradation of their standards of living and the spaces they inhabit.

It is certainly possible that some of the bank's internal policies and operational directives might be invoked to challenge some aspect or another of a particular structural adjustment loan. However, any chal-

lenge going directly to the question whether structural adjustment loan conditions violate fundamental international human rights would be beyond the scope of the Inspection Panel's jurisdiction, as currently established. Proposals to expand the panel's jurisdiction to address such complaints would immediately confront the opposition of precisely those states whose interests are served by the imposition of structural adjustment on borrower states, that is, the rich capital exporting states of the North, whose power in the inter-state system is reflected in the weighted voting rights structure through which the bank is governed. These states are unlikely to give the panel the power to review the policies they themselves are promoting through the bank— particularly given that they have not even given it the power to make binding determinations about the staff's compliance with the bank's own policies.

Thus, whatever the impact of the Inspection Panel on the conflict between government officials and the peoples they govern, it is clear that this conflict is embedded within a broader conflict between rich and poor across many institutional contexts organized by both domestic and international law. As with the CRA, a definitive discursive victory over the economic–political dichotomy would be worthwhile. If nothing else, this kind of victory would make asymmetrical allocations of institutional power more immediately apparent, thus enabling more informed responses. Just as my institutional class analysis of the CRA suggests reasons why legal reform efforts should aim at keeping and expanding "the action" at the negotiating table between banks and communities, my analysis of the Inspection Panel regime suggests reasons why "the action" over World Bank lending practices is still lodged in the legislative forums and executive apparatus of First World governments. While I certainly would welcome a reinvigorated

grassroots mobilization of the American people intent on reclaiming the power of the U.S.
government on behalf of our fundamental
commitments to basic humanity and global
justice—in the meantime—I simply want to
suggest that the purpose of deconstructing
the economic–political dichotomy is to promote the development of alternative legal
regimes and institutional mechanisms,
regimes and mechanisms that will move "the
action" out of the U.S. Departments of Treasury and Commerce and into some other
space, where the effective participation and
adequate representation of affected communities will be better positioned to put the
World Bank out of the business of producing racial spaces.

Conclusion

I would like to conclude with a few remarks
about the kind of legal theory I think is well
worth our efforts and energies. First, there is
no question that power relations are central
to the production of racial spaces, nor that
these relations of power and powerlessness
are mapped across the economic and political institutions of the state and the market.
There is likewise no question that we are
every day in the process of discovering new
aspects, dynamics and expressions of power.
As legal scholars, RaceCrits and LatCrits
have a particular role to play in contributing
to progressive social transformation, which
includes the production of theoretical work
that increases our understanding of the way
power relations are established through the
legal organization of the social, political and
economic institutions that build the racialized environments we both inhabit and seek
to transform.

The call for institutional-class analysis is,
thus, first a call for detailed understanding of
the kinds of decision processes law institutionalizes in different contexts and the way

authority over these decisions is allocated
among competing groups within any particular institutional context. The emphasis here
is on concrete rather than generalized explanations of the way power is constructed,
because concrete and particularized analysis
can enable us to envision how relations of
power and powerlessness can be reconstructed in specific institutions.[58]

Second, analyzing the terms of the struggle over institutional structures is a practice
that quickly moves into an analysis of law as
a discursive universe constructed by and
manipulated through the deployment of
dichotomies such as economics–politics and
special interests–common good. Thus,
analysis of the discursive structures that
organize legal doctrine and political rhetoric is critical to analysis of law's role in the
production of institutional-class structures.

Finally, the call for institutional-class
analysis is a call to move beyond the
race–class dichotomy and domestic myopia
that have disorganized and demobilized so
many progressive coalitions.[59] The major
obstacle to community control of capital is
not some supposed conflict between class
struggles against economic exploitation and
the racial struggle against white supremacy.
Racial spaces are produced by both, in the
United States and abroad. Instead, the problem is that every legislative intervention, regulatory reform, or new strategy of direct
political action is eventually filtered through
legal discourses in which the dichotomiza-
tion of economics and politics is strategically manipulated to maintain structures of
privilege and resist the democratization of
both the state and the economy.

This is to say that Critical Race Theory
is best understood as an antisubordination
project in the production of legal scholarship. However removed from or immediate
to the struggle against subordination legal
scholarship may be, the fact is that the production of legal scholarship would go on

without Critical Race Theory if RaceCrits were ever misguided enough to abandon the field. It would go on because legal scholarship serves the important function of rationalizing, synthesizing, and disseminating the decision outcomes and doctrinal formulations through which legal institutions simultaneously deploy their own unique forms of power and organize the relations of power and powerlessness that operate in virtually every other social institution that mediates human interaction. From the public institutions of local, state, and federal governments, to private institutions such as banks, corporations, labor unions, to even the most supposedly intimate relations of family and sexuality, law is everywhere implicated in the organization of power and powerlessness. Critical Race Theory thus has had and will continue to have significant impact on the struggle for social racial justice, precisely because law is about power, and legal scholarship is about the rationalization of power. To the extent that CRT increases our collective understanding of the ways in which law, legal process, and legal institutions participate in the reproduction of subordination, it will help to reveal the stakes in the production of legal knowledge. The stakes are very high indeed.

Notes

Epigraphs: U. S. Anderson, *Three Magic Words* (North Hollywood, Calif.: Wilshire Book, 1954), 91. Karl Marx, "The German Ideology," in *Marx and Engels Reader,* ed. Robert C. Tucker (New York: Norton Publishing, 1972), 64.

1. See Jonathan R. Macey and Geoffrey P. Miller, "The Community Reinvestment Act: An Economic Analysis," *Virginia Law Review* 79 (1993): 291, 301, n. 65.

2. For a phenomenological account of the way racism inhibits minority movement through racialized spaces, see Anthony Paul Farley's chapter in this volume.

3. See, for example, "Nowhere to Go," *Christian Science Monitor,* December 10, 1986, 22, reporting on the forced relocation of Guatemalan Indians from their villages to "model villages" as part of the Guatemalan army's counter-insurgency strategy based on the Vietnam model; "Little Hope: Human Rights in Guatemala," *Americas Watch Report* (January 1984–January 1985), 25, reporting that "after the military's massive scorched earth tactics and massacres of 1982 and early 1983, thousands of Indians displaced from their lands ... were resettled in model villages.... The army represents the ultimate authority in the village; and the residents were not free to go"; "Indians Reoriented at Model Village," *Washington Post,* November 23, 1986 (final edition), A22, reporting the advantages of living in the model villages).

4. See, for example, Brian McAllister, "The United Nations Conference on Environment and Development: An Opportunity to Forge a New Unity in the Work of the World Bank among Human Rights, the Environment, and Sustainable Development," *Hastings International and Comparative Law Review* 16 (1993): 689

5. Hernando De Soto, *The Other Path: The Invisible Revolution in the Third World,* trans. June Abbott (New York: Harper and Row, 1989).

6. Ibid, xxiv.

7. I am thinking here of the way the enactment of Title VII must have appeared to the minority union workers whose unions were destroyed and whose collective power was diluted by the Title VII cases ordering the compulsory merger of their unions into the larger, all-white unions in which they were to become a powerless minority. For an extensive analysis of how decentralized adjudication hides the structural violence produced through legal interpretation, see also Elizabeth M. Iglesias, "Structures of Subordination: Women of Color at the Intersection of Title VII and the NLRA. Not!" *Harvard Civil Rights–Civil Liberties Law Review* 28 (1993): 395.

8. Ibid., revealing how the structural intersections of Title VII of the Civil Rights Act of 1964, 42 U.S.C. § 2000e *et seq.,* and the National Labor Relations Act, 29 U.S.C. § 151 *et seq.,* suppress the avenues of legal agency available for women of color to engage lawfully in transformative struggle over the terms and conditions of work.

9. These three themes have been central in the emergent body of LatCrit scholarship, which reflects a concerted, collective project "to reinvigorate the antisubordination agenda of Critical Race Theory, revive its ethical aspirations, and expand its sub-

stantive scope": See idem, "Foreword: International Law, Human Rights and LatCrit Theory," *University of Miami Inter-American Law Review* 28 (1996–97): 177–8, exploring the significance of international human rights in the articulation of LatCrit anti-subordination agendas both within and beyond the United States. For more extensive accounts of the way LatCrit theory is reimagining the parameters of Critical Race Theory along multiple dimensions, see idem, "Out of the Shadow: Marking Intersections in and between Asian Pacific American Critical Legal Scholarship and Latina/o Critical Theory," *Boston College Law Review* 40 (1998): 349, and *Boston College Third World Law Journal* 19 (1998): 349; idem, "Foreword: Identity, Democracy, Communicative Power, Inter/National Labor Rights and Evolution of LatCrit Theory and Community," *University of Miami Law Review* 53 (1999): 575; Elizabeth M. Iglesias and Francisco Valdes, "Religion, Gender, Sexuality, Race and Class in Coalitional Theory: A Critical and Self-Critical Analysis of LatCrit Social Justice Agendas," *Chicano–Latino Law Review* 19 (1998): 503.

10. See Orin Starn, Carlos Degregori, and Robin Kirk, eds., *The Peru Reader: History, Culture, Politics* (Durham, N.C.: Duke University Press, 1995), for an account of the contradictory theories about the who and the why of the Shining Path.

11. See De Soto, *The Other Path*, n.p., quoting Michael Novak: "The big argument among Latin America's Catholics today may be symbolized thus: Gustavo (Gutierrez: *The Theology of Liberation*) vs. Hernando (De Soto: [*The Other Path*]). . . . Hernando speaks for the poor [and] makes a revolutionary critique of elites both of the right and left."

12. When I presented this paper at the CRT conference at Yale in November 1997, my friend Enrique Carrasco took issue with my use of the term "neo-liberal conservatives" by asking me whether there was such a thing as a "neo-liberal radical." I answered that indeed there is such a thing: "The neo-liberal radical is, in effect, a communist." Embedded in both his question and my answer is the paradox of the way ideologies converge at their extremes. Indeed, a careful reading of Marx's *The German Ideology* might lead anyone with half a(n open) mind to conclude that "the final stage of communism" would be a neo-liberal paradise of flexible production and unrestricted circulation of goods, capital and labor—a postmodern paradise of personal freedom, for, according to Marx: "In communist society, where nobody has one exclusive sphere of activity but each can become accomplished in any branch he wishes, society regulates the general production and

thus makes it possible for me to do one thing today and another tomorrow, to hunt in the morning, fish in the afternoon, rear cattle in the evening, criticize after dinner, just as I have a mind, without ever becoming hunter, fisherman, shepherd or critic": Marx, "German Ideology," 124.

13. Jane Kaufman Winn, "How To Make Poor Countries Rich and How to Enrich Our Poor" (review of De Soto, *The Other Path*), *Iowa Law Review* 77 (1992): 899. Winn quotes Reagan's Address to the United Nations General Assembly, New York, September 21, 1987. Like his predecessor, President George Bush was also much impressed. Addressing the annual meeting of the World Bank and the International Monetary Fund (IMF) in September 1989, Bush referred to De Soto's work this way: "De Soto's great contribution has been to point out what in retrospect may seem obvious: people everywhere want the same things. . . . De Soto's prescription offers a clear and promising alternative to economic stagnation in Latin America and other parts of the world. Government must bring the "informal" workers into the regular economy and then get out of the way and let individual enterprise flourish." See President George Bush, Speech to the World Bank–IMF Annual Meeting, September 27, 1989, as quoted in ibid., 899, n. 2. President Richard Nixon was yet another fan.

14. De Soto, *The Other Path*, 132–4.

15. Ibid, 135. De Soto provides a graph of the average length of the various procedures required in formalizing the business. The purpose and outcome of these procedures was to acquire some required license, certificate, or registration.

16. See Hernando De Soto, "The Informals Pose an Answer to Marx," *Washington Quarterly* 12 (Winter 1989): 165; Kaufman Winn, "How to Make Poor Countries Rich."

17. See, for example, Elizabeth M. Iglesias, "Institutionalizing Economic Justice: A LatCrit Perspective on the Imperatives of Linking the Reconstruction of 'Community' to the Transformation of Legal Structures that Institutionalize the Depoliticization and Fragmentation of Labor/Community Solidarity," *University of Pennsylvania Journal of Labor and Employment Law* 2 (2000): 773, 797–79, urging that the measure of a regime's legitimacy is not the fact that justice can be achieved through the extraordinary efforts and agency of otherwise marginalized persons but, rather, the extent to which the regime enables the achievement of justice *on a routine basis.*

18. See, for example, Alan Mabin, "On the Problems and Prospects of Overcoming Segregation and

Fragmentation in Southern Africa's Cities in the Postmodern Era," in *PostModern Cities and Spaces*, ed. Sophie Watson and Katherine Gibson (Malden: Blackwell Publishers, 1995).

19. Ibid., 188.

20. Ibid., 189–90.

21. Laurence Harris, "The Political Economy of Reform in South Africa," in *Marxism in the Post Modern Age: Confronting the New World Order*, ed. Antonio Callari, Stephen Cullenberg and Carole Biewener (New York: Guilford Press, 1995), 315.

22. Ibid., 316. Harris explains that the economic agenda initially embraced within the Congress of South African Trade Unions (COSATU), South African Communist Party (SACP), and African National Congress (ANC), and referred to by the slogan "Growth Through Redistribution," emphasized that "the state should take a strong role in redistributing income and wealth toward the masses, simultaneously developing domestic industry's production to meet the demand for increased living standards, and essentially growing on the basis of the domestic market, while seeking simultaneously to increase the competitiveness of export industries": ibid. This prescription should be familiar to Latin American development economists, as well as to LatCrit scholars. See, for example, Enrique R. Carrasco, "Opposition, Justice, Structuralism, and Particularity: Intersections Between LatCrit Theory and Law and Development Studies," *University of Miami Inter-American Law Review* 28 (1996–97): 313, taking critical perspective on the failure of radical development economics to achieve any meaningful transformation in Latin America; but see also Iglesias, "Foreword: International Law," 177, 200, suggesting alternative reasons for this failure. In either event, Growth Through Redistribution promotes an agenda that is distinct from both the right-wing trickle-down alternative of "growth and redistribution" and the World Bank's approach focusing on "growth with distribution."

23. See, for example, Elizabeth M. Iglesias, "Rape, Race and Representation: The Power of Discourse, Discourses of Power and the Reconstruction of Heterosexuality," *Vanderbilt Law Review* 49 (1996): 869, 929–43, n. 174, exploring the problem of designing effective legal strategies for eliminating rape in the absence of a positive substantive vision of what heterosexual autonomy means to women.

24. Iglesias, "Structures of Subordination," locating the legal production of structural violence in the interpretative manipulation of fundamental conceptual structures such as the individual-collective rights dichotomy, special interests-common good, group membership as prerequisite (or not) of representational authority.

25. I address these points more fully in a longer work in progress entitled, "Structural Violence: Law and the Anti-Political Economy" (forthcoming).

26. According to De Soto, "The findings of *The Other Path* challenge those who assert that Latin American culture, particularly the Indian and mestizo traditions, is incompatible with the entrepreneurial spirit and the democratic and economic systems of the more economically advanced nations of the world Contrary to this preconception, ILD research has found that informals maintain private regimes through extralegal norms that they have created, and that these norms allow for healthy competition in which contractual rights are enforced": De Soto, *The Other Path*, xxiv.

27. According to De Soto, "The ILD has looked at the actual experience in Peru and has found that it is not the elimination of the entrepreneurial class that the poor want On the contrary, *they want the state to remove the obstacles that it has constructed* that handicap their entrepreneurial efforts": ibid., xxvi.

28. See, for example, Margaret Beebe Held, "Developing Micro-Businesses in Public Housing: Notes from the Field," *Harvard Civil Rights–Civil Liberties Law Review* 31 (1996): 473.

29. See, for example, Julia Ann Parzen and Michael Hall Kieschnick, eds., *Credit Where It's Due: Development Banking for Communities* (Philadelphia: Temple University Press, 1992), 47, which notes that "today, the great majority of business lending is done by financial intermediaries that have formal methods to compare the local business loan to finance inventory with a loan to finance the latest megamerger, or a loan to finance construction of a power plant in Brazil, or a loan to finance the purchase of mortgages made in a distant state. Increasingly, every investment is compared to every other investment on the basis of risk, return and liquidity and priced accordingly."

30. See William Greider, *Secrets of the Temple* (New York: Simon and Schuster Trade, 1987), 144–5, 189–90, recounting how the "free-market" decisions of U.S. banks and brokerages participated in financing one of the most outrageous conspiracies to establish a monopoly.

31. See Martin Mayer, *The Greatest-Ever Bank Robbery: The Collapse of the Savings and Loan Industry* (New York: Simon and Schuster Trade, 1990), recounting the consequences of deregulation on the savings-and-loan industry.

32. See generally Sylvia Maxfield, *Governing Capital: International Finance and Mexican Politics* (Ithaca, N.Y.: Cornell University Press, 1990).

33. See, for example, Jorge Dominguez, *Capital Flows in Minority Areas* (Lexington, Mass.: Lexington Books, 1976), 22. Studying the flow of capital in minority communities, Dominguez makes the following observations about the role of "price" in the allocation of capital: "A statistical survey of minority businessmen was conducted in which the businessmen were asked to list the factors that determined whether or not they received investment funds from lending institutions. Most respondents placed little emphasis upon the cost of borrowing, since they normally expected to pay higher rates of interest than borrowers outside the inner city, and since changes in the rate of interest did not affect the availability of capital. Also most of the businessmen stated that their expected returns for a given venture were usually substantially above the negotiated rate of interest. The principle problem they identified was the acquisition of funds from financial institutions which were generally reluctant to make loans in the ghetto—not the level of interest rates."

34. Kaufmann Winn, "How to Make Poor Countries Rich," providing economic analysis of situation of informals after deregulation.

35. See, for example, Sylvia Maxfield, "National Business, Debt-Led Growth and Political Transition in Latin America," in *Debt and Democracy in Latin America*, ed. Barbara Stallings and Robert Kaufman (Boulder, Colo.: Westview Press, 1989).

36. Iglesias, "Structures of Subordination," contrasting the relative impact on minority interests and the transformative potential of legal strategies aimed at reforming the substantive elements of the NLRA's duty of fair representation or Title VII's antidiscrimination mandates, on the one hand, as compared with legal strategies aimed at reorganizing the institutional arrangements of majoritarian power that currently structure the processes of collective bargaining, on the other.

37. In a longer work in progress, I map out the strategic manipulation of the separation and interpenetration of politics and economics across various regulatory frameworks and institutional contexts to deconstruct the institutional class structures of the neo-liberal political economy: Iglesias, "Structural Violence."

38. See, for example, Iglesias, "Institutionalizing Economic Justice," exploring this point through a case study of labor and community activism involving coercive police intervention.

39. Richard Marsico, "A Guide to Enforcing the Community Reinvestment Act," *Fordham Urban Law Journal* 20 (1993): 165, 170, n. 4, describing the four federal regulatory agencies.

40. Congress strengthened the statute in 1989 by requiring bank regulators to prepare a public, written evaluation of the applicant's CRA performance and establishing a new system for rating the level of compliance with CRA requirements. The 1989 amendments also required that CRA ratings be made public for the first time. In 1995, federal regulatory agencies finalized a series of new regulations making important changes, including new evaluation criteria. See, for example, E. L. Baldinucci, "The Community Reinvestment Act: New Standards Provide New Hope," *Fordham Urban Law Journal* 23 (1996): 831. Nevertheless, the act remains the subject of controversy, and Congressional efforts to repeal it are sustained and persistent: ibid.

41. Calvin Bradford and Gale Cincotta, "The Legacy, the Promise, and the Unfinished Agenda," in *From Redlining to Reinvestment*, ed. Gregory D. Squires (Philadelphia: Temple University Press, 1992); Allen J. Fishbein, "The Community Reinvestment Act after Fifteen Years: It Works, but Strengthened Federal Enforcement Is Needed," *Fordham Urban Law Journal* 20 (1993): 293, 298: "The CRA is credited with resulting in total commitments in excess of $30 billion to poor communities throughout the country, far exceeding whatever conditions would have been imposed by regulators." Cf. Macey and Miller, "The Community Reinvestment Act," arguing that the dollar values are not as significant as they appear at first glance.

42. 12 U.S. C. § 2903. An application to acquire a depository facility includes applications for national-bank or thrift-institution charters; deposit insurance in connection with a newly chartered depository institution; the establishment of a domestic branch; the relocation of a home or branch office; merger or consolidation with, the acquisition of the assets of, or the assumption of the liabilities of a depository institution; and the acquisition of shares in a depository institution requiring approval under the federal Bank Holding Company Act or Savings Association Holding Company Act: ibid., § 2902(3).

43. Fishbein, "Community Reinvestment Act after Fifteen Years," 293, 298.

44. See Credit Opp Amend Act of 1997, 143 *Congressional Record* E72-01 (statement of Representative Bill McCollum).

45. The Financial Services Modernization Act of 1999 was officially enacted as the Gramm-Leach-Bliley Act of 1999, Public Law 106-102, 1999 U.S.C.C.A.N. (113 Stat.) 1338. This legislation, which has been called "the granddaddy of all financial deregulation," significantly lowers barriers between the banking and securities industries established by the Glass-Steagall Act of 1933 as well as barriers the Bank Holding Company Act of 1956 established between the banking and insurance industries. See Ralph Nader, "The Democrats Bow to the Megabanks," *The Progressive* (January 2000), 24, noting that the financial sector tossed in $155 million to Congressional candidates in the 1998 election while the "House-Senate conferees, who made the critical decisions on the final shape of the legislation, received more than $16 million among themselves."

46. See, for example, Iglesias, "Structural Violence."

47. Idem, "Structures of Subordination."

48. See Daniel D. Bradlow, "International Organizations and Private Complaints: The Case of the World Bank Inspection Panel," *Virginia Journal of International Law* 34 (1994): 553; Ellen Hey, "The World Bank Inspection Panel: Towards the Recognition of a New Legally Relevant Relationship in International Law," *Hofstra Law and Policy Symposium* 2 (1997): 61.

49. Daniel D. Bradlow, "The World Bank, the IMF, and Human Rights," *Transnational Law and Contemporary Problems* 6 (1996): 47, 54, noting that the Articles of both the International Bank for Reconstruction and Development and the International Development Association state that, "The Bank and its officers shall not interfere in the political affairs of any member, nor shall they be influenced in their decisions by the political character of the member or members concerned. Only economic considerations shall be relevant to their decisions."

50. "World Bank Energy Complex Creates Hell on Earth for Indian Citizens," Probe International (Website). Available from: <http://www.probeinternational.org/pi/wb/index.cfm?DSP-content&ContentID=1208> (visited August 30, 1998), citing Catherine Caufield, *Masters of Illusion: The World Bank and the Poverty of Nations* (New York: Henry Holt, 1996).

51. Ibid.

52. See "Request No 10: India: National Thermal Power Corporation Project," *World Bank Inspection Panel Annual Report, 1996–1997.*

53. See "World Bank Energy Complex."

54. See "Request for Inspection 2: Compensation for Expropriation of Foreign Assets in Ethiopia 1995," *World Inspection Panel Annual Report 1994–96* (request rejected on grounds that requestor had not exhausted local remedies and that requester failed to show how failure to compensate was consequence of bank actions or omissions); and "Request for Inspection 8: Jute Sector Adjustment Credit, Bangladesh, 1996," *World Inspection Panel Annual Report, 1996–97* (rejecting management's claim that it had no responsibility for the implementation of sectoral-adjustment claims).

55. See Development Group for Alternative Policies (DGAP), "Structural Adjustment and the Spreading Crisis in Latin America" (1995), Website, 16–7, available from: <http://www.igc.apc.org/dgap/crisis.html> (visited March 9, 1998).

56. Diana E. Moller, "Intervention, Coercion, or Justifiable Need? A Legal Analysis of Structural Adjustment Lending in Costa Rica," *Southwestern Journal of Law and Trade in the Americas* 2 (Fall 1995): 483.

57. See DGAP, "Structural Adjustment," reporting on the 1994 World Bank–IMF consultations in which the Nicaraguan government arranged to include several non-governmental organizations and academic groups: "NGOs, many of whom came to the sessions with their own analyses and alternative proposals, reported that the meetings on the adjustment package were little more than briefings on the programs planned by the Bank and the Fund with scant opportunity for constructive dialogue Whatever the government's intentions in organizing the meetings, in reality it had little latitude to change the nature of the adjustment program, given the loan conditions of the international financial institutions and its own desperate need for foreign exchange."

58. See Carrasco, "Opposition, Justice," urging LatCrit scholars to master and engage the language of economic analysis and finance theory in order to equip themselves for the radical monitoring necessary to combat the structural discrimination that neo-liberal policies and institutional arrangements tend to produce.

59. See, for example, Iglesias, "Out of the Shadow."

CHAPTER FOURTEEN

Global Feminism at the Local Level: The Criminalization of Female Genital Surgeries

Isabelle R. Gunning

THIS CHAPTER on the local impact of a set of domestic laws targeting African-born resident and citizen women is part of a set of essays that use Critical Race Theory to analyze transnational law. In particular, this essay uses a child of CRT, Critical Race Feminism (CRF), which focuses on the perspectives of and effects on women of color to examine these laws, the political maneuvering involved in the enactment of these laws, and the social impact of these laws on their targets: women of color.

CRT has not been widely understood to encompass international and transnational legal approaches, but its ideological heritage is clearly consistent with a global critique.[1] CRT has both intellectual and activist roots that encompass traditional notions of using law as a tool for struggle and to go beyond that approach to include the action of producing knowledge as an additional site of political engagement.[2]

The early scholars in the CRT movement were molded by the intellectual and political ideas and actions of the Civil Rights Movement—especially the Black Power movement.[3] This progressive intellectual and activist heritage was marked by leaders and organizations—from Dr. Martin Luther King, Jr., to Malcolm X and the Black Panther Party—who consciously understood and articulated the fact that domestic political analysis and action were inextricably intertwined with international politics and struggle.[4] This progressive tradition informed CRT's legal analyses and included the influence of international legal scholars.[5] The impact of women of color in this progressive intellectual and activist tradition has been profound, if unheralded until recently. The emergence of CRF as a related CRT approach in analyzing international and transnational law in general and in the context of political practice was inevitable, given this history.[6]

International law has not historically been designed to address or respond to the concerns and needs of women of color. Like law in the domestic context, international law is the law of the victors, the powerful. The origins of international law dealt exclusively with the law that governed nations—and only those nations that were considered "civilized" (read, Western), at that. The decolonization process expanded the list of nations that could be considered members of the international community; it also introduced the concept of "peoples" or colonized peoples. People's rights came along with a notion of individual human rights. And internationally, "human" has meant what it has long meant domestically—men, generally elite, powerful men. It is out of that history that women have engaged in a struggle to get our interests and perspectives recognized so we can begin to talk about and ask about the contours of a global feminism.

Increasingly, issues affecting women have been put or pushed to the center stage of international discussion. The Convention on the Elimination of All Forms of Discrimination Against Women (1981) and its related committee, which monitors the global status of women, is but one example of the ways in which women's issues have attained a global status and but one of the forums in which a "global feminism" has been developing. I will not attempt to define the contours of this emerging global feminism. But I do think—however it has begun to be defined—that we see the same problems of essentialism that CRT and CRF scholars have criticized in domestic notions of feminism (put simply, that the experiences and perspectives of elite, Western women are privileged). So when women of color attempt to use law as a tool to improve our lives and as a symbolic space in which to create a true expression of our condition, we are often caught in a fundamental contradiction. What I will explore is the complicated impact on women of color of laws that derive from this global feminist movement.

Why Female Genital Surgeries Legislation?

I will examine these contradictions or effects in the context of recent anti–female-genital-surgeries (FGS) legislation enacted by a number of states and the federal government of the United States—in particular, the federal bill and the California bill.[7] I use FGS as an example because it allows an exploration of the problematics of global feminism from a CRF perspective. FGS is a practice that apparently is performed only in a few cultures other than the United States. These FGS activities have become a global issue—a symbol of a range of what are often characterized as "harmful traditional practices" that affect women and that feminists in the international context have been fighting to get moved from the margins of acceptable cultural norms to the center stage of political oppression and human-rights violations. As part of that international movement, individual nations—largely, but not exclusively, First World or Western—have begun to address the issue by passing various laws that criminalize these practices. Accordingly, this is a good place to explore how what seems to be a positive political move to put women's issues—perhaps, women-of-color issues—on the international agenda has actually affected the lives of women of color in one particular domestic context the United States.

I have also chosen FGS because it is an area in which I have worked. Five years ago, I published an article on FGS that largely deconstructed the language and approach of Western feminists to FGS and identified an arrogant perception in the Western gaze. In that article, I constructed a three-part model to combat this.[8] I addressed the use of law to combat the surgeries. Although I then suggested that the law's symbolic prescriptions might have some use, I determined that its coercive punishment aspects were highly problematic. Thus, it was with some irony that I have found myself heavily involved politically, of late, with anti-FGS criminal statutes. But this is fertile ground for exposing the contradictions.

What Is Wrong with the Law?

My continuing unease with the use of the law as a tool and as a representational symbol for the benefit of women of color probably is not surprising. Women of color so rarely have any input into the makings of laws that do or are designed to affect us. Indeed, the colonial history of anti-FGS laws reveals how troublesome and ineffective imposing foreign values on people can be. However, there is a way in which the domestic anti-FGS bills have their origins in the global feminist movement, with which women of color—in this instance, African women—particularly have been involved. African activists and feminists, who are often but not exclusively from nations or groups that are most directly affected by these practices, have been participants in the diverse array of individuals and groups who have struggled for world attention to abolish the surgeries. However, their presence has not resolved the problem women of color often face of having laws demean and damage us, their intended or claimed beneficiaries. Clearly, part of the reason stems from the diversity within essentialist-sounding terms such as "women of color" and "African feminists." Class, educational, and cultural gaps often exist among the African women who have the means to work in international organizations and those who are most directly involved with FGS—that is, the circumcisers and midwives, the grandmothers and mommas, who live more modest, family-centered lives in African villages and immigrant African communities in Western cities.

Part of the problem lies in the law itself. In part, there is debate over whether law as a tool—that is, a method of change involving force—is effective or respectful of non-white women and their concerns. At the level of international "law," this issue is secondary. Because the international community relies on nations to effectuate the law as they see fit, the focus typically falls on the creation of norms and on law in its symbolic value. But a complex issue is involved in the symbolic value of law and its language. What should we call this "illegal" thing? And who are we talking to?

At the international level, the term "female genital mutilation" has its virtues. At United Nations-related conferences and committees, using severe language that invokes uncontested international human-rights violations such as torture is an effective approach to moving the surgeries from private cultural norm to public political practice. Being recognized as a human-rights violation has the symbolic effect of taking women's lives seriously and the practical effect of possibly attracting resources from international organizations. However, it is not at all clear that using as inflammatory a term as "female genital mutilation" is effective in persuading those who most need to change their ways.

The participation of women of color and of African feminists in the continuing process of bringing about a norm against the FGS is a positive thing. But the complications and contradictions of using the law continue down to the national level when one looks at the ways in which anti-FGS laws have come about in the United States.

Why Do We Have Anti-FGS Laws, and Who Are They Talking To?

When I became involved with the African Community Resources Center (ACRC) in

Los Angeles, an African refugee and immigrant community group,[9] its members were already burdened with a multiplicity of problems, including English-language training, job training, culture clash, citizenship classes, and domestic violence. At the same time, they were reeling from the news of the passage of California's anti-FGS bill. Members of the Center's women's focus group, which was and remains most involved in the legislation, asked, "Why are they passing this law? We have been performing circumcision for generations. We have been battling against the surgeries for generations. Why are they attacking us now?"

These are interesting questions. In part, I suppose, I have answered them: As I said earlier, FGS has become something of an international symbol of harmful traditional practices at the international level, and typically, once a practice or situation is recognized as an international human-rights violation or a problem of some kind, the aim is to get individual nations to take action to "enforce" that global norm or determination. But it is interesting that the response to the international concern about FGS—given the problems and moral valuations involved in coercing people to change and the complexities of what kind of a symbol such a law would provide, given the nature of the problem—would lie in criminal legislation as opposed to, say, a health-care and educational plan and program, as one sees in many African countries. When the American Academy of Pediatrics determined some twenty-five years ago that male circumcision has no health benefits whatsoever,[10] why was no law passed prohibiting that practice, under threat of fines and imprisonment? Perhaps the option was raised, but because of the deep-seated religious, aesthetic, and cultural norms surrounding male circumcision, an educational approach was chosen. For FGS, the chosen approach has been criminalization.

I am sure that the complete answer is very complex. But although I recognize that compelling arguments exist for criminalization, I think that criminalization has gained great popularity in the United States because it is a safe and easy way to pretend to address race and gender issues at a time when those of us who continue to care about such things are sneered at as "politically correct" and those who have never cared feel as if they are getting America "back." These bills have passed with ease, with little debate, discussion, research, mark-up, or controversy in Sacramento or Washington, D.C. (These capitals are places where elite white women occasionally can get their needs met. They are not places where women of color, immigrants, or poor people have been welcome in recent years, if they ever were.)

The ease with which these bills pass means that conservatives who are otherwise busy trashing welfare, health care—you name it—have suddenly found concern for colored women. That is, the bills have a cynical symbolic value: Supporting such a bill is one way for a conservative whose voting record has demonstrated little interest in women or people of color to claim that he indeed has racial and gender concerns. Moreover, voting for the bills provides opportunities for the conservative to make speeches in which he (or she) can safely and comfortably denounce African culture and people—for example, to label Africans as the most egregious of child abusers, as was done both in California and at the federal level. In addition, such a vote is cost-free: No resources are taken away from one's constituents when such legislation is passed. Although the California and federal bills call for further study of the problem and the creation of health and educational material, no monies have been allocated for these programs.

Along with conservative legislators who vote for the bills are the liberals who, sometimes at the behest of feminist groups, often propose this legislation. Although these feminist groups and legislators are well meaning, in contrast with their conservative brethren, they are largely white and almost exclusively American. Being a woman of color but American—I am thinking here of Carol Mosely Braun, a sponsor and supporter of the federal bill—apparently created blind spots in thinking through the actual impact of the legislation. The white feminists suffered a similar fate, but multiplied, because white feminists have a need to make symbolic gestures around their concerns for race matters within feminism.

White feminists still have a tendency to be essentialist about what a real woman is, and they remain indifferent to the multiple circumstances and perspectives of women of color. They find it difficult to be truly in coalition with women of color. The anti-FGS bills did not raise that problem for white feminists, who apparently felt that they did not have to "talk" to anyone, viewing, as I think they did, the targeted or affected African refugee and immigrant communities as people who do not speak English and probably do not vote—or, in other words, people they have to take care of because "they are not yet able to speak for themselves."[11] Had the issue been viewed as one that affected "indigenous," or native-born, African Americans, there would have been Black legislators and major civil-rights organizations to approach and persuade, fight with, and kowtow to. FGS was outside such traditional political practices.

When you look at the list of organizations that sponsored the California anti-FGS bill, you will see no African American organizations—not even specifically black women's organizations—and only one African organization, which, though affiliated with a large international group, is actually extremely small and new in California. There are other African immigrant

groups throughout the state, typically in the big cities such as Los Angeles, San Diego, and the San Francisco Bay area, but none of these was informed or questioned. The executive director of the Los Angeles group with which I work was one African community leader at the helm of one such group that was ignored. She is well known in Sacramento and Washington, D.C., circles dealing with refugee and African matters, yet none of her contacts and colleagues thought to inform her or ask her opinion about the California bill as it made its way through the legislative process. However, not one but several largely white feminist and community organizations were consulted or contacted for input and support.

The federal bill includes no list of supporting organizations. The federal government gathered experts and concerned activists in more of a conference than a congressional hearing to provide information and various perspectives on the problem that the bill is designed to address. The array of invitees to this symposium was far more diverse than California's supporters and included several African feminists—including the executive director of the Los Angeles center. Unfortunately, the symposium was held on the very day that the president signed the bill into law, so the participants clearly had little if any impact on the creation and substance of the bill.

What Is the Result of the Absence of African Women's Input?

Although these bills are touted as representing a serious American response to an international human-rights issue that affects women—African women—and about which African women themselves have concerns, the reality of their passage is that the process has excluded the voices of most African women who are living in this country and connected to the targeted communities. This means that no serious discussion of the efficacy of a criminalization approach versus a public-health and educational approach has taken place, as we see raging, for example, in the context of AIDS.[12] There has also been no full discussion on the social import and weight of language. Should we call the practice female genital mutilation, female genital surgeries, or female circumcision? What will the impact be of using only one or all of these terms? The lack of a resolution to these questions has contributed to the contradictory position in which many African feminists find themselves—that of being forced to attack a part of their culture that they dislike by denouncing the entire culture that they love.

My work in Los Angeles with the ACRC has involved crafting a revision of the California anti-FGS bill in response to the concerns of various representatives of the African communities in Los Angeles and San Diego. Not all of the women whom I have met have been opposed to the surgeries. I have talked with women who have invoked, in all sincerity, the health, sexuality, cleanliness, aesthetic, and religious rationales that are usually used to support the surgeries. Others have been quite opposed to the surgeries, although the tenor of their opposition would be considered muted by Western standards. Sometimes the quietness of their opposition reflects a general discomfort with speaking about such matters. Sometimes it reflects fear of being criticized or ostracized by the remnants of the familiar African community that they have managed to piece together in their new and often hostile home, America. Sometimes the opposition is gentle because the opponents are leaders who are so concerned about getting too far ahead of the people they lead, love, and connect with that they are willing to slow down and speak in understandable terms so that their friends, families, and constituents will hear what they

are saying. Whatever the approach, though, the consensus was to support the law. Some did so because they opposed the surgeries and, although this approach would not be their first choice of method, they supported the symbol of opposition. Others who might otherwise have supported the surgeries were clear about being "good citizens." I use that term not in the legalistic sense of naturalization, but in the true social sense: They felt that they wanted to be part of this new home, and that involves responsibility for respecting the law.

However, they did have concerns. First, they objected to the use of the term "female genital mutilation." This was not an easy decision. There was a loud and sometimes angry debate among the ACRC board members—all of whom present were immigrant or refugee African—over the choice of language. Some women felt that "female genital mutilation" was the correct characterization of the procedures and the proper political symbol to project. Others felt that the term "mutilation" would be so offensive to so many members of the African immigrant and refugee communities that they would be repelled from getting the available educational and health-care information. Ultimately, the group agreed—and several other California groups concurred—that the term "female circumcision" would be more appropriate. The board members were also concerned about the validity of the one study that had been done in California to support the proposition that cuttings of children was going on with some regularity in the state. They wanted another study—preferably one in which African and African American scholars were more intimately involved. And they were concerned about the location of the new bill in the California child-abuse statutes. All found the characterization of their parents and grandparents as child abusers offensive and disrespectful, and a few were fearful of the impact of child welfare and protective services in the lives of immigrant African families.

After a series of meetings not only with the ACRC board, but also with members of the Center's women's focus group and, more generally, with members of the communities that the organization serves, I drew up a draft of a new bill and, along with staff members, some talking points about female circumcision. The organization then decided to do two things: 1) to participate in whatever meetings the California Department of Health's Office of Women's Health, the agency designated to implement the new bill, would hold in its effort to gather information and create educational materials; and 2) to lobby for a change in the actual bill. We are currently engaged in both of these projects, but our presence has been greeted with discomfort and hostility.

We struggle within a binary oppositionality: If you are willing to call the practices female genital mutilation, then it follows that you are against the surgeries and for the rights and health of girls and women. If you call the practices female circumcision, no matter what else you say, you must be characterized as for the surgeries and, consequently, if unwittingly, against the rights and health of girls and women. So if you want government and societal support—and possibly money, because it is also clear that much of the jockeying among groups and academics is about who will receive funding that the Office of Women's Health promises will come down the pike—to combat the surgeries, you must ignore the disrespect that the process and language shows toward African women as intelligent and self-actualizing adults and parents; you must be blind to the denigration of your culture; and you must remain uncritical of—rather, you must be grateful for—whatever attentions and plans, however ill fitting, are made for you.

These anti-FGS bills, which are consistent with one level of the international struggle

to end the surgeries, focus on law as symbol. Although law as a tool is a reality at the national and domestic level, the focus of the bills' legislators and supporters seems largely to be on what supporting the bill can stand for. That is, "I as a legislator or feminist activist support this bill; therefore, I stand for certain racial and gender positions." Those who are using these symbols do so largely to speak to one another, not to or with African women. After all, in passing these bills, few African women were consulted or even informed.

Does Law as a Tool Work? Have the Surgeries Stopped?

The true measure of one's concern for women of color would seem to be less symbols, speeches, and profiling than substance and result. At the domestic level, law is a tool, a method of change. So the question to ask is: In spite of my complaints and concerns about the symbolism, are the laws working and stopping the surgeries in the United States?

The answer is unclear. But it never was clear how prevalent the surgeries were in this country to begin with. I have seen only one study cited in the statutes or anywhere else, and its methodology is questionable. Still, the presence of these laws may well discourage people from having the surgeries performed here. It is not clear that the process of enaction or the language used in these statutes has the moral authority and persuasive power to educate people against performing the surgeries at all. Maybe that will come when these promised but unfunded educational programs are developed. In the meantime, the California bill has created a lot of anxiety and anger in African immigrant and refugee communities. Microaggressions appear to be on the rise: There are more stories of strangers stopping African women to ask whether they are mutilated, and doctors are increasingly deciding to perform genital exams on the children of African immigrants, even if the health problem they present is a sore throat. African women at all class and educational levels express growing reluctance to seek out any kind of medical attention.

For the supporters of criminalization who were interested in more than profiling and self-aggrandizement, these results are probably not what they intended. But they are not unexpected when the voices, experiences, and views of African women, women of color, are left out.

Notes

1. In one of the major collected essays of CRT writings, the editors note in their "Introduction" that CRT intends to bring a "useful perspective" to liberal and left discourse over the role of the United States in the globalization process: Kimberlé W. Crenshaw, Neil Gotanda, Gary Peller, and Kendall Thomas, "Introduction," in *Critical Race Theory: The Key Writings That Formed the Movement*, ed. Kimberlé W. Crenshaw, Neil Gotanda, Gary Peller, and Kendall Thomas (New York: New Press, 1995), xxx.

2. Ibid., xxii.

3. Ibid., xx.

4. See, for example, Malcolm X, "Not Just an American Problem, but a World Problem," in *February 1965: The Final Speeches of Malcolm X*, ed. Malcolm X (New York: Pathfinder Press, 1992), 143; Connie Matthews, "The Struggle Is a World Struggle," in *The Black Panthers Speak*, ed. Philip Foner (St. Louis: Da Capa Press, 1995), 154; Eldridge Cleaver, "The Black Man's Stake in Vietnam," in Foner, *Black Panthers*, 100; and Kathleen Neal Cleaver, "Back to Africa: 'The International Section of the Black Panther Party,'" *The Black Panther Party Reconsidered*, ed. Charles Jones (Baltimore: Black Classic Press, 1998).

5. One of the early political actions taken by the Harvard law students who formed part of the core of the scholars of color who founded the CRT movement was the organization of the "Alternative Course," a course designed to provide the students with the racially conscious legal approach they sought after Professor Derrick Bell left Harvard: See Crenshaw et al., "Introduction." Although he is not

mentioned in that introduction, Henry J. Richardson III, the prominent African American international legal scholar, was one of the guest speakers invited to participate in the Alternative Course. Professor Richardson has written many scholarly works in the area of international law and has often raised in academic and scholarly forums the connection between international law and domestic law and politics. See, for example, Henry J. Richardson III, "The International Implications of the Los Angeles Riots," *Denver University Law Review* 70 (1993): 213.

6. Although the relationship between legal analysis and political practice has always formed a piece of the CRT legacy and approach, the interconnectedness between scholarship and resistance was perhaps most concretely articulated in the introduction to the only collected works on Critical Race Feminism: See Adrien K. Wing, "Introduction," in *Critical Race Feminism: A Reader*, ed. Adrien K. Wing (New York: New York University Press, 1997), 5.

7. These surgeries are also known as female genital mutilation or female circumcision The naming itself contains contradictions that I have discussed elsewhere: See Isabelle R. Gunning, "Arrogant Perception, World-Traveling and Multicultural Feminism: The Case of Female Genital Surgeries," *Columbia Human Rights Law Review* 23 (1992): 189, 193.

8. Ibid. In brief, I outlined a three-part approach to analyzing culturally challenging practices such as female genital surgeries. The approach involved: 1) seeing yourself (Westerners) historically; 2) seeing oneself as other might see you; and, 3) seeing the other as she might see herself.

9. The ACRC is involved in a broad range of social-service activities designed to ease the transition of immigrant and refugee people who are largely, but not exclusively, from the African continent.

10. See "Reconsidering Circumcision: North Dakota Woman Challenges Male Circumcision," *Star Tribune* (Minneapolis), May 19, 1997, 7A. The American Academy of Pediatrics now takes a position of neutrality, having acknowledged a study that suggests that male circumcision may prevent a few rare diseases.

11. Karen Hughes, "The Criminalization of Female Genital Mutilation in the United States," *Journal of Law and Policy* 4 (1995): 321.

12. I realize that here, too, issues of race, gender, and class arise when one explores whose voices are heard at the legislative level, but it still serves as an example of what happens when at least a portion of the targeted or affected group is part of the conversation.

CHAPTER FIFTEEN

Breaking Cycles of Inequality: Critical Theory, Human Rights, and Family In/justice

Berta Esperanza Hernández-Truyol

People have the right to be equal whenever difference makes them inferior, but they also have the right to be different whenever equality jeopardizes their identity.
—Boaventura De Sousa Santos

For feminists to sign on to [a whole network of liberal concepts—rights, interests, contracts, individualism, representative government, negative liberty] may be to obscure rather than to illuminate a vision of politics, citizenship, and "the good life." ... Feminist scholars have revealed the inegalitarianism behind the myth of equal opportunity.
—Mary G. Dietz

It has frequently been acknowledged by those concerned with real equality of opportunity that the family presents a problem. ... Disparity [exists] within the family, ... its gender structure is itself a major obstacle to equality of opportunity. ... So much of the social construction of gender takes place in the family.
—Susan Moller Okin

THE 1997 CELEBRATION of the tenth anniversary of Critical Race Theory commemorated the birth of a movement that, at its core, is committed to humanitarian conceptions of personhood.[1] These conceptions transcend the limitations of current equality doctrine.[2] The human-rights norms that further these conceptions were first articulated comprehensively in the Universal Declaration of Human Rights, a revolutionary document that embraces a plethora of individual rights that are central to personhood—not only civil and political rights but also social, economic, cultural, and solidarity rights.

This chapter posits that a co-celebration of the CRT enterprise on its tenth anniversary and the Universal Declaration on the fiftieth anniversary of its adoption is an appropriate event to mark the commencement of work that aspires to break global and local cycles of inequality.[3] This work would seek both to "globalize a localism" and "localize a globalism."[4] By globalizing a localism, I mean a venture that takes the exciting, but to date domestic, critical theory movement global by using domestic critical theory to develop and transform the context, meaning, and application of international human-rights norms.

The "localizing a globalism" aspect of this proposal entails the simultaneous utilization of theoretical and substantive dimensions of human-rights norms to develop and transform the context, meaning, and reach of domestic critical discourses.

This chapter takes the first steps in these complementary directions by exploring the relationships of CRT to international law and, more specifically, to human-rights law. The basic goals of this project are to globalize critical theory and localize human-rights norms concerning personhood in order to redefine notions of participation so that all people, wherever located, can exercise rights of full citizenship. The globalization of domestic critical theory seeks to reconstruct human-rights norms to render them more inclusive. Simultaneously, localizing international human-rights norms and principles into domestic critical discourse may bring about a paradigm shift in which the United States' language of citizenship and equality comes to incorporate international human-rights notions of personhood and human dignity.

Beyond the State

Because of their common aspirations for liberation and justice, human-rights and critical theories can provide opportunities for mutual enrichment. For instance, critical theoretical movements that address subaltern communities in the United States have flourished in the past fifteen years. These movements parallel significant human-rights developments regarding individual rights and, more recently, the rights of marginalized groups (indigenous/First Nations peoples, women, children) and the rights of peripheral states in the worldwide sphere. Like international human-rights discourses, critical theoretical movements engage notions of dignity and rights in relation to the state, but they go beyond statism.

Human-rights law is an important component of a project of liberation because in its short formal existence it has effectively reconstituted the doctrine of sovereignty, that formerly omnipotent power of the state to do as it wished with its subjects wherever they might be and even with anyone who found himself or herself within its territorial jurisdiction. Human-rights law is revolutionary from a statist perspective in that it renders individuals subjects, rather than just objects, of international law. Human-rights norms demand accountability for the state's treatment of all people within its jurisdiction—citizens and non-citizens alike. No one would any longer dispute, for example, that sovereignty cannot and will not shield a state from accountability for human-rights violations such as genocide, torture, or apartheid. Moreover, the concept of accountability may be extended to sectors of society, hitherto viewed as "private," that effectively regulate their members if these sectors erect barriers to personhood with respect to some of their less powerful members. Human-rights language, then, is a morally compelling tool for denouncing sovereign actions that derogate the dignity and integrity of personhood and citizenship.[5]

The fifty years since the emergence of the international human-rights framework have witnessed an exponential growth in its structures and the numbers of documents that reflect and implement its aspirations. In this time, moreover, the world has also undergone revolutions in science and technology. At present, movements of people and capital across borders are de-emphasizing nationality as the axis on which individual-rights claims may be based, creating new challenges to concepts of sovereignty. These movements reshape the link among territory and states and citizenship, requiring conceptions of sovereignty to be reconstituted even further. Even the increased access of nongovernmental organizations and individuals to the human-rights system helps to redefine the significance of state boundaries to claims of rights. In this regard, the human-rights framework is very useful in helping to move global society beyond traditional concepts of rights, space, and geography, and toward the creation of new structures of justice *sin fronteras* that will enable all people to fulfill their full potential for personhood.

Globalizing the Local: Human Rights, Sex, and Race

Although the human-rights model can go far in enabling the aspiration to full personhood for all, it is important not to romanticize the human-rights regime that currently exists. Before it can serve its emancipatory function, the human-rights vision itself must be reconstructed—a task in which critical theory is of immense utility.

There is a basic level at which the international human-rights system and its norms would greatly benefit from a critical theoretical intervention. Since relatively early in their development, human-rights norms have been criticized as embedding the very Western/Northern hegemonic foundation[6] that critical scholars have denounced in domestic law—norms that were articulated by and crafted in the image of Western/Northern power elites. In the domestic arena, "Crits" have challenged the objectivity and fairness of a system of laws designed with the interests of a few, homogeneous, powerful political actors. Similarly, in the international arena it has been the so-called developing or peripheral states— states of the South and East—that have resisted universalizing the vision of human rights of the industrial states of the North and West.

Since its inception, critical theory in the United States—in particular, feminist theory and CRT—has attempted to deconstruct the legal master narrative to reveal its rootedness in a specific class (wealthy, propertied, educated), race (white), and sex (male).[7] Critical theory can insist that a substantive reconstruction of the human-rights model requires contextualization. For example, critical analysis can show how supposedly universal norms were crafted within specific and narrow social, economic, historical, and cultural spaces. Such contextualization underscores the effective imposition on many states of the perspective and experience of a few powerful ones.

An example of the exclusionary process for defining human rights is the adoption of the Universal Declaration of Human Rights. The Universal Declaration was signed by only forty-eight states, with eight states abstaining (including Saudi Arabia, the USSR, South Africa, and Yugoslavia). Today, with 185 independent states belonging to the community of nations, the majority of which never voted on the declaration, this document is nevertheless broadly accepted as embodying a plethora of customary universal human-rights norms.[8] Critical theory can question the validity of the universalization of customary normative standards that were formulated prior to the entrance of the former colonies into the community of nations. It can influence a post-colonial perspective for reconstituting appropriate standards rather than support the acceptance of the interpretation that patently fostered the interests of the colonizers. Critical theory can be a lens through which international human-rights documents are subjected to scrutiny to reveal the hegemonic influences and control in their formulation. Such analysis can lead to a reconstruction exercise that transforms the rules in an inclusive and just fashion.

The adoption of the Universal Declaration reflected a commitment by states to enter into one treaty incorporating a collection of indivisible, interdependent, and inviolable rights that include not only civil and political rights, but also social, economic, cultural, and solidarity rights.[9] The aspiration that this holistic human-rights ideal would be incorporated into a single convention, however, was short-lived. Historical events resulted in the bifurcation of rights into two separate treaties—the International Covenant on Civil and Political Rights (ICCPR) and the International Covenant on Economic, Social, and Cultural Rights (Economic Covenant). Critical theorists could explain the failure of this original vision by first unmasking the power imbalance among the actors.

During deliberations on the human-rights convention, the Western/Northern states were comfortable only with the granting of negative civil and political rights—that is, the right of individuals to be free from governmental interference with respect to civil and political rights, an approach that is grounded in the "equal access" thinking of the liberal tradition.[10] These states were resistant to granting positive social, economic, and cultural rights, and consequently resisted undertaking state obligations with respect to such rights.[11]

However, newly emerging states (the so-called Third World states or underdeveloped/peripheral states) and communist states (the then Second World) saw negative rights simply as preserving colonialism and maintaining the already powerful bourgeoisie's power over the masses. The former colonies' vision was that the masses could and would be liberated only by the granting of positive social and economic rights.

Not surprisingly, the North/West resisted this perspective. Thus, the covenants were bifurcated. To date, the United States remains steadfast, although virtually alone, in its refusal to ratify the Economic Covenant. Even those Western states that have ratified the Economic Covenant, however, for the most part view it not as an obligation to create economic rights but, rather, simply to enforce those rights the state recognizes in a nondiscriminatory manner.[12] A critical evaluation of this process leads to the conclusion that the resulting structure simply reflects the institutionalization of the West's narrative and that a reconstruction is needed.

Indeed, pursuant to the dominant Western interpretation, only civil and political rights, the so-called first-generation rights, are considered synonymous with international human rights. But as critical theorists would emphasize, a comprehensive review of the documents makes plain that economic, social, and cultural rights are not, and should not be, a second class of rights. Moreover, a critical analysis of the blueprints for the Universal Declaration explains and clarifies the divergent viewpoints of the North and South, East and West, with respect to rights. The declaration's roots lie in the American Declaration of Independence and the French *Declaration des Droits de L'Homme* (Declaration of the Rights of Man)—documents that resulted from the late-eighteenth-century political and social uprisings that sought to identify impermissible governmental intrusions into individual lives. Yet, as critical thinkers have underscored, it is important to recall that these eighteenth-century social and political revolutions coexisted with slavery and with women's status as chattel—hardly positions of equality or equal access.[13] Thus, although all agree that civil and political rights such as the rights to nondiscrimination, liberty, and security of the person are not only desirable but necessary, current interventions into equality discourses require a recognition of their exclusionary beginnings in order to ensure that, in the present, all people benefit from this uneven historical legacy.

Critical theoretical interventions could be invaluable to inform global discourses. First, they provide the tools for exposing the hegemonic foundations of human-rights norms. Second, they can assist in the counter-hegemonic, multidimensional, multicultural reconstruction of human-rights norms. In these reconstructive efforts it is imperative to ensure that new notions of justice with paramount respect for personhood do not become synonymous with Westernization, with the privileging of elites from the peripheral spaces, with the visible portions of global market economies, or with economic growth.[14] Toward this end, the process of reconstruction must be transformational, dynamic, and ongoing—*un*hegemonic.

Critical theory can help inform the debate surrounding other particular norms. For example, human-rights instruments, including the United Nations Charter, mandate nondiscrimination on the basis of sex in their general nondiscrimination clauses. However, if one looks beyond those clauses to some of the substantive provisions granting specific rights, one finds, disturbingly, that some of the provisions exclude sex as the basis of protection. For example, although Article 2(1) of the ICCPR mandates sex equality, Article 20 of the same treaty provides that "any advocacy of national, racial or religious hatred that constitutes incitement to discrimination, hostility or violence shall be prohibited by law." On its face, Article 20 does not proscribe sex-based advocacy of hatred. Canons of construction—both domestic, from contract law, and international, from the Vienna Convention on the Law of Treaties—provide that the general cedes to the specific. Therefore, the omission of sex from Article 20 signifies that the advocacy of sex-based "hatred that constitutes incitement to discrimination, hostility, or violence—is not proscribed."[15] This interpretation suggests that sex-based violence—a global problem of such proportions that it succeeded in uniting women from the North and South, East and West, at the 1993 Human Rights Conference in Vienna to bring the subject to the forefront of the Human Rights meeting (a meeting that at the outset did not even include women on the agenda)—if bad at all, is not as bad as ethnic-, race-, or religion-based hatred.

Certainly, a feminist reevaluation and reinterpretation of the prohibitions against sex-based violence is in order. In addition, critical race feminism and feminist discourse are vital tools in the reconstruction of these norms in a fashion sensitive to the intersections of race, sex, ethnicity, class, religion, language, and sexuality. Such critical theoretical interventions are not only appropriate but necessary for a truly workable human-rights model to emerge.

The hegemonic foundations of international human-rights norms are also evident in the way that the International Convention on the Elimination of All Forms of Racial Discrimination (Race Convention) constructs sex, race, and racial power. This treaty contains a general nondiscrimination provision that does not include sex. In its preambular message, it refers to a provision of the Universal Declaration that includes sex. Yet somehow, the Race Convention manages to delete sex from the reference. Moreover, the very definition of race in the Race Convention is emblematic of its Northern/Western viewpoint. The convention defines racial discrimination as "any distinction, exclusion, restriction or preference based on race, color, *descent, or national or ethnic origin* which has the purpose or effect of nullifying or impairing the recognition, enjoyment or exercise, on an equal footing, of human rights and fundamental freedoms in the political, economic, social, cultural or any other field or public life."[16] This definition effectively internationalizes and institutionalizes the U.S. construction of race—the binary black–white paradigm. It racializes ethnicity and national origin and has the potential to effect erasures of classifications that are not black or white.

The LatCrit movement has specifically challenged the conflation of many and varied identity factors. Race as a generic term for all differences is a wholly inadequate construct for Latinas/os, whose multidimensionality within the U.S. borderlands can render them both racial and ethnic others. An interpretation that equates difference with race and race with the black–white binary not only reflects the dominance of but also adopts as "neutral, rational, ... just," and international the Northern/Western perspective."[17] Such an epistemology presents as normative the monolingualism of the white, straight, moneyed, educated, able-bodied (male) person—the "perpetrator perspective." Once critically refashioned, however, the indivisibility–interdependence structure of the human-rights model, which recognizes and mandates the recognition of rights as holistic, indivisible, and interdependent, becomes invaluable as a tool to eradicate injustice.

Other vestiges of these foundational inequalities are yet to be eliminated. Women are still far from attaining full citizenship rights and benefits in any geography in the global community. Racial, sexual, and ethnic minorities within First World states, all people in Third World states, and indigenous peoples in all states—North and South, East and West—are similarly deprived of full citizenship rights. All these populations, regardless of their status as citizens under the current liberal conception, are experiencing a widespread pattern of inequality in access to education; health care; nutrition; participation in the social, political, and economic spheres; and recognition as full persons. Similarly, both core and peripheral states experience a widespread pattern of inequality in access to wealth, resources, technology, and wages. These conditions provide a clear opportunity to cultivate critical theoretical discourses that can transform international principles into just ones.[18]

Another outgrowth of the foundational inequalities of the human-rights structure that provides a valuable entry for a critical theoretical intervention into human-rights conversations is the tremendous polarization of the economic development of states. Understanding the historical underpinnings of human-rights norms explains why the international arena flourishes with the inequalities attendant to market economies and the economic locations of states as core or peripheral, developed or underdeveloped, North or South.[19]

Earlier, I discussed how polarization of the political interests of states resulted in the severance of the human-rights vision into civil and political rights, on the one hand, and social, economic, and cultural rights, on the other. More recently, the economic-globalization movement has rendered this schism more patent, particularly in the failed programs of aid to underdeveloped states. Such programs were destined for failure, as they were not only highly bureaucratized but also implemented without a thorough comprehension of the various cultures and needs of diverse peoples and of the problems in the societies receiving aid.[20] Recent post-Cold War events reveal great discord resulting, at least in part, from economic instability and polarization. The attendant consequences are increased nationalism, ethnic strife, civil war, and human-rights abuses—challenges that the international community is struggling to resolve, regrettably without marked success.[21]

A critical perspective on these conflicts could yield valuable information to address these myriad problems. For instance, many different states and communities could benefit from the application of an appropriately globalized version of the U.S. race discourse. Effectively, every First World state has an internal Third World—inner cities, "new underclasses," racial and ethnic minorities, the disfranchised, economically marginalized people, and second-class citizens whose race, sex, sexuality, class, linguistic ability, or nationality "others" them. Critical theorists concerned with social justice and issues of race, sex, class, sexuality, ethnicity, and their intersections have been analyzing these concerns. Their vast and rich literature offers valuable suggestions for corrective measures and can be a phenomenal resource for global challenges and conversations.

Similarly, critical analyses could develop, expand, and transform the globalization discourse and provide it with a broader mission, one that could work to eradicate barriers in the understanding of globalization's positive and negative consequences. Current conversations about economic globalization are limited to opening and broadening financial markets, disregarding the impact of the market on individual lives. If the economic-globalization discourse were refocused with a critical perspective, relevant narratives would include stories beyond those about the massive capital transfers in the world geography that now monopolize the conversation. A critical chronicle also would consider up-to-now invisible transmigrations related to economic globalization, such as the flow of labor—often undocumented—almost exclusively from ethnic and racial minority groups, and frequently female.[22] This flow of labor is related to the flow of capital and goods. A critical evaluation of the globalized economy takes into account low-wage workers who service the demands generated by industries—the service workers who clean up the glamorous buildings where the money travels, the hotels where global financiers stay, and the *restaurantes* at which they eat.

A critical lens would render visible and analyze the meanings of movements of people in the geography of the global economy.

It would include an interrogation of the social and economic byproducts and consequences of these movements—such as the migration of customs, languages, and religious and cultural practices that follow the flow of people. Consider, for instance, the different culinary traditions that result in the desire and need for "ethnic" foods. Such demand causes industries to emerge to meet the demand. These new businesses range from food-importing startups to the ethnic restaurants that originally spring up to feed the service workers and eventually are discovered by the traders. This perspective includes *all* the service industries necessary to support both the visible and invisible cities, not only the big-money concerns. Such a changed vision of globalized economies could transform the conversations about globalization from an emphasis on transnational capitalism to a broader forum in which to evaluate economic justice.

Beyond reconceptualizing the discourse of economic globalization, critical theory may have valuable input into crafting the solutions for other conflicts that involve diverse peoples. Critical movements can be instrumental in ensuring that human-rights discourse does not simply become an echo of the master narrative but, rather, ensures that it incorporates respect and appreciation for different cultures.

An appropriate methodology for these conversations and exchanges—one that comfortably fits both the critical theoretical model and the human-rights ideology—is one that recognizes the need for and insists on broad and pluralistic participation. The approach must be pliable and dynamic. It needs to include input and evaluation from diverse cultures, cultural perspectives, languages, ethnicities, social origins (classes), religions, races, sexes, sexualities, and national origins. This approach must provide a voice for the interests, issues, and concerns of these groups in deliberations about rights, self-determination, autonomy, invest-ments, change, and obligations.[23] Absent such an inclusive approach, the legitimacy of the process itself, as well as its outcomes, can and should be called into question.

To be sure, such a process is more easily envisioned than instituted into practice. Any implementation of a theoretical model must be flexible to accommodate and accept the changes that are needed as stresses and exclusions are revealed. Such a critically informed human-rights model has the potential, however, to result in broad-based, inclusive, diverse, and multicultural politi-cal formations. These formations can ensure that majorities do not use differences as a sword to eviscerate or obscure minori-ties and that such differences, in turn, are not used as a shield against accountability for human-rights abuses by any community.

Localizing the Global: Interdependence and Critical Theories

Critical theory can contribute to the devel-opment and transformation of human-rights discourse. Similarly, the international human-rights complex can provide a valu-able and useful intervention into critical theory discourse in numerous ways.

First, the human-rights framework helps move beyond a comparativistic same-ness–difference approach to equality by pro-viding a construct in which rights are indi-visible and interdependent.[24] International human-rights norms provide classifications that constitute a more expansive and, con-sequently, more useful measure than U.S. (and other local) measures of an individual's attainment of dignity, integrity, and full cit-izenship. For example, the global standards for nondiscrimination include categories such as language, culture, and social ori-gin—categories that are contested and rejected in many local environments, includ-

ing the United States and the European Union, as providing the bases for any pro-tections at all.[25] Moreover, human-rights indivisibility and interdependence analysis requires that these categories as a whole, rather than the single-trait fragmented analysis of U.S. jurisprudence, be the meas-ure of an individual's equality.

Second, although critical theory scruti-nizes and rejects normative concepts that have institutionalized the perpetrator per-spective, it has not always succeeded in its enterprise without imposing another perpe-trator's viewpoint. To be sure, critical theory has provided invaluable insights into the consequences of normalizing the dominant viewpoint: the exclusion of all women, racial, ethnic, religious, class, and sexual minori-ties. For example, CRT was founded on the desire to effect "a left intervention into race discourse and race intervention into left dis-course."[26] The resulting implementation of this approach, however, was under-inclusive and marginalized women of color (for whom race interventions into the critical discourse obscured gender and sex issues) and Lati-nas/os (and others) whose multidimensional identities, including sex, race, color, ethnic-ity, religion, sexuality, national origin, lan-guage, citizenship, and culture (to name a few) may alienate them not only from the norm, but also from a single-dimensional view of the "other." Thus, just as structural debates persist about the nature and extent of human rights, some fundamental struc-tural debates are engaging the Crits, as well.

Indeed, the appearance of various schools of critical thinking makes it evident that a transition away from the liberal binary paradigm of difference (black–white, male–female) is indispensable. In this regard, local critical discourses can be expanded by incorporating the Universal Declaration's recognition of the indivisi-ble—inseparable, interdependent, and invi-olable—nature of civil, political, social, economic, and cultural rights. Human-rights discourse benefits from a recognition of the need to work together and share experiences successfully to promote rights for all peoples.

This international human-rights prototype provides a blueprint for a multidimensional critical paradigm that can be used to bring about a participatory society in which all people can fully exercise and enjoy their rights and obligations as equal citizens. Lack of participation by any particular group, which may render a citizenry subordinate or second class, renders questionable the legitimacy of the process itself, and of the body guiding or implementing the process—be it the state or another community, such as the family, a school, or an ethnic, racial, or religious community.[27] After all, a truly legitimate civil and pluralistic society is one that seeks the opinions and entertains the desires of all of the governed peoples and that, in promoting their equality, respects their differences.

Moreover, the multilingualism of the international human-rights tradition is a useful addition to domestic critical theory. A body that listens to only one language from its people silences not only groups within its realm that speak different tongues but also outside groups who share the language. Thus, importing the human-rights discourse's acceptance of multilingualism serves to promote local acceptance of the voices of othered groups.

Paradigmatic Transformations: The Family In/justice

Both critical theory and international human-rights formulations seek to eradicate structures of domination. These disciplines engage and promote notions of justice and of participation by all people in the enjoyment of life as members of society—

not only as individuals but also within various and varied communities. Critical theory furthers those goals by exposing how many groups were excluded from the formulation of notions of law and justice that govern society and by urging ways to remedy historical exclusions. Human-rights principles, however, articulate the rights—civil, political, social, cultural, and economic—inherent in the fulfillment and enjoyment of full personhood.

The previous sections of this chapter have revealed both the need to inform human-rights norms with U.S. critical theory so that they may be truly universalized and the need to expand the vision of critical theories to reach a global scope. This section discusses how concepts of justice have been absent from one community to which all people belong—the family—and suggests how critical internationalist legal interpretations, based on attributes of human beings as human beings, will serve to place the family in justice.[28]

Critically informed human-rights principles provide a rich basis on which to interrogate the gendered, hierarchical assumptions of family so deeply embedded in society, law, and religion that to date have created and cemented women's second-class-citizenship status. Unlike U.S. domestic law, international human-rights norms expressly protect both privacy and family life and protect against interference with the home, while also providing that people have equal rights to marriage, both during marriage and after its dissolution.[29] Based on such concepts, international norms provide that the family is entitled to protection by society and the state.

Human-rights principles also include broad protections against discrimination on grounds of race, sex, religion, political or other opinion, national or social origin, property, birth, or other status. These provisions protect the liberal ideal of rights to life, liberty, security of the person, and property. Such rights coincide with traditional notions of personhood and are useful to critical scholars who want to redefine conceptions of the family and locate that structure within the sphere of justice.

Any construct that seeks truly to eradicate inequalities must confront and challenge existing, systemic social, economic, and political privileges and account for varied cultural circumstances within which real people lead their lives. The core of the critical internationalist vision is that the fulfillment of personhood is indivisibly connected to the entitlement not only to individual rights, but also to membership and participation in varied and various communities. These positions include political communities as well as economic and social locations such as the family, religious affiliations, and places of employment.[30] Thus, this conception of full personhood regards the liberal individualistic and communitarian traditions not as irreconcilable visions but, rather, as interdependent dimensions of human existence. Full personhood not only requires individual freedoms and dignity; it also promotes community support and affiliation, cultural protections, individual autonomy, and self-determination.

Families Engendered

Concepts of justice within the family have been wholly lacking in traditional Western thinking. This vacuum reflects a family structure that is neither equal nor just; rather, it is a major contributor to the structures of domination that persist in most (if not all) world cultures. A critically reformed human-rights construct can be central to placing the family in justice by insisting that privacy and equality, community and individualism, be coexisting forces in a struc-

ture that aims to free both individuals and communities to attain the ideal of full citizenship.

There is no doubt that the family is a gendered institution. In the United States (as elsewhere), gendered roles in families always have existed. The eighteenth-century legal model of family was based on coverture—the notion that, on marriage, husband and wife became one, with the one being the husband. The wife (and children) had no separate legal personality or rights.

At the start of industrialization, when the center of production shifted from inside to outside the home, the "domestic code" emerged. This model of the nuclear family, which continues to fix the parameters of the propriety of gendered behavior, carved out wholly separate spheres of existence for the sexes.[31] It located the female as mother and wife, inside the home, laboring for love not money; placed her on a private pedestal, away from state scrutiny or protection; and obligated her to nurture and provide moral education. At the same time, the code located the husband in the paid labor force, the "market"—outside the home. Although for the man this role is fully consonant with the liberal ideals of individualism and autonomy, for the woman, the result is dependency, subordination, and self-abnegation.

Critical analysis exposes this construction of family as a social and political fabrication. The traditional family framework is fraught with sexism and infected with racist and classist assumptions that are contrary to the spirit, if not the letter, of human-rights equality and nondiscrimination mandates. This framework defines work exclusively as paid work, rendering women's unpaid work invisible and treating it as irrelevant to the market. The rhetoric of the family as a separate "private" realm not only disregards, but also fully discounts, the value of women's unpaid work—work that can be crucial for the family's well-being.

The result of this public–private dichotomy is the country's historic denial of women's basic human rights.[32]

In embracing the ideology of separate, different, and unequal spheres, Western political thought, in derogation of women's civil, social, and economic rights, has completely excluded the existence of women from discourses on justice and equality; has taken their inferior, subordinated, second-class citizenship for granted; and has assumed their exclusive location in the home. Throughout history and in contemporary times, the "'individual' who is the basic subject of the theories is the male head of a patriarchal household.... [The theories are] about men with wives at home."[33] Justice theories "*assume*, though they do not discuss, the traditional, gender-structured family."[34] They also assume that the structure is just.

Significantly, some theorists acknowledge the unjust nature of the gendered division of labor in families yet justify it as "grounded in nature and necessary."[35] Others simply claim that, because of the nature of the family, justice is not an appropriate or applicable standard. In all cases, justice and family are not viewed as necessarily coexistent.

Rather than assuming the existing concept of family as "just," accepting family injustice as natural law, or denying the propriety of justice in the family, a critical analysis reveals the family structure as fraught with inequalities. The existing model simply ignores the unequal burden for unpaid labor borne by women and the resultant unequal "distribution of power, responsibility and privilege"—the injustice—within families.[36] Considering the central role the family plays in society, a just family should be a precondition to a just society, and thus principles of justice must be applied to the family structure.[37] Justice is a necessary ideal in the family narrative

because constructions and gendered expectations within families have consequences that reach far beyond the family and into the market, resulting at best in unequal treatment, and at worst in wholesale exclusion of women from economic spheres. Public market disparities inevitably will affect the power balance in the private realm.[38]

Moreover, the ideological location of women at home ignores the reality of working-class women, Latinas, Black women, and immigrant women, many of whom spend long hours toiling outside their homes, often performing domestic work for low pay in the homes of the privileged. A critical lens also unearths the racist consequences of the separate-spheres ideology. During slavery, Black families—fathers, mothers, and children—were property to be sold or used as labor, including for sexual labor, for which there was no desert.[39] These market facts, disregarded by the dominant ideology, underscore two significant realities. One is that housework has a real market cost, even if grossly devalued or simply taken. The other is that women's unpaid work is not recognized in the market notwithstanding its *real* market cost. Critical internationalists should join the feminist interrogation of the justice in concepts of individual autonomy that for women presume subservience; of "productive" labor that ignores women's non-wage work; and of productivity that devalues even paid work along gender lines.

Critical analysis challenges and unmasks legal practice's validation of the traditional family model. Law has reinforced and perpetuated the separate-spheres ideology that diminishes women's citizenship in the family and in society.[40] Claiming the lauded (but separate) position of the mother and wife to be natural, and the superior public position and private needs of the husband to be rational, courts have excluded women from opportunities in the labor force and denied women their economic rights, giving the separate-spheres ideology the force of law.[41]

Throughout history, U.S. courts have upheld rules banning women from certain professions. Women are now admitted into most of the paid labor force, but their opportunities and earning potential continue to be limited by their unchanged and unchanging domestic roles and their concomitant responsibilities; by the gendered nature of the workplace, which largely relegates them to low-paying jobs; and the gendered assumptions of the workplace.[42] Moreover, women's family-based exclusion from public life has resulted in other wholesale denial of rights, including the rights and duties of citizens. As late as 1961, women were excluded from juries because "woman is still regarded as the center of home and family life."[43]

At present, more than 57 percent of all married women work outside the home, a figure that rises to 73.5 percent for the 35–44 age group. However, the real, gendered market consequences of the separate spheres persist. Married women earn less than their husbands—only 65 percent of their husbands' average incomes; they are also disproportionately represented in the part-time and seasonal work forces (particularly when they have children at home), and do far more of the unpaid child-care and household tasks than their partners.[44]

In fact, 125 years after *Bradwell v. Illinois*, it is plain that although the law may have changed to suggest women's entitlement to participate in the public realm, social reality reinforces the assumptions about women's proper location as wives and mothers. On the eve of the twenty-first century, religious groups have become increasingly vocal about the "truth" of women's proper, subordinated position in the home sphere. In his Apostolic Letter titled, "On the Dignity of Women," Pope Paul II echoed

the socially and legally dictated gendered roles for women and "refer[red] to women's special capacity to care for others in arguing for confining them to motherhood or celibacy."[45]

Similarly, in June 1998, the Southern Baptist Convention in Salt Lake City adopted a statement, based on a supposed biblically based hierarchy for the family, providing that wives are subordinate to their husbands and are their husbands' helpers. Embracing the so-called traditional family form, the convention not only rejected any notion of marriage that is not monogamous and heterosexual, but narrowly defined family to exclude widows, widowers, and single people as expressions of family. The statement blurs social, religious, and legal formulations and reifies women's subordinated status.[46] Ironically, echoing existing policy, the statement also provides that women should stay out of combat because "the idea of women in combat rejects [the] gender-based designation established by God and undermines the 'male headship' in the family."[47]

These examples—more than a century apart—expose the social, religious, and legal underpinnings of women's second-class status in contravention of human-rights norms. One feminist scholar has explained that the mandated private location of women "cripples women's citizenship [as] it inhibits the authoritative speech and dialogue that derive from self-determination and thus impairs the successful participation of women in democratic life."[48]

To engage in a project of reconstruction, it is necessary to understand the myriad locations beyond the family in which this private–public ideology has crafted and sustained structures of domination. One place where gender-subordinating consequences of the public–private double standard are exposed is in courts' general refusal to enforce individualized terms of marriage contracts, reasoning that the terms—gendered and hierarchical—have already been set by social norms that the individual parties are not permitted to change.[49] Judicial rulings transmogrify social norms into legal obligations—the man's being to support the family during marriage; the woman's to take care of the home and the husband; and the mother's to fulfill the biologically ordained duty to bear children and socially ordained duty to rear them.

The effects of these generally understood terms of the marriage contract have market consequences. The social and legal orders "create a cycle in which the division of labor between the sexes (with wives performing a far greater share of the unpaid labor of the family, and tending to subordinate their outside work lives to the needs of their husbands and children) reinforces and increases over time the asymmetric power relation between them."[50] Should the woman reject the stay-at-home model and opt for market participation—that is, work outside the home for pay, a decision that could equalize power imbalances within the family—both society and law are likely to punish her for being a gender outlaw. In a recent custody dispute, an attorney in a high-powered practice lost her children to an unemployed husband. Quite poignant in elucidating the gendered roles of parents in the family is her estranged husband's comment that "Dads can be Moms too."[51]

Even at the end of marriage, women's social and economic inequality is exacerbated by the patriarchal family model. Ignoring the parties' patently unequal market positions, current divorce law (ironically crafted pursuant to a feminist pursuit of sameness as equality) treats men and women as if they were equally situated in the market. Thus, even an equal division of property and walking papers would not place a woman, whose share of the family work was unpaid and who might not have

the training to support herself and her children, in an equal place.

In all cases, equal division of property is not the norm. Judges view the marketplace laborer's income—the husband's income—as solely his own. On divorce, in dividing property, decision-makers plainly note that equal divisions are not warranted, as the accumulation of goods is a result of the wage worker's labor and thus his just dessert. This ideology was patent in the recent popular-press coverage of a Connecticut case involving an extremely wealthy executive with General Electric. After more than three decades of marriage, he was awarded more because he had earned it in the market; the wife and mother was given less because all she did was care for the home, the husband, and the children. With this prevalent judicial philosophy, it is not surprising that, after divorce, the husband's standard of living goes up while that of the wife, who is most frequently the custodial parent, and the children declines.[52] These inequities fly in the face of international human-rights social and economic protection of family.

Another example of the double standard of the public-private dichotomy is tort law's historical inapplicability to harms inflicted by family members, although in the past thirty-five years, at least half of the states have done away with interspousal tort immunity. Similarly, at common law a husband could not rape his wife—the marriage was license for unlimited sexual access. Even today, many jurisdictions exclude a husband's forced sex with his wife from the definition of rape.[53] These gendered norms contradict the combined rights to equality in, during, and after marriage that the human-rights construct embraces.

The law books are replete with other examples that show institutional acceptance and support of the normative family model. Tax laws support this model, as do Social

Security laws (for example, the two–wage-earner tax penalty as well as the higher rate of Social Security taxes paid when two persons, rather than one, are subject to the regressive tax), welfare and other social insurance programs, and the prohibitions against same-sex marriages.[54] Under the U.S. Social Security system, middle-class children whose source of support is affected by the wage-earning parent's death or disability are entitled to rather generous benefits that are not meansbased. However, for children from nontraditional families—poor or single-mother families—social benefits not only are means-tested; they are also are contingent on the family's pursuing corrective behavior as dictated by the state. So-called welfare recipients are viewed as undeserving drains on public coffers.

The most recent welfare reforms in the United States provide evidence of the persistent support for the traditional family model. This new legislation reveals discrimination based on the intersections of class, sex, and privacy—all categories protected from discrimination in the human-rights model. The "reforms" demonize single mothers, punish women whose families do not include a "male" head of household as breadwinner, and characterize the father-less-family structure as deviant.

The welfare solution for "deviant" families (whose deviance is simply their need for public assistance) is to find a man to head the home. Laws require that child support—a symbolic male presence—be established where the father is known. In circumstances in which the identity of the father is unknown, the law conditions eligibility for benefits on the mother's cooperation in establishing the father's identity, including requiring her to reveal the name of sexual partners who might be the biological father of the child needing assistance.[55] This demand flies in the face of sex equality, individual autonomy, and family privacy. The

legislation plainly notes that it is intended to promote marriage and eliminate out-of-wedlock births. Thus, in derogation of human-rights protection of private family life, this new federal legislation intrudes into women's reproductive and sexual lives as well as into their maternal activity.[56]

Intrusions into reproductive matters have continued for all women. Biological sex differences and claimed (but largely contested) psychological and psychosocial differences are used as pretexts to perpetuate women's systemic inequalities in their various communities, including at home, at work, in schools, and in the church. In fact, a critical analysis reveals that inserting women into the realm of legal analysis has shown the deficiency of norms crafted with the male form as the sole model.

Women's childbearing capacity continues to be a legal misfit that has complicated the dichotomy of the rights to individual autonomy and to life, has revealed the complexities of the equality debate, and has provided continuing excuses for treating women differently.[57] In *Geduldig v. Aiello*, the Supreme Court reached the amazing conclusion that discrimination on the basis of pregnancy is not discrimination on the basis of sex.[58] Then, notwithstanding the *Roe v. Wade* decision, which reinforced women's right to autonomy even against a contrary claim of life, *Planned Parenthood of Southeastern Pennsylvania v. Casey* and *Webster v. Reproductive Health Services* work to deny that autonomy by limiting access to public venues and funds for purposes of abortion and allowing state-mandated conditions that make the exercise of that autonomy contingent.[59]

As the examples of family law (including divorce), welfare, and reproduction have shown, differentiated roles for women—particularly the gendered assumptions about women's roles in and obligations to the family—have brought about and perpetuate a subordinated, second-class-citizen status for all women. Human-rights norms that protect against discrimination on the basis of sex and choice of family structure can inform domestic analysis to avoid these inequitable results.

The Promise of a Critically Informed Human-Rights Model

Women's historical social, legal, and economic narratives reflect the power of the family as a traditional structure that has colonized women and legitimized liberalism's hierarchical gender order. Without critical reconstruction, the international protection of family would reinforce gendered social norms and perpetuate women's subordination. A critically informed human-rights reconstruction, however, would demand that the individual civil and political rights to equality, liberty, autonomy, and integrity of the person exist within the family unit so that it is reimagined as a just system. In this regard, the right to life, together with both the right of families to decide on the number and spacing of their children and the right to nondiscrimination on the bases of race and social origin, provide strong grounds to challenge regulations, such as the recent U.S. welfare reforms, that aim at controlling reproduction.

The fact that human-rights norms protect both family and privacy is a helpful tool for a critical analysis that seeks to transform the family into a just institution within which women will be able to enjoy full citizenship rights. Individual privacy and autonomy are central tenets of Western political and philosophical thought about personhood and citizenship. Yet the application of these principles to the family unit has resulted in a hierarchical, gendered, classed, and racialized notion of the legitimate family. Legal institutions have justified non-intervention, even in light of injus-

tices that have included rape, battery, and other forms of violence by hiding behind the veil of the separate private sphere.

On the other end of the spectrum, society, law, and religion normalized the notion of (gendered) family and interfamilial dependence only for units that were economically independent. Having rendered the notion of support a private one, the legal establishment pierces the privacy veil when a particular form of family needs public assistance. Thus, law has used family privacy both as a shield from any threatened change to the established order and as a sword to punish and impose order on those structures that deviate from the traditional normative mold—such as poor families and the aberrant "female-headed households."

Since the 1970s, the U.S. courts have expanded the notion of individual privacy to the family, resulting in protection of such intimate decisions as marriage, reproduction, and parenting. Simultaneously, states have contracted the privacy realm to intervene against domestic violence. Notwithstanding legal changes, however, both societal and religious norms persist in classifying conduct within the home as private, and the state still is hesitant to intrude into every man's castle—his home—even to handle violence between intimates. Further, as the recent welfare reforms reveal, the state will intrude on decisions it considers illegitimate—*non*-marriage and reproduction out of wedlock. These social and legal assumptions render the human right to individual autonomy within the context of certain family forms an illusion.

Using a critically informed human-rights approach allows for the development of signposts to redefine the state's proper location with respect to family privacy. While the state, along with society at large, would retain the obligation to protect the family, the coexistent right to privacy would impede the invasive reach of the state into matters of reproduction, sexuality, and family composition. In particular, critically informed human-rights concepts of family integrity and family privacy can be used to challenge state regulation that seeks information about or collaboration with efforts to establish paternity by conditioning health and welfare benefits (including food and shelter) on divulging information about intimate relations.

A critical reconstruction of the family entails recognition of the interdependence of the coexisting and indivisible rights of individual autonomy and of family. This bundle of rights protects an individual's decision as to her family form and provides that any family form is entitled to respect and dignity equal to that afforded the traditional or normative family.

Critical inquiry also requires a sensitive interrogation of the reasons for families' poverty and rejects making poverty tantamount to deviance. Such contestation will reveal the patriarchal, hierarchical, gendered, racialized, and classed underpinnings of the pathology narrative. Indeed, the popular-deviance model, which simply assists the "othering" of the poor, is in direct contravention of the human-rights mandate of nondiscrimination on the bases of social class, sex, and race.

Rather, critical interrogation exposes that the foundations of poverty in female-headed households include myriad reasons that can be traced to the patriarchal family structure and its dependence on normed gender, social, and economic hierarchies. One reason for the low earning capacity of mothers—single and married alike—is the market's reflection of the normative family values that women stay at home to be supported by their husbands. Another is the workplace's lack of accommodation for the real needs of childrearing, such as flexible work hours and, in the United States, adequate child care and maternity leaves. A

related problem is the legal system's view that, once out of the home, the salary is *his*, not the family unit's, notwithstanding the significance of the mother's unpaid contribution to the family's well-being and standard of living.

The ideology behind the normative family is rooted in myths that reduce the family to a male-dominated reproductive unit and women to their wombs.[60] This architecture mirrors the locations of power in society at large, re-creating in the family the structural frameworks of male domination that exist in other institutions, such as the church, educational system, legislatures, and judiciary.

Although the patently patriarchal structure of family law has given way to a more egalitarian model, the shift is but a rhetorical trope. Far from representing progress, the semantic movement obscures the persistent inequality and subordination that is revealed by critical interrogations. Moreover, the so-called equality model emphasizes individual autonomy, creating tension with the reality of the family as a community. The critically informed human-rights paradigm is helpful in alleviating these tensions by insisting on protections and celebrations of both individuals and communities, privacy and family, autonomy and interdependence (social and political status), and difference and equality.

Because of women's traditional location in the family, the human-rights system's protection of family, if applied without the suggested critical reformations, would simply reinforce and entrench women's positions as second-class citizens. It also could insulate family structures from the scrutiny of justice, except in instances in which public economic supports create pretexts for public intrusion. Critical theory informs a reconstruction of the family forum that enables family rights to become an emancipatory script. This example of the family illustrates the imperative of cross-fertilization of local critical theories and global human-rights norms.

Notes

Acknowledgments: Portions of this essay were presented at the 1997 Critical Race Theory Conference at Yale University and at a University of Wisconsin Law School Faculty Workshop. Thanks are due to many who attended the presentations for their helpful questions and comments. Special thanks are due to friends who offered invaluable insights: Enrique Carrasco, Lisa Iglesias, Jane Larson, Johanna Niemi, Hank Richardson III, and Celina Romany. Muchisimas gracias a Boaventura De Sousa Santos for his generosity not only for reading an earlier version of the chapter, but also for being a commenter at the Wisconsin presentation, and to the faculty and staff at the University of Wisconsin Law School for their hospitality. Linda Ryan, acting director of the St. John's University (SJU) Law Library, provided invaluable support in providing sources for this work, and Christina Gleason (SJU '98 and continuing past her graduation), Amy Kyle Parker (SJU '99), Rebecca Deconcillio (University of Florida Levin College of Law '02), and Shelbi D. Day (University of Florida Levin College of Law '02) did the same in research and editing assistance. Finally, I am very grateful to the SJU Law School and to my new institution, the University of Florida Levin College of Law, for the research-support programs that gave me the time and resources to undertake this project.

Epigraphs: Boaventura De Sousa Santos, "Toward a Multicultural Conception of Human Rights," 18.1 *Zeitschrift für Rechts-Soziologie* (1997): 1, 8–9. Mary G. Dietz, "Context Is All: Feminism and Theories of Citizenship," *Daedalus* (Fall 1987): 1, 6. Professor Dietz continues to explain that scholars have unveiled how the presumptions behind the myth of equal opportunity "deny the social reality of unequal treatment, sexual discrimination, cultural stereotypes, and women's subordination both at home and in the marketplace": Dietz, "Context Is All": 6–7. For various feminist critiques of liberalism, see Dietz, "Context Is All": 21, n. 18, and the sources cited therein. Susan Moller Okin, *Justice, Gender, and the Family* (Princeton, N.J.: Princeton University Press, 1989).

1. Critical Race Theory Conference, Yale University Law School, November 13–15, 1997.

2. See, for example, Berta Esperanza Hernández-Truyol, "Borders (En)gendered: Normativities, Latinas, and a LatCrit Paradigm," *New York University of Law Review* 72 (1997): 882, discussing the normative perspective of equality doctrine. Equality narratives in the United States appear fixated on an "equality-as-sameness" model. This paradigm has generated an awkward jurisprudence on issues of race (particularly in the affirmative-action context), sex (especially in the ongoing pregnancy debate), and gendered family hierarchies (notably in discussions about the public and private, including essential but unpaid work). See James Carney, "Why Talk Is Not Cheap: The Turmoil of Clinton's Race Initiative Is the Latest Evidence of America's Black–White Distrust," *Time,* December 22, 1997, 32, citing strife among members of the initiative's advisory board, critics, and even White House staff members over the makeup and goals of the President's Initiative on Race; Charles Lawrence and Mari J. Matsuda, *We Won't Go Back: Making the Case for Affirmative Action* (Boston: Houghton Mifflin, 1997). See also *Geduldig v. Aiello,* 417 U.S. 484 (1974); Ann C. Scales, "Towards a Feminist Jurisprudence," *Indiana Law Journal* 56 (1981): 375; and Berta E. Hernández, "To Bear or Not to Bear: Reproductive Freedom as an International Human Right," *Brooklyn Journal of International Law* 17 (1991): 309. Critical race and feminist theorists have challenged the validity and authority of an equality jurisprudence that aspires to and insists on blindness with respect to race, sex, and class differences—a patently unworkable approach. A realistic reconsideration of the equality paradigm would acknowledge both sameness and difference and serve to resolve concerns about fairness and (in)justice, explain the real incongruity between the goals of full participation in society by all people and the reality of the invisibility and marginalization of many individuals and groups, and unite, rather than divide, varied but often interdependent communities. See Berta E. Hernández-Truyol, "Building Bridges—Latinas and Latinos at the Crossroads: Realities, Rhetoric and Replacement," *Columbia Human Rights Law Review* 25 (1994): 369; idem, "Building Bridges: Bringing International Human Rights Home," *La Raza Law Journal* 9 (1996): 69; idem, "Building Bridges III—Personal Narratives, Incoherent Paradigms, and Plural Citizens," *Chicano–Latino Law Review* 19 (1998): 303.

3. "Universal Declaration of Human Rights," General Assembly Resolution 217, United Nations General Assembly Organization Resolution, 3rd Session, Part 1, adopted December 10, 1948.

4. See Boaventura De Sousa Santos, *Toward a New Common Sense: Law Science and Politics in the Paradigmatic Transition* (New York: Routledge, 1995), 263, defining "globalized localism" as "the processes by which a given local phenomenon is successfully globalized, be it the worldwide operation of TNCs (transnational corporations), the transformation of the English language into lingua franca, the globalization of American fast food or popular music, or the worldwide adoption of American copyright laws on computer software" and explaining a "localized globalism" as "the specific impact of transnational practices and imperatives on local conditions that are thereby destructured and restructured in order to respond to transnational imperatives." My use of the term "globalized localism" refers to the use of a domestic critical concepts to inform international norms. My turn of the localized globalism phrase in this work refers to the use of an international human-rights concept to develop, expand, and transform the context, concept, meaning, and application of critical theoretical constructs. Currently, in both international and domestic spheres, it is virtually impossible to travel through a day without being repeatedly confronted with the term "globalization." However, one seldom encounters remotely similar definitions: See ibid. Professor Santos defines globalization as the "process by which a given local condition or entity succeeds in extending its reach over the globe and, by doing so, develops the capacity to designate a rival condition or entity as local": See Santos, "Multicultural Conception," 3. See also Aihwa Ong, "Strategic Sisterhood or Sisters in Solidarity? Questions of Communitarianism and Citizenship in Asia," *Indiana Journal of Global Legal Studies* 4 (1996): 107, defining globalization as "the intensified capitalist integration of the world." I use the term "globalization" to refer to the processes by which inter-, intra-, and transboundary movements of capital, information, and people serve to influence, affect, and change norms, traditions and processes of learning, the exchange of information and goods, and lifestyles.

5. See Celina Romany, "Women as Aliens: A Feminist Critique of the Public/Private Distinction in International Human Rights Law," *Harvard Human Rights Journal* 6 (1993): 87.

6. See Santos, *Paradigmatic Transition*, 346.

7. See Lisa C. Ikemoto, "Traces of the Master Narrative in the Story of African American/Korean American Conflict: How We Constructed 'Los Angeles,'" *South California Law Review* 66 (1993): 158. See also Hernández-Truyol, "Borders (En)gendered."

8. See "Universal Declaration," Res. 257-79, describing customary norms and international human-rights law. See also "Statute of the International Court of Justice," annexed to the U.N. Charter June 26, 1945, entered into force October 24, 1945, Art. 38, citing custom as one of the primary sources of international law.

9. The Universal Declaration included rights to life, liberty, nondiscrimination, and more, including the prohibition of slavery, inhuman treatment, arbitrary arrest, and arbitrary interference with privacy that is considered civil and political in nature. See also "International Covenant on Civil and Political Rights" (ICCPR), adopted December 16, 1996, 999 U.N.T.S. 171, entered into force March 23, 1976, Arts. 6, 7, 8(1)-(2), 15, 16, 18, which includes rights such as the right to life; freedom from torture or cruel, inhuman, or degrading treatment or punishment; freedom from slavery and servitude; nonapplicability of retroactive laws; right to recognition as a person before the law; and the right to freedom of thought, conscience, and religion. The Universal Declaration also included the right to social security, full employment, fair working conditions, an adequate standard of living, and participation in the cultural life of the community, which are considered economic, social and cultural in nature. See also "International Covenant on Social, Cultural, and Economic Rights," adopted December 16, 1966, 993 U.N.T.S. 3, entered into force January 3, 1976.

10. See Dietz, "Context Is All": 4-5. Interestingly, and perhaps ironically, the liberal vision, while stuck on civil and political rights even at the expense of the greater societal good, recognized the inviolability premise: "Each person possesses an inviolability founded on justice that even the welfare of society as a whole cannot override.... The rights secured by justice are not subject to political bargaining or the calculus of social interests": See ibid.: 4, quoting John Rawls, *A Theory of Justice* (London: Oxford University Press, 1971).

11. See Berta E. Hernández-Truyol, "Human Rights Through a Gendered Lens: Emergence, Evolution, Revolution," in *Women and International Human Rights Law*, ed. Kelly Askin and Dorean Koenig (New York: Transnational, 1999); Dietz, "Context Is All": 4: "The life of liberalism ... began in capitalist market societies, and as Marx argued, it can only be fully comprehended in terms of the social and economic institutions that shaped it."

12. See *Feldbrugge v. The Netherlands*, European Court of Human Rights, Series A, No. 99, May 29,

1986; see also Martin Scheinin, "Economic and Social Rights as Legal Rights," in *Economic, Social and Cultural Rights*, ed. Asbjorn Eide, Catarina Krause, and Allan Rosas (Norwell, Mass.: Martinus Nijhoff Publishers, 1995), 41, 43.

13. See Romany, "Women as Aliens': "The presence of patriarchy in these emancipatory structures [of liberalism] reveals the gap between liberal concepts and reality." See also Ursula Vogel, "Marriage and the Boundaries of Citizenship," *The Condition of Citizenship*, ed. Bart van Steenbergen (Thousand Oaks, Calif.: Sage Publications, 1994): 79.

14. See Iris Marion Young, "Polity and Group Difference: A Critique of the Ideal of Universal Citizenship," in *Theorizing Citizenship*, ed. Ronald Beiner (Albany: State University of New York Press, 1995), 184-95, proposing a principle of group representation. See also Ong, "Strategic Sisterhood."

15. See United Nations General Assembly Resolution 220A (XXI), U.N. Doc. A/6316 (1966), 999 U.N.T.S. 171, entered into force March 23, 1976.

16. See "Convention on the Elimination of All Forms of Racial Discrimination," 660 U.N.T.S. 195, Art. 1(1), entered into force January 4, 1969, ratified by the United States June 24, 1994. The italics are added for emphasis.

17. See Kimberlé W. Crenshaw, Neil Gotanda, Gary Peller, and Kendall Thomas, "Introduction," in *Critical Race Theory: The Key Writings That Formed the Movement*, ed. Kimberlé W. Crenshaw, Neil Gotanda, Gary Peller, and Kendall Thomas (New York: New Press, 1995), xiv.

18. See Ralf Dahrendorf, "The Changing Quality of Citizenship," in van Steenbergen, *Condition of Citizenship*, 16: "There is a deep similarity between the underclass problem in rich countries and the problem of poor countries.... They too are economically 'not needed' and politically harmless, but challenge our moral foundations." See also Romany, "Women as Aliens, " n.p.: "International society can thus be viewed as a blown-up liberal state which legislates in accordance with liberal humanistic values and which accepts as part of a social contract those values which refer to the essential dignity and freedom of human beings."

19. See, for example, Santos, *Paradigmatic Transition*, 427: "The core-periphery hierarchy in the world system is the result of unequal exchange, a mechanism of trade imperialism by means of which surplus-value is transferred from the periphery to the core."

20. See, for example, David M. Trubek, " Back to the Future: The Short, Happy Life of the Law and Society Movement," *Florida State University Law Review* 18 (1990): 1, 23-4.

21. Dahrendorf, "Changing Quality," 16-7, noting that post-communist states do not have a "bourgeoisie" that is concerned about both civil rights and economic growth, which results in a confusion that, in turn, makes people seek a "citizenship" that is formulated on a desire to belong to a homogeneous group—a "deplorable" result, as "the true test of the strength of citizenship rights is heterogeneity."

22. See Saskia Sassen, "Toward a Feminist Analytics of the Global Economy," *Indiana Journal Global Legal Studies* 4 (1996): 7.

23. See, for example, Jurgen Habermas, "Citizenship and National Identity," in van Steenbergen, *Condition of Citizenship*, 32.

24. See Rhonda Copelon, "The Indivisible Framework of International Human Rights: Bringing It Home," *The Politics of Law*, 3rd ed., ed. David Kairys (New York: Pantheon Books, 1998), 216-7.

25. See *Rust v. Sullivan*, 500 U.S. 173 (1990), refusing to extend constitutional protections regarding the right to abortion to include public funding for the same; *Hernández v. New York*, 500 U.S. 352 (1991), addressing issues of language-based discrimination; *Hopwood v. Texas*, 84 F. 3d 720 (5th Cir. 1996), concerning race and culture.

26. See Crenshaw et al., *Key Writings*, xiv.

27. See Thomas Franck, *The Power of Legitimacy Amongst Nations* (New York: Oxford University Press, 1990); Sassen, "Feminist Analytics"; Thomas Franck, "The Emerging Rights to Democratic Governance," *American Journal of International Law* 86 (1992): 46. See also Berta E Hernández-Truyol, "Women's Rights as Human Rights—Rules, Realities and the Role of Culture: A Formula for Reform," *Brooklyn Journal of International Law* 21 (1996): 605.

28. See, for example, Martha C. Nussbaum, "Nature, Function, and Capability: Aristotle on Political Distribution," in *Oxford Studies in Ancient Philosophy*, supp., ed. Julia Annas and Robert H. Grimm (New York: Oxford University Press, 1988).

29. See, for example, "Universal Declaration," Art. 16; *Report of the International Conference on Population and Development*, chap. 2 II, princ. I, Art. 14, U.N. Doc. A/CONF.171/13 (1994).

30. See Will Kymlicka and Wayne Norman, "Return of the Citizen: A Survey of Recent Work on Citizenship Theory," *Ethics* 104 (1994): 352, 363: "Emphasiz[ing] the necessity of civility and self restraint to a healthy democracy but deny that either the market or political participation is sufficient to

teach these virtues. Instead, it is in the voluntary organizations of civil society—churches, families, unions, ethnic associations, cooperatives, environmental groups, neighborhood associations, women's support groups, charities—that we learn the virtues of mutual obligations." Michael Walzer refers to these geographies as "associational networks": See Michael Walzer, "The Civil Society Argument," in *Dimensions of Radical Democracy: Pluralism, Citizenship and Community*, ed. Chantal Moutteed (New York: Routledge, 1992), 104.

31. M. M. Slaughter, review of *Fantasies: Single Mothers and Welfare Reform—The Neutered Mother, the Sexual Family and other Twentieth Century Tragedies*, ed. Martha Albertson Fineman, *Columbia Law Review* 95 (1995): 2156-7.

32. Nadine Taub and Elizabeth M. Schneider, eds., *Women's Subordination* (New York: Basic Books, 1998), 343: "Throughout this country's history, women have been denied the most basic rights of citizenship, allowed only limited participation in the market place, and otherwise denied access to power, dignity, and respect. Women have instead been largely occupied with providing the personal and household services necessary to sustain family life." See also *Mueller v. Oregon*, 208 U.S. 412, 421-2 (1908): "That woman's physical structure and the performance of maternal functions place her at a disadvantage in the struggle for subsistence is obvious. This is especially true when the burdens of motherhood are upon her.... [C]ontinuance for a long time on her feet at work, repeating this from day to day, tends to injurious effects upon the body, and as healthy mothers are essential to vigorous offspring, the physical well-being of woman becomes an object of public interest and care in order to preserve the strength and vigor of the race.... Still again history discloses the fact that woman has always been dependent upon man."

33. Okin, *Justice*, 13-4.

34. Ibid., 8.

35. Ibid., 26, discussing the views of Allan Bloom, author of *The Closing of the American Mind* (New York: Simon and Schuster, 1987).

36. Ibid., 9, 25. Okin argues that "a just family is [a just society's] essential foundation.... Unless the first and most formative example of adult interaction usually experienced by children is one of justice and reciprocity, rather than one of domination and manipulation or of unequal altruism and one-sided sacrifice, and unless they themselves are treated with concern and respect, they are likely to be considerably hindered in becoming people who

are guided by principles of justice.... [The family] is potentially, a place where we can learn to be just": Ibid., 17-8. See also Hans Adriaansens, "Citizenship, Work and Welfare," in van Steenbergen, *Condition of Citizenship*, 67, suggesting that the discussion of citizenship move from a moral order to the "social structural prerequisites underlying the moral discourse" and urging the individualization of the wage structure that was geared to traditional and gendered visions of work divisions.

37. Okin, *Justice*, 22: "In a just society, the structure and practices of families must give women the same opportunities as men to develop their capacities, to participate in political power and influence social choices, and to be economically secure."

38. Okin, *Justice*, 95: "The resulting disparities in the earnings of men and women, and the economic dependence of women on men, are likely to affect power relations within the household, as well as access to leisure, prestige, political power, and so on, among its adult members."

39. See Barbara Allen Babcock, Ann E. Freedman, Wendy Webster Williams, Rhonda Copelan, Deborah Rhodes, and Nadine Taub, *Sex Discrimination and the Law: History, Practice, and Theory* (New York: Little, Brown, 1996).

40. See generally Katherine O'Donovan, "Sexual Divisions in Law," in *Women's Studies—Essential Readings*, ed. Stevi Jackson, Karen Atkinson, Deirdre Beddoe, Jane Prince, and Sue Faulkner (New York: New York University Press, 1993).

41. *Bradwell v. Illinois*, 83 U.S. (16 Wall.) 130 (1873): "The civil law[,] as well as nature itself, has always recognized a wide difference in the respective spheres and destinies of man and woman. Man is, or should be woman's protector and defender. The natural and proper timidity and delicacy which belongs to the female sex evidently unfits if for many of the occupations of civil life.... The constitution of the family organization, which is founded in the divine ordinance, as in the nature of things, indicates the domestic sphere as that which properly belongs to the domain and function of womanhood. The harmony, not to say identity, of interests and views which belong or should belong, to the family institution is repugnant to the idea of a woman adopting a distinct and independent career from that of her husband.... The paramount destiny and mission of woman are to fulfill the noble and benign offices of wife and mother. This is the law of the Creator."

42. See *Dothard v. Rawlinson*, 433 U.S. 321 (1977); *EEOC v. Sears*, 839 F. 2d 302, 313, 356, n. 57 (7th Cir.

1988), arguing that women prefer less stressful and demanding jobs because of their domestic obligation.

43. See *Hoyt v. Florida*, 368 U.S. 57, 61 (1961). *Taylor v. Louisiana*, 419 U.S. 522 (1975), implicitly overruled *Hoyt*.

44. Okin, *Justice*, 134–69.

45. Ibid., 15, cites extracts from "Apostolic Letter," in *New York Times*, October 1, 1988, A1, A6.

46. Judy H. Longshaw, "Church's Stance on Spouses Reaffirms, Embarrasses [*sic*]," *The Herald* (Rock Hill, S.C.), June 11, 1998, 4A: "God has ordained the family as the foundational institution of human society. It is composed of people related to one another by marriage, blood or adoption. Marriage is the uniting of one man and one woman in covenant commitment for a lifetime.... A husband ... has the God-given responsibility to provide for, protect and to lead his family. A wife is to submit herself graciously to the servant leadership of her husband [and] has the God-given responsibility to respect her husband and to serve as his helper in managing the household and nurturing the next generation."

47. Pat Gilliland, "Women in Combat Shunned by Baptists," *Daily Oklahoman*, June 12, 1998, 12. See also 10 U.S.C. 6015, 8549; see also Taub and Schneider, *Women's Subordination*, 330, suggesting that the right to combat is a right of citizenship. Cf. *Massachusetts v. Feeny*, 442 U.S. 256 (1978), upholding a veteran preference.

48. See Okin, *Justice*, 131–3. Okin has detailed four major ways in which the public–private dichotomy is central to women's subordination. First, power, including violence, is not only a matter of public concern; it is also a matter critical to family dynamics and thus should be a matter of public regulation. Second, public—hence, political—decisions (such as family laws, divorce laws, and other state interventions, including the limitation of women from certain spheres of work) govern much of the domestic sphere and thus should be subject to public challenge, not private protection. Third, the family is the first place in which all people learn about social conduct and roles (including gendered roles). Thus, as an equality concern, family justice is properly in the public view. And fourth, sex segregation of the workplace is part of the reason women become primary parents; the consequent family division of labor causes additional barriers for

women in other spheres. These fiscal barriers exist in the public sector and thus should not be hidden from public review: See ibid., 111, 124–33.

49. See, for example, *Graham v. Graham*, 33 F. Supp. 936 (E.D. Mich. 1940), holding that based on the marriage contract the husband has a duty to support and the wife must follow him if he opts to change domicile and that any private attempts to change such "essential obligations" would be void and unenforceable as against public policy. See generally Jana B. Singer, "The Privatization of Family Law," *Wisconsin Law Review* (1992): 1443.

50. Okin, *Justice*, 123.

51. Melody Petersen, "The Short End of Long Hours: A Female Lawyer's Job Puts Child Custody at Risk," *New York Times*, July 18, 1998, D1.

52. Okin, *Justice*, 160–7.

53. Taub and Schneider, *Women's Subordination*, 332.

54. See, for example, *Beher v. Lewin*, 852 P. 2d 44 (Haw, 1993), which lists more than a dozen benefits of traditional marriage.

55. Slaughter, review of *Fantasies*, 2170–1, describing the interplay of federal and state law and citing the book (*passim*) and discussions of pending legislation.

56. See Hernández, "To Bear," discussing reproductive freedom as an international human right.

57. See, for example, *Michael M. v. Sonoma County*, 450 U.S. 464, 471 (1981), upholding, against challenge by a man, statutory-rape laws that punish men for having sex with women younger than 18 because "only women may become pregnant and they suffer disproportionately the profound physical, emotional and psychological consequences of sexual activity." The Supreme Court continued to explain that "detrimental" gender-based classifications do not always violate the constitution because of the differences between men and women, particularly noting in this regard women's ability to become pregnant.

58. *Geduldig* (1974).

59. See *Planned Parenthood of Southeastern Pennsylvania v. Casey*, 510 U.S. 1309 (1994); *Rust v. Sullivan*, 500 U.S. 173 (1991); *Webster v. Reproductive Health Services*, 492 U.S. 490 (1989).

60. See generally Martha L. Fineman, "Images of Mothers in *Poverty Discourses*," *Duke Law Journal* (1991): 274.

CHAPTER SIXTEEN

Critical Race Theory and Post-Colonial Development: Radically Monitoring the World Bank and the IMF

Enrique R. Carrasco

IN THIS CHAPTER, I explore how Critical Race Theory might help us monitor the development policies of multilateral institutions, particularly those of the World Bank and the International Monetary Fund (IMF) (collectively known as the Bretton Woods Institutions, or BWIs), from a radical perspective. This task is vital in light of the troublesome paradox we face in today's increasingly interconnected and globalized economy. On the one hand, the technologically driven phenomenon of globalization has significantly increased trade and capital flows throughout the world, creating promising opportunities for economic growth. On the other hand, globalization has also led to increased poverty, unemployment, and social disintegration, the last of which is most graphically manifested in violence. We can call this post-colonial paradox "growth with marginalization."

For decades, the BWIs, as well as others involved in "law and development" matters, have devised policies and programs intended to promote economic growth and social welfare in developing countries. In so doing, they have adhered to a hopeful and thoroughly modernist approach, believing that properly structured legal institutions along with appropriate economic policies can help resolve the paradox and lead to human fulfillment, social justice, and peace.[1] Although this approach has met with some success, I doubt that it will enjoy long-term viability without a rigorous exploration of the racial aspects of growth with marginalization on a global scale.

The evidence of racialized marginalization is abundant. In the United States, poverty rates for Latinos/as and African Americans are higher than they are for whites. In Guatemala, unemployment and lower earnings are more common among indigenous than nonindigenous people; the same economic relationship holds true as between blacks and whites in Brazil. The economic and social conditions on the African continent, particularly in Sub-Saharan Africa, compare poorly with those of developing countries as a whole. In Eastern Europe, dark-skinned Gypsies, often called "niggers," live in poverty and suffer racially motivated violence, especially at the hands of white skinheads. Anti-immigrant racism is also alive and well in Western Europe, as countries there struggle to restructure their economies to meet the conditions of the European Monetary Union. And the Asian financial crisis has reignited racial violence in the region, especially in Indonesia, where growth with marginalization is most evident.[2]

Yet an examination of the mountains of research and literature produced by the World Bank and the IMF reveals a large lacuna relating to problems of race and development. The lacuna must be filled if the BWIs wish to defend their legitimacy and relevancy. They are unlikely, however, to embrace potentially explosive racial issues as quickly and wholeheartedly as they have other issues, such as poverty alleviation and corruption. Even if they do jump in eagerly, there is no guarantee that they will address race and development effectively.

Using CRT as a starting point, this chapter suggests principles in which "outsiders" can monitor law and development policies to ensure that the World Bank and the IMF are sensitive to race, law, and economic growth. The first part of this chapter provides the project's foundation by exploring modernity's narrative of development. Using a CRT-inspired technique, I trace the various hopeful and optimistic themes that have contributed both to the narrative's popularity and to its recent condemnation, especially in light of the persistence of the growth-with-marginalization paradox.

In part two, I identify four principles that should inform a general framework for the monitoring project. Collectively, they call

for a hopeful approach to development that does not abandon the teleological quest for the good and just world. But as the postmodern vein of CRT has demonstrated, the struggle for justice should be informed by the contingent nature of post-colonial development policy and its racial roots.

The Rise and Fall of Modernity's Narrative of Development

One of CRT's important contributions has been its careful and revealing analysis of narrative in law. CRT has demonstrated that law is essentially a story that reflects and legitimates the (racial) viewpoints and interests of those in power. The story retains its popularity and persuasiveness as long as it explains the world in logical, positive, and universal terms that justify the status quo. With this in mind, I will briefly trace modernity's narrative of development. It is a familiar and compelling story, filled with great hope, optimism, and despair.

Controlling One's Destiny and Pursuing Material Progress

Relying on H. W. Arndt's observations for the purposes of this chapter, we can trace the narrative's beginnings to the interest in measuring time through the use of the clock in the thirteenth century and to increased interest in the natural world during the same period. Copernicus and Galileo later added to the narrative by stressing the importance of understanding the universe. The Protestant Reformation then produced an ethic that encouraged worldly progress. And the work of Francis Bacon and Isaac Newton in the seventeenth century stressed the importance of science to material progress and to the manipulation of nature.[3] A century later in Britain, development was defined largely as material progress and had evolved into a hopeful and self-sustaining concept with universal justifications.[4] By this time, the nation-state, which had arisen from the ruins of feudalism, had become primarily responsible for legitimizing the narrative.

Optimism in Political Economy

The evolution of political economy reinforced the optimistic tone of the development narrative. For instance, in the eighteenth century the idea that one could achieve material progress through manipulation of one's environment was reflected in the classical political economy of Adam Smith and David Ricardo, who posited that international trade could overcome internal obstacles in the economy and lead to greater productivity. For Karl Marx, progress meant "the development of the productive power of man and the transformation of material production into a scientific domination of natural agencies."[5] Neo-classical thought in the nineteenth century was equally optimistic. Focusing on the theory of equilibrium, Alfred Marshall and others argued that orderly and efficient economic growth could be promoted by examining the microeconomic phenomena relating to pricing and supply and demand. The deracinated consumer, fully informed and rational, became the center of attention; the market was assumed to be perfect; and production techniques and consumer preferences were given. Marshall was so taken with his theories that he predicted capitalism would lead to a classless society.

Then came John Maynard Keynes, the great twentieth-century engineer of economics, who argued that state intervention via government spending and taxation could help avoid recessions and secure full employment. His ideas laid the groundwork for the rise of the welfare state after the Great Depression. Governments around the world acted upon Keynesian optimism by pursuing state-led development policies.

Optimism in Post-World War II International Institutions

After World War II, policymakers hoped that development would be pursued by nations agreeing to abide by the rules of international organizations such as the United Nations, the World Bank, and the IMF. By doing so, the community of nations would reap the benefits of seemingly unlimited progress. Speaking at the Bretton Woods Conference in 1944, U.S. Treasury Secretary Henry Morgenthau, Jr., described the postwar narrative in poetic terms when he proclaimed:

> We are to concern ourselves here with essential steps in the creation of a dynamic world economy in which the people of every nation will be able to realize their potentialities in peace; will be able, through their industry, their inventiveness, their thrift, to raise their own standards of living and enjoy, increasingly, the fruits of material progress on an earth infinitely blessed with natural riches. This is the indispensable cornerstone of freedom and security. All else must be built upon this. For freedom of opportunity is the foundation for all other freedoms.[6]

With the creation of the World Bank and the IMF (and later the General Agreement on Tariffs and Trade), the liberal narrative of peace and prosperity secured a multilateral institutional source which was crucial to the narrative's survival in the post-colonial world. Lower trade barriers, stable exchange rates, and an aggressive assault on what became known as "underdevelopment" in the Third World became the means by which the narrative's happy ending would be reached.

Of course, the themes and storyline were controlled by the rich industrialized countries, especially the United States. This enabled the liberal narrative to withstand the attacks of counter-narratives such as the New International Economic Order (NIEO) of the 1970s. In that movement, developing countries called for negotiations with industrialized countries to modify the philosophical, juridical, and institutional structures that made up postwar liberalism. The project collapsed, however, because its goal of radical and contextual change could not be achieved within liberalism's moderate, state-centered, universal narrative. In international law, the collapse was manifested in distinctions between the "hard law" of the liberal narrative and the "soft law" of the NIEO embodied in U.N. resolutions.

Another radical counter-narrative emanated from neo-Marxists in the late 1960s. They argued that "peripheral" (developing) countries were stuck in a state of underdevelopment and unequal exchange with the "center" (advanced capitalist countries). Under such circumstances, the periphery could not possibly reach the advanced stage of capitalism required for a socialist revolution. Neo-Marxists thus called for an immediate revolution to capture the economic surplus for equitable development.

The Neo-Marxists were provocative but ineffectual. Other voices in development claimed that neo-Marxist solutions, such as autarky, were unrealistic. Much of neo-Marxist theory proved to be incomplete or empirically incorrect. Ironically, in their zeal to create an effective counter-narrative, neo-Marxists espoused theories that became too grand and fatally formalistic.

The Development Narrative Today

Today's approach to law and development continues to reflect the hopeful narrative that began in the thirteenth century. The IMF, the World Bank, and the World Trade Organization, along with the regional development banks (for example, the Asian Development Bank), continue to operate on the premise that they, along with their member states, can help humankind overcome obstacles blocking the path to sustainable development. Their substantive agenda is frequently labeled "neo-liberalism"[7] because of its general rejection of state-dominated development and the great faith policymakers place in the long-term benefits of market-friendly policies and the Rule of Law.

After the fall of the Soviet Union, nearly every region of the globe began some form of neo-liberal reform. Changes in economic law and policy have concentrated on non-inflationary growth, fiscal discipline, high savings and investment, trade and foreign-investment liberalization, privatization, and domestic-market deregulation. The Asian financial crisis has highlighted regulatory transparency and financial-market reform, two recent additions to the list of neo-liberal prescriptions. In many instances, economic changes have been accompanied by pushes for "democratization," with pro-democracy advocates arguing that political freedoms must accompany economic liberalization.

Post-Modernism and the Death of the Grand Narrative

The optimistic narrative I have described is nevertheless under considerable strain today. The transitions to market economies occurring in many regions of the world have accentuated already glaring and often racialized dualities in the global order. Supporters of neo-liberalism believe that marginalization is a temporary phenomenon that countries must endure as they shed discredited socialist or statist development models; they also argue that different people become marginalized at different times for different reasons.

Others attribute the persistence of the paradox to the work of the IMF and the World Bank. Critics claim that the BWIs, along with domestic government elites, have pursued overly ambitious development policies and projects, resulting in massive environmental degradation and forced displacement of communities. They also believe that structural-adjustment policies have hit the most vulnerable populations the hardest and widened the gap between the rich and the poor. Thus, during the fiftieth anniversary of the creation of the BWIs in 1994, critics accused the modern development narrative of being morally and intellectually bankrupt. This led some to proclaim the death of the Grand Narrative of Development.

Going Forward: A Framework for Radical Monitoring of the BWIs

I am not so sure we have witnessed the death of the Grand Narrative. The modernist approach, which is now embodied in pragmatic neo-liberalism (that is, fewer official references to ontological justifications and ideology), appears to be alive and well, especially among policymakers. Does this mean that those who oppose it face a postmodern abyss of despair and cynicism? Should we abolish the World Bank and the IMF and otherwise wage a frontal assault on neo-liberalism? The answers to both questions should be "no." The BWIs and their neo-liberal prescriptions cannot easily be dismissed as evil or useless. Accordingly, what we really need to do is critically and radically monitor neo-liberalism to ensure a more equitable development process.[8] Our task should be informed by the following closely linked principles.

Contingency's Hope

First, we need to recognize that we have moved into a post-Hegelian world, where the visions and beliefs we hold, such as those relating to the promises of the law and development agenda, are contingent and, if we look closely enough, fractured and incoherent. As Jurgen Habermas has stated, "The specific languages of science and technology, law and morality, economics, political science, etc. . . . live off the revivifying power of metaphorical tropes."[9] At first blush, one might conclude that hope for a better life may be hard to sustain under such circumstances.

But we can find hope in the despair of incoherency. As Richard Rorty has argued, by showing us the contingency of our language, beliefs, and institutions, that postmodernism provides us with the freedom to redefine ourselves as our conversations evolve. We can do this and still seek to agree on public principles, such as solidarity and the condemnation of cruelty.[10] We must not, therefore, abandon modernism's emphasis on principled struggle for human liberation. After all, marginalized groups throughout the world have sustained themselves on the conviction that principles matter and that liberation is worth a good fight.

This cautions against overplaying the distinction between modernism and postmodernism. Rather than dwelling on the modern–postmodern dichotomy, our energy can be better used to examine carefully the ways in which the modernist approach to law and development has prevented us from formulating alternative visions of and mechanisms for human liberation. Put another way, in the era of globalization we should pursue an international version of Angela Harris's proposed "jurisprudence of reconstruction." Taking this type of CRT-inspired approach will compel us "to live in the tension between modernism and postmodernism, transforming political modernism in the process."[11]

Focus on the Constructedness of "Law and Development"

The task of reconstruction leads to the second principle. Instead of debating whether the Grand Narrative of Development is dead, we should focus on the constructed nature of the law-and-development enterprise, realizing that the discourse of law and development provides the language through which the social subject is constituted, and through which identities in relation to others are formed. As CRT has demonstrated, the words "nigger," "spik," "honky," "black," "Hispanic," "white," "African American," "Latino/a," and "European American" are all part of a familiar discourse relating to law and development in the United States. The discourse necessarily structures our conversations regarding our projects, legitimating some views and speakers while marginalizing others (that is, Othering).

Once we recognize and interrogate the constitutive nature of law and development discourse and the power and knowledge links that give the discourse meaning and form, we can begin to reconstruct a path toward sustained social justice through radical monitoring of the neo-liberal paradigm. In other words, understanding the constructedness of the law-and-development enterprise will help us detect, analyze, and address the dominant narrative's process of Othering, a phenomenon that is intimately linked to growth with marginalization.

The Rule of Law Is Not Necessarily Liberating

Third, we should be wary of believing that the Rule of Law itself can be liberating. This is not to suggest that we should adopt a Nietzschean view of law as an unwanted obstacle to the will to power. Yet we should recognize, as did Nietzsche, that the Rule of Law also performs a conservative function—namely, securing and preserving states of equilibrium.

This dynamic has played itself out repeatedly in history. In the nineteenth century, for example, Sir Henry Maine viewed law as liberating, arguing that progressive societies were moving from status to contract.[12] Some one hundred years later, Friedrick Kessler observed that the law had come to protect unequal distribution of property and power in the world of monopolistic capitalism, thus constituting a returning to a new feudal order based on status.[13]

In the United States, civil-rights law, including the concept of affirmative action, was originally considered a liberating force. RaceCrits, however, have compellingly argued that such law has been manipulated by white majoritarians to prevent further progress in the realm of racial socioeconomic equality in the United States.[14]

The law-and-development movement has also experienced this phenomenon. During the Cold War, academics and practitioners undertook to modernize Third World nations through legal reform. Inspired by the work of Max Weber, these individuals believed that an autonomous, consciously designed, and universal system could help replicate the development path of Western industrialized societies. By the early 1970s, some scholars—notably, David Trubek—began to doubt the efficacy of the "liberal legalist model." They realized that exporting U.S. institutions to developing countries could actually retard development.[15]

The realm of human rights and development provides yet another example of law's conservative function. Human-rights arguments, particularly relating to civil and political human rights, typically have relied on Western notions of individual rights. Although these rights are viewed by many as immensely liberating, they have been used to oppose claims for group rights, the so-called third generation of solidarity rights that includes the right to development.

Addressing Race and Racism Self-Consciously and Explicitly

The first three principles are closely related to the fourth principle: We should revisit the role of race in law and development throughout the world. One of CRT's important contributions to the study of law and society in the United States is its insistence on discussing race and racism in explicit and self-conscious terms. As noted earlier, RaceCrits have used narratives in law as an analytic tool to promote what is often a painful and controversial discussion. Scholars such as Thomas Ross, for example, have explored racialized narratives in judicial opinions. Others, such as Gerald Torres and Kathryn Milun, have looked at how the "idiom of legal discourse" privileges the storytelling of the dominant group while de-legitimizing and silencing competing stories emanating from subaltern populations, such as Indian tribes in the United States.[16] Narrative in law is thus the mechanism by which the dominant group is able to transform an otherwise contingent view of the world into a universal system, while simultaneously marginalizing competing views through the use of a "dominant gaze" that perpetuates racial inequality.[17] Although the RaceCrit approach is controversial, it has helped heighten the awareness of pervasive racial privileging in the United States—that is, the privileging of whiteness in U.S. law and society.

Has there been a similar privileging in the narrative of law and development? Let us return to the narrative outlined in part one. Generally speaking, the narrative is based on a bundle of inter-related normative propositions: that we should achieve some control or mastery over nature; that it is important to stimulate economic growth, which leads to higher living standards; that

we should eradicate poverty, meet basic human needs, and promote equitable growth; and that we should create and maintain legal and political institutions that will help humans achieve the good life, in both its material and spiritual manifestations. Few policymakers would disagree with the utility of these propositions or seek to discredit the optimistic narrative of which they are part. Indeed, the contrary is true. At the international level, many have sought to sanctify the narrative by demanding fulfillment of the "right to development."[18] Query, though, whether the "right" at issue leads inevitably to growth with *racialized* marginalization, given the following racial aspects embedded in the development narrative.

Even before European colonialism, the ruling classes in Europe practiced racism by constructing biologically based explanations of their superiority over the "savages" or "barbarians" of the lower classes, who were commonly thought to belong to a different "race." Racism then accompanied the liberal narrative of economic development as it spread throughout the Americas, Africa, and Southeast Asia.[19]

The colonial narrative legitimated itself in the same way the ruling elite had legitimated their power over the lower classes within Europe—by the process of Othering ("those populations are fundamentally different from us and inferior") and by appealing to the civilizing mission of the colonizers. European law and institutions played a dual role of promoting colonial exploitation while simultaneously lifting the colonized out of their abyss of barbarism and into a peaceful, more enlightened world. Thus, in his treatise on India, Charles Grant, former chair of the East India Company, considered it the Christian duty of the West to "diffuse among [India's] inhabitants, long sunk in darkness, vice and misery, the light and benign influence of the truth, the blessings of a well-regulated society, [and] the improvements and comforts of active industry."[20]

In the early nineteenth century, the British utilitarians viewed poverty as causing "the vices and defects of the masses of mankind" in India. Poverty in their view was the product of "bad law and government."[21] Later, during the era of imperialism, moral justification for colonial policy gave rise to the rhetoric of social justice and welfare, which was articulated in paternalistic notions of "the White Man's Burden" and trusteeship. By the early twentieth century, colonial law, such as the British Colonial Development and Welfare Act, reflected the "need for minimum standards of nutrition, health and education."[22]

As noted earlier, by the time the World Bank and the IMF were established, the narrative of development had acquired a sweet, poetic universality. Blatant racial references gave way to supposedly race-neutral rhetoric of economic theory and euphemisms such as "underdevelopment" in the former colonies. Racism and its problems were officially, if indirectly, severed from the BWIs through charter provisions that prohibit the institutions from interfering in the domestic political affairs of member nations.

So today, racism is considered a domestic matter that is beyond the reach of the BWIs. They are nevertheless very busy in former colonial regions helping to implement a modernist agenda that explicitly thrived on racial oppression prior to World War II.[23] The World Bank strives more than ever today to eradicate poverty. Both the World Bank and the IMF in their post-debt crisis approach of "adjustment with a human face" now stress targeted social spending and safety nets in order to meet basic human needs and to promote equitable growth. The narrative's emphasis on effective legal and political institutions is now manifested in widespread efforts by the World Bank and regional development banks to eradicate corruption and implement legal and judicial reforms in developing countries. And the IMF has expanded conditionality (the conditions by which member countries are expected to abide in exchange for IMF funds) to include good-governance criteria.[24]

In sum, although the modernist narrative appears to be spectacularly liberating, prompting many to demand a right to participate fully in it, the core themes or propositions of the narrative actually help reinforce a global structure that thrives on marginalization, much of it racial. The BWIs cannot effectively change the structure because they are part of it and they help perpetuate it, even if they mean well. Real change, then, can begin with a self-conscious examination of race and development.

Conclusion

I am not arguing that race and racism are the sole explanations of the growth-with-marginalization paradox; other factors such as gender and class can intensify and complicate the phenomenon's mechanisms of oppression. Nor am I suggesting that pushing the World Bank and the IMF to take race and racism into account in their policies and operations will magically fix all of their perceived problems. Moreover, both institutions have plenty of work to do, and other organizations, such as the United Nations Development Program and the International Labor Organization, address law-and-development matters.

Still, the World Bank and the IMF are the big players in development, and their activities are readily felt in many regions of the world. Although CRT can help us grapple with the paradox of growth with marginalization in post-colonial development, the key question is whether outsiders can successfully persuade institutional bastions of neo-liberal development, such as the World Bank and the IMF, to address self-consciously and directly racial aspects of the paradox. The framework I have proposed for radically monitoring the BWIs should help us push them in the right direction.

Fortunately, we do not have to start from scratch. We can take advantage of evolving notions of the good life based on "a political, economic, ethical and spiritual vision for social development that is based on human dignity, human rights, equality, respect, peace, democracy, mutual responsibility and cooperation, and full respect for the various religious and ethical values and cultural backgrounds of people."[25] This expanding notion of social development will inevitably lead to discussion and analysis of racial constructs. And although the IMF and World Bank charters only narrowly refer to development (largely in economic terms), they have made some attempt to be sensitive to human-rights issues,[26] which presents us with an opening through which we can embark on the project of radical monitoring of the BWIs.

Notes

Acknowledgments: Many thanks to Angela Harris for providing very useful commentary on an earlier draft of this piece. The chapter has benefited tremendously from many conversations I have had with fellow LatCrits.

1. Ann Seidman and Robert B. Seidman, *State and Law in the Development Process* (New York: St. Martin's Press, 1994), 11–26.

2. Coverage of the Asian financial crisis can be found on my Website, The E-Book on International Finance and Development. Available from: <http://www.uiowa.edu/ifdebook>.

3. H. W. Arndt, *Economic Development: The History of an Idea* (Chicago: University of Chicago Press, 1987), 10–1.

4. Adam Smith, *The Wealth of Nations* (New York: Colliier, 1961), 91.

5. Karl Marx, "The Consequences of British Rule in India," in *Marxism and Asia,* ed. Hélène Carrère

d'Encausse and S. R. Schram (New York: Allen Lane, 1969), 119.

6. U.S. Department of State, *Proceedings and Documents of the United Nations Monetary and Financial Conference,* vol. 1 (Washington, D.C.: U.S. Government Printing Office, 1948), 80.

7. The term "neo-liberal" has many different definitions and connotations. I use the term to connote the ideological underpinnings of market-based policies in today's global economy. The following definition of neo-liberalism is suitable: "[Traditional economic development] embraces traditional neoliberal economic development, updated to include the role of the new global economic forces. This approach seeks to convert centralized command economies into market economies; to stabilize the growth of developing countries in ways that facilitate further expansion and access to global markets; and to enhance continued growth and financial stability of postindustrial economies. Growth will be led by the private sector, facilitated by a political environment structured around the goals of trade liberalization and minimal state intervention in the market" (Stanley Foundation, *United Nations–Bretton Woods Collaboration: How Much Is Enough?* [Muscatine, Iowa: Stanley Foundation, 1995], 20).

8. Antonio Gramsci described "a process of differentiation and change in the relative weight that the elements of the old ideologies used to possess. What was previously secondary and subordinate ... is now taken to be primary and becomes the nucleus of a new ideological and theoretical complex": Antonio Gramsci, *Selections from the Prison Notebooks,* ed. Quintin Hoare and Geoffrey Nowell Smith (New York: International Publishers, 1971), 195.

9. Jurgen Habermas, *The Philosophical Discourse of Modernity* (Cambridge, Mass.: MIT Press, 1987), 209.

10. Richard Rorty, *Contingency, Irony, and Solidarity* (New York: Cambridge University Press, 1989), 3–69, 73–198. On p. 189, Rorty argues that "a belief can still regulate action, can still be thought worth dying for, among people who are quite aware that this belief is caused by nothing deeper than contingent historical circumstances."

11. Angela P. Harris, "Foreword: The Jurisprudence of Reconstruction," *California Law Review* 82 (1994): 741, 760.

12. Henry Maine, *Ancient Law* (Buffalo, N.Y.: W. S. Hein Press, 1864), 163–5.

13. Friedrick Kessler, "Contracts of Adhesion—Some Thoughts about Freedom of Contract," *Columbia Law Review* (1943): 629, 640.

14. Kimberlé W. Crenshaw, Neil Gotanda, Gary Peller, and Kendall Thomas, "Introduction," in *Critical Race Theory: The Key Writings That Formed the Movement*, ed. Kimberlé W. Crenshaw, Neil Gotanda, Gary Peller, and Kendall Thomas (New York: New Press, 1995).

15. See Enrique R. Carrasco, "Opposition, Justice, Structuralism, and Particularity: Intersections Between LatCrit Theory and Law and Development Studies," *University of Miami Inter-American Law Review* 28 (Winter 1996–97): 313, 325.

16. Thomas Ross, "The Richmond Narratives," *Texas Law Review* 68 (1989): 381; Gerald Torres and Kathryn Milun, trans., "Yonnondio by Precedent and Evidence: The Mashpee Indian Case," *Duke Law Journal* (1990): 625.

17. Margaret M. Russell, "Race and the Dominant Gaze: Narratives of Law and Inequality in Popular Film," *Legal Studies* 15 (1991): 243.

18. See generally Subrata Roy Chowdhury, Erik M. G. Denters, and Paul J.I.M. de Waart, eds., *The Right to Development in International Law* (Dordrecht, Netherlands, and Boston: Martinus Nijhoff Publisher, 1992).

19. Robert Miles, *Racism after "Race Relations"* (New York: Routledge, 1993), 80–104.

20. Eric Stokes, *The English Utilitarians and India* (New York: Clarendon Press, 1959), 34; Ronald Robinson et al., *Africa and the Victorians: The Official Mind and Imperialism* (New York: St. Martin's Press, 1961), 1. Marx addressed economic development outside Europe, particularly in Asia, out of a conviction that capitalism was the best cure for the "barbarism" and "stagnation" in Asia and non-European countries: Arndt, *Economic Development*, 30.

21. Arndt, *Economic Development*, quoting James Mill.

22. W. K. Hancock, "Survey of British Commonwealth Affairs," in *Problems of Economic Policy II* (London: Oxford University Press, 1942), 267; see also Arndt, *Economic Development*, 27.

23. For op-ed pieces published by the author relating to the neo-liberal narrative and the Asian crisis, see Enrique R. Carrasco, "Tough Sanctions: The Asian Crisis and New Colonialism," *Chicago Tribune*, February 3, 1998; idem, "Rhetoric, Race and the Asian Financial Crisis," *San Diego Union-Tribune*, January 9, 1998; and idem, "Rhetoric Fuels Racism in the Crises," *Los Angeles Times*, January 1, 1998.

24. IMF Survey, "IMF Adopts Guidelines Regarding Governance Issues," U.S. Government Printing Office, Washington, D.C. (August 1997), 233.

25. "Copenhagen Declaration on Social Summit," Report of the U.N. World Summit for Social Development, U.N. Doc. A/CONF.166/9 (1995), para. 14.

26. Enrique R. Carrasco and M. Ayhan Kose, "Income Distribution and the Bretton Woods Institutions: Promoting an Enabling Environment for Social Development," *Transnational Law and Contemporary Problems* 6 (1996): 1.

PART III

Directions

CHAPTER SEVENTEEN

Critical Coalitions: Theory and Praxis

Julie A. Su and Eric K. Yamamoto

WHY ARE PROGRESSIVE law professors so often absent from the in-the-trenches legal struggles of communities of color—where trial courts, community halls, city councils, churches, corporate-accountability campaigns, government bureaucracies, and state initiatives are the terrain for race controversies? And why are political lawyers so often missing from gatherings of progressive academics—where critiques of race, culture, and law provide critical insight into the limitations and possibilities of contemporary civil-rights practice in pursuit of racial justice? Of course, progressive scholars and political lawyers do interact. But in our estimation, not nearly enough.

We write in the hope of blurring the line, to explore both the power and difficulty of collapsing categories of political lawyer and scholar.[1] We write as a front-line civil-rights lawyer who is also engaged in race and coalitional theory development, and as a scholar–teacher who is also practicing civil-rights and human-rights law.

Why is it so hard for scholars and front-line lawyers to collaborate, to translate their work for one another, to directly inform each others' efforts? Eric's writing on a crit-ical race praxis begins to address this larger question.[2] In this chapter, we take on a more discrete task—to sketch the complex dynamics of one particular coalitional effort and assess its implications for the development of critical coalitional theory.

Intellectually and politically, we agree on the potential, as well as the sharp limitations, of civil-rights law and litigation practice in contemporary America. Where we disagree, mildly, concerns what to do in light of these limitations. For Julie, a pressing question is, "Given the concrete realities facing subordinated communities, what strategies work best and how can those strategies help individuals gain the power to make real changes in their lives?"[3] For Eric, a primary question is, "How can we, over time, remake civil-rights law and practice into a viable instrument for progressive change?"

For both of us, an important question is, "What might Critical Race Theory offer to and learn from groups engaged in forging alliances and building coalitions?" In framing this question we are implicitly making several assertions about the development of critical coalitional theory. Theory development should be forward-looking—that is, it should explore how race-theory insights illuminate and aid ongoing and future coalition-building efforts. Developments should integrate theory and action—reflecting our belief that theory-building both shapes and is shaped by coalitional practice and that theory solely for its own sake is of limited efficacy in progressive social-change work. Issues of gender, class, sexual orientation, disability, and multiracialism are crucial to the dynamics of racial coalition-building in a political climate that is hostile to the civil rights of subordinated peoples. And finally, we are asserting that among coalition partners, intergroup healing and reconciliation are sometimes a necessary first step to, and always an ongoing process in, forging lasting alliances.

We ground these assertions, this chapter's thematic points, and our call for continuing development of critical coalitional theory in the following, more detailed account of the explosive, frustrating, and empowering coalition-building struggles of Thai and Latina garment workers in Los Angeles. The account reflects Julie's own experiences.

Thai and Latina Garment Workers in Los Angeles

The Thai Garment Workers

On August 2, 1995, federal, state, and local law-enforcement officials in a suburb of Los Angeles uncovered seventy-one Thai garment workers behind a barbed-wire compound, posted with armed guards. The discovery sent shock waves across America and around the world. From impoverished rural Thailand, these garment workers dreamed the immigrant dream: a life of hard work with fair pay, decency, self-sustenance, and hope. What they found instead was an industry—the garment industry—that thrives on oppressive sweatshop labor, while closing its eyes to inhumane treatment of workers. What these workers also found were government bureaucracies so intent on maintaining the status quo and on self-promotion that they contributed to the exploitation of these immigrant workers.

The Thai workers were enslaved in a two-story apartment complex in El Monte, California. There they were forced to work, live, eat, and sleep for as long as seven years, sewing garments that were later sold in the nation's top retail stores. Eighteen-hour days laboring over sewing machines were the norm. The workers consumed large quantities of coffee or splashed water on their faces to stay awake. When they were permitted to go upstairs to sleep, they crowded on thin mats on the floor, eight or ten to a small room, while rats and roaches crawled over them. Their pay was less than a dollar an hour, and whatever they made, they sent to parents, siblings, and children in Thailand.

A ring of razor wire and inward-pointing iron spikes surrounded the apartment complex. Their captors threatened that if they tried to resist or escape, the workers would be beaten, their homes in Thailand burned, and their families murdered. To prove their point, the captors showed a photo of the battered face of a worker caught trying to escape. The workers were also told that if they reported these abuses, they would be imprisoned and then deported by the Immigration and Naturalization Service (INS); they, not their captors, would be punished.

The Thai workers were denied medical attention. Many were found with vision impairment, including near-blindness, respiratory illnesses, and repetitive-motion disorders. Others were found with tumors that required immediate surgery. While confined at El Monte, one worker extracted eight of his own teeth without anesthesia after his periodontal disease went untreated.

Even upon discovery of the slave-labor sweatshop, however, the workers remained incarcerated. The INS immediately took them to a federal penitentiary, where the workers found themselves again behind barbed wire, facing an uncertain period of confinement. The INS forced the workers to wear prison uniforms and shackled them each time they were transported. The workers waited interminably, confused and frightened, as INS prisoners in humid holding tanks.

A small group of activists, mostly young Asian Americans, including attorneys, demanded their release. The activists argued that INS detention of these workers was bad public policy. It confirmed the common threats of sweatshop operators that workers were the ones at risk if abuses were brought to light. The detention discouraged immigrant workers from reporting exploitation and pushed sweatshops and El Monte-type slave shops further underground. The INS, the activists insisted, should not become a tool of exploitative employers.[4]

The activists quickly learned that the INS is not moved by policy arguments and set up a makeshift office in the INS basement waiting room, using INS pay phones as their primary means of outside communication. Julie's account captures the feeling of the time:

> We filled out endless forms until we realized the forms were means of delay and diversion. We banged on doors that were slammed in our faces and sat in offices they wanted to close. We told our story to the local, national and international media. After nine long days, the pay phones were broken, our bodies fatigued and the INS beleaguered. And the Thai workers gained their freedom. We succeeded in just over a week in part because we refused to accept excuses such as, "It doesn't work that way" and "There are more appropriate channels."[5]

The Criminal Prosecution and Civil Lawsuit

The U.S. Department of Justice, led by the U. S. Attorney's Office in Los Angeles, charged the operators with criminal conspiracy, involuntary servitude, kidnaping by trick, and smuggling and harboring individuals in violation of U.S. immigration law. For the workers, the criminal case embodied the first of many conflicts between the mandates of traditional "legal justice" (with narrow notions of redress) and the goals of progressive political and social activism (emphasizing changes in living conditions and institutional power structures). Because the workers were the key witnesses in the criminal case, the U.S. attorney warned them not to speak out about the abuses they had endured. While this restriction made some sense in the context of the criminal prosecution, it restricted the workers' control over their own lives and prevented them from telling their stories. To satisfy the demands of criminal-law enforcement—that is, to punish the workers' captors—an important opportunity for the workers to express themselves, to learn, to heal, to challenge, and to feel empowered was lost.

Soon after the Thai workers gained their freedom from the INS, they filed a federal civil lawsuit in Los Angeles. Upon the conclusion of the criminal case, the workers' civil lawsuit began. The lawsuit charged the immediate operators of the El Monte compound with false imprisonment, civil racketeering, and labor-law and civil-rights violations. The suit also asserted claims against the clothing manufacturers and retailers for whom the workers had sewn.

On one level, the civil lawsuit was significant because workers had gained access to the legal system. Immigrant workers seldom find the legal system open to them. In the large majority of situations, legal protections for exploited workers and redress for violations are wholly illusory.

On another level, the lawsuit was significant for its call for corporate accountability. Not only does the legal system too seldom give workers of color the opportunity to tell their stories, but there is an additional barrier that poor people of color face: the hostility of the law and the courts to calling those in power to account. Once in court, the workers asserted three theories of corporate liability. First, the manufactureres and retailers, as "joint employers" of the workers, violated federal and state labor laws, including minimum-wage and overtime requirements. Second, the manufacturers and retailers violated federal and state laws prohibiting them from using industrial homeworkers for garment production, from doing business with unregistered entities, and from placing into the stream of commerce products produced in violation of minimum-wage and overtime laws. Third, the manufacturers and retailers negligently hired and supervised sweatshop operators.

The Latina Garment Workers

During the case, the plaintiffs found that the manufacturers and retailers had been dealing directly with a second sweatshop, operated and owned by the same family that enslaved the Thai workers. This sweatshop, located in downtown Los Angeles, employed twenty-some Latina garment workers in "typical" sweatshop conditions—that is, conditions that characterize the Los Angeles garment industry. The Latina workers worked ten- to twelve-hour days, six days a week, though the operators kept time records indicating that they worked only forty hours a week. The Latina workers in the downtown sweatshop were paid cash, subminimum wages, and no overtime, although they received pay stubs documenting legal wages.

The manufacturers and retailers sent their orders and detailed specifications to the downtown shop. From there, the work was sent to two sewing facilities: the El Monte apartment complex where the Thai workers sewed, and a sweatshop where another group of Latina workers sewed. Although they were not forced into physical servitude, the Latina

workers also lived in economic servitude. Despite full-time, year-round work, they were unable to rise above poverty. The Latina workers, like the Thai workers, were legally entitled to hundreds of thousands of dollars in unpaid minimum wages and overtime.

The Latina workers also endured daily indignities from the sweatshop operators. The Latina workers were sometimes denied permission to use the bathroom. They were verbally and physically assaulted. They were punished for inquiring about their rights or taking a day to tend to a sick child. Lunch breaks were short or nonexistent; workers often ate at their machines. Workers who ironed clothes stood all day until their legs were numb, their feet swollen, and their backs sore.

Joining the Latina garment workers as plaintiffs in the lawsuit was legally significant, politically important, and practically challenging. Exposure of the Thai workers' enslavement posed double risks. Enslavement was so outrageous that the public might view it as a terrible but nevertheless isolated incident. In addition, people might no longer be outraged by ordinary sweatshop oppression. Despite the workers' overcrowding in dark warehouses, long hours for subminimum wages, and constant harassment, the industry might say, without irony, "at least they weren't held behind barbed wire, and there were no armed guards." By uniting through their lawsuit, however, the Thai and Latina workers sent a compelling message to garment manufacturers, retailers, and the public: Their case was not just about slave labor, it was also about the hundreds of thousands of garment workers laboring in oppressive sweatshops throughout the United States.

Coalition Litigation as Political Activism

Although the Thai and Latina garment workers all experienced exploitation for years, and although they all were skeptical of the legal system, the act of pursuing a single lawsuit provided a concrete opportunity for them to unite. The strategic value of this coalitional litigation was confirmed by the defendants' persistent efforts to distinguish the Thai and Latina workers. The manufacturers and retailers argued that public opprobrium should be focused on the illegal enslavement of this one Thai immigrant group in this one compound. Why this tack? The potential impact of collaborative litigation on the garment industry was enormous. The workers' joint lawsuit compelled the industry and the public to view abuses not as isolated incidents, but as structural deficiencies. Corporate decision-making, profits, and indifference were responsible for the creation and maintenance of these and other sweatshops.

By exposing the workers to both the power and the limitations of the law, the lawsuit encouraged them to join together not only as litigants, but as social activists. The workers learned that for poor, non-English-speaking, documented and undocumented women of color, compassion, dignity, rights, and equality—even in the United States—are not givens. They are not even necessarily "the law"; they are the ephemeral rewards of hard, continuing struggle.

The Thai and Latina workers' lawsuit also challenged the notion that social justice is obtained through court victories engineered by lawyers. Lawyers file pleadings, write briefs, make oral arguments, take depositions, and respond to discovery requests as components of every litigation strategy. But if lawyers, and the litigation itself, are the focal point, while communities stand on the sidelines, the struggle for social justice withers. Even as we lawyers play the game, we must ask, What do workers gain from a litigation process that reinforces their marginalization? What is lost by discouraging community participation in the process, and what do legal victories mean, if anything, in terms of concrete, tangible improvements in the daily lives of community members? Can

litigation be a process through which individuals learn about rights and responsibilities and participate actively in the decisions affecting their lives? How do lawyers learn to be facilitators of, rather than barriers to, that potential?

In October 1997, after two years of litigation, several manufacturers and retailers—including Mervyn's (Dayton Hudson), Montgomery Ward, Miller's Outpost (Hub Distributing, Inc.), B.U.M. Equipment, and L.F. Sportswear—paid the workers nearly $3 million to settle the lawsuit.[6] In May 1999, nearly four years after the case began, the last defendant manufacturer, Tomato, Inc., agreed to pay $1.2 million.[7] The workers jointly made the decisions to settle after attending numerous court hearings and status conferences about their case; participating in countless group meetings, weekend gatherings, depositions, and interactive workshops; and working to understand the evidence, legal theories, risks, and possible litigation outcomes. Joint participation in all phases of the litigation generated a sense of their ownership of the settlements.

The litigation, by design, was also a vehicle for public education and social and economic pressure for broader changes in industry practices. In this, the media was critical. Media can be a crucial ally in social-justice work. The local, national, and international coverage of the Thai workers' slave compound and its connection to a highly exploitative and often lawless industry generated public awareness and, more important, public understanding.

But media visibility risks distortion of the lives of poor communities of color. The media likes simplistic stories—isolated heroes and nameless groups of victims. Some media portrayed the workers only as hapless victims, and that generated the false impression that they were not human agents engaged in a struggle to improve their lives. Those portrayals suggested, and sometimes explicitly stated, that heroes—

lawyers and government agents, usually straight, white men—were the ones working to save the downtrodden.

In its distaste for complexity, the media also adamantly resisted covering the union of Asian and Latina workers. Although racial discord between communities of color is newsworthy, particularly in Los Angeles, interracial solidarity is not. The Thai and Latina coalition of working poor women, crucial to the actual struggle, did not exist in the minds of print and electronic journalists and, therefore, in the public eye. The Latina workers in particular remained largely invisible. This, in turn, fueled animosity between the Thai and Latina workers.

The workers shared a common enemy, common purpose, and common space on the plaintiff's side of the caption to a legal brief. This alone, however, was not enough to make them see one another as true coalitional allies. The fact that Julie was their attorney and advocate also was not, in the abstract, enough to forge the coalitional bonds that would transform a civil-rights attorney–community-client relationship into a genuine partnership. The challenge of building these coalitions in the face of existing and often deeply entrenched conflicts between potential partners raises important questions. Should internal coalitional tensions be avoided or ignored in the interest of presenting a unified political front or embraced and addressed as integral to the struggle for coalitional formation and action? If coalitions across differences are so fraught with difficulties and so vulnerable to internal division, should we reassess the value of these coalitions in progressive work?

Critical Race Theory and Emerging Alliances

What does Critical Race Theory have to say about these new alliances and the struggles they encounter? Both a lot and not enough.

As many have observed, traditional civil-rights alliances have disintegrated.[8] In the late 1950s and 1960s, an alliance of labor, the Democratic Party, and organizers of the Civil Rights Movement collectively triggered school desegregation, the 1964 Civil Rights Act, the Voting Rights Act, the Fair Housing Act, the War on Poverty, and affirmative action. That alliance of primarily blacks, white liberals, and workers has splintered. The fractured politics of California's Propositions 187 (immigration) and 209 (affirmative action) is evidence. What accounts for the defection of white workers, many white liberals, and significant numbers of African Americans, Latino/as, and Asian Americans from the traditional progressive alliance? There are, of course, many reasons. Some are obvious. Unrelenting conservative attacks by Republican presidents, legislative majorities, and federal and state judges on civil rights, affirmative action, and desegregation, with the complicity and active participation of so-called liberal leaders and Democratic Party members, have rolled back many civil-rights gains. Economic hard times also breed insecurity, distrust, and a search for scapegoats, all of which threaten fragile progressive coalitions.[9]

What is less openly acknowledged is the splintering effect of conflicts among participants in the traditional progressive alliance. For example, organized labor has long faced charges of racism, sexism, and homophobia.[10] Established civil-rights organizations representing people of color have been criticized by the poor and by workers as increasingly irrelevant to their communities. Traditional alliances, facing continuing external hostility from traditional enemies, are also severely stressed by unresolved internal conflicts.

Another reason for the breakdown of traditional civil-rights alliances is the destabilizing effect of the absence of certain groups from those alliances and, particularly, from positions of leadership within them: women, especially women of color; other racial and ethnic groups; gay men and lesbians; and immigrants. In the early twenty-first century when even the term "civil rights" has been distored and misappropriated—when workers are blamed for their exploitation, affirmative action is equated with racism, and segregation passes for just social policy—it is these latter groups that are also claiming a place at the progressive coalitional table. We thus see the emergence of Cleveland's Women for Racial and Economic Equality; Oakland's multiracial People for Bread, Work and Justice; New York's Black–Korean Mediation Project; Los Angeles's Metropolitan Alliance (including multiracial immigrant workers' advocates); and the Civil Rights Consortium (including Latinos/as, Asian Americans, Native Americans, gays and lesbians, and the disabled).[11]

Critical Race Theory writing has begun to explore the new multifaceted coalitions. It has pioneered the concept of intersectionality to explain the confluence of race, class, gender, and sexual orientation and the law's often hidden contribution to the maintenance of interconnecting forms of social oppression.[12] This concept of intersectionality has evolved in several directions. A critical race feminism focuses on women of color,[13] and an emerging, dynamic LatCrit theory crosses borders of gender (Latina/o), ethnicity (Chicano/Cuban), race (with African Americans and Asian Americans), and citizenship (immigrants/citizens).[14]4

In this fashion, Critical Race Theory and its related schools have provided a framework for diverse alliances to combat the anti–affirmative-action assault, to challenge resegregation in housing and schools, to stop immigrant- and gay-bashing, and to stem racial and gender violence. The Society of American Law Teachers (SALT), for example, formed such an alliance of professors, workers, teachers, organizers, attorneys, students, and gay and lesbian leaders to march at the 1998 American Association of Law Schools' Annual Convention to protest California's implementation of Proposition 209. The preamble to the SALT resolution challenging the anti–affirmative-action initiative "acknowledges the connections among forms of oppression that exclude us from equal citizenship."

> Attacks on affirmative action, immigration, welfare, and gay and lesbian equality must be understood as interrelated, mean-spirited policies of exclusion. Therefore, each struggle against Prop 209, Prop 187, the "Welfare-to-Work" law, or the Defense of Marriage Act must be seen as a part of a larger movement for social transformation and justice.[15]

Many critical race scholars also have much to say about alliances across academic disciplines. Rejecting "law as an autonomous discipline," they have urged border crossing among disciplines—law, sociology, psychology, cultural anthropology, literary theory, political science, history, feminist theory, queer theory, religion.[16] They have urged multidisciplinarity as a way of understanding the sharp constraints and subtle potential of law in progressive politics.

Of particular importance to this chapter, critical race scholarship has begun to critique the limitations of the "common-interest" theoretical model of coalition-building. Eric has argued that much of the recent writing on coalition-building tends toward the a-historical and misses the complex dynamics of intergroup tensions that both enliven and enervate coalitional efforts.[17]7 That writing focuses tightly on the social or economic interests of coalition members. By encouraging those members to stay fixed on common ground (usually resisting white racism or monopoly capitalism or obtaining governmental benefits), "common-interest" coalitional theory ignores the salience of group differences and underplays the disruptive effects of intergroup grievances on coalition formation.

In related fashion, Eric has critiqued recent writing on coalition-building that focuses predominantly on culture. That writing insightfully calls for sensitivity to culture-based behaviors and modes of communication, thereby limiting intergroup misunderstandings. In doing so, however, the culture-based theory tends to overlook the impact of external factors—social, economic, or political structures, for example—in the generation of intergroup conflicts.[18]

Finally, critical race scholars such as Harlon Dalton have begun to explore the healing of racial grievances. That exploration is particularly important to racial communities facing both common ground and mutual disaffection. It speaks to reconciliation among communities of color as predicates to long-term alliances.[19]

Despite these contributions, Critical Race Theory has yet to explore the difficult dynamics and racialized settings of coalition formation and action. The complexity and full potential of critical coalitions are subjects ripe for further inquiry.

Beyond Common Ground

How does a diverse coalition challenging, for instance, "English Only" voter initiatives, immigration "reform," or discriminatory admissions policies at public universities identify and then move beyond "common ground" politics when a challenged law appears to benefit or hurt different groups differently? Is the appeal to abstract legal or moral principles? To the banner of fighting racist, heterosexist patriarchy? To practical deal-making (my turn, then your turn)? These questions bring to mind the internal debates of a race-based organization, the Japanese American Citizens League in Hawaii, during the struggles of gay men and lesbians for the right to same-sex marriage. Should a Japanese American civil-rights group take a public stand against heterosexism as matters of both resource alloca-

tion and intra-community dynamics? Although it is oversimplified, this real-life example has echoes in innumerable civil-rights battles. Moving beyond "common ground" to form progressive coalitions is fraught with tension, difficulty, and internal and external conflict. However, coalitions that rely solely on "common ground" risk approaching civil-rights issues narrowly and defensively so as to miss important opportunities for collective action.

Constricted Civil-Rights Law Paradigm

The current paradigm by which civil-rights struggles are conceived and debated—a devotion to colorblindness and individuality[20]—constricts and at the same time requires the productive framing and handling of coalitional claims against dominant white interests. Something more than the language of traditional civil-rights law and traditional civil-rights tools is needed to drive coalitional efforts. We are reminded of the Thai and Latina garment workers, their deployment of civil-rights rhetoric and their use of the courts as part of a larger political strategy—recognizing both the sharp limitations and focused potential of a civil-rights legal approach to their situation. But their alliance was not without tension, frustration, and sometimes outright animosity.

Underlying Intergroup Grievances

Deep, often unacknowledged grievances among racial communities can transform seemingly minor face-to-face conflicts into intergroup controversies. In addition, group members from traditionally disfranchised communities too often redeploy oppressive strategies and structures against one another, generating grievances that undermine coalition-building efforts. What is the importance of addressing and redressing those grievances, of healing and reconciliation, as predicates to coalition?[21] A number of organizations appear to answer that question by their very existence: Los Angeles's Leadership Development in Inter-ethnic Relations (LDIR) and New York's Black–Korean Mediation Project, for example, are designed specifically to deal with interracial tensions and healing. All too often, the dangers of explicitly acknowledging intergroup tensions seem too threatening, but in neglecting to deal with them honestly and self-critically, we miss important opportunities for building real coalitions that are the basis for building a true community of justice.

Scholars as Practitioners: Praxis

These issues also arise in coalitional efforts between scholars and front-line activists, which returns us to our initial question. In what ways can race scholars and political lawyers, working together, contribute to a progressive social-justice movement? What is our role, not only in the academy and the courts, but also in neighborhoods, schools, workplaces, churches, city councils, and legislatures? In forward-looking terms, how can scholars connect with, learn from, translate our work for, and assist progressive lawyers, teachers, social workers, therapists, politicians, clergy, and community organizers? And how can civil-rights lawyers draw more deeply from the well of critical race insights to energize and sometimes refocus efforts in the trenches? In sum, as a form of praxis, how can we better become "scholars as justice practitioners" and "activist lawyers as theorists"?[22]

Critical Coalitions

The coalition forged between the Asian and Latina workers and their Asian American attorney and advocates underscores the need for further inquiry into these areas. It provides a glimpse of the pitfalls, triumphs, and potentially transformative nature of new, albeit difficult, progressive coalitions. The efforts in Los Angeles to form a cross-racial, cross-cultural, and cross-class alliance between Asian and Latina workers and Asian American civil-rights attorneys reflect the difficulties and enormous potential of justice work in a hostile, conservative environment. An alliance of individuals and communities who were not part of the traditional progressive alliance—and who did not consider one another natural allies—formed to wage a compelling campaign against sweatshop exploitation and corporate greed.

What made this coalition much more difficult than many others was that it was not about privileged people coming together across their differences, or activists seeking more effective, broad-based means of advancing a common cause. This was about coalitions between people who did not speak the same language, who did not know whether they would have enough to pay the month's rent or phone bill, for whom paying bus fare to come to a meeting was expensive, and for whom the prospect of long-term social change was far too distant. This was coalition work among people who could hardly afford to do anything more than survive. They had much in common—poverty, low wages, harsh daily working conditions, language barriers. It was precisely those similarities, however, that made the coalition so unlikely.

This was a coalition that seemed destined to fail. First, the structure of the garment industry severely hampers the formation of an interracial, interethnic alliance. Sweatshop owners are often Asian immigrants eking out a living in the face of downward pressures imposed by manufacturers and retailers. For this reason, Latina workers view Asians generally not as friends or even strangers, but as enemies—the very source of their daily subjugation. Owners and executive officers of large corporations, who are primarily white, appear to remain above the fray. They can blame interracial conflict at the bottom for the workers' problems, even though in large part they created and maintain the conditions for that conflict.[23] In this way, individual divisions are entrenched, interracial group hostility solidified, and white corporate racism absolved. The economic structure of the garment industry militates against coalition-building among those at the bottom.

Second, Asian–Latina tensions are exacerbated, and coalition-building prospects undermined, by the government and media. Government agencies seeking credit and good publicity for "helping" the enslaved Thai workers purposely excluded the Latina workers from their services. The media, consistent in its continual refusal to report interracial coalition efforts, ignored the Latina workers. Even the large Spanish-language paper *La Opinion* ran a front-page article about the lawsuit and failed to mention the Latina workers.[24] Julie had spoken to the reporter for forty minutes emphasizing the importance of the cross-racial alliance. When the news article appeared, there was no mistaking that the Latina workers blamed Julie, the Asian American attorney, for their exclusion.

Third, Asians and Latinas often experience intercultural discomfort. They suffer similar exploitation in the underworld of American garment-industry sweatshops. They often labor side by side. But their difficulty in communicating across language and cultural differences, exacerbated by the daily indignities they suffer, make them turn on one another. The Thai workers, while confined against their will and barred from contact with anyone outside their apartment complex-turned-sweatshop compound, did hold stereotypes and harbor deep prejudices of their own. Clearly, institutional racism permeated their daily experience, both before and after their arrival in the United States. Although the El Monte

compound prevented them from having daily contact with racial "others," and that lack of contact limited their viewing themselves in racial terms (they identified as "Thai people" primarily as a matter of national identity), it did not shield them from animosity based on ethnicity (their captors were ethnically Chinese) and race (they were told to fear Latinos and African Americans in the United States).

The Latina workers, however, had been exposed to the racialized environment of Los Angeles's low-wage workforce, many for years, and in varying degrees had internalized it. At the first meeting between the workers, one of the Thai workers, addressing the Latinas, expressed her hope and gratitude that freedom would now permit them to work together. The Latinas, both in relation to the Thai workers and to Julie, approached coalitional prospects with open trepidation, skepticism, and, at times, outright hostility. For them, Asians—or "*chinas*," as they referred to all Asians—were unnatural allies and perhaps even enemies.

These perceptions signal a phenomenon Eric has described as the "redeployment of structures of oppression."[25] Even as communities of color struggle against white racism and corporate domination, they at times tend to replicate oppressive social and economic structures to oppress others. They thereby become, in limited fashion, oppressors as well as the oppressed, excluders as well as the excluded. Asian sweatshop owners are an example. They feel relatively powerless in the face of corporate industry control, a mysterious legal system, and American racism that derides their looks, accents, and cultures. Those sweatshop operators simultaneously redeploy those oppressive structures—economic, racist, legal (recall threats of deportation)—to subject Latina and other Asian immigrant workers to inhumane working and living conditions.

In turn, the treatment Latina workers receive from their Asian employers translates into Latina hostility and distrust of Asian Americans. The redeployment of oppressive structures thus occurs at both the class and racial levels: Workers and sweatshop operators turn their economic powerlessness into anger at one another as a class; Asians and Latinos turn the racial oppression they suffer into racial antipathy toward the other as a race. Individual conflicts at the workplace translate into group disaffection. All of this profoundly affects coalition-building.

The first time the Latina workers came to see Julie, they took one look and said, "Si eres china, porque quiere ayudarnos?" (If you are Chinese, why do you want to help us?) and "Si ayuda los tailendeses, porque quiere ayudarnos?" (If you're helping the Thais, why do you want to help us?). "Porque creo en justicia," Julie said, "y la lucha es muy grande. La explotación de los trabajadores y los latinos es la explotación de todos de nosotros. Si no luchamos juntos, no podemos ganar" (Because I believe in justice, and the struggle is a big one. The exploitation of workers and of Latina/os is the exploitation of us all. If we do not fight together, we will not win). It was the first time they had heard this from someone who looked like Julie, speaking their language, and who was also a lawyer, seeking to join their fight. Building coalitions for Julie meant creating linkages across not only race and gender but also class. To make those linkages, the Thai and Latina workers needed to deal with the barriers to coalition erected by a racialized corporate and class structure, by government and media, and by their own perceptions. And they needed a safe place where the workers could struggle to address grievances against one another (and each other's groups) without threatening the existence of the fragile alliance.

After one particularly bitter meeting, one Latina worker finally admitted that shouting at Julie and the Thai workers gave her satisfaction because it felt like she was yelling at the supervisor in the factories where she had worked. Julie finally told her she needed to get over that; that if she had problems with Julie, she should say so. But if she wanted Julie as an Asian American to answer for all the pain and indignity inflicted by people with Asian faces, they needed instead to create a more productive way for handling those deep group-to-group grievances. Over time and with persistence, humility, and patience, the Thai and Latina workers and their lawyer developed a sense for how to be critical coalition members. While fighting corporations and legal and economic systems, the workers and Julie learned to analyze oppressive class, race, and political structures, to deal with individual conflicts among coalition members face-to-face, and to struggle jointly to address deeper group-to-group grievances.

These experiences reveal that critical coalitions can be sources of both intense struggle and great joy. A genuine sense of community often emerges only through engagement in, rather than avoidance of, nitty-gritty efforts to align. There is the exhilaration of a march outside a fancy department store or a chant done in three languages; the shared stories about families, hopes, and dreams; the worker talking through two translators to another about how she wants so much more than her current situation, and the other expressing agreement, while her face gives away her surprise that this is what she wants, too; the twelve-year-old daughter of one of the Latina workers who said she now wants to be "a lawyer like Julie," because lawyers help people fight.

Conclusion: Making Critical Coalitional Theory

Communities in crisis cannot await elegant legal theories. Immediate action and practical solutions addressed to real-life exploitation and suffering, however imperfect, are crucial. The attack by some that

Critical Race Theory is about race, power, and politics but not about law tells us that it is law—or, more specifically, how we traditionally do law—that needs to change.[26] Lawyers cannot become so invested in the technical practice of lawyering—even public-interest, civil-rights lawyering—that we fail to challenge the ways that it *and we* redeploy oppressive structures. Critical Race Theory helps us understand this.

The critique, from the inside, that much of Critical Race Theory is no longer about real, concrete experiences in our communities is more troublesome. We believe that to the extent the critique rings true, Critical Race Theory needs to move. Greater attention to critical coalitions is one area for movement.

Critical coalitions are real, fragile, and vibrant. They grow out of strategic community attempts to change the material conditions of peoples' lives, often at great risk to community members. They reflect a refusal to limit coalitions to alliances based solely on short-term common interests or to alliances only among activists and civil-rights lawyers. And they compel rethinking of traditional civil-rights approaches to justice.

Critical coalitions thus present a dynamic realm for the expansion of Critical Race Theory. Although critical race scholarship has extensively examined the black–white race-relations paradigm and also sought to refashion it in multiracial terms, it is only beginning to explore how diverse communities of color can coalesce over legal-political issues in a virulently hostile, largely anti–civil-rights climate.

Critical Race Theory also needs to examine how coalitions addressing progressive legal and political issues, once formed, survive in the face of unrelenting opposition. Critical coalition work is hard, messy, and time-consuming. It is usually underfunded, particularly in comparison with the financial resources of its conservative adversaries.

This creates practical survival pressures. In addition, individuals in coalition may find themselves fighting for something of indirect, or long-term, benefit. Can coalitions be sustained beyond members' immediate self-interest? To answer that question, critical coalitional theory needs to address the concrete challenges communities face in approaching progressive alliances: Do we build coalitions even if they do not directly advance our present position, even if they are difficult and force us to face new foes, and even if they cannot ensure successful outcomes? The Thai and Latina workers' experience tells us, yes. We build critical coalitions not only because of the enhanced potential for favorable outcomes, but also because the process of coalition-building itself sometimes changes each of us. It is a process, small and large, of building a community. It may contribute to the end of sweatshops, the dismantling of white racism, and the eradication of sexism and homophobia. Or it may not. The process nevertheless allows us to know and define ourselves, our friends, and, in turn, our visions of a just society.

Critical Race Theory might also productively explore how critical coalitions explode the constricted, colorblind civil-rights paradigm. When multiracial communities are fighting white racism and when mainstream America subconsciously acts on race in myriad daily decisions, can racism be fought without acknowledging both racial diversity and convergence? And if multiracial color-consciousness adds power, richness, and depth to coalitions, should we not encourage deeper understanding of one another not only as individuals but also as members of racial communities? Critical coalitions tell us about our racial selves and the role of racial identity, as well as class, gender, and sexual identity, in building alliances.

Finally, Critical Race Theory's interrogation of critical coalitions will be productive only to the extent that it is accessible to all of the communities about whom it speaks—including the poor, urban racial communities and immigrant workers. How can Critical Race Theory make real its connection to the material conditions of peoples' lives? For example, race scholars did not join the coalition efforts of the Thai and Latina garment workers in Los Angeles. Why not? How could they have done so? Low-wage people of color do not regularly attend conferences, read legal scholarship, or grace the halls of elite academic institutions. The development of critical coalitional theory can provide strategies for alliances between progressive scholars and subordinated communities. One measure of the quality of critical race scholarship is the response by the academy. Another, equally important measure is whether garment workers in some fashion know that Critical Race Theory is talking about their liberation, their justice, too.

Notes

1. See generally Gerald López, *Rebellious Lawyering* (Boulder, Colo.: Westview Press, 1991).
2. Eric K. Yamamoto, "Critical Race Praxis: Race Theory and Political Lawyering Practice in Post–Civil Rights America," *Michigan Law Review* 95 (1997): 821.
3. In attempting a beginning answer to this question at the Critical Race Theory Conference in November 1997, Julie offered suggestions for what critical race scholars might do to aid front-line activist work. "Make your theories into arguments that stand up in court and into foundation proposals that will get us funding for front-line activism; make them into sound bites, media pieces, press releases, position papers, summaries and flyers for community education; talk about front-line activism and in-your-face street work in your conferences, faculty meetings, classrooms and give your students opportunities to do them": Julie A. Su, Critical Coalitions Plenary Session, Critical Race Theory Conference, Yale University Law School, November 13–15, 1997.

4. Idem, "Making the Invisible Visible: The Garment Industry's Dirty Laundry," *Iowa Journal of Gender, Race and Justice* 1 (1998): 405. See also Gary Delgado, "How the Empress Gets Her Clothes: Asian Immigrant Women Fight Fashion Designer Jessica McClintock," in *Beyond Identity Politics: Emerging Social Justice Movements in Communities of Color* (Boston: South End Press, 1996). See George White and Patrick McDonnell, "Sweatshop Workers to Get $2 Million," *Los Angeles Times*, October 24, 1997, D1.
5. Julie A. Su, personal recollections, notes on file with Julie Su.
6. White and McDonnell, "Sweatshop," D1.
7. See K. Connie Kang, "Final $1.2 Million Added to Thai Workers' Settlement," *Los Angeles Times*, July 29, 1999, A1.
8. See Richard W. Thomas, *Understanding Interracial Unity* (Oklahoma City: Sage Press, 1997), 105–33. See also A. Meier and E. Rudwick, eds., *Core: A Study in the Civil Rights Movement* (Champaign: University of Illinois Press, 1975).
9. See Fred L. Pincus and Howard J. Ehrlich, eds., *Race and Ethnic Conflict* (Boulder, Colo.: Westview Press, 1994), describing connections between economic conditions and racial and ethnic conflict; see Michael Omi and Howard Winant, *Racial Formation in the United States*, 2nd ed. (New York: Routledge, 1994), describing the socioeconomic conditions supporting the rise of neo-conservatism and the impact on traditional liberal alliances.
10. Troy Duster, "Individual Fairness, Group Preferences, and the California Strategy," *Representations* 55 (1996): 41, 45. The AFL-CIO recently reversed its position on immigrants and, in a historic move, has called for the legalization of undocumented immigrant workers as a matter of basic fairness and worker empowerment.
11. Manning Marable, "Black (Community) Power!" *The Nation*, December 22, 1997, 21, describing emergent multiracial, community-based coalitions. See also John Anner, ed., "Having the Tools at Hand: Building Successful Multicultural Social Justice Organizations," in *Beyond Identity Politics*, 153.
12. Kimberlé W. Crenshaw, "Mapping the Margins: Intersectionality, Identity, Politics and Violence Against Women of Color," *Stanford Law Review* 43 (1991): 1241. See also Mari J. Matsuda, "Beside My Sister, Facing the Enemy: Legal Theory out of Coalition," *Stanford Law Review* 43 (1991): 1183; Haunani-Kay Trask, "Coalition-building Between Natives and Non-natives," *Stanford Law Review* 43 (1991): 1197.
13. See Adrien K. Wing, ed., *Critical Race Feminism* (New York: New York University Press, 1996).

14. See Francisco Valdes, "Poised at the Cusp: LatCrit Theory, Outsider Jurisprudence and Latina/o Self-Empowerment," *Harvard Latino Law Review* 2 (1997): 1; Berta Esperanza Hernández-Truyol, "Borders (En)gendered: Normativities, Latinas, and a LatCrit Paradigm," *New York University Law Review* 72 (1997): 882.

15. Board of the Society of American Law Teachers, "Resolution in Support of the SALT C.A.R.E March," Washington, D.C., September 28, 1997, on file with Eric Yamamoto.

16. See Mari J. Matsuda, Charles R. Lawrence III, Richard Delgado, and Kimberlé W. Crenshaw, eds., *Words That Wound: Critical Race Theory, the First Amendment and Assaultive Speech* (Boulder, Colo.: Westview Press, 1993), describing Critical Race Theory's disciplinary border crossing; Francisco Valdes, "Queers, Sissies, Dykes, and Tomboys: Deconstructing the Conflation of 'Sex,' 'Gender,' and 'Sexual Orientation' in Euro-American Law and Society," *California Law Review* 83 (1995): 1. See generally Richard Delgado, ed., *Critical Race Theory: The Cutting Edge* (Philadelphia: Temple University Press, 1995); Kimberlé W. Crenshaw, Neil Gotanda, Gary Peller, and Kendall Thomas, eds., *Critical Race Theory: The Key Writings That Formed the Movement* (New York: New Press, 1995).

17. Eric K. Yamamoto, "Rethinking Alliances: Agency, Responsibility and Interracial Justice," *UCLA Asian Pacific American Law Journal* 3 (1995): 33, 35.

18. Ibid., 33-4. See Omi and Winant, *Racial Formation*.

19. Harlon Dalton, *Racial Healing: Confronting the Fear Between Blacks and Whites* (New York: Doubleday, 1995). See also Elizabeth M. Iglesias, "The Intersubjectivity of Objective Justice: A Theory and Praxis for Constructing LatCrit Coalitions," *Harvard Latino Law Review* 2 (1997): 467; Laura Padilla, "LatCrit Praxis to Heal Fractured Communities," *Harvard Latino Law Review* 2 (1997): 375; Yamamoto, "Rethinking Alliances."

20. Kimberlé W. Crenshaw, "Race, Reform and Retrenchment: Transformation and Legitimation in Anti-discrimination Law," *Harvard Law Review* 101 (1988): 1331.

21. Yamamoto, "Rethinking Alliances," 47.

22. Idem, "Critical Race Praxis," 821.

23. In one case in which the Asian Pacific American Legal Center represented a Chinese garment worker against three manufacturers, including the well-known company City Girl, Inc., Ronald Perilman, president of City Girl, commented: "If Julie Su really wants to be a champion of justice, why doesn't she go after unregistered contractors in her backyard—and I'll take her hand and show them to her. Why doesn't she go after contractors and manufacturers in the Asian community who aren't paying people" (as quoted in Jerry Sullivan, "Settlement Leaves City Girl Unsettled," *California Apparel News,* May 2000, 1).

24. Mary Ballesteros-Coronel, "Victoria Judicial Para Costureras," *La Opinion,* March 4, 1997, 1.

25. Yamamoto, "Rethinking Alliances," 47.

26. According to some critics, postmodernism exerts too strong an influence on critical race scholarship, focusing on legal deconstruction without an affirmative program and thereby divorcing that scholarship from the concrete justice problems of racial communities Many of the original Critical Race Theory writings and some of the recent critical race writing, however, emphasize development of a "jurisprudence of reconstruction." That reconstructive jurisprudence seeks to critique law and liberal legalism while drawing on those aspects of law and legal process that assist racial communities in their real world struggles against subordination: See Angela P. Harris, "Foreword: The Jurisprudence of Reconstruction," *California Law Review* 82 (1994): 741, 744; Robert L. Hayman, Jr., "The Color of Tradition: Critical Race Theory and Postmodern Constitutional Traditionalism," *Harvard Civil Rights–Civil Liberties Law Review* 30 (1995): 57. We endorse continued emphasis on the developing reconstructive jurisprudence.

CHAPTER EIGHTEEN

Beyond, and Not Beyond, Black and White: Deconstruction Has a Politics

Mari Matsuda

A PRESIDENT'S CONVERSATION on race is going on right now, accompanied by a new McCarthyism that excludes a radical critique of American racism. No one affiliated with Critical Race Theory sits on the President's Commission, and that is not an accident. It is impossible to have a conversation about race in America without critical race theorists unless the omission is deliberate. Our work is a looming absence as the national conversation grows in confusion.

I heard the confusion all of this week. On Monday, I was discussing the President's Initiative on Race with an Asian American civil-rights lawyer. She said that she was worried that the President's Initiative had gotten stuck on the Black-white paradigm. On Tuesday, I ran into a prominent African American veteran of the Civil Rights Movement, and she said, "If you are going to talk about race in America you can't avoid the Black-white paradigm, and I wish you'd explain this to people, since you are so good at explaining things." On Wednesday, I went to a meeting with a group of people who are

trying to advise the President's Initiative. At the first opportunity to speak, I said, "It's your job to assert that there is racism in America, because there are still a lot of people out there who believe that racism doesn't exist. You have to make it plain to them that it is not a colorblind world." Immediately after I spoke, a Native American activist jumped into the conversation to say, "Well, I hope you understand that racial discrimination is not the first problem that my people face. Our first issue is sovereignty." On Thursday, I came to Yale for the CRT Conference, and I met with Asian American students. They were angry because there is no Asian American studies program at one of the so-called finest universities in the so-called free world. One of the students said to me, "How do you ever figure out if your work is any good when none of your professors are in a position to evaluate your work because they don't know anything about what you are trying to do? If they talk about race here at Yale, all they know is Black and white." Now it's Friday, and I need to discuss this racial-paradigm business as a challenge for CRT generally, as the challenge and the politics of deconstruction.

We in CRT made a choice to put race at the center of our analysis for reasons historical, political, and analytical, and that meant that initially we were talking primarily about African American history and experience. Several years ago at Yale, Professor Harlon Dalton introduced me as "someone who knows more about my people than I could ever hope to know about her people." This was a profound compliment. It also included a little bit of the self-critique that is just one page out of the Harlon Dalton school-of-charm book. The reason his compliment resonated so deeply is embedded in the social history of Japanese Americans of a certain age.

A streetwise cousin of mine, when he was a teenager, showed me sketch books he was developing through participation in the Yellow Brotherhood, which, depending on your perspective, was either a gang or a political formation. He had sketched Malcolm, Frederick Douglass, Ho Chi Minh, and Che in profile, marching off into the future, facing a big rising sun. This was an iconic, early 1970s vision shared not just by intellectuals.

In this particular time, people you might call the grassroots, the lumpen, shared the politics of liberation. We were children in Los Angeles when Black nationalist graffiti first started appearing on the walls and we heard phrases like "Black is beautiful." For Asian Americans, this remarkable inversion meant yellow was also, possibly, beautiful. This was a time when young Asian girls were saving money to get their eyelids slit by plastic surgeons so they could look more white. On television, Asian men were portrayed as bucktoothed, idiotic houseboys. The idea that someone could say, "I'm Black and I'm proud," was deeply subversive not just in the African American community, but also in the Chicano community and in the Asian American community. Travel around the world and talk to people my age, in corners of Africa, the Pacific, Asia. Go to Aotearoa (New Zealand) and talk to the Maori people, and they will tell you, "We heard this message, 'I'm Black and I'm proud,' and we translated it and formed our own struggle of liberation around it." The idea that one can develop self-respecting love of Blackness, tie it to a broader, popularized culture, transmute it over to politics so that it teaches a critique of colonialism, of capitalism, and of racism, created the most exciting personal and political moment of my lifetime.[1]

Out of this confluence of culture and politics came the Asian American Movement, Asian American Studies, and Asian American membership in the Third World coalition. The Black-white paradigm therefore feels like the old home to me. I read W.E.B. Du Bois and Paul Robeson and others in the Black intellectual tradition and feel validated by their analysis of what happened in this country, not just in the late twentieth century, but if you look back to what they were writing about in the nineteenth and earlier twentieth century: They included Asians. They talked about what was then called "Coolie Labor," and they understood that the quasi-chattel status of contract laborers from Asia was the global equivalent of the quasi-chattel status of Black sharecroppers in the American South. They critiqued this as part of a critique of global capitalism, and they tied these forms of indentured servitude to the history of slavery. These intellectual links are quite powerful for understanding not just the Black experience but the Asian experience, as well.

We cannot understand American racism unless we understand African American history as American history. Asian Americans need to know how the fear of a Black planet was real for planters in many areas of the South where the enslaved far outnumbered the free, and how the fear of Blackness burrowed into the collective unconscious of this nation. There have been times in my own life when I transgressed boundaries and found that I was feared as a Black person. In the fifth grade, I defied a teacher because she made a pronouncement that was unfair. She said to me in a bitter tone that I was not used to hearing from her, "I thought you were different." I had become to her like the Black kids in the class. This is no inconsequential position for Asians, because fear of Blackness kills. When the Los Angeles Police Department gunned down a Korean American traffic violator;[2] when police in Northern California murdered an unarmed Chinese American man who was drunk on his own front lawn;[3] when a Louisiana jury acquitted a Louisiana homeowner who had shot a Japanese teenager who came to the door to ask for directions[4]—these are real instances, not metaphors, of fear of Blackness killing somebody. This is not to say that xenophobic, yellow-peril, Asian-specific forms of racism are absent in these cases. Rather, I submit that the quick finger on the trigger traces back in history to a whispered name, Nat Turner, and a legacy of terror inflicted by the terrified. It says "shoot first," and White Supremacy shoots in fear of what its own evil has wrought on this continent.

When I say "fear of Blackness," I don't mean that this is all we need to understand. I don't want to use up what little time I have left to say it five times, but I must be understood as though I said it five times: That's not all we need to understand. We need to see the blood soaking our land from the genocide that strips sovereignty, home, and family from Indian people. We need to see that without U.S. imperial campaigns of westward expansion that intended to go all the way to Asia, we would be speaking Spanish at half the panels at this conference. Without that imperialism, the nations of

Hawaii, Guam, Micronesia, Okinawa, and the Philippines—all these places that don't have independence from U.S. military domination today—would have true sovereignty. We need to know how racism in all its variant forms has played out in our history, how inter- and intragroup oppression makes a people-of-color coalition a fantasy in many contemporary parts of the United States, and as we complexify, we have a challenge.

When we say we need to move beyond Black and white, this is what a whole lot of people say or feel or think: "Thank goodness we can get off that paradigm, because those Black people made me so uncomfortable. I know all about Blacks, but I really don't know anything about Asians, and while we're deconstructing that Black–white paradigm, we also need to reconsider the category of race all together, since race, as you know, is a constructed category, and thank God I don't have to take those angry Black people seriously anymore."

I am an intellectual. Theory is important. I don't want my comments taken as anti-intellectual, anti-theory, or anti-deconstruction in particular. My attack is on deconstruction that comes without a progressive politics and without a material component. Professor Lawrence speaks of *Griggs*[5] as the doctrinal culmination of the Civil Rights struggle, a high point before we sank back to where we are now. I am a material girl, and *Griggs* is my case. For those of you who are not lawyers, let me just explain briefly: The *Griggs* case says that if we see an end result of racial exclusion, we will presume that racism is there, and we're not going to require proof that someone intended to get to this racist place. If you have 500 job openings and you haven't hired any of the 500 qualified Black people who applied, your statement that this exclusion just happened by accident is not tenable. We're going to take the result as evidence of what you intended.

The *Griggs* test is how to achieve equality if you believe that the real world counts. I want to look at the effects of any given deconstruction, whether it's of the Black–white paradigm or of the notion of race itself. Is the effect of your deconstruction to give aid and comfort to the enemies of racial justice? Is your deconstruction of race further obfuscating deep racial stratification and white supremacy? If so, you're engaging in reactionary politics, whether you intend to or not. Similarly, when I speak loudly and clearly on behalf of racial justice and I'm attacked, I notice that the same people who are attacking me are attacking Catharine MacKinnon when she speaks loudly and clearly on the subject of the sexual abuse of women. When the same people are attacking us, when we have the same enemies, we are allies. Working backward from that and working very hard to understand Professor MacKinnon's work, I have come to see why her work is true in theoretical terms. I start from a material place. The people who want to annihilate her also want to annihilate me when we demand an end to their position of domination. Therefore, she is my sister.

I have come to a *Griggs* test for deconstruction theory out of my struggle around the issue of affirmative action. When I'm defending affirmative action, as I've tried to do in my writing and in speaking to all kinds of groups all over the country, I find that deconstruction walks into the room, and usually not in ways that are useful to the project of racial justice. I run into liberals questioning whether affirmative action makes any sense, because only privileged people of color get to take advantage of it. By the way, in empirical terms, this is a lie. I run into people who question inclusion of Asian Americans in affirmative-action programs because "Asian" is an artificial category comprising diverse and oppositional groups. I run into the *Hopwood* court[6] that does an antiessentialist analysis of race, challenging the university's goal of diversity. By bringing in Black people or bringing in Latino/Latina people, you don't get diversity, the court says, because those groups themselves are diverse to the point of being non-existent. The court concluded by criminalizing any further efforts to integrate the University of Texas. Admit a Mexican, go to jail is the result; antiessentialism is the justification.

This *Hopwood* form of deconstruction and antiessentialism is, of course, simplistic and reactionary, but I think too often it is aligned with more sophisticated theoretical forms. I see a similar groundswell happening with gender. When structuralist thinkers identify patriarchy and describe the subordination of women, they immediately face the charges of "vulgar," "simplistic," or simply "excluding my experience." To the extent that this critique is used against a writer such as MacKinnon, I think it misreads her work. The power of her model is that it encompasses a multiplicity, and it still exists. The women in this room, as diverse as they are, or the women on this panel, as diverse and individually unique as they are, are nevertheless understood by the broader powers of patriarchy as available for use and abuse by men. They are systematically devalued as social, economic, intellectual, and political agents because of that reality. That many of us manage to rise above in one way or another doesn't erase the reality.

The reluctance to accept this powerful description of patriarchy within CRT sometimes, I think, comes from the same affinity that I articulated earlier for myself around the Black–white paradigm. To do cross-cutting analysis, as critical race feminists have tried to do, feels like a dilution to people who have struggled all their lives for liberation of their people, as constructed by race, not gender. In other words, when Professor MacKinnon says, "It's sex, it's sex, it's sex," that's heard as saying, "It's not race, it's not race, it's not race." She never said, "It's not race," and if you read her work you can underline and highlight all the places in which she says, "And if you think that this is bad try multiplying it by racial oppression and see what you get." But maybe she can't physically say that enough times in a world in which any move to gender is taken as an excuse to drop race, and vice versa.

Disaggregation, antiessentialism, post-structuralism—whatever theoretical move you make, I'll be watching you. A sophisticated, nuanced, thick understanding of human life may call for breaking out of categories and examining exceptionality. Read MacKinnon. She does this. Any theory that seeks structure, that can call oppression just that, lacks power if it cannot account for the outlier. And what if we are all outliers— if race is nothing but variability and gender nothing but theater? What if we could choose, invent, and dance up, down, and all around categories? If you love human beings, you see this transcendent potential. If you love them under present political circumstances, you see their unbearable vulnerability. Count the bodies as they fall, even as you imagine freedom from the template they fall through.

What does this mean for the future of CRT? I see an emerging consensus among the progressive wing of this band that race, gender, class, ethnicity, and sexuality are complex, interlinked and indisputable locations of oppression, and any attempt to erase or dilute one analysis in order to do another is a reactionary move. This makes our work incredibly hard, but the theoretical practice of disaggregation for its own sake, without attention to political effects, is ultimately going to serve interests that are not our own. If you think that sexual abuse of women is a side issue, please read MacKinnon again. If you think you know every-thing you need to know about white over Black as a metaphenomenon, you need to go back to CRT 101. If you think that you've done that and that's all you need to do, the train is leaving the station; please get on board. If you are tired of pulling others out of their ignorance about your own liberation struggle, all I can say is, I'm sorry, but that burden is your gift. You'll have to find some place to rest when weary, and you will have to come back to the table and ask, "Whom can I struggle with who will bring their ignorance in good faith and hear what they can learn from me as this train pulls away?" Can you do two things that are different at the same time? Can you drive while you talk on your cellular phone? No. Can you say, "I love you, and I am angry at you?" Yes. Can you say, "The institution of slavery is foundational in American racism, and the struggle against American racism encompasses much beyond the Black–white paradigm"? Can you say, "The sexual abuse of women and girls of all races is an epidemic in this country, and the present rate of incarceration of Black men is genocidal, and the fact that these two are gendered phenomena indicates that patriarchy is after Black men as well as all women, and just because I said 'Black' does not mean you should forget about Asian, Latino, Latina, gay, Indian, poor, working class, disabled, and, this is not a laundry list?" This is somebody's body, and at the end of the line there is liberation, and that is what gives meaning to all we do.

Notes

Editor's note: This chapter is a transcription of remarks given at the November 1997 CRT Conference at Yale University while President Bill Clinton's Initiative on Race was conducting a national inquiry into the state of race relations in America: See President's Advisory Board, *One America in the 21st Century: Forging a New Future* (Washington, D.C.:

U.S. President's Advisory Board, 1998). It should be read with the chapters by Professor Catharine MacKinnon and Professor Kimberlé Crenshaw in this book as part of an organic whole on the question of theory, community, and power.

1. For an account of this period by an African American who became active in the Puerto Rican liberation movement, see James Early, "An African-American Puerto Rican Connection," in Andres Torres and José E. Velazques, *The Puerto Rican Movement* (Philadelphia: Temple University Press, 1998), 316-28.

2. See Renee Tawa, "Korean Groups Want Answers on Police Killing," *Los Angeles Times*, February 17, 1997, B1.

3. See Rohnert Park, "Man Fatally Shot by Cops," *San Francisco Chronicle*, April 30, 1997, A18.

4. See Adam Nossiter, "Student's Trust in People Proved Fatal," *New York Times*, October 23, 1992, A12.

5. *Griggs v. Duke Power Company,* 401 U.S. 424 (1971), as discussed in Charles R. Lawrence III's Foreword in this volume.

6. *Hopwood v. Texas,* 78 F. 3d 932 (5th Cir. 1996).

CHAPTER NINETEEN

Outsider Scholars, Critical Race Theory, and "OutCrit" Perspectivity: Postsubordination Vision as Jurisprudential Method

Francisco Valdes

THIS CHAPTER considers the relationship of Critical Race Theory[1] to the concept and potential of postsubordination vision as jurisprudential method. But as presented later, postsubordination is both a means and an end. It also comprises both method and content, for it describes the project of articulating and producing the sociolegal conditions necessary to the attainment of substantive security by outsider communities.

By "substantive security" I mean specifically outgroup attainment of safe, secure, and continuous access to the basic rights, goods, and services that are substantially necessary to human well-being. More doctrinally, and perhaps somewhat simply, I mean by "substantive security" the overall state of affairs that is possible only after outgroups *qua* outgroups finally accrue and enjoy the "three generations" of civil and political, economic, social and cultural, and group rights that international covenants already recognize and promise to us all.[2]

Postsubordination vision grounded in substantive security thus conjures a time and place wherein people of color, women, sexual minorities, and other traditionally subordinated groups no longer are the targets of social disdain, hate crime, and backlash democracy.[3] It imagines a society wherein these traditionally marginalized populations are well represented in popular culture, Congress, and the corridors of the corporate world. It describes a nation of peaceably and multiply diverse playgrounds, schools, workplaces, neighborhoods, and governments. It demands the restructuring of social, legal, and economic conditions to eradicate the systematic imposition of poverty, violence, and exploitation based on racism, sexism, xenophobia, homophobia, and similar ideologies of prejudice and repression.

By offering postsubordination vision as jurisprudential method this chapter also strives to recast extant sameness and difference questions as relevant, but not threshold or conclusive, determinants of the possibility for critical coalitions as vehicles of social justice and substantive security. By "critical coalitions" I mean "alliances based on a thoughtful and reciprocal interest in the goals or purpose(s) of a collaborative and collective project."[4] Critical coalitions signify intergroup collaborations grounded explicitly and substantively in joint convictions and mutual commitments rather than in the happenstance of coinciding self-interest. Critical coalitions therefore stand in sharp contrast to the convergence of White–Black group interests that produced yesteryears' civil-rights triumphs.[5] Though this chapter obviously is only one step in the longer and larger journey of CRT's second decade toward a postsubordination society, these words aim to make it more likely that our coming work will bring multiply diverse OutCrit scholars closer to a progressive postsubordination era marked by substantive social justice for all.

By "OutCrit" I mean "those scholars that identify and align themselves with outgroups in this country, as well as globally."[6] Therefore, among them are the legal scholars who in recent times have launched CRT, feminist, queer, and LatCrit legal discourses, including critical race feminists and Asian American and Native American scholars. But this OutCrit denomination also is a conscious effort to conceptualize and operationalize a mutual and proactive interconnection of the social-justice analyses and struggles of varied and overlapping—yet "different"—subordinated groups in the United States and globally. My hope and purpose are that a broader identification among outsider and progressive legal scholars as "OutCrits" will enhance our collective and individual understanding of the needs and goals that must underpin critical exchanges and collaborative projects among and between people of color, sexual minorities, women, and other outgroups. Ideally,

this chapter's framing and focus around postsubordination vision, substantive security, and critical coalitions will help promote a culture of antisubordination community, convocation, and collaboration among multiply diverse OutCrit legal theorists as a form of praxis.

Postsubordination Vision as Jurisprudential Method: Identities, Ideals, and Ideas

The cumulative experience and record of outsider jurisprudence illustrates how CRT, feminist, queer, and LatCrit experiments in critical legal theory converge and diverge in numerous significant ways, both substantively and structurally.[7] In different ways and to different degrees, these outsider discourses strive similarly to represent certain marginalized viewpoints; espouse critical, egalitarian, progressive, diverse antisubordination projects; accept discursive subjectivity, political consciousness, and social responsibility; recognize postmodernism; favor praxis; and seek community.[8] In addition, these outsider discourses have imagined and alluded to, but have not explicitly described, their vision of a *post*subordination order to orient our collective antisubordination work.[9]

The rhetorics and ambitions of outsider scholars indicate that we are striving collectively toward a sociolegal alternative to the Euroheteropatriarchal status quo,[10] which by definition must entail some vision of a postsubordination alternative. Yet no such vision has been expressly denoted in CRT or similar outsider venues. Accordingly, among the pending and interrelated queries for all OutCrit scholars and activists are: How does the post-homophobic society appear from today's QueerCrit perspective? How does the post-White supremacy society appear from today's RaceCrit and

LatCrit positions? How does the post-patri-archal society appear from today's FemCrit viewpoint? How do these visions overlap? How can legal theory and praxis help to engineer such transformation? Clearly, these questions of vision implicate at the threshold issues of "sameness" and "differ-ence" in outsider jurisprudence.

Sameness and Difference: Toward Critical Coalitions

In part to address intergroup issues of per-ceived or actual sameness and difference, CRT and other OutCrit legal scholars have turned in recent years to a critical and cross-disciplinary re-evaluation of historic group experiences with, and struggles against, var-ied but similar forms of privilege and prej-udice. Focused to date primarily on race and gender, the turn to group experience and struggle arose to help transcend the dis-abling essentialisms of historical analyses rooted in single-axis conceptions or percep-tions of current "identities" and related communities. In linking past and present, this turn to group experience and struggle has helped to bring forth the now perennial conversation among outgroup scholars about the antisubordination relevance of "sameness" and "difference" in and across various contemporary identity categories.[11]

This focus on experience and struggle is salutary because it helps to historicize cur-rent sociolegal or socioeconomic arrange-ments. This history reminds all OutCrits that today's antisubordination struggles, like yesterday's, are important, regardless of the odds that confront us,[12] because resist-ance always makes some difference, even if not readily discernible. As process, the dia-logue that this turn has brought forth is useful and necessary, in part because it forces legal scholars of all stripes to listen, read, and learn about the varied experiences and struggles of our (putative?) sisters and brothers. Substantively, this sameness-and-difference dialogue is useful and necessary because it can help to expand our under-standing of subordinationist structures and systems, both quantitatively and qualita-tively. This dialogue is useful and necessary because mapping difference can help to pro-mote egalitarian pluralism in and through our ongoing struggles for a just social order.

This effort to transcend through the experience and history of struggle the limi-tations of conventional outgroup identity politics in turn has initiated a tentative, ongoing shift toward substantive justice commitments (and away from essentializ-ing identity markers such as race and gen-der) as platforms for antisubordination communities and critical coalitions. Pro-ducing calls to move from "essential" to "political" identities and interests,[13] this shift challenges the parameters and pur-poses of pre-existing outsider jurispruden-tial formations, including, in some respects, those of CRT. Ultimately, this shift honors CRT's commitment to postmodern multi-dimensional analyses of injustice and con-centrates CRT's political pragmatism on actual social transformation. This shift and call are valuable because over time they can help animate substantive cross-group affini-ties in the service of antiessentialist com-munity and antisubordination solidarity.

In fact, some of the foundational insights produced during CRT's first decade are asso-ciated with this exploration of sameness and difference. Concepts such as intersectionality, multiplicity, antiessentialism, and multiple consciousness arise from issues of sameness and difference in critical legal analysis, anti-subordination discourse and, contemporary identity politics.[14] These concepts have pro-vided strong foundations, helping CRT and other OutCrit scholars to elucidate multidi-mensional analyses that foster interconnec-tion of antisubordination insights and projects.[15] Thus, this turn to outgroup experience and struggle no doubt has helped to illuminate important issues and mediate some of the tensions between sameness and difference. Indeed, this potential utility explains why OutCrit scholars must continue to learn lessons from self-critical assessments of our collective jurisprudential experience.[16]

But the focus on experience and struggle in effect has asked: How can outsider scholars join forces and share consciousness now due mainly to our historic experiences with and struggles against past and present oppression? With this historical focus, CRT and other OutCrit scholars basically have queried how experience and struggle around the structure of victimhood can bring together varied groups or people. Analytically, this focus calls for resolution of sameness-and-difference issues to help decide whether OutCrit experiences and struggles are sufficiently the "same" or "different" to justify collaborative antisubordination exertions. In part because this inquiry is necessarily backward-focused, this approach inadvertently has invited the inconclusive sameness-and-difference debates along various identity axes.

Though this discourse usefully has reminded critical legal theorists that outgroup commonality cannot be assumed or claimed cavalierly in antisubordination analyses, this debate must be understood as ultimately limited. One limitation comes about because this approach tends to isolate and highlight for comparison's sake single-axis identity markers such as "gender" versus "race" versus "sexual orientation." This comparison in effect questions whether the histories and positions of "women" and "people of color" and "sexual minorities" are the "same" or "different." Given this framing, they of course always will be "different" in various and sundry respects. Ironically, the net effect of single-axis categorical comparison to delineate "sameness" and "difference" may be to recycle various essentialisms within outsider discourse and praxis based on these and similar identity constructs—or, at least, to occlude the multiple and overlapping diversities within each of those categories.

In addition, and perhaps more important, this focus necessarily looks to past or present circumstances as the principal fountainhead of coalitional possibilities. While antisubordination criticality requires us collectively to learn from the past, the danger with this approach is in permitting sameness-and-difference "dilemmas" to become a comparative quagmire or to instill a sense of impasse. If so, this historical focus ultimately cannot satisfy OutCrits' need for expansive multidimensional analyses that recognize the holistic, cosynthetic, and interconnected character of subordination,[17] analyses that can provide strong but flexible frames for critical coalitions capable of dismantling Euroheteropatriarchy in law and society and delivering substantive security to the traditionally subordinated among us.

If outsider theorists are serious about using critical legal theory to catalyze social transformation, this potentially powerful dialogue about identity and continuity and discontinuity cannot become an impediment to, or a substitute for, acts of solidarity through theory in the service of antisubordination community and action. Depending on its use, this dialogue can be, but is neither automatically nor always, a form of progressive or effective jurisprudential method. Thus, sameness-and-difference dialogue is empowering *only* if deployed to ensure substantive security for the socially or legally subordinated.

Postsubordination Vision and Euroheteropatriarchy: Substantive Security for All

Postsubordination vision expands the prevailing focus of OutCrit inquiry beyond experience and struggle to include aspiration and hope[18] as another way of approaching and assessing the efficacy and design of critical coalitions. But this method also can help OutCrit scholars begin to delineate as concretely as possible the substance of critical coalitions grounded in the pursuit of substantive security for all. Postsubordination vision can help to provide the principles and purposes of intergroup cooperation and coalescence. And by providing a fundamentally different point of entry for coalitional enterprise, vision as method may activate political analyses and dynamics that may aid intergroup collaboration where history and experience might not.

This expanded, forward-looking focus asks: Regardless of where we have been, where do we want to go? Have we arrived at similar conclusions and aspirations even though we may have traveled different routes to these conclusions and aspirations? Though our hopes and aims partially may be shaped by past and present circumstances, this expanded focus provides a different entry point toward critical coalitions because it asks OutCrits a different question: Whether we can join forces now due to the hopes or aspirations that we harbor and perhaps share. This focus thus asks not whether OutCrit scholars and outgroup communities can travel together based first and foremost on present or past positions, but whether overlapping yet distinct outgroups can work together to arrive at a common destination.

Rather than prompting outsiders to determine whether our past and present are sufficiently alike to create a common path toward social justice and substantive security, postsubordination vision prompts us to determine first and foremost whether our destination coordinates are compatible—whether our critical conceptions of substantive social justice match, or can be made to. By shifting the focus to visions, agendas, and projects of substantive security, post-

subordination vision may help coalition-building where backward-looking assessments of sameness and difference may not. By emphasizing a forward-looking basis for intergroup coalescence toward substantive security, the shift from victimhood to vision can advance mutual recognition and accommodation of continuities and discontinuities within and across multiply diverse outgroups. Postsubordination vision therefore is best viewed as a complement to, not a substitute for, constructive and progressive sameness-and-difference dialogue.

Postsubordination vision also may be useful as OutCrit method because it sometimes is helpful to begin a project by first envisioning as concretely as possible where one wants to be at its end, and then working back from that vision to plan the journey. And it sometimes is useful to imagine and spell out for oneself (and others) not only what the project is "against" but what also it is "for." This utility is magnified when the project or journey is long, controversial, complex, or arduous. Because coalitional antisubordination projects and journeys are each of these, and more, critical legal scholars from varied subject positions constructively can begin coalitional OutCrit theorizing by imagining and articulating the substantive end goal of our respective yet collective antisubordination activities and communities.

The move to progressive postsubordination vision thereby may occasion another possibility for theoretical and political advancement: Postsubordination vision pushes for the continual linkage of identities to ideas and ideals and supports the move from reactive to proactive antisubordination theory and praxis. Plainly, the attainment of a postsubordination society requires RaceCrits, FemCrits QueerCrits, LatCrits, and other "Crits" to expose and dismantle entrenched rules, structures, and conditions that breed injustice and inequality. But the composition of postsubordination vision goes beyond critique, beyond unpacking and deconstructing. Postsubordination discourse entails a positive articulation of substantive visions about reconstructed social relations and legal fields. By focusing attention on the specific sociolegal character of a postsubordination era, this move encourages identity critiques to go beyond oppositional criticism and to set forth the alternative(s) to the status quo that motivate our work.

Postsubordination vision as jurisprudential method therefore calls for some hard thinking and honest talking about the type of postsubordination society that "we" are struggling toward. This concreteness might reveal differences of vision and produce conflict, as our collective record of comparative jurisprudential experience already illustrates.[19] But as ongoing outsider experiments in critical legal theory also illustrate, this engagement is precisely the crucible that forges progress.[20] To transcend as well as test the limits of past injustices and present practices, antisubordination theory and praxis must in part be organized around the need to join other and varied OutCrit scholars in imaginative and productive ways to articulate successfully, and produce materially, a postsubordination order that actually delivers substantive social justice across the many troubled categories of life and hope that law and policy daily affect.[21]

Postsubordination vision as jurisprudential method thus calls for OutCrit scholars to focus on an omnipresent sociolegal formation that appropriately might be called "Euroheteropatriarchy." This term signifies the commingling and conflation of various supremacies: White supremacy, Anglo supremacy, male supremacy, and straight supremacy. This term therefore seeks to capture the interlocking operation of dominant forms of racism, ethnocentrism, androsexism, and heterocentrism—all of which operate in tandem in the United States and beyond it to produce identity hierarchies that subordinate people of color, women, and sexual minorities in different yet similar and familiar ways.

In this way, Euroheteropatriarchy also encompasses issues of language, religion, and other features of "culture" and community that help to produce and sustain hierarchical social and legal relations.[22] Euroheteropatriarchy, therefore, denotes a specific form of subordination in a specific context, which encompasses and enforces White racism and Anglo ethnocentrism, as well as androsexism and heterosexism, normatively, politically, and legally. Precisely because Euroheteropatriarchy is a system of interlocking rules, traditions, and structures that jointly legitimate and perpetuate today's sociolegal status quo, its dismantling is a prerequisite common to the postsubordination hopes and visions of *all* OutCrits and outgroups.

Only through this dismantling of Euroheteropatriarchy will society be ready to restructure itself substantively and be able to embrace transformative policies and practices to secure social justice for "people of color," "women," "sexual minorities," and other overlapping outgroups. Only after Euroheteropatriarchy's dismantling is a postsubordination order possible because Euroheteropatriachy, by definition, demands and imposes unjust hierarchies based on race–ethnicity, sex–gender, sexuality–sexual orientation, and other identity fault lines. Only then will this nation's traditionally subordinated outgroups move in significant numbers and in structural ways from the neglected and impoverished margins of law and society created for us by Euroheteropatriarchal elites and toward the realization of substantive security for all regardless of race, ethnicity, gender, sexuality, class, and other target identities.

But to get from here to there—to get from oppressive Euroheteropatriarchal realities to egalitarian postsubordination ideals—

OutCrit scholars must help to foster a difference-friendly approach to social and legal relations. We must use the gains achieved through sameness-and-difference dialogue not only to map historic or current sources of difference and learn antisubordination lessons from that effort, but also to bring into existence a culture of affinity and understanding among us in relationship to the past and present, as represented by the dominance of Euroheteropatriarchal imperatives, as well as in relationship to the future, as represented by the postsubordination visions and goals we articulate. By focusing on Euroheteropatriarchy as an integrated phenomenon or formation, and by underscoring the interconnectivity of the myriad oppressions that it represents historically and in the present, an OutCrit lesson of central importance to the cultivation of critical coalitions and to the attainment of substantive security comes to the fore: We must embrace and marshal the enduring fact of human difference and diversity to strengthen, and not only question, antisubordination collaboration.

To that end, the vision I pursue here and elsewhere is a society where "difference" is not only tolerated and accepted but cultivated and celebrated, a society where legal principles and cultural practices accommodate and affirm, rather than burden or disdain, the public performance of difference across multiple axes of social and legal personhood. Rather than utopian, this vision seeks to reclaim and apply the demand for human agency and dignity proclaimed stirringly at the founding of this nation but betrayed since then by the many acts of de jure or de facto domination and exploitation that have wracked the nation's soul, and that still do.[23] Thus, for legal scholars of whatever affiliation willing to share and toil for this progressive postsubordination vision, the pressing question is: How do we help to theorize and materialize this vision of a multiply diverse and socially just national and international community?

The means are several, if not numerous, as suggested both by the gains and limits of CRT's first decade: CRT, and outsider jurisprudence more generally, teach that OutCrits must move beyond single-axis projects; we must rise above essentialist habits; we must blend theory with practice; we must come together periodically for intellectual and human sustenance; we must engage in careful but caring self-critique; we must remain dedicated to pushing beyond hard-fought gains and despite daunting limits.[24] Yet another concrete and immediate step toward our collective creation of an egalitarian postsubordination culture is our proactive nurturing of critical coalitions among all OutCrit scholars and throughout our larger communities.

By and through critical coalitions, OutCrits can dedicate ourselves jointly not only to the dismantling of Euroheteropatriarchy as an interlocking scheme that (still) oppresses us all, even if differently, but also to the process of learning about both the continuities and discontinuities of our multiple identities. Critical coalitions can help bring together OutCrits who identify principally with "different" communities or struggles in a process of convocation, exchange, accommodation, and collaboration that can aid us mutually to learn both about the histories of struggles and the substance of visions. Indeed, through convocation and communication, critical coalitions can help OutCrits to learn not only about experience and aspiration but also about the antisubordination insights of "different" perspectives as applied critically to varying sociolegal contexts. Critical coalitions thereby can help us to map the interconnections of the particular with the universal within and throughout Euroheteropatriarchy, helping us collaboratively and perhaps synergistically to theorize, strategize, and realize the establishment of a postsubordination society.[25] Critical coalitions can help bring together the many particularities from which patterns of oppression may be discerned.

By bringing us together in antisubordination criticality and discourse, this type of coalition can help multiply diverse OutCrit scholars and outgroup communities to understand and accept the differences that both define and delineate our respective yet multiple positions, perspectives, experiences, and identities. By bringing us together in a critical yet collaborative setting, critical coalitions can help all OutCrits to see better the interconnection of "different" oppressions. Critical coalitions thereby can be the vehicles that enable us to learn from and reinforce various antisubordination drives, to celebrate and activate "difference" as a source of insight, accommodation and collaboration. Critical coalitions in this way can help to transport us to a postsubordination order under which all outgroups can claim and enjoy the fruits of substantive security.

Even while helping to map and marshal "difference" as antisubordination praxis, critical coalitions also can help bring into sharp relief a crucial and often neglected link in CRT's array of insights: To get there from here, every one of us must own the struggle against White and Anglo supremacies, as well as against male and straight supremacies. In time, and ideally, critical coalitions can help us all to see that: To realize a progressive vision of social justice for all, I personally must resist oppression in all its permutations and on multiple fronts and levels at once; I personally must resist a single-axis conflation of identity, conviction, and community. And so must you. And so must every OutCrit committed to social justice for all persons and groups.

Consequently, and in conjunction with critical coalitions, progressive vision can help to bring into sharp relief the relational and interdependent present operation of "different" histories, identities, and hierarchies, highlighting the importance of *practicing* intersectionality, multiplicity, interconnectivity, and multidimensionality in consistent and expansive ways to produce antiessentialist communities and antisubordination coalitions. Critical coalitions supported by postsubordination vision may generate an intergroup "blueprint" of sorts that espouses and pursues social justice and substantive security for all. Vision as method thereby can help outsider scholars to join forces and synergistically build OutCrit solidarity around outgroup struggles that otherwise we might not appreciate as personal— or, at minimum, as linked to our own. Over time, vision as method can help to place a premium on a wide-scale recognition that all of us *personally* must own the struggles against all forms of unjust privilege—a premium that over time can help to address and overcome the lingering effects of CRT's historic ambivalence toward multidimensional antisubordination collaboration.[26]

This personal commitment to and expansive vision of postsubordination life is the touchstone of OutCrit positionality, as well as the baseline of critical coalitions devoted to substantive security for all. Our common and everyday project must be "fighting for a world where we *all* have seats at the table."[27] By using vision to animate critical coalitions and unite antisubordination projects, this forward-looking approach can help to ground, consolidate, and advance antisubordination theory and praxis.

In sum, progressive postsubordination vision can help OutCrits imagine and animate critical coalitions by underscoring how "different" forms of hegemony or supremacy may combine to produce mutually reinforcing vectors of oppression that mutate in myriad ways, time and again, to oppose or co-opt any effort toward material transformation on any single front. In this way, postsubordination vision may help to interconnect the historic quests for substantive security that many OutCrits and outgroups continue to pursue today. If Out-Crit scholars practice critical legal theory in this way, and if we do so responsibly, insistently, collectively, and mutually, our respective and shared visions of a progressive postsubordination order just may help bring us together during CRT's second decade to build a common table of justice, dignity, and prosperity for all.

Conclusion

CRT, like outsider jurisprudence generally, is a product of its time and context. But times and contexts always change. So must jurisprudential movements that, like CRT, are in search of substantive social justice. Its adherents must theorize and re-theorize CRT in both structure and substance as the pre-eminent genre of OutCrit jurisprudence to ensure that CRT's first decade also will be not its best. Ensuring a second decade of ever-greater relevance and potency is the challenge that awaits us all.

To help meet this challenge, this chapter urges outsider scholars to embrace an "Out-Crit" identification, and to do so as part of the larger antisubordination project of outsider jurisprudence that CRT has helped to pioneer during the past decade. As Out-Crits, we can take up the serious business of defining and committing ourselves to an egalitarian vision of a postsubordination society, an undertaking that effectively requires all OutCrits personally to embrace the struggle against all forms of oppression under today's Euroheteropatriarchal status quo. By expanding the focus of outgroup coalitions beyond issues of sameness and difference with forward-looking assessments of hopes and aspirations, postsubor-

dination vision as jurisprudential method can help OutCrits to organize critical coalitions chiefly around the progressive principles and policies that will ensure social justice and substantive security for all.

Notes

Acknowledgments: I thank Marc Spindelman for prompting some initial thoughts included in this chapter. I thank also Angela Harris, Jerome Culp, and Harlon Dalton for conceiving, and leading the organization of, the conference at which I delivered a preliminary version of these thoughts. Finally, I thank Bob Chang, Sumi Cho, Angela Harris, and Robert Westley for valuable feedback that improved the final version of this chapter; Jerome Culp for superb editing; and Angela Harris and Jerome Culp for an enriching collaboration on every facet of this project. All defects are mine.

1. Though it is not susceptible to any one definition, Critical Race Theory has been described as the genre of critical legal scholarship that "focuses on the relationship between law and racial subordination in American society": Kimberlé W. Crenshaw, "A Black Feminist Critique of Antidiscrimination Law and Politics," in *The Politics of Law: A Progressive Critique,* rev. ed., ed. David Kairys (New York: Pantheon Books, 1990), 195, 213, n. 7; see generally Angela P. Harris, "Foreword—The Jurisprudence of Reconstruction," *California Law Review* 82 (1994): 741. Two recently released book anthologies provide good compilations of the literature: See Richard Delgado, ed., *Critical Race Theory: The Cutting Edge* (Philadelphia: Temple University Press, 1995), and Kimberlé W. Crenshaw, Neil Gotanda, Gary Peller, and Kendall Thomas, eds., *Critical Race Theory: The Key Writings That Formed the Movement* (New York: New Press, 1995). Even though CRT in fact comprises many voices and viewpoints, I discuss it as a collectivity in this chapter for the sake of simplicity.

2. For a succinct critical primer, see Natsu Taylor Saito, "Beyond Civil Rights: Considering 'Third Generation' International Human Rights Law in the United States," *University of Miami Inter-American Law Review* 28 (1996–97): 387. This interconnection of the "domestic" and the "international" has prompted calls for outsider jurisprudence to synthesize "civil" and "human" rights in the United

States. See Berta Esperanza Hernández-Truyol, "Building Bridges: Bringing International Human Rights Home," *La Raza Law Journal* 9 (1996): 69.

3. See generally Francisco Valdes, "Beyond Sexual Orientation in Queer Legal Theory: Majoritarianism, Multidimensionality and Responsibility in Social Justice Scholarship," *Denver Law Review* 75 (1998): 1409, 1426–43.

4. Idem, "Afterword—Theorizing 'OutCrit' Theories: Coalitional Method and Comparative Jurisprudential Experience—RaceCrits, QueerCrits and LatCrits," *University of Miami Law Review* 53 (1998): 1265.

5. See generally Derrick A. Bell, Jr., "*Brown v. Board of Education* and the Interest-Convergence Dilemma," *Harvard Law Review* 93 (1980): 518; Mary L. Dudziak, "Desegregation as a Cold War Imperative," *Stanford Law Review* 41 (1988): 61.

6. OutCrit positionality is framed around the need to confront in collective and coordinated ways the mutually reinforcing tenets and effects of two sociolegal macro-structures that currently operate both domestically and internationally: Euroheteropatriarchy and neo-liberal globalization For more on this point, see Francisco Valdes, "Unpacking Hetero-Patriarchy: Tracing the Conflation of Sex, Gender and Sexual Orientation to its Origins," *Yale Journal of Law and the Humanities* 8 (1996): 161.

7. For a discussion of comparative jurisprudential experience, see Valdes, "Afterword."

8. See generally Francisco Valdes, "Foreword—Poised at the Cusp: LatCrit Theory, Outsider Jurisprudence and Latina/o Self Empowerment," *Harvard Latino Law Review* 2 (1997): 1, 52–9.

9. This sense of "vision" is embedded in various works, which collectively manifest an expansive and activist antisubordination purpose regarding both theory and community: See, for example, n. 1 and the sources cited therein. As with CRT and other jurisprudential formations generally, references to a single collective vision necessarily oversimplify the matter: see n. 1. My chief effort here, therefore, is to center vision as method and to invoke its antisubordination utility.

10. For a critical discussion of some key elements that help to constitute Euroheteropatriarchy, see Valdes, "Unpacking Hetero-Patriarchy": 161.

11. See generally Martha Minow, *Making All the Difference: Inclusion, Exclusion and American Law* (Ithaca, N.Y.: Cornell University Press, 1990); see also Regina Austin, "Black Women, Sisterhood, and the Difference/Deviance Divide," *New England Law Review* 26 (1992): 877; Martha Albertson Fineman,

"Feminist Theory in Law: The Difference It Makes," *Columbia Journal of Gender and Law* 2 (1992): 1; Joan C. Williams, "Dissolving the Sameness/Difference Debate: A Post-Modern Path Beyond Essentialism in Feminist and Critical Race Theory," *Duke Law Journal*, 1991, 296.

12. For powerful invocations of experience and struggle as key bases of CRT projects, see Harris, "Foreword"; Charles R. Lawrence, III, "Foreword—Race, Multiculturalism, and the Jurisprudence of Transformation," *Stanford Law Review* 47 (1995): 819, 835.

13. See, for example, Robert S. Chang, "The End of Innocence, or Politics after the Fall of the Essential Subject," *American University Law Review* 45 (1996): 687, 690–1.

14. For readings on these and similar concepts, see Kimberlé W. Crenshaw, "Mapping the Margins: Intersectionality, Identity Politics, and Violence Against Women of Color," *Stanford Law Review* 43 (1991): 1241; idem, "Demarginalizing the Intersection of Race and Sex: A Black Feminist Critique of Antidiscrimination Doctrine, Feminist Theory and Antiracist Politics," *University of Chicago Legal Forum*, 1989, 139; Angela P. Harris, "Race and Essentialism in Feminist Legal Theory," *Stanford Law Review* 42 (1990): 581; Mari J. Matsuda, "When the First Quail Calls: Multiple Consciousness as Jurisprudential Method," *Women's Rights Law Reporter* 11 (1989): 7.

15. See Darren Lenard Hutchinson, "Ignoring the Sexualization of Race: Heteronormativity, Critical Race Theory and Antiracist Politics," *Buffalo Law Review* 47 (1999): 1; Francisco Valdes, "Queer Margins, Queer Ethics: A Call to Account for Race and Ethnicity in the Law, Theory and Politics of 'Sexual Orientation,'" *Hastings Law Journal* 48 91997): 1293, 1315–8.

16. For one effort, see Valdes, "Afterword."

17. For readings on these concepts, see e. christi cunningham, "The Rise of Identity Politics I: The Myth of the Protected Class in Title VII Disparate Treatment Cases," *University of Connecticut Law Review*, 30 (1998): 441; Peter Kwan, "Jeffrey Dahmer and the Cosynthesis of Categories," *Hastings Law Journal* 48 (1997): 1257; Francisco Valdes, "Sex and Race in Queer Legal Culture: Ruminations on Identities and Interconnectivities," *Southern California Review of Law and Women's Studies* 5 (1995): 25.

18. For a discussion of hope and law in another context, see Jennifer Gerarda Brown, "The Role of Hope in Negotiations," *UCLA Law Review* 44 (1997): 1661.

19. See Valdes, " Afterword," and Elizabeth M. Iglesias and Francisco Valdes, "Afterword—Religion,

Gender, Sexuality, Race and Class in Coalitional Theory: A Critical and Self-Critical Analysis of Lat-Crit Social Justice Agendas," *UCLA Chicano–Latino Law Review* 19 (1998): 503.

20. See generally Elizabeth M. Iglesias, "Fore-word—Identity, Democracy, Communicative Power, Inter/National Labor Rights and the Evolution of LatCrit Theory and Community," *University of Miami Law Review* 53 (1998): 575.

21. Antisubordination theory and praxis also has to be organized around recognition and ameliora-tion of intergroup injustice among outsiders. See Eric K. Yamamoto, "Critical Race Praxis: Race The-ory and Political Lawyering Practice in Post Civil Rights America," *Michigan Law Review* 95 (1997): 821; Eric K. Yamamoto, "Rethinking Alliances: Agency, Responsibility and Interracial Justice," *UCLA Asian Pacific American Law Journal* 3 (1995): 33.

22. In recent years LatCrit theorists have delved into these areas. See Symposium, "LatCrit Theory: Naming and Launching a New Discourse of Criti-cal Legal Scholarship," *Harvard Latino Law Review* 2 (1997): 1; Symposium, "Difference, Solidarity and Law: Building Latina/o Communities Through Lat-Crit Theory," *UCLA Chicano–Latino Law Review* 19 (1998): 1; Colloquium, "Representing Latina/o Com-munities: Critical Race Theory and Practice," *La Raza Law Journal* 9 (1996): 1; Colloquium, "Interna-tional Law, Human Rights and LatCrit Theory," *University of Miami Inter-American Law Review* 28 (1997): 177; Symposium, "Comparative Latinas/os: Identity, Law and Policy in LatCrit Theory," *Uni-versity of Miami Law Review* 53 (1998): 575; Sympo-sium, "Rotating Centers, Expanding Frontiers: Lat-Crit Theory and Marginal Intersections," *Davis Law Review* 23 (2000): 751. These publications correspond to the LatCrit colloquia and conferences held in various locales since LatCrit theory's inception in 1995. For more information, see <http://www.lat-crit.org>. In addition to these conference-based publications, two independent symposia have been published: See Joint Symposium, "LatCrit Theory: Latinas/os and the Law," *California Law Review* 85 (1997): 1087, and *La Raza Law Journal* 10 (1998): 1; Joint Symposium, "Culture, Language, Sexuality and Law: LatCrit Theory and the Construction of the Nation," *University of Michigan Journal of Law Reform* 33 (2000): 203, and *Michigan Journal of Race and Law* 5 (2000): 787.

23. Cultural war is the latest and ongoing out-come of this history: See Valdes, "Beyond Sexual Orientation": 1426–43.

24. See generally Iglesias and Valdes, "Afterword": 503.

25. Ibid., 555–61.

26. See Valdes, "Afterword."

27. See Lawrence, "Foreword": 819, 835 (emphasis added).

The Handmaid's Truth

Derrick A. Bell

MANY YEARS AFTER having read the book, I remain fascinated by the similarities between the dangers faced by those of us writing in the Critical Race Theory mode and those faced by the heroine of Margaret Atwood's 1985 novel, *The Handmaid's Tale*. Atwood's story recalls the Old Testament story of Rachel, whose child was fathered by her husband Jacob but born to her handmaid, Bilhad. But her narrative takes place in a post-nuclear world in which a dictatorial regime forces women still able to bear children to serve as breeders for leaders whose wives are barren. Offred, the heroine, is such a handmaid; the book is about the extraordinary measures and enormous risks she takes to retain her sanity and some remnants of her self-esteem. Deprived of books and writing materials, she forces herself to remember all that she has undergone; quite literally, she keeps herself alive in order to tell her story. Generations later, anthropologists uncover the recordings she has made, but because her record does not contain information of interest, they misconstrue and trivialize it. Their rejection serves as a despairing answer to Offred's sacrifice and perseverance.

Some may scoff at comparing the difficulties of those whose writings fit the broad category of Critical Race Theory to the totalitarian regime of Atwood's novel, in which the slightest deviation from official orthodoxy is punished by a death both quick and cruel. Few will deny, however, that our challenge to social injustice is cause for consternation by defenders of the status quo. Academic faculties either ban us from their midst entirely or ensure that our numbers do not exceed one or two. Critical race theorists are seldom invited to take part in public debate. When published, our views are more ridiculed than engaged. Indeed, those who condemn our work receive more attention than we who create it.

Undeterred, we continue to identify and critique the entrenched and enduring evils many would prefer to ignore. Considering the difficulty of our work and the resistance to its acceptance, we have reason for satisfaction with the rich bibliography we have produced over the past decade. Some book publishers and law-review editors recognize the forthrightness and timeliness of our writing. They, at least, see our unorthodoxy as appropriate, even indispensable, to our craft. The readers who hail our work may not be powerful, but they do exist, and their positive response and welcome encouragement reassures us that what we do is not without value in our time.

The fate of Offred's record, however, poses a dramatic question: How will historians view our efforts a hundred years hence? The question cannot be answered for the future, but it is essential for our work today that we pose it regularly to ourselves, and to one another.

Evaluation is not easy. If the lives of those we most respect are any indication, our effectiveness may best be measured by the mainstream's rejection. Certainly, too much public recognition may be cause for concern and a re-examination of our goals. The desire for general acceptance—to have our writing read by many rather than the faithful few—is normal. But in striving for readership, the temptation is ever present to soften our critiques and rationalize rather than rant against the injustices in our midst.

Fortunately, the works published in this anthology confirm our collective capacity and determination to resist such temptations. Employing varied forms, tools, and methods, the essays in this volume uniformly and eloquently oppose both the multiple permutations of racism and their intersection with other virulent forces of oppression. This timely collection keeps the critical race edge razor sharp.

As this book illustrates, our writing is our art. Like all art, it may come in many forms, but it must be grounded in truth as we see it. That truth may and will evolve with our understanding and come to reflect the wisdom that emerges with experiences. The chapters in this volume adhere to this basic credo. They offer unusual perspectives and unfailing insights into the evils of our time. That is our mission in life, and our contribution to the future.

About the Contributors

DERRICK A. BELL is Visiting Professor of Law, New York University School of Law, New York.

DEVON W. CARBADO is Acting Professor of Law, University of California at Los Angeles School of Law.

ENRIQUE R. CARRASCO is Professor of Law, University of Iowa College of Law, Iowa City.

ROBERT S. CHANG is Professor of Law, Loyola Law School, Loyola Marymount University, Los Angeles.

SUMI CHO is Associate Professor of Law, DePaul University College of Law, Chicago.

KIMBERLÉ WILLIAMS CRENSHAW is Professor of Law, University of California at Los Angeles and Columbia University Law School, New York, N.Y.

JEROME McCRISTAL CULP is Professor of Law, Duke University, Durham, N.C.

JENNIFER ELROD, teacher, social activist, and lawyer, is pursuing a doctoral degree at Columbia University Law School, New York, N.Y.

ANTHONY PAUL FARLEY is Professor of Law, Boston College School of Law.

ISABELLE R. GUNNING is Professor of Law, Southwestern University School of Law, Los Angeles.

ANGELA P. HARRIS is Professor of Law, Boalt Hall School of Law, University of California at Berkeley.

ROBERT L. HAYMAN, JR., is Associate Professor of Law, Widener University School of Law, Wilmington, Del.

BERTA ESPERANZA HERNÁNDEZ-TRUYOL is Professor of Law, University of Florida College of Law, Gainesville.

ELIZABETH M. IGLESIAS is Professor of Law, University of Miami Law School.

KEVIN R. JOHNSON is Associate Dean for Academic Affairs and Professor of Law, University of California at Davis School of Law.

CHARLES R. LAWRENCE III is Professor of Law, Georgetown University Law Center, Washington, D.C.

NANCY LEVIT is Associate Professor of Law, University of Missouri–Kansas City School of Law.

CATHARINE A. MACKINNON is Professor of Law, University of Michigan, Ann Arbor.

MARI MATSUDA is Professor of Law, Georgetown University Law Center, Washington, D.C.

MARGARET E. MONTOYA is Professor of Law, University of New Mexico School of Law, Albuquerque.

PATRICIA MONTURE-ANGUS is Professor of Native Studies, University of Saskatchewan, Canada, and Special Assistant to the Dean on Indigenous Initiatives.

VICTORIA ORTIZ is Dean of Students, Boalt Hall School of Law, University of California at Berkeley.

SHERENE H. RAZACK is Professor of Sociology and Equity Studies in Education, Ontario Institute for Studies in Education, University of Toronto.

HENRY J. RICHARDSON III is Professor of Law, Temple Univesrity Law School, Philadelphia.

CELINA ROMANY is an attorney in private practice in San Juan, Puerto Rico, and former Professor of Law, City University of New York, School of Law at Queens College.

THOMAS ROSS is Professor of Law, University of Pittsburgh School of Law.

JULIE A. SU is an attorney, Asian Pacific American Legal Center, Los Angeles.

FRANCISCO VALDES is Professor of Law, University of Miami School of Law.

ROBERT WESTLEY is Associate Professor of Law, Tulane University School of Law, New Orleans.

STEPHANIE M. WILDMAN is Professor of Law, Santa Clara University School of Law, Santa Clara, Calif.

ERIC K. YAMAMOTO is Professor of Law, University of Hawaii at Manoa.